ARIS & PHILLIPS CLAS

The *Athenian Constitution*

Written in the School of ARISTOTLE

With an introduction, translation and notes by

P. J. Rhodes

LIVERPOOL UNIVERSITY PRESS

First published 2017 by
Liverpool University Press
4 Cambridge Street
Liverpool
L69 7ZU

www.liverpooluniversitypress.co.uk

British Library Cataloguing-in-Publication data
A British Library CIP record is available

ISBN 978-1-78694-070-4 cased
ISBN 978-1-78694-837-3 paperback

Typeset by Tara Evans
Printed and bound by CPI Group (UK) Ltd, Croydon CR0 4YY

Cover image: Model of Klepsydra in action. Photo reproduced with permission from The American School of Classical Studies at Athens: Agora Excavations.

CONTENTS

PREFACE

I published a very large commentary on this text in 1981 (revised addenda 1993), and a Penguin Classics translation with notes in 1984 (corrections 2002). Recently I have edited the Greek text, and written an introduction and a more up-to-date but more modest commentary to be translated into Italian, for the Fondazione Lorenzo Valla's volume *Democrazia in Grecia*, iii (Milan: Mondadori, 2016). I am very grateful to the Fondazione for giving its permission for, and to Oxbow Books and Liverpool University Press as successive heirs to Aris & Phillips for accepting and producing, this edition based on my materials for the Fondazione's volume, to Prof. T. Gargiulo, who translated my English for the Fondazione's volume and pointed the way to several corrections and improvements, and to Dr. W. J. B. G. Mack, for inciting me to publish this edition. The English translation given here has been newly made for this volume: it is more punctilious than my translation for Penguin; and, in particular, where Penguin asked me to give English equivalents of most technical terms, here I mostly give a transliteration of the technical term in the translation and an explanation in the commentary.

University of Durham
Michaelmas Term 2016 P.J.R.

REFERENCES

Ancient authors and their works are in general abbreviated as in the fourth edition of the *Oxford Classical Dictionary*, but I occasionally use a fuller form of reference, and in particular I cite speeches both by number and by short title. I refer to the work edited here and to its author as *A.P.*

The following collections of texts (* and translations, references to which are preceded by ~) of inscriptions are cited:

Agora	*The Athenian Agora: Results of Excvavations Conducted by the American School of Classical Studies at Athens*
C. Delphes	*Corpus des Inscriptions de Delphes*
Fornara	Fornara, C. W. *Translated Documents of Greece and Rome*, i. *Archaic Times to the End of the Peloponnesian War* (Cambridge U. P., [2]1983)
Harding	Harding, P. E. *Translated Documents of Greece and Rome*, ii. *From the End of the Peloponnesian War to the Battle of Ipsus* (Cambridge U. P., 1985)
I. Délos	*Inscriptions de Délos*
IG	*Inscriptiones Graecae*
ML	Meiggs, R., & Lewis, D. M. *A Selection of Greek Historical Inscriptions to the End of the Fifth Century BC* (Oxford U. P., 1969; reprinted with addenda 1988)
OGIS	Dittenberger, W. *Orientis Graeci Inscriptiones Selectae* (Leipzig: Hirzel, 1903–5)
Reinmuth	Reinmuth, O. W. *The Ephebic Inscriptions of the Fourth Century BC* (*Mnemosyne* Supp. 14 [1971]).
RO	Rhodes, P. J., & Osborne, R. G. *Greek Historical Inscriptions, 404–323 BC* (Oxford U. P., 2003; corrected reprint 2007)
SEG	*Supplementum Epigraphicum Graecum*

The following collections of fragmentary texts are cited:

FIR	Bruns, C. G. *Fontes Iuris Romani Antiqui* (Tübingen: Mohr, [7]1919)
FIRA	Riccobono, S. *Fontes Iuris Romani Anteiustiniani* (Florence: Barbera, [2]1940–3)
FGrH	Jacoby, F., *et al.* *Die Fragmente der griechischen Historiker* (Berlin: Weidmann Leiden: Brill, 1926–)
Kassel & Austin	Kassel, R. & Austin, C. F. L. *Poetae Comici Graeci* (Berlin: De Gruyter, 1983–)
Müller	Müller, K. O. *Fragmenta Historicorum Graecorum* (Paris: Firmin-Didot, 1878–85)
Sauppe	fragments in Baiter, J. G., & Sauppe, H. *Oratores Attici* (Zurich: Höhr, 1850)
Szegedy-Maszak	Szegedy-Msazak, A. *The Nomoi of Theophrastus* (New York: Arno, 1981)
TrGF	Snell, B., *et al.* *Tragicorum Graecorum Fragmenta* (Göttingen: Vandenhoeck & Ruprecht, 1971–2004)
West	West, M. L. *Iambi et Elegi Graeci ante Alexandrum Cantati* (Oxford U. P., [2]1989–92)

Otherwise, details are given in the Bibliography of modern books which are cited frequently (with abbreviations for some which are cited very frequently), and at the point of citation of modern books which are cited occasionally. Details of articles in periodicals are given where they are cited. The titles of periodicals are given as follows; superior figures (e.g. *CQ*²) denote the second and subsequent series.

Bhft.	Beiheft
Einz.	Einzelschriften
Supp.	Supplement

AA	*Archäologischer Anzeiger*
AC	*L'Antiquité Classique*
Acme	*Acme*
AGR	*Akten der Gesellschaft für griechische und hellenistische Rechtsgeschichte*

AJA	*American Journal of Archaeology*
AJP	*American Journal of Philology*
AM	*Athenische Mitteilungen (Mitteilungen des Deutschen Archäologischen Instituts, Athenische Abteilung)*
Antichthon	*Antichthon*
Anz. Wien	*Anzeiger (Österreichische Akademie der Wissenschaften, Philosophisch–Historische Klasse)*
AR	*Archaeological Reports*
ASNP	*Annali della Scuola Normale Superiore di Pisa, Classe di Lettere e Filosofia*
Athenaeum	*Athenaeum*
BCH	*Bulletin de Correspondance Hellénique*
BICS	*Bulletin of the Institute of Classical Studies (London)*
BSA	*Annual of the British School at Athens*
C&M	*Classica et Mediaevalia*
CCJ	*Cambridge Classical Journal*
Chiron	*Chiron*
CP	*Classical Philology*
CQ	*Classical Quarterly*
CR	*Classical Review*
CSCA	*California Studies in Classical Antiquity*
Dike	*Dike*
Eirene	*Eirene*
Eranos	*Eranos*
G&R	*Greece and Rome*
GRBS	*Greek, Roman and Byzantine Studies*
Hermathena	*Hermathena*
Hermes	*Hermes*
Hesperia	*Hesperia*
Historia	*Historia*
HSCP	*Harvard Studies in Classical Philology*
HZ	*Historische Zeitschrift*
Incid. Antico	*Incidenza del Antico*
JHS	*Journal of Hellenic Studies*
Klio	*Klio*
LCM	*Liverpool Classical Monthly*

LEC	*Les Études Classiques*
LSKP	*Leipziger Studien zur klassischen Philologie*
LZB	*Literarisches Zentralblatt für Deutschland*
Maia	*Maia*
MH	*Museum Helveticum*
Mnemosyne	*Mnemosyne*
NC	*Numismatic Chronicle*
NJA	*Neue Jahrbücher für das klassische Altertum, Geschichte und deutsche Literatur und für Pädagogik*
NJPhP	*Neue Jahrbücher für Philologie und Paedagogik*
Opus	*Opus*
PAPS	*Proceedings of the American Philosophical Society*
PCPS	*Proceedings of the Cambridge Philological Society*
Philologus	*Philologus*
Phoenix	*Phoenix*
PP	*La Parola del Passato*
Proc. Mass. Hist. Soc.	*Proceedings of the Massachusetts Historical Society*
RA	*Revue Archéologique*
REA	*Revue des Études Anciennes*
REC	*Revista de Estudios Clásicos*
REG	*Revue des Études Grecques*
RH	*Revue Historique*
RIDA	*Revue Internationale des Droits de l'Antiquité*
RM	*Rheinisches Museum*
RPh	*Revue de Philologie*
SSAC	*Studi Storici per l'Antichità Classica*
TAPA	*Transactions of the American Philological Society*
TAPhS	*Transactions of the American Philosophical Society*
ZPE	*Zeitschrift für Papyrologie und Epigraphik*

ΑΔ	*Ἀρχαιολογικὸν Δελτίον*
Ἀθηνᾶ	*Ἀθηνᾶ*
Ἀρχ. Ἐφ.	*Ἀρχαιολογικὴ Ἐφημερίς*
Γραμματεῖον	*Γραμματεῖον*
hόρος	*hόρος*

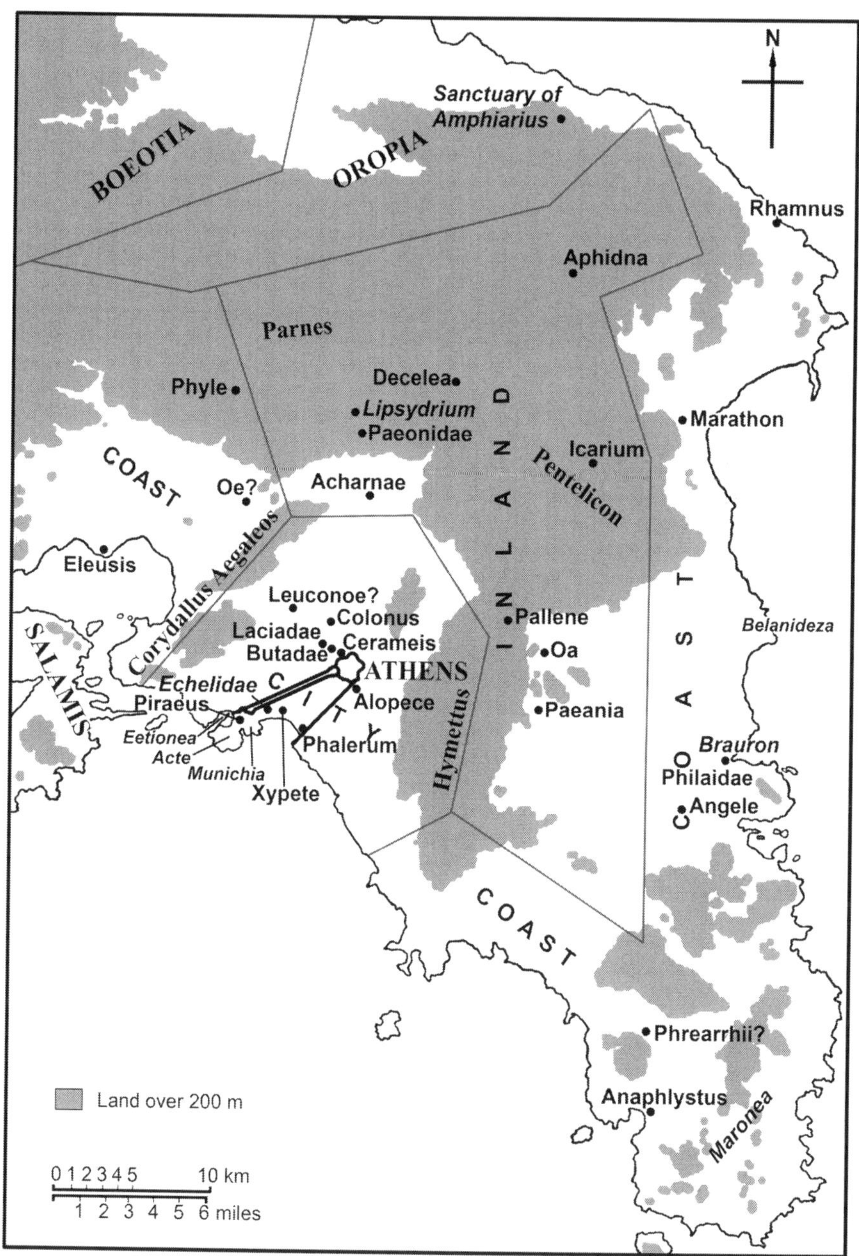

Map 1. Map of Attica. Names of demes are in sanserif roman capital and lower case letters; names of Cleisthenes' three regions are in sanserif roman capitals. Regional boundaries are purely schematic.

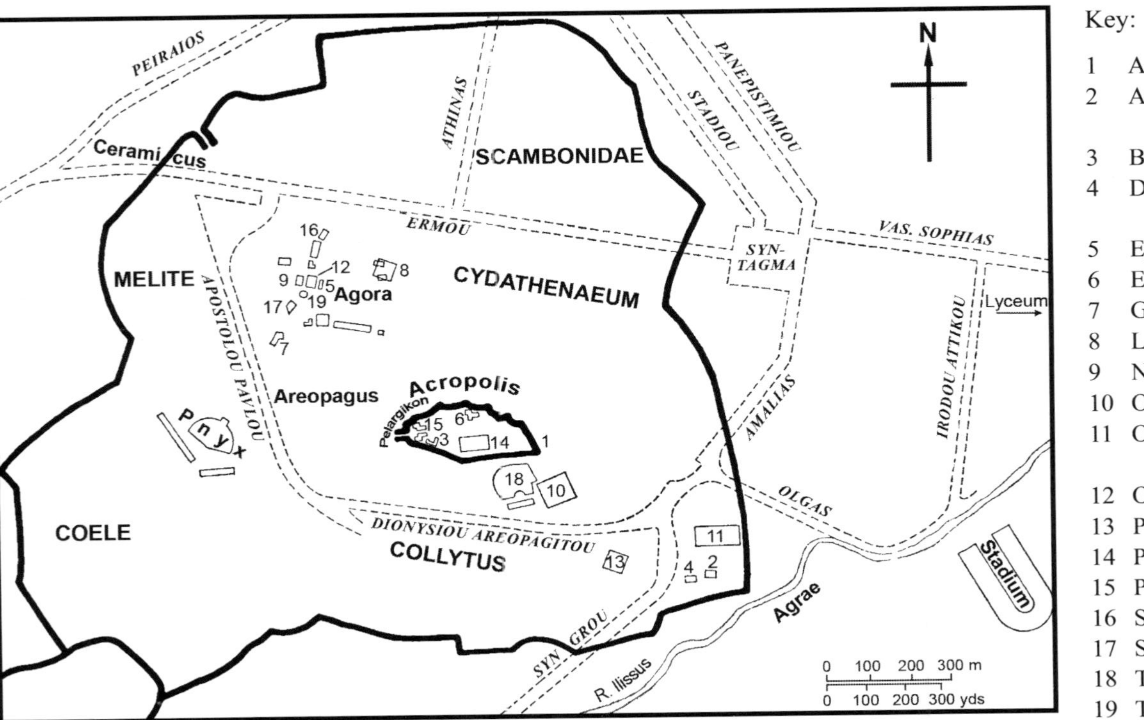

Key:

1 Aglaurus, shrine of
2 Apollo Delphinios, temple of
3 Brauronium
4 Delphinium, court at the
5 Eponymi, statues of
6 Erechtheum
7 Gaol (?)
8 Lawcourts
9 New Bouleuterion
10 Odeum
11 Olympian Zeus, temple of
12 Old Bouleuterion
13 Palladium, court at the
14 Parthenon
15 Propylaea
16 Stoa of the Basileus
17 Strategeion (?)
18 Theatre of Dionysus
19 Tholos

Map 2. Athens. Names of demes are in capital letters; principal modern streets are shown in pecked lines.

INTRODUCTION

1. Aristotle and the Athenaion Politeia

This work, preserved not through the western manuscript tradition but only on papyrus, is the only survivor from a collection of Greek constitutions (together with a constitution of Carthage) attributed to Aristotle. Certainly it was written in Aristotle's school in Athens, but it was probably not written by Aristotle himself. However, it is a work of great interest and importance. The first part, about two thirds of the whole, gives a history of the constitution to the end of the fifth century, and, while based not on documentary research but on a range of sources, preserves a good deal of material which has not survived in other ways, and shows how a fourth-century writer tried to make sense of the material available; the second part, the remaining third, is unprecedented in giving an account of the constitution's working in the author's own time, and was based on the laws currently in force and on direct observation.

Aristotle was born at Stagirus, in Chalcidice, in 384. He was in Athens, as a pupil of Plato, from 367 until Plato's death in 347; he then left Athens, and after periods elsewhere was appointed by Philip of Macedon to be tutor to his son Alexander the Great. In 336 Alexander succeeded Philip, and in 335 Alexander returned to Athens and opened a philosophical school there. In 323, on the death of Alexander, Athens embarked on the Lamian War against Macedon, and Aristotle left the city; in 322 he died, and Athens and her allies were defeated in the war; in 321 the settlement after the war involved the overthrow of Athens' democratic constitution. We shall see that it was between 335 and 323, when Aristotle was working in Athens, that *A.P.* was originally written and was revised (§6, below).

Aristotle's *Nicomachean Ethics* ends with a passage leading to the *Politics*, which is to be based on the works of his predecessors and 'the collection of constitutions', τῶν συνηγμένων πολιτειῶν (*E.N.* X. 1180 B

20–1181 B 24). A collection of constitutions, most probably 158, appears in lists of Aristotle's works (Diog. Laert. V. 27 = V. Rose, *Aristotelis ... Fragmenta*, pp. 8–9; Hesychius Illustrius s.v. Ἀριστοτέλης = Rose, p. 16; cf. Ptolemy nos 81, 89 ap. Rose, pp. 21–2). A man called Heraclides, probably Heraclides Lembus of Alexandria in the second century BC, produced a set of excerpts from the collection; and later somebody else produced a set of excerpts from the excerpts, which survives as the *Epitome of Heraclides* (fr. 611 Rose):[1] this gives a brief summary of *A.P.*, followed by briefer excerpts from forty-three other *politeiai*. None of the *politeiai* has survived through the western manuscript tradition, though there are many quotations from and references to them by later writers (frs. 381–603 Rose), but papyrus texts of *A.P.* were found in the late nineteenth century, and it was quickly seen that this work was what the ancient world knew as Aristotle's *Athenaion Politeia* (cf. §2, below).

Aristotle says that the *Politics* will be based on 'the collection of constitutions'. He and his school collected information on particular states for the study of politics in the same way as they collected information on particular plants and animals for the study of biology,[2] and in the *Politics* the generalisations are indeed illustrated by examples from the history and constitutions of various states. We know also of various other historical works undertaken by the school.

We might therefore expect *A.P.* and the other *politeiai* to be comparatively early works of the school and the *Politics* to be comparatively late. In fact, however, we shall see that even the original version of *A.P.* was not completed until the late 330s (cf. §6, below), whereas the latest unambiguous reference in the *Politics* is to the murder of Philip of Macedon in 336 (Arist. *Pol.* V. 1311 B 1–3). It has often been thought that different parts of the *Politics* represent different stages in the development of Aristotle's thought,[3] and that remains attractive in principle though it has proved hard to secure agreement on what material is early and what is late. There are some factual disagreements between the *Politics* and *A.P.* (cf. below), where

1 A recent edition: Dilts, *Heraclidis Lembi Excerpta Politiarum*; ch. 1 of this is included in my frs 1–5.

2 See particularly G. Huxley, *GRBS* 13 (1972), 157–69.

3 Jaeger, *Aristoteles*, anticipated by Wilamowitz, *A.u.A.* i. 355–9.

on the evidence available to us we must assume that what is stated in the *Politics* was written before *A.P.* Clearly Aristotle did not first have the collection of *politeiai* made and afterwards write the *Politics*: we should assume that from the beginning he did think that the general study of politics, like his other general studies, should be based on knowledge of particular examples; as he and his pupils collected more information he fitted more information into his general treatment of the subject; but the text of the *Politics* which we have seems not to have benefited from information acquired in the final years of his life.

We shall see (in §3, below), that the first part of *A.P.* cites the poems of Solon, a dedication on the acropolis and scolia, and quotes documents. It argues for conclusions which are reasonable (e.g. 'more reasonable', εὐλογώτερον, 7. 4) and cites familiar facts as evidence to support a conclusion (e.g. 'indication', σημεῖον, 8. 1). This is in keeping with what we know of the other historical works of the school,[4] and indeed of Greek historians more generally, but I argue that in most cases (though he may have added such material as the scolia from his own direct knowledge) the author did not obtain his evidence by his own researches but found it already deployed by the sources which he was using. What is distinctive about the first part of *A.P.* is its purpose: to provide not a universal history or a history of a war or a history of Athens, but a history of the *politeia*, showing the stages by which it had developed to its present and (the author supposed) final form. As a historian the author was mediocre – he could make sensible judgments but he had difficulties when his sources disagreed – but he is important to us because of the material which he has preserved which would not have been available to us without *A.P.* The second part (cf. §4, below) is the more original: it provides, as no earlier work is known to have provided, a factual account of the working of Athens' *politeia* in the author's own time, and it is based on direct research in the laws and direct observation of the *politeia* in practice. While the first part is Aristotelian in its purpose, the second part in its organisation uses the kinds of category that are used in the *Politics* (but those categories are

4 Cf. Huxley, *GRBS* 13 (1972), 157–69; also 12 (1971), 505–15, 14 (1973), 271–86, 15 (1974), 203–13.

not peculiar to Aristotle, and it may well have derived its categories from the laws on which it was based rather than from Aristotelian doctrine)

Beyond that, however, the work does not seem to be strongly conditioned by Aristotelian theories. Also the language is very different from that of the other works in the Aristotelian corpus (cf. §5, below), but that may be explained by the nature of the work and the sources on which it is based; and, while some distinctively Aristotelian expressions are used, some other Aristotelian expressions are conspicuously absent.

In content, there is a tendency towards 'middling' political views of the kind which we associate with Aristotle, though I argue that our author tends to repeat views found in his sources rather than to express his own views spontaneously. There are some significant agreements between *A.P.* and the *Politics*: notably, that Solon was one of the 'middling citizens', μέσοι πολῖται, and that he did not intend everything which was later built on his foundations; that the battle of Salamis led both to a more oligarchic constitution under the control of the Areopagus and to the strengthening of Athens' naval power and the democracy (cf. p. 11, below). However, there are also some striking disagreements. *Pol.* II. 1274 B 15–16 says that Draco enacted laws for the existing constitution, whereas *A.P.* 4 reports a 'constitution of Draco' (but we shall see in §6, below, that is an insertion made by the reviser, and the original text may well have been compatible with the *Politics* on this point). *Pol.* II. 1273 B 40–1274 A 2 (cf. 1274 A 16–17) and III. 1281 B 25–34 say that Solon left unaltered the appointment of magistrates by election, but according to *A.P.* 8. 1–2 and 22. 5 for the nine archons Solon introduced *klerosis ek prokriton*, allotment from an elected short list, in place of election by the Areopagus, and this was abandoned by the tyranny but revived in 487/6. On the oligarchy of the Four Hundred, *Pol.* V. 1304 B 12–15 states explicitly that those who offered the prospect of Persian help against Sparta were deceitful, which is compatible with *A.P.* 29. 1 but is not actually stated there; and 1305 B 22–7 mentions the demagogy of Phrynichus within the Four Hundred, whereas the surviving text of *A.P.* does not mention Phrynichus at all.[5] If the *Politics* is in its

5 However, I suspect that the omission of Phrynichus from the list of oligarchic

substance earlier than *A.P.*, there is no difficulty in believing that further information was discovered in the course of work on *A.P.* which had not been available when the corresponding passage in the *Politics* was written, but that Aristotle did not then revise that passage. The reviser's additions of the 'constitution of Draco' and the story of Themistocles and Ephialtes were changes for the worse (cf. §6, below), but we can accept that further work on Solon had shown that what was said in the *Politics* about Solon and the appointment of archons was wrong (though appointment by the Areopagus before Solon's reforms may be simply a guess).

This leads inevitably to the much-discussed question, whether the author of *A.P.* was Aristotle himself or somebody else. The work was certainly the *A.P.* which in antiquity was attributed to Aristotle, was written in the 330s and revised in the 320s when Aristotle was in Athens, and is a product of his school. Whether he was himself the author is more important to the student of Aristotle than to the student of Athenian history.

That *A.P.*, together with all the other *Politeiai*, was attributed to Aristotle in antiquity is not sufficient proof of authorship, since he can hardly have written on his own all the works which were attributed to him, but must have set his pupils to work collecting material in the various fields in which he was interested. Some have argued that the Athenian constitution was particularly important, so Aristotle must have reserved that for himself;[6] but he was not an Athenian and was not an admirer of extreme democracy, so the Athenian constitution may not have seemed particularly important to him.[7] As we have seen above, the stylistic differences between *A.P.* and the rest of the corpus may be due simply to the different nature of this work, and the factual disagreements between *A.P.* and the *Politics* may be due simply to the discovery of further material after the relevant passage in the *Politics* had been written. The first part of *A.P.* is mediocre as a work of history and does not display the breadth of treatment which

leaders in *A.P.* 32. 3, based on Thuc. VIII. 68, which does include him, is due not to our author but to a copyist: see *ad loc.*

6 E.g. Busolt, *G.G.* ii^2. 29.

7 Cf. Hignett, *Constitution*, 30.

we find in the *Politics*,[8] but *A.P.* did not require breadth of treatment as the *Politics* does, and it could be that despite his other merits Aristotle was not a great historian.[9] However, I am impressed by the absence of several characteristically Aristotelian expressions which we might have expected to find in *A.P.*, and by the small number of passages in *A.P.* which have a strongly Aristotelian flavour. Those few Aristotelian passages could indicate either that in writing them a pupil was particularly conscious of his master's teaching, or that the master read his pupil's text and occasionally intervened.[10] On the evidence which we have Aristotle could have written *A.P.* himself, but I think it is much more likely that *A.P.* is the work of a pupil.

In this volume I shall refer to the work and to its author as *A.P.*

2. The survival of the text

The text is not contained in any manuscripts in the western tradition, but a little of it is preserved in a papyrus in Berlin, and almost the whole work is preserved in a papyrus in London.

The **Berlin papyrus** was originally P. Berol. 163, of the Ägyptisches Museum, Berlin, and is now P. 5009 in the Ägyptisches Museum und Papyrussammlung, Berlin.[11] It was a codex written probably in the fourth century AD, and two leaves survive: (IA) 12. 3–4, (IB) 13. 1–5, (IIA) 21. 4–22. 3, (IIB) 22. 4–7.

The **London papyrus** is P. Lond. 131, originally of the British Museum and now of the British Library.[12] It was written at the end of

8 Cf. Hignett, *Constitution*, 29.

9 Cf. Wilamowitz, *Au.A.* i. 373.

10 For the second possibility cf. L. Whibley, *CR* 5 (1891), 223.

11 Acquired in 1879; published by F. W. Blass, *Hermes* 15 (1880), 366–82; identified as *A.P.* by T. Bergk, *RM*[2] 36 (1881), 87–115; re-edited by M. Chambers, *TAPA* 98 (1967), 49–66; restudied by M. Stroppa, in *Proceedings of the XXVth International Congress of Papyrology … 2007*, 747–56. I thank Dr. F. Reiter for information on its current location.

12 Acquired in 1888–9; identified as *A.P.* by F. G. Kenyon on 26 February 1890; first public announcement in *The Times* 19 January 1891, 9. i–ii, iv–v; facsimile published, with preface by Scott (London: British Museum, 1 March 1891; 2nd edition 1891); included in Milne, *Catalogue of the Literary Papyri in the British*

the first or the beginning of the second century AD, on the reverse of accounts dated AD 77–9,[13] and consists of four rolls, containing the complete work apart from a section at the beginning, judged from the Berlin fragments to be equivalent to four to six pages of that, or about five of the chapters into which Kenyon divided the surviving text,[14] which since the surviving text starts at the beginning of a roll must have been missing from the exemplar which was being copied. The ending of the preserved text is abrupt, but there is no reason to think that further material has been lost and that it is not the end of *A.P.* The work was divided between four scribes (with the third doing a second stretch of work, at the end, and the fourth making corrections throughout). This text was quickly identified, and confirmed that the identification of the Berlin fragments as belonging to *A.P.* was correct.

A small fragment from Oxyrhynchus was restored by M. Chambers to give a version of 7. 3, but the extent to which it diverges from the London papyrus indicates that, if it is correctly identified, it gives not the text of *A.P.* but a paraphrase.[15]

The *editio princeps* was published by F. G. Kenyon on 30 January 1891; his final editions were his punctilious Berlin edition of 1903 and his O.C.T. of 1920; the most recent Teubner edition was published by Chambers in 1986 (second edition 1994); Kenyon's Berlin edition and the second edition of J. E. Sandys (which consolidated the first generation of work on *A.P.*) have the fullest collections of *testimonia* and indexes; the most recent major commentaries are by P. J. Rhodes in English and by Chambers in German.[16]

Museum (P. Lit. Lond.), p. 84 no. 108. It has been digitised and can be viewed on line: http://www.bl.uk/manuscripts/FullDisplay.aspx?ref=Papyrus_131&index=4. For an account of its acquisition see M. Chambers, in *Transitions to Empire … E. Badian*, 211–8.

13 After Σοφωνίδου in 25. 1 the text is interrupted by 1½ columns, written earlier in the opposite direction and deleted when *A.P.* was copied, containing a *hypothesis* to and scholia on Dem. XXI. *Midias*: see Kenyon³, 86–7, 215–9.

14 Sandys², p. lxv, Chambers, *TAPA* 98 (1967), 63–5.

15 Chambers, *TAPA* 102 (1971), 43; cf. commentary *ad loc.* There has not yet been a further publication of this fragment (I thank Dr. N. Gonis for confirming this).

16 See Bibliography.

3. *The first part of the work*

The contents of *A.P.* fall into two parts: from the lost beginning to ch. 41, a history of the *politeia* to its last *metabole*, 'change', the restoration of the democracy in 403; and chs 42–69, an account of the working of the *politeia* in the author's own time. We do not know whether any of the other *politeiai* were organised in the same way.

The first part may be analysed as follows; the letters on the left denote the main subject sections into which the commentary in this volume is divided; the roman numerals and short headings on the right denote the *metabolai* of 41. 2.

A	—	The lost beginning from the foundation of the monarchy to the annual archonship		I Ion; II Theseus
B	1	Cylon		
C	2–4	Between Cylon and Solon		
		2	causes of strife: poor enslaved to rich	
		3	causes of strife: ancient constitution	
		4	Draco [see commentary]	– Draco
D	5–12	Solon		III Solon
		5	Solon's background	
		6	*seisachtheia*	
		7–8	laws and *politeia*	
		9	Solon and democracy	
		10	measures, weights, coinage	
		11. 1	Solon's travels	
		11. 2–12	Solon in middle ground	
E	13	Between Solon and Pisistratus		
		13. 1–2	*stasis* over archonship	
		13. 3–5	the three parties	
F	14–19	The tyranny		IV Pisistratus
		14–15	the rise of Pisistratus	
		16	the rule of Pisistratus	
		17–18	the end of the tyranny: Hipparchus	
		19	the end of the tyranny: Hippias	

G	20–2	From Cleisthenes to Xerxes' invasion		V Cleisthenes
		20. 1–3	Cleisthenes and Isagoras	
		20. 4–5	the Alcmaeonids and the end of the tyranny	
		21	reforms of Cleisthenes	
		22	from Cleisthenes to Xerxes' invasion	
H	23–8	The mid fifth century		
		23. 1–2	ascendancy of the Areopagus	VI Areopagus
		23. 2–24	naval power	VII Aristides
		25	reform of Ephialtes	...
		26. 1	Cimon	... and
		26. 2–4	changes of the 450s	Ephialtes
		27	Pericles	
		28	deterioration after Pericles; aristocratic and democratic leaders	
I	29–34. 1	The Four Hundred and the Five Thousand		VIII The Four Hundred
		29	The institution of the Four Hundred	
		30	'future' constitution	
		31	'immediate' constitution	
		32	the rule of the Four Hundred	
		33–34. 1	the intermediate régime	
J	34–41. 1	The Thirty and the Ten		
		34. 1–2	the restored democracy	IX Democracy
		34. 3	the institution of the Thirty	X The Thirty
		35	the rule of the Thirty	...
		36	the opposition of Theramenes	
		37	Theramenes eliminated	
		38	the democrats at Munichia	
		39	terms of reconciliation	... and the Ten
		40	moderation of the restored democracy	
		41. 1	the democracy restored	
				XI Democracy
K	41. 2–3	Conclusion to first part		
		41. 2	changes in the constitution	
		41. 3	payment for attending the assembly	

41. 2 indicates that the author's intention was to list the changes which the Athenian constitution had undergone between the earliest times and the achievement of its present form. Aristotle believed that the *polis* exists by nature and man is a *polis* kind of creature (*Pol.* I. 1252 B 27–1253 A 18, III. 1278 B 15–30), and that nature does nothing without a purpose (e.g. *Pol.* I. 1253 A 9, 1256 B 20–1). Human and political phenomena could therefore be explained in the same way as other natural phenomena. Democracy was not a 'straight' form of constitution but a 'perversion', *parekbasis* (*Pol.* III. 1279 A 22–B 10); it was therefore not conducive to the final cause, *telos*, of the *polis*, which is the good life (*Pol.* III. 1278 B 15–30, 1280 A 31–1281 A 8), but it could be said that any form of constitution has its own *telos*, and that the *telos* of democracy is freedom (*Rhet.* I. 1366 A 2–7). The history of the constitution should therefore show how the constitution had arrived at the goal to which it had been aiming. On the other hand, Aristotle knew that history does not in fact proceed steadily and tidily in one direction, and that a state can change either from a first form to a second or from the second to the first (cf. *Pol.* V. 1316 A 1–B 27); and both *Pol.* II. 1273 B 35–1274 A 21 and *A.P.* 9. 2 maintain that Solon did not intend everything which was later built on his foundations. When *A.P.* was written, the author believed that there had been no *metabole* for seventy years, but there were in fact to be further changes subsequently, some away from democracy and some towards democracy. If the constitution of the author's time was thought to be the final form, it too had been achieved by changes towards democracy and changes away from democracy, as the list in 41. 2 shows.

A.P. does not use the words *telos* and *physis* with teleological implications, and does not claim that the present form of Athens' constitution is the 'final' form, but in 41. 2 each move towards democracy takes the constitution further than the previous such move had taken it. It is then claimed (though many scholars would consider the claim mistaken) that since the *metabole* of 403 the constitution had continued to grow ever more democratic, and 41. 3 gives the introduction of payment for attending the assembly (very soon after

403) as an example of that. With no identifiable major change after 403 Athens will in the 330s and 320s have seemed remarkably stable, and the author may be forgiven for thinking that the constitution of his own time was the final form.

A.P. does not express a consistent political viewpoint, but follows different sources which had different viewpoints. However, in various places 'moderate' views are expressed which are consonant with (but not peculiar to) the views expressed by Aristotle in the *Politics*: for instance, that after Ephialtes' reform the *politeia* became 'more loosened' because of the demagogues, and the Athenians did not adhere to the laws as they had done in the past (26. 1–2); that under Pericles' leadership things were not too bad, but after his death they became much worse as less respectable men became leaders of the *demos* (28. 1). There are a few (but only a few) passages which are very close to the *Politics*: Solon was one of the 'middling citizens', μέσοι πολῖται (5. 3 ~ IV. 1296 A 18–20); Solon did not intend all that was built on his foundations (cf. above); the battle of Salamis led both to a more oligarchic constitution under the control of the Areopagus and to the strengthening of Athens' naval power and the democracy (23–4 ~ V. 1304 A 20–4); both write of the régime of the Thirty without mentioning one of the most notorious oligarchs, Plato's relative Critias (34–40 ~ V. 1305 B 22–7). To that extent *A.P.* gives us an Aristotelian view of Athens' political history, and it is entirely credible that *A.P.* is a product of the Aristotelian school; but the attempt by J. Day and M. Chambers to see in *A.P.* a much closer and more thorough exemplification of Aristotle's theories[17] was forced, and the historical part of *A.P.* seems to me to be influenced much more by the sources used than by Aristotelian theory. Overt expressions of a political opinion, such as that on the intermediate régime of 411/0 (33. 2 ~ Thuc. VIII. 97. 2), while they are opinions of a kind which we might expect to find in Aristotle and his followers, tend to be taken over with approval from a source rather than expressed spontaneously by our author.

17 Day & Chambers, *Aristotle's History of Athenian Democracy*; cf. J. Day, *TAPA* 92 (1961), 52–65.

There has inevitably been much discussion of the sources of the first part of *A.P.* Poems of Solon are quoted in chs 5 and 12, scolia in 19. 3 and 20. 5, a dedication on the acropolis in 7. 4 and documents in 30–1 and 39 (while there is material elsewhere which must ultimately be derived from documents). Herodotus was used on the rise of Pisistratus, the expulsion of Hippias and the conflict between Cleisthenes and Isagoras (14–15, 19, 20. 1–3), and Thucydides on the killing of Hipparchus and the revolutions of 411 (17–18, 29–33); but except on those periods they do not report much that would be useful to a historian of the Athenian constitution. There is much material in *A.P.* which is not likely to have come from any general historians, and two other kinds of writing in particular have been suggested: the *Atthides*, histories of Athens, and especially that of Androtion, written not long before *A.P.*; and partisan political writings of the late fifth and early fourth centuries.

Wilamowitz soon after the publication of *A.P.* argued that the material with an oligarchic bias came from a pamphlet written in 404 by Theramenes, and the factual and democratic material from the *Atthides* and mostly from Androtion.[18] Some scholars have taken up the idea of a pamphlet, if not by Theramenes himself, by a supporter of his, and many have considered Androtion and the other Atthidographers. Jacoby was prepared to allow some use of the other Atthidographers and of writings of other kinds, but considered Androtion to be an exponent of moderate political views and to be overwhelmingly the main source of *A.P.*,[19] and versions of that judgment have been widespread. However, G. Mathieu limited use of the Atthidographers to the most austerely factual and chronological material, and thought that *A.P.* made far more use of a range of partisan writings, not always succeeding in resolving the contradictions between them;[20] while more recently P. Harding has denied that any of the Atthidographers wrote from a distinctive political standpoint.[21]

Partisan writings undoubtedly did exist. Some historians were

18 Wilamowitz, *A.u.A.* i, esp. 161–9.

19 Jacoby, *Atthis*; *FGrH* IIIb. Supp.

20 Mathieu, *Aristote, Constitution d'Athènes*.

21 Harding, *Androtion and the Atthis*, 1–51, preceded by a series of articles.

biased, even if the Atthidographers were less biased than was once supposed: writers such as Stesimbrotus of Thasos and Theopompus of Chios, and (later than *A.P.*) Idomeneus of Lampsacus.[22] Of pamphlets, the *Athenaion Politeia* of the 'Old Oligarch', arguing that democracy is bad in principle but in Athens is appropriate and stable, preserved with the works of Xenophon but almost certainly written in the 420s and not by him, has long been known;[23] and a Heidelberg papyrus seems to be a fragment of a similar work, of similar date.[24] Thucydides and others knew and admired Antiphon's defence of himself under the intermediate régime of 411/0 (Thuc. VIII. 68. 2, Arist. *E.E.* III. 1232 B 6–9, [Plut.] *X Or.* 833 B), and there are some papyrus fragments which, if they do not belong to this speech, belong to a defence of one of the extremists of 411.[25] However, an additional fragment of the 'Theramenes papyrus' has strengthened the view originally put forward that, while its author knew Lys. XII. *Eratosthenes* 68–70 and XIII. *Agoratus* 8–11, the papyrus contains a fragment of a history rather than of a posthumous defence of Theramenes.[26]

Documents are most obviously used in chs 30–1 and 39, and lie behind other parts of 29–39. On the whole it seems likely that the inclusion of this material is not the result of our own author's research in the archives, but will have been found by him in a source which he was using. That is probably true also of the quotations from Solon's poems in 5 and 12, and in 7. 4 the dedication on the acropolis is part of the evidence cited by 'some people', ἔνιοι. Old comedy may have contributed to the lists in 24. 3 and 28. 2–3, but is not likely to have been used directly by our author in compiling his lists. However, it is

---

22 See on Stesimbrotus K. Meister, *Historia* 17 (1978), 274–94; on Theopompus Connor, *Theopompus*.

23 See Marr & Rhodes (eds), *The 'Old Oligarch'*.

24 P. Heid. 182 with M. Gigante, *Maia* 9 (1957), 68–74.

25 Nicole, *L'Apologie d'Antiphon*; against Antiphon see G. Pasquali, *SSAC* 1 (1908), 46–57, P. Roussel, *REA* 27 (1925), 5–10.

26 P. Mich. 5982: *editio princeps* H. C. Youtie & R. Merkelbach *ZPE* 2 (1968), 161–9; defence of Theramenes A. Henrichs, *ZPE* 3 (1968), 101–8 (a possibility), A. Andrewes, *ZPE* 6 (1970), 35–8 (more certainly), J. Engels, *ZPE* 99 (1993), 125–55; additional fragment A. Loftus, *ZPE* 133 (2000), 11–20.

possible that the ancient laws in 8. 3 and 16. 10, and the scolia in 19. 3 and 20. 5, were inserted into the narrative by our author from his own knowledge, and there may be other passages where our author was not reproducing a source, such as the inaccurate passage in 34. 1 which bridges the gap between 410 and 404.

The truth probably lies somewhere between the views of Mathieu and of Jacoby at his most cautious: our author used Herodotus and Thucydides where they provided material which he could use; beyond that he used whatever he could find – including the *Atthides*, and particularly that of Androtion, for dated and factual material; including, I argue, a detailed work on Solon which served as a common source for *A.P.* and for Plutarch's *Solon*;[27] and a variety of less sober sources as well. Not all his sources had the same political viewpoint: 25. 1–2 gives the democratic view of Ephialtes, while Plutarch gave the anti-democratic view; but 26. 1 reads as an anti-democratic apology for failing to prevent the advance of democracy. Often his sources disagreed, and he did not always succeed in resolving the disagreements: on the rise of Pisistratus (14–15) he combines a narrative based on Herodotus, which implies that Pisistratus' first two periods in power were short, with a chronological scheme in which they were not short; in 23. 3–4 Themistocles and Aristides are personal opponents but are on the same side as champions of the people, but in 28. 2 (I believe) while Themistocles is a champion of the people Aristides is on the aristocratic side.

Sometimes, always on what are for his purpose secondary issues, our author indicates that there was a difference of opinion, and in some but not all of these cases he states his own preference: e.g. in 6. 2–4 it is agreed that Solon gave advance notice of the *seisachtheia* to some of his friends, who profited from the knowledge; it is disputed whether Solon himself was guilty or was naïve and innocent; *A.P.* thinks the latter. Sometimes he characterises the different sources (for instance, as 'democratic', 6. 2–3, 18. 5), but only in 14. 4 he names one, Herodotus; in 18. 4 he explicitly rejects a version which we know but he does not say was given by Thucydides. Sometimes there are

27 On this cf. p. 15, below.

disagreements which we know of but to which he does not alert us: most strikingly, between 8. 1–2 and Arist. *Pol.* II. 1273 B 40–1274 A 2 on Solon's rules for the appointment of the nine archons.[28] When our author not only expresses a preference but gives his reason, he tends to say not that he has evidence (though his silence should not be taken as proof that there was no evidence) but that one version is more reasonable: in 6. 2–4 it is not likely that Solon would behave dishonourably in small things when he behaved honourably in great (but here modern scholars tend to think that the whole story is a later invention and neither version can be true). Frustratingly, when he insists that Hippias cannot have detected Hipparchus' murderers by telling the members of the Panathenaic procession to stand aside from their arms, because the armed procession was not instituted until later (18. 4), he does not tell us how he knows that – and we therefore cannot know whether he or Thucydides was right.

He used a variety of sources, but for this first part of his work he did not engage in original research: he relied on earlier writings of historical and other kinds, and where they quoted documents and other forms of evidence he was happy to follow them, but he did not look for further evidence himself. He gave details where he had a detailed source (for instance, on Solon), and did not where he did not have a detailed source (for instance, on Ephialtes). Where he was conscious of a disagreement between his sources, he followed the one which he considered more reasonable, and sometimes he failed to notice or failed to resolve a disagreement. Sometimes his judgments were sensible, for instance that Solon is not likely to have made his laws deliberately ambiguous in order to give discretion to jurors (9. 2); sometimes he judged badly, as when he embarked on an account of the killing of Hipparchus which would make him the Pisistratid who loved Harmodius, but combined that with an account of Pisistratus' sons in which Thessalus was an alternative name of Hegesistratus, and then changed the story to make it that man rather than Hipparchus who loved Harmodius (17. 3–18. 2).The value of this first part of *A.P.* to present-day historians is that it preserves material which would

28 On this cf.p. 4, above, and commentary *ad loc.*

otherwise have been lost, and shows us how a fourth-century writer tried to reconcile conflicting sources and to solve historical problems.

4. The second part of the work[29]

Chs 42–69 are devoted to an account of the constitution in the author's own time. This second part may be analysed as follows; the letters on the left denote the main subject sections into which the commentary in this volume is divided.

L	42	REGISTRATION AND TRAINING OF CITIZENS	
M	43–62	OFFICES, SORTITIVE AND ELECTIVE	
	43. 2–49	The council	
		43. 2–44	*prytaneis*, *epistates*; meetings of council and assembly
		45. 1–3	powers of council: judicial (not *kyria*)
		45. 4	*probouleusis*
		46. 1	navy
		46. 2	public works
		47–8	financial offices
		49	*dokimasiai*
N	50–4	Sortitive annual offices	
		50–1	concerned with city facilities
		52–3	concerned with justice
		54	various
O	55–9	The archons	
		55–56. 1	appointment
		56. 2–7	*archon*
		57	*basileus*
		58	*polemarchos*
		59. 1–6	*thesmothetai*
		59. 7	the whole college
P	60	The *athlothetai* (sortitive, quadrennial)	
Q	61	Elective military offices	
R	62	Concluding note on offices	

29 For a modern account of the constitution in the author's own time see Hansen, *Democracy*, based on a large number of detailed studies.

S	63–9	Jury-courts	
		63–5	allotment of jurors to courts
		66. 1	allotment of magistrates to courts
		66. 2–3	allotment of courtroom officials
		67	timing of trials
		68. 1	size of juries
		68. 2–69. 1	voting
		69. 2	*timesis*; payment of jurors

After beginning this part with the registration and training of young citizens (42), the author subdivides his analysis of the *politeia* by authorities: first sortitive annual offices, beginning with the council and, together with that, financial offices working under the supervision of the council, and continuing with other sortitive annual offices, ending with the nine archons; then the *athlothetai*, treated separately as a sortitive quadrennial office; finally military offices, elective and annual; and the analysis ends with the jury-courts. Similar but not identical frameworks can be found in other fourth-century texts. [Dem.] XXV. *Aristogeiton i.* 20 mentions as the four main manifestations of the state's working the meeting of the council, the assembling of the *demos*, the manning of the jury-courts and the succession of one year's *archai* by the next. Arist. *Pol.* IV, in discussing the best form of constitution, treats first the citizen body (1296 B 13–1297 B 34) and then the 'three parts of all *politeiai*', τρία μόρια τῶν πολιτειῶν πασῶν (1297 B 35–1298 A 9): 'that which deliberates about common matters', τὸ βουλευόμενον περὶ τῶν κοινῶν (1298 A 9–1299 A 2), 'that concerned with the offices', τὸ περὶ τὰς ἀρχάς (1299 A 3–1300 B 12), and 'that which judges', τὸ δικάζον (1300 B 13–1301 A 15) – similar to but not identical with the modern distinction between the legislative, executive and judicial powers.[30] Also, at the end of Arist. *Pol.* VI there is a survey of the kinds of official needed by a *polis* (1321 B 4–1323 A 10), which at some points reflects Athenian practice but is not directly based on Athens.

30 This modern distinction is enshrined in Articles I–III of the constitution of the USA. The Baron de Montesquieu had recommended it and had claimed to detect it in the (unwritten) constitution of England: *De l'Esprit des loix*, livre XI chapitre vi.

A.P.'s second part uses the same kind of categories as Aristotle in the *Politics*, but neither work is in this respect directly dependent on the other. *A.P.* has no separate treatment of the deliberative element, attaching what it does say about this to the council and including that under the offices (so that the *nomothetai* and the fourth-century procedure for enacting laws are omitted altogether); and, although it ends with the jury-courts, that section focuses on the procedures followed during a day in the courts, and many other aspects of justice are treated in connection with the various offices. If we allow for those features, *A.P.*'s analysis is systematic and coherent, though the placing of the nine archons after the other sortitive annual offices and before the concluding chapters on offices is less than ideal.

In theory our author could have obtained his information from a study of the laws of Athens, or from observation of current practice (he could have participated in current practice if he was an Athenian citizen aged eighteen or over, but could not if he was not), or from earlier analyses of the constitution. However, there is no evidence that any earlier analyses existed (the *Athenaion Politeia* of the 'Old Oligarch' was a very different kind of work[31]), whereas the existence of an organised code of laws revised at the end of the fifth century (cf. on 35. 2) will have made direct study of the laws concerning the constitution in the fourth century a fairly easy task. There are indeed some indications that the organisation of that code of laws may have provided the pattern for *A.P.*'s chapters on the offices: *IG* i^3 105 seems to have contained a collection, made in the early stages of that process of revision, of the laws concerning the council. A supposed law providing for the annual review of the new code divides the laws of Athens into four categories: 'those of the council, those which are common [i.e. common to all offices?], those established for the nine archons, those of the other offices', τῶν βουλευτικῶν, τῶν κοινῶν, οἳ κεῖνται τοῖς ἐννέα ἄρχουσιν, τῶν ἄλλων ἀρχῶν;[32] and various texts

31 Cf. p. 13, above.

32 Document *ap.* Dem. XXIV. *Timocrates* 20. The authenticity of this and other documents may be challenged (see particularly Canevaro, *The Documents in the Attic Orators*, rejecting this document at pp. 94–102), but even if they are later inventions their inventors may have worked on the basis of some authentic

mention laws in more restricted sub-categories, such as the law of the *basileus* (Ath. VI. 235 c) and the law about *eisangelia* (Hyp. IV. *Euxenippus* 3). If the 'common' laws were of a kind which need not be included in an analysis of the *politeia*, the other three categories correspond to the three main categories of *A.P.* 43–62 (but suggest that 55–9, on the nine archons, would be better placed before 50–4), and may help to explain why the assembly and the offices supervised by the council are treated together with the council in 43. 2–49. This may also explain other features, such as the omission of the *nomothetai*, and of the important financial office held by Lycurgus and his friends at the time when the work was written,[33] and the appearance of the council of the Areopagus only in a few casual mentions.

Some topics are treated at unexpected length. Most striking is the detailed account of the organisation of the jury-courts in 63–9: by the author's time the Athenians had developed an extremely elaborate system of judicial allotments, using the latest technology and designed to ensure that nobody could predict which jurors would sit together under which magistrate to try which case, and we may guess that the Athenians were proud of this system and the author was fascinated by it, and that that is the reason for his giving so much detail. Another perhaps surprisingly detailed section is that devoted to the *epheboi* in 42. 2–5, and here the reason for the detail may be that the ephebic system had been reorganised *c.* 335/4, immediately before this work was written (if the author was an Athenian, he may himself have been one of the first men to serve under the new system).

In *A.P.* 56. 7 we have a summary of the law quoted in Dem. XLIII. *Macartatus* 75, transposed into the indicative mood,[34] and similarly 57. 3 summarises the extracts from the homicide law which are quoted in Dem. XXIII. *Aristocrates* 22 with 24, 53, 57. In general *A.P.*'s language in this second part does not prescribe what should be done but states what is done, but often such expressions as 'the law/s prescribe/s', ὁ

knowledge.

33 For this cf. on 43. 1.

34 Cf. Wilamowitz, *A.u.A.* i. 256–9. Wilamowitz created a complication – shown by Jacoby, *Atthis*, to be unfounded – by supposing that there was an earlier analysis in a lost *Atthis* of *c.* 380 and that our author was following that.

νόμος κελεύει / οἱ νόμοι κελεύουσιν, are inserted (e.g. 49. 4 singular, 43. 6 plural), and there is also frequent use of such expressions as 'must', δεῖ, and 'is not permitted', οὐκ ἔξεστιν (e.g. 44. 3, 44. 1). There are notes on differences between past practice and current practice, which might be derived either from the original law and an amending law or from the author's general knowledge (e.g. 45. 3): most of these read as integral parts of the text, but 54. 7, which gives the date 329/8 and probably drives from its author's direct knowledge of the change, must be one of the items inserted when the text was revised.[35] Occasionally, by contrast, we find expressions of a kind which are not likely to be derived from a law, such as 'this man is called the inserter', οὗτος δὲ καλεῖται ἐμ[πήκτ]ης (64. 2). Mostly, however, we may assume that the author has done what he demonstrably did in 56. 7 and 57. 3, and has given a summary, transposed into indicative statements of what is done, of the laws concerning the *politeia*.

In this second part the author keeps strictly to his task of describing the *politeia* as it worked in his own time. There is only one anecdote (45. 1); outside that, no men are named except Solon (47. 1), Harmodius and Aristogeiton (58. 1), and Cephisophon, the archon of 329/8 (in the insertion in 54. 7). Argument is rarer than in the first part, but there are instances at 47. 4 and 54. 3; there are two cross references to the first part (47. 1, 54. 3); 3. 3 and 57. 1 disagree on the distribution of festivals among the archons, and 57. 1 is more likely to be correct; on the circumstances in which an archon may be required to dedicate a statue 55. 5 is more specific than 7. 1 and is probably correct. There is no comment on the merits and defects of the system described, and no comparison between Athens and other states.

While the first part of *A.P.* was based on historians and other literary sources, this second part is based on direct research in the laws, probably combined with some direct observation of current practice. As far as we know, nobody had attempted this before, either for Athens or for any other state (and we should much like to know if there was a similar analysis in some or all of the other Aristotelian *politeiai*). It is thus of very great importance both for its factual content,

35 On this cf. p. 29, below.

the correctness of which we have no reason to doubt (though there are omissions: for instance, apart from the silence on the *nomothetai* and on the financial office held by Lycurgus, mentioned above, 54. 3–5 lists three public secretaries when contemporary inscriptions mention six), and as evidence that this new kind of investigation was one of the many kinds of investigation undertaken in Aristotle's school.

5. Language and style

A.P. is utterly different from the other surviving works of the Aristotelian corpus. It is not a speculative work, in which the author addresses a series of *aporiai* (and the distinctive vocabulary of such a work is conspicuously absent), and it is not like the biological works, which generalise from a large number of observed instances (though the end of the *Nicomachean Ethics*, cited on pp. 1–2, suggests that this and the other *politeiai* provided the body of observed instances from which the *Politics* would generalise[36]). The history of the *politeia* in the first part uses earlier writings, not in order to criticise them or give the author's own views, as is done elsewhere in the corpus, but as sources in order to extract from them a coherent narrative. The analysis of the current *politeia* in the second part is not a generalisation from many instances but an account of one instance, based on the laws which regulated its working and observation of its working. In view of its objectives, it is not surprising that the general manner of this work is much more straightforward than that of the rest of the corpus, and in view of its dependence on sources it is not surprising that its language shows the influence of those sources.

When we can compare *A.P.* with its sources (e.g. in the first part 14–15 and 19–20. 3 with Herodotus, in the second part 56. 7 and 57. 3 with the laws), we can see that it follows them closely, and this fact explains some features of the vocabulary. For instance, in the first part, 'when his rule had not yet taken root', οὔπω δὲ τῆς ἀρχῆς ἐρριζωμένης (14. 3), repeats ἐρριζωμένην from Hdt. I. 60. 1, and 'Cleisthenes, since he was getting the worse of the struggle for supporters, tried

36 But on this see pp. 2–3, above.

to win over the *demos* to his side', ἡττώμνος δὲ ταῖς ἑταιρείαις … προσηγάγετο τὸν δῆμον (20. 1) is a refashioning of ἑσσούμενος … τὸν δῆμον προσεταιρίζεται in Hdt. V. 66. 2. In the second part, 56. 7 follows the law (as quoted in Dem. XLIII. *Macartatus* 75) in using such terms as 'take care', ἐπιμελεῖσθαι, 'orphans', ὀρφανοί, 'heiresses', ἐπίκληροι, 'impose a summary penalty', ἐπιβάλλειν, but substitutes the commoner fourth-century terms σκήπτεσθαι ('claim') for φάσκειν ('assert') and δικαστήριον for ἡλιαία ('lawcourt'). 61. 1 does not use what came to be the standard terminology for the regular postings of particular generals, but it is possible that its language is the language used in the laws instituting those postings and what came to be the standard terminology differed from that.

Because of the subject matter and the dependence on sources, it is not surprising that *A.P.* uses many words which are not found elsewhere in the Aristotelian corpus or in other fourth-century prose. It is more surprising that, apart from constitutional technicalities such as προεδρικός, 'against *proedroi*' (59. 2) and quantitative terms such as ἑπτάχους, 'of seven *choes*' (67. 2), there are many words and usages in *A.P.* which are found elsewhere not at all or only much later: e.g. παραστρατηγεῖν, 'outgeneral', already metaphorical (6. 2); δεσποτικωτέρως, 'in a more despotic way' (24. 2); οὐκ οἷον … ἀλλὰ καὶ as a way of expressing 'not only … but also' (40. 3). There are some expressions which are distinctly Aristotelian, such as τάξις τῆς πολιτείας, 'structure of the constitution' (3. 1, 5. 1, cf. 41. 2); ἀμφισβήτησις, 'dispute' (9. 2, 28. 5, cf. 3. 4, 5. 2, 35. 2); μήτε … ἀλλὰ as a way of expressing 'not … but' (16. 3); but apart from distinctively philosophical terms many more ordinary terms which were favourites of Aristotle are absent from *A.P.*, such as εὐλαβεῖσθαι for 'take care' and ἐφίεσθαι and ὀρέγεσθαι for 'reach out for'. There are also some expressions in *A.P.* which are characteristic of Isocrates, and which may be derived from him either directly or through an intermediary, such as κολάζουσα … τοὺς ἀκοσμοῦντας, 'chastise … the disorderly' (3. 6); βλασφημεῖν, 'slander' (6. 2).

Even before computers made such investigations easy, early commentators studied *A.P.*'s use of particles and conjunctions. In general, particles are used far more sparingly than in the rest of the Aristotelian corpus (though the use of particular particles is not consistent within the corpus): for instance, ἄρα, γε and γοῦν, κἂν εἰ, τε γάρ, τοίνυν and τοίγαρ are not found at all, and μήν only in οὐ μὴν ἀλλά; but there is one instance of δή after a superlative (40. 3), which is not found elsewhere in the corpus. But this feature too may be explained as a consequence of the nature of the work and its dependence on sources, and stylometric exercises will not help us to decide whether Aristotle himself was the author of *A.P.*

Our author aimed not merely to set out the facts in a straightforward way but to write readable Greek. Where he could easily do so, he avoided hiatus, though not as determinedly as Isocrates; but hiatus does occur in passages in the first part which are derived from a documentary original, and increasingly as we proceed through the second part.

There are signs of a liking for balanced elements within a sentence. The most striking instance is in 38. 4 (which may be derived from a source early enough to have been written under the influence of Gorgias):

a^1 οἱ δὲ περὶ τὸν ῾Ρίνωνα
b^1 διά τε τὴν εὔνοιαν τὴν εἰς τὸν δῆμον ἐπῃνέθησαν,
c^1 καὶ λαβόντες τὴν ἐπιμέλειαν ἐν ὀλιγαρχίᾳ
c^2 τὰς εὐθύνας ἔδοσαν ἐν δημοκρατίᾳ,
b^2 καὶ οὐδεὶς οὐδὲν ἐνεκάλεσεν αὐτοῖς
d^1 οὔτε τῶν ἐν ἄστει μεινάντων
d^2 οὔτε τῶν ἐκ Πειραιέως κατελθόντων,
a^2 ἀλλὰ διὰ ταῦτα καὶ στρατηγὸς εὐθὺς ᾑρέθη ῾Ρίνων.

a^1 Rhinon and his colleagues
b^1 were praised for their good will towards the *demos*:
c^1 they received their charge under the oligarchy
c^2 but submitted their *euthynai* under the democracy,
b^2 and nobody made any complaint against them
d^1 either of those who had stayed in the city
d^2 or by those who had been reinstated from Piraeus;
a^2 but because of this Rhinon was immediately elected general.

There is a balanced sentence in 6. 1 in which the balance is interrupted and the sense is disturbed by the words καὶ νόμους ἔθηκε, 'and he enacted laws'. Kaibel & Wilamowitz deleted the words,[37] but I think it more likely that the words were inserted here by our author in a clumsy attempt to foreshadow the non-economic reforms which are to follow in 7–8. Often he began a sentence with a balanced structure but failed to maintain it: for instance, in 5. 3 the sentence beginning ἦν δ' ὁ Σόλων, 'Solon was', begins with balanced clauses but has nothing to balance the final element, παραινῶν τοῖς πλουσίοις μὴ πλεονεκτεῖν, 'when he urges the rich not to be greedy'.

In some passages metrical patterns have been detected, which may sometimes have been intended by the author:[38] for instance (55. 4):

	ἐπειδὰν	
a^1	δὲ παράσχηται τοὺς μάρτυρας,	⏑ ⏑ – – – – – – ⏑ ⏓
a^2	ἐπερωτᾷ "τούτου βούλεταί	⏑ ⏑ – – – – – – ⏑ ⏓
b^1	τις κατηγορεῖν;" κἂν μὲν ᾖ	– ⏑ – ⏑ – – ⏑ –
b^2	τις κατήγορος, δοὺς κατη-	– ⏑ – ⏑ – – ⏑ –
	γορίαν.	

There are some instances of verse rhythm, which we may assume the author did not intend: the iambic trimeters λαβὼν δὲ τοὺς κορυνηφόρους καλουμένους (14. 1) and εἰ μή τι παρεωρᾶτο τῶν ἐν τοῖς νόμοις (26. 2), or the dactylic hexameter οὓς πρότερον μὲν ὁ δῆμος ἐχειροτόνει δέκα ὄντας (56. 4).

In the choice and arrangement of words it would be easy to produce a very high degree of monotony, particularly in the annalistic passages, the summaries in 28. 2–3 and 41. 2, and the lists of offices in 47–8 and 50–4. Our author has done a little to mitigate this: for instance, what is said of the appointment of the treasurers of Athena in 47. 1 is matched almost exactly by what is said of the *poletai* in 47. 2, but the formulation is then varied for the *apodektai* (48. 1), the *logistai* (48. 3) and the *euthynoi* (48. 4). In the first part attempts to avoid monotony

37 Cf. Kaibel, *Stil und Text*, 81–2, 134 (discussion of balance within sentences 81–6).

38 Cf. Kaibel, *Stil und Text*, 87–95.

have sometimes led to ambiguity. In the list of democratic and upper-class *prostatai* in 28. 2, Xanthippus and Miltiades are assigned one to each category, and so are Ephialtes and Cimon, with the democratic *prostates* named first in each case, but between them we have the bald ἔπειτα Θεμιστοκλῆς καὶ Ἀριστείδης, 'then Themistocles and Aristides'. In context the natural interpretation, and I believe the correct interpretation, would be that Themistocles was the democratic and Aristides the upper-class *prostates* – but in 23. 3 both men are said to be *prostatai* of the *demos*, and many scholars have assumed that our author could not have contradicted himself over so short a space and have assumed that what is stated in 23. 3 must be what is meant in 28. 2. I think it more likely that the two passages are derived from different sources and our author failed to notice the contradiction. However, as Kaibel remarked, he could have done much more to avoid monotony if he had set a high priority on doing so: for instance, in 7. 1–2 νόμοι, 'laws', appears three times in the accusative and once in the genitive in four consecutive sentences, although the meaning could easily have been expressed without such repetition.[39]

The most obvious style for presenting a historical narrative is a sequential style, such as we find in 22: in one year A happened; in a second year B, and also C; in a third year D. The summary in 41. 2 shows that our author thought of his first part as a review of a series of changes, some of them advances and others setbacks, by which the constitution had arrived at its final form; and the underlying pattern of the first part is sequential. On the other hand, an account of how the constitution now works calls for an analytic style, which does not simply list one law after another, but divides and subdivides to produce a coherent arrangement. This is what has been done in the second part, and to a limited extent the principal divisions and subdivisions are marked by the device of ring composition, as used frequently by Herodotus, where an expression opening a section is echoed by an expression closing it.[40] For instance, the section on the council begins

39 Cf. Kaibel, *Stil und Text*, 50–1.

40 On ring composition in *A.P.* cf. J. J. Keaney, *AJP* 90 (1969), 406–23; *Composition*, 72–89.

βουλὴ δὲ…, 'The council…' (43. 2), and ends τὰ μὲν οὖν ὑπὸ τῆς βουλῆς διοικούμενα ταῦτ' ἐστίν, 'That, then, is the administration done by the council' (50. 1), while in the last three chapters of that section there is a subsidiary ring beginning συνδιοικεῖ δὲ καὶ ταῖς ἄλλαις ἀρχαῖς τὰ πλεῖστα, 'It also joins in administration with the other officials for the most part' (47. 1), and ending συνδιοικεῖ δὲ καὶ ταῖς ἄλλαις ἀρχαῖς τὰ πλεῖσθ', ὡς ἔπος εἰπεῖν, 'It also joins in administration with the other officials for the most part, so to say' (49. 5). In the first part there is less use of this style, but it is not wholly absent. An elaborate ring with subsidiary rings inside it begins at συνέβη στασιάσαι τούς τε γνωρίμους καὶ τὸ πλῆθος πολὺν χρόνον, 'there occurred dissension between the notables and the masses for a long time' (2. 1), and ends at ἀντέστη τοῖς γνωρίμοις ὁ δῆμος. ἰσχυρᾶς δὲ τῆς στάσεως οὔσης καὶ πολὺν χρόνον ἀντικαθημένων ἀλλήλοις, 'the *demos* rose up against the notables. Since the dissension was powerful and they were opposed to each other for a long time' (5. 1–2). Keaney from his analysis of ch. 2 argued that the economic background was enclosed within and thus shown to be less important than the political background, but one could as well argue from his analysis of 2. 1–5. 1 that the political background was enclosed within and thus shown to be less important than the economic background, and I suspect that neither conclusion would be justified. Rather, *A.P.* announces that there were two causes of dissatisfaction, one political and one economic, and then proceeds *hysteron proteron* to deal first with the economic and afterwards with the political.

A.P. uses ring composition but does not do so systematically, and if we set out all the principal and subsidiary rings which can be detected we are probably being more self-conscious about it than our author was. But, if he did not often deliberately construct elaborate ring schemes, he was like many Greek writers a man to whom it came naturally to present complex material in this way; and appreciating that can help us to understand, for instance, the placing of the Alcmaeonids at the end of 20, which to a reader who thinks sequentially seems illogical but which closes a ring opened at the beginning of that chapter.

However, in contrast to the signs that our author took some care over the composition of his work, there are many passages which are awkward in language, logic or both. In 6. 1 καὶ νόμους ἔθηκε, 'and he enacted laws', interrupts both the sense and the balance of the sentence (cf. above); 10 interrupts what is otherwise a well-organised account of Solon; 22. 1 arouses the expectation that the law of ostracism will be discussed, but §2 deals with the council's oath and the election of generals, and we return to ostracism only in §3. 22. 4–6 reports the ostracisms of Hipparchus and Megacles, and then says that 'friends of the tyrants' were ostracised for three years but does not name the third victim; and, in the second part, 57. 3–4 distinguishes between the different kinds of homicide trial, and in each case except the last specifies the court (in that last case we know from other evidence that the court was the *prytaneion*). In both of those passages some scholars have suspected a lacuna in the text, but more probably there is a lacuna in our author's composition, and he failed to give information which he should have given and could have given. In 43. 6 the author frustratingly mentions *procheirotonia* only to say that sometimes it is not used; and in 63–9 the complicated material on the organisation of the jury-courts is not set out in the best order for the reader's understanding, but the author has to turn aside to explain something not explained earlier, presumably because he had not thought carefully enough about what would be the best order.

In 24. 2–3 there are several oddities of grammar and sense: editors have tried to correct these, and in some cases may be right to do so (it is at least likely that the repeated εἰς ἑπτακοσίους, 'seven hundred', is due to a copyist), but probably much that is unsatisfactory here is due to our author's failing to condense successfully what was provided in greater detail by his source. It is certainly our author who is at fault in 17. 3–18. 2, through failing to reconcile conflicting sources, when what seems to be the beginning of the story in which Hipparchus loved Harmodius becomes instead a story in which Thessalus loved Harmodius (cf. above). Copyists do sometimes make nonsense of sensible texts, but too much of *A.P.* shows failings of this kind for us to blame all the failings on copyists and reconstruct a pure *A.P.* which has suffered badly in transmission.

A.P. is thus a very uneven work. There are passages where the sequence of thought has been carefully worked out, where there are guiding phrases to help readers to follow the sequence, and where attention has been given to such matters as variation and balance in expression, and perhaps even rhythm; but there are also passages where monotony has not been avoided, passages which are inconsistent with one another, passages where the meaning is obscure and a few passages which are grammatically incoherent. Some scholars supposed that *A.P.* is an unfinished work, perhaps left unfinished by Aristotle and published after his death by a friend or pupil,[41] but it is better simply to accept that what we have is what the author wrote, and that the carelessness and the care are both part of his own work. For this reason, I suspect that the elaborate study by Keaney of the language and structure of *A.P.*, by assuming that the work has been carefully composed throughout, has sometimes indeed uncovered what the author was intentionally doing but at other times has imagined an intended effect where none was intended.[42]

6. The date of **A.P.***; insertions and revisions*

In the first part of *A.P.* there is no allusion to anything later than the increase in assembly pay to 3 obols, which occurred earlier than Aristophanes' *Ecclesiazusae* of the late 390s (41. 3: see *ad loc.*). Although I do not accept the view of Keaney that the material in the second part is selected and presented in order to support the conclusion drawn at the end of the first part,[43] I see no reason to suppose that the two parts were composed at significantly different times.[44]

41 For this suggestion see Kaibel, *Stil und Text*, 27, cf. 21–2.

42 Keaney, *Composition.*

43 Keaney, *HSCP* 67 (1963), 121–2, 136; *AJP* 90 (1969), 412; *Composition*, 43–9.

44 Zürcher, *Aristoteles' Werk und Geist*, 257–8, accepted the evidence for a late date for the second part, but regarded the first part as a youthful work of Aristotle. D. Whitehead, in Piérart (ed.), *Aristote et Athènes*, 25–38, suggested that the two parts are so different that they might have been written by different men, but I think the differences in subject-matter and sources are enough to explain the differences.

In the second part, 42. 2–5 describes the *ephebeia* as refashioned *c.* 335/4, and 53. 4 mentions a change probably linked to that; 54. 4 mentions the secretary 'in charge of the laws', ἐπὶ τοὺς νόμους, who is not included in a list of secretaries in 335/4 (*Agora* xv 43. 227–31) or any earlier list; the specific postings for *strategoi* in 61. 1 include one 'in charge of the *symmoriai*', ἐπὶ τὰς συμμορίας, and two for the Piraeus, whereas there was none in charge of the *symmoriai* in 334/3 (*IG* ii^2 1623. 147–59) and only one for the Piraeus in 333/2 (Reinmuth 9. ii. 9–10). None of those passages looks like a revision of the original text, so the original text should have been completed after 333/2. The text describes in the present tense the working of the constitution which was superseded at the beginning of 321/0, and refers in 62. 2 to Samos, which Athens lost at the end of 322 (Diod. Sic. XVIII. 18. 9), so the text should have been completed before then.

There are some passages which point to a date in the 320s, but each of these seems to be an insertion made in order to revise the original text. 46. 1 begins and ends with triremes but awkwardly at one point mentions quadriremes (but not quinqueremes): the earliest surviving navy list which mentions quadriremes is that of 330/29 (*IG* ii^2 1627. 275–8), while quinqueremes are still not mentioned in 326/5 but are mentioned in 325/4 (1628. 495–7, 1629. 808–12). 54. 7 gives a list of quadrennial festivals, stating at the end that another 'has been added also', [νῦ]ṿ δὲ πρόσκειται, in the year 329/8. 51. 3 contrasts the number of *sitophylakes* in the past with the number 'now', νῦν, the increase is likely to have been made during the grain shortages of the 330s–320s, and Harp. σ 19 Keaney σιτοφύλακες cites *A.P.* and gives only the earlier number, so there may be another revision here. 61. 7 gives the names of the sacred triremes as Paralus and Ammonos, but that passage does not in itself appear to have been revised, the latest reference to the Salaminia is in 373 (Xen. *Hell.* VI. 2. 14), and the change of name need not be as late as the reign of Alexander.[45] The best conclusion is that the original text of *A.P.* was completed in the late 330s, and the version which we have results from a revision in the

45 W. Bubelis, *Historia* 59 (2010), 385–411, argues from an inscription of that year, *SEG* xxi 241, for 363/2.

first half of the 320s (whcther by the original author or by somebody else, we cannot say).

There are signs of revision in the first part also. It is widely agreed that the 'constitution of Draco', from 4. 1 ('The structure...', ἡ δὲ τάξις αὕτη...) to the end of 4. 4 (with 4. 5 written to ease the insertion by recalling ch. 2) both is a later invention and was absent from the text of *A.P.* which was generally known in antiquity (although *A.P.* was widely used by other writers, no other writer shows knowledge of this 'constitution'). There are also awkward passages elsewhere in which it seems that the original text has been modified to accommodate this 'constitution': there is a reference to 'The structure of the ancient constitution before Draco', ἡ τάξις τῆς ἀρχαίας πολιτείας τῆς πρὸ Δράκοντος (3. 1); in the numbered list of constitutional changes in 41. 2, the first is that of Ion, that of Theseus is 'The second, and first after that', δευτέρα δέ, καὶ πρώτη μετὰ ταύτην, then that of Draco is unnumbered, and the list continues with Solon's change as the third; and, since the property classes appear in the 'constitution of Draco' (4. 3), some have suspected another modification in the statement that Solon divided the citizen body into four classes, 'as they had already been divided before', καθάπερ διῄρητο καὶ πρότερον (7. 3). Another probable insertion is the story of Themistocles and Ephialtes in 25. 3–4, which appears elsewhere only in the *hypothesis* to Isoc. VII. *Areopagitic* (which cites *A.P.*) and seems chronologically impossible, and where the last sentence of the chapter, about the assassination of Ephialtes, fits awkwardly with what precedes. Other insertions have been suspected in the first part, such as ch. 10, which interrupts the structure of the section on Solon, but here I suspect that we are dealing not with a later insertion into the original text but with the awkward incorporation of material from a different source at the time when the text was originally written (cf. above).

The text preserved in the London papyrus has thus had revisions made in both parts, but, whereas in the second part there is no need to doubt the factual accuracy of the revisions, in the first part the reviser was unfortunate, since he seems in both cases to have been deceived into adding false material. The absence of references to the added material in later literature suggests that he version of *A.P.* which was generally current in antiquity was the original version, not the revised version preserved for us.

7. This Edition

As in Kenyon[5] (his Oxford Classical Text), in order to produce a more readable text, I have not used brackets for editorial supplements or dots under letters which are not wholly clear in cases where there is no doubt what the correct text should be.

In the *apparatus*, a report such as 'τ̣α[ῦ]τ' Herwerden & Leeuwen, Wilcken, Kenyon[4], West, Chambers' indicates that all those named read the same word, but not necessarily that they all apply brackets and dots to it in the same way. I have tried to attribute all supplements and emendations to their authors, but particularly in the case of foreign periodicals I have not thought it necessary for the purposes of this edition to indicate where each suggestion was published (references can be found regularly in my 1981 *Commentary*, and in some cases in the commentary in this edition). I cite the two papyri (on which see above, pp. 6–7) as

B Berlin P. 5009.
L P. Lond. 131.

The editors whom I cite most often (on whom see the Bibliography, pp. 33–7) are

Gentili & Prato: *Poetarum Elegiacorum Testimonia et Fragmenta*, i.

Herwerden (& Leeuwen), (Herwerden &) Leeuwen: suggestion attributed to one or to the other in the edition of Herwerden & Leeuwen.

Hommel: *Heliaia*.

Kenyon[4]: Kenyon's Berlin edition (1903).

Kenyon[5]: Kenyon's Oxford Classical Text (1920).

Thomas: J. D. Thomas, quoted in Rhodes, *Comm. Ath. Pol.*.

West: *Iambi et Elegi Graeci*, ii.

Wilcken: U. Wilcken, quoted in Kaibel & Wilamowitz[3].

CR: without further specification indicates a suggestion published for the first time or republished in *CR* 5 (1891).

In the translation I have been more punctilious than in my Penguin Classics translation (but I hope not so much so as to make the result unreadable): I use figures rather than spell out a number where the papyrus does likewise; I commonly give a transliteration of technical terms in the translation and an explanation in the commentary; although I regard it as most important to convey the meaning accurately, where consistently with that I can use the same English word for the same Greek word and a different English word for a different Greek word I do so.

BIBLIOGRAPHY

Some standard modern works are abbreviated as in the fourth edition of the *Oxford Classical Dictionary* (e.g. *C.A.H.*).

In the Bibliography which follows, abbreviations by which certain works are cited are given in square brackets at the end of an entry

1. Select list of editions of and commentaries on A.P. *(in chronological order).*

Kenyon, F. G. English introduction; text; *apparatus* (3rd edn only); commentary; *testimonia* (London: British Museum, 30 January 1891; ^{2}1891; ^{3}1892).

Scott, E. J. L. Facsimile of London papyrus (London: British Museum, 1 March 1891; ^{2}1891).

Kaibel, G., & von Wilamowitz-Moellendorff, U. Latin introduction; text; *apparatus*; *testimonia* (3rd edn only) (Berlin: Weidmann, July 1891; ^{2}1891; reporting readings of U. Wilcken, ^{3}1898).

van Herwerden, H., & van Leeuwen, J. Latin introduction; line-by-line transcription; text; *apparatus*; full indexes (Leiden: Sijthoff, 1891 [preface August]).

Blass, F. W. Latin introduction; text; *testimonia*; *apparatus.* Bibl. Teubneriana (Leipzig: Teubner, 1892; ^{2}1895; ^{3}1898; ^{4}1903; reprinted with *addenda nova* after publication of Kenyon's Berlin edn).

Hude, K. K. T. Danish introduction; text; commentary (1–41 only) (Copenhagen: Klein, 1892); German introduction; text; commentary (1st edn 1–41 only) (Leipzig: Teubner, 1892; ^{2}1916).

Thalheim, T. Latin introduction; text; *testimonia*; *apparatus*. Bibl. Teubneriana (Leipzig: Teubner, 1909; ^{2}1914).

Sandys, J. E. English introduction; text; *apparatus*; *testimonia*; commentary; full indexes (London: Macmillan, 1893; ^{2}1912).

Kenyon, F. G. Latin introduction; text; *apparatus*; *testimonia* (by Kenyon

& Wentzel, G.); full indexes (by Neustadt, E.). Supplementum Aristotelicum III. ii. (Berlin: Reimer, 1903) [Kenyon[4]].

Kenyon, F. G. Latin introduction; text; *apparatus*. O.C.T. (Oxford U. P., 1920) [Kenyon[5]].

Mathieu, G., & Haussoullier, B. French introduction; translation; notes; text; *apparatus*. Coll. Budé (Paris: Les Belles Lettres, 1922); minimal revision, with introduction and notes by C. Mossé, Classiques en Poche (Paris: Les Belles Lettres, 1996).

Oppermann, H. Latin introduction; text; *testimonia*; *apparatus*; full indexes. Bibl. Teubneriana. (Leipzig: Teubner, 1928; reprinted with *addenda* to bibliography Stuttgart: Teubner, 1961, 1968).

von Fritz, K., & Kapp, E. English introduction; translation; notes; selection of other texts. Hafner Library of Classics (New York, 1950).

Rhodes, P. J. *A Commentary on the Aristotelian Athenaion Politeia*: English introduction; commentary (Oxford U. P., 1981; reprinted with *addenda* 1993) [*Comm. Ath. Pol.*].

Chambers, M. Latin introduction; text; *testimonia*; *apparatus*; full indexes. Bibl. Teubneriana (Leipzig: Teubner, 1986; Stuttgart: Teubner, [2]1994).

Chambers, M.: German translation; commentary. Aristoteles' Werke in deutscher Übersetzung x. i (Berlin: Akademie-Verlag, 1990).

2. Other books

I list here all other books cited in the Introduction, and books cited frequently in the commentary

Badian, E. *Transitions to Empire ... E. Badian* (U. of Oklahoma P., 1996).

Beloch, K. J. *Griechische Geschichte* (Strassburg: Trübner / Berlin & Leipzig: de Gruyter, [2]1912–27) [*G.G.*[2]].

Brenne, S. *Ostrakismos und Prominenz in Athen* (*Tyche* Supp. iii 2001) [*Ostrakismos*].

Bugh, G. R. *The Horsemen of Athens* (Princeton U. P., 1988) [*Horsemen*].

Busolt, G. *Griechische Geschichte* (Gotha: Perthes, 1893–1904) [*G.G.*].

Camp, J. McK., II, *The Athenian Agora: Site Guide* (Princeton: Am. Sch. Class. Stud. Ath., [5]2010) [*Site Guide*].

Canevaro, M. *The Documents in the Attic Orators* (Oxford U. P., 2013).

Cloché, P. *La Restauration démocratique à Athènes en 403 avant J.-C.* (Paris: Leroux, 1915) [*Restauration*].

Connor, W. R. *Theopompus and Fifth-Century Athens* (Harvard U. P. for Center for Hellenic Studies, 1968) [*Theopompus*].

Davies, J. K. *Athenian Propertied Families, 600–300 BC* (Oxford U. P., 1971) [*A.P.F.*].

Day, J., & Chambers, M. *Aristotle's History of Athenian Democracy* (U. of California P., 1962).

Deubner, L., rev. Doer, B. *Attische Feste* (Hildesheim: Olms, ^{2}1966) [*Attische Feste*].

Dilts, M. R. *Heraclidis Lembi Excerpta Politiarum*. (*GRBMon.* v 1971).

Gentili, B., & Prato, C. *Poetarum Elegiacorum Testimonia et Fragmenta*, i. Bibl. Teubneriana (Leipzig: Teubner, 1979) [Gentili & Prato].

Hammond, N. G. L. *Studies in Greek History* (Oxford U. P., 1973) [*Studies*].

Hansen, M. H. *Eisangelia: The Sovereignty of the People's Court in Athens in the Fourth Century BC and the Impeachment of Generals and Politicians* (Odense U. P., 1975) [*Eisangelia*].

— *The Athenian Democracy in the Age of Demosthenes* (London: Duckworth, ^{2}1999) [*Democracy*].

Harding, P. *Androtion and the Atthis* (Oxford, 1994).

Harrison, A. R. W. *The Law of Athens* (Oxford, 1968–71) [*L.A.*]

Hignett, C. *A History of the Athenian Constitution to the End of the Fifth Century BC* (Oxford U. P., 1952) [*Constitution*].

Hommel, H. *Heliaia: Untersuchungen zur Verfassung und Prozessordnung des athenischen Volksgerichts, insbesondere zum Schlussteil der Ἀθηναίων Πολιτεία des Aristoteles* (*Philologus* Supp. XIX. ii 1927). [*Heliaia*].

Jacoby, F. *Atthis*, Oxford, 1949

— *FGrH* IIIb. Supp. (Leiden: Brill, 1954).

Jaeger, W. W. *Aristoteles: Grundlegung einer Geschichte seiner Entwicklung* (Berlin: Weidmann, 1923); translated by Robinson, R., as *Aristotle: Fundamentals of the History of His Development* (Oxford U. P., ^{2}1948).

Kaibel, G. *Stil und Text der Πολιτεία Ἀθηναίων des Aristoteles* (Berlin: Weidmann, 1893) [*Stil und Text*].

Keaney, J. J. *The Composition of Aristotle's Athenaion Politeia: Observation and Explanation* (New York: Oxford U. P., 1992) [*Composition*].

Krentz, P. *The Thirty at Athens* (Cornell U. P., 1982) [*Thirty*].

Lewis, D. M. *Selected Papers on Greek and Near Eastern History* (Cambridge U. P., 1997) [*Selected Papers*].

Lipsius, J. H. *Das attische Recht und Rechtsverfahren* (Leipzig: Reisland, 1905–15) [*A.R.*].

MacDowell, D. M. *Athenian Homicide Law in the Age of the Orators* (Manchester U. P., 1963) [*Homicide*].

— *The Law in Classical Athens* (London: Thames & Hudson, 1978) [*Law*].

Marr, J. L., & Rhodes, P. J. (eds), *The 'Old Oligarch': The Constitution of the Athenians Attributed to Xenophon* (Oxford: Oxbow, 2008).

Mathieu, G. *Aristote, Constitution d'Athènes: essai sur la méthode suivi par Aristote dans la discussion des textes* (Paris: Champion, 1915).

Milne, H. J. M. *Catalogue of the Literary Papyri in the British Museum (P. Lit. Lond.)* (London: British Museum, 1927).

Nicole, J. *L'Apologie d'Antiphon* (Geneva & Basle: Georg, 1907).

Osborne, M. J. *Naturalization in Athens* (Brussels: Royal Academy, 1981–3) [*Naturalization*].

Parker, R. *Polytheism and Society at Athens* (Oxford U. P., 2005) [*Polytheism*].

Piérart, M. (ed.), *Aristote et Athènes / Aristoteles and Athens* (Paris: De Boccard for U. de Fribourg, 1993).

Pritchett, W. K. *The Greek State at War* (U. of California P., 1974–91; vol. i first published as *Ancient Greek Military Practices*, i, 1971) [*War*].

Proceedings of the XXVth International Congress of Papyrology ... 2007 (U. of Michigan P., 2010: http://quod.lib.umich.edu/i/icp/).

Rhodes, P. J. *The Athenian Boule* (Oxford U. P., 1972) [*A.B.*].

Rose, V. *Aristotelis qui Ferebantur Librorum Fragmenta*. Bibl. Teubneriana (Leipzig: Teubner, 1886).

Ruschenbusch, E. *Kleine Schriften zur Alten Geschichte* (Wiesbaden: Harrassowitz, 2014) [*Kleine Schriften A.G.*].

— *Kleine Schriften zur griechischen Rechtsgeschichte* (Wiesbaden: Harrassowitz, 2005), [*Kleine Schriften G. R.*].

Samuel, A. E. *Greek and Roman Chronology* (Munich: Beck, 1972) [*Chronology*].

Travlos, J. *Pictorial Dictionary of Ancient Athens* (London: Thames & Hudson for D.A.I., 1971) [*Pictorial Dictionary*].

Wade-Gery, H. T. *Essays in Greek History* (Oxford: Blackwell, 1958) [*Essays*].

West, M. L. *Iambi et Elegi Graeci*, ii (Oxford U. P., ^{2}1992).

von Wilamowitz-Moellendorff, U. *Aristoteles und Athen*. (Berlin: Weidmann, 1893) [Wilamowitz, *A.u.A.*].

Zürcher, J. *Aristoteles' Werk und Geist* (Paderborn: Schöningh, 1952).

REFERENCES IN *APPARATUS*

Papyri (cf. pp. 6–7, 31)

B Berlin P. 5009.

L P. Lond. 131.

Editors (cf. pp. 31–2)

CR: without further specification indicates a suggestion published for the first time or republished in *CR* 5 (1891).

Gentili & Prato: *Poetarum Elegiacorum Testimonia et Fragmenta*, i.

Herwerden (& Leeuwen), (Herwerden &) Leeuwen: suggestion attributed to one or to the other in the edition of Herwerden & Leeuwen.

Hommel: *Heliaia.*

Kenyon[4]: Kenyon's Berlin edition (1903).

Kenyon[5]: Kenyon's Oxford Classical Text (1920).

Thomas: J. D. Thomas, quoted in Rhodes, *Comm. Ath. Pol.*

West: *Iambi et Elegi Graeci*, ii.

Wilcken: U. Wilcken, quoted in Kaibel & Wilamowitz[3].

This edition follows the papyrologists' conventions, by which a dot under a letter indicates an uncertain reading, [square brackets] enclose letters supplied by the editor where none can be read, <angle brackets> enclose letters added by the editor and {braces} enclose letters deleted by the editor.

CONSTITUTION OF THE ATHENIANS

ΑΘΗΝΑΙΩΝ ΠΟΛΙΤΕΙΑ

FRAGMENTA DEPERDITAE PARTIS PRIMAE

1

Epitoma Heraclidis 1: Ἀθηναῖοι τὸ μὲν ἐξ αρχῆς ἐχρῶντο βασιλείᾳ, συνοικήσαντος δὲ Ἴωνος αὐτοῖς τότε πρῶτον Ἴωνες ἐκλήθησαν. Πανδίων δὲ βασιλεύσας μετα Ἐρεχθέα διένειμε τὴν ἀρχὴν τοῖς υἱοῖς. καὶ διετέλουν οὗτοι στασιάζοντες.

Harpocration (α 194 Keaney): **Ἀπόλλων πατρῷος ὁ Πύθιος.** προσηγορία τίς ἐστι τοῦ θεοῦ, πολλῶν καὶ ἄλλων οὐσῶν. τὸν δὲ Ἀπόλλωνα κοινῶς πατρῷον τιμῶσιν Ἀθηναῖοι ἀπὸ Ἴωνος· τούτου γὰρ οἰκίσαντος τὴν Ἀττικήν, ὡς Ἀριστοτέλης φησί, τοὺς Ἀθηναίους Ἴωνας κληθῆναι καὶ Ἀπόλλωνα πατρῷον αὐτοῖς ὀνομασθῆναι.

Schol. Ar. *Av.* 1527: **ὅθεν ὁ πατρῷος.** [...] πατρῷον δὲ τιμῶσιν Ἀπόλλωνα Ἀθηναῖοι, ἐπεὶ Ἴων ὁ πολέμαρχος Ἀθηναίων ἐξ Ἀπόλλωνος καὶ Κρεούσης τῆς Ξούθου <γυναικὸς> ἐγένετο.

2

Lex. Patm. (*Lexica Graeca Minora*, p. 162): **γεννῆταί.** πάλαι τό τῶν Ἀθηναίων πλῆθος, πρὶν ἢ Κλεισθένη διοικήσασθαι τὰ περὶ τὰς φυλάς, διῃρεῖτο εἰς γεωργοὺς καὶ δημιουργούς. καὶ φυλαὶ τούτων ἦσαν δ΄· τῶν δὲ φυλῶν ἑκάστη μοίρας εἶχε γ΄, ἃς φατρίας καὶ τριττύας ἐκάλουν· τούτων δὲ ἑκάστη συνειστήκει ἐκ τριάκοντα γενῶν, καὶ γένος ἕκαστον ἄνδρας εἶχε τριάκοντα, τοὺς εἰς τὰ γένη τεταγμένους, οἵτινες γενvηταὶ ἐκαλοῦντο. <ἐξ> ὧν αἱ ἱερωσύναι <αἱ> ἑκάστοις προσήκουσαι ἐκληροῦντο, οἷον Εὐμολπίδαι καὶ Κήρυκες καὶ Ἐτεοβουτάδαι, ὡς ἱστορεῖ ἐν τῇ Αθηναίων Πολιτείᾳ Ἀριστοτέλης, λέγων οὕτως· "φυλὰς δὲ αὐτῶν συννενεμῆσθαι δ΄, ἀπομιμησαμένων τὰς ἐν τοῖς ἐνιαυτοῖς ὥρας· ἑκάστην δὲ διῃρῆσθαι εἰς τρία μέρη τῶν φυλῶν, ὅπως γένηται τὰ πάντα δώδεκα μέρη, καθάπερ οἱ μῆνες εἰς τὸν ἐνιαυτόν, καλεῖσθαι δὲ αὐτὰ τριττῦς καὶ φατρίας· εἰς δὲ τὴν φατρίαν τριάκοντα γένη διακεκοσμῆσθαι, καθάπερ αἱ ἡμέραι εἰς τὸν μῆνα, τὸ δὲ γένος εἶναι τριάκοντα ἀνδρῶν." [...]

FRAGMENTS OF THE LOST BEGINNING

1

Epitome of Heraclides 1: The Athenians from the beginning used kingship, and when Ion settled with them they were first called Ionians. Pandion who was king after Erechtheus distributed the rule among his sons; and these continued in dissension.

Harpocration (α 194 Keaney): **Ancestral Apollo is the Pythian.** This is a title of the god: there are many others, but the Athenians in common have been honouring Apollo as Ancestral since Ion: for when he settled Attica, as Aristotle says, the Athenians were called Ionians and Apollo was called Ancestral for them.

Schol. Ar. *Birds* 1527: **Whence Ancestral.** [...] The Athenians honour Ancestral Apollo, since Ion the Athenians' polemarch was born from Apollo and Creusa the wife of Xuthus.

2

Patmos Lexicon (*Lexica Graeca Minora*, p. 162): ***Gennetai.*** Long ago, before Cleisthenes arranged matters with regard to the tribes, the mass of the Athenians was divided into farmers and craftsmen. And there were 4 tribes of these; each of the tribes had 3 parts, which they called *phratriai* and *trittyes*; each of these was composed of thirty *gene*; and each *genos* had thirty men, those assigned to the *gene*, who were called *gennetai*. From these they allotted the priesthoods belonging to each, such as the Eumolpidae and the Kerykes and the Eteobutadae, as Aristotle reports in his *Athenian Constitution*, saying as follows: '4 tribes of them were put together, imitating the seasons in the years; each of the tribes was divided into three parts, so that there were altogether twelve parts, like the months in the year, and they were called *trittys* and *phatriai*; in the *phatriai* thirty *gene* were arranged, as the days are arranged in the month; and the *genos* was of thirty men.' [...]

Schol. [Pl.] *Axioch.* 371 E: **γεννήτῃ.** Ἀριστοτέλης φησὶ τοῦ ὅλου πλήθους διῃρημένου Ἀθήνησιν εἴς τε τοὺς γεωργοὺς καὶ τοὺς δημιουργοὺς φυλὰς αὐτῶν εἶναι δ΄, τῶν δὲ φυλῶν ἑκάστης μοίρας εἶναι τρεῖς, ἃς τριττύας τε καλοῦσι καὶ φρατρίας, ἑκάστης δὲ τούτων τριάκοντα εἶναι γένη, τὸ δὲ γένος ἐκ τριάκοντα ἕκαστον ἀνδρῶν συνεστάναι. τούτους δὴ τοὺς εἰς τὰ γένη τεταγμένους γεννήτας καλοῦσιν.

Harpocration (τ 34 Keaney): **τριττύς.** [...] τριττύς ἐστι τὸ τρίτον μέρος τῆς φυλῆς· αὕτη γὰρ διῄρηται εἰς τρία μέρη, τριττῦς καὶ ἔθνη καὶ φατρίας, ὥς φησιν Ἀριστοτέλης ἐν τῇ Ἀθηναίων Πολιτείᾳ.

3

Pergit *Epitoma Heraclidis* 1: Θησεὺς δὲ ἐκήρυξε καὶ συνεβίβασε τούτους ἐπ᾽ ἴσῃ καὶ ὁμοίᾳ μοίρᾳ.

Plut. *Thes.* 25: (*1*) ἔτι δὲ μᾶλλον αὐξῆσαι τὴν πόλιν βουλόμενος ἐκάλει πάντας ἐπὶ τοῖς ἴσοις, καὶ τὸ "δευρ᾽ ἴτε πάντες λεῴ" κήρυγμα Θησέως γενέσθαι φασὶ πανδημίαν τινα καθίσταντος. (*2*) οὐ μὴν ἄτακτον οὐδὲ μεμειγμένην περιεῖδεν ὑπὸ πλήθους ἐπιχυθέντος ἀκρίτου γενομένην τὴν δημοκρατίαν, ἀλλὰ πρῶτος ἀποκρίνας χωρὶς εὐπατρίδας καὶ γεωμόρους καὶ δημιουργούς, εὐπατρίδαις δὲ <τὸ> γινώσκειν τὰ θεῖα καὶ παρέχειν <τοὺς> ἄρχοντας ἀποδοὺς καὶ νόμων διδασκάλους εἶναι καὶ ὁσίων καὶ ἱερῶν ἐξηγήτας, τοῖς ἄλλοις πολίταις ὥσπερ εἰς ἴσον κατέστησε, δόξῃ μὲν εὐπατριδῶν χρείᾳ δὲ γεωμόρων πλήθει δὲ δημιουργῶν ὑπερέχειν δοκούντων. (*3*) ὅτι δὲ πρῶτος ἀπέκλινε πρὸς τὸν ὄχλον, ὡς Ἀριτοτέλης φησί, καὶ ἀφῆκε τὸ μοναρχεῖν, ἔοικε μαρτυρῶν καὶ Ὅμηρος ἐν νεῶν καταλογῇ μόνους Ἀθηναίους δῆμον προσαγορεύσας.

4

Pergit *Epitoma Heraclidis* 1: οὗτος ἐλθὼν εἰς Σκῦρον ἐτελεύτησεν ὠσθεὶς κατὰ πετρῶν ὑπὸ Λυκομήδους, φοβηθέντος μὴ σφετερίσηται τὴν νῆσον. Ἀθηναῖοι δὲ ὕστερον περὶ τὰ Μηδικὰ μετεκόμισαν αὐτοῦ τὰ ὀστᾶ.

Scholium on [Pl.] *Axioch.* 371 E: ***Gennetes.*** Aristotle says that when the whole mass at Athens was divided into the farmers and craftsmen there were 4 tribes of them, and there were three parts of each tribe, which they called *trittyes* and *phratriai*, and belonging to each of these there were thirty *gene*, and each *genos* was composed of thirty men. These men who are assigned to the *gene* they call *gennetai.*

Harpocration (τ 34 Keaney): ***Trittys.*** [...] A *trittys* is the third part of the tribe: for this [i.e. the tribe] is divided into three parts, *trittys* and *ethne* and *phatriai*, as Aristotle says in his *Athenian Constitution.*

3

Epitome of Heraclides 1 continues: Theseus made a proclamation and brought these men together on the basis of an equal and like share.

Plut. *Thes.* 25: (*1*) Wanting to increase the city still further, he summoned them all on equal terms, and they say that 'Come hither all you folk' was a proclamation of Theseus when he established a totality of the people. (*2*) He did not, indeed, allow the democracy to be disorderly or mixed up by the influx of an indiscriminate mass, but first he distinguished separately the *eupatridai*, the farmers and the craftsmen, granting to the *eupatridai* to know about divine matters, to provide officials and to be teachers of laws and expounders of profane and sacred matters; but he placed them in a kind of equality with the other citizens, the *eupatridai* seeming to excel in repute, the farmers in utility and the craftsmen in numbers. (*3*) That he was the first to incline towards the mob, as Aristotle says, and to renounce monarchic rule, Homer also seems to attest, since in his Catalogue of Ships he calls only the Athenians a *demos*.

4

Epitome of Heraclides 1 continues: He went to Scyros and died there, pushed down from the cliffs by Lycomedes, who was afraid that he would make the island his own. Later, after the Persian Wars, the Athenians brought back his bones.

Schol. Vat. ad Eur. *Hipp.* 11: **ἁγνοῦ Πιτθέως.** Ἀριστοτέλης ἱστορεῖ ὅτι ἐλθὼν Θησεὺς εἰς Σκῦρον ἐπὶ κατασκοπὴν εἰκότως διὰ τὴν Αἰγέως συγγένειαν ἐτελεύτησεν ὠσθεὶς κατὰ πετρῶν, φοβηθέντος τοῦ Λυκομήδους τοῦ βασιλεύοντος – – – Ἀθηναῖοι δὲ μετὰ τὰ Μηδικὰ κατὰ μαντείαν ἀνελόντες τὰ ὀστᾶ αὐτοῦ ἔθαψαν.

5

Pergit *Epitoma Heraclidis* 1: ἀπὸ δὲ Κοδριδῶν οὐκέτι βασιλεῖς ῃροῦντο διὰ τὸ δοκεῖν τρυφᾶν καὶ μαλακοὺς γεγονέναι. Ἱππομένης δὲ εἷς τῶν Κοδριδῶν, βουλόμενος ἀπώσασθαι τὴν διαβολήν, λαβὼν ἐπὶ τῇ θυγατρὶ Λειμώνῃ μοιχόν, ἐκεῖνον μὲν ἀνεῖλεν ὑποζεύξας [μετὰ τῆς θυγατρὸς] τῷ ἅρματι, τὴν δὲ ἵππῳ συνέκλεισεν ἕως ἀπόληται.

6

Pergit *Epitoma Heraclidis* 2: τοὺς μετὰ Κύλωνος διὰ τὴν τυραννίδα ἐπὶ τὸν βωμὸν τῆς θεοῦ πεφευγότας οἱ περὶ Μεγακλέα ἀπέκτειναν. καὶ τοὺς δράσαντας ὡς ἐναγεῖς ἤλαυνον.

Vatican scholium on Eur. *Hipp.* 11: **of holy Pittheus.** Aristotle reports that Theseus went to Scyros to prospect, reasonably on account of his kinship with Aegeus, but was pushed down from the cliffs and died, because Lycomedes the king was afraid of him – – – After the Persian Wars the Athenians in accordance with an oracle brought back his bones and buried them.

5

Epitome of Heraclides 1 continues: After the Codridae they no longer appointed kings, because they seemed to be given to luxury and to have become soft. But Hippomenes, one of the Codridae, wanting to rebut the slander, when he caught an adulterer with his daughter Leimone, killed him by yoking him to his chariot, and shut her up with a horse until she died.

6

Epitome of Heraclides 2 continues: Because of the tyranny those with Cylon took refuge at the altar of the Goddess but were killed by the associates of Megacles. Those who did that they expelled as accursed.

ΑΘΗΝΑΙΩΝ ΠΟΛΙΤΕΙΑ

(**1**) … <κατηγοροῦντος> Μύρωνος καθ᾽ ἱερῶν ὀμόσαντες ἀριστίνδην. καταγνωσθέντος δὲ τοῦ ἄγους, αὐτοὶ μὲν ἐκ τῶν τάφων ἐξεβλήθησαν, τὸ δὲ γένος αὐτῶν ἔφυγεν ἀειφυγίαν. Ἐπιμενίδης δ᾽ ὁ Κρὴς ἐπὶ τούτοις ἐκάθηρε τὴν πόλιν.

(**2**) μετὰ δὲ ταῦτα συνέβη στασιάσαι τούς τε γνωρίμους καὶ τὸ πλῆθος πολὺν χρόνον {τὸν δῆμον}. (*2*) ἦν γὰρ αὐτῶν ἡ πολιτεία τοῖς τε ἄλλοις ὀλιγαρχικὴ πᾶσι, καὶ δὴ ἐδούλευον οἱ πένητες τοῖς πλουσίοις καὶ αὐτοὶ καὶ τὰ τέκνα καὶ αἱ γυναῖκες. καὶ ἐκαλοῦντο πελάται καὶ ἑκτήμοροι· κατὰ ταύτην γὰρ τὴν μίσθωσιν ἠργάζοντο τῶν πλουσίων τοὺς ἀγρούς. ἡ δὲ πᾶσα γῆ δι᾽ ὀλίγων ἦν· καὶ εἰ μὴ τὰς μισθώσεις ἀποδιδοῖεν, ἀγώγιμοι καὶ αὐτοὶ καὶ οἱ παῖδες ἐγίγνοντο. καὶ οἱ δανεισμοὶ πᾶσιν ἐπὶ τοῖς σώμασιν ἦσαν μέχρι Σόλωνος· οὗτος δὲ πρῶτος ἐγένετο τοῦ δήμου προστάτης. (*3*) χαλεπώτατον μὲν οὖν καὶ πικρότατον ἦν τοῖς πολλοῖς τῶν κατὰ τὴν πολιτείαν τὸ δουλεύειν· οὐ μὴν ἀλλὰ καὶ ἐπὶ τοῖς ἄλλοις ἐδυσχέραινον· οὐδενὸς γάρ, ὡς εἰπεῖν, ἐτύγχανον μετέχοντες.

(**3**) ἦν δ᾽ ἡ τάξις τῆς ἀρχαίας πολιτείας τῆς πρὸ Δράκοντος τοιάδε. τὰς μὲν ἀρχὰς καθίστασαν ἀριστίνδην καὶ πλουτίνδην· ἦρχον δὲ τὸ μὲν πρῶτον διὰ [βίου], μετὰ δὲ ταῦτα δεκαέτειαν. (*2*) μέγισται δὲ καὶ πρῶται τῶν ἀρχῶν ἦσαν βασιλεὺς καὶ πολέμαρχος καὶ ἄρχων· τούτων δὲ πρώτη μὲν ἡ τοῦ βασιλέως (αὕτη γὰρ ἦν πάτριος), δευτέρα δ᾽ ἐπικατέστη πολεμαρχία, διὰ τὸ γενέσθαι τινὰς τῶν βασιλέων τὰ πολέμια μαλακούς· ὅθεν καὶ τὸν Ἴωνα μετεπέμψαντο χρείας καταλαβούσης. (*3*) τελευταία δ᾽ ἡ τοῦ ἄρχοντος· οἱ μὲν γὰρ πλείους ἐπὶ Μέδοντος, ἔνιοι δ᾽ ἐπὶ Ἀκάστου φασὶ γενέσθαι ταύτην· τεκμήριον δ᾽ ἐπιφέρουσιν ὅτι οἱ ἐννέα ἄρχοντες ὀμνύουσι[ν ὥ]σ̣π̣ε̣ρ̣ ἐπὶ Ἀκάστου τὰ ὅρκια ποιήσειν, ὡς ἐπὶ τούτου τῆς βασιλείας παραχωρησάντων τῶν Κοδριδῶν ἀντὶ τῶν δοθεισῶν τῷ ἄρχοντι δωρεῶν. τοῦτο μὲν οὖν ὁποτέρως ποτ᾽ ἔχει, μικρὸν ἂν παραλλάττοι τοῖς χρόνοις. ὅτι δὲ τελευταία τούτων ἐγένετο

2. 1. τὸν δῆμον L: deleted Kenyon[1].

3. 1. διὰ [βίου] Kaibel & Wilamowitz.

3. 3. ὥ]σ̣π̣ε̣ρ̣ Kenyon[4]: η̣ιτα Wilcken, traces do not fit either Thomas, traces illegible Chambers.

ATHENIAN CONSTITUTION

(**1**) … on the prosecution of Myron, chosen on an aristocratic basis and swearing over holy victims. When they had been condemned as accursed, they themselves were expelled from their tombs, and their descendants incurred permanent exile. Epimenides the Cretan purified the city on these terms.

(**2**) After that there occurred dissension between the notables and the masses for a long time. (*2*) For the constitution was oligarchic in all other respects, and in particular the poor were enslaved to the rich – themselves and their children and their wives. They were called *pelatai* and *hektemoroi*, for it was on the basis of this rent of a sixth that they worked the fields of the rich. All the land was in the hands of a few, and if they did not pay their rents they themselves and their children were subject to seizure. And loans for all of them were on the security of the person until Solon: he was the first champion of the *demos*. (*3*) What was most harsh and bitter for the many in the constitution was their enslavement; but they were discontented about the other aspects too, for so to speak they found that they had a share in nothing.

(**3**) The structure of the ancient constitution before Draco was as follows. They appointed the officials on the basis of aristocratic birth and wealth. They held office at first for life, and afterwards for ten years. (*2*) The greatest and first of the offices were the *basileus*, the polemarch and the archon. Of these the first was the *basileus* (for this was the traditional ruling office). Secondly the office of polemarch was instituted in addition, because some of the kings became soft in matters to do with warfare – which is why they sent for Ion when need came upon them. (*3*) Last was the office of archon. Most say that this happened in the time of Medon, but some say the time of Acastus, and the latter adduce as supporting evidence that the nine archons swear that they will fulfil their oaths as in the time of Acastus, suggesting that it was in his time that the Codridae withdrew from the kingship in exchange for the grants made to the archon. But, whichever of these is the case, it makes little difference to the chronology. That this was the last of the offices is indicated by

τῶν ἀρχῶν, σημεῖον καὶ τὸ μηδὲν τῶν πατρίων τὸν ἄρχοντα διοικεῖν, ὥσπερ ὁ βασιλεὺς καὶ ὁ πολέμαρχος, ἀλλ’ ἁπλῶς τὰ ἐπίθετα· διὸ καὶ νεωστὶ γέγονεν ἡ ἀρχὴ μεγάλη, τοῖς ἐπιθέτοις αὐξηθεῖσα. (*4*) θεσμοθέται δὲ πολλοῖς ὕστερον ἔτεσιν ᾑρέθησαν, ἤδη κατ’ ἐνιαυτὸν αἱρουμένων τὰς ἀρχάς, ὅπως ἀναγράψαντες τὰ θέσμια φυλάττωσι πρὸς τὴν τῶν ἀμφισβητούντων κρίσιν· διὸ καὶ μόνη τῶν ἀρχῶν οὐκ ἐγένετο πλείων ἐνιαυσίας. (*5*) τοῖς μὲν οὖν χρόνοις τοσοῦτον προέχουσιν ἀλλήλων. ἦσαν δ’ οὐχ ἅμα πάντες οἱ ἐννέα ἄρχοντες, ἀλλ’ ὁ μὲν βασιλεὺς εἶχε τὸ νῦν καλούμενον Βουκολεῖον, πλησίον τοῦ πρυτανείου (σημεῖον δέ· ἔτι καὶ νῦν γὰρ τῆς τοῦ βασιλέως γυναικὸς ἡ σύμμειξις ἐνταῦθα γίγνεται τῷ Διονύσῳ καὶ ὁ γάμος), ὁ δὲ ἄρχων τὸ πρυτανεῖον, ὁ δὲ πολέμαρχος τὸ Ἐπιλύκειον (ὃ πρότερον μὲν ἐκαλεῖτο πολεμαρχεῖον, ἐπεὶ δὲ Ἐπίλυκος ἀνῳκοδόμησε καὶ κατεσκεύασεν αὐτὸ πολεμαρχήσας, Ἐπιλύκειον ἐκλήθη), θεσμοθέται δ’ εἶχον τὸ θεσμοθετεῖον. ἐπὶ δὲ Σόλωνος ἅπαντες εἰς τὸ θεσμοθετεῖον συνῆλθον. κύριοι δ’ ἦσαν καὶ τὰς δίκας αὐτοτελεῖς [κρίν]ειν, καὶ οὐχ ὥσπερ νῦν προανακρίνειν. τὰ μὲν οὖν περὶ τὰς ἀρχὰς τοῦτον εἶχε τὸν τρόπον. (*6*) ἡ δὲ τῶν Ἀρεοπαγιτῶν βουλὴ τὴν μὲν τάξιν εἶχε τοῦ διατηρεῖν τοὺς νόμους, διῴκει δὲ τὰ πλεῖστα καὶ τὰ μέγιστα τῶν ἐν τῇ πόλει, καὶ κολάζουσα καὶ ζημιοῦσα πάντας τοὺς ἀκοσμοῦντας κυρίως. ἡ γὰρ αἵρεσις τῶν ἀρχόντων ἀριστίνδην καὶ πλουτίνδην ἦν, ἐξ ὧν οἱ Ἀρεοπαγῖται καθίσταντο. διὸ καὶ μόνη τῶν ἀρχῶν αὕτη μεμένηκε διὰ βίου καὶ νῦν.

(**4**) ἡ μὲν οὖν πρώτη πολιτεία ταύτην εἶχε τὴν ὑπογραφήν. μετὰ δὲ ταῦτα χρόνου τινὸς οὐ πολλοῦ διελθόντος, ἐπ’ Ἀρισταίχμου ἄρχοντος, Δράκων τοὺς θεσμοὺς ἔθηκεν· ἡ δὲ τάξις αὐτοῦ τόνδε τὸν τρόπον εἶχε. (*2*) ἀπεδέδοτο μὲν ἡ πολιτεία τοῖς ὅπλα παρεχομένοις· ᾑροῦντο δὲ τοὺς μὲν ἐννέα ἄρχοντας καὶ τοὺς ταμίας οὐσίαν κεκτημένους οὐκ ἐλάττω δέκα μνῶν ἐλευθέραν, τὰς δ’ ἄλλας ἀρχὰς <τὰς> ἐλάττους ἐκ τῶν ὅπλα παρεχομένων, στρατηγοὺς δὲ καὶ ἱππάρχους οὐσίαν ἀποφαίνοντας οὐκ ἔλαττον ἢ ἑκατὸν μνῶν ἐλευθέραν, καὶ παῖδας ἐκ γαμετῆς γυναικὸς γνησίους ὑπὲρ δέκα ἔτη γεγονότας· τούτους δ’ ἔδει διεγγυᾶν τοὺς πρυτάνεις καὶ τοὺς στρατηγοὺς καὶ τοὺς ἱππάρχους τοὺς ἕνους μέχρι εὐθυνῶν, ἐγγυητὰς δ΄ ἐκ τοῦ αὐτοῦ τέλους δεχομένους οὗπερ οἱ στρατηγοὶ

4. 1. αὐτοῦ Wilcken, Chambers: αὕτη Kenyon.

the fact that the archon administers none of the traditional matters, as the *basileus* and polemarch do, but simply the added ones. This is how it has become the major office, augmented by the additions. (*4*) The *thesmothetai* were appointed many years later, when the archons were already appointed annually, with the function of writing up the statutes and keeping them for decisions between disputants. For that reason this alone of the offices has never lasted for more than a year. (*5*) This is the chronological precedence among them. At first the nine archons were not all together, but the *basileus* had what is now called the *Boukoleion*, near the *prytaneion* (here is an indication: for even now the ritual encounter and marriage of the *basileus*' wife with Dionysus takes place there), the archon the *prytaneion* and the polemarch the *Epilykeion* (which was first called the *polemarcheion*, but after Epilycus rebuilt and furbished it when he was polemarch it was called the *Epilykeion*), and the *thesmothetai* had the *thesmotheteion*. In the time of Solon they all joined together at the *thesmotheteion*. They had the power to decide lawsuits on their own authority, and not as now simply to hold the preliminary *anakrisis*. (*6*) The council of the Areopagites had the task of watching over the laws, and it administered most and the greatest of the affairs in the city, with full power to chastise and punish all the disorderly. For the election of the archons was on the basis of aristocratic birth and wealth, and the Areopagites were appointed from these. For that reason this alone of the offices has continued to be held for life even now.

(**4**) That is the outline of the first constitution. When not a long time had passed after this, in the archonship of Aristaechmus, Draco enacted his statutes. The structure of his constitution had the following form. (*2*) Political rights had been given to those who provided arms. They elected the nine archons and the treasurers, men owning unencumbered property worth not less than ten minas, and the other, lesser, officials from those providing arms; and as generals and hipparchs men declaring unencumbered property worth not less than a hundred minas, with legitimate children over ten years old by a wedded wife. These had to take guarantors from thc previous *prytaneis*, generals and hipparchs until their *euthynai*, accepting as guarantors for each 4 men of the same

καὶ οἱ ἵππαρχοι. (*3*) βουλεύειν δὲ τετρακοσίους καὶ ἕνα τοὺς λαχόντας ἐκ τῆς πολιτείας. κληροῦσθαι δὲ καὶ ταύτην καὶ τὰς ἄλλας ἀρχὰς τοὺς ὑπὲρ τριάκοντ' ἔτη γεγονότας, καὶ δὶς τὸν αὐτὸν μὴ ἄρχειν πρὸ τοῦ πάντας δ[ι]ελθεῖν· τότε δὲ πάλιν ἐξ ὑπαρχῆς κληροῦν. εἰ δέ τις τῶν βουλευτῶν, ὅταν ἕδρα βουλῆς ἢ ἐκκλησίας ᾖ, ἐκλείποι τὴν σύνοδον, ἀπέτινον ὁ μὲν πεντακοσιομέδιμνος τρεῖς δραχμάς, ὁ δὲ ἱππεὺς δύο, ζευγίτης δὲ μίαν. (*4*) ἡ δὲ βουλὴ ἡ ἐξ Ἀρείου πάγου φύλαξ ἦν τῶν νόμων, καὶ διετήρει τὰς ἀρχάς ὅπως κατὰ τοὺς νόμους ἄρχωσιν. ἐξῆν δὲ τῷ ἀδικουμένῳ πρὸς τὴν τῶν Ἀρεοπαγιτῶν βουλὴν εἰσαγγέλλειν, ἀποφαίνοντι παρ' ὃν ἀδικεῖται νόμον. (*5*) ἐπὶ δὲ τοῖς σώμασιν ἦσαν οἱ δανεισμοί, καθάπερ εἴρηται, καὶ ἡ χώρα δι' ὀλίγων ἦν.

(**5**) τοιαύτης δὲ τῆς τάξεως οὔσης ἐν τῇ πολιτείᾳ, καὶ τῶν πολλῶν δουλευόντων τοῖς ὀλίγοις, ἀντέστη τοῖς γνωρίμοις ὁ δῆμος. (*2*) ἰσχυρᾶς δὲ τῆς στάσεως οὔσης καὶ πολὺν χρόνον ἀντικαθημένων ἀλλήλοις, εἵλοντο κοινῇ διαλλακτὴν καὶ ἄρχοντα Σόλωνα, καὶ τὴν πολιτείαν ἐπέτρεψαν αὐτῷ, ποιήσαντι τὴν ἐλεγείαν ἧς ἐστὶν ἀρχή·

γιγνώσκω, καί μοι φρενὸς ἔνδοθεν ἄλγεα κεῖται,
  πρεσβυτάτην ἐσορῶν γαῖαν Ἰαονίας
καινομένην·

ἐν ᾗ πρὸς ἑκατέρους ὑπὲρ ἑκατέρων μάχεται καὶ διαμφισβητεῖ, καὶ μετὰ ταῦτα κοινῇ παραινεῖ καταπαύειν τὴν ἐνεστῶσαν φιλονικίαν. (*3*) ἦν δ' ὁ Σόλων τῇ μὲν φύσει καὶ τῇ δόξῃ τῶν πρώτων, τῇ δ' οὐσίᾳ καὶ τοῖς πράγμασι τῶν μέσων, ὡς ἔκ τε τῶν ἄλλων ὁμολογεῖται, καὶ αὐτὸς ἐν τοῖσδε τοῖς ποιήμασιν μαρτυρεῖ, παραινῶν τοῖς πλουσίοις μὴ πλεονεκτεῖν·

ὑμεῖς δ' ἡσυχάσαντες ἐνὶ φρεσὶ καρτερὸν ἦτορ,
  οἳ πολλῶν ἀγαθῶν ἐς κόρον ἠλάσατε,
ἐν μετρίοισι τίθεσθε μέγαν νόον· οὔτε γὰρ ἡμεῖς
  πεισόμεθ', οὔθ' ὑμῖν ἄρτια ṭα[ῦ]τ' ἔσεται.

4. 3. δ[ι]ελθεῖν Wilcken, Chambers, approved Thomas: ẹξελθεῖν Kenyon.

5. 2. καινομένην Blass[4], Kenyon[4–5], Chambers, approved Thomas: κλινομένην Wilcken, West, Gentili & Prato.

5. 3. ṭα[ῦ]τ' Herwerden (& Leeuwen), Wilcken, Kenyon[4], West, Gentili & Prato, Chambers, approved Thomas: πά[ντ'] Kaibel & Wilamowitz, Kenyon[5].

financial class as the generals and hipparchs. (*3*) The council comprised four hundred and one men appointed by sortition from those with political rights. This appointed by lot to the other offices men over thirty years old, and the same man could not hold an office for a second time until all had gone through; then they made allotments again from the beginning. If any of the councillors, when there was a session of the council or assembly, missed the meeting, a *pentakosiomedimnos* had to pay three drachmae, a *hippeus* two and a *zeugites* one. (*4*) The council of the Areopagus was guardian of the laws, and it kept watch over the officials to see that they conducted their office in accordance with the laws. It was possible for a man who was wronged to make an *eisangelia* to the council of the Areopagites, indicating the law in contravention of which he was wronged. (*5*) Loans were on the security of the person, as has been said, and the land was in the hands of a few.

(**5**) When that was the kind of structure in the constitution, and the many were enslaved to the few, the *demos* rose up against the notables. (*2*) Since the dissension was powerful and they were opposed to each other for a long time, they jointly chose Solon as reconciler and archon, and entrusted the constitution to him, because he had written the elegy which begins:

> I know, and anguish of heart lies within me,
>   When I look and see the eldest land of Ionia
> Being slain.

In this he fights and disputes against each side on behalf of the other side, and after that he urges them to put an end jointly to the rivalry which besets them. (*3*) Solon was by birth and repute one of the leading men, but in his property and his station in life one of those in the middle: this is agreed on other grounds, and he himself bears witness to it in these verses, when he urges the rich not to be greedy:

> But you must quieten the strong passion in your hearts,
>   You who have forced your way to an excess of many good things,
> And must settle your great thoughts in moderation. For we shall not
>   Allow you, nor will these things be fitting for you.

καὶ ὅλως αἰεὶ τὴν αἰτίαν τῆς στάσεως ἀνάπτει τοῖς πλουσίοις· διὸ καὶ ἐν ἀρχῇ τῆς ἐλεγείας δεδοικέναι φησὶ "τήν τε φιλ̣[οπλο]υ̣τ̣ίαν τήν θ' ὑπερηφανίαν", ὡς διὰ ταῦτα τῆς ἔχθρας ἐνεστώσης.

(**6**) κύριος δὲ γενόμενος τῶν πραγμάτων Σόλων τόν τε δῆμον ἠλευθέρωσε καὶ ἐν τῷ παρόντι καὶ εἰς τὸ μέλλον, κωλύσας δανείζειν ἐπὶ τοῖς σώμασιν, καὶ νόμους ἔθηκε καὶ χρεῶν ἀποκοπὰς ἐποίησε, καὶ τῶν ἰδίων καὶ τῶν δημοσίων, ἃς σεισάχθειαν καλοῦσιν, ὡς ἀποσεισάμενοι τὸ βάρος. (*2*) ἐν οἷς πειρῶνταί τινες διαβάλλειν αὐτόν· συνέβη γὰρ τῷ Σόλωνι μέλλοντι ποιεῖν τὴν σεισάχθειαν προειπεῖν τισι τῶν γνωρίμων, ἔπειθ', ὡς μὲν οἱ δημοτικοὶ λέγουσι, παραστρατηγηθῆναι διὰ τῶν φίλων, ὡς δ' οἱ βουλόμενοι βλασφημεῖν, καὶ αὐτὸν κοινωνεῖν. δανεισάμενοι γὰρ οὗτοι συνεπρίαντο πολλὴν χώραν, καὶ μετ' οὐ πολὺ τῆς τῶν χρεῶν ἀποκοπῆς γενομένης ἐπλούτουν· ὅθεν φασὶ γενέσθαι τοὺς ὕστερον δοκοῦντας εἶναι παλαιοπλούτους. (*3*) οὐ μὴν ἀλλὰ πιθανώτερος ὁ τῶν δημοτικῶν λόγος· οὐ γὰρ εἰκὸς ἐν μὲν τοῖς ἄλλοις οὕτω μέτριον γενέσθαι καὶ κοινόν, ὥστ' ἐξὸν αὐτῷ τοὺς ἑτέρους ὑποποιησάμενον τυραννεῖν τῆς πόλεως, ἀμφοτέροις ἀπεχθέσθαι καὶ περὶ πλείονος ποιήσασθαι τὸ καλὸν καὶ τὴν τῆς πόλεως σωτηρίαν ἢ τὴν αὑτοῦ πλεονεξίαν, ἐν οὕτω δὲ μικροῖς καὶ φανεροῖς καταρρυπαίνειν ἑαυτόν. (*4*) ὅτι δὲ ταύτην ἔσχε τὴν ἐξουσίαν, τά τε πράγματα νοσοῦντα μαρτυρεῖ, καὶ ἐν τοῖς ποιήμασιν αὐτὸς πολλαχοῦ μέμνηται, καὶ οἱ ἄλλοι συνομολογοῦσι πάντες. ταύτην μὲν οὖν χρὴ νομίζειν ψευδῆ τὴν αἰτίαν εἶναι.

(**7**) πολιτείαν δὲ κατέστησε καὶ νόμους ἔθηκεν ἄλλους, τοῖς δὲ Δράκοντος θεσμοῖς ἐπαύσαντο χρώμενοι πλὴν τῶν φονικῶν. ἀναγράψαντες δὲ τοὺς νόμους εἰς τοὺς κύρβεις ἔστησαν ἐν τῇ στοᾷ τῇ βασιλείῳ καὶ ὤμοσαν χρήσεσθαι πάντες. οἱ δ' ἐννέα ἄρχοντες ὀμνύντες πρὸς τῷ λίθῳ κατεφάτιζον ἀναθήσειν ἀνδριάντα χρυσοῦν, ἐάν τινα παραβῶσι τῶν νόμων· ὅθεν ἔτι καὶ νῦν οὕτως ὀμνύουσι. (*2*) κατέκλεισεν δὲ τοὺς νόμους εἰς ἑκατὸν ἔτη. καὶ διέταξε τὴν πολιτείαν τόνδε <τὸν> τρόπον. (*3*) τιμήματι διεῖλεν εἰς τέτταρα τέλη, καθάπερ διῄρητο καὶ

5. 3. φιλ̣[οπλο]υ̣τ̣ίαν Blass[3], Chambers, υ̣τ̣ίαν possible Thomas: φι[λαργυρί]αν Kenyon, φιλοχρηματίαν Plut. *Sol.* 14. 3, Gentili & Prato, φ[. .] . . [. .] . .τ̣ιαν (= φιλοχρηματίαν?) West

θ' J. B. Mayor and H. Jackson (*CR*): τε L, Kaibel & Wilamowitz, Kenyon[4].

6. 1. καὶ νόμους ἔθηκε: deleted Kaibel & Wilamowitz.

And in general he everywhere attaches the blame for the dissension to the rich. So at the beginning of his elegy he says that he was afraid of 'their love of wealth and their arrogance', since it was on account of this that the hostility had arisen.

(**6**) When Solon had gained control of affairs, he liberated the *demos* both in the present and for the future, forbidding loans on the security of the person, and he enacted laws, and he made a cancellation of debts both private and public, which they call the *seisachtheia*, because their burden was shaken off. (*2*) In this matter some people try to slander him. For it happened that when Solon was about to enact the *seisachtheia* he mentioned it in advance to some of the notables; and then, as the democrats say, he was outgeneralled by his friends, or, as those who want to malign him say, he himself took part. For these men raised loans and conspired to buy large quantities of land, and not long afterwards the cancellation of debts occurred and they were enriched. This is said to be the origin of those who were later considered 'rich from long ago'. (*3*) Nevertheless, the democrats' account is more credible. For it is not likely that, when in other respects Solon was so moderate and public-spirited, so that he could have outwitted the others and become tyrant of the city, but accepted the hatred of both sides and valued honour and the salvation of the city above his own selfish advantage, he would have defiled himself in such a small and blatant matter. (*4*) That he had this possibility of becoming tyrant the diseased state of affairs attests, in his verses he has often mentioned it, and all the others agree. This accusation must therefore be judged false.

(**7**) He established a constitution and enacted other laws, and they ceased using the statutes of Draco except those on homicide. They wrote up the laws on the *kyrbeis* and placed them in the Stoa of the *Basileus*, and all swore to use them. The nine archons when swearing at the stone declared that they would dedicate a gold statue if they transgressed any of the laws: consequently they still swear in this way now. (*2*) He locked in his laws for a hundred years, and organised the constitution in the following way. (*3*) He divided them by an assessment into four classes,

πρότερον, εἰς πεντακοσιομέδιμνον καὶ ἱππέα καὶ ζευγίτην καὶ θῆτα. καὶ τὰς μεγ̣ά̣λ̣α̣ς ἀρχὰς ἀπένειμεν ἄρχειν ἐκ πεντακοσιομεδίμνων καὶ ἱππέων καὶ ζευγιτῶν, τοὺς ἐννέα ἄρχοντας καὶ τοὺς ταμίας καὶ τοὺς πωλητὰς καὶ τοὺς ἕνδεκα καὶ τοὺς κωλακρέτας, ἑκάστοις ἀνάλογον τῷ μεγέθει τοῦ τιμήματος ἀποδιδοὺς τὴν ἀρχήν· τοῖς δὲ τὸ θητικὸν τελοῦσιν ἐκκλησίας καὶ δικαστηρίων μετέδωκε μόνον. (*4*) ἔδει δὲ τελεῖν πεντακοσιομέδιμνον μὲν ὃς ἂν ἐκ τῆς οἰκείας ποιῇ πεντακόσια μέτρα τὰ συνάμφω ξηρὰ καὶ ὑγρά, ἱππάδα δὲ τοὺς τριακόσια ποιοῦντας, ὡς δ' ἔνιοί φασι τοὺς ἱπποτροφεῖν δυναμένους. σημεῖον δὲ φέρουσι τό τε ὄνομα τοῦ τέλους, ὡς ἂν ἀπὸ τοῦ πράγματος κείμενον, καὶ τὰ ἀναθήματα τῶν ἀρχαίων· ἀνάκειται γὰρ ἐν ἀκροπόλει εἰκὼν {Διφίλου}, ἐφ' ᾗ ἐπιγέγραπται τάδε·

Διφίλου Ἀνθεμίων τήνδ' ἀνέθηκε θεοῖς,
θητικοῦ ἀντὶ τέλους ἱππάδ' ἀμειψάμενος.

καὶ παρέστηκεν ἵππος ἐκμαρτυρῶν, ὡς τὴν ἱππάδα τοῦτο σημαίνουσαν. οὐ μὴν ἀλλ' εὐλογώτερον τοῖς μέτροις διῃρῆσθαι, καθάπερ τοὺς πεντακοσιομεδίμνους. ζευγίσιον δὲ τελεῖν τοὺς διακόσια τὰ συνάμφω ποιοῦντας· τοὺς δ' ἄλλους θητικόν, οὐδεμιᾶς μετέχοντας ἀρχῆς. διὸ καὶ νῦν ἐπειδὰν ἔρηται τὸν μέλλοντα κληροῦσθαί τιν' ἀρχήν, ποῖον τέλος τελεῖ, οὐδ' ἂν εἷς εἴποι θητικόν.

(**8**) τὰς δ' ἀρχὰς ἐποίησε κληρωτὰς ἐκ προκρίτων, οὓς ἑκάστη προκρίνειε τῶν φυλῶν. προὔκρινεν δ' εἰς τοὺς ἐννέα ἄρχοντας ἑκάστη δέκα, καὶ τούτου̣ς ἐ̣κ̣λήρουν· ὅθεν ἔτι διαμένει ταῖς φυλαῖς τὸ δέκα κληροῦν ἑκάστην, εἶτ' ἐκ τούτων κυαμεύειν. σημεῖον δ' ὅτι κληρωτὰς ἐποίησεν ἐκ τῶν τιμημάτων ὁ περὶ τῶν ταμιῶν νόμος, ᾧ χρώμενοι διατελοῦσιν ἔτι καὶ νῦν· κελεύει γὰρ κληροῦν τοὺς ταμίας ἐκ πεντακοσιομεδίμνων. (*2*) Σόλων μὲν οὖν οὕτως ἐνομοθέτησεν περὶ τῶν ἐννέα ἀρχόντων. τὸ δ̣' ἀρχαῖον ἡ ἐν Ἀ[ρεί]ῳ̣ [πάγῳ̣ βου]λὴ ἀνακαλεσαμένη καὶ κρίνασα καθ'

7. 3. μεγ̣ά̣λ̣α̣ς Chambers after Fritz & Kapp, approved Thomas: μὲ[ν ἄλλ]ας Wilcken, {με[γίστ]ας} Blass[1].

7. 4. Διφίλου deleted E. S. Thompson (*CR*).

8. 1. καὶ τούτους ἐ̣κ̣λήρουν Kenyon[1], Chambers: καὶ <ἐκ> τού[των ἐκ]λήρουν Kaibel & Wilamowitz[1], Kenyon[4] (noting correction in papyrus).

8. 2. τὸ δ' ἀρχαῖον Herwerden & Leeuwen, Wilcken, Chambers: γὰρ Kenyon, γ with no mark of abbreviation Thomas.

as they had already been divided before: the *pentakosiomedimnoi*, the *hippeis*, the *zeugitai* and the *thetes*. He assigned the holding of the great offices – the nine archons and the treasurers and the *poletai* and the Eleven and the *kolakretai* – to men from the *pentakosiomedimnoi*, *hippeis* and *zeugitai*, granting offices to each in proportion to the size of their assessment. To those in the *thetes*' class he gave a share only in the assembly and the lawcourts. (*4*) A man had to be classed as a *pentakosiomedimnos* if from his own property he produced five hundred measures, dry and wet together; men were classed as *hippeis* if they produced three hundred – or as some say if they were able to maintain a horse. These cite as an indication the name of the class, as derived from the underlying facts, and the dedications of the ancients. For there has been set up on the acropolis a statue on which this text has been inscribed:

> Diphilus' son Anthemion dedicated this to the gods,
> Having exchanged the *thetes*' class for the *hippeis*'.

And beside it a horse has been placed, suggesting that this is what *hippeis* means. Nevertheless it is more reasonable that the distinction should have been based on measures, as in the case of the *pentakosiomedimnoi*. The men belonging to the *zeugitai*'s class were those who produced two hundred measures of the two kinds. The others belonged to the *thetes*' class and had a share in no offices. For that reason even now, when a man is about to undergo allotment for any office and is asked which class he belongs to, nobody would say the *thetes*'.

(**8**) He had the officials appointed by allotment from a list of men pre-elected by the tribes. Each tribe pre-elected ten for the nine archons, and they made the allotment from these. Consequently it still remains the practice for the tribes each to allot ten, and then for the lots to be drawn from these. An indication that he had appointments made by allotment from those satisfying the assessments is the law about the treasurers, which they still continue to use even now: for that orders the treasurers to be appointed by allotment from the *pentakosiomedimnoi*. (*2*) This was the law which Solon enacted about the nine archons: for in antiquity the council of the Areopagus called up and judged by itself

αὐτὴν τὸν ἐπιτήδειον ἐφ’ ἑκάστῃ τῶν ἀρχῶν ἐπ’ [ἐν]ια[υτ]ὸν δ̣[ιατάξ]α̣σ̣α ἀπέστελλεν. (*3*) φυλαὶ δ’ ἦσαν δ´ καθάπερ πρότερον, καὶ φυλοβασιλεῖς τέτταρες. [ἐκ] δὲ τῆς φυλῆς ἑκάστης ἦσαν νενεμημέναι τριττύες μὲν τρεῖς, ναυκραρίαι δὲ δώδεκα καθ’ ἑκάστην. [ἦ]ν [δ’ ἐπὶ] τῶν ναυκραριῶν ἀρχὴ καθεστηκυῖα ναύκραροι, τεταγμένη πρός τε τὰς εἰσφορὰς καὶ τὰς δαπάνας τὰς γιγνομένας· διὸ καὶ ἐν τοῖς νόμοις τοῖς Σόλωνος οἷς οὐκέτι χρῶνται πολλαχοῦ γέγραπται “τοὺς ναυκράρους εἰσπράττειν”, καὶ “ἀναλίσκειν ἐκ τοῦ ναυκραρικοῦ ἀργυρίου”. (*4*) βουλὴν δ’ ἐποίησε τετρακοσίους, ἑκατὸν ἐξ ἑκάστης φυλῆς, τὴν δὲ τῶν Ἀρεοπαγιτῶν ἔταξεν ἐπὶ τὸ νομοφυλακεῖν, ὥσπερ ὑπῆρχεν καὶ πρότερον ἐπίσκοπος οὖσα τῆς πολιτείας, καὶ τά τε ἄλλα τὰ πλεῖστα καὶ τὰ μέγιστα τῶν πολιτ<ικ>ῶν διετήρει, καὶ τοὺς ἁμαρτάνοντας ηὔθυνεν κυρία οὖσα καὶ ζημιοῦν καὶ κολάζειν, καὶ τὰς ἐκτίσεις ἀνέφερεν εἰς πόλιν, οὐκ ἐπιγράφουσα τὴν πρόφασιν †δ̣[ιὰ] τ̣ὸ̣ [ε]ὐ̣θύ[ν]εσ̣θαι†, καὶ τοὺς ἐπὶ καταλύσει τοῦ δήμου συνισταμένους ἔκρινεν, Σόλωνος θέντος νόμον εἰσαγγελίας περὶ αὐτῶν. (*5*) ὁρῶν δὲ τὴν μὲν πόλιν πολλάκις στασιάζουσαν, τῶν δὲ πολιτῶν ἐνίους διὰ τὴν ῥαθυμίαν [ἀγα]πῶντας τὸ αὐτόματον, νόμον ἔθηκεν πρὸς αὐτοὺς ἴδιον, ὃς ἂν στασιαζούσης τῆς πόλεως μὴ θῆται τὰ ὅπλα μηδὲ μεθ’ ἑτέρων, ἄτιμον εἶναι καὶ τῆς πόλεως μὴ μετέχειν.

(9) τὰ μὲν οὖν περὶ τὰς ἀρχὰς τοῦτον εἶχε τὸν τρόπον. δοκεῖ δὲ τῆς Σόλωνος πολιτείας τρία ταῦτ’ εἶναι τὰ δημοτικώτατα· πρῶτον μὲν καὶ μέγιστον τὸ μὴ δανείζειν ἐπὶ τοῖς σώμασιν, ἔπειτα τὸ ἐξεῖναι τῷ βουλομένῳ τιμωρεῖν ὑπὲρ τῶν ἀδικουμένων, τρίτον δέ, <ᾧ> μάλιστά φασιν ἰσχυκέναι τὸ πλῆθος, ἡ εἰς τὸ δικαστήριον ἔφεσις· κύριος γὰρ ὢν ὁ δῆμος τῆς ψήφου κύριος γίγνεται τῆς πολιτείας. (2) ἔτι δὲ καὶ διὰ τὸ μὴ γεγράφθαι τοὺς νόμους ἁπλῶς μηδὲ σαφῶς, ἀλλ’ ὥσπερ ὁ περὶ τῶν κλήρων καὶ ἐπικλήρων, ἀνάγκη πολλὰς ἀμφισβητήσεις γίγνεσθαι καὶ πάντα βραβεύειν καὶ τὰ κοινὰ καὶ τὰ ἴδια τὸ δικαστήριον. οἴονται

8\. 2. δ̣[ιατάξ]α̣σ̣α Kenyon (‘not certain’ Kenyon[4]), Chambers, approved Thomas: [ἄρξον]τα Kaibel & Wilamowitz[3].

8\. 4. πολιτ<ικ>ῶν H. Richards (*CR*), 177: πολιτ´ L.

†δ̣[ιὰ] τ̣ὸ̣ [ε]ὐ̣θύ[ν]εσ̣θαι† Wilcken (deleted Kaibel & Wilamowitz[3]), Chambers (obelising), approved Thomas: πρόφασι[ν τοῦ εὐθύν]εσθαι Blass (*LZB* 1891, 303), δι’ ὃ [τὸ ἐ]κτ[ίν]εσθαι Kenyon[4–5] (‘doubtful’).

9\. 1. <ᾧ> (Herwerden &) Leeuwen.

which man was appropriate for each of the offices, and appointed and dispatched him for the year. (*3*) There were four tribes, as before, and four *phylobasileis*. From each tribe three *trittyes* were distributed, and there were twelve *naukrariai* in each. The officials appointed to have charge of the *naukrariai* were the *naukraroi*, with duties concerning the income and expenditure which occurred: for that reason also in the laws of Solon which they no longer use it is often written, 'The *naukraroi* shall exact', and, 'expend from the naucraric silver'. (*4*) He created a council of four hundred, one hundred from each tribe. And to the council of the Areopagus he gave the task of law-guarding, just as previously it had been overseer of the constitution; and it watched over most and the greatest of the city's affairs, and it called offenders to account, having full power to punish and chastise, and took up the payments to the acropolis without recording the reason for calling to account; and it tried those who combined for the overthrow of the *demos*, since Solon enacted the law of *eisangelia* concerning them. (*5*) Seeing that the city was often in a state of dissension, and that some of the citizens through apathy were content with whatever happened, he enacted a particular law aimed at these, that when the city was in a state of dissension anybody who did not place his arms at the disposal of one side or the other should be *atimos* and not participate in the city.

(**9**) That was the manner of his arrangements for the officials. These seem to be the three most democratic features of Solon's political dispensation: first and greatest, that loans should not be on the security of the person; next, the possibility for whoever wished to obtain vengeance for those who were wronged; and thirdly, the point by which they say the masses were strengthened most, appeal to the lawcourt: for when the *demos* has power over the vote it has power over the political régime. (*2*) In addition, because his laws were not written simply and clearly, but were like that about inheritance and *epikleroi*, it was inevitable that many disputes occurred and that the lawcourt acted as umpire of everything both common and individual. Some people think that he

μὲν οὖν τινες ἐπίτηδες ἀσαφεῖς αὐτὸν ποιῆσαι τοὺς νόμους, ὅπως ᾖ τῆς κρίσεως ὁ δῆμος κύριος. οὐ μὴν εἰκός, ἀλλὰ διὰ τὸ μὴ δύνασθαι καθόλου περιλαβεῖν τὸ βέλτιστον· οὐ γὰρ δίκαιον ἐκ τῶν νῦν γιγνομένων ἀλλ' ἐκ τῆς ἄλλης πολιτείας θεωρεῖν τὴν ἐκείνου βούλησιν.

(**10**) ἐν μὲν οὖν τοῖς νόμοις ταῦτα δοκεῖ θεῖναι δημοτικά, πρὸ δὲ τῆς νομοθεσίας ποιήσας τὴν τῶν χρεῶν ἀποκοπὴν καὶ μετὰ ταῦτα τήν τε τῶν μέτρων καὶ σταθμῶν καὶ τὴν τοῦ νομίσματος αὔξησιν. (*2*) ἐπ' ἐκείνου γὰρ ἐγένετο καὶ τὰ μέτρα μείζω τῶν Φειδωνείων, καὶ ἡ μνᾶ πρότερον ἄ̣γ[ο]υσα σταθμὸν ἑβδομήκοντα δραχμὰς ἀνεπληρώθη ταῖς ἑκατόν· ἦν δ' ὁ ἀρχαῖος χαρακτὴρ δίδραχμον. ἐποίησε δὲ καὶ σταθμὰ πρὸς τὸ νόμισμα τρεῖς καὶ ἑξήκοντα μνᾶς τὸ τάλαντον ἀγούσας, καὶ ἐπιδιενεμήθησαν αἱ τρεῖς μναῖ τῷ στατῆρι καὶ τοῖς ἄλλοις σταθμοῖς.

(**11**) διατάξας δὲ τὴν πολιτείαν ὅνπερ εἴρηται τρόπον, ἐπειδὴ προσιόντες αὐτῷ περὶ τῶν νόμων ἐνώχλουν, τὰ μὲν ἐπιτιμῶντες τὰ δὲ ἀνακρίνοντες, βουλόμενος μήτε ταῦτα κινεῖν μήτ' ἀπεχθάνεσθαι παρών, ἀποδημίαν ἐποιήσατο κατ' ἐμπορίαν ἅμα καὶ θεωρίαν εἰς Αἴγυπτον, εἰπὼν ὡς οὐχ ἥξει δέκα ἐτῶν· οὐ γὰρ οἴεσθαι δίκαιον εἶναι τοὺς νόμους ἐξηγεῖσθαι παρών, ἀλλ' ἕκαστον τὰ γεγραμμένα ποιεῖν. (2) ἅμα δὲ καὶ συνέβαινεν αὐτῷ τῶν τε γνωρίμων διαφόρους γεγενῆσθαι πολλοὺς διὰ τὰς τῶν χρεῶν ἀποκοπάς, καὶ τὰς στάσεις ἀμφοτέρας μεταθέσθαι διὰ τὸ παράδοξον αὐτοῖς γενέσθαι τὴν κατάστασιν. ὁ μὲν γὰρ δῆμος ᾤετο πάντ' ἀνάδαστα ποιήσειν αὐτόν, οἱ δὲ γνώριμοι πάλιν εἰς τὴν αὐτὴν τάξιν ἀποδώσειν ἢ μ[ικ]ρ[ὸ]ν παραλλάξ[ειν]. <ὁ δὲ> Σόλων ἀμφοτέροις ἠναντιώθη, καὶ ἐξὸν αὐτῷ μεθ' ὁποτέρων ἐβούλετο συστάντα τυραννεῖν εἵλετο πρὸς ἀμφοτέρους ἀπεχθέσθαι, σώσας τὴν πατρίδα καὶ τὰ βέλτιστα νομοθετήσας.

(**12**) ταῦτα δ' ὅτι τοῦτον <τὸν> τρόπον ἔσχεν οἵ τ' ἄλλοι συμφωνοῦσι πάντες, καὶ αὐτὸς ἐν τῇ ποιήσει μέμνηται περὶ αὐτῶν ἐν τοῖσδε·

10. 1. ποιήσας Kaibel & Wilamowitz, Chambers: ποιῆσαι Kenyon.

10. 2. ἄ̣γ[ο]υσα conjectured W. Wyse (*CR*), 108, read Chambers: ἔχ[ο]υσα Wilcken, Kenyon[4–5].

11. 2. <ὁ δὲ> Blass.

ἀπεχθέσθαι W.Wyse (*CR*): απεχθεσθηναι L.

12. 1. <τὸν> Kenyon[1].

made his laws unclear deliberately, in order that the *demos* should be master of the judgment. However, that it not likely, but the reason is that it is impossible to circumscribe what is best overall: for it is not just to make conjectures about his intention from what happens now, but rather from the rest of his political dispensation.

(**10**) These appear to be the democratic features of the laws which he enacted; and before his legislation he made the cancellation of debts, and after that the increase in the measures, weights and coinage. (*2*) For under him the measures were made larger than those of Pheidon, and the mina, which previously had a weight of seventy drachmae, was filled up to the hundred. The ancient standard coin was the two-drachmae. He created as weights with regard to the coinage sixty-three minas weighing a talent; and the three minas were distributed in proportion to the stater and the other weights.

(**11**) After he had organised the constitution in the manner which has been stated, men took to approaching him and pestering him about his laws, complaining about some matters and interrogating him about others. Since he did not want to interfere with the laws or to remain present and incur hostility, he made a foreign journey to Egypt, for trade and at the same time to see the sights, saying that he would not return for ten years: for he did not think it just that he should remain present and expound the laws, but rather that everybody should do what had been written. (*2*) At the same time it happened that many of the notables had been alienated by his cancellation of debts, and that both factions had changed their stance, because the upshot was contrary to their expectation: for the *demos* had expected him to make a redistribution of everything, but the notables had thought he would restore things to the previous arrangement or make only a small change. But Solon was opposed to both; and, when it was possible for him to take a stand with whichever faction he chose and become tyrant, he chose to be hated by both but to save the country and enact laws for the best.

(**12**) That this is the way he acted all the others agree, and he himself has recorded it in his poetry, in the following:

δήμῳ μὲν γὰρ ἔδωκα τόσον γέρας ὅσσον ἀπαρκεῖ<ν>,
  τιμῆς οὔτ' ἀφελὼν οὔτ' ἐπορεξάμενος·
οἳ δ' εἶχον δύναμιν καὶ χρήμασιν ἦσαν ἀγητοί,
  καὶ τοῖς ἐφρασάμην μηδὲν ἀεικὲς ἔχειν.
ἔστην δ' ἀμφιβαλὼν κρατερὸν σάκος ἀμφοτέροισι,
  νικᾶν δ' οὐκ εἴασ' οὐδετέρους ἀδίκως.

(*2*) πάλιν δ' ἀποφαινόμενος περὶ τοῦ πλήθους, ὡς αὐτῷ δεῖ χρῆσθαι·

δῆμος δ' ὧδ' ἂν ἄριστα σὺν ἡγεμόνεσσιν ἕποιτο,
  μήτε λίαν ἀνεθεὶς μήτε βιαζόμενος.
τίκτει γὰρ κόρος ὕβριν, ὅταν πολὺς ὄλβος ἕπηται
  ἀνθρώποισιν ὅσοις μὴ νόος ἄρτιος ᾖ.

(*3*) καὶ πάλιν δ' ἑτέρωθί που λέγει περὶ τῶν διανείμασθαι τὴν γῆν βουλομένων·

οἳ δ' ἐφ' ἁρπαγαῖσιν ἦλθον, ἐλπίδ' εἶχον ἀφνεάν,
κἀδόκουν ἕκαστος αὐτῶν ὄλβον εὑρήσειν πολύν,
καί με κωτίλλοντα λείως τραχὺν ἐκφανεῖν νόον.
χαῦνα μὲν τότ' ἐφράσαντο, νῦν δέ μοι χολούμενοι
λοξὸν ὀφθαλμοῖσ' ὁρῶσι πάντες ὥστε δήιον.
οὐ χρεών· ἃ μὲν γὰρ εἶπα, σὺν θεοῖσιν ἤνυσα,
ἄ[λλ]α δ' ο[ὐ] μάτην ἔερδον, οὐδέ μοι τυραννίδος
ἁνδάνει βίᾳ τι [ῥέζ]ειν, οὐδὲ πιείρας χθονὸς
πατρίδος κακοῖσιν ἐσθλοὺς ἰσομοιρίαν ἔχειν.

12. 1. ἀπαρκεῖ<ν> (Herwerden &) Leeuwen, K. Ziegler: ἀπαρκεῖ L, κράτος ὅσσον ἐπαρκεῖ Plut., ἐπαρκεῖν Brunck, West.

12. 2. λίαν L: λίην (et η for ᾱ throughout) West.

βιαζόμενος L: πιεζόμενος Plut.

12. 3. οἳ edd.: οἱ West, perhaps rightly.

κἀδόκουν L: κἀδόκ[ε]ον West.

τι [ῥέζ]ειν Kenyon[1]: [κιν]εῖν J. B. Bury (*CR*), τι[. .] . ε[ι]ν West.

ἐσθ[λοὺς] … ἐχει[ρώθη] (12. 4) present in B, fr. Ia.

I gave the *demos* as much prerogative as would suffice,
Not detracting from its honour or reaching out for it;
While, as for those who had power and were admired for their possessions,
I pronounced to them also that they should have nothing unseemly.
I stood holding my stout buckler against both,
And did not allow either an unjust victory.

(*2*) Again, another passage about the masses, revealing how they ought to be treated:

This is how the *demos* would best follow its leaders:
Neither let loose too far nor constrained.
For excess generates insolence, when great wealth attends
Men who do not possess a sound mind.

(*3*)And again somewhere else he says about those who wanted the land to be distributed:

They came for plunder and had lavish hopes,
And each of them expected to find great wealth,
And that I though chattering smoothly should reveal a harsh mind.
Their supposition then was vain; but now they are angry with me
And their eyes all look askance at me as if I were a foe.
It should not be. What I said, I accomplished with the help of the gods;
I did nothing without reason; nor does it please me
Violently to do any of the deeds of tyranny, or that of the rich land
Of our country the good should have equal shares with the bad.

(*4*) [π]ἀ̣λ̣ιṿ δὲ καὶ περὶ τῆς ἀποκοπῆς τῶν χρεῶν καὶ τῶν δουλευόντων μὲν πρότερον, ἐλευθερωθέντων δὲ διὰ τὴν σεισάχθειαν·

ἐγὼ δὲ τῶν μὲν οὕνεκα ξυνήγαγον
δῆμον, τί τούτων πρὶν τυχεῖν ἐπαυσάμην;
συμμαρτυροίη ταῦτ' ἂν ἐν δίκῃ χρόνου
μήτηρ μεγίστη δαιμόνων Ὀλυμπίων
ἄριστα, Γῆ μέλαινα, τῆς ἐγώ ποτε
ὅρους ἀνεῖλον πολλαχῇ πεπηγότας,
πρόσθεν δὲ δουλεύουσα, νῦν ἐλευθέρα.
πολλοὺς δ' Ἀθήνας, πατρίδ' εἰς θεόκτιτον,
ἀνήγαγον πραθέντας, ἄλλον ἐκδίκως,
ἄλλον δικαίως, τοὺς δ' ἀναγκαίης ὑπὸ
χρειοῦς φυγόντας, γλῶσσαν οὐκέτ' Ἀττικὴν
ἱέντας, ὡς ἂν πολλαχῇ πλανωμένους·
τοὺς δ' ἐνθάδ' αὐτοῦ δουλίην ἀεικέα
ἔχοντας, ἤθη δεσποτῶν τρομευμένους,
ἐλευθέρους ἔθηκα. ταῦτα μὲν κράτει,
ὁμοῦ βίαν τε καὶ δίκην συναρμόσας,
ἔρεξα, καὶ διῆλθον ὡς ὑπεσχόμην.
θεσμοὺς δ' ὁμοίως τῷ κακῷ τε κἀγαθῷ,
εὐθεῖαν εἰς ἕκαστον ἁρμόσας δίκην,
ἔγραψα. κέντρον δ' ἄλλος ὡς ἐγὼ λαβών,
κακοφραδής τε καὶ φιλοκτήμων ἀνήρ,
οὐκ ἂν κατέσχε δῆμον. εἰ γὰρ ἤθελον

12. 4. [π]ἀ̣λ̣ιṿ Chambers, [πάλιν] Kenyon ('fitting traces sufficiently'), cf. §§2, 3, 5: . . . ει Wilcken.

πρόσθεν δὲ all sources: γε H. Stadtmüller, J. B. Mayor (*CR*), Chambers.

χρειοῦς φυγόντας L: χρεῶν B, χρησμὸν λέγοντας Aristides.

ὡς ἂν: all sources: ὥστε A. Platt, ὡς δὴ West.

κράτει, ὁμοῦ Aristid., West, Gentili & Prato, Chambers: κρατεει νόμου L (whence κράτει νόμου Kenyon), κράτη ὁμοῦ B, ὁμοῦ (without the previous line) Plut.

θεσμοὺς δ' ὁμοίως West, Gentili & Prato: θεσμοὺς θ' ὁμοίως L (θ above τε), θεσμὸν δ' ὁμοίως B, θεσμοὺς θ' ὁμοίως vel ὁμοίους Aristides.

τῷ κακῷ τε κἀγαθῷ L: καλῷ B.

(*4*) And again, about the cancellation of debts and those who were previously enslaved but freed through the *seisachtheia*:

Of the things for which I called together
The *demos*, did I cease before I had achieved any?
I might call as best witness, in the justice which time brings,
The great mother of the Olympian deities,
Black Earth, from which I
Took up the markers which were fixed in many places.
The Earth which previously was enslaved but now is free.
Many men to Athens, to their divinely-founded country,
I brought back, who had been sold, some unjustly
And some justly, some who under compelling need
Had fled, no longer uttering the Attic
Tongue, but straying in many places.
And those right here, suffering unseemly
Slavery, trembling at the ways of their masters,
I made free. This I did by might,
Harnessing force and justice together,
And I persevered as I promised.
Statutes for bad and good alike,
Applying straight justice to each man,
I wrote. Another man, taking up the goad as I did,
A man of evil counsel and love of possessions,
Would not have restrained the *demos*. For if I had been willing

ἃ τοῖς ἐναντίοισιν ἥνδανεν τότε,
αὖθις δ' ἃ τοῖσιν οὕτεροι φρασαίατο,
πολλῶν ἂν ἀνδρῶν ἥδ' ἐχηρώθη πόλις.
τῶν οὕνεκ' ἀλκὴν πάντοθεν ποιούμενος
ὡς ἐν κυσὶν πολλαῖσιν ἐστράφην λύκος.

(*5*) καὶ πάλιν ὀνειδίζων πρὸς τὰς ὕστερον αὐτῶν μεμψιμοιρίας ἀμφοτέρων·

δήμῳ μὲν εἰ χρὴ διαφάδην ὀνειδίσαι,
ἃ νῦν ἔχουσιν οὔποτ' ὀφθαλμοῖσιν ἂν
εὕδοντες εἶδον.
ὅσοι δὲ μείζους καὶ βίαν ἀμείνονες
αἰνοῖεν ἄν με καὶ φίλον ποιοίατο.

εἰ γάρ τις ἄλλος, φησί, ταύτης τῆς τιμῆς ἔτυχεν,

οὐκ ἂν κατέσχε δῆμον, οὐδ' ἐπαύσατο
πρὶν ἀνταράξας πῖαρ ἐξεῖλεν γάλα.
ἐγὼ δὲ τούτων ὥσπερ ἐν μεταιχμίῳ
†ὅρος† κατέστην.

(**13**) τὴν μὲν οὖν ἀποδημίαν ἐποιήσατο διὰ ταύτας τὰς αἰτίας. Σόλωνος δ' ἀποδημήσαντος, ἔτι τῆς πόλεως τεταραγμένης, ἐπὶ μὲν ἔτη τέτταρα διῆγον ἐν ἡσυχίᾳ· τῷ δὲ πέμπτῳ μετὰ τὴν Σόλωνος ἀρχὴν οὐ κατέστησαν ἄρχοντα διὰ τὴν στάσιν, καὶ πάλιν ἔτει πέμπτῳ διὰ τὴν αὐτὴν αἰτίαν ἀναρχίαν ἐποίησαν. (*2*) μετὰ δὲ ταῦτα διὰ τῶν αὐτῶν χρόνων Δαμασίας αἱρεθεὶς ἄρχων ἔτη δύο καὶ δύο μῆνας ἦρξεν, ἕως ἐξηλάθη βίᾳ τῆς ἀρχῆς. εἶτ' ἔδοξεν αὐτοῖς διὰ τὸ στασιάζειν ἄρχοντας ἑλέσθαι δέκα, πέντε μὲν

12. 4. ἃ τοῖς … ἃ τοῖσιν B, Aristides: αὐτοῖς … αὐτοῖσιν L.
αὖθις Aristides: αὖτις B, West, Gentili & Prato, αυ[. .]ς L.
12. 5. πῖαρ Plut.: πῦαρ L.
†ὅρος† I obelise: <δ>όρος W. W. Jaeger, οὖρος T. C. W. Stinton.
13. 1. τῷ δὲ [πέμπ]τῳ … [καθαροὶ] δ̣ι̣ὰ̣ (13. 5) present in B, fr. Ib.
διὰ τὴν αὐτὴν αἰτίαν: διὰ omitted L, διὰ ταύτην τὴν [αἰτίαν] B.
13. 2. ἐξηλάθη Herwerden (& Leeuwen): ἐξηλάσθη B, L.

To do what pleased the *demos*' opponents then,
Or again to do what the other side planned against them,
This city would have been widowed of many men.
On that account I set up a defence on all sides,
And turned about like a wolf among many bitches.

(*5*) And again, reproaching the subsequent fault-finding of both sides:

If I am to reproach the *demos* openly,
What they have now their eyes would never
Have seen in their sleep.
And those who are greater and better in strength
Should raise me and make me their friend.

For if another man, he says, had obtained this position,

He would not have restrained the *demos*, or have ceased
Until he had stirred up the milk and taken off the cream.
But as if in the no man's land between them
I stood as a boundary marker (?).

(**13**) Solon made his foreign journey for that reason. While he was journeying, and the city was still in a state of upheaval, they remained at peace for four years, but in the fifth year after Solon's archonship they did not appoint an archon because of their dissension; and again in the fifth year after that for the same reason they had a year without an archon. (*2*) After the same interval of time after that Damasias when appointed archon held office for two years and two months, until he was ejected from his office by force. Then they decided on account of their dissension to appoint ten archons, five from the *eupatridai*, three from

εὐπατριδῶν, τρεῖς δὲ ἀγροίκων, δύο δὲ δημιουργῶν, καὶ οὗτοι τὸν μετὰ Δαμασίαν ἦρξαν ἐνιαυτόν. ᾧ καὶ δῆλον ὅτι μεγίστην εἶχεν δύναμιν ὁ ἄρχων· φαίνονται γὰρ αἰεὶ στασιάζοντες περὶ ταύτης τῆς ἀρχῆς. (*3*) ὅλως δὲ διετέλουν νοσοῦντες τὰ πρὸς ἑαυτούς, οἱ μὲν ἀρχὴν καὶ πρόφασιν ἔχοντες τὴν τῶν χρεῶν ἀποκοπήν (συνεβεβήκει γὰρ αὐτοῖς γεγονέναι πένησιν), οἱ δὲ τῇ πολιτείᾳ δυσχεραίνοντες διὰ τὸ μεγάλην γεγονέναι μεταβολήν, ἔνιοι δὲ διὰ τὴν πρὸς ἀλλήλους φιλονικίαν. (*4*) ἦσαν δ' αἱ στάσεις τρεῖς· μία μὲν τῶν παραλίων, ὧν προειστήκει Μεγακλῆς ὁ Ἀλκμέωνος, οἵπερ ἐδόκουν μάλιστα διώκειν τὴν μέσην πολιτείαν· ἄλλη δὲ τῶν πεδιακῶν, οἳ τὴν ὀλιγαρχίαν ἐζήτουν, ἡγεῖτο δ' αὐτῶν Λυκοῦργος· τρίτη δ' ἡ τῶν διακρίων, ἐφ' ᾗ τεταγμένος ἦν Πεισίστρατος, δημοτικώτατος εἶναι δοκῶν. (*5*) προσεκεκόσμηντο δὲ τούτοις οἵ τε ἀφῃρημένοι τὰ χρέα διὰ τὴν ἀπορίαν καὶ οἱ τῷ γένει μὴ καθαροὶ διὰ τὸν φόβον· σημεῖον δ', ὅτι μετὰ τὴν τῶν τυράννων κατάλυσιν ἐποίησαν διαψηφισμόν, ὡς πολλῶν κοινωνούντων τῆς πολιτείας οὐ προσῆκον. εἶχον δ' ἕκαστοι τὰς ἐπωνυμίας ἀπὸ τῶν τόπων ἐν οἷς ἐγεώργουν.

(**14**) δημοτικώτατος δ' εἶναι δοκῶν ὁ Πεισίστρατος καὶ σφόδρ' εὐδοκιμηκὼς ἐν τῷ πρὸς Μεγαρέας πολέμῳ, κατατραυματίσας ἑαυτὸν συνέπεισε τὸν δῆμον, ὡς ὑπὸ τῶν ἀντιστασιωτῶν ταῦτα πεπονθώς, φυλακὴν ἑαυτῷ δοῦναι τοῦ σώματος, Ἀριστίωνος γράψαντος τὴν γνώμην. λαβὼν δὲ τοὺς κορυνηφόρους καλουμένους, ἐπαναστὰς μετὰ τούτων τῷ δήμῳ κατέσχε τὴν ἀκρόπολιν, ἔτει δευτέρῳ καὶ τριακοστῷ μετὰ τὴν τῶν νόμων θέσιν, ἐπὶ Κωμέου ἄρχοντος. (*2*) λέγεται δὲ Σόλωνα, Πεισιστράτου τὴν φυλακὴν αἰτοῦντος, ἀντιλέξαι καὶ εἰπεῖν ὅτι τῶν μὲν εἴη σοφώτερος, τῶν δ' ἀνδρειότερος· ὅσοι μὲν γὰρ ἀγνοοῦσι Πεισίστρατον ἐπιτιθέμενον τυραννίδι, σοφώτερος εἶναι τούτων, ὅσοι δ' εἰδότες κατασιωπῶσιν, ἀνδρειότερος. ἐπεὶ δὲ λέγων [οὐκ ἔ]πειθεν, ἐξαράμενος τὰ ὅπλα πρὸ τῶν θυρῶν αὐτὸς μὲν ἔφη βεβοηθηκέναι τῇ πατρίδι καθ' ὅσον ἦν δυνατός (ἤδη γὰρ σφόδρα πρεσβύτης ἦν), ἀξιοῦν δὲ καὶ τοὺς ἄλλους ταὐτὸ τοῦτο ποιεῖν. (*3*) Σόλων μὲν οὖν οὐδὲν ἤνυσεν τότε παρακαλῶν. Πεισίστρατος δὲ λαβὼν τὴν ἀρχὴν διῴκει τὰ κοινά πολιτικῶς μᾶλλον ἢ τυραννικῶς.

13. 2. ἀγροίκων L: ἀποίκων B.

13. 5. διαψηφισμόν Sandys (*CR*): δ(ια)φημισμό(ν) L.

the rustics and two from the craftsmen; and these held office for the year after Damasias. From this it is clear that the archon had the greatest power, for it is evident that their dissension was always focused on this office. (*3*) Altogether they continued in a diseased state with regard to relations between one another, some having as origin and explanation the cancellation of debts (since it had turned out that they had become poor), others discontented with the political régime because of the great change which had occurred, and some because of their rivalry with one another. (*4*) The factions were three in number: one of the coastal men, over which presided Megacles son of Alcmeon, a group which seemed particularly to be aiming for a middling régime; another of the men of the plain, who sought oligarchy, and their leader was Lycurgus; and the third that of the *Diakrioi*, in charge of which was Pisistratus, who seemed to be most democratic. (*5*) There were added to adorn these last those who had been deprived of the debts due to them, because of their hardship, and those of impure ancestry, because of their fear: an indication is that after the overthrow of the tyranny they held a review vote, because there were many participating in the régime who were not qualified to do so. The three factions each took their names from the places where they farmed.

(**14**) Pisistratus seemed to be most democratic, and had gained a very good reputation in the war against Megara. He wounded himself, and as if this has been done to him by his opponents he persuaded the *demos* to give him a bodyguard; the proposal was made by Aristion. Taking those who were called club-bearers, he rose up against the *demos* with these and seized the acropolis, in the thirty-second year after the enactment of the laws, in the archonship of Comeas. (*2*) It is said that when Pisistratus asked for his bodyguard Solon spoke against it, and said that he was wiser than some and braver than others: wiser than those who did not recognise that Pisistratus was aiming at tyranny and braver than those who knew but kept quiet. When he had spoken but failed to persuade, he set up his arms in front of his house, and said that he had supported his country as far as he was able (for he was now a very old man) but called on the others to do this same thing also. (*3*) But Solon had no success in making this appeal. Pisistratus assumed a ruling position, and

οὔπω δὲ τῆς ἀρχῆς ἐρριζωμένης, ὁμοφρονήσαντες οἱ περὶ τὸν Μεγακλέα καὶ τὸν Λυκοῦργον ἐξέβαλον αὐτόν, ἕκτῳ ἔτει μετὰ τὴν πρώτην κατάστασιν, ἐφ' Ἡγησίου ἄρχοντος. (*4*) ἔτει δὲ πέμπτῳ μετὰ ταῦτα περιελαυνόμενος ὁ Μεγακλῆς τῇ στάσει πάλιν ἐπικηρυκευσάμενος πρὸς τὸν Πεισίστρατον, ἐφ' ᾧ τε τὴν θυγατέρα αὐτοῦ λήψεται, κατήγαγεν αὐτὸν ἀρχαίως καὶ λίαν ἁπλῶς. προδιασπείρας γὰρ λόγον ὡς τῆς Ἀθηνᾶς καταγούσης Πεισίστρατον, καὶ γυναῖκα μεγάλην καὶ καλὴν ἐξευρών, ὡς μὲν Ἡρόδοτός φησιν ἐκ τοῦ δήμου τῶν Παιανιέων, ὡς δ' ἔνιοι λέγουσιν ἐκ τοῦ Κολλυτοῦ στεφανόπωλιν Θρᾷτταν, ᾗ ὄνομα Φύη, τὴν θεὸν ἀπομιμησάμενος τῷ κόσμῳ συνεισήγαγεν μετ' αὐτοῦ· καὶ ὁ μὲν Πεισίστρατος ἐφ' ἅρματος εἰσήλαυνε παραιβατούσης τῆς γυναικός, οἱ δ' ἐν τῷ ἄστει προσκυνοῦντες ἐδέχοντο θαυμάζοντες.

(**15**) ἡ μὲν οὖν πρώτη κάθοδος ἐγένετο τοιαύτη. μετὰ δὲ ταῦτα ὡς ἐξέπεσε τὸ δεύτερον, ἔτει μάλιστα ἑβδόμῳ μετὰ τὴν κάθοδον, (οὐ γὰρ πολὺν χρόνον κατέσχεν, ἀλλὰ διὰ τὸ μὴ βούλεσθαι τῇ τοῦ Μεγακλέους θυγατρὶ συγγίγνεσθαι φοβηθεὶς ἀμφοτέρας τὰς στάσεις ὑπεξῆλθεν), (*2*) καὶ πρῶτον μὲν συνῴκισε περὶ τὸν Θερμαῖον κόλπον χωρίον ὃ καλεῖται Ῥαίκηλος, ἐκεῖθεν δὲ παρῆλθεν εἰς τοὺς περὶ Πάγγαιον τόπους, ὅθεν χρηματισάμενος καὶ στρατιώτας μισθωσάμενος ἐλθὼν εἰς Ἐρέτριαν ἑνδεκάτῳ πάλιν ἔτει τό<τε> πρῶτον ἀνασώσασθαι βίᾳ τὴν ἀρχὴν ἐπεχείρει, συμπροθυμουμένων αὐτῷ πολλῶν μὲν καὶ ἄλλων, μάλιστα δὲ Θηβαίων καὶ Λυγδάμιος τοῦ Ναξίου, ἔτι δὲ τῶν ἱππέων τῶν ἐχόντων ἐν Ἐρετρίᾳ τὴν πολιτείαν. (*3*) νικήσας δὲ τὴν ἐπὶ Παλληνίδι μάχην καὶ λαβὼν τὴν πόλιν καὶ παρελόμενος τοῦ δήμου τὰ ὅπλα, κατεῖχεν ἤδη τὴν τυρρανίδα βεβαίως· καὶ Νάξον ἑλὼν ἄρχοντα κατέστησε Λύγδαμιν. (*4*) παρείλετο <δὲ> τοῦ δήμου τὰ ὅπλα τόνδε τὸν τρόπον. ἐξοπλασίαν

14. 4. πέμπτῳ Wilamowitz, *A.u.A.* i. 22–3: δωδεκάτῳ L.

15. 1. ὡς deleted Kaibel & Wilamowitz: αὖθις A. Gennadios (*CR*), perhaps 15. 2 {καὶ} πρῶτον μὲν Kenyon[5].

15. 2. τό<τε> Blass: τὸ L.

15. 4. παρείλετο <δὲ> Chambers: παρεῖλε<το> δὲ W. G. Rutherford (*CR*), cf. 15. 3 παρελόμενος, παρεῖλε retained Thalheim.

administered public affairs in a citizen's rather than a tyrant's manner. But, when his rule had not yet taken root, the factions of Megacles and Lycurgus came to an agreement and drove him out, in the sixth year after his first establishment, in the archonship of Hegesias. (*4*) In the fifth year after that Megacles, who was under pressure in the factional rivalry, made overtures to Pisistratus, on condition that Pisistratus should marry his daughter, and installed him in an archaic and over-simple manner. For he circulated in advance a story that Athena was reinstalling Pisistraus; and he found a tall and handsome woman whose name was Phye – as Herodotus says, from the deme of Paeania, but as some say, a Thracian garland-seller from Collytus – adorned her in imitation of the goddess, and brought her in with Pisistratus; and Pisistratus drove in a chariot with the woman standing at his side. And the people in the city received them with reverence and wonder.

(**15**) His first return happened like that. After this he was expelled for the second time, about the seventh year after his return: for he did not hold down his position for a long time, but because he was unwilling to have intercourse with Megacles' daughter he became afraid of both factions and withdrew. (*2*) First he joined in settling a place near the Thermaic Gulf called Rhaecelus; from there he arrived at the locality around Pangaeum, and after obtaining funds and hiring soldiers he went to Eretria, in the eleventh year again. This was when he first tried to recover his rule by force, with the enthusiastic support of many others and in particular the Thebans and Lygdamis of Naxos, and also the cavalry who controlled the régime in Eretria. (*3*) He won the battle at Pallenis and took control of the city, and he deprived the *demos* of its arms, and then held down the tyranny firmly. Also he captured Naxos and installed Lygdamis as its ruler. (*4*) He deprived the *demos* of its arms

ἐν τῷ Θησείῳ ποιησάμενος ἐκκλησιάζειν ἐπεχ̣ε̣ίρει, καὶ [χρόνον προσηγό]ρευεν μικρόν· οὐ φασκόντων δὲ κατακούειν, ἐκέλευσεν αὐτοὺς προσαναβῆναι πρὸς τὸ πρόπυλον τῆς ἀκροπόλεως, ἵνα γεγωνῇ μᾶλλον. ἐν ᾧ δ᾽ ἐκεῖνος διέτριβε δημηγορῶν, ἀνελόντες οἱ ἐπὶ τούτῳ τεταγμένοι τὰ ὅπλα καὶ [κατα]κλείσαντες εἰς τὰ πλησίον οἰκήματα τοῦ Θησείου διεσήμηναν ἐλθόντες πρὸς τὸν Πεισίστρατον. (*5*) ὁ δὲ ἐπεὶ τὸν ἄλλον λόγον ἐπετέλεσεν, εἶπε καὶ περὶ τῶν ὅπλων τὸ γεγονός, ὡς οὐ χρὴ θαυμάζειν οὐδ᾽ ἀθυμεῖν, ἀλλ᾽ ἀπελθόντας ἐπὶ τῶν ἰδίων εἶναι, τῶν δὲ κοινῶν αὐτὸς ἐπιμελήσεσθαι πάντων.

(**16**) ἡ μὲν οὖν Πεισιστράτου τυραννὶς ἐξ ἀρχῆς τε κατέστη τοῦτον τὸν τρόπον, καὶ μεταβολὰς ἔσχεν τοσαύτας. (*2*) διῴκει δ᾽ ὁ Πεισίστρατος, ὥσπερ εἴρηται, τὰ περὶ τὴν πόλιν μετρίως καὶ μᾶλλον πολιτικῶς ἢ τυραννικῶς. ἔν τε γὰρ τοῖς ἄλλοις φιλάνθρωπος ἦν καὶ πρᾶος καὶ τοῖς ἁμαρτάνουσι συγγνωμονικός, καὶ δὴ καὶ τοῖς ἀπόροις προεδάνειζε χρήματα πρὸς τὰς ἐργασίας, ὥστε διατρέφεσθαι γεωργοῦντας. (*3*) τοῦτο δ᾽ ἐποίει δυοῖν χάριν, ἵνα μήτε ἐν τῷ ἄστει διατρίβωσιν ἀλλὰ διεσπαρμένοι κατὰ τὴν χώραν, καὶ ὅπως εὐποροῦντες τῶν μετρίων καὶ πρὸς τοῖς ἰδίοις ὄντες μήτ᾽ ἐπιθυμῶσι μήτε σχολάζωσιν ἐπιμελεῖσθαι τῶν κοινῶν. (*4*) ἅμα δὲ συνέβαινεν αὐτῷ καὶ τὰς προσόδους γίγνεσθαι μείζους ἐξεργαζομένης τῆς χώρας. ἐπράττετο γὰρ ἀπὸ τῶν γιγνομένων δεκάτην. (*5*) διὸ καὶ τοὺς κατὰ δήμους κατεσκεύασε δικαστάς, καὶ αὐτὸς ἐξῄει πολλάκις εἰς τὴν χώραν, ἐπισκοπῶν καὶ διαλύων τοὺς διαφερομένους, ὅπως μὴ καταβαίνοντες εἰς τὸ ἄστυ παραμελῶσι τῶν ἔργων. (*6*) τοιαύτης γάρ τινος ἐξόδου τῷ Πεισιστράτῳ γιγνομένης, συμβῆναί φασι τὰ περὶ τὸν ἐν τῷ Ὑμηττῷ γεωργοῦντα τὸ κληθὲν ὕστερον χωρίον ἀτελές. ἰδὼν γάρ τινα παντελῶς πέτρας σκάπτοντα καὶ ἐργαζόμενον, διὰ τὸ θαυμάσαι τὸν παῖδα ἐκέλευσεν ἐρέσθαι τί γίγνεται ἐκ τοῦ χωρίου. ὁ δ᾽ "ὅσα κακὰ καὶ ὀδύναι" ἔφη, "καὶ τούτων τῶν κακῶν καὶ τῶν ὀδυνῶν Πεισίστρατον δεῖ λαβεῖν τὴν δεκάτην." ὁ μὲν οὖν ἄνθρωπος ἀπεκρίνατο ἀγνοῶν, ὁ δὲ

15. 4. κ(αὶ) [χρ(όνον) προσηγό]ρευεν μικρόν Kenyon [4–5] ('extremely uncertain'), approved Thomas: κ(αὶ) [χρ(όνον) μὲν ἠκκλησί[ασεν Thalheim (]ασεν Kenyon[1–3], possible Kenyon[4]), γ^{ω} δ̣ε̣σ̣τ̣ε̣γεν Wilcken, rejected Thomas, traces illegible Chambers.

τούτῳ W. G. Rutherford and J. E. B. Mayor (*CR*): τούτ(ων) L.

[κατα]κλείσαντες (ηι L) Blass[2].

16. 2. πρᾶος L, cf. 22. 4: πρᾷος Kaibel & Wilamowitz.

in the following way. Holding an armed parade in the Theseum, he tried to address the assembled men, and continued speaking for a short time. When the men claimed that they could not hear him, he instructed them to go up to the entrance gate of the acropolis so that he could make himself heard better; and while he spent time haranguing them the men who had been given that task took up the arms, shut them in the nearby buildings of the Theseum and went and signalled this to Pisistratus. (*5*) When he had completed the rest of his speech, he told them also what had been done with their arms, and said that they should not be surprised or despondent but should go back and focus on their individual affairs, and he would take care of all public matters.

(**16**) That is the way in which Pisistratus' tyranny was established from the beginning, and that is the series of changes which it underwent. (*2*) As has been said, Pisistratus administered affairs in the city moderately, and in a citizen's rather than a tyrant's manner. Among other things he was humane, mild and disposed to forgive offenders; and in particular he lent funds to the needy for their working, so that they could maintain themselves by farming. (*3*) He did this for two reasons: so that they should spend their time not in the city but dispersed across the countryside, and in order that they should be provided with their modest needs and be focused on their individual affairs without having either the desire or the leisure to care for public affairs. (*4*) At the same time this resulted in his revenues' becoming greater, as the land was thoroughly worked: for he exacted a tithe of the produce. (*5*) For that reason also he devised the deme justices, and he himself often went out into the countryside, inspecting, and reconciling men who were involved in disputes, so that they should not go down to the city and neglect their work. (*6*) When Pisistratus was making one of his excursions of this kind there is said to have occurred the incident concerning the man who was farming what was afterwards called the tax-free plot, in the region of Hymettus. He saw a man digging and working what was entirely stones, and because he was surprised he told his attendant to ask what was produced from the plot. The man said, 'Just evil and pain, and of this evil and pain Pisistratus has to take a tithe'. The man gave this answer without recognising him,

Πεισίστρατος ἡσθεὶς διὰ τὴν παρρησίαν καὶ τὴν φιλεργίαν ἀτελῆ πάντων ἐποίησεν αὐτόν. (*7*) οὐδὲν δὲ τὸ πλῆθος οὐδ’ ἐν τοῖς ἄλλοις παρώχλει κατὰ τὴν ἀρχήν, ἀλλ’ αἰεὶ παρεσκεύαζεν εἰρήνην καὶ ἐτήρει τὴν ἡσυχίαν· διὸ καὶ πολλὰ κλέ[α ἐ]θρ[ύλλο]υν ὡς ἡ Πεισιστράτου τυραννὶς ὁ ἐπὶ Κρόνου βίος εἴη· συνέβη γὰρ ὕστερον δια[δε]ξ[α]μένων τῶν υἱέων πολλῷ γενέσθαι τραχυτέραν τὴν ἀρχήν. (*8*) μέγιστον δὲ πάντων ἦν τῶν ε[ἰρη]μένων τὸ δημοτικὸν εἶναι τῷ ἤθει καὶ φιλάνθρωπον. ἔν τε γὰρ τοῖς ἄλλοις ἐβούλετο πάντα διοικεῖν κατὰ τοὺς νόμους, οὐδεμίαν ἑαυτῷ πλεονεξίαν διδούς, καί ποτε προσκληθεὶς φόνου δίκην εἰς Ἄρειον πάγον αὐτὸς μὲν ἀπήντησεν ὡς ἀπολογησόμενος, ὁ δὲ προσκαλεσάμενος φοβηθεὶς ἔλιπεν. (*9*) διὸ καὶ πολὺν χρόνον ἔμεινεν <ἐν> [τῇ ἀρ]χ[ῇ], καὶ ὅτ’ ἐκπέσοι πάλιν ἀνελάμβανε ῥᾳδίως. ἐβούλοντο γὰρ καὶ τῶν γνωρίμων καὶ τῶν δημοτικῶν οἱ πολλοί· τοὺς μὲν γὰρ ταῖς ὁμιλίαις, τοὺς δὲ ταῖς εἰς τὰ ἴδια βοηθείαις προσήγετο, καὶ πρὸς ἀμφοτέρους ἐπεφύκει καλῶς. (*10*) ἦσαν δὲ καὶ τοῖς Ἀθηναίοις οἱ περὶ τῶν τυράννων νόμοι πρᾶοι κατ’ ἐκείνους τοὺς καιρούς, οἵ τ’ ἄλλοι καὶ δὴ καὶ ὁ μάλιστα καθήκων πρὸς τὴν τῆς τυραννίδος <κατάστασιν>. νόμος γὰρ αὐτοῖς ἦν ὅδε· “θέσμια τάδε Ἀθηναίων ἐστὶ καὶ πάτρια· ἐάν τινες {τυραννεῖν} ἐπανιστῶνται ἐπὶ τυραννίδι ἢ συγκαθιστῇ τὴν τυραννίδα, ἄτιμον εἶναι καὶ αὐτὸν καὶ γένος.”

16. 7. παρώχλει L, cf. Theophr. *Caus. Pl.* III. 10. 5: παρ<ην>ώχλει J. B. Mayor and W. Wyse (*CR*).

πολλὰ κλέ[α ἐ]θρ[ύλλο]υν Kenyon[4–5] (‘not certain but fits traces sufficiently’), approved Thomas: πολλάκ[ις ἐ]θρ[ύλλουν] Thalheim (πολλάκις Kenyon[1–3]), πολλα̣ . ε̣λει̣ετο̣υ̣ . . ιν Wilcken (whence πολλ . . ἐλέγετο . . . . . Kaibel & Wilamowitz[3]), traces illegible Chambers.

16. 9. ἔμεινεν <ἐν> [τη̣ ἀρ]χ[ῇ] Kenyon[4–5] (conjectured Blass), ἀ[ρ]χ[ῇ] Wilcken: ἔμεινεν [ἡ] ἀ[ρ]χ[ὴ] Blass[4], Chambers.

ἀνελάμβανε H. Richards (*CR*): ἐπελάμβανε L.

16. 10. πρᾶοι Chambers, cf. 16. 2, 22. 4: πρᾳ̃οι L.

<κατάστασιν> Kaibel & Wilamowitz (in *apparatus*).

Ἀθηναίων (ἐστὶ) Kenyon[4–5], Chambers: (ἐστὶ) not read Blass[2–4], Wilcken.

τυραννεῖν deleted N. C. Conomis: ἐπὶ τυραννίδι deleted Kenyon, but present in RO 79 = *IG* ii[3] 320. 7.

ἢ συγκαθιστῇ Kaibel & Wilamowitz: τι or rather ἢ συγκαθιστῇ L: τι<ς> συγκαθιστῇ Kenyon[1], συγκαθιστῇ <τις> Sandys[2].

but Pisistratus was pleased at his free speech and devotion to work, and made him free of all taxes. (*7*) During his rule he did nothing to trouble the masses in any other respect either, but always secured peace and was careful to maintain calm. For that reason many good reports were spread that Pisistratus' tyranny was the life of the age of Cronus: for it happened that later when his sons took over the régime became much harsher. (*8*) Greatest of all the points mentioned was that he was democratic in his character and humane. For in other respects he was willing to administer everything in accordance with the laws, not giving himself any advantage; and once when he was summoned to the Areopagus for a homicide trial he presented himself to answer the charge but the summoner took fright and abandoned it. (*9*) For that reason he continued in his rule for a long time, and on the occasions when he was expelled he recovered it easily. For he had the consent of many both of the notables and of the democratic: he won over the notables by his friendly dealing with them and the democratic with his support for their individual concerns, and he inclined well to both. (*10*) Also the Athenians' laws about tyrants were mild at that time, in general and in particular the law applying to the establishment of tyranny; for this was their law: 'These are statutory and traditional rules of the Athenians: if any men rise up for tyranny or he joins in establishing the tyranny, he shall be *atimos*, both himself and his descendants'.

(**17**) Πεισίστρατος μὲν οὖν ἐγκατεγήρασε τῇ ἀρχῇ, καὶ ἀπέθανε νοσήσας ἐπὶ Φιλόνεω ἄρχοντος, ἀφ' οὗ μὲν κατέστη τὸ πρῶτον τύραννος ἔτη τριάκοντα καὶ τρία βιώσας, ἃ δ' ἐν τῇ ἀρχῇ διέμεινεν ἑνὸς δέοντα εἴκοσι· ἔφευγε γὰρ τὰ λοιπά. (*2*) διὸ καὶ φανερῶς ληροῦσι<ν οἱ> φάσκοντες ἐρώμενον εἶναι Πεισίστρατον Σόλωνος, καὶ στρατηγεῖν ἐν τῷ πρὸς Μεγαρέας πολέμῳ περὶ Σαλαμῖνος· οὐ γὰρ ἐνδέχεται ταῖς ἡλικίαις, ἐάν τις ἀναλογίζηται τὸν ἑκατέρου βίον καὶ ἐφ' οὗ ἀπέθανεν ἄρχοντος. (*3*) τελευτήσαντος δὲ Πεισιστράτου κατεῖχον οἱ υἱεῖς τὴν ἀρχήν, προάγοντες τὰ πράγματα τὸν αὐτὸν τρόπον. ἦσαν δὲ δύο μὲν ἐκ τῆς γαμετῆς, Ἱππίας καὶ Ἵππαρχος, δύο δ' ἐκ τῆς Ἀργείας, Ἰοφῶν καὶ Ἡγησίστρατος, ᾧ παρωνύμιον ἦν Θέτταλος. (*4*) ἔγημεν γὰρ Πεισίστρατος ἐξ Ἄργους ἀνδρὸς Ἀργείου θυγατέρα, ᾧ ὄνομα ἦν Γοργίλος, Τιμώνασσαν, ἣν πρότερον ἔσχεν γυναῖκα Ἀρχῖνος ὁ Ἀμπρακιώτης τῶν Κυψελιδῶν· ὅθεν καὶ ἡ πρὸς τοὺς Ἀργείους ἐνέστη φιλία, καὶ συνεμαχέσαντο χίλιοι τὴν ἐπὶ Παλληνίδι μάχην, Ἡγησιστράτου κομίσαντος. γῆμαι δέ φασι τὴν Ἀργείαν οἱ μὲν ἐκπεσόντα τὸ πρῶτον, οἱ δὲ κατέχοντα τὴν ἀρχήν.

(**18**) ἦσαν δὲ κύριοι μὲν τῶν πραγμάτων διὰ τὰ ἀξιώματα καὶ διὰ τὰς ἡλικίας Ἵππαρχος καὶ Ἱππίας, πρεσβύτερος δὲ ὢν ὁ Ἱππίας καὶ τῇ φύσει πολιτικὸς καὶ ἔμφρων ἐπεστάτει τῆς ἀρχῆς. ὁ δὲ Ἵππαρχος παιδιώδης καὶ ἐρωτικὸς καὶ φιλόμουσος ἦν (καὶ τοὺς περὶ Ἀνακρέοντα καὶ Σιμωνίδην καὶ τοὺς ἄλλους ποιητὰς οὗτος ἦν ὁ μεταπεμπόμενος), (*2*) Θέτταλος δὲ νεώτερος πολὺ καὶ τῷ βίῳ θρασὺς καὶ ὑβριστής, ἀφ' οὗ καὶ συνέβη τὴν ἀρχὴν αὐτοῖς γενέσθαι πάντων τῶν κακῶν. ἐρασθεὶς γὰρ τοῦ Ἁρμοδίου καὶ διαμαρτάνων τῆς πρὸς αὐτὸν φιλίας οὐ κατεῖχε τὴν ὀργήν, ἀλλ' ἔν τε τοῖς ἄλλοις ἐνεσημαίνετο πικρῶς, καὶ τὸ τελευταῖον μέλλουσαν αὐτοῦ τὴν ἀδελφὴν κανηφορεῖν Παναθηναίοις ἐκώλυσεν, λοιδορήσας τι τὸν Ἁρμόδιον ὡς μαλακὸν ὄντα, ὅθεν συνέβη παροξυνθέντα τὸν Ἁρμόδιον καὶ τὸν Ἀριστογείτονα πράττειν τὴν πρᾶξιν μετεχόντων πολλῶν. (*3*) ἤδη δὲ παρατηροῦντες ἐν ἀκροπόλει τοῖς Παναθηναίοις Ἱππίαν (ἐτύγχανεν γὰρ οὗτος μὲν δεχόμενος, ὁ δ' Ἵππαρχος ἀποστέλλων τὴν πομπήν), ἰδόντες τινὰ τῶν κοινωνούντων τῆς πράξεως φιλανθρώπως ἐντυγχάνοντα τῷ Ἱππίᾳ, καὶ νομίσαντες μηνύειν, βουλόμενοί τι δρᾶσαι πρὸ τῆς συλλήψεως,

17. 2. ληροῦσι<ν οἱ> Kaibel & Wilamowitz.

18. 2. μετεχόντων πολλῶν L: <οὐ> πολλῶν Kaibel (*Stil und Text*, 167).

(**17**) Pisistratus, then, grew old in his rule, and he died from illness in the archonship of Philoneos: he had lived thirty-three years from when he was first established as tyrant, and had remained in power for nineteen; for he had been in exile for the remainder. (*2*) For that reason those people are uttering palpable nonsense who allege that Pisistratus was loved by Solon and was a general in the war against the Megarians for Salamis: for it does not fit their ages, if one reckons the life of each and the archon under whom each died. (*3*) When Pisistratus had died his sons proceeded to hold down the rule, carrying affairs forward in the same way. There were two sons from his wedded wife, Hippias and Hipparchus, and two from his Argive wife, Iophon and Hegesistratus, of whom the latter had the alternative name Thettalus. (*4*) For Pisistratus married from Argos Timonassa, the daughter of an Argive man whose name was Gorgilus, who had previously been the wife of Archinus of Ambracia, of the Cypselids. That was the origin of his friendship with the Argives, and a thousand of them joined him in fighting the battle at Pallenis, brought by Hegesistratus. Some say he married the Argive woman when he was expelled for the first time, others when he obtained his rule for the first time.

(**18**) Hippias and Hipparchus were in control of affairs because of their reputation and because of their age. Hippias, being the older and by nature politically-minded and sensible, was in charge of the régime, but Hipparchus was childish, amorous and fond of culture (it was he who sent for such men as Anacreon, Simonides and the other poets). (*2*) Thettalus was much younger, and in his life-style bold and insolent, and that turned out to be the beginning of all their troubles. For he was in love with Harmodius, but failed to gain his affection, and did not restrain his anger but in other respects gave bitter signs of it and finally, when Harmodius' sister was about to serve as basket-bearer at the Panathenaea, he forbade that, and disparaged Harmodius somewhat as effeminate. It was as a result of this that Harmodius and Aristogeiton were provoked, and did their deed, with many collaborators. (*3*) When at the Panathenaea they were already on the acropolis watching Hippias (for it happened that he was to receive the procession and Hipparchus was to dispatch it), they saw one of their accomplices in the affair encountering Hippias in a friendly way, and, thinking that he was informing on them and wanting

καταβάντες καὶ προεξαναστάντες τῶν [ἄλλω]ν, τὸν μὲν Ἵππαρχον διακοσμοῦντα τὴν πομπὴν παρὰ τὸ Λεωκόρειον ἀπέκτειναν, τὴν δ᾽ ὅλην ἐλυμήναντο πρᾶξιν. (*4*) αὐτῶν δ᾽ ὁ μὲν Ἁρμόδιος εὐθέως ἐτελεύτησεν ὑπὸ τῶν δορυφόρων, ὁ δ᾽ Ἀριστογείτων ὕστερον συλληφθεὶς καὶ πολὺν χρόνον αἰκισθείς. κατηγόρησεν δ᾽ ἐν ταῖς ἀνάγκαις πολλῶν οἳ καὶ τῇ φύσει τῶν ἐπιφανῶν καὶ φίλοι τοῖς τυράννοις ἦσαν. οὐ γὰρ ἐδύναντο παραχρῆμα λαβεῖν οὐδὲν ἴχνος τῆς πράξεως, ἀλλ᾽ ὁ λεγόμενος λόγος ὡς ὁ Ἱππίας ἀποστήσας ἀπὸ τῶν ὅπλων τοὺς πομπεύοντας ἐφώρασε τοὺς τὰ ἐγχειρίδια ἔχοντας οὐκ ἀληθής ἐστιν· οὐ γὰρ ἔπεμπον τό<τε> μεθ᾽ ὅπλων, ἀλλ᾽ ὕστερον τοῦτο κατεσκεύασεν ὁ δῆμος. (*5*) κατηγόρει δὲ τῶν τοῦ τυράννου φίλων, ὡς μὲν οἱ δημοτικοί φασιν ἐπίτηδες, ἵνα ἀσεβήσαιεν ἅμα καὶ γένοιντο ἀσθενεῖς, ἀνελόντες τοὺς ἀναιτίους καὶ φίλους ἑαυτῶν, ὡς δ᾽ ἔνιοι λέγουσιν οὐχὶ πλαττόμενος ἀλλὰ τοὺς συνειδότας ἐμήνυεν. (*6*) καὶ τέλος ὡς οὐκ ἐδύνατο πάντα ποιῶν ἀποθανεῖν, ἐπαγγειλάμενος ὡς ἄλλους μηνύσων πολλούς, καὶ πείσας αὐτῷ τὸν Ἱππίαν δοῦναι τὴν δεξιὰν πίστεως χάριν, ὡς ἔλαβεν, ὀνειδίσας ὅτι τῷ φονεῖ τἀδελφοῦ τὴν δεξιὰν δέδωκε, οὕτω παρώξυνε τὸν Ἱππίαν ὥσθ᾽ ὑπὸ τῆς ὀργῆς οὐ κατέσχεν ἑαυτὸν ἀλλὰ σπασάμενος τὴν μάχαιραν διέφθειρεν αὐτόν.

(**19**) μετὰ δὲ ταῦτα συνέβαινεν πολλῷ τραχυτέραν εἶναι τὴν τυραννίδα· καὶ γὰρ διὰ τὸ τιμωρεῖν τἀδελφῷ καὶ διὰ τὸ πολλοὺς ἀνῃρηκέναι καὶ ἐκβεβληκέναι, πᾶσιν ἦν ἄπιστος καὶ πικρός. (*2*) ἔτει δὲ τετάρτῳ μάλιστα μετὰ τὸν Ἱππάρχου θάνατον, ἐπεὶ κακῶς εἶχεν τὰ ἐν τῷ ἄστει, τὴν Μουνιχίαν ἐπεχείρησε τειχίζειν, ὡς ἐκεῖ μεθιδρυσόμενος. ἐν τούτοις δ᾽ ὢν ἐξέπεσεν ὑπὸ Κλεομένους τοῦ Λακεδαιμονίων βασιλέως, χρησμῶν γιγνομένων ἀεὶ τοῖς Λάκωσι καταλύειν τὴν τυραννίδα διὰ τοιάνδ᾽ αἰτίαν. (*3*) οἱ φυγάδες ὧν οἱ Ἀλκμεωνίδαι προειστήκεσαν, αὐτοὶ μὲν δι᾽ αὑτῶν οὐκ ἐδύναντο ποιήσασθαι τὴν κάθοδον, ἀλλ᾽ αἰεὶ προσέπταιον. ἔν τε γὰρ τοῖς ἄλλοις οἷς ἔπραττον διεσφάλλοντο, καὶ τειχίσαντες ἐν τῇ χώρᾳ Λειψύδριον τὸ ὑπὸ Πάρνηθος, εἰς ὃ συνεξῆλθόν τινες τῶν ἐκ τοῦ ἄστεως,

19. 2. Μουνιχίαν Kaibel & Wilamowitz: Μουνυχίαν here and throughout L.

19. 3. ὑπὸ Πάρνηθος J. H. Wright (cf. *E.M.* 361. 31 ἐπὶ Λειψυδρίῳ μάχη): ὑπὲρ L. εἰς ταύτην Kaibel & Wilamowitz (cf. Suda ε 2440, *E.M.* 361. 31, also *A.P.* 20. 5): μ(ετὰ) L.

to do something before they were arrested, they went down and, acting ahead of the others, they killed Hipparchus while he was organising the procession by the Leocoreum. This ruined the whole affair. (*4*) Their fate was that Harmodius was killed immediately by the spear-bearers, and Aristogeiton was captured later and tortured for a long time. In his agony he denounced many men who by birth were among the distinguished and who were friends of the tyrants. For they could not immediately pick up any trace of the affair; but the prevalent story that Hippias separated the members of the procession from their arms and caught those with daggers is not true: for at that time they did not take part in the procession under arms, but that was arranged later by the democracy. (*5*) Aristogeiton denounced the friends of the tyrants, deliberately according to the democrats, so that the tyrants should at the same time be polluted and be weakened, by removing men who were innocent and friends of theirs; but as some say this was not a fiction but those denounced were members of the conspiracy. (*6*) In the end, when whatever he did could not bring about his death, he offered to denounce many others, persuaded Hippias to give him his right hand as a mark of good faith, and then as he took it rebuked him for giving his right hand to his brother's killer. This so provoked Hippias that in his rage he did not restrain himself but drew his dagger and destroyed him.

(**19**) What happened after this was that the tyranny became much harsher: for because of his vengeance for his brother and his killing and exiling many men Hippias became untrusting and bitter towards everybody. (*2*) About the fourth year after the death of Hipparchus, when things in the city were in a bad way, he tried to fortify Munichia with the intention of migrating there. While he was engaged in this he was expelled by Cleomenes the king of the Spartans, since the Spartans were always receiving oracles to overthrow the tyranny, for the following reason. (*3*) The exiles, of whom the Alcmaeonids were the leaders, were not able to bring about their own restoration by their own efforts, but always stumbled: for they were unsuccessful in the other actions which they took, and, when they had fortified Lipsydrium, in the countryside below Parnes, where they were joined by some of the men from the city,

ἐξεπολιορκήθησαν ὑπὸ τῶν τυράννων, ὅθεν ὕστερον μετὰ ταύτην τὴν συμφορὰν ᾖδον ἐν τοῖς σκολιοῖς {αἰεί}·

αἰαῖ Λειψύδριον προδωσέταιρον,
οἵους ἄνδρας ἀπώλεσας μάχεσθαι
ἀγαθούς τε καὶ εὐπατρίδας,
οἳ τότ' ἔδειξαν οἵων πατέρων ἔσαν.

(*4*) ἀποτυγχάνοντες οὖν ἐν ἅπασι τοῖς ἄλλοις, ἐμισθώσαντο τὸν ἐν Δελφοῖς νεὼν οἰκοδομεῖν, ὅθεν εὐπόρησαν χρημάτων πρὸς τὴν τῶν Λακώνων βοήθειαν. ἡ δὲ Πυθία προέφερεν αἰεὶ τοῖς Λακεδαιμονίοις χρηστηριαζομένοις ἐλευθεροῦν τὰς Ἀθήνας εἰς τοῦθ' ἕως προύτρεψε τοὺς Σπαρτιάτας, καίπερ ὄντων ξένων αὐτοῖς τῶν Πεισιστρατιδῶν· συνεβάλλετο δὲ οὐκ ἐλάττω μοῖραν τῆς ὁρμῆς τοῖς Λάκωσιν ἡ πρὸς τοὺς Ἀργείους τοῖς Πεισιστρατίδαις ὑπάρχουσα φιλία. (*5*) τὸ μὲν οὖν πρῶτον Ἀγχίμολον ἀπέστειλαν κατὰ θάλατταν ἔχοντα στρατιάν. ἡττηθέντος δ' αὐτοῦ καὶ τελευτήσαντος διὰ τὸ Κινέαν βοηθῆσαι τὸν Θετταλὸν ἔχοντα χιλίους ἱππεῖς, προσοργισθέντες τῷ γενομένῳ Κλεομένην ἐξέπεμψαν τὸν βασιλέα στόλον ἔχοντα μείζω κατὰ γῆν, ὃς ἐπεὶ τοὺς τῶν Θετταλῶν ἱππεῖς ἐνίκησεν κωλύοντας αὐτὸν εἰς τὴν Ἀττικὴν παριέναι, κατακλείσας τὸν Ἱππίαν εἰς τὸ καλούμενον Πελαργικὸν τεῖχος ἐπολιόρκει μετὰ τῶν Ἀθηναίων. (*6*) προσκαθημένου δ' αὐτοῦ, συνέπεσεν ὑπεξιόντας ἁλῶναι τοὺς τῶν Πεισιστρατιδῶν υἱεῖς· ὧν ληφθέντων ὁμολογίαν ἐπὶ τῇ τῶν παίδων σωτηρίᾳ ποιησάμενοι καὶ τὰ ἑαυτῶν ἐν πένθ' ἡμέραις ἐκκομισάμενοι παρέδωκαν τὴν ἀκρόπολιν τοῖς Ἀθηναίοις, ἐπὶ Ἁρπακτίδου ἄρχοντος, κατασχόντες τὴν τυραννίδα μετὰ τὴν τοῦ πατρὸς τελευτὴν ἔτη μάλιστα ἑπτακαίδεκα, τὰ δὲ σύμπαντα σὺν οἷς ὁ πατὴρ ἦρξεν τριάκοντα ἕξ.

(**20**) καταλυθείσης δὲ τῆς τυραννίδος ἐστασίαζον πρὸς ἀλλήλους Ἰσαγόρας ὁ Τεισάνδρου φίλος ὢν τῶν τυράννων καὶ Κλεισθένης τοῦ γένους ὢν τῶν Ἀλκμεωνιδῶν. ἡττώμενος δὲ ταῖς ἑταιρείαις ὁ Κλεισθένης προσηγάγετο τὸν δῆμον, ἀποδιδοὺς τῷ πλήθει τὴν πολιτείαν. (*2*) ὁ δὲ Ἰσαγόρας ἐπιλειπόμενος τῇ δυνάμει πάλιν ἐπικαλεσάμενος τὸν

19. 3. {αἰεί} deleted Hude.

19. 6. τριάκοντα ἕξ G. V. Sumner: ἑνὸς δεῖ πεντήκοντα L.

they were besieged and taken by the tyrants, in consequence of which later after this disaster they used to sing in their drinking-songs:

> Alas, Lipsydrium the betrayer of comrades,
> What men you lost, good
> At fighting and well born,
> Who showed then what kind of fathers they were from.

(*4*) After failing in everything else, they took the contract to build the temple at Delphi, from which they gained an abundance of funds with a view to securing the Spartans' help. For when the Spartans consulted the oracle the Pythia always added that they should liberate Athens, persisting until she convinced the Spartiates, although the Pisistratids were guest-friends of theirs; and no less a contribution to the Spartans' impulse was made by the Pisistratids' current friendship towards the Argives. (*5*) First they sent Anchimolus with a force by sea. When he had been defeated and killed, because Cineas the Thessalian came to support the Pisistratids with a thousand cavalry, they became more angry at what had happened and sent their king Cleomenes with a larger force by land. He defeated the Thessalian cavalry, who tried to prevent him from entering Attica, and then shut Hippias into what was called the Pelargic wall and together with the Athenians laid siege to him. (*6*) While he was proceeding with the siege, it happened that he captured the sons of the Pisistratids when they were trying to escape. When these had been taken the Pisistratids made an agreement to secure the boys' safety, and within five days they conveyed their property away and handed over the acropolis to the Athenians. This was in the archonship of Harpactides, when they had held down the tyranny for about seventeen years after their father's death, the total with their father's rule being thirty-six.

(**20**) After the tyranny had been overthrown Isagoras the son of Teisandrus, a friend of the tyrants, and Cleisthenes, of the Alcmaeonid family, engaged in dissension with each other. Cleisthenes, since he was getting the worse of the struggle for supporters, tried to win over the *demos* to his side, by offering political power to the masses. (*2*) Isagoras, falling behind in power, invited back Cleomenes, who was a

Κλεομένην, ὄντα ἑαυτῷ ξένον, συνέπεισεν ἐλαύνειν τὸ ἄγος, διὰ τὸ τοὺς Ἀλκμεωνίδας δοκεῖν εἶναι τῶν ἐναγῶν. (*3*) ὑπεξελθόντος δὲ τοῦ Κλεισθένους <ἀφικόμενος ὁ Κλεομένης> μετ' ὀλίγων ἠγηλάτει τῶν Ἀθηναίων ἑπτακοσίας οἰκίας· ταῦτα δὲ διαπραξάμενος τὴν μὲν βουλὴν ἐπειρᾶτο καταλύειν, Ἰσαγόραν δὲ καὶ τριακοσίους τῶν φίλων μετ' αὐτοῦ κυρίους καθιστάναι τῆς πόλεως. τῆς δὲ βουλῆς ἀντιστάσης καὶ συναθροισθέντος τοῦ πλήθους οἱ μὲν περὶ τὸν Κλεομένην καὶ Ἰσαγόραν κατέφυγον εἰς τὴν ἀκρόπολιν, ὁ δὲ δῆμος δύο μὲν ἡμέρας προσκαθεζόμενος ἐπολιόρκει, τῇ δὲ τρίτῃ Κλεομένην μὲν καὶ τοὺς μετ' αὐτοῦ πάντας ἀφεῖσαν ὑποσπόνδους, Κλεισθένην δὲ καὶ τοὺς ἄλλους φυγάδας μετεπέμψαντο. (*4*) κατασχόντος δὲ τοῦ δήμου τὰ πράγματα, Κλεισθένης ἡγεμὼν ἦν καὶ τοῦ δήμου προστάτης. αἰτιώτατοι γὰρ σχεδὸν ἐγένοντο τῆς ἐκβολῆς τῶν τυράννων οἱ Ἀλκμεωνίδαι, καὶ στασιάζοντες τὰ πολλὰ διετέλεσαν. (*5*) ἔτι δὲ πρότερον τῶν Ἀλκμεωνιδῶν Κήδων ἐπέθετο τοῖς τυράννοις, διὸ καὶ ᾖδον καὶ εἰς τοῦτον ἐν τοῖς σκολιοῖς·

ἔγχει καὶ Κήδωνι, διάκονε, μηδ' ἐπιλήθου,
εἰ χρὴ τοῖς ἀγαθοῖς ἀνδράσιν οἰνοχοεῖν.

(**21**) διὰ μὲν οὖν ταύτας τὰς αἰτίας ἐπίστευεν ὁ δῆμος τῷ Κλεισθένει. τότε δὲ τοῦ πλήθους προεστηκώς, ἔτει τετάρτῳ μετὰ τὴν τῶν τυράννων κατάλυσιν, ἐπὶ Ἰσαγόρου ἄρχοντος, (*2*) πρῶτον μὲν οὖν <συν>ένειμε πάντας εἰς δέκα φυλὰς ἀντὶ τῶν τεττάρων, ἀναμεῖξαι βουλόμενος, ὅπως μετάσχωσι πλείους τῆς πολιτείας· ὅθεν ἐλέχθη καὶ τὸ μὴ φυλοκρινεῖν πρὸς τοὺς ἐξετάζειν τὰ γένη βουλομένους. (*3*) ἔπειτα τὴν βουλὴν πεντακοσίους ἀντὶ τετρακοσίων κατέστησεν, πεντήκοντα ἐξ ἑκάστης φυλῆς· τότε δ' ἦσαν ἑκατόν. διὰ τοῦτο δὲ οὐκ εἰς δώδεκα φυλὰς συνέταξεν, ὅπως αὐτῷ μὴ συμβαίνῃ μερίζειν πρὸς τὰς προϋπαρχούσας τριττῦς· ἦσαν γὰρ ἐκ δ΄ φυλῶν δώδεκα τριττύες, ὥστ' οὐ συνέπιπτεν <ἂν>

20. 3 <ἀφικόμενος ὁ Κλεομένης> Kaibel & Wilamowitz[2].

20. 5. εἰ χρὴ L: εἰ δὴ χρὴ Athenaeus.

21. 2. πρῶτον μὲν οὖν <συν>ένειμε: μ΄ ο΄ ἔνειμε L: μὲν συνένειμε W. L. Newman (*CR*), πρῶτον μὲν οὖν <συν>ένειμε after a lacuna Kaibel & Wilamowitz, without lacuna H. Diels *ap.* Kenyon[4].

guest-friend of his, and persuaded him to drive out the curse, since it appeared that the Alcmaeonids were among the accursed. (*3*) Cleisthenes withdrew; and Cleomenes arrived with a few men and solemnly expelled seven hundred Athenian households. After completing this he tried to overthrow the council and establish Isagoras with three hundred friends of his with power over the city. But the council resisted and the masses came together. The suppporters of Cleomenes and Isagoras fled to the acropolis, and the *demos* settled down to besiege them for two days but on the third allowed Cleomenes and all the men with him to leave under a truce, and recalled Cleisthenes and the other exiles. (*4*) When the *demos* was in control of affairs, Cleisthenes was the leader and the champion of the *demos.* For in effect the Alcmaeonids were most responsible for the expulsion of the tyrants, and for most of the time they had continued in dissension with them. (*5*) Even earlier, Cedon of the Alcmaeonids had attacked the tyrants, as a result of which they sang of him too in their drinking-songs:

> Pour to Cedon also, steward, and do not forget,
> If we are to pour wine to good men.

(**21**) So for these reasons the *demos* placed its trust in Cleisthenes. Then, as champion of the masses, in the fourth year after the overthrow of the tyrants, in the archonship of Isagoras, (*2*) first he distributed them all in ten tribes instead of the four, wanting to mix them up, so that more men would have a share in political power: that is why they said, 'Don't judge by tribes' in response to those who wanted to enquire into men's ancestry. (*3*) Then he established the council as a body of five hundred instead of four hundred, fifty from each tribe (at that time there were a hundred from each old tribe). The reason why he did not organise them in twelve tribes is this, that he should not end up by apportioning them on the basis of the pre-existing *trittyes*: for there were twelve *trittyes* from 4 tribes, so that if he had done that the result would not have been to mix

ἀναμίσγεσθαι τὸ πλῆθος. (*4*) διένειμε δὲ καὶ τὴν χώραν κατὰ δήμους τριάκοντα μέρη, δέκα μὲν τῶν περὶ τὸ ἄστυ, δέκα δὲ τῆς παραλίας, δέκα δὲ τῆς μεσογείου, καὶ ταύτας ἐπονομάσας τριττῦς ἐκλήρωσεν τρεῖς εἰς τὴν φυλὴν ἑκάστην, ὅπως ἑκάστη μετέχῃ πάντων τῶν τόπων. καὶ δημότας ἐποίησεν ἀλλήλων τοὺς οἰκοῦντας ἐν ἑκάστῳ τῶν δήμων, ἵνα μὴ πατρόθεν προσαγορεύοντες ἐξελέγχωσιν τοὺς νεοπολίτας, ἀλλὰ τῶν δήμων ἀναγορεύωσιν· ὅθεν καὶ καλοῦσιν Ἀθηναῖοι σφᾶς αὐτοὺς τῶν δήμων. (*5*) κατέστησε δὲ καὶ δημάρχους, τὴν αὐτὴν ἔχοντας ἐπιμέλειαν τοῖς πρότερον ναυκράροις· καὶ γὰρ τοὺς δήμους ἀντὶ τῶν ναυκραριῶν ἐποίησεν. προσηγόρευσε δὲ τῶν δήμων τοὺς μὲν ἀπὸ τῶν τόπων, τοὺς δὲ ἀπὸ τῶν κτισάντων· οὐ γὰρ ἅπαντες ὑπῆρχον ἔτι τοῖς τόποις. (*6*) τὰ δὲ γένη καὶ τὰς φρατρίας καὶ τὰς ἱερωσύνας εἴασεν ἔχειν ἑκάστους κατὰ τὰ πάτρια. ταῖς δὲ φυλαῖς ἐποίησεν ἐπωνύμους ἐκ τῶν προκριθέντων ἑκατὸν ἀρχηγετῶν, οὓς ἀνεῖλεν ἡ Πυθία, δέκα.

(**22**) τούτων δὲ γενομένων δημοτικωτέρα πολὺ τῆς Σόλωνος ἐγένετο ἡ πολιτεία· καὶ γὰρ συνέβη τοὺς μὲν Σόλωνος νόμους ἀφανίσαι τὴν τυραννίδα διὰ τὸ μὴ χρῆσθαι, καινοὺς δ᾽ ἄλλους θεῖναι τὸν Κλεισθένη στοχαζόμενον τοῦ πλήθους, ἐν οἷς ἐτέθη καὶ ὁ περὶ τοῦ ὀστρακισμοῦ νόμος. (*2*) πρῶτον μὲν οὖν ἔτει ὀγδόῳ μετὰ ταύτην τὴν κατάστασιν, ἐφ᾽ Ἑρμοκρέοντος ἄρχοντος, τῇ βουλῇ τοῖς πεντακοσίοις τὸν ὅρκον ἐποίησαν ὃν ἔτι καὶ νῦν ὀμνύουσιν. ἔπειτα τοὺς στρατηγοὺς ᾑροῦντο κατὰ φυλάς, ἐξ ἑκάστης φυλῆς ἕνα, τῆς δὲ ἁπάσης στρατιᾶς ἡγεμὼν ἦν ὁ πολέμαρχος. (*3*) ἔτει δὲ μετὰ ταῦτα δωδεκάτῳ νικήσαντες τὴν ἐν Μαραθῶνι μάχην, ἐπὶ Φαινίππου ἄρχοντος, διαλιπόντες ἔτη δύο μετὰ τὴν νίκην, θαρροῦντος ἤδη τοῦ δήμου τότε πρῶτον ἐχρήσαντο τῷ νόμῳ τῷ περὶ τὸν ὀστρακισμόν, ὃς ἐτέθη διὰ τὴν ὑποψίαν τῶν ἐν ταῖς δυνάμεσιν, ὅτι Πεισίστρατος δημαγωγὸς καὶ στρατηγὸς ὢν τύραννος κατέστη.

21. 4. ἀ̣γ̣α̣γορεύουσιν … Κ]λ̣ε̣ι̣σ̣θ̣έ̣[νης (22. 4) present in B, fr. IIa.

21. 5. ἔτι L: ἐν B, ἔτι ἐν P. N. Papageorgios.

21. 6. φρατρίας B: φατρίας L.

22. 1. χρῆσθαι L: χρ̣ᾶ̣σθαι B.

22. 2. ὀγδόῳ Kenyon[1–3] (i.e. η´ for ε´): πέμπτ̣ῳ L, B.

Ἑρμοκρέοντος W. G. Rutherford (*CR*): Ἑρμουκρέοντ° L, –]ρέοντος B.

ἐξ ἑκάστης φυλῆς L: ἀ]π̣ὸ̣ φυλῆς ἑ̣κ̣ά̣στης B; the author's usage varies.

22. 3. ὅτι Kenyon[1] from Androtion, ὅ̣τ̣ι̣ B: ὅτε L.

up the masses. (*4*) He distributed them over the countryside by demes in thirty sections – ten of demes in the city region, ten of the coast and ten inland – and, calling these *trittyes*, he assigned by lot three to each tribe, so that each tribe should have a share in all of the regions. And he made fellow-demesmen of one another the men living in each of the demes, so that they should not be designated by their fathers' names and expose the new citizens but should be identified by their demes. (*5*) Also he instituted demarchs, with the same responsibility as the former *naukraroi*; for he created the demes as a replacement for the *naukrariai*. Of the demes he designated some from their localities and some from their founders (for not all the founders of the places were still known). (*6*) The *gene*, the *phratriai* and the priesthoods he allowed to remain in accordance with tradition in each case. For the tribes he created eponymous heroes, ten chosen by the Pythia from a hundred pre-elected leaders.

(**22**) When this had occurred the constitution became much more democratic than that of Solon: for it happened that the tyranny had consigned Solon's laws to oblivion by not using them, and Cleisthenes enacted other new laws in reaching out to the masses, among which was his enactment of the law about ostracism. (*2*) First, in the eighth year after this settlement, in the archonship of Hermocreon, they created for the council of five hundred the oath which they still swear now. Next they elected the generals by tribes, one from each tribe, but the leader of the whole army was the polemarch. (*3*) In the twelfth year after this they won the battle of Marathon, in the archonship of Phaenippus. After waiting for two years after their victory, when the *demos* was now confident, they then first used the law about ostracism, which had been enacted because of their suspicion of the men in powerful positions, because Pisistratus from being a demagogue and general had been

(*4*) καὶ πρῶτος ὠστρακίσθη τῶν ἐκείνου συγγενῶν Ἵππαρχος Χάρμου Κολλυτεύς, δι' ὃν καὶ μάλιστα τὸν νόμον ἔθηκεν ὁ Κλεισθένης, ἐξελάσαι βουλόμενος αὐτόν. οἱ γὰρ Ἀθηναῖοι τοὺς τῶν τυράννων φίλους, ὅσοι μὴ συνεξαμαρτάνοιεν ἐν ταῖς ταραχαῖς, εἴων οἰκεῖν τὴν πόλιν, χρώμενοι τῇ εἰωθυίᾳ τοῦ δήμου πραότητι· ὧν ἡγεμὼν καὶ προστάτης ἦν Ἵππαρχος. (*5*) εὐθὺς δὲ τῷ ὑστέρῳ ἔτει, ἐπὶ Τελεσίνου ἄρχοντος, ἐκυάμευσαν τοὺς ἐννέα ἄρχοντας κατὰ φυλὰς ἐκ τῶν προκριθέντων ὑπὸ τῶν δημοτῶν πεντακοσίων τότε μετὰ τὴν τυραννίδα πρῶτον· οἱ δὲ πρότεροι πάντες ἦσαν αἱρετοί. καὶ ὠστρακίσθη Μεγακλῆς Ἱπποκράτους Ἀλωπεκῆθεν. (*6*) ἐπὶ μὲν οὖν ἔτη γ´ τοὺς τῶν τυράννων φίλους ὠστράκιζον, ὧν χάριν ὁ νόμος ἐτέθη, μετὰ δὲ ταῦτα, τῷ τετάρτῳ ἔτει, καὶ τῶν ἄλλων εἴ τις δοκοίη μείζων εἶναι μεθίσταντο· καὶ πρῶτος ὠστρακίσθη τῶν ἄπωθεν τῆς τυραννίδος Ξάνθιππος ὁ Ἀρίφρονος. (*7*) ἔτει δὲ τρίτῳ μετὰ ταῦτα, Νικοδήμου ἄρχοντος, ὡς ἐφάνη τὰ μέταλλα τὰ ἐν Μαρωνείᾳ καὶ περιεγένετο τῇ πόλει τάλαντα ἑκατὸν ἐκ τῶν ἔργων, συμβουλευόντων τινῶν τῷ δήμῳ διανείμασθαι τὸ ἀργύριον Θεμιστοκλῆς ἐκώλυσεν, οὐ λέγων ὅ τι χρήσεται τοῖς χρήμασιν ἀλλὰ δανεῖσαι κελεύων τοῖς πλουσιωτάτοις Ἀθηναίων ἑκατὸν ἑκάστῳ τάλαντον, εἶτ' ἐὰν μὲν ἀρέσκῃ τὸ ἀνάλωμα, τῆς πόλεως εἶναι τὴν δαπάνην, εἰ δὲ μή, κομίσασθαι τὰ χρήματα παρὰ τῶν δανεισαμένων. λαβὼν δ' ἐπὶ τούτοις ἐναυπηγήσατο τριήρεις ἑκατόν, ἑκάστου ναυπηγουμένου τῶν ἑκατὸν μίαν, αἷς ἐναυμάχησαν ἐν Σαλαμῖνι πρὸς τοὺς βαρβάρους. ὠστρακίσθη δ' ἐν τούτοις τοῖς καιροῖς Ἀριστείδης ὁ Λυσιμάχου. (*8*) τρίτῳ δ' ἔτει κατεδέξαντο πάντας τοὺς ὠστρακισμένους, ἄρχοντος Ὑψιχίδου, διὰ τὴν Ξέρξου στρατιάν· καὶ τὸ λοιπὸν ὥρισαν τοῖς

22. 4. εἰωθ]υί[ᾳ … κατοι]κ̣ε̣ῖ̣ν̣ (22. 8) present in B, fr. IIb.

πραότητι L: πρᾳότητι Kaibel & Wilamowitz.

22. 5. δημοτ(ῶν) L: δήμων B.

22. 7. Νικοδήμου B, cf. Dion. Hal.: Νικομήδους L.

τάλαντα ἑκατὸν ἐκ τῶν ἔργων L: ẹκ τῷṿ [ἔ]ρ̣γῳṿ ἑκαṭ[ὸν τάλαντα] B.

τὴν δαπάνην added by another hand in L, seems to have been reading of B.

22. 8. τρίτῳ δ' ἔτει Kaibel & Wilamowitz[2], cf. Plut. *Arist.* 8. 1: τετάρτῳ L, not present in B but τετάρτῳ would fit the space better.

Ὑψιχίδου corrrection of Ὑψηχίδου L, –]χίδου B.

στρατιάν L: σ]ṭρ̣α̣ṭε̣ί̣α̣ṿ B.

established as tyrant. The first man ostracised was one of his relatives, Hipparchus son of Charmus, of Collytus; and it was because of him in particular that Cleisthenes had enacted the law, wanting to drive him out. For the Athenians allowed those of the tyrants' friends who had not joined in wrongdoing during the disturbances to live in the city, following the *demos*' customary mildness; and the leader and champion of these men was Hipparchus. (*5*) Immediately in the next year, in the archonship of Telesinus, they appointed the nine archons by drawing lots by tribe among the five hundred men pre-elected by the demesmen, for the first time since the tyranny: the previous archons were all elected. And Megacles son of Hippocrates, of Alopece, was ostracised. (*6*) For 3 years, then, they proceeded to ostracise the friends of the tyrants, on account of whom the law had been enacted, but after that, in the fourth year, they took to removing any of the others who seemed to be too great; and the first of those unconnected with the tyranny to be ostracised was Xanthippus son of Ariphron. (*7*) In the third year after that, in the archonship of Nicodemus, when the mines at Maronea were revealed and the city gained a surplus of a hundred talents from the workings, some men proposed that the money should be distributed to the *demos*, but Themistocles prevented that: he did not say what he would do with the money, but told them to lend to the hundred richest Athenians a talent each, and if they were satisfied with the outlay the expenditure should count as the city's, but if not they should recover the money from those who had borrowed it. Taking the money on these terms, he had a hundred triremes built, each of the hundred men building one; and with these they fought the naval battle at Salamis against the barbarians. At this juncture Aristides son of Lysimachus was ostracised. (*8*) In the third year they received back all the men who had been ostracised, in the archonship of Hypsichides, on account of Xerxes' campaign; and for the future they

ὀστρακιζομένοις ἐντὸς Γεραιστοῦ καὶ Σκυλλαίου κατοικεῖν ἢ ἀτίμους εἶναι καθάπαξ.

(**23**) τότε μὲν οὖν μέχρι τούτου προῆλθεν ἡ πόλις ἅμα τῇ δημοκρατίᾳ κατὰ μικρὸν αὐξανομένη· μετὰ δὲ τὰ Μηδικὰ πάλιν ἴσχυσεν ἡ ἐν Ἀρείῳ πάγῳ βουλὴ καὶ διῴκει τὴν πόλιν, οὐδενὶ δόγματι λαβοῦσα τὴν ἡγεμονίαν ἀλλὰ διὰ τὸ γενέσθαι τῆς περὶ Σαλαμῖνα ναυμαχίας αἰτία· τῶν γὰρ στρατηγῶν ἐξαπορησάντων τοῖς πράγμασι, καὶ κηρυξάντων σῴζειν ἕκαστον ἑαυτόν, πορίσασα δραχμὰς ἑκάστῳ ὀκτὼ διέδωκε καὶ ἐνεβίβασεν εἰς τὰς ναῦς. (*2*) διὰ ταύτην δὴ τὴν αἰτίαν παρεχώρουν αὐτῆς τῷ ἀξιώματι, καὶ ἐπολιτεύθησαν Ἀθηναῖοι καλῶς {καὶ} κατὰ τούτους τοὺς καιρούς. συνέβη γὰρ αὐτοῖς περὶ τὸν χρόνον τοῦτον τά τε εἰς τὸν πόλεμον ἀσκῆσαι καὶ παρὰ τοῖς Ἕλλησιν εὐδοκιμῆσαι καὶ τὴν τῆς θαλάττης ἡγεμονίαν λαβεῖν, ἀκόντων Λακεδαιμονίων. (*3*) ἦσαν δὲ προστάται τοῦ δήμου κατὰ τούτους τοὺς καιροὺς Ἀριστείδης ὁ Λυσιμάχου καὶ Θεμιστοκλῆς ὁ Νεοκλέους, ὁ μὲν τὰ πολέμια δοκῶν <ἀσκεῖν>, ὁ δὲ τὰ πολιτικὰ δεινὸς εἶναι καὶ δικαιοσύνῃ τῶν καθ᾽ ἑαυτὸν διαφέρειν· διὸ καὶ ἐχρῶντο τῷ μὲν στρατηγῷ, τῷ δὲ συμβούλῳ. (*4*) τὴν μὲν οὖν τῶν τειχῶν ἀνοικοδόμησιν κοινῇ διῴκησαν, καίπερ διαφερόμενοι πρὸς ἀλλήλους, ἐπὶ δὲ τὴν ἀπόστασιν τὴν τῶν Ἰώνων ἀπὸ τῆς τῶν Λακεδαιμονίων συμμαχίας Ἀριστείδης ἦν ὁ προτρέψας, τηρήσας τοὺς Λάκωνας διαβεβλημένους διὰ Παυσανίαν. (*5*) διὸ καὶ τοὺς φόρους οὗτος ἦν ὁ τάξας ταῖς πόλεσιν τοὺς πρώτους, ἔτει τρίτῳ μετὰ τὴν ἐν Σαλαμῖνι ναυμαχίαν, ἐπὶ Τιμοσθένους ἄρχοντος, καὶ τοὺς ὅρκους ὤμοσεν τοῖς Ἴωσιν ὥστε τὸν αὐτὸν ἐχθρὸν εἶναι καὶ φίλον, ἐφ᾽ οἷς καὶ τοὺς μύδρους ἐν τῷ πελάγει καθεῖσαν.

(**24**) μετὰ δὲ ταῦτα θαρρούσης ἤδη τῆς πόλεως, καὶ χρημάτων

22. 8. ἐντὸς L, B: ἐκτὸς W. Wyse (*CR*), <μὴ> κατοικεῖν Kaibel (*Stil und Text*, 177).

23. 2. αὐτῆς W. G. Rutherford (*CR*): αὐτ(ὴν) L.

{καὶ} suspected Kenyon[1], deleted Kaibel & Wilamowitz.

πε(ρὶ) another hand in L: κ(ατὰ) first hand.

ἀκόντων L: ἑκόντων J. E. B. Mayor (*CR*), <οὐκ> ἀκόντων W. Vollgraff.

23. 3. πολέμια L: πολεμικὰ Blass.

δοκῶν <ἀσκεῖν> Kenyon[3] (in *apparatus*): ἀσκῶν L, δοκῶν H. Richards and E. S. Thompson (*CR*).

defined for the ostracised that they should settle between Geraestus and Scyllaeum, or else they should be completely *atimoi*.

(**23**) So then the city advanced to this point, increasing gradually with the democracy. But after the Persian Wars the council of the Areopagus became strong again and administered the city, gaining its leadership not by any formal decision but because it was responsible for the naval battle near Salamis. For, when the generals were unable to cope with the situation and had proclaimed that everybody should save himself, it provided and allocated eight drachmae to each man and embarked them on the ships. (2) For this reason they gave way to its reputation, and Athens' politics were in a good condition at this juncture. It happened at this time that they gained practice in waging war, won a good reputation among the Greeks and acquired the leadership at sea against the wishes of the Spartans. (*3*) The champions of the *demos* at this juncture were Aristides son of Lysimachus and Themistocles son of Neocles, of whom the latter was judged to be a practitioner of warfare and the former to be clever in political matters and to surpass his contemporaries in uprightness: for that reason they used the one as a general and the other as an adviser. (*4*) The rebuilding of the walls, then, they administered together, although they were at variance with each other; but it was Aristides who prompted the defection of the Ionians from the Spartans' alliance, noticing that the Spartans were criticised on account of Pausanias. (*5*) For that reason it was he who fixed the first tribute for the cities, in the third year after the battle of Salamis, in the archonship of Timosthenes; and he swore the oaths with the Ionians to have the same enemies and friends, to confirm which they sank the molten iron in the sea.

(**24**) After this, when the city was now confident and a great deal of

ἠθροισμένων πολλῶν, συνεβούλευεν ἀντιλαμβάνεσθαι τῆς ἡγεμονίας καὶ καταβάντας ἐκ τῶν ἀγρῶν οἰκεῖν ἐν τῷ ἄστει· τροφὴν γὰρ ἔσεσθαι πᾶσι, τοῖς μὲν στρατευομένοις, τοῖς δὲ φρουροῦσι, τοῖς δὲ τὰ κοινὰ πράττουσι, εἶθ' οὕτω κατασχήσειν τὴν ἡγεμονίαν. (*2*) πεισθέντες δὲ ταῦτα καὶ λαβόντες τὴν ἀρχὴν τοῖς τε συμμάχοις δεσποτικωτέρως ἐχρῶντο, πλὴν Χίων καὶ Λεσβίων καὶ Σαμίων· τούτους δὲ φύλακας εἶχον τῆς ἀρχῆς, ἐῶντες τάς τε πολιτείας παρ' αὐτοῖς καὶ ἄρχειν ὧν ἔτυχον ἄρχοντες. (*3*) κατέστησαν δὲ καὶ τοῖς πολλοῖς εὐπορίαν τροφῆς, ὥσπερ Ἀριστείδης εἰσηγήσατο. συνέβαινεν γὰρ ἀπὸ τῶν φόρων καὶ τῶν τελῶν καὶ τῶν συμμάχων πλείους ἢ δισμυρίους ἄνδρας τρέφεσθαι. δικασταὶ μὲν γὰρ ἦσαν ἑξακισχίλιοι, τοξόται δ' ἑξακόσιοι καὶ χίλιοι, καὶ πρὸς τούτοις ἱππεῖς χίλιοι καὶ διακόσιοι, βουλὴ δὲ πεντακόσιοι, καὶ φρουροὶ νεωρίων πεντακόσιοι, καὶ πρὸς τούτοις ἐν τῇ πόλει φρουροὶ ν´, ἀρχαὶ δ' ἔνδημοι μὲν εἰς ἑπτακοσίους ἄνδρας, ὑπερόριοι δ' εἰς †ἑπτακοσίους†· πρὸς δὲ τούτοις, ἐπεὶ συνέστήσαν <τὰ εἰς> τὸν πόλεμον ὕστερον, ὁπλῖται μὲν δισχίλιοι καὶ πεντακόσιοι, νῆες δὲ φρουρίδες εἴκοσι, †ἄλλαι δὲ νῆες αἱ τοὺς φόρους ἄγουσαι τοὺς ἀπὸ τοῦ κυάμου δισχιλίους ἄνδρας†, ἔτι δὲ πρυτανεῖον καὶ ὀρφανοὶ καὶ δεσμωτῶν φύλακες· ἅπασι γὰρ τούτοις ἀπὸ τῶν κοινῶν ἡ διοίκησις ἦν.

24. 1. ἠθροισμένων πολλῶν: πολλῶν ἠθροισμένων with the letters β and α written above L.

24. 2. τοῖς {τε} συμμάχοις Blass, lacunaa after ἄρχοντες Kaibel & Wilamowitz.

<τὰς> παρ' αὐτοῖς G. A. Papabasileios, <τὰς> παρ' αὐτοῖς <ἔχειν> H. Richards (*CR*).

24. 3. καὶ τῶν τελῶν καὶ deleted Herwerden & Leeuwen, καὶ τῶν συμμάχων deleted Kaibel & Wilamowitz[1–2], {καὶ} τῶν <ἀπὸ τῶν> συμμάχων Hude, perhaps τελῶν ἀπὸ τῶν συμμάχων but more probably L preserves the author's words Rhodes.

ὑπερόριοι δ' εἰς †ἑπτακοσίους†: ἑπτακοσίους wrongly repeated Kaibel & Wilamowitz.

συνέστησαν Leeuwen: συνεστήσαντο L.

<τὰ εἰς> τὸν πόλεμον Kaibel & Wilamowitz [1–2].

†ἄλλαι δὲ νῆες … δισχιλίους ἄνδρας† I obelise: φρουροὺς Blass; <ἐπὶ> τοὺς φόρους J. B. Mayor (*CR*), ἄγουσαι <καὶ> Matthieu & Haussoullier; lacuna after ἄγουσαι Wilamowitz (*A.u.A.* ii. 205–6).

money had been accumulated, he advised them to grasp the leadership and to go down from the fields and live in the city: for there would be sustenance for all, while some were on campaign, others were on guard duty and others were attending to public affairs, and in this way they would hold down their leadership. (*2*) Persuaded of this, and taking the ruling position, they proceeded to treat their allies in a more despotic way, apart from the Chians, Lebsians and Samians: these they kept as guardians of their rule, allowing them to retain the constitutions which they had and to rule those whom they happened to be ruling. (*3*) For the many they established an abundance of sustenance, as Aristides had proposed: for the upshot was that from the tribute, the taxes and the allies more than twenty thousand men received sustenance. For there were six thousand jurors, one thousand six hundred archers; in addition to these one thousand two hundred cavalry, five hundred men in the council, five hundred guards of the dockyards; in addition to these 50 guards on the acropolis, internal officials about seven hundred men and abroad †seven hundred†. In addition to these, when later they set up their arrangements for war, two thousand five hundred hoplites, twenty guard ships, †other ships bringing the tribute two thousand men picked by drawing lots†; then the *prytaneion*, orphans and guards of prisoners. For all of these the finance was from public funds.

(**25**) ἡ μὲν οὖν τροφὴ τῷ δήμῳ διὰ τούτων ἐγίγνετο. ἔτη δὲ ἑπτακαίδεκα μάλιστα μετὰ τὰ Μηδικὰ διέμεινεν ἡ πολιτεία προεστώτων <τῶν> Ἀρεοπαγιτῶν, καίπερ ὑποφερομένη κατὰ μικρόν. αὐξανομένου δὲ τοῦ πλήθους, γενόμενος τοῦ δήμου προστάτης Ἐφιάλτης ὁ Σοφωνίδου, δοκῶν καὶ ἀδωροδόκητος εἶναι καὶ δίκαιος πρὸς τὴν πολιτείαν, ἐπέθετο τῇ βουλῇ. (*2*) καὶ πρῶτον μὲν ἀνεῖλεν πολλοὺς τῶν Ἀρεοπαγιτῶν, ἀγῶνας ἐπιφέρων περὶ τῶν διῳκημένων· ἔπειτα τῆς βουλῆς ἐπὶ Κόνωνος ἄρχοντος ἅπαντα περιεῖλε τὰ ἐπίθετα δι' ὧν ἦν ἡ τῆς πολιτείας φυλακή, καὶ τὰ μὲν τοῖς πεντακοσίοις, τὰ δὲ τῷ δήμῳ καὶ τοῖς δικαστηρίοις ἀπέδωκεν. (*3*) ἔπραξε δὲ ταῦτα συναιτίου γενομένου Θεμιστοκλέους, ὃς ἦν μὲν τῶν Ἀρεοπαγιτῶν, ἔμελλε δὲ κρίνεσθαι μηδισμοῦ. βουλόμενος δὲ καταλυθῆναι τὴν βουλὴν ὁ Θεμιστοκλῆς πρὸς μὲν τὸν Ἐφιάλτην ἔλεγεν ὅτι συναρπάζειν αὐτὸν ἡ βουλὴ μέλλει, πρὸς δὲ τοὺς Ἀρεοπαγίτας ὅτι δείξει τινὰς συνισταμένους ἐπὶ καταλύσει τῆς πολιτείας. ἀγαγὼν δὲ τοὺς {ἀφ}αιρεθέντας τῆς βουλῆς οὗ διέτριβεν ὁ Ἐφιάλτης, ἵνα δείξῃ τοὺς ἀθροιζομένους, διελέγετο μετὰ σπουδῆς αὐτοῖς. ὁ δ' Ἐφιάλτης ὡς εἶδεν καταπλαγεὶς καθίζει μονοχίτων ἐπὶ τὸν βωμόν. (*4*) θαυμασάντων δὲ πάντων τὸ γεγονός, καὶ μετὰ ταῦτα συναθροισθείσης τῆς βουλῆς τῶν πεντακοσίων, κατηγόρουν τῶν Ἀρεοπαγιτῶν ὅ τ' Ἐφιάλτης καὶ <ὁ> Θεμιστοκλῆς, καὶ πάλιν ἐν τῷ δήμῳ τὸν αὐτὸν τρόπον, ἕως περιείλοντο αὐτῶν τὴν δύναμιν. καὶ * * * ἀνῃρέθη δὲ καὶ ὁ Ἐφιάλτης δολοφονηθεὶς μετ' οὐ πολὺν χρόνον δι' Ἀριστοδίκου τοῦ Ταναγραίου.

(**26**) ἡ μὲν οὖν τῶν Ἀρεοπαγιτῶν βουλὴ τοῦτον τὸν τρόπον ἀπεστερήθη τῆς ἐπιμελείας. μετὰ δὲ ταῦτα συνέβαινεν ἀνίεσθαι μᾶλλον τὴν πολιτείαν διὰ τοὺς προθύμως δημαγωγοῦντας. κατὰ γὰρ τοὺς καιροὺς τούτους συνέπεσε μηδ' ἡγεμόνα ἔχειν τοὺς ἐπιεικεστέρους,

25. 1. <τῶν> not read in L Wilcken, Chambers.
δοκῶν καὶ Kaibel (*Stil und Text*, 182); καὶ δοκῶν L.
περιεῖλε: περιείλε<το> H. Richards (*CR*).
25. 3. {ἀφ}αιρεθέντας Kenyon[1].
25. 4. <ὁ> Θεμιστοκλῆς Kaibel & Wilamowitz.
περιείλοντο: περιεῖλον, with the letters το added, L.
καὶ * * * ἀνῃρέθη: lacuna Kaibel & Wilamowitz.
26. 1. ἡγεμόνα <σπουδαῖον> A Gennadios (*CR*), other suggestions have been made.

(**25**) That is how sustenance for the *demos* was provided. For about seventeen years after the Persian Wars the constitution continued under the predominance of the Areopagites, though declining gradually. As the masses were increasing, Ephialtes son of Sophonides became champion of the *demos*, a man who appeared to be incorruptible and upright in his political stance, and he attacked the council. (*2*) First he removed many of the Areopagites, bringing them to trial in connection with their administration. Then in the archonship of Conon he stripped off from the council all the additions through which it had acquired its guardianship of the constitution, giving some to the Five Hundred and others to the *demos* and the lawcourts. (*3*) He did this with Themistocles as jointly responsible. Themistocles was one of the Areopagites, and was about to be tried for medism. Wanting the council to be overthrown, he said to Ephialtes that the council was intending to arrest him and to the Areopagites that he would reveal men who were combining to overthrow the constitution. He took men chosen from the council to where Ephialtes was spending his time, in order to reveal the men gathering there, and engaged in urgent conversation with the men from the Areopagus. Ephialtes on seeing this was terrified, and went to sit as a suppliant at the altar wearing only his undergarment. (*4*) Everybody was amazed at what had happened, and after this Ephialtes and Themistocles denounced the Areopagites when the council of the Five Hundred met, and again in the assembly, until they had stripped off their power. And [*lacuna*] and Ephialtes was removed by being murdered, not long afterwards, through the agency of Aristodicus of Tanagra.

(**26**) In that way the council of the Areopagites was deprived of its responsibility. What happened after this was that the constitution became more loosened, on account of those engaging enthusiastically in demagogy. For it happened that at that juncture the more respectable men had no leader, but the man who acted as their champion was Cimon

ἀλλ' αὐτῶν προεστάναι Κίμωνα τὸν Μιλτιάδου, νεώτερον ὄντα καὶ πρὸς τὴν πόλιν ὀψὲ προσελθόντα, πρὸς δὲ τούτοις ἐφθάρθαι τοὺς πολλοὺς κατὰ πόλεμον· τῆς γὰρ στρατείας γιγνομένης ἐν τοῖς τότε χρόνοις ἐκ καταλόγου, καὶ στρατηγῶν ἐφισταμένων ἀπείρων μὲν τοῦ πολεμεῖν, τιμωμένων δὲ διὰ τὰς πατρικὰς δόξας, αἰεὶ συνέβαινεν τῶν ἐξιόντων ἀνὰ δισχιλίους ἢ τρισχιλίους ἀπόλλυσθαι, ὥστε ἀναλίσκεσθαι τοὺς ἐπιεικεῖς καὶ τοῦ δήμου καὶ τῶν εὐπόρων. (*2*) τὰ μὲν οὖν ἄλλα πάντα διῴκουν οὐχ ὁμοίως καὶ πρότερον τοῖς νόμοις προσέχοντες, τὴν δὲ τῶν ἐννέα ἀρχόντων αἵρεσιν οὐκ ἐκίνουν, ἀλλ' ἕκτῳ ἔτει μετὰ τὸν Ἐφιάλτου θάνατον ἔγνωσαν καὶ ἐκ ζευγιτῶν προκρίνεσθαι τοὺς κληρωσομένους τῶν ἐννέα ἀρχόντων, καὶ πρῶτος ἦρξεν ἐξ αὐτῶν Μνησιθείδης. οἱ δὲ πρὸ τούτου πάντες ἐξ ἱππέων καὶ πεντακοσιομεδίμνων ἦσαν, οἱ <δὲ> ζευγῖται τὰς ἐγκυκλίους ἦρχον, εἰ μή τι παρεωρᾶτο τῶν ἐν τοῖς νόμοις. (*3*) ἔτει δὲ πέμπτῳ μετὰ ταῦτα, ἐπὶ Λυσικράτους ἄρχοντος, οἱ τριάκοντα δικασταὶ κατέστησαν πάλιν οἱ καλούμενοι κατὰ δήμους. (*4*) καὶ τρίτῳ μετὰ τοῦτον, ἐπὶ Ἀντιδότου, διὰ τὸ πλῆθος τῶν πολιτῶν Περικλέους εἰπόντος ἔγνωσαν μὴ μετέχειν τῆς πόλεως ὃς ἂν μὴ ἐξ ἀμφοῖν ἀστοῖν ᾖ γεγονώς.

(**27**) μετὰ δὲ ταῦτα πρὸς τὸ δημαγωγεῖν ἐλθόντος Περικλέους, καὶ πρῶτον εὐδοκιμήσαντος ὅτε κατηγόρησε τὰς εὐθύνας Κίμωνος στρατηγοῦντος νέος ὤν, δημοτικωτέραν ἔτι συνέβη γενέσθαι τὴν πολιτείαν· καὶ γὰρ τῶν Ἀρεοπαγιτῶν ἔνια παρείλετο, καὶ μάλιστα προύτρεψεν τὴν πόλιν ἐπὶ τὴν ναυτικὴν δύναμιν, ἐξ ἧς συνέβη θαρρήσαντας τοὺς πολλοὺς ἅπασαν τὴν πολιτείαν μᾶλλον ἄγειν εἰς αὑτούς. (*2*) μετὰ δὲ τὴν ἐν Σαλαμῖνι ναυμαχίαν ἑνὸς δεῖ πεντηκοστῷ ἔτει, ἐπὶ Πυθοδώρου ἄρχοντος, ὁ πρὸς Πελοποννησίους ἐνέστη πόλεμος, ἐν ᾧ κατακλεισθεὶς ὁ δῆμος ἐν τῷ ἄστει καὶ συνεθισθεὶς ἐν ταῖς στρατιαῖς μισθοφορεῖν, τὰ μὲν ἑκὼν τὰ δὲ ἄκων προῃρεῖτο τὴν

26. 1. νεώτερον: νωθρότερον K. S. Kontos, ἐνεώτερον H. Weil, other suggestions have been made.

26. 2. οἱ <δὲ> ζευγῖται Kenyon[1].

Before τῶν ἐν τοῖς νόμοις L has ὑπὸ τ(ῶν) δήμων deleted.

27. 1. πρῶτον W. G. Rutherford and L. Campbell (*CR*): πρώτου L, πρὸ τοῦ H. Jackson (*CR*).

27. 2. στρατιαῖς: στρατείαις Kaibel & Wilamowitz[1].

son of Miltiades, who was fairly young and had only recently come forward to political engagement, and in addition that many of these men had perished in war. For campaigns at that time were based on registers, and, since the generals in command were inexperienced in warfare but honoured because of their forebears' reputations, the result was that repeatedly two or three thousand of the men who went out were killed, so that the respectable men both among the *demos* and among the well-off were used up. (*2*) In all the other aspects of their administration they did not pay heed to the laws as they had done previously, but they did not interfere with the appointment of the nine archons. But in the sixth year after the death of Ephialtes they resolved that the men among whom the allotment was to be made for the nine archons should be pre-elected from the *zeugitai* also, and the first from these to hold office was Mnesithides. Before him they had all been from the *hippeis* and *pentakosiomedimnoi*, while the *zeugitai* had held the routine offices, except when some stipulation in the laws had been neglected. (*3*) In the fifth year after that, in the archonship of Lysicrates, the thirty justices called deme justices were re-instituted. (*4*) And in the third after that, under Antidotus, because of the large number of citizens they resolved on the proposal of Pericles that a man should not participate in the city unless he was born from two citizens.

(**27**) After that Pericles embarked on demagogy, and first gained a good reputation when, while still young, he prosecuted the general Cimon in his *euthynai*; and so the constitution became still more democratic. For he stripped off some powers of the Areopagites, and particularly steered the city towards naval power, as a result of which the many became confident and increasingly drew towards themselves the whole control of the state. (*2*) In the forty-ninth year after the naval battle at Salamis, in the archonship of Pythodorus, the war against the Peloponnesians broke out, and in this the *demos* was shut up in the city and grew accustomed to earning stipends on campaign, and, intentionally in some matters and unintentionally in others, it chose to administer the

πολιτείαν διοικεῖν αὐτός. (*3*) ἐποίησε δὲ καὶ μισθοφόρα τὰ δικαστήρια Περικλῆς πρῶτος, ἀντιδημαγωγῶν πρὸς τὴν Κίμωνος εὐπορίαν. ὁ γὰρ Κίμων, ἅτε τυραννικὴν ἔχων οὐσίαν, πρῶτον μὲν τὰς κοινὰς λῃτουργίας ἐλῃτούργει λαμπρῶς, ἔπειτα τῶν δημοτῶν ἔτρεφε πολλούς· ἐξῆν γὰρ τῷ βουλομένῳ Λακιαδῶν καθ' ἑκάστην τὴν ἡμέραν ἐλθόντι παρ' αὐτὸν ἔχειν τὰ μέτρια, ἔτι δὲ τὰ χωρία πάντα ἄφρακτα ἦν, ὅπως ἐξῇ τῷ βουλομένῳ τῆς ὀπώρας ἀπολαύειν. (*4*) πρὸς δὴ ταύτην τὴν χορηγίαν ἐπιλειπόμενος ὁ Περικλῆς τῇ οὐσίᾳ, συμβουλεύσαντος αὐτῷ Δαμωνίδου τοῦ Οἴηθεν (ὃς ἐδόκει τῶν πολλῶν εἰσηγητὴς εἶναι τῷ Περικλεῖ· διὸ καὶ ὠστράκισαν αὐτὸν ὕστερον), ἐπεὶ τοῖς ἰδίοις ἡττᾶτο, διδόναι τοῖς πολλοῖς τὰ αὐτῶν, κατεσκεύασε μισθοφορὰν τοῖς δικασταῖς· ἀφ' ὧν αἰτιῶνταί τινες χείρω γενέσθαι, κληρουμένων ἐπιμελῶς ἀεὶ μᾶλλον τῶν τυχόντων ἢ τῶν ἐπιεικῶν ἀνθρώπων. (*5*) ἤρξατο δὲ μετὰ ταῦτα καὶ τὸ δεκάζειν, πρώτου καταδείξαντος Ἀνύτου μετὰ τὴν ἐν Πύλῳ στρατηγίαν· κρινόμενος γὰρ ὑπό τινων διὰ τὸ ἀποβαλεῖν Πύλον, δεκάσας τὸ δικαστήριον ἀπέφυγεν.

(**28**) ἕως μὲν οὖν Περικλῆς προειστήκει τοῦ δήμου, βελτίω τὰ κατὰ τὴν πολιτείαν ἦν, τελευτήσαντος δὲ Περικλέους πολὺ χείρω. πρῶτον γὰρ τότε προστάτην ἔλαβεν ὁ δῆμος οὐκ εὐδοκιμοῦντα παρὰ τοῖς ἐπιεικέσιν· ἐν δὲ τοῖς πρότερον χρόνοις ἀεὶ διετέλουν οἱ ἐπιεικεῖς δημαγωγοῦντες. (*2*) ἐξ ἀρχῆς μὲν γὰρ καὶ πρῶτος ἐγένετο προστάτης τοῦ δήμου Σόλων, δεύτερος δὲ Πεισίστρατος, τῶν <δὲ> εὐγενῶν καὶ γνωρίμων <Λυκοῦργος>· καταλυθείσης δὲ τῆς τυραννίδος Κλεισθένης, τοῦ γένους ὢν τῶν Ἀλκμεωνιδῶν, καὶ τούτῳ μὲν οὐδεὶς ἦν ἀντιστασιώτης, ὡς ἐξέπεσον οἱ περὶ τὸν Ἰσαγόραν. μετὰ δὲ ταῦτα τοῦ μὲν δήμου προειστήκει Ξάνθιππος, τῶν δὲ γνωρίμων Μιλτιάδης· ἔπειτα Θεμιστοκλῆς καὶ Ἀριστείδης· μετὰ δὲ τούτους Ἐφιάλτης μὲν τοῦ δήμου, Κίμων δ' ὁ

27. 4. Δαμωνίδου τοῦ Οἴηθεν: <Δάμωνος τοῦ> Δαμωνίδου {τοῦ} Ὄαθεν W. Wyse (*CR*), cf. Steph. Byz.

δικασταῖς: δικαστηρίοις Blass, H. Richards (*CR*).

χείρω: χείρους W. L. Newman (*CR*).

27. 5. Ἀνύτου Kenyon[1] cf. Harp. δ 13 Keaney δεκάζων: αὐτοῦ L.

28. 2. τῶν <δὲ> εὐγενῶν καὶ γνωρίμων <Λυκοῦργος>, accepted Chambers, or else <Λυκοῦργος καὶ Μεγακλῆς>, A. W. Gomme; τῶν εὐγενῶν καὶ γνωρίμων deleted Kaibel & Wilamowitz; εὐγενῶν <ὢν> H. Richards (*CR*), εὐγενῶν <ὄντες> T. Gomperz; text of L retained Kenyon.

state itself. (*3*) Also it was Pericles who was first to provide a stipend for the lawcourts, as an act of demagogy to counter the lavishness of Cimon. For Cimon, whose property was like that of a tyrant, first was outstanding in his performance of the public liturgies, and next sustained many of his fellow-demesmen: for any of the Laciadae who wished was able to go each day and receive a modest livelihood from him, and also all his land was unfenced, so that anybody who wished could benefit from the fruit. (*4*) Since Pericles' property fell short for that service, on the advice of Damonides of Oë (who seems to have suggested most of Pericles' measures to him: because of that they later ostracised him), that since he was being worsted through private resources he should give the many their own, he devised the payment of a stipend for the jurors. Some say that in consequence of this the jurors became worse, as it was always run-of-the-mill men rather than respectable men who were careful to present themselves for allotment. (*5*) After this the practice of judicial bribery began, first introduced by Anytus after his generalship at Pylos: for he was brought to trial by some men for losing Pylos but bribed the lawcourt and was acquitted.

(**28**) While Pericles was champion of the *demos* matters with regard to the constitution were better, but after Pericles' death they were much worse. For then for the first time the *demos* took a champion who was not of good repute among the respectable men; but in the previous times it was always the respectable who continued to be popular leaders. (*2*) For from the beginning it was Solon who was the first champion of the *demos*; and secondly Pisistratus, and Lycurgus of the well-born and notable. After the overthrow of the tyranny it was Cleisthenes, of the Alcmaeonid family, and there was no factional leader opposed to him, since the circle of Isagoras had gone into exile. After this Xanthippus was champion of the *demos*, and Miltiades of the notables; then Themistocles and Aristides respectively; after them Ephialtes was champion of the *demos*

Μιλτιάδου τῶν εὐπόρων· εἶτα Περικλῆς μὲν τοῦ δήμου, Θουκυδίδης δὲ τῶν ἑτέρων, κηδεστὴς ὢν Κίμωνος. (*3*) Περικλέους δὲ τελευτήσαντος, τῶν μὲν ἐπιφανῶν προειστήκει Νικίας ὁ ἐν Σικελίᾳ τελευτήσας, τοῦ δὲ δήμου Κλέων ὁ Κλεαινέτου, ὃς δοκεῖ μάλιστα διαφθεῖραι τὸν δῆμον ταῖς ὁρμαῖς, καὶ πρῶτος ἐπὶ τοῦ βήματος ἀνέκραγε καὶ ἐλοιδορήσατο, καὶ περιζωσάμενος ἐδημηγόρησε, τῶν ἄλλων ἐν κόσμῳ λεγόντων. εἶτα μετὰ τούτους τῶν μὲν ἑτέρων Θηραμένης ὁ Ἅγνωνος, τοῦ δὲ δήμου Κλεοφῶν ὁ λυροποιός, ὃς καὶ τὴν διωβελίαν ἐπόρισε πρῶτος· καὶ χρόνον μέν τινα διεδίδοτο, μετὰ δὲ ταῦτα κατέλυσε Καλλικράτης Παιανιεύς, πρῶτον ὑποσχόμενος ἐπιθήσειν πρὸς τοῖν δυοῖν ὀβολοῖν ἄλλον ὀβολόν. τούτων μὲν οὖν ἀμφοτέρων θάνατον κατέγνωσαν ὕστερον· εἴωθεν γὰρ κἂν ἐξαπατηθῇ τὸ πλῆθος ὕστερον μισεῖν τούς τι προαγαγόντας ποιεῖν αὐτοὺς τῶν μὴ καλῶς ἐχόντων. (*4*) ἀπὸ δὲ Κλεοφῶντος ἤδη διεδέχοντο συνεχῶς τὴν δημαγωγίαν οἱ μάλιστα βουλόμενοι θρασύνεσθαι καὶ χαρίζεσθαι τοῖς πολλοῖς, πρὸς τὰ παραυτίκα βλέποντες. (*5*) δοκοῦσι δὲ {οἱ} βέλτιστοι γεγονέναι τῶν Ἀθήνησι πολιτευσαμένων μετὰ τοὺς ἀρχαίους Νικίας καὶ Θουκυδίδης καὶ Θηραμένης. καὶ περὶ μὲν Νικίου καὶ Θουκυδίδου πάντες σχεδὸν ὁμολογοῦσιν ἄνδρας γεγονέναι οὐ μόνον καλοὺς κἀγαθούς, ἀλλὰ καὶ πολιτικοὺς καὶ τῇ πόλει πάσῃ πατρικῶς χρωμένους· περὶ δὲ Θηραμένους διὰ τὸ συμβῆναι κατ᾽ αὐτὸν ταραχώδεις τὰς πολιτείας ἀμφισβήτησις τῆς κρίσεώς ἐστι. δοκεῖ μέν<τοι> τοῖς μὴ παρέργως ἀποφαινομένοις οὐχ ὥσπερ αὐτὸν διαβάλλουσι πάσας τὰς πολιτείας καταλύειν, ἀλλὰ πάσας προάγειν ἕως μηδὲν παρανομοῖεν, ὡς δυνάμενος πολιτεύεσθαι κατὰ πάσας, ὅπερ ἐστὶν ἀγαθοῦ πολίτου ἔργον, παρανομούσαις δὲ οὐ συγχωρῶν ἀλλ᾽ ἀπεχθανόμενος.

28. 2–3. Θουκυδίδης δὲ τῶν ἑτέρων … τῶν μὲν ἑτέρων Θηραμένης: ἐσθλῶν W. Wyse (*CR*), ἐπιεικῶν J. E. B. Mayor (*CR*), εὐπόρων H. Richards (*CR*), other suggestions have been made.

28. 3. διεδίδοτο W. Wyse, W. G. Rutherford (*CR*): διεδίδου L.

κατέλυσε: κατηύξησε L. Whibley (*CR*), other suggestions have been made.

πρῶτον (Herwerden &) Leeuwen: πρῶτος L.

28. 5. δὲ {οἱ} βέλτιστοι Kaibel & Wilamowitz: δοι with the letter ε written above L.

μέν<τοι> τοῖς Kenyon[1]: μ(ὲν) τοῖς L, μέντοι without τοῖς Kaibel & Wilamowitz.

and Cimon son of Miltiades of the well-off; then Pericles of the *demos* and Thucydides of the others, a relative of Cimon. (*3*) After Pericles' death the champion of the distinguished was Nicias, who died in Sicily, and of the *demos* Cleon son of Cleaenetus: Cleon seems particularly to have corrupted the *demos* by his wild impulses, and was the first to shout and utter abuse on the platform, and to speak with his clothes hitched up, when the others spoke in an orderly manner. Then after these the champion of the others was Theramenes son of Hagnon, and of the *demos* Cleophon the lyre-maker, who was also the first man to provide the two-obol grant. (That continued to be paid for a time, but then it was abolished by Callicrates of Paeania, though he first promised to add another obol to the two obols.) Both of these were afterwards condemned to death; for it was the masses' custom, particularly if they were deceived, to hate those who had incited them at all to do anything improper. (*4*) After Cleophon there was a continual succession in demagogy of those who most wanted to be outrageous and to gratify the masses, looking only to the short term. (*5*) It seems that the best of the Athenian politicians after the ancients were Nicias, Thucydides and Theramenes. About Nicias and Thucydides almost all agree that they were not only fine gentlemen but civic-minded, and treated the whole city in a fatherly manner. But about Theramenes, because in his time there were disturbances with regard to the constitution, the judgment is disputed. However, it seems to those who do not express their opinions casually that he did not overthrow all the constitutions, as his detractors allege, but supported them all as long as they did nothing illegal, since he was able to take part in political life under all (which is the duty of a good citizen), but when they did act illegally he did not acquiesce but incurred their hatred.

(**29**) ἕως μὲν οὖν ἰσόρροπα τὰ πράγματα κατὰ τὸν πόλεμον ἦν, διεφύλαττον τὴν δημοκρατίαν. ἐπεὶ δὲ μετὰ τὴν ἐν Σικελίᾳ γενομένην συμφορὰν ἰσχυρότερα τὰ τῶν Λακεδαιμονίων ἐγένετο διὰ τὴν πρὸς βασιλέα συμμαχίαν, ἠναγκάσθησαν κε[ινήσα]ντες τὴν δημοκρατίαν καταστῆσαι τὴν ἐπὶ τῶν τετρακοσίων πολιτείαν, εἰπόντος τὸν μὲν πρὸ τοῦ ψηφίσματος λόγον Μηλοβίου, τὴν δὲ γνώμην γράψαντος Πυθοδώρου το[ῦ Ἀναφ]λυ[σ]τίου, μάλιστα δὲ συμπεισθέντων τῶν πολλῶν διὰ τὸ νομίζειν βασιλέα μᾶλλον ἑαυτοῖς συμπολεμήσειν ἐὰν δι᾽ ὀλίγων ποιήσωνται τὴν πολιτείαν. (*2*) ἦν δὲ τὸ ψήφισμα τοῦ Πυθοδώρου τοιόνδε· τὸν δῆμον ἑλέσθαι μετὰ τῶν προϋπαρχόντων δέκα προβούλων ἄλλους εἴκοσι ἐκ τῶν ὑπὲρ τετταράκοντα ἔτη γεγονότων, οἵτινες ὀμόσαντες ἦ μὴν συγγράψειν ἃ ἂν ἡγῶνται βέλτιστα εἶναι τῇ πόλει συγγράψουσι περὶ τῆς σωτηρίας· ἐξεῖναι δὲ καὶ τῶν ἄλλων τῷ βουλομένῳ γράφειν, ἵν᾽ ἐξ ἁπάντων αἱρῶνται τὸ ἄριστον. (*3*) Κλειτοφῶν δὲ τὰ μὲν ἄλλα καθάπερ Πυθόδωρος εἶπεν, προσαναζητῆσαι δὲ τοὺς αἱρεθέντας ἔγραψεν καὶ τοὺς πατρίους νόμους οὓς Κλεισθένης ἔθηκεν ὅτε καθίστη τὴν δημοκρατίαν, ὅπως ἀκούσαντες καὶ τούτων βουλεύσωνται τὸ ἄριστον (ὡς οὐ δημοτικὴν ἀλλὰ παραπλησίαν οὖσαν τὴν Κλεισθένους πολιτείαν τῇ Σόλωνος). (*4*) οἱ δ᾽ αἱρεθέντες πρῶτον μὲν ἔγραψαν ἐπάναγκες εἶναι τοὺς πρυτάνεις ἅπαντα τὰ λεγόμενα περὶ τῆς σωτηρίας ἐπιψηφίζειν, ἔπειτα τὰς τῶν παρανόμων γραφὰς καὶ τὰς εἰσαγγελίας καὶ τὰς προσκλήσεις ἀνεῖλον, ὅπως ἂν οἱ ἐθέλοντες Ἀθηναίων συμβουλεύωσι περὶ τῶν προκειμένων· ἐὰν δέ τις τούτων χάριν ἢ ζημιοῖ ἢ προσκαλῆται ἢ εἰσάγῃ {ἢ} εἰς δικαστήριον, ἔνδειξιν αὐτοῦ εἶναι καὶ ἀπαγωγὴν πρὸς τοὺς στρατηγούς, τοὺς δὲ στρατηγοὺς παραδοῦναι τοῖς ἕνδεκα θανάτῳ ζημιῶσαι. (*5*) μετὰ δὲ ταῦτα τὴν πολιτείαν διέταξαν

29. 1. πράγματα deleted (Herwerden &) Leeuwen.
συμφορὰν H. Richards (*CR*) *et al.*: δ(ια)φορὰν L.
ἰσχυρότερα J. B. Mayor (*CR*) *et al.*: ἰσχυρότατα L.
κε[ινήσα]ντες Kaibel & Wilamowitz.
Πυθοδώρου το[ῦ Ἀναφ]λυ[σ]τίου Blass (λ read by Chambers).
29. 2. τοῦ Πυθοδώρου: τὸ Blass[2].
29. 3. ὅπως: ὅπως <ἂν> Kaibel & Wilamowitz.
29. 4. εἰσάγῃ {ἢ} Kenyon[1].

(**29**) While affairs were evenly balanced in the war, they preserved the democracy. But when, after the disaster which occurred in Sicily, the Spartans' position became stronger on account of their alliance with the King, they were compelled to interfere with the democracy and establish the constitution centred on the Four Hundred. The speech introducing the decree was made by Melobius, the formal proposal was made by Pythodorus of Anaphlystus, and the many were persuaded to accept it particularly because they thought that the King would be more likely to fight on their side if they based the constitution on a few men. (*2*) Pythodorus' decree was of this nature: the assembly should elect together with the ten *probouloi* already in existence twenty others from those over the age of forty, who should swear to draft what they thought best for the city and should draft proposals for their salvation; anybody else who wished could make proposals, so that they could choose the best from all. (*3*) Cleitophon proposed in other respects as Pythodorus, but that those who were elected should also search out the traditional laws which Cleisthenes enacted when he established the democracy, so that they could hear these too and arrive at the best policy. (His point was that Cleisthenes' constitution was not populist but much like that of Solon.) (*4*) Those who were elected proposed first that it should be obligatory for the *prytaneis* to put to the vote all proposals that were made about salvation. Then they suspended the *graphai paranomon*, the *eisangeliai* and the *proskleseis*, so that those Athenians who wanted could deliberate about what was laid before them; if anybody on account of this imposed a penalty or made a *prosklesis* or brought a man before a lawcourt, he should be liable to *endeixis* and *apagoge* before the generals, and the generals should hand him over to the Eleven for the death penalty. (*5*) After that they organised the constitution in the following way. The

τόνδε <τὸν> τρόπον· τὰ μὲν χρήματα <τὰ> προσιόντα μὴ ἐξεῖναι ἄλλοσε δαπανῆσαι ἢ εἰς τὸν πόλεμον, τὰς δ' ἀρχὰς ἀμίσθους ἄρχειν ἁπάσας ἕως ἂν ὁ πόλεμος ᾖ̣, πλὴν τῶν ἐννέα ἀρχόντων καὶ τῶν πρυτάνεων οἳ ἂν ὦσιν· τούτους δὲ φέρειν τρεῖς ὀβολοὺς ἕκαστον τῆς ἡμέρας. τὴν δ' ἄλλην πολιτείαν ἐπιτρέψαι πᾶσαν Ἀθηναίων τοῖς δυνατωτάτοις καὶ τοῖς σώμασιν καὶ τοῖς χρήμασιν λ̣ητουργεῖν, μὴ ἔλαττον {ἢ} πεντακισχιλίων, ἕως ἂν ὁ πόλεμος ᾖ̣· κυρίους δ' εἶναι τούτους καὶ συνθήκας συντίθεσθαι πρὸς οὓς ἂν ἐθέλωσιν. ἑλέσθαι δὲ καὶ τῆς φυλῆς ἑκάστης δέκα ἄνδρας ὑπὲρ τετταράκοντα ἔτη γεγονότας, οἵτινες καταλέξουσι τοὺς πεντακισχιλίους ὀμόσαντες καθ' ἱερῶν τελείων.

(**30**) οἱ μὲν οὖν αἱρεθέντες ταῦτα συνέγραψαν. κυρωθέντων δὲ τούτων εἵλοντο σφῶν αὐτῶν οἱ πεντακισχίλιοι τοὺς ἀναγράψοντας τὴν πολιτείαν ἑκατὸν ἄνδρας. οἱ δ' αἱρεθέντες ἀνέγραψαν καὶ ἐξήνεγκαν τάδε. (*2*) βουλεύειν μὲν κατ' ἐνιαυτὸν τοὺς ὑπὲρ τριάκοντα ἔτη γεγονότας ἄνευ μισθοφορᾶς· τούτων δ' εἶναι τοὺς στρατηγοὺς καὶ τοὺς ἐννέα ἄρχοντας καὶ τὸν ἱερομνήμονα καὶ τοὺς ταξιάρχους καὶ ἱππάρχους καὶ φυλάρχους καὶ ἄρχοντας εἰς τὰ φρούρια καὶ ταμίας τῶν ἱερῶν χρημάτων τῇ θεῷ̣ καὶ τοῖς ἄλλοις θεοῖς δέκα καὶ ἑλληνοταμίας καὶ τῶν ἄλλων ὁσίων χρημάτων ἁπάντων εἴκοσιν οἳ διαχειριοῦσιν, καὶ ἱεροποιοὺς καὶ ἐπιμελητὰς δέκα ἑκατέρους· αἱρεῖσθαι δὲ πάντας τούτους ἐκ προκρίτων, ἐκ τῶν ἀεὶ βουλευόντων πλείους προκρίνοντας· τὰς δ' ἄλλας ἀρχὰς ἁπάσας κληρωτὰς εἶναι καὶ μὴ ἐκ τῆς βουλῆς· τοὺς δὲ ἑλληνοταμίας οἳ ἂν διαχειρίζωσι τὰ χρήματα μὴ συμβουλεύειν. (*3*) βουλὰς δὲ ποιῆσαι τέτταρας ἐκ τῆς ἡλικίας τῆς εἰρημένης εἰς τὸν λοιπὸν χρόνον, καὶ τούτων

29. 5. τόνδε <τὸν> τρόπον J. B. Mayor *et al.* (*CR*).

τὰ μὲν χρήματα <τὰ> προσιόντα Kenyon[1]: τὰ μὲν {χρήματα} προσιόντα H. Richards (*CR*).

μὴ ἔλαττον {ἢ} πεντακισχιλίων Kaibel & Wilamowitz: ἢ πεντακισχιλίοις with the letters ων written above L, ἢ πεντακισχιλίοις Kenyon[1].

30. 2. θεῷ̣ Kenyon[1]: θεῷ̣[ι] L, better θεᾷ̣[ι] Wilcken, Thomas, traces would fit either ω or α Kenyon[4].

οἳ ἂν διαχειρίζωσι Kaibel & Wilamowitz: ἐὰν L.

30. 3. βουλὰς: φυλὰς E. M. Harris.

money received as revenue it should not be permitted to spend for any purpose other than the war; all the officials should hold office without stipend as long as the war continued, apart from the nine archons and whatever *prytaneis* there might be, who should each be paid three obols a day. All the remaining political power should be entrusted to those Athenians who were most able to serve with their bodies and their possessions, not fewer than five thousand, as long as the war continued, and these should have power to make treaties with whoever they wanted. There should be elected from each tribe ten men over the age of forty, who were to register the Five Thousand after swearing an oath over full-grown victims.

(**30**) That, then, is what was drafted by those who had been elected. When it had been ratified, the Five Thousand elected from among themselves a hundred men to write up the constitution, and those who were elected wrote up and brought forward the following. (*2*) The council year by year should comprise those over the age of thirty, without stipend. From these should come the generals and the nine archons and the *hieromnemon*, and the taxiarchs and hipparchs and phylarchs and garrison commanders, and ten treasurers of the sacred funds of the Goddess and the Other Gods and twenty *hellenotamiai* to handle all the other proper funds, and *hieropoioi* and *epimeletai* ten each. All of these should be elected from pre-elected candidates, pre-electing a larger number from those currently in the council. The *hellenotamiai* who handled the funds should not join in deliberation. (*3*) Four councils should be created for the future from the stated age range, and of these

τὸ λαχὸν μέρος βουλεύειν, νεῖμαι δὲ καὶ τοὺς ἄλλους πρὸς τὴν λῆξιν ἑκάστην· τοὺς δ' ἑκατὸν ἄνδρας διανεῖμαι σφᾶς τε αὐτοὺς καὶ τοὺς ἄλλους τέτταρα μέρη ὡς ἰσαίτατα καὶ διακληρῶσαι, καὶ εἰς ἐνιαυτὸν βουλεύειν. (*4*) <βουλεύεσθαι> δὲ ᾗ ἂν δοκῇ αὐτοῖς ἄριστα ἕξειν περί τε τῶν χρημάτων, ὅπως ἂν σῶα ᾖ καὶ εἰς τὸ δέον ἀναλίσκηται, καὶ περὶ τῶν ἄλλων ὡς ἂν δύνωνται ἄριστα· κἄν τι θέλωσιν βουλεύσασθαι μετὰ πλειόνων, ἐπεισκαλεῖν ἕκαστον ἐπείσκλητον ὃν ἂν ἐθέλῃ τῶν ἐκ τῆς αὐτῆς ἡλικίας. τὰς δ' ἕδρας ποιεῖν τῆς βουλῆς κατὰ πενθήμερον, ἐὰν μὴ δέωνται πλειόνων. (*5*) πληροῦν δὲ τὴν βουλὴν τοὺς ἐννέα ἄρχοντας· τὰς δὲ χειροτονίας κρίνειν πέντε τοὺς λαχόντας ἐκ τῆς βουλῆς, καὶ ἐκ τούτων ἕνα κληροῦσθαι καθ' ἑκάστην ἡμέραν τὸν ἐπιψηφιοῦντα. κληροῦν δὲ τοὺς λαχόντας πέντε τοὺς ἐθέλοντας προσελθεῖν ἐναντίον τῆς βουλῆς, πρῶτον μὲν ἱερῶν, δεύτερον δὲ κήρυξιν, τρίτον πρεσβείαις, τέταρτον τῶν ἄλλων· τὰ δὲ τοῦ πολέμου ὅταν δέῃ ἀκληρωτὶ προσαγαγόντας τοὺς στρατηγοὺς χρηματίζειν. (*6*) τὸν δὲ μὴ ἰόντα εἰς τὸ βουλευτήριον τῶν βουλευόντων τὴν ὥραν τὴν προρρηθεῖσαν ὀφείλειν δραχμὴν τῆς ἡμέρας ἑκάστης, ἐὰν μὴ εὑρισκόμενος ἄφεσιν τῆς βουλῆς ἀπῇ.

(**31**) ταύτην μὲν οὖν εἰς τὸν μέλλοντα χρόνον ἀνέγραψαν τὴν πολιτείαν, ἐν δὲ τῷ παρόντι καιρῷ τήνδε. βουλεύειν μὲν τετρακοσίους κατὰ τὰ πάτρια, τετταράκοντα ἐξ ἑκάστης φυλῆς, ἐκ προκρίτων οὓς ἂν ἕλωνται οἱ φυλέται τῶν ὑπὲρ τριάκοντα ἔτη γεγονότων. τούτους δὲ τάς τε ἀρχὰς καταστῆσαι, καὶ †περὶ τοῦ ὅρκου ὅντινα χρὴ ὀμόσαι γράψαι†, <καὶ> περὶ τῶν νόμων καὶ τῶν εὐθυνῶν καὶ τῶν ἄλλων πράττειν ᾗ ἂν ἡγῶνται

30. 3–4 βουλεύειν. <βουλεύεσθαι> δὲ Sandys[1]: βουλεύειν <τοὺς λαχόντας. πράττειν> δὲ Kaibel & Wilamowitz, βουλεύειν <του\ς λαχόντας. βουλεύεσθαι> δὲ Blass[1–3].

30. 4. σῶα: σῷα Kaibel & Wilamowitz.

30. 5. πληροῦν H. Weil: κληροῦν L.

καθ' ἑκάστην <τὴν> ἡμέραν Blass.

ἐναντίον τῆς βουλῆς: afterwards βουλὰς δ´ ποιῆσαι τεττάρας repeated and deleted L.

πρεσβείαις W. Wyse (*CR*): πρεσβειαι L.

χρηματίζειν Kaibel & Wilamowitz[3]: χρηματίζεσθαι L.

31. 1. †περὶ τοῦ ὅρκου ὅντινα χρὴ ὀμόσαι γράψαι† I obelise: perhaps καὶ τὸν ὅρκον …, other suggestions have been made.

<καὶ> περὶ τῶν νόμων Kenyon[1].

a part picked by sortition should serve as council. The other men also should be distributed to each section; the hundred men should distribute themselves and the others in four parts as equally as possible and make an allotment, and the council should serve for a year. (*4*) They should deliberate as they judged would be best with regard to the funds, so that they should be safe and spent on what was necessary, and concerning the other matters as best they could. And, if they wanted to deliberate with a larger number, each member should coopt one coopted member, whoever he wanted, from the same age range. They should hold meetings of the council at five-day intervals, unless they needed more. (*5*) The council should be convened by the nine archons; the votes by hand should be judged by five men picked by sortition from the council, and of these one should be picked by lot each day to put motions to the vote. These five men picked by sortition should pick by lot those who wanted to appear before the council, first on sacred matters, secondly for heralds, thirdly for embassies, fourthly on other matters; on matters of war when necessary they should bring forward the generals to do business without allotment. (*6*) A member of the council who did not go to the council house at the time specified should owe a drachma for each day, unless he received leave from the council and was absent.

(**31**) That is the constitution which they wrote up for the time to come, but for the present juncture the following. There should be a council of four hundred in accordance with tradition, forty from each tribe, from pre-elected candidates elected by the tribesmen from those over thirty years old. These should institute the officials, and †make a proposal about the oath which was to be sworn†, and with regard to the laws, *euthynai* and other matters do what they thought advantageous. (*2*) The

συμφέρειν. (*2*) τοῖς δὲ νόμοις οἳ ἂν τεθῶσιν περὶ τῶν πολιτικῶν χρῆσθαι, καὶ μὴ ἐξεῖναι μετακινεῖν μηδ᾽ ἑτέρους θέσθαι. τῶν δὲ στρατηγῶν τὸ νῦν εἶναι τὴν αἵρεσιν ἐξ ἁπάντων ποιεῖσθαι τῶν πεντακισχιλίων, τὴν δὲ βουλὴν ἐπειδὰν καταστῇ ποιήσασαν ἐξέτασιν <ἐν> ὅπλοις ἑλέσθαι δέκα ἄνδρας καὶ γραμματέα τούτοις, τοὺς δὲ αἱρεθέντας ἄρχειν τὸν εἰσιόντα ἐνιαυτὸν αὐτοκράτορας, καὶ ἐάν τι δέωνται συμβουλεύεσθαι μετὰ τῆς βουλῆς. (*3*) ἑλέσθαι δὲ καὶ ἵππαρχον ἕνα καὶ φυλάρχους δέκα· τὸ δὲ λοιπὸν τὴν αἵρεσιν ποιεῖσθαι τούτων τὴν βουλὴν κατὰ τὰ γεγραμμένα. τῶν δ᾽ ἄλλων ἀρχῶν πλὴν τῆς βουλῆς καὶ τῶν στρατηγῶν μὴ ἐξεῖναι μήτε τούτοις μήτε ἄλλῳ μηδενὶ πλέον ἢ ἅπαξ ἄρξαι τὴν αὐτὴν ἀρχήν. εἰς δὲ τὸν ἄλλον χρόνον, ἵνα νεμηθῶσιν οἱ τετρακόσιοι εἰς τὰς τέτταρας λήξεις, ὅταν {τοῖς} αὐτοῖς γίγνηται μετὰ τῶν ἄλλων βουλεύειν, διανειμάντων αὐτοὺς οἱ ἑκατὸν ἄνδρες.

(**32**) οἱ μὲν οὖν ἑκατὸν οἱ ὑπὸ τῶν πεντακισχιλίων αἱρεθέντες ταύτην ἀνέγραψαν τὴν πολιτείαν. ἐπικυρωθέντων δὲ τούτων ὑπὸ τοῦ πλήθους, ἐπιψηφίσαντος Ἀριστομάχου, ἡ μὲν βουλὴ <ἡ> ἐπὶ Καλλίου πρὶν διαβουλεῦσαι κατελύθη μηνὸς Θαργηλιῶνος τετράδι ἐπὶ δέκα, οἱ δὲ τετρακόσιοι εἰσῄεσαν ἐνάτῃ φθίνοντος Θαργηλιῶνος· ἔδει δὲ τὴν εἰληχυῖαν τῷ κυάμῳ βουλὴν εἰσιέναι δʹ ἐπὶ δέκα Σκιροφοριῶνος. (*2*) ἡ μὲν οὖν ὀλιγαρχία τοῦτον κατέστη τὸν τρόπον, ἐπὶ Καλλίου μὲν ἄρχοντος, ἔτεσιν δ᾽ ὕστερον τῆς τῶν τυράννων ἐκβολῆς μάλιστα ἑκατὸν, αἰτίων μάλιστα γενομένων Πεισάνδρου καὶ Ἀντιφῶντος <καὶ Φρυνίχου> καὶ Θηραμένους, ἀνδρῶν καὶ γεγενημένων εὖ καὶ συνέσει καὶ γνώμῃ δοκούντων διαφέρειν. (*3*) γενομένης δὲ ταύτης τῆς πολιτείας, οἱ μὲν πεντακισχίλιοι λόγῳ μόνον ᾑρέθησαν, οἱ δὲ τετρακόσιοι μετὰ τῶν δέκα τῶν αὐτοκρατόρων εἰσελθόντες εἰς τὸ βουλευτήριον ἦρχον τῆς πόλεως,

31. 2. ἐξέτασιν <ἐν> ὅπλοις W. Wyse (*CR*).

καὶ ἐάν Herwerden (& Leeuwen): καὶ ἄν L, κἄν Sandys[1].

31. 3. ἵππαρχον ἕνα <καὶ ταξιάρχους δέκα> Wilamowitz (*A.u.A.* ii. 115 n. 9, Kaibel & Wilamowitz[3]).

{τοῖς} αὐτοῖς Sandys[1]: τοῖς ἀστοῖς L, τοῖς αὐτοῖς R. Y. Tyrrell (*CR*).

32. 1. <ἡ> ἐπὶ Καλλίου W. G. Rutherford (*CR*).

32. 2. Ἀντιφῶντος <καὶ Φρυνίχου> καὶ Rhodes.

laws which they enacted about constitutional matters they should follow, and it should not be permitted to interfere with these or to enact others. For now the election of the generals should be made from all the Five Thousand; but when the council had been established it should hold an armed review and elect ten men and a secretary for them, and the men elected should hold office with full power for the coming year and if they needed anything should deliberate together with the council. (*3*) They should elect also one hipparch and ten phylarchs; and for the future the election of these should be made by the council in accordance with what had been written. For the other officials apart from the council and the generals, it should not be permitted either to these or to anybody else to hold the same office more than once. For the rest of the time, so that the Four Hundred should be distributed into the four sections, when it became possible for them to deliberate with the others, the hundred men were to distribute them.

(**32**) That constitution was written up by the hundred men elected by the Five Thousand. When that had been ratified by the masses, put to the vote by Aristomachus, the council of the year of Callias was dissolved without completing its term of office, on the fourteenth of the month Thargelion, and the Four Hundred were inaugurated on the twenty-second of Thargelion. The council appointed by lot was due to be inaugurated on 14 Scirophorion. (*2*) That is the manner in which the oligarchy was instituted, in the archonship of Callias, about a hundred years after the expulsion of the tyrants. The men particularly responsible were Pisandrus, Antiphon, Phrynichus and Theramenes, men who both were well born and appeared outstanding in intelligence and judgment. (*3*) With that constitution in being, the Five Thousand were elected only in name, and the Four Hundred together with the ten men with full power were inaugurated in the council house and began ruling the city. And

καὶ πρὸς Λακεδαιμονίους πρεσβευσάμενοι κατελύοντο τὸν πόλεμον ἐφ' οἷς ἑκάτεροι τυγχάνουσιν ἔχοντες. οὐχ ὑπακουόντων δ' ἐκείνων, εἰ μὴ καὶ τὴν ἀρχὴν τῆς θαλάττης ἀφήσουσιν, οὕτως ἀπέστησαν.

(**33**) μῆνας μὲν οὖν ἴσως τέτταρας διέμεινεν ἡ τῶν τετρακοσίων πολιτεία, καὶ ἦρξεν ἐξ αὐτῶν Μνασίλοχος δίμηνον ἐπὶ Θεοπόμπου ἄρχοντος, <ὃς> ἦρξε τοὺς ἐπιλοίπους δέκα μῆνας. ἡττηθέντες δὲ τῇ περὶ Ἐρέτριαν ναυμαχίᾳ καὶ τῆς Εὐβοίας ἀποστάσης ὅλης πλὴν Ὠρεοῦ, χαλεπῶς ἐνεγκόντες ἐπὶ τῇ συμφορᾷ μάλιστα τῶν προγεγενημένων (πλείω γὰρ ἐκ τῆς Εὐβοίας ἢ τῆς Ἀττικῆς ἐτύγχανον ὠφελούμενοι), κατέλυσαν τοὺς τετρακοσίους, καὶ τὰ πράγματα παρέδωκαν τοῖς πεντακισχιλίοις τοῖς ἐκ τῶν ὅπλων, ψηφισάμενοι μηδεμίαν ἀρχὴν εἶναι μισθοφόρον. (*2*) αἰτιώτατοι δ' ἐγένοντο τῆς καταλύσεως Ἀριστοκράτης καὶ Θηραμένης, οὐ συναρεσκόμενοι τοῖς ὑπὸ τῶν τετρακοσίων γιγνομένοις· ἅπαντα γὰρ δι' αὑτῶν ἔπραττον, οὐδὲν ἐπαναφέροντες τοῖς πεντακισχιλίοις. δοκοῦσι δὲ καλῶς πολιτευθῆναι κατὰ τούτους τοὺς καιρούς, πολέμου τε καθεστῶτος καὶ ἐκ τῶν ὅπλων τῆς πολιτείας οὔσης.

(**34**) τούτους μὲν οὖν ἀφείλετο τὴν πολιτείαν ὁ δῆμος διὰ τάχους. ἔτει δ' ἑβδόμῳ μετὰ τὴν τῶν τετρακοσίων κατάλυσιν, ἐπὶ Καλλίου τοῦ Ἀγγελῆθεν ἄρχοντος, γενομένης τῆς ἐν Ἀργινούσαις ναυμαχίας, πρῶτον μὲν τοὺς δέκα στρατηγοὺς τοὺς τῇ ναυμαχίᾳ νικῶντας συνέβη κριθῆναι μιᾷ χειροτονίᾳ πάντας, τοὺς μὲν οὐδὲ συνναυμαχήσαντας, τοὺς δ' ἐπ' ἀλλοτρίας νεὼς σωθέντας, ἐξαπατηθέντος τοῦ δήμου διὰ τοὺς παροργίσαντας· ἔπειτα βουλομένων Λακεδαιμονίων ἐκ Δεκελείας ἀπιέναι καὶ ἐφ' οἷς ἔχουσιν ἑκάτεροι εἰρήνην ἄγειν, ἔνιοι μὲν ἐσπούδαζον, τὸ δὲ πλῆθος οὐχ ὑπήκουσεν ἐξαπατηθέντες ὑπὸ Κλεοφῶντος, ὃς ἐκώλυσε γενέσθαι τὴν εἰρήνην, ἐλθὼν εἰς τὴν ἐκκλησίαν μεθύων καὶ θώρακα

33. 1. Μνασίλοχος Kenyon[1]: Μνασίμαχος with the letters λο written above L, Μνησιλοχος Kaibel & Wilamowitz.

<ὃς> ἦρξε Kenyon[1].

33. 2. πολέμου τε another hand in L: δὲ first hand, γε J. B. Bury *ap.* Sandys[2].

34. 1. ἑβδόμῳ L: ἕκτῳ Kaibel & Wilamowitz[2], κατάστασιν for κατάλυσιν Kaibel & Wilamowitz[1].

Ἀργινούσαις Kenyon[1]: Ἀργινούσας with the letters σαις written above L, Ἀργινούσσαις Blass[1].

ἑκάτεροι εἰρήνην Kenyon[1]: ἰρήνην ἑκάτεροι L, other suggestions have been made.

they sent envoys to Sparta to try to end the war on the basis of what each side possessed; but when the Spartans would not acquiesce unless the Athenians also gave up their rule of the sea they abandoned the attempt.

(**33**) The constitution of the Four Hundred lasted, then, about four months; and from their number Mnesilochus was archon for two months in the archonship of Theopompus, who was archon for the remaining ten months. When the Athenians had been defeated in the battle near Eretria and the whole of Euboea had defected apart from Oreus, they were dejected at this disaster to a greater extent than at what had gone before (for they happened to be deriving more benefit from Euboea than from Attica), and they overthrew the Four Hundred and entrusted their affairs to the Five Thousand based on the hoplite qualification, decreeing that no office should attract a stipend. (*2*) The men most responsible for the overthrow were Aristocrates and Theramenes, who were not satisfied with what was being done by the Four Hundred: for they did everything on their own and referred nothing to the Five Thousand. Their political affairs seem to have been run well at this juncture, when they were in a state of war and the constitution was based on the hoplites.

(**34**) The *demos*, then, soon deprived these of their political control. In the seventh year after the overthrow of the Four Hundred, in the archonship of Callias of Angele, the naval battle at Arginusae occurred, and what happened then was, first, that the ten generals who had been victorious in the battle were all judged in a single vote, even though some had not taken part in the battle and others had been saved on another man's ship, because the *demos* was deceived by those who inflamed its anger. Next, when the Spartans were willing to withdraw from Decelea and make peace on the condition that each side should possess what it currently had, some were eager for that but the masses refused it, since they were deceived by Cleophon: he prevented peace by going into the assembly drunk and wearing a breastplate, saying that he would not

ἐνδεδυκώς, οὐ φάσκων ἐπιτρέψειν ἐὰν μὴ πάσας ἀφῶσι Λακεδαιμόνιοι τὰς πόλεις. (*2*) οὐ χρησάμενοι δὲ καλῶς τότε τοῖς πράγμασι, μετ' οὐ πολὺν χρόνον ἔγνωσαν τὴν ἁμαρτίαν. τῷ γὰρ ὕστερον ἔτει, ἐπ' Ἀλεξίου ἄρχοντος, ἠτύχησαν τὴν ἐν Αἰγὸς ποταμοῖς ναυμαχίαν, ἐξ ἧς συνέβη κύριον γενόμενον τῆς πόλεως Λύσανδρον καταστῆσαι τοὺς τριάκοντα τρόπῳ τοιῷδε. (*3*) τῆς εἰρήνης γενομένης αὐτοῖς ἐφ' ᾧ τε πολιτεύσονται τὴν πάτριον πολιτείαν, οἱ μὲν δημοτικοὶ διασῴζειν ἐπειρῶντο τὸν δῆμον, τῶν δὲ γνωρίμων οἱ μὲν ἐν ταῖς ἑταιρείαις ὄντες καὶ τῶν φυγάδων οἱ μετὰ τὴν εἰρήνην κατελθόντες ὀλιγαρχίας ἐπεθύμουν, οἱ δ' ἐν ἑταιρείᾳ μὲν οὐδεμιᾷ συγκαθεστῶτες ἄλλως δὲ δοκοῦντες οὐδενὸς ἐπιλείπεσθαι τῶν πολιτῶν τὴν πάτριον πολιτείαν ἐζήτουν· ὧν ἦν μὲν καὶ Ἀρχῖνος καὶ Ἄνυτος καὶ Κλειτοφῶν καὶ Φορμίσιος καὶ ἕτεροι πολλοί, προειστήκει δὲ μάλιστα Θηραμένης. Λυσάνδρου δὲ προσθεμένου τοῖς ὀλιγαρχικοῖς, καταπλαγεὶς ὁ δῆμος ἠναγκάσθη χειροτονεῖν τὴν ὀλιγαρχίαν. ἔγραψε δὲ τὸ ψήφισμα Δρακοντίδης Ἀφιδναῖος.

(**35**) οἱ μὲν οὖν τριάκοντα τοῦτον τὸν τρόπον κατέστησαν, ἐπὶ Πυθοδώρου ἄρχοντος. γενόμενοι δὲ κύριοι τῆς πόλεως, τὰ μὲν ἄλλα τὰ δόξαντα περὶ τῆς πολιτείας παρεώρων, πεντακοσίους δὲ βουλευτὰς καὶ τὰς ἄλλας ἀρχὰς καταστήσαντες ἐκ προκρίτων {ἐκ τῶν} χιλίων, καὶ προσελόμενοι σφίσιν αὐτοῖς τοῦ Πειραιέως ἄρχοντας δέκα καὶ τοῦ δεσμωτηρίου φύλακας ἕνδεκα καὶ μαστιγοφόρους τριακοσίους ὑπηρέτας κατεῖχον τὴν πόλιν δι' ἑαυτῶν. (*2*) τὸ μὲν οὖν πρῶτον μέτριοι τοῖς πολίταις ἦσαν καὶ προσεποιοῦντο διώκειν τὴν πάτριον πολιτείαν, καὶ τούς τ' Ἐφιάλτου καὶ Ἀρχεστράτου νόμους τοὺς περὶ τῶν Ἀρεοπαγιτῶν καθεῖλον ἐξ Ἀρείου πάγου, καὶ τῶν Σόλωνος θεσμῶν ὅσοι διαμφισβητήσεις εἶχον καὶ τὸ κῦρος ὃ ἦν ἐν τοῖς δικασταῖς κατέλυσαν, ὡς ἐπανορθοῦντες καὶ ποιοῦντες ἀναμφισβήτητον τὴν πολιτείαν· οἷον περὶ τοῦ δοῦναι τὰ ἑαυτοῦ ᾧ ἂν ἐθέλῃ κύριον ποιήσαντες καθάπαξ, τὰς δὲ προσούσας δυσκολίας, "ἐὰν μὴ μανιῶν ἢ γήρως <ἕνεκα> ἢ γυναικὶ

35. 1. {ἐκ τῶν} χιλίων Herwerden: other suggestions have been made.

35. 2. διώκειν K. S. Kontos: διοικεῖν L.

πάγου, καὶ … εἶχον καὶ punctuated thus A. W. Gomme (*CR* xl 1926, 11).

μανιῶν ἢ γήρως <ἕνεκα> W. Wyse (*CR*, cf. [Dem.] XLVI): μανιῶν ἢ γηρῶν L, μανιῶν ἢ γήρως Blass.

πιθόμενος L: πειθόμενος W. Wyse (*CR*, cf. [Dem.] XLVI).

allow it unless the Spartans relinquished all the cities. (*2*) They did not manage affairs well then, and not long afterwards they recognised their error. For in the next year, in the archonship of Alexias, they failed in the naval battle at Aegospotami, and the result of that was that Lysander gained power over the city, and he installed the Thirty in the following manner. (*3*) Peace was made for them on condition that they should live under the traditional constitution. The democrats were trying to save the *demos*, those of the notables in the clubs and those of the exiles who had returned after the peace were eager for oligarchy, and those who were not involved in any of the clubs and who otherwise seemed not to be inferior to any of the citizens were aiming for the traditional constitution: among these last were Archinus, Anytus, Cleitophon, Phormisius and many others, but their particular leader was Theramenes. When Lysander gave his support to the oligarchs, the *demos* was terrified and was compelled to vote for the oligarchy; the proposer of the decree was Dracontides of Aphidna.

(**35**) That is the way in which the Thirty were installed, in the archonship of Pythodorus. When they had gained power over the city, they overlooked the other decisions which had been taken about the constitution, but appointed five hundred councillors and the other officials from a thousand pre-elected men; and, choosing in order to reinforce themselves ten governors of the Piraeus, eleven guards of the prison and three hundred attendants armed with whips, they held down the city in their own hands. (*2*) At first they were moderate towards the citizens and pretended that their goal was the traditional constitution. They took down from the Areopagus the laws of Ephialtes and Archestratus about the Areopagites; and they cancelled those laws of Solon which contained scope for disputes, and the power which resided in the jurors, claiming that they were correcting the constitution and rendering it free from disputes. For instance, in the case of bequeathing property to whoever one wants they gave men absolute power, removing the attached difficulties – 'unless under the influence of insanity or senility, or induced by a

πιθόμενος”, ἀφεῖλον, ὅπως μὴ ᾖ τοῖς συκοφάνταις ἔφοδος· ὁμοίως δὲ τοῦτ’ ἔδρων καὶ ἐπὶ τῶν ἄλλων. (*3*) κατ’ ἀρχὰς μὲν οὖν ταῦτ’ ἐποίουν, καὶ τοὺς συκοφάντας καὶ τοὺς τῷ δήμῳ πρὸς χάριν ὁμιλοῦντας παρὰ τὸ βέλτιστον καὶ κακοπράγμονας ὄντας καὶ πονηροὺς ἀνῄρουν, ἐφ’ οἷς ἔχαιρεν ἡ πόλις γιγνομένοις, ἡγούμενοι τοῦ βελτίστου χάριν ποιεῖν αὐτούς. (*4*) ἐπεὶ δὲ τὴν πόλιν ἐγκρατέστερον ἔσχον, οὐδενὸς ἀπείχοντο τῶν πολιτῶν, ἀλλ’ ἀπέκτειναν τοὺς καὶ ταῖς οὐσίαις καὶ τῷ γένει καὶ τοῖς ἀξιώμασιν προέχοντας, ὑπεξαιρούμενοί τε τὸν φόβον καὶ βουλόμενοι τὰς οὐσίας διαρπάζειν· καὶ χρόνου διαπεσόντος βραχέος, οὐκ ἐλάττους ἀνῃρήκεσαν ἢ χιλίους πεντακοσίους.

(**36**) οὕτως δὲ τῆς πόλεως ὑποφερομένης, Θηραμένης ἀγανακτῶν ἐπὶ τοῖς γιγνομένοις τῆς μὲν ἀσελγείας αὐτοῖς παρῄνει παύσασθαι, μεταδοῦναι δὲ τῶν πραγμάτων τοῖς βελτίστοις. οἱ δὲ πρῶτον ἐναντιωθέντες, ἐπεὶ διεσπάρησαν οἱ λόγοι πρὸς τὸ πλῆθος καὶ πρὸς τὸν Θηραμένην οἰκείως εἶχον οἱ πολλοί, φοβηθέντες μὴ προστάτης γενόμενος τοῦ δήμου καταλύσῃ τὴν δυναστείαν, καταλέγουσιν τῶν πολιτῶν τρισχιλίους ὡς μεταδώσοντες τῆς πολιτείας. (*2*) Θηραμένης δὲ πάλιν ἐπιτιμᾷ καὶ τούτοις, πρῶτον μὲν ὅτι βουλόμενοι μεταδοῦναι τοῖς ἐπιεικέσι τρισχιλίοις μόνοις μεταδιδόασι, ὡς ἐν τούτῳ τῷ πλήθει τῆς ἀρετῆς ὡρισμένης, ἔπειθ’ ὅτι δύο τὰ ἐναντιώτατα ποιοῦσιν, βίαιόν τε τὴν ἀρχὴν καὶ τῶν ἀρχομένων ἥττω κατασκευάζοντες. οἱ δὲ τούτων μὲν ὠλιγώρησαν, τὸν δὲ κατάλογον τῶν τρισχιλίων πολὺν μὲν χρόνον ὑπερεβάλλοντο καὶ παρ’ αὐτοῖς ἐφύλαττον τοὺς ἐγνωσμένους, ὅτε δὲ καὶ δόξειεν αὐτοῖς ἐκφέρειν τοὺς μὲν ἐξήλειφον τῶν <ἐγ>γεγραμμένων, τοὺς δ’ ἀντενέγραφον τῶν ἔξωθεν.

(**37**) ἤδη δὲ τοῦ χειμῶνος ἐνεστῶτος, καταλαβόντος Θρασυβούλου μετὰ τῶν φυγάδων Φυλήν, καὶ κατὰ τὴν στρατιὰν ἣν ἐξήγαγον οἱ τριάκοντα κακῶς ἀποχωρήσαντες, ἔγνωσαν τῶν μὲν ἄλλων τὰ ὅπλα παρελέσθαι, Θηραμένην δὲ διαφθεῖραι τόνδε <τὸν> τρόπον. νόμους

35. 3. ἔχαιρεν A. Sidgwick and W. G. Rutherford (*CR*); ἔχαιρον L.

36. 1. τρισχιλίους Kenyon[3], cf. Kenyon [1–2] in *apparatus*: δισχιλίους L, defended P. Krentz (*Thirty*, 57 n. 1), cf. Chambers in *apparatus*.

36. 2. <ἐγ>γεγραμμένων Herwerden (& Leeuwen).

37. 1. τόνδε <τὸν> τρόπον J. B. Mayor *et al.* (*CR*).

woman' – so that there should be no way in for malicious prosecutors. And they did likewise in all the other cases. (*3*) That is how they acted at the beginning; and they eliminated the malicious prosecutors and those who associated with the *demos* to curry favour with it contrary to what was best, and were evildoers and wicked; and the city was glad that that was happening and thought they were acting for the best. (*4*) But when they had a stronger grip on the city they held off from none of the citizens, but killed those who were outstanding for their possessions, family and reputation, cunningly removing those they were afraid of and wishing to plunder their possessions; and after a short time had passed they had killed no fewer than one thousand five hundred.

(**36**) When the city was declining in this way Theramenes, annoyed at what was happening, urged them to cease their brutality and to give a share in affairs to the best men. They opposed him at first; and, when the news had seeped out to the masses and the many were well disposed towards Theramenes, they were afraid that he would become champion of the *demos* and overthrow their clique, and so they proceeded to enrol three thousand of the citizens with a view to giving them a share in political power. (*2*) Again Theramenes objected to this too, first because they wished to give a share to the respectable men but were giving it only to three thousand, as if good qualities were limited to that number, and next because they were doing two totally incompatible things, devising a violent form of rule but making themselves weaker than those whom they were ruling. They took no notice of this, but for a long time they delayed the register of the Three Thousand and kept to themselves those whom they had decided on, and when they thought they might bring it out they deleted some of the men written in it and entered instead some of those excluded.

(**37**) Once winter had set in Thrasybulus with the exiles seized Phyle, and the Thirty had a bad outcome with the expedition which they sent out. They then decided to deprive the others of their arms, and to destroy Theramenes in the following way. They introduced two laws

εἰσήνεγκαν εἰς τὴν βουλὴν δύο κελεύοντες ἐπιχειροτονεῖν, ὧν ὁ μὲν εἷς αὐτοκράτορας ἐποίει τοὺς τριάκοντα τῶν πολιτῶν ἀποκτεῖναι τοὺς μὴ τοῦ καταλόγου μετέχοντας τῶν τρισχιλίων, ὁ δ' ἕτερος ἐκώλυε κοινωνεῖν τῆς παρούσης πολιτείας ὅσοι τυγχάνουσιν τὸ ἐν Ἠετιωνείᾳ τεῖχος κατασκάψαντες ἢ τοῖς τετρακοσίοις ἐναντίον τι πράξαντες {ἢ} τοῖς κατασκευάσασι τὴν προτέραν ὀλιγαρχίαν· ὧν ἐτύγχανεν ἀμφοτέρων κεκοινωνηκὼς ὁ Θηραμένης, ὥστε συνέβαινεν ἐπικυρωθέντων τῶν νόμων ἔξω τε γίγνεσθαι τῆς πολιτείας αὐτόν καὶ τοὺς τριάκοντα κυρίους εἶναι θανατοῦντας. (*2*) ἀναιρεθέντος δὲ Θηραμένους, τά τε ὅπλα παρείλοντο πάντων πλὴν τῶν τρισχιλίων, καὶ ἐν τοῖς ἄλλοις πολὺ πρὸς ὠμότητα καὶ πονηρίαν ἐπέδοσαν. πρέσβεις <δὲ> πέμψαντες εἰς Λακεδαίμονα τοῦ τε Θηραμένους κατηγόρουν καὶ βοηθεῖν αὐτοῖς ἠξίουν· ὧν ἀκούσαντες οἱ Λακεδαιμόνιοι Καλλίβιον ἀπέστειλαν ἁρμοστὴν καὶ στρατιώτας ὡς ἑπτακοσίους, οἳ τὴν ἀκρόπολιν ἐλθόντες ἐφρούρουν.

(**38**) μετὰ δὲ ταῦτα, καταλαβόντων τῶν ἀπὸ Φυλῆς τὴν Μουνιχίαν καὶ νικησάντων μάχῃ τοὺς μετὰ τῶν τριάκοντα βοηθήσαντας, ἐπαναχωρήσαντες μετὰ τὸν κίνδυνον οἱ ἐκ τοῦ ἄστεως καὶ συναθροισθέντες εἰς τὴν ἀγορὰν τῇ ὑστεραίᾳ τοὺς μὲν τριάκοντα κατέλυσαν, αἱροῦνται δὲ δέκα τῶν πολιτῶν αὐτοκράτορας ἐπὶ τὴν τοῦ πολέμου κατάλυσιν. οἱ δὲ παραλαβόντες τὴν ἀρχήν ἐφ' οἷς μὲν ᾑρέθησαν οὐκ ἔπραττον, ἔπεμπον δ' εἰς Λακεδαίμονα βοήθειαν μεταπεμπόμενοι καὶ χρήματα δανειζόμενοι. (*2*) χαλεπῶς δὲ φερόντων ἐπὶ τούτοις τῶν ἐν τῇ πολιτείᾳ, φοβούμενοι μὴ καταλυθῶσιν τῆς ἀρχῆς, καὶ βουλόμενοι καταπλῆξαι τοὺς ἄλλους (ὅπερ ἐγένετο), συλλαβόντες Δημάρετον οὐδενὸς ὄντα δεύτερον τῶν πολιτῶν ἀπέκτειναν, καὶ τὰ πράγματα βεβαίως εἶχον, συναγωνιζομένου Καλλιβίου τε καὶ τῶν Πελοποννησίων τῶν παρόντων, καὶ πρὸς τούτοις ἐνίων τῶν ἐν τοῖς ἱππεῦσι· τούτων γάρ τινες μάλιστα τῶν πολιτῶν ἐσπούδαζον μὴ κατελθεῖν τοὺς ἀπὸ Φυλῆς. (*3*) ὡς δ' οἱ τὸν Πειραιέα καὶ τὴν Μουνιχίαν ἔχοντες, ἀποστάντος ἅπαντος τοῦ δήμου πρὸς αὐτούς, ἐπεκράτουν τῷ πολέμῳ, τότε καταλύσαντες τοὺς δέκα τοὺς πρώτους αἱρεθέντας ἄλλους εἵλοντο δέκα τοὺς βελτίστους εἶναι δοκοῦντας, ἐφ' ὧν συνέβη

37. 1. {ἢ} τοῖς κατασκευάσασι Herwerden (& Leeuwen): other suggestions have been made.

37. 2. πρέσβεις <δὲ> J. B. Mayor and A. Sidgwick (*CR*).

to the council and ordered it to vote them through: one of these gave the Thirty full authority to execute those who were not included in the register of the Three Thousand, and the other banned from participating in the current régime those who happened to have demolished the fort at Eëtionea or to have done anything against the Four Hundred who had devised the previous oligarchy. It happened that Theramenes had done both of those things; so the result was that when the laws were ratified he was outside the régime and the Thirty had the power to execute him. (*2*) When Theramenes had been eliminated, they deprived all except the Three Thousand of their arms, and in other respects advanced a long way in the direction of savagery and wickedness. They sent envoys to Sparta and both denounced Theramenes and asked the Spartans to come to their support; and on hearing them the Spartans sent Callibius as *harmostes* and about seven hundred soldiers, who went to the acropolis and mounted guard there.

(**38**) After that the men from Phyle seized Munichia and defeated in battle those who rallied against them with the Thirty. The men from the city withdrew after their dangerous encounter, and the next day they crowded into the agora, overthrew the Thirty and elected ten of the citizens with full authority to resolve the war. But on taking over the ruling position they did not do the task for which they had been elected, but sent to Sparta to summon a supporting force and borrow money. Those in the citizen body were dejected at this; but the Ten, afraid that they would be overthrown from their ruling position, and wanting to strike terror into the others (which did indeed happen), arrested and executed Demaenetus, who was second to none of the citizens, and kept a firm hold on affairs, with the cooperation of Callibius and the Peloponnesians who were present, and in addition to them of some men among the cavalry – for some of them were the most determined of the citizens that the men from Phyle should not be reinstated. (*3*) But the whole *demos* defected to the men occupying the Piraeus and Munichia, they got the upper hand in the war, and then they overthrew the Ten who had been elected first and elected another ten, whom they judged to be the best men, with the result that under them the settlement took

καὶ τὰς διαλύσεις γενέσθαι καὶ κατελθεῖν τὸν δῆμον, συναγωνιζομένων καὶ προθυμουμένων τούτων. προειστήκεσαν δ' αὐτῶν μάλιστα Ῥίνων τε ὁ Παιανιεὺς καὶ Φάϋλλος ὁ Ἀχερδούσιος· οὗτοι γὰρ πρίν {ἢ} <τε> Παυσανίαν {τ'} ἀφικέσθαι διεπέμποντο πρὸς τοὺς ἐν Πειραιεῖ, καὶ ἀφικομένου συνεσπούδασαν τὴν κάθοδον. (*4*) ἐπὶ πέρας γὰρ ἤγαγε τὴν εἰρήνην καὶ τὰς διαλύσεις Παυσανίας ὁ τῶν Λακεδαιμονίων βασιλεύς μετὰ τῶν δέκα διαλλακτῶν τῶν ὕστερον ἀφικομένων ἐκ Λακεδαίμονος, οὓς αὐτὸς ἐσπούδασεν ἐλθεῖν. οἱ δὲ περὶ τὸν Ῥίνωνα διά τε τὴν εὔνοιαν τὴν εἰς τὸν δῆμον ἐπῃνέθησαν, καὶ λαβόντες τὴν ἐπιμέλειαν ἐν ὀλιγαρχίᾳ τὰς εὐθύνας ἔδοσαν ἐν δημοκρατίᾳ, καὶ οὐδεὶς οὐδὲν ἐνεκάλεσεν αὐτοῖς, οὔτε τῶν ἐν ἄστει μεινάντων οὔτε τῶν ἐκ Πειραιέως κατελθόντων, ἀλλὰ διὰ ταῦτα καὶ στρατηγὸς εὐθὺς ᾑρέθη Ῥίνων.

(**39**) ἐγένοντο δ' αἱ διαλύσεις ἐπ' Εὐκλείδου ἄρχοντος κατὰ τὰς συνθήκας τάσδε. τοὺς βουλομένους Ἀθηναίων τῶν ἐν ἄστει μεινάντων ἐξοικεῖν ἔχειν Ἐλευσῖνα ἐπιτίμους ὄντας καὶ κυρίους καὶ αὐτοκράτορας ἑαυτῶν καὶ τὰ αὑτῶν καρπουμένους. (*2*) τὸ δ' ἱερὸν εἶναι κοινὸν ἀμφοτέρων, ἐπιμελεῖσθαι δὲ Κήρυκας καὶ Εὐμολπίδας κατὰ τὰ πάτρια. μὴ ἐξεῖναι δὲ μήτε τοῖς Ἐλευσινόθεν εἰς τὸ ἄστυ μήτε τοῖς ἐκ τοῦ ἄστεως Ἐλευσινάδε ἰέναι, πλὴν μυστηρίοις ἑκατέρους. συντελεῖν δὲ ἀπὸ τῶν προσιόντων εἰς τὸ συμμαχικὸν καθάπερ τοὺς ἄλλους Ἀθηναίους. (*3*) ἐὰν δέ τινες τῶν ἀπιόντων οἰκίαν λαμβάνωσιν Ἐλευσῖνι, συμπείθειν τὸν κεκτημένον· ἐὰν δὲ μὴ συμβαίνωσιν ἀλλήλοις, τιμητὰς ἑλέσθαι τρεῖς ἑκάτερον, καὶ ἥντιν' ἂν οὗτοι τάξωσιν τιμὴν λαμβάνειν. Ἐλευσινίων δὲ συνοικεῖν οὓς ἂν οὗτοι βούλωνται. (*4*) τὴν δ' ἀπογραφὴν εἶναι τοῖς βουλομένοις ἐξοικεῖν, τοῖς μὲν ἐπιδημοῦσιν ἀφ' ἧς ἂν ὀμόσωσιν τοὺς ὅρκους δέκα ἡμερῶν, τὴν δ' ἐξοίκησιν εἴκοσι, τοῖς δ' ἀποδημοῦσιν ἐπειδὰν ἐπιδημήσωσιν κατὰ ταὐτά. (*5*) μὴ ἐξεῖναι δὲ ἄρχειν μηδεμίαν ἀρχὴν τῶν ἐν τῷ ἄστει τὸν Ἐλευσῖνι κατοικοῦντα, πρὶν ἂν ἀπογράψηται

38. 3. πρίν {ἢ} <τε> Παυσανίαν {τ'} ἀφικέσθαι H. Richards (*CR*).

39. 1. τοὺς βουλομένους Ἀθηναίων Blass: Ἀθηναίων written above L.

39. 2. In the margin L has δ εισιεν|ετει, which Kenyon[3] took to mean δ´ εἰσὶ ἐν ἔτει (*sc.* μυστήρια).

ἑκατέρους: ἑκατέροις H. Jackson (*CR*).

39. 3. οὗτοι βούλωνται: αὐτοὶ H. Richards (*CR*).

place and the *demos* was reinstated, helped by these men's efforts and enthusiasm. Their leaders were particularly Rhinon of Paeania and Phaÿllus of Acherdus: before Pausanias arrived they made overtures to those at Piraeus, and after he had arrived they joined in eagerness for the reinstatement. (*4*) For Pausanias the Spartan king brought the peace and settlement to fruition, together with the ten reconcilers who arrived afterwards from Sparta, for whose coming he had himself been eager. Rhinon and his colleagues were praised for their good will towards the *demos*: they received their charge under the oligarchy but submitted their *euthynai* under the democracy, and nobody made any complaint against them, either of those who had stayed in the city or of those who had been reinstated from Piraeus; but because of this Rhinon was immediately elected general.

(**39**) The settlement was made in the archonship of Euclides, in accordance with the following agreement. Of the Athenians who had remained in the city those who wished to emigrate should occupy Eleusis, retaining their civic rights, with power and authority over their own property and receiving their revenue. (*2*) The sanctuary should be the common property of both parties, and the Kerykes and Eumolpidae should have care of it in accordance with tradition. It should not be permitted either to those from Eleusis to go to the city or to those from the city to go to Eleusis, except to each party for the Mysteries. Those at Eleusis should contribute to the alliance from their income in the same way as the other Athenians. (*3*) If any of those departing took a house at Eleusis, they must persuade the owner; if they could not agree with one another, each must choose three assessors, and whatever price they fixed must be accepted. Those of the Eleusinians whom the migrants wished could live with them. (*4*) The registration for those wishing to emigrate should take place, for those at home, within ten days from when they swore the oath, and their emigration within twenty days, and for those away, on the same terms from when they arrived home. (*5*) It should not be permitted to a man living at Eleusis to hold any of the offices in the city until he had registered to live in the city again. Trials for

πάλιν ἐν τῷ ἄστει κατοικεῖν. τὰς δὲ δίκας τοῦ φόνου εἶναι κατὰ τὰ πάτρια, εἴ τίς τινα αὐτοχειρίᾳ ἔκτεινεν ἢ ἔτρωσεν. (*6*) τῶν δὲ παρεληλυθότων μηδενὶ πρὸς μηδένα μνησικακεῖν ἐξεῖναι, πλὴν πρὸς τοὺς τριάκοντα καὶ τοὺς δέκα καὶ τοὺς ἕνδεκα καὶ τοὺς τοῦ Πειραιέως ἄρξαντας, μηδὲ πρὸς τούτους ἐὰν διδῶσιν εὐθύνας. εὐθύνας δὲ δοῦναι τοὺς μὲν ἐν Πειραιεῖ ἄρξαντας ἐν τοῖς ἐν Πειραιεῖ, τοὺς δ' ἐν τῷ ἄστει ἐν τοῖς τὰ τιμήματα παρεχομένοις. εἶθ' οὕτως ἐξοικεῖν τοὺς <μὴ> ἐθέλοντας. τὰ δὲ χρήματα ἃ ἐδανείσαντο εἰς τὸν πόλεμον ἑκατέρους ἀποδοῦναι χωρίς.

(**40**) γενομένων δὲ τοιούτων τῶν διαλύσεων, καὶ φοβουμένων ὅσοι μετὰ τῶν τριάκοντα συνεπολέμησαν, καὶ πολλῶν μὲν ἐπινοούντων ἐξοικεῖν ἀναβαλλομένων δὲ τὴν ἀπογραφὴν εἰς τὰς ἐσχάτας ἡμέρας, ὅπερ εἰώθασιν ποιεῖν ἅπαντες, Ἀρχῖνος συνιδὼν τὸ πλῆθος καὶ βουλόμενος κατασχεῖν αὐτούς ὑφεῖλε τὰς ὑπολοίπους ἡμέρας τῆς ἀπογραφῆς, ὥστε συναναγκασθῆναι μένειν πολλοὺς ἄκοντας ἕως ἐθάρρησαν. (*2*) καὶ δοκεῖ τοῦτό τε πολιτεύσασθαι καλῶς Ἀρχῖνος, καὶ μετὰ ταῦτα γραψάμενος τὸ ψήφισμα τὸ Θρασυβούλου παρανόμων, ἐν ᾧ μετεδίδου τῆς πολιτείας πᾶσι τοῖς ἐκ Πειραιέως συγκατελθοῦσι, ὧν ἔνιοι φανερῶς ἦσαν δοῦλοι, καὶ τρίτον, ἐπεί τις ἤρξατο τῶν κατεληλυθότων μνησικακεῖν, ἀπαγαγὼν τοῦτον ἐπὶ τὴν βουλὴν καὶ πείσας ἄκριτον ἀποκτεῖναι, λέγων ὅτι νῦν δείξουσιν εἰ βούλονται τὴν δημοκρατίαν σῴζειν καὶ τοῖς ὅρκοις ἐμμένειν· ἀφέντας μὲν γὰρ τοῦτον προτρέψειν καὶ τοὺς ἄλλους, ἐὰν δ' ἀνέλωσιν, παράδειγμα ποιήσειν ἅπασιν. ὅπερ καὶ συνέπεσεν· ἀποθανόντος γὰρ οὐδεὶς πώποτε ὕστερον ἐμνησικάκησεν. (*3*) ἀλλὰ δοκοῦσιν κάλλιστα δὴ καὶ πολιτικώτατα ἁπάντων καὶ ἰδίᾳ καὶ κοινῇ χρήσασθαι ταῖς προγεγενημέναις συμφοραῖς· οὐ γὰρ μόνον τὰς περὶ τῶν προτέρων αἰτίας ἐξήλειψαν, ἀλλὰ καὶ τὰ χρήματα Λακεδαιμονίοις, ἃ οἱ τριάκοντα πρὸς τὸν πόλεμον ἔλαβον, ἀπέδοσαν κοινῇ, κελευουσῶν τῶν συνθηκῶν ἑκατέρους ἀποδιδόναι χωρίς τούς τ' ἐκ τοῦ ἄστεως καὶ τοὺς ἐκ τοῦ Πειραιέως, ἡγούμενοι τοῦτο πρῶτον ἄρχειν δεῖν τῆς ὁμονοίας·

39. 5. αὐτοχειρίᾳ ἔκτεινεν ἢ ἔτρωσεν Kaibel & Wilamowitz: αυτοχιραεκτισιοτρωσασ L, with ε above ι[1], ε above ι[2], οτ deleted and ιε written above, αὐτόχειρ ἀπέκτεινεν Blass[1–3], perhaps rightly, τρώσας W. Wyse (*CR*).

39. 6. ἐν τοῖς τὰ τιμήματα: ἐν τοῖς <ἐν τῷ ἄστει> τὰ τιμήματα Kenyon [1–3].

εἶθ' … τοὺς <μὴ> ἐθέλοντας Blass[3–4]: εἶθ' … τοὺς ἐθέλοντας many editors, εἴθ' … τοὺς ἐθέλοντας A. P. Dorjahn, perhaps rightly.

homicide should be in accordance with tradition, if anybody had killed or wounded anybody by his own hand. (*6*) For past actions nobody should be permitted to recall wrongs against anybody, except against the Thirty, the Ten, the Eleven and the men who had ruled the Piraeus, and not even against these if they submitted *euthynai. Euthynai* should be submitted by those who had ruled Piraeus among those at Piraeus, and by those in the city among those satisfying a property assessment. Or on this basis those who did not want to comply should emigrate. The funds which they borrowed for the war each party should repay separately.

(**40**) When the settlement had been made on these lines, those who had fought on the side of the Thirty were afraid, and many were thinking of emigrating but delaying their registration until the final days, as everybody is apt to do. Archinus, conscious of the numbers and wishing to keep the men back, withdrew the remaining days for the registration, so that many were compelled to remain, against their will until they grew confident. (*2*) It seems that Archinus followed a good policy in this respect; and also when he attacked in a *graphe paranomon* the decree of Thrasybulus which gave a share in citizenship to all those who had joined in the return from Piraeus, some of whom were blatantly slaves; and thirdly, when somebody began to recall wrongs against those who had returned, by haling him before the council and persuading it to execute him without trial. He said that now they could show if they were willing to save the democracy and abide by their oaths: for if they acquitted him they would encourage the others too, but if they killed him they would set an example to all. And that is what happened; for when he had been executed nobody ever afterwards recalled wrongs. (*3*) But they seem to have dealt with their previous misfortune in the finest and most civic-minded way of all, bith individually and collectively: for not only did they wipe out accusations about previous matters, but also they collectively repaid to the Spartans the funds which the Thirty had received for the war, although the agreement stipulated that each party, that of the city and that of the Piraeus, should repay separately, because they thought that that should be the first beginning of their concord. But

ἐν δὲ ταῖς ἄλλαις πόλεσιν οὐχ οἷον ἔτι προστιθέασιν τῶν οἰκείων οἱ δῆμοι κρατήσαντες, ἀλλὰ καὶ τὴν χώραν ἀνάδαστον ποιοῦσιν. (*4*) διελύθησαν δὲ καὶ πρὸς τοὺς ἐν Ἐλευσῖνι [κατο]ικήσαντας, ἔτει τρίτῳ μετὰ τὴν ἐξοίκησιν, ἐπὶ Ξεναινέτου ἄρχοντος. (**41**) ταῦτα μὲν οὖν ἐν τοῖς ὕστερον συνέβη γενέσθαι καιροῖς, τότε δὲ κύριος ὁ δῆμος γενόμενος τῶν πραγμάτων ἐνεστήσατο τὴν νῦν οὖσαν πολιτείαν, ἐπὶ Πυθοδώρου μὲν ἄρχοντος, †δοκοῦντος δὲ δικαίως τοῦ δήμου λαβεῖν τὴν πολιτείαν διὰ τὸ ποιήσασθαι τὴν κάθοδον δι' αὑτοῦ τὸν δῆμον.†

(*2*) ἦν δὲ τῶν μεταβολῶν ἑνδεκάτη τὸν ἀριθμὸν αὕτη. πρώτη μὲν γὰρ ἐγένετο μετά<σ>τασις τῶν ἐξ ἀρχῆς Ἴωνος καὶ τῶν μετ' αὐτοῦ συνοικησάντων· τότε γὰρ πρῶτον εἰς τὰς τέτταρας συνενεμήθησαν φυλάς, καὶ τοὺς φυλοβασιλέας κατέστησαν. δευτέρα δέ, καὶ πρώτη μετὰ ταύτην, ἔχουσα πολιτείας τάξιν, ἡ ἐπὶ Θησέως γενομένη, μικρὸν παρεγκλίνουσα τῆς βασιλικῆς. μετὰ δὲ ταύτην ἡ ἐπὶ Δράκοντος, ἐν ᾗ καὶ νόμους ἀνέγραψαν πρῶτον. τρίτη δ' ἡ μετὰ τὴν στάσιν ἡ ἐπὶ Σόλωνος, ἀφ' ἧς ἀρχὴ δημοκρατίας ἐγένετο. τετάρτη δ' ἡ ἐπὶ Πεισιστράτου τυραννίς. πέμπτη δ' ἡ μετὰ <τὴν> τῶν τυράννων κατάλυσιν ἡ Κλεισθένους, δημοτικωτέρα τῆς Σόλωνος. ἕκτη δ' ἡ μετὰ τὰ Μηδικά, τῆς ἐξ Ἀρείου πάγου βουλῆς ἐπιστατούσης. ἑβδόμη δὲ καὶ μετὰ ταύτην, ἣν Ἀριστείδης μὲν ὑπέδειξεν, Ἐφιάλτης δ' ἐπετέλεσεν, καταλύσας τὴν Ἀρεοπαγῖτιν βουλήν· ἐν ᾗ πλεῖστα συνέβη τὴν πόλιν διὰ τοὺς δημαγωγοὺς ἁμαρτάνειν διὰ τὴν τῆς θαλάττης ἀρχήν. ὀγδόη δ' ἡ τῶν τετρακοσίων κατάστασις, καὶ μετὰ ταύτην, ἐνάτη δέ, <ἡ> δημοκρατία πάλιν. δεκάτη

40. 3. δῆμοι κρατήσαντες (Herwerden &) Leeuwen: δημοκρατήσαντες L.

40. 4. ἐν Ἐλευσῖνι: ἐν written above L, deleted Herwerden & Leeuwen.

41. 1. ἐπὶ Πυθοδώρου μὲν ἄρχοντος, † δοκοῦντος δὲ δικαίως τοῦ δήμου λαβεῖν τὴν πολιτείαν διὰ τὸ ποιήσασθαι τὴν κάθοδον δι' αὑτοῦ τὸν δῆμον. † : αὑτοῦ J. B. Mayor (*CR*), αὐτὸν Kenyon[1–3], υ above a doubtful letter in L Kenyon[4]; other suggestions have been made.

41. 2. μετά<σ>τασις Wilcken.

μετὰ ταύτην, ἔχουσα Kenyon[3]: μετὰ ταῦτα (with the letters η[ν] written above) ἔχουσαι (ι deleted) L.

μετὰ <τὴν> Kenyon[1].

ἁμαρτάνειν διὰ: <καὶ> διὰ (Herwerden &) Leeuwen, other suggestions have been made.

in other cities not only do democrats when they come to power refuse to make additional payments from their own property, but they engage in a redistribution of the land. (*4*) They made a settlement with those who had gone to live at Eleusis in the third year after their emigration, in the archonship of Xenaenetus. (**41**) That is what happened at a later juncture; but at this point the *demos* gained power over affairs and instituted the now existing constitution, in the archonship of Pythodorus, †when the *demos* seemed to be justified in taking political power because the *demos* had achieved its return by its own action.†

(*2*) That was the eleventh in number of the changes. For the first modification of the original arrangement was that of Ion and those who settled with him: for that was when they were first distributed through the four tribes, and they instituted the *phylobasileis*. The second, and first after that, involving a structuring of the constitution, was that which occurred under Theseus, inclining slightly away from the kingly. After that, the change under Draco, in which they first wrote up laws. The third was that after the dissension, under Solon, from which came the beginning of democracy. Fourth was the tyranny under Pisistratus. Fifth, after the overthrow of the tyrants, that of Cleisthenes, which was more democratic than that of Solon. Sixth, that after the Persian Wars, with the council of the Areopagus presiding. Seventh and after that, the one pointed to by Aristides and completed by Ephialtes when he overthrew the Areopagite council: in this what happened was that through the demagogues the city made its worst mistakes on account of its rule of the sea. Eighth, the establishment of the Four Hundred; and after that, ninth, democracy again. Tenth, the tyranny of the Thirty and the Ten.

δ' ἡ τῶν τριάκοντα καὶ ἡ τῶν δέκα τυραννίς. ἑνδεκάτη δ' ἡ μετὰ τὴν ἀπὸ Φυλῆς καὶ ἐκ Πειραιέως κάθοδον, ἀφ' ἧς διαγεγένηται μέχρι τῆς νῦν, ἀεὶ προσεπιλαμβάνουσα τῷ πλήθει τὴν ἐξουσίαν. ἁπάντων γὰρ αὐτὸς αὑτὸν πεποίηκεν ὁ δῆμος κύριον, καὶ πάντα διοικεῖται ψηφίσμασιν καὶ δικαστηρίοις, ἐν οἷς ὁ δῆμός ἐστιν ὁ κρατῶν. καὶ γὰρ αἱ τῆς βουλῆς κρίσεις εἰς τὸν δῆμον ἐληλύθασιν. καὶ τοῦτο δοκοῦσι ποιεῖν ὀρθῶς· εὐδιαφθορώτεροι γὰρ <οἱ> ὀλίγοι τῶν πολλῶν εἰσιν καὶ κέρδει καὶ χάρισιν. (*3*) μισθοφόρον δ' ἐκκλησίαν τὸ μὲν πρῶτον ἀπέγνωσαν ποιεῖν· οὐ συλλεγομένων δ' εἰς τὴν ἐκκλησίαν, ἀλλὰ πολλὰ σοφιζομένων τῶν πρυτάνεων ὅπως προσιστῆται τὸ πλῆθος πρὸς τὴν ἐπικύρωσιν τῆς χειροτονίας, πρῶτον μὲν Ἀγύρριος ὀβολὸν ἐπόρισεν, μετὰ δὲ τοῦτον Ἡρακλείδης ὁ Κλαζομένιος ὁ βασιλεὺς ἐπικαλούμενος διώβολον, πάλιν δ' Ἀγύρριος τριώβολον.

(**42**) ἔχει δ' ἡ νῦν κατάστασις τῆς πολιτείας τόνδε τὸν τρόπον. μετέχουσιν μὲν τῆς πολιτείας οἱ ἐξ ἀμφοτέρων γεγονότες ἀστῶν, ἐγγράφονται δ' εἰς τοὺς δημότας ὀκτωκαίδεκα ἔτη γεγονότες. ὅταν δ' ἐγγράφωνται, διαψηφίζονται περὶ αὐτῶν ὀμόσαντες οἱ δημόται, πρῶτον μὲν εἰ δοκοῦσι γεγονέναι τὴν ἡλικίαν τὴν ἐκ τοῦ νόμου, κἂν μὴ δόξωσι, ἀπέρχονται πάλιν εἰς παῖδας, δεύτερον δ' εἰ ἐλεύθερός ἐστι καὶ γέγονε κατὰ τοὺς νόμους. ἔπειτ' ἂν μὲν ἀποψηφίσωνται μὴ εἶναι ἐλεύθερον, ὁ μὲν ἐφίησιν εἰς τὸ δικαστήριον, οἱ δὲ δημόται κατηγόρους αἱροῦνται πέντε ἄνδρας ἐξ αὑτῶν, κἂν μὲν μὴ δόξῃ δικαίως ἐγγράφεσθαι, πωλεῖ τοῦτον ἡ πόλις· ἐὰν δὲ νικήσῃ, τοῖς δημόταις ἐπάναγκες ἐγγράφειν. (*2*) μετὰ δὲ ταῦτα δοκιμάζει τοὺς ἐγγραφέντας ἡ βουλή, κἄν τις δόξῃ νεώτερος ὀκτωκαίδεκ' ἐτῶν εἶναι, ζημιοῖ τοὺς δημότας τοὺς ἐγγράψαντας. ἐπὰν δὲ δοκιμασθῶσιν οἱ ἔφηβοι, συλλεγέντες οἱ πατέρες αὐτῶν κατὰ φυλάς ὀμόσαντες αἱροῦνται τρεῖς ἐκ τῶν φυλετῶν τῶν ὑπὲρ τετταράκοντα ἔτη γεγονότων, οὓς ἂν ἡγῶνται βελτίστους εἶναι καὶ ἐπιτηδειοτάτους ἐπιμελεῖσθαι τῶν ἐφήβων, ἐκ δὲ τούτων ὁ δῆμος ἕνα τῆς φυλῆς ἑκάστης χειροτονεῖ σωφρονιστήν, καὶ κοσμητὴν ἐκ τῶν ἄλλων Ἀθηναίων ἐπὶ

41. 2. ἡ τῶν δέκα: ἡ deleted Kaibel & Wilamowitz, perhaps rightly.
<οἱ> ὀλίγοι M. Gennadios (*CR*).
41. 3. μισθοφόρον δ' ἐκκλησίαν: δ<ὲ τὴν> Kaibel & Wilamowitz.
ἀλλὰ πολλὰ: perhaps ἄλλα.
42. 1. ἀποψηφίσωνται W. Wyse (*CR*): ἐπιψηφίσωνται L.

Eleventh, that after the return from Phyle and Piraeus, from which it has persisted until that in force now, continually extending the competence of the masses: for the *demos* has itself made itself master of everything, and it administers everything through decrees and lawcourts, in which it is the *demos* which has the power; for also the judgments of the council have come to the *demos*. And in this they seem to be acting rightly, for the few are more easily corrupted than the many by profit and favours. (*3*) At first they refused to attach a stipend to the assembly; but when men were not gathering in the assembly, and the *prytaneis* attempted various devices to make the masses attend for the ratification of the votes, first Agyrrhius provided an obol, after him Heraclides of Clazomenae, known as 'king', two obols, and Agyrrhius again three obols.

(**42**) The present disposition of the constitution is in the following manner. Men participate in the citizen body if they are born of two citizen parents, and they are registered among their demesmen when they have reached the age of eighteen. When they are registered, the demesmen vote over them after swearing an oath: first, whether they are judged to have reached the age prescribed by the law, and if they are judged not to have done so they revert to the rank of boys again; secondly, if he is free and has been born in accordance with the laws. Then if they vote to reject him as not being free, he appeals to the lawcourt, and the demesmen elect five men from their own number as prosecutors, and if he is judged not to have been registered justly the city sells him as a slave; if he wins, it is obligatory for the demesmen to register him. (*2*) After this the council vets those who have been registered, and if anybody is judged to be below the age of eighteen it punishes the demesmen who registered him. When the *epheboi* have been vetted, their fathers assemble by tribes and after swearing an oath elect three of the tribesmen over forty years old, who they think are the best and most suitable to take care of the *epheboi*, and the *demos* elects from these one man from each tribe as *sophronistes* and from the rest of the Athenians a *kosmetes* over all of

πάντας. (*3*) συλλαβόντες δ' οὗτοι τοὺς ἐφήβους, πρῶτον μὲν τὰ ἱερὰ περιῆλθον, εἶτ' εἰς Πειραιέα πορεύονται, καὶ φρουροῦσιν οἱ μὲν τὴν Μουνιχίαν, οἱ δὲ τὴν Ἀκτήν. χειροτονεῖ δὲ καὶ παιδοτρίβας αὐτοῖς δύο, καὶ διδασκάλους οἵτινες ὁπλομαχεῖν καὶ τοξεύειν καὶ ἀκοντίζειν καὶ καταπάλτην ἀφιέναι διδάσκουσιν. δίδωσι δὲ καὶ εἰς τροφὴν τοῖς μὲν σωφρονισταῖς δραχμὴν α΄ ἑκάστῳ, τοῖς δ' ἐφήβοις τέτταρας ὀβολοὺς ἑκάστῳ· τὰ δὲ τῶν φυλετῶν τῶν αὑτοῦ λαμβάνων ὁ σωφρονιστὴς ἕκαστος ἀγοράζει τὰ ἐπιτήδεια πᾶσιν εἰς τὸ κοινόν (συσσιτοῦσι γὰρ κατὰ φυλάς), καὶ τῶν ἄλλων ἐπιμελεῖται πάντων. (*4*) καὶ τὸν μὲν πρῶτον ἐνιαυτὸν οὕτως διάγουσι· τὸν δ' ὕστερον ἐκκλησίας ἐν τῷ θεάτρῳ γενομένης, ἀποδειξάμενοι τῷ δήμῳ τὰ περὶ τὰς τάξεις καὶ λαβόντες ἀσπίδα καὶ δόρυ παρὰ τῆς πόλεως, περιπολοῦσι τὴν χώραν καὶ διατρίβουσιν ἐν τοῖς φυλακτηρίοις. (*5*) φρουροῦσι δὲ τὰ δύο ἔτη χλαμύδας ἔχοντες, καὶ ἀτελεῖς εἰσι πάντων· καὶ δίκην οὔτε διδόασιν οὔτε λαμβάνουσιν, ἵνα μὴ πρόφασις ᾖ τοῦ ἀπιέναι, πλὴν περὶ κλήρου καὶ ἐπικλήρου, κἄν τινι κατὰ τὸ γένος ἱερωσύνη γένηται. διεξελθόντων δὲ τῶν δυοῖν ἐτῶν ἤδη μετὰ τῶν ἄλλων εἰσίν.

(**43**) τὰ μὲν οὖν περὶ τὴν τῶν πολιτῶν ἐγγραφὴν καὶ τοὺς ἐφήβους τοῦτον ἔχει τὸν τρόπον. τὰς δ' ἀρχὰς τὰς περὶ τὴν ἐγκύκλιον διοίκησιν ἁπάσας ποιοῦσι κληρωτάς, πλὴν ταμίου στρατιωτικῶν καὶ τῶν ἐπὶ τὸ θεωρικὸν καὶ τοῦ τῶν κρηνῶν ἐπιμελητοῦ. ταύτας δὲ χειροτονοῦσιν, καὶ οἱ χειροτονηθέντες ἄρχουσιν ἐκ Παναθηναίων εἰς Παναθήναια. χειροτονοῦσι δὲ καὶ τὰς πρὸς τὸν πόλεμον ἁπάσας.

(*2*) βουλὴ δὲ κληροῦται φ΄, ν΄ ἀπὸ φυλῆς ἑκάστης. πρυτανεύει δ' ἐν μέρει τῶν φυλῶν ἑκάστη καθ' ὅ τι ἂν λάχωσιν, αἱ μὲν πρῶται τέτταρες ἓξ καὶ λ΄ ἡμέρας ἑκάστη, αἱ δὲ ς΄ αἱ ὕστεραι ε΄ καὶ λ΄ ἡμέρας ἑκάστη· κατὰ σελήνην γὰρ ἄγουσιν τὸν ἐνιαυτόν. (*3*) οἱ δὲ πρυτανεύοντες αὐτῶν πρῶτον μὲν συσσιτοῦσιν ἐν τῇ θόλῳ, λαμβάνοντες ἀργύριον παρὰ τῆς πόλεως, ἔπειτα συνάγουσιν καὶ τὴν βουλὴν καὶ τὸν δῆμον· τὴν μὲν οὖν βουλὴν ὅσαι ἡμέραι, πλὴν ἐάν τις ἀφέσιμος ᾖ, τὸν δὲ δῆμον τετράκις τῆς πρυτανείας ἑκάστης. καὶ ὅσα δεῖ χρηματίζειν τὴν βουλήν καὶ ὅ τι ἐν ἑκάστῃ

42. 3. καταπάλτην Kaibel & Wilamowitz: κατην with the letters απελτην written above L.

διδάσκουσιν: διδάξουσιν W. G. Rutherford (*CR*).

42. 5 δυοῖν Kaibel & Wilamowitz[2]: δυεῖν L.

them. (*3*) These take the *epheboi*, first make a tour of the sanctuaries, and then proceed to Piraeus, where some guard Munichia and some guard Acte. The *demos* elects two physical trainers for them, and teachers who teach them to fight as hoplites, to shoot arrows, to throw javelins and to fire catapults. For sustenance they give the *sophronistai* 1 drachma each and the *epheboi* four obols each; each *sophronistes* takes the grant for his own tribesmen and buys provisions for all of them in common (for they eat together by tribes), and takes care of everything else. (*4*) That is how they spend the first year. In the next an assembly is held in the theatre, they demonstrate to the *demos* their skills in manoeuvring and receive a shield and spear from the city, and they patrol the countryside and spend their time in the guard-posts. (*5*) They act as guards for two years, wearing short cloaks, and they are free from all impositions; and so that they shall have no excuse for absence they do not defend or prosecute in lawsuits, except concerning inheritance and *epikleroi*; and absence is allowed if a priesthood in his *genos* falls to anybody. After the two years gave passed they join the others.

(**43**) That is the manner of the arrangements for the registration of the citizens and for the *epheboi*. All the officials for the regular administration they appoint by allotment, apart from the treasurer of the stratiotic fund and the men in charge of the theoric fund and the *epimeletai* of the fountains: these they elect, and the men elected hold office from Panathenaea to Panathenaea. They also elect all the officers for warfare.

(*2*) The council is of 500 appointed by lot, 50 from each tribe. Each of the tribes serves in turn as prytany as determined by sortition, the first four 36 days each and the subsequent 6 35 days each (for the year is regulated by the moon). (*3*) Those who are in prytany first eat together in the *tholos*, receiving money from the city, and then convene both the council and the *demos*: the council every day, except when there is a day of exemption, and the *demos* four times in each prytany. And they prescribe what business the council is to transact, what on each day and

τῇ ἡμέρᾳ καὶ ὅπου καθίζειν οὗτοι προγράφουσι. (*4*) προγράφουσι δὲ καὶ τὰς ἐκκλησίας οὗτοι· μίαν μὲν κυρίαν, ἐν ᾗ δεῖ τὰς ἀρχὰς ἐπιχειροτονεῖν εἰ δοκοῦσι καλῶς ἄρχειν, καὶ περὶ σίτου καὶ περὶ φυλακῆς τῆς χώρας χρηματίζειν, καὶ τὰς εἰσαγγελίας ἐν ταύτῃ τῇ ἡμέρᾳ τοὺς βουλομένους ποιεῖσθαι, καὶ τὰς ἀπογραφὰς τῶν δημευομένων ἀναγιγνώσκειν καὶ τὰς λήξεις τῶν κλήρων καὶ τῶν ἐπικλήρων {ἀναγινώσκειν}, ὅπως μηδένα λάθῃ μηδὲν ἔρημον γενόμενον. (*5*) ἐπὶ δὲ τῆς ἕκτης πρυτανείας πρὸς τοῖς εἰρημένοις καὶ περὶ τῆς ὀστρακοφορίας ἐπιχειροτονίαν διδόασιν εἰ δοκεῖ ποιεῖν ἢ μή, καὶ συκοφαντῶν προβολὰς τῶν Ἀθηναίων καὶ τῶν μετοίκων μέχρι τριῶν ἑκατέρων, κἄν τις ὑποσχόμενός τι μὴ ποιήσῃ τῷ δήμῳ. (*6*) ἑτέραν δὲ ταῖς ἱκετηρίαις, ἐν ᾗ θεὶς ὁ βουλόμενος ἱκετηρίαν [ὑπὲρ] ὧν ἂν βούληται καὶ ἰδίων καὶ δημοσίων διαλέξεται πρὸς τὸν δῆμον. αἱ δὲ δύο περὶ τῶν ἄλλων εἰσίν, ἐν αἷς κελεύουσιν οἱ νόμοι τρία μὲν ἱερῶν χρηματίζειν, τρία δὲ κήρυξιν καὶ πρεσβείαις, τρία δὲ ὁσίων· χρηματίζουσιν δ' ἐνίοτε καὶ ἄνευ προχειροτονίας. προσέρχονται δὲ καὶ οἱ κήρυκες καὶ οἱ πρέσβεις τοῖς πρυτάνεσιν πρῶτον, καὶ οἱ τὰς ἐπιστολὰς φέροντες τούτοις ἀποδιδόασι.

(**44**) ἔστι δ' ἐπιστάτης τῶν πρυτάνεων εἷς ὁ λαχών. οὗτος δ' ἐπιστατεῖ νύκτα καὶ ἡμέραν, καὶ οὐκ ἔστιν οὔτε πλείω χρόνον οὔτε δὶς τὸν αὐτὸν γενέσθαι. τηρεῖ δ' οὗτος τάς τε κλεῖς τὰς τῶν ἱερῶν ἐν οἷς τὰ χρήματ' ἐστὶν καὶ <τὰ> γράμματα τῇ πόλει, καὶ τὴν δημοσίαν σφραγῖδα, καὶ μένειν ἀναγκαῖον ἐν τῇ θόλῳ τοῦτόν ἐστιν καὶ τριττὺν τῶν πρυτάνεων ἣν ἂν οὗτος κελεύῃ. (*2*) καὶ ἐπειδὰν συναγάγωσιν οἱ πρυτάνεις τὴν βουλὴν ἢ τὸν δῆμον, οὗτος κληροῖ προέδρους ἐννέα, ἕνα ἐκ τῆς φυλῆς ἑκάστης πλὴν τῆς πρυτανευούσης, καὶ πάλιν ἐκ τούτων ἐπιστάτην ἕνα, καὶ παραδίδωσι τὸ πρόγραμμα αὐτοῖς· (*3*) οἱ δὲ παραλαβόντες τῆς τ' εὐκοσμίας ἐπιμελοῦνται, καὶ ὑπὲρ ὧν δεῖ χρηματίζειν προτιθέασιν, καὶ

43. 4. {ἀναγινώσκειν} deleted A. Gennadios (*CR*), not present in the lexica.

43. 5 ἐπιχειροτονίαν L, cf. *Lex. Rhet. Cant.* κυρία ἐκκλησία: προχειροτονίαν Kaibel & Wilamowitz cf. *Lex. Rhet. Cant.* ὀτρακισμοῦ τρόπος, but διαχειροτονίαν would be better, cf. 49. 2.

43. 6. [ὑπὲρ]: [ὑ(πὲρ)] (Herwerden &) Leeuwen, [περὶ] K. S. Kontos.

44. 1. <τὰ> Kaibel & Wilamowitz cf. *Lex. Patm.*, Eust.

τοῦτόν <τ'> Kaibel & Wilamowitz, <καὶ> τοῦτόν P. N. Papageorgios.

44. 3. οἱ δὲ: οἳ δὲ Kaibel & Wilamowitz.

where it is to meet. (*4*) It is they also who prescribe the assemblies. One is the *ekklesia kyria*, in which they have to hold a vote of confidence to decide whether the officials are conducting their offices well, and to transact business about grain and about the defence of the territory, and on this day those who wish are to make *eisangeliai*, and they are to read out schedules of confiscated property and applications for the assignment of inheritances and *epikleroi*, so that none should go unclaimed without anybody's noticing. (*5*) In the sixth prytany, in addition to what has been stated, they also provide a vote on ostracism, whether the assembly should decide to hold one or not, and *probolai* against *sykophantai* both Athenian and metic, up to three of each, and whether anybody has made a promise to the *demos* and has failed to keep it. (*6*) A second assembly is devoted to supplications, in which whoever wishes makes a supplication about whatever he wishes, whether individual or public, and addresses the *demos*. The other two are for other matters, and the laws prescribe that they should transact three sacred items, three for heralds and embassies and three proper. But sometimes they transact business without a *procheirotonia*. Heralds and envoys approach the *prytaneis* first, and those bringing letters deliver them to them.

(**44**) There is a chairman of the *prytaneis* appointed by sortition. He serves as chairman for a night and a day, and it is not possible to serve for a longer time or for the same man to serve twice. He keeps watch over the keys of the sanctuaries in which the city's funds and documents are kept, and the public seal, and it is obligatory to remain in the *tholos* for him and for a *trittys* of the *prytaneis* ordered by him. (*2*) And when the *prytaneis* convene the council or the *demos* he picks by lot nine *proedroi*, one from each tribe except the tribe in prytany, and again from these one chairman, and he gives the agenda to them. (*3*) They take it over, and they take care of good order, and put forward the business which they

τὰς χειροτονίας κρίνουσιν, καὶ τὰ ἄλλα πάντα διοικοῦσιν, καὶ τοῦ {τ'} ἀφεῖναι κύριοί εἰσιν. καὶ ἐπιστατῆσαι μὲν οὐκ ἔξεστιν πλέον ἢ ἅπαξ ἐν τῷ ἐνιαυτῷ, προεδρεύειν δ' ἔξεστιν ἅπαξ ἐπὶ τῆς πρυτανείας ἑκάστης.

(*4*) ποιοῦσι δὲ καὶ {δεκ} ἀρχαιρεσίας στρατηγῶν καὶ ἱππάρχων καὶ τῶν ἄλλων τῶν πρὸς τὸν πόλεμον ἀρχῶν ἐν τῇ ἐκκλησίᾳ, καθ' ὅ τι ἂν τῷ δήμῳ δοκῇ· ποιοῦσι δ' οἱ μετὰ τὴν ϛ΄ πρυτανεύοντες ἐφ' ὧν ἂν εὐσημία γένηται. δεῖ δὲ προβούλευμα γενέσθαι καὶ περὶ τούτων.

(**45**) ἡ δὲ βουλὴ πρότερον μὲν ἦν κυρία καὶ χρήμασιν ζημιῶσαι καὶ δῆσαι καὶ ἀποκτεῖναι. καὶ Λυσίμαχον αὐτῆς ἀγαγούσης ὡς τὸν δήμιον, καθήμενον ἤδη μέλλοντα ἀποθνῄσκειν, Εὐμηλίδης ὁ Ἀλωπεκῆθεν ἀφείλετο, οὐ φάσκων δεῖν ἄνευ δικαστηρίου γνώσεως οὐδένα τῶν πολιτῶν ἀποθνῄσκειν· καὶ κρίσεως ἐν δικαστηρίῳ γενομένης, ὁ μὲν Λυσίμαχος ἀπέφυγεν καὶ ἐπωνυμίαν ἔσχεν ὁ ἀπὸ τοῦ τυπάνου, ὁ δὲ δῆμος ἀφείλετο τῆς βουλῆς τὸ θανατοῦν καὶ δεῖν καὶ χρήμασι ζημιοῦν, καὶ νόμον ἔθετο, ἄν τινος ἀδικεῖν ἡ βουλὴ καταγνῷ ἢ ζημιώσῃ, τὰς καταγνώσεις καὶ τὰς ἐπιζημιώσεις εἰσάγειν τοὺς θεσμοθέτας εἰς τὸ δικαστήριον, καὶ ὅ τι ἂν οἱ δικασταὶ ψηφίσωνται, τοῦτο κύριον εἶναι.

(*2*) κρίνει δὲ τὰς ἀρχὰς ἡ βουλὴ τὰς πλείστας, καὶ μάλισθ' ὅσαι χρήματα διαχειρίζουσιν· οὐ κυρία δ' ἡ κρίσις, ἀλλ' ἐφέσιμος εἰς τὸ δικαστήριον. ἔξεστι δὲ καὶ τοῖς ἰδιώταις εἰσαγγέλλειν ἣν ἂν βούλωνται τῶν ἀρχῶν μὴ χρῆσθαι τοῖς νόμοις· ἔφεσις δὲ καὶ τούτοις ἐστὶν εἰς τὸ δικαστήριον ἐὰν αὐτῶν ἡ βουλὴ καταγνῷ.

(*3*) δοκιμάζει δὲ καὶ τοὺς βουλευτὰς τοὺς τὸν ὕστερον ἐνιαυτὸν βουλεύσοντας καὶ τοὺς ἐννέα ἄρχοντας. καὶ πρότερον μὲν ἦν ἀποδοκιμάσαι κυρία, νῦν δὲ τούτοις ἔφεσίς ἐστιν εἰς τὸ δικαστήριον.

(*4*) τούτων μὲν οὖν ἄκυρός ἐστιν ἡ βουλή· προβουλεύει δ' εἰς τὸν δῆμον, καὶ οὐκ ἔξεστιν οὐδὲν ἀπροβούλευτον οὐδ' ὅ τι ἂν μὴ προγράψωσιν οἱ πρυτάνεις ψηφίσασθαι τῷ δήμῳ· κατ' αὐτὰ γὰρ ταῦτα ἔνοχός ἐστιν ὁ νικήσας γραφῇ παρανόμων.

44. 3. {τ'} Kaibel & Wilamowitz.
44. 4. {δεκ} Sandys (*CR*).
45. 1. Lacuna before καὶ Λυσίμαχον Kaibel & Wilamowitz.
καθήμενον: perhaps καθη<λω>μένον L. Gernet.

must transact, and they judge the votes by show of hands and administer everything else, and they have the power of dismissal. And it is not permitted to be chairman more than once in the year, but it is permitted to be *proedros* once in each prytany.

(*4*) They also hold elections of generals, hipparchs and the other officers for warfare in the assembly, in accordance with whatever the *demos* decides: this is done by those *prytaneis* after the 6th in whose term there are good omens. There has to be a *probouleuma* about this also.

(**45**) The council formerly had the power to punish with fines, to imprison and to execute. And when it was taking Lysimachus to the public servant, and he was already sitting and waiting to be executed, Eumelides of Alopece took him away, saying that none of the citizens ought to be executed without the judgment of a lawcourt; and when judgment was passed in a lawcourt Lysimachus was acquitted, and he came to be known as the man who came back from the garrotte. And the *demos* took away from the council the right to put to death and imprison and punish with fines, and enacted a law that if the council convicted anybody of wrongdoing or proposed to fine him the convictions and proposals for punishment should be introduced by the *thesmothetai* to the lawcourt, and that whatever the jurors voted that should be definitive.

(*2*) The council judges most of the officials, and particularly those who handle funds; but the judgment is not decisive but subject to reference to the lawcourt. It is also permitted to private individuals to make an *eisangelia* against any of the officials whom they wish on a charge of not complying with the laws; and there is reference to the lawcourt for these also if the council convicts.

(*3*) It also vets the councillors who are to hold office in the following year and the nine archons: previously it had the power to reject them, but now for these there is reference to the lawcourt.

(*4*) In these matters the council lacks definitive power. But it conducts *probouleusis* for the *demos*, and it is not permitted to the *demos* to decree anything without *probouleusis* or not prescribed by the *prytaneis*; for on these matters the man who succeeded with a proposal is liable to the *graphe paranomon*.

(**46**) ἐπιμελεῖται δὲ καὶ τῶν πεποιημένων τριήρων καὶ τῶν σκευῶν καὶ τῶν νεωσοίκων, καὶ ποιεῖται καινὰς {δὲ} τριήρεις ἢ τετρήρεις, ὁποτέρας ἂν ὁ δῆμος χειροτονήσῃ, καὶ σκεύη ταύταις καὶ νεωσοίκους· χειροτονεῖ δ' ἀρχιτέκτονας ὁ δῆμος ἐπὶ τὰς ναῦς. ἂν δὲ μὴ παραδῶσιν ἐξειργασμένα ταῦτα τῇ νέᾳ βουλῇ, τὴν δωρεὰν οὐκ ἔστιν αὐτοῖς λαβεῖν· ἐπὶ γὰρ τῆς ὕστερον βουλῆς λαμβάνουσιν. ποιεῖται δὲ τὰς τριήρεις, δέκα ἄνδρας ἐξ αὐτ[ῆ]ς ἑλομένη τριηροποιούς. (*2*) ἐξετάζει δὲ καὶ τὰ οἰκοδομήματα τὰ δημόσια πάντα, κἄν τις ἀδικεῖν αὐτῇ δόξῃ, τῷ τε δήμῳ τοῦτον ἀποφαίνει, καὶ καταγνοῦσα παραδίδωσι δικαστηρίῳ.

(**47**) συνδιοικεῖ δὲ καὶ ταῖς ἄλλαις ἀρχαῖς τὰ πλεῖστα. πρῶτον μὲν γὰρ οἱ ταμίαι τῆς Ἀθηνᾶς εἰσὶ μὲν δέκα, κλ[ηρο]ῦται δ' εἷς ἐκ τῆς φυλῆς, ἐκ πεντακοσιομεδίμνων κατὰ τὸν Σόλωνος νόμ[ον (ἔτι γὰρ ὁ] νόμος κύριός ἐστιν), ἄρχει δ' ὁ λαχὼν κἂν πάνυ πένης ᾖ. παραλαμβάνουσι δὲ τό τε ἄγαλμα τῆς Ἀθηνᾶς καὶ τὰς Νίκας καὶ τὸν ἄλλον κόσμον καὶ τὰ χρήματα ἐναντίον τῆς βουλῆς.

(*2*) ἔπειθ' οἱ πωληταὶ ι´ μέν εἰσι, κληροῦται δ' εἷς ἐκ τῆς φυλῆς. μισθοῦσι δὲ τὰ μισθώματα πάντα, καὶ τὰ μέταλλα πωλοῦσι καὶ τὰ τέλη μετὰ τοῦ ταμίου τῶν στρατιωτικῶν καὶ τῶν ἐπὶ τὸ θεωρικὸν ᾑρημένων ἐναντίον τῆς [βουλῆς]· καὶ κυροῦσιν ὅτῳ ἂν ἡ βουλὴ χειροτονήσῃ καὶ τὰ πραθέντα μέταλλα, τά̣ τ̣' ἐργάσιμα τὰ εἰς τρία ἔτη πεπραμένα, καὶ τὰ συγκεχωρημένα τὰ εἰς ζ´ ἔτη πεπραμένα. καὶ τὰς οὐσίας τῶν ἐξ Ἀρείου πάγου φευγόντων καὶ τῶν ἄ̣λ̣λ̣[ων] ἐν̣α̣ν̣τ̣[ίον τῆς] βουλῆς πωλοῦσιν, κατακυροῦσι δ' οἱ θ´ ἄρχοντες. καὶ τὰ τέλη τὰ εἰς ἐνιαυτὸν πεπραμένα, ἀναγράψαντες εἰς λελευκωμένα γραμματεῖα τόν τε πριάμενον καὶ ὅ[σ]ου

46. 1. {δὲ} Kenyon[1]: δ´ (= 4) B. Keil, δέκα W. Kolbe.
αὐτ[ῆ]ς read by Chambers: αὐ[τ]ῆς Wilcken.
46. 2. καταγνοῦσα L, cf. Aeschin. I. *Timarchus* 111: καταγνόντος Kaibel & Wilamowitz.
47. 1. κλ[ηρο]ῦται read by Chambers: κλ[ηροῦται] M. C. Gertz.
47. 2. [βουλῆς] Kenyon[1].
καὶ κυροῦσιν … χειροτονήσῃ transposed to follow πεπραμένα A. A. Sakellarios.
καὶ κυροῦσιν: καὶ <κατα>κυροῦσιν Kaibel & Wilamowitz[3], cf. P. N.Pagageorgios.
ζ´ Chambers: γ´ read in L Wilcken, Chambers.
ἄ̣λ̣λ̣[ων] ἐν̣α̣ν̣τ̣[ίον τῆς] read by Chambers, cf. Kenyon[4].
ὅ[σ]ου Kaibel & Wilamowitz[1–2], cf. Kaibel (*Stil und Text*, 211–20: ὅ[σ]α L.

(**46**) The council also takes care of the triremes which have been built, the equipment and the shipsheds, and it builds new triremes or quadriremes, whichever the *demos* votes, and equipment and shipsheds for these. The *demos* elects architects for the ships. If they do not hand over these ships completed to the new council, it is not permitted to them to take their award; for they take it under the subsequent council. It builds the triremes, electing ten men from itself as *trieropoioi*. (*2*) Also it inspects all the public buildings, and if it judges anybody guilty of wrongdoing it reports him to the *demos*, and after convicting him hands him over to a lawcourt.

(**47**) It also joins in administration with the other officials for the most part. For first the treasurers of Athena are ten in number, one appointed by lot per tribe, from the *pentakosiomedimnoi* in accordance with the law of Solon (for the law is still valid), and the man picked in the sortition holds office even if he is really poor. They take over the image of Athena and the Victories and the rest of the paraphernalia and the money, in the presence of the council.

(*2*) Next the *poletai* are 10 in number, one appointed by lot per tribe. They let all the leases, and they sell the rights to mines and taxes, together with the treasurer of the stratiotic fund and the men elected to take charge of the theoric fund, in the presence of the council. And they ratify for whoever the council votes the mines which are sold, those which are in working order sold for three years and those which have been abandoned sold for 7 years, and they sell the properties of those exiled after trial by the Areopagus and the others, in the presence of the council, and the 9 archons ratify them. And the taxes sold for a year they hand to the council, writing up on whitened boards the purchasers and the prices for

ἂν πρίηται, τῇ βουλῇ παραδιδόασιν. (*3*) ἀναγράφουσιν δὲ χωρὶς μὲν οὓς δεῖ κατὰ πρυτανείαν ἑκάστην καταβάλλειν, εἰς δέκα γραμματεῖα, χωρὶς δὲ οὓς τρὶς τοῦ ἐνιαυτοῦ, γραμματεῖον κατὰ τὴν καταβολὴν ἑκάστην ποιήσαντες, χωρὶς δ' οὓς ἐπὶ τῆς ἐνάτης πρυτανείας. ἀναγράφουσι δὲ καὶ τὰ χωρία καὶ τὰς οἰκίας τἀπογραφέντα καὶ πραθέντα ἐν τῷ δικαστηρίῳ· καὶ γὰρ ταῦθ' οὗτοι πωλ[οῦσιν. ἐστὶ] δὲ τῶν μὲν οἰκιῶν ἐν ε΄ ἔτεσιν ἀνάγκη τὴν τιμὴν ἀποδοῦναι, τῶν δὲ χωρίων ἐν δέκα· καταβάλλουσιν δὲ ταῦτα ἐπὶ τῆς ἐνάτης πρυτανείας. (*4*) εἰσφέρει δὲ καὶ ὁ βασιλεὺς τὰς μισθώσεις τῶν τεμενῶν, ἀναγράψας ἐν γραμματείοις λελευκωμένοις. ἔστι δὲ καὶ τούτων ἡ μὲν μίσθωσις εἰς ἔτη δέκα, καταβάλλεται δ' ἐπὶ τῆς θ̣΄ πρυτανείας. διὸ καὶ πλεῖστα χρήματα ἐπὶ ταύτης συλλέγεται τῆς πρυτανείας. (*5*) εἰσφέρεται μὲν οὖν εἰς τὴν βουλὴν τὰ γραμματεῖα κατὰ τὰς καταβολὰς ἀναγεγραμμένα, τηρεῖ δ' ὁ δημόσιος· ὅταν δ' ᾖ χρημάτ[ων κ]α̣τ̣αβολή, παραδίδωσι τοῖς ἀποδέκταις αὐτὰ ταῦτα καθελὼν ἀπὸ [τῶν] ἐπιστυλίων ὧν ἐν ταύτῃ τῇ ἡμέρᾳ δεῖ τὰ χρήματα καταβληθῆναι καὶ ἀπαλειφθῆναι· τὰ δ' ἄλλα ἀπόκειται χωρίς, ἵνα μὴ προεξαλειφθῇ.

(**48**) εἰσὶ δ' ἀποδέκται δέκα κεκληρωμένοι κατὰ φυλάς· οὗτοι δὲ παραλαβόντες τὰ γραμματεῖα ἀπαλείφουσι τὰ καταβαλλόμενα χρήματα ἐναντίον τ[ῆς βουλῆς] ἐν τῷ βουλευτηρίῳ, καὶ πάλιν ἀποδιδόασιν τὰ γραμματεῖα τῷ δημοσίῳ. κἄν τις ἐλλίπῃ καταβολήν, ἐνταῦθ' ἐγγέγραπται, καὶ διπλάσιον ἀνάγκη τὸ ἐλλειφθὲν καταβάλλειν ἢ δεδέσθαι, καὶ ταῦτα εἰσπράττειν ἡ βουλὴ καὶ δῆσαι κυρία κατὰ τοὺς νόμους ἐστίν. (*2*) τῇ μὲν οὖν προτεραίᾳ δέχονται τὰς π[άσα]ς καὶ μερίζουσι ταῖς ἀρχαῖς, τῇ δ' ὑστεραίᾳ τόν τε μερισμὸν εἰσφ[έρο]υσι γράψαντες ἐν σανίδι καὶ καταλέγουσιν ἐν τῷ βουλευτηρίῳ, καὶ προ[τιθ]έασιν ἐν τῇ βουλῇ εἴ τίς τινα οἶδεν ἀδικοῦντα περὶ τὸν μερισμὸν ἢ ἄρχοντα ἢ ἰδιώτην, καὶ γνώμας ἐπιψηφίζουσιν ἐάν τίς τι δοκῇ ἀδικεῖν.

(*3*) κληροῦσι δὲ καὶ λογιστὰς ἐξ αὑτῶν οἱ βουλευταὶ δέκα τοὺς λογιουμένους ταῖς ἀρχαῖς κατὰ τὴν πρυτανείαν ἑκάστην. (*4*) κληροῦσι δὲ καὶ εὐθύνους ἕνα τῆς φυλῆς ἑκάστης, καὶ παρέδρους β΄ ἑκάστῳ τῶν

48. 2. π[άσα]ς Kaibel & Wilamowitz[3].
προ[τιθ]έασιν J. E. Sandys (*CR*).

which they are purchased. (*3*) They write up separately those who have to pay each prytany, on ten boards, those who have to pay three times in the year, creating a board for each payment, and those who have to pay in the ninth prytany. They write up also the lands and houses which have been registered and put up for sale in the lawcourt: for they sell these also. For houses the price has to be paid in 5 years. and for lands they pay in ten years: these payments are made in the ninth prytany. (*4*) The *basileus* introduces the leases of sacred lands, writing them up on whitened boards: the lease of these also is for ten years, and the payment is made in the 9th prytany. For that reason most of the money is collected in this prytany. (*5*) The boards, then, are brought in to the council, written up in accordance with the payments, and the public slave keeps watch over them. When there is a payment of money, he gives these particular boards to the *apodektai*, taking down from the racks the records of the men whose monies are to be paid and wiped off on this day. The rest are kept separately, so that they shall not be wiped out prematurely.

(**48**) There are ten *apodektai*, allotted by tribes. These take over the boards, and wipe off the monies paid, in the presence of the council in the council house, and they give back the boards to the public slave. And if anybody misses a payment he is written in there, and he is obliged to pay double the amount missed or to be imprisoned, and the council has the power to exact this and to imprison, in accordance with the laws. (*2*) On the first day, then, they receive all the payments and make the *merismos* to the officials; and on the next day they introduce the *merismos*, after writing it on a tablet, and read it out in the council house, and in the council they call for anybody who knows that anybody, whether an official or a private citizen, is guilty of wrongdoing with regard to the *merismos*, and they put to the vote proposals that anybody should be judged to be in the wrong in any respect.

(*3*) Also the councillors allot from themselves ten *logistai* to check accounts for the officials in each prytany. (*4*) They also allot *euthynoi*, one for each tribe, and 2 *paredroi* for each of the *euthynoi*, who are

εὐθύνων, οἷς ἀναγκαῖόν ἐστι ταῖς ἀ[γορ]αῖς κατὰ τὸν ἐπώνυμον τὸν τῆς φυλῆς ἑκάστης καθῆσθαι· κἄν τις βούληταί τινι τῶν τὰς εὐθύνας ἐν τῷ δικαστηρίῳ δεδωκότων ἐντὸς λ΄ ἡμ[ε]ρῶν ἀφ' ἧς ἔδωκε τὰς εὐθύνας εὔθυναν ἄν τ' ἰδίαν ἄν τε δημοσίαν ἐμβαλέσθαι, γράψας εἰς πινάκιον λελευκωμένον τοὔνομα τό [θ' αὑτο]ῦ καὶ τὸ τοῦ φεύγοντος καὶ τὸ ἀδίκημ' ὅ τι ἂν ἐγκαλῇ, καὶ τίμημα ἐ[πιγρα]ψάμενος ὅ τι ἂν αὐτῷ δοκῇ, δίδωσιν τῷ εὐθύνῳ. (*5*) ὁ δὲ λαβὼν τοῦτο καὶ ἀν[αγνού]ς, ἐὰν μὲν καταγνῷ, παραδίδωσιν τὰ μὲν ἴδια τοῖς δικασταῖς τοῖς κατὰ δήμ[ους τοῖς] τὴν φυλὴν ταύτην δικάζουσιν, τὰ δὲ δημόσια τοῖς θεσμοθέται[ς συν]ạγạγράφει. οἱ δὲ θεσμοθέται, ἐὰν παραλάβωσιν, πάλιν εἰσάγουσιν ṭ[ὴ]ṿ [ε]ὔθυναν εἰς τὸ δικαστήριον, καὶ ὅ τι ἂν γνῶσιν οἱ δικασταί, [τοῦτο κύ]ριόν ἐστιν.

(**49**) δοκιμάζει δὲ καὶ τοὺς ἵππους ἡ βουλή, κἂν μέν τις καλ[ὸν ἵππον ἔχ]ων κακῶς δοκῇ τρέφειν, ζημιοῖ τῷ σίτῳ· τοῖς δὲ μὴ δυναμέν[ο]ις [ἀκολ]ουθεῖν, ἢ μὴ θέλουσι μένειν ἀναγ<ώγοις> οὖσι, τροχὸν ἐπὶ τὴν γνάθον ἐπιβάλλει, καὶ ὁ τοῦτο παθὼν ἀδόκιμός ἐστι. δοκιμάζει δὲ καὶ τοὺς προδρόμους οἵτινες ἂν αὐτῇ δοκῶσιν ἐπιτήδειοι προδρομεύειν εἶναι, κἄν τιν' ἀποχειροτονήσῃ καταβέβηκεν οὗτος. δοκιμάζει δὲ καὶ τοὺς ἁμίππους, κἄν τιν' ἀποχειροτονήσῃ πέπαυται μισθοφορῶν οὗτος. (*2*) τοὺς δ' ἱππέας

48. 4. ἀ[γορ]αῖς Kenyon[1]: αγ̣ . . . λ̣αις vel σ̣αις Wilcken, α . . . σ̣αις Chambers, ἀν[ατο]λαῖς A. Rehm, <ἐπὶ> ταῖς σ[τήλ]αις A. A. Efstathiou, *ZPE* 187 (2013), 84–6.

λ΄ possible Kenyon[4–5], cf. J. H. Lipsius: γ΄ Kenyon, Chambers, Efstathiou, τ΄ Wilcken.

48. 5. ἀν[αγνού]ς Blass: ἀν[ακρίνα]ς W. Wayte (*CR*).

δικάζουσιν H. Richards and E. S. Thompson (*CR*): εἰσάγουσιν L.

θεσμοθέται[ς συν]ạγạγράφει Wilcken, Chambers: θεσμοθέτα[ις ἀ]ναγράφει Kenyon.

ἐὰν παραλάβωσιν: ἐπὰν K. S. Kontos, perhaps.

ṭ[ὴ]ṿ [ε]ὔθυναν Chambers, cf. Kenyon[1]: [ταύτ(ην) τ(ὴν)] Blass[2].

[τοῦτο κύ]ριόν Kaibel & Wilamowitz.

49. 1. καλ[ὸν ἵππον ἔχ]ων Kaibel & Wilamowitz[1]: καλ[ὸ]ν [δυ/νατο]ς ὢν Blass[3], but too long for the space.

ἀναγ<ώγοις> οὖσι (Herwerden &) Leeuwen cf. Xen. *Mem.* IV. 1. 3: αναγουσι with the letters λλ written above να L, whence ἀλλ' ἀνάγουσι Blass[1].

ἀποχειροτονήσῃ *bis* J. B. Mayor and L. Campbell (*CR*).

ἁμίππους W. Wyse and W. L. Newman (*CR*).

obliged to sit by the eponymous hero of each tribe in market hours; and if anybody wishes to invoke either a private or a public *euthyna* against any of those who have submitted *euthynai* in the lawcourt, within 30 days of his submitting *euthynai*, he writes on a whitened tablet his own name, that of the defendant and the offence of which he accuses him, adds the assessment which he judges right, and gives it to the *euthynos*. (*5*) He takes this and reads it; and if he convicts he hands private matters to the deme justices who are serving for that tribe, and reports public matters to the *thesmothetai*. The *thesmothetai* if they take it over introduce the *euthyna* into the lawcourt again, and whatever the jurors deciude is definitive.

(**49**) Also the council vets the horses, and if anybody who has a good horse is judged to be maintaining it badly it fines him the fodder grant. Those horses which are not able to keep up, or do not want to stay in position and are unmanageable, it brands with a wheel on their jaw, and the horse to which this is done is rejected. It also vets the *prodromoi* to judge which are fit to serve, and if it votes anybody out he is expelled. It also vets the *hamippoi*, and if it votes anybody out his paid service is ended. (*2*)

καταλέγουσι μὲν οἱ καταλογεῖς, οὓς ἂν ὁ δῆμος χειροτονήσῃ δέκα ἄνδρας· οὓς δ' ἂν καταλέξωσι, παραδιδόασι τοῖς ἱππάρχοις καὶ φυλάρχοις, οὗτοι δὲ παραλαβόντες εἰσφέρουσι τὸν κατάλογον εἰς τὴν βουλήν, καὶ τὸν πίνακ' ἀνοίξαντες ἐν ᾧ κατασεσημασμένα τὰ ὀνόματα τῶν ἱππέων ἐστί, τοὺς μὲν ἐξομνυμένους τῶν πρότερον ἐγγεγραμμένων μὴ δυνατοὺς εἶναι τοῖς σώμασιν ἱππεύειν ἐξαλείφουσι, τοὺς δὲ κατειλεγμένους καλοῦσι, κἂν μέν τις ἐξομόσηται μὴ δύνασθαι τῷ σώματι ἱππεύειν ἢ τῇ οὐσίᾳ, τοῦτον ἀφιᾶσιν, τὸν δὲ μὴ ἐξομνύμενον διαχειροτονοῦσιν οἱ βουλευταί πότερον ἐπιτήδειός ἐστιν ἱππεύειν ἢ οὔ· κἂν μὲν χειροτονήσωσιν, ἐγγράφουσιν εἰς τὸν πίνακα, εἰ δὲ μή, καὶ τοῦτον ἀφιᾶσιν.

(*3*) ἔκρινεν δέ ποτε καὶ τὰ παραδείγματα καὶ τὸν πέπλον ἡ βουλή, νῦν δὲ τὸ δικαστήριον τὸ λαχόν· ἐδόκουν γὰρ οὗτοι καταχαρίζεσθαι τὴν κρίσιν. καὶ τῆς ποιήσεως τῶν Νικῶν καὶ τῶν ἄθλων τῶν εἰς τὰ Παναθήναια συνεπιμελεῖται μετὰ τοῦ ταμίου τῶν στρατιωτικῶν.

(*4*) δοκιμάζει δὲ καὶ τοὺς ἀδυνάτους ἡ βουλή· νόμος γάρ ἐστιν ὃς κελεύει τοὺς ἐντὸς τριῶν μνῶν κεκτημένους καὶ τὸ σῶμα πεπηρωμένους ὥστε μὴ δύνασθαι μηδὲν ἔργον ἐργάζεσθαι δοκιμάζειν μὲν τὴν βουλήν, διδόναι δὲ δημοσίᾳ τροφὴν δύο ὀβολοὺς ἑκάστῳ τῆς ἡμέρας. καὶ ταμίας ἐστὶν αὐτοῖς κληρωτός.

(*5*) συνδιοικεῖ δὲ καὶ ταῖς ἄλλαις ἀρχαῖς τὰ πλεῖσθ' ὡς ἔπος εἰπεῖν.

(**50**) τὰ μὲν οὖν ὑπὸ τῆς βουλῆς διοικούμενα ταῦτ' ἐστίν. κληροῦνται δὲ καὶ ἱερῶν ἐπισκευασταὶ δέκα ἄνδρες, οἳ λαμβάνοντες τριάκοντα μνᾶς παρὰ τῶν ἀποδεκτῶν ἐπισκευάζουσιν τὰ μάλιστα δεόμενα τῶν ἱερῶν. (*2*) καὶ ἀστυνόμοι δέκα· τούτων δὲ ε´ μὲν ἄρχουσιν ἐν Πειραιεῖ, πέντε δ' ἐν ἄστει, καὶ τάς τε αὐλητρίδας καὶ τὰς ψαλτρίας καὶ τὰς κιθαριστρίας οὗτοι σκοποῦσιν ὅπως μὴ πλείονος ἢ δυοῖν δραχμαῖν μισθωθήσονται, κἂν πλείους τὴν αὐτὴν σπουδάζωσι λαβεῖν, οὗτοι διακληροῦσι καὶ τῷ λαχόντι μισθοῦσιν. καὶ ὅπως τῶν κοπρολόγων μηδεὶς ἐντὸς ι´ σταδίων τοῦ τείχους καταβαλεῖ κόπρον ἐπιμελοῦνται. καὶ τὰς ὁδοὺς κωλύουσι κατοικοδομεῖν καὶ δρυφάκτους ὑπὲρ τῶν ὁδῶν ὑπερτείνειν καὶ ὀχετοὺς μετεώρους εἰς τὴν ὁδὸν ἔκρουν ἔχοντας ποιεῖν καὶ τὰς θυρίδας εἰς

49. 2. τοῖς σώμασιν: <ἢ ταῖς οὐσίαις> P. N. Papageorgios.
50. 2. δυοῖν δραχμαῖν Herwerden & Leeuwen: δυεῖν δραχμαῖς L.
σπουδάζωσι Blass[2]: σπουδάσωσι L.

The cavalrymen are registered by the *katalogeis*, ten men elected by the *demos*. They give the names of those whom they register to the hipparchs and the phylarchs, and these take them over and introduce the register to the council. They open the tablet in which have been sealed up the names of the cavalrymen: those who had been entered before but swear an oath of exemption, that they are unable to serve with their bodies, they wipe out; and they summon those who have been enrolled, and if anybody swears an oath of exemption, that he is unable to serve either with his body or with his property, they release him; and for a man who does not swear an oath of exemption the councillors vote on whether he is fit to serve or not. If they vote that he is, they enter him on the tablet; if not, they release him also.

(*3*) The council used to judge the patterns and the *peplos*; but now it is done by a lawcourt picked by sortititon, since it was thought that the councillors were using favouritism in their judgment. And it joins with the treasurer of the stratiotic fund in taking care of the making of the Victories and the prizes for the Panathenaea.

(*4*) The council also vets the invalids; for there is a law which prescribes that those who possess less than three minas, and are maimed in their bodies so that they cannot do any work, are to be vetted by the council and each given two obols per day for sustenance. And they have an allotted treasurer.

(*5*) It also joins in administration with the other officials for the most part, so to say.

(**50**) That, then, is the administration done by the council. There are also allotted ten men as *hieron episkeuastai*, who take thirty minas from the *apodektai* and repair the sanctuaries most in need of it. (*2*) And ten *astynomoi*: of these 5 hold office in Piraeus and five in the city, and they supervise the pipe-girls, harp-girls and lyre-girls to see that they are not hired for more than two drachmae, and if several men are eager to employ the same girl they hold a lottery and hire her to the man picked by sortition. And they take care that none of the dung-collectors deposits the dung within 10 stades of the wall. And they prevent men from building to encroach on the streets and extending balconies over the streets and creating overhead drainpipes which discharge into the street and opening

τὴν ὁδὸν ἀνοίγειν. καὶ τοὺς ἐν ταῖς ὁδοῖς ἀπογιγνομένους ἀναιροῦσιν, ἔχοντες δημοσίους ὑπηρέτας.

(**51**) κληροῦνται δὲ καὶ ἀγορανόμοι <ι´>, πέντε μὲν εἰς Πειραιέα, ε´ δ' εἰς ἄστυ. τούτοις δὲ ὑπὸ τῶν νόμων προστέτακται τῶν ὠνίων ἐπιμελεῖσθαι πάντων, ὅπως καθαρὰ καὶ ἀκίβδηλα πωλήσεται. (*2*) κληροῦνται δὲ καὶ μετρονόμοι <ι´>, πέντε μὲν εἰς ἄστυ, ε´ δὲ εἰς Πειραιέα, καὶ οὗτοι τῶν μέτρων καὶ τῶν σταθμῶν ἐπιμελοῦνται πάντων, ὅπως οἱ πωλοῦντες χρήσονται δικαίοις. (*3*) ἦσαν δὲ καὶ σιτοφύλακες κληρωτοὶ <ι´>, πέντε μὲν εἰς Πειραιέα, πέντε δ' εἰς ἄστυ, νῦν δ' εἴκοσι μὲν εἰς ἄστυ, πεντεκαίδεκα δ' εἰς Πειραιέα. οὗτοι δ' ἐπιμελοῦνται πρῶτον μὲν ὅπως ὁ ἐν ἀγορᾷ σῖτος ἀργὸς ὤνιος ἔσται δικαίως, ἔπειθ' ὅπως οἵ τε μυλωθροὶ πρὸς τὰς τιμὰς τῶν κριθῶν τὰ ἄλφιτα πωλήσουσιν καὶ οἱ ἀρτοπῶλαι πρὸς τὰς τιμὰς τῶν πυρῶν τοὺς ἄρτους, καὶ τὸν σταθμὸν ἄγοντας ὅσον ἂν οὗτοι τάξωσιν· ὁ γὰρ νόμος τούτους κελεύει τάττειν. (*4*) ἐμπορίου δ' ἐπιμελητὰς δέκα κληροῦσιν· τούτοις δὲ προστέτακται τῶν τ' ἐμπορίων ἐπιμελεῖσθαι, καὶ τοῦ σίτου τοῦ καταπλέοντος εἰς τὸ σιτικὸν ἐμπόριον τὰ δύο μέρη τοὺς ἐμπόρους ἀναγκάζειν εἰς τὸ ἄστυ κομίζειν.

(**52**) καθιστᾶσι δὲ καὶ τοὺς ἕνδεκα κλήρῳ, τοὺς ἐπιμελησομένους τῶν ἐν τῷ δεσμωτηρίῳ, καὶ τοὺς ἀπαγομένους κλέπτας καὶ τοὺς ἀνδραποδιστὰς καὶ τοὺς λωποδύτας, ἂν μὲν [ὁμ]ολ[ο]γῶ]σι, θανάτῳ ζημιώσοντας, ἂν δ' ἀμφισβητῶσιν, εἰσάξοντας εἰς τὸ δικαστήριον, κἂν μὲν ἀποφύγωσιν, ἀφήσοντας, εἰ δὲ μή, τότε θανατώσοντας· καὶ τὰ ἀπογραφόμενα χωρία καὶ οἰκίας εἰσάξοντας εἰς τὸ δικαστήριον, καὶ τὰ δόξαντα δημόσια εἶναι παραδώσοντας τοῖς πωληταῖς· καὶ τὰς ἐνδείξεις εἰσάξοντας, καὶ γὰρ ταύτας εἰσάγουσιν οἱ ἕνδεκα. εἰσάγουσι δὲ τῶν ἐνδείξεών τινας καὶ οἱ θεσμοθέται.

51. 1. <ι´> P. N. Papageorgios.

πωλήσεται Kaibel (*Stil und Text*, 220–1): πωλῆται L.

51. 2. <ι´> P. N. Papageorgios.

χρήσονται A. Sidgwick and W. G. Rutherford (*CR*): χρήσωνται L.

51. 3. <ι´> Kaibel & Wilamowitz.

52. 1. κλήρῳ, τοὺς Kaibel (*Stil und Text*, 223): κληρωτοὺς Kenyon[1–3] cf. [4]corrigenda, Chambers, κληρωτοὺς, <τοὺς> W. G. Rutherford (*CR*).

[ὁμ]ολ[ο]γῶ]σι Chambers: [ὁμολογῶ]σι Kenyon[1].

shutters into the street. And those who pass away in the streets they retrieve, using public attendants.

(**51**) There are also allotted 10 *agoranomoi*, five for Piraeus and five for the city. These are enjoined by the laws to take care of everything that is sold, so that goods shall be sold pure and genuine. (*2*) There are also allotted 10 *metronomoi*, five for the city and 5 for Piraeus, and these take care of all measures and weights, so that the sellers use just standards. (*3*) There used to be 10 allotted *sitophylakes*, five for Piraeus and five for the city, but now there are twenty for the city and fifteen for Piraeus. These take care, first, that the unground grain in the agora is sold justly, and, next, that the millers sell the meal in accordance with the price paid for the barleycorns and that the breadsellers sell their loaves in accordance with the price paid for the wheat, and at the weight which the *sitophylakes* fix: for the law enjoins them to fix it. (*4*) They allot ten *emporiou epimeletai*: these are instructed to take care of the wholesale markets, and to compel the wholesalers to convey to the city two thirds of the grain brought by sea to the grain market.

(**52**) They appoint by lot the Eleven, who are to take care of those in the prison, and to punish with death the robbers, kidnappers and highwaymen brought by *apagoge*, if they confess; but if they dispute it they introduce them into the lawcourt, and if they are acquitted are to release them but if not are then to put them to death. They are also to introduce into the lawcourt lands and houses registered for confiscation, and those that are judged to be public property they are to hand over to the *poletai*. And they are to introduce the *endeixeis*, for it is the Eleven who introduce these also; but the *thesmothetai* introduce some of the *endeixeis*.

(*2*) κληροῦσι δὲ καὶ εἰσαγωγέας ε´ ἄνδρας, οἳ τὰς ἐμμήνους εἰσάγουσι δίκας, δυοῖν φυλαῖν ἕκαστος. εἰσὶ δ’ ἔμμηνοι προικός, ἐάν τις ὀφείλων μὴ ἀποδῷ, κἄν τις ἐπὶ δραχμῇ δανεισάμενος ἀποστερῇ, κἄν τις ἐν ἀγορᾷ βουλόμενος ἐγράζεσθαι δανείσηται παρά τινος ἀφορμήν· ἔτι δ’ αἰκείας καὶ ἐρανικαὶ καὶ κοινωνικαὶ καὶ ἀνδραπόδων καὶ ὑποζυγίων καὶ τριηραρχι<κ>αὶ καὶ τραπεζιτικαί. (*3*) οὗτοι μὲν οὖν ταύτας δικάζουσιν ἐμμήνους εἰσάγοντες, οἱ δ’ ἀποδέκται τοῖς τελώναις καὶ κατὰ τῶν τελωνῶν, τὰ μὲν μέχρι δέκα δραχμῶν ὄντες κύριοι, τὰ δ’ ἄλλ’ εἰς τὸ δικαστήριον εἰσάγοντες ἔμμηνα.

(**53**) κληροῦσι δὲ καὶ <τοὺς> τετταράκοντα, τέτταρας ἐκ τῆς φυλῆς ἑκάστης, πρὸς οὓς τὰς ἄλλας δίκας λαγχάνουσιν· οἳ πρότερον μὲν ἦσαν τριάκοντα καὶ κατὰ δήμους περιόντες ἐδίκαζον, μετὰ δὲ τὴν ἐπὶ τῶν τριάκοντα ὀλιγαρχίαν τετταράκοντα γεγόνασιν. (*2*) καὶ τὰ μὲν μέχρι δέκα δραχμῶν αὐτοτελεῖς εἰσι δ[ικ]άζε[ι]ν, τὰ δ’ ὑπὲρ τοῦτο τὸ τίμημα τοῖς διαιτηταῖς παραδιδόασιν. οἱ δὲ παραλαβόντες, ἐὰν μὴ δύνωνται διαλῦσαι, γιγνώσκουσι, κἂν μὲν ἀμφοτέροις ἀρέσκῃ τὰ γνωσθέντα καὶ ἐμμένωσιν ἔχει τέλος ἡ δίκη. ἂν δ’ ὁ ἕτερος ἐφῇ τῶν ἀντιδίκων εἰς τὸ δικαστήριον, ἐμβαλόντες τὰς μαρτυρίας καὶ τὰς προκλήσεις καὶ τοὺς νόμους εἰς ἐχίνους, χωρὶς μὲν τὰς τοῦ διώκοντος χωρὶς δὲ τὰς τοῦ φεύγοντος, καὶ τούτους κατασημηνάμενοι καὶ τὴν γνῶσιν τοῦ διαιτητοῦ γεγραμμένην ἐν γραμματείῳ προσαρτήσαντες παραδιδόασι τοῖς δ´ τοῖς τὴν φυλὴν τοῦ φεύγοντος δικάζουσιν. (*3*) οἱ δὲ παραλαβόντες εἰσάγουσιν εἰς τὸ δικαστήριον, τὰ μὲν ἐντὸς χιλίων εἰς ἕνα καὶ διακοσίους, τὰ δ’ ὑπὲρ χιλίας εἰς ἕνα καὶ τετρακοσίους. οὐκ ἔξεστι δ’ οὔτε νόμοις οὔτε προκλήσεσι οὔτε μαρτυρίαις ἀλλ’ ἢ ταῖς παρὰ τοῦ διαιτητοῦ χρῆσθαι ταῖς εἰς τοὺς ἐχίνους ἐμβεβλημέναις. (*4*) διαιτηταὶ δ’ εἰσὶν οἷς ἂν ἑξηκοστὸν ἔτος ᾖ· τοῦτο δὲ δῆλον ἐκ τῶν ἀρχόντων καὶ τῶν ἐπωνύμων. εἰσὶ γὰρ ἐπώνυμοι δέκα μὲν οἱ τῶν φυλῶν, δύο δὲ καὶ τετταράκοντα οἱ

52. 2. ἐρανικαὶ καὶ κοινωνικαὶ … τριηραρχι<κ>αὶ καὶ τραπεζιτικαί J. B. Bury (*CR*): ἐρανικὰς καὶ κοινωνικὰς … τριηραρχιὰς καὶ τραπεζιτικάς L.

53. 1. <τοὺς> Kaibel & Wilamowitz[1].

περιόντες L: περι<ι>όντες Kenyon[1–3].

ἐπὶ τῶν τριάκοντα: ἐπὶ written above L.

53. 2. δ[ικ]άζε[ι]ν Wilcken.

ἐμμεν<εῖν ὁμολογ>ῶσιν D. M. Lewis (*ap.* Rhodes, *Comm. Ath. Pol.* 589).

(*2*) They allot as *eisagogeis*, who introduce the monthly suits, five men, each one for two tribes. The monthly suits are: for a dowry, if a man owes it and fails to pay; and if anybody borrows at a drachma interest and defaults; and if anybody wishing to work in the agora borrows capital from somebody; also for battery, friendly loans, associations, concerning slaves and yoke-animals, trierarchic suits and banking suits. (*3*) They introduce these and try them as monthly suits. But the *apodektai* introduce suits by and against tax-collectors, having definitive power up to ten drachmae, and introducing the others into the lawcourts as monthly suits.

(**53**) They allot also the Forty, four from each tribe, before whom plaintiffs obtain their hearing in the other private suits. Previously they were thirty, and went round the demes trying cases, but after the oligarchy of the Thirty they have become forty. (*2*) The cases up to ten drachmae they have independent authority to try, but those over that assessment they hand over to the *diaitetai.* These take them over, and if they are not able to make a settlement they decide, and if both parties are satisfied with the decision and abide by it the case is completed. But if either of the opposing litigants appeals to the lawcourt, they insert in jars the testimonies, challenges and laws, those of the plaintiff and of the defendant separately, and they seal these, attach the decision of the *diaitetes* written on a board, and hand them over to the 4 who are trying cases for the defendant's tribe. (*3*) These take them over and introduce them into the lawcourt, those up to a thousand a court of two hudred and one, and those over a thousand four hundred and one. It is not permitted to use laws, challenges or testimonies except those inserted in the jars from the *diaitetes*. (*4*) The *diaitetai* are those in their sixtieth year. This is clear from the archons and the eponymous heroes: for there are ten eponymous heroes of the tribes and forty-two of the age-classes. The

τῶν ἡλικιῶν· οἱ δὲ ἔφηβοι ἐγγραφόμενοι πρότερον μὲν εἰς λελευκωμένα γραμματεῖα ἐνεγράφοντο, καὶ ἐπεγράφοντο αὐτοῖς ὅ τ' ἄρχων ἐφ' οὗ ἐνεγράφησαν καὶ ὁ ἐπώνυμος ὁ τῷ προτέρῳ ἔτει δεδιαιτηκώς, νῦν δ' εἰς στήλην χαλκῆν ἀναγράφονται, καὶ ἵσταται ἡ στήλη πρὸ τοῦ βουλευτηρίου παρὰ τοὺς ἐπωνύμους. (*5*) τὸν δὲ τελευταῖον τῶν ἐπωνύμων λαβόντες οἱ τετταράκοντα διανέμουσιν αὐτοῖς τὰς διαίτας καὶ ἐπικληροῦσιν ἃς ἕκαστος διαιτήσει· καὶ ἀναγκαῖον ἃς ἂν ἕκαστος λάχῃ διαίτας ἐκδιαιτᾶν. ὁ γὰρ νόμος, ἄν τις μὴ γένηται διαιτητὴς τῆς ἡλικίας αὐτῷ καθηκούσης ἄτιμον εἶναι κελεύει, πλὴν ἐὰν τύχῃ ἀρχὴν ἄρχων τινὰ ἐν ἐκείνῳ τῷ ἐνιαυτῷ ἢ ἀποδημῶν· οὗτοι δ' ἀτελεῖς εἰσὶ μόνοι. (*6*) ἔστιν δὲ καὶ εἰσαγγέλλειν εἰς τοὺς διαιτητάς ἐάν τις ἀδικηθῇ ὑπὸ τοῦ διαιτητοῦ, κἄν τινος καταγνῶσιν, ἀτιμοῦσθαι κελεύουσιν οἱ νόμοι· ἔφεσις δ' ἔστι καὶ τούτοις. (*7*) χρῶνται δὲ τοῖς ἐπωνύμοις καὶ πρὸς τὰς στρατείας, καὶ ὅταν ἡλικίαν ἐκπέμπωσι προγράφουσιν ἀπὸ τίνος ἄρχοντος καὶ ἐπωνύμου μέχρι τίνων δεῖ στρατεύεσθαι.

(**54**) κληροῦσι δὲ καὶ τάσδε τὰς ἀρχάς· ὁδοποιοὺς πέντε, οἷς προστέτακται δημοσίους ἐργάτας ἔχουσι τὰς ὁδοὺς ἐπισκευάζειν.

(*2*) καὶ λογιστὰς δέκα καὶ συνηγόρους τούτοις δέκα, πρὸς οὓς ἅπαντας ἀνάγκη τοὺς τὰς ἀρχὰς ἄρξαντας λόγον ἀπενεγκεῖν. οὗτοι γάρ εἰσι μόνοι <οἱ> τοῖς ὑπευθύνοις λογιζόμενοι καὶ τὰς εὐθύνας εἰς τὸ δικαστήριον εἰσάγοντες. κἂν μέν τινα κλέπτοντ' ἐξελέγξωσι, κλοπὴν οἱ δικασταὶ καταγιγνώσκουσι, καὶ τὸ γνωσθὲν ἀποτίνεται δεκαπλοῦν· ἐὰν δέ τινα δῶρα λαβόντα ἐπιδείξωσιν καὶ καταγνῶσιν οἱ δικασταί, δώρων τιμῶσιν, ἀποτίνεται δὲ καὶ τοῦτο δεκαπλοῦν. ἂν δ' ἀδικεῖν καταγνῶσιν, ἀδικίου τιμῶσιν, ἀποτίνεται δὲ τοῦθ' ἁπλοῦν, ἐὰν πρὸ τῆς θ´ πρυτανείας ἐκτ<ε>ίσῃ τις, εἰ δὲ μή, διπλοῦται. τὸ <δὲ> δεκαπλοῦν οὐ διπλοῦται.

(*3*) κληροῦσι δὲ καὶ γραμματέα τὸν κατὰ πρυτανείαν καλούμενον, ὃς τῶν γραμμάτων ἐστὶ κύριος, καὶ τὰ ψηφίσματα τὰ γιγνόμενα φυλάττει καὶ τἆλλα πάντα ἀντιγράφεται, καὶ παρακάθηται τῇ βουλῇ. πρότερον μὲν οὖν οὗτος ἦν χειροτονητός, καὶ τοὺς ἐνδοξοτάτους καὶ πιστοτάτους

53. 6. εἰς τοὺς διαιτητάς L: δικαστάς some lexica.

54. 2. μόνοι <οἱ>J. B. Mayor (*CR*): εἰσι<ν οἱ> Blass[2–3], perhaps {μον}οἱ Rhodes.

ἐκτ<ε>ίσῃ Kaibel & Wilamowitz[1].

τὸ <δὲ> δεκαπλοῦν Kenyon[1].

epheboi when they were entered used to be entered on whitened boards, and the names were written on them of the archon under whom they were entered and the eponymous hero of the previous year's *diaitetai;* but now they are written up on a bronze *stele*, and the *stele* is erected in front of the council house by the eponymous heroes. (5) The Forty take the last of the eponymous heroes and distribute the arbitrations among the men, drawing lots for which cases each is to arbitrate; and it is obligatory for each man to complete the arbitrations of whichever cases fall to him. For the law enjoins that if anybody fails to act as a *diaitetes* when his age-class has come he is to be *atimos*, unless he happens to be holding some office or to be abroad: only these are exempt. (*6*) It is possible to make an *eisangelia* to the *diaitetai* if one is wronged by the *diaitetes*, and if they convict anybody the laws enjoin *atimia*; but it is possible for these to appeal. (*7*) They use the eponymous heroes also for military campaigns, and when they send out an age range they prescribe from which archon and hero to which the men must go on the campaign.

(**54**) They allot also the following officials: five road-builders, who are instructed with public workmen to repair the roads.

(*2*) And ten *logistai* and ten advocates for them, before whom all who have held offices are obliged to bring their accounts; for it is these alone who check the accounts for those subject to *euthynai* and introduce their *euthynai* into the lawcourt. And if they establish that a man is an embezzler, the jurors convict him of embezzlement, and the amount decided is repaid tenfold; if they demonstrate that a man has taken bribes and the jurors convict him, they make an assessment for bribery, and this also is repaid tenfold; if they convict him of misdemeanour, they make an assessment for misdemeanour, and this is repaid simply if a man pays before the 9th prytany, or if he does not it is doubled. The tenfold payment is not doubled.

(*3*) They allot also the secretary called the secretary by the prytany, who has power over the documents, guards the decrees which are enacted and copies everything else, and he sits in attendance on the council. Previously this man was elected, and they used to elect the most

ἐχειροτόνουν· καὶ γὰρ ἐν ταῖς στήλαις πρὸς ταῖς συμμαχίαις καὶ προξενίαις καὶ πολιτείαις οὗτος ἀναγράφεται. νῦν δὲ γέγονε κληρωτός. (*4*) κληροῦσι δὲ καὶ ἐπὶ τοὺς νόμους ἕτερον, ὃς παρακάθηται τῇ βουλῇ καὶ ἀντιγράφεται καὶ οὗτος πάντας. (*5*) χειροτονεῖ δὲ καὶ ὁ δῆμος γραμματέα τὸν ἀναγνωσόμενον αὐτῷ καὶ τῇ βουλῇ, καὶ οὗτος οὐδενός ἐστι κύριος ἀλλὰ τοῦ ἀναγνῶναι.

(*6*) κληροῖ δὲ καὶ ἱεροποιοὺς δέκα, τοὺς ἐπὶ τὰ ἐκθύματα καλουμένους, οἳ τά τε μαντευτὰ ἱερὰ θύουσιν, κἄν τι καλλιερῆσαι δέῃ καλλιεροῦσι μετὰ τῶν μάντεων. (*7*) κληροῖ δὲ καὶ ἑτέρους δέκα, τοὺς κατ' ἐνιαυτὸν καλουμένους, οἳ θυσίας τέ τινας θύουσι καὶ τὰς πεντετηρίδας ἁπάσας διοικοῦσιν πλὴν Παναθηναίων. εἰσὶ δὲ πεντετηρίδες μία μ[ὲν ἡ εἰ]ς Δῆλον (ἔστι δὲ καὶ ἑπτετηρὶς ἐνταῦθα), δευτέρα δὲ Βραυρώνια, τρίτη [δ' Ἡράκλ]ẹια, τετάρτη δ' Ἐλευσίνια, ε´ δὲ Παναθήναια, καὶ τούτων οὐδεμία ἐν τῷ αὐτῷ ἐγγίγνετ[αι. νῦ]ṇ δὲ πρόσκειται καὶ Ἡφαίστια, ἐπὶ Κηφισοφῶντος ἄρχοντος.

(*8*) κληροῦσι δὲ καὶ εἰς Σαλαμῖνα ἄρχοντα, καὶ εἰς Πειραιέα δήμαρχον, οἳ τά τε Διονύσια ποιοῦσιν ἑκατέρωθι καὶ χορηγοὺς καθιστᾶσιν. ἐν Σαλαμῖνι δὲ καὶ τοὔνομα τοῦ ἄρχοντος ἀναγράφεται.

(**55**) αὗται μὲν οὖν αἱ ἀρχαὶ κληρωταί τε καὶ κύριαι τῶν εἰρημένων [πάν]των εἰσίν. οἱ δὲ καλούμενοι ἐννέα ἄρχοντες τὸ μὲν ἐξ ἀρχῆς ὃν τρόπον καθίσταντο εἴρηται· [νῦν] δὲ κληροῦσιν θεσμοθέτας μὲν ἓξ καὶ γραμματέα τούτοις, ἔτι δ' ἄρχοντα καὶ βασιλέα καὶ πολέμαρχον, κατὰ μέρος ἐξ ἑκάστης φυλῆς. (*2*) δοκιμάζονται δ' οὗτοι πρῶτον μὲν ἐν τῇ βουλῇ τοῖς φ´ πλὴν τοῦ γραμματέως. οὗτος δ' ἐν δικαστηρίῳ μόνον ὥσπερ οἱ ἄλλοι ἄρχοντες (πάντες γὰρ καὶ οἱ κληρωτοὶ καὶ οἱ χειροτονητοὶ δοκιμασθέντες ἄρχουσιν)·

54. 5. ἀλλὰ τοῦ L: ἀλλ' ἢ H. Richards (*CR*) *et al.*

54. 7. μ[ὲν ἡ εἰ]ς Kenyon[1].

τρίτη [δ' Ἡράκλ]ẹια Kenyon[1] e Poll. VIII. 107, cf. Chambers: . . . . . ṭα Wilcken.

ἐν τῷ αὐτῷ ἐγγίγνετ[αι (γινετ[with the letters εν written above) L: τῷ αὐτῷ ἐν[ιαυτῷ] γίγνε[ται Kaibel & Wilamowitz[1–2] *et al.*

[καὶ Ἡ]φαίσ[τια] Blass[2], confirmed by Wilcken, Kenyon[4–5], Chambers: Ἀμφιάραια P. Foucart *et al.*, not the text of L but perhaps the author's text.

55. 1. [πάν]των Chambers: [πραγμάτ]ων Kenyon[1–3], [ἁπάντ]ων P. N. Papageorgios, [πράξε]ων Kaibel & Wilamowitz[3], [πάντ]ων Kenyon[4–5].

[νῦν] Kenyon[1].

distinguished and reliable men: for in *stelai* concerned with alliances, proxenies and citizenship grants this man is written up. But now he has become allotted. (*4*) They allot also another secretary, in charge of the laws: he sits in attendance on the council, and he also copies them all. (*5*) And the *demos* elects the secretary who is to read documents to itself and the council, and he has no power except that of reading.

(*6*) The *demos* allots ten *hieropoioi*, called those in charge of expiatory sacrifices, who perform the sacrificial rites ordered by oracles, and if there is a need to seek good omens they seek them together with the soothsayers. (*7*) It also allots ten others, those called yearly, who perform some sacrifices and administer all the quadrennial festivals except the Panathenaea. The five-yearly festivals are: first, that to Delos (there is also a seven-yearly festival there); second, the Brauronia; third, the Heraclea; fourth, the Eleusinia; 5th, the Panathenaea; and none of these falls in the same year. Now there has been added also the Hephaestia, in the archonship of Cephisophon.

(*8*) They allot also an archon for Salamis and a demarch for Piraeus, who conduct the Dionysia in each place and appoint the *choregoi*. In Salamis in addition the name of the archon is written up.

(**55**) Those offices are allotted, and have power over all the matters stated. As for the so-called nine archons, the manner in which they were appointed from the beginning has been stated. Now they allot six *thesmothetai* and a secretary for them, and also the archon, *basileus* and polemarch, in turn from each tribe. (*2*) These are vetted first in the council of 500 apart from the secretary. He like the other officials is vetted in a lawcourt only (for all allotted and elected officials serve after being vetted); but the nine archons

οἱ δ' ἐννέα ἄρχοντες ἔν τε τῇ βουλῇ καὶ πάλιν ἐν δικαστηρίῳ, καὶ πρότερον μὲν οὐκ ἦρχεν ὅντιν' ἀποδοκιμάσειεν ἡ βουλή, νῦν δ' ἔφεσίς ἐστιν εἰς τὸ δικαστήριον, καὶ τοῦτο κύριόν ἐστι τῆς δοκιμασίας. (*3*) ἐπερωτῶσιν δ', ὅταν δοκιμάζωσιν, πρῶτον μὲν "τίς σοι πατὴρ καὶ πόθεν τῶν δήμων, καὶ τίς πατρὸς πατήρ, καὶ τίς μήτηρ, καὶ τίς μητρὸς πατὴρ καὶ πόθεν τῶν δήμων;" μετὰ δὲ ταῦτα, εἰ ἔστιν αὐτῷ Ἀπόλλων Πατρῷος καὶ Ζεὺς Ἑρκεῖος, καὶ ποῦ ταῦτα τὰ ἱερά ἐστιν, εἶτα ἠρία εἰ ἔστιν καὶ ποῦ ταῦτα, ἔπειτα γονέας εἰ εὖ ποιεῖ, καὶ τὰ τέλη <εἰ> τελεῖ, καὶ τὰς στρατείας εἰ ἐστράτευται. ταῦτα δ' ἀνερωτήσας, "κάλει" φησὶν "τούτων τοὺς μάρτυρας." (*4*) ἐπειδὰν δὲ παράσχηται τοὺς μάρτυρας, ἐπερωτᾷ "τούτου βούλεταί τις κατηγορεῖν;" κἂν μὲν ᾖ τις κατήγορος, δοὺς κατηγορίαν καὶ ἀπολογίαν οὕτω δίδωσιν ἐν μὲν τῇ βουλῇ τὴν ἐπιχειροτονίαν, ἐν δὲ τῷ δικαστηρίῳ τὴν ψῆφον· ἐὰν δὲ μηδεὶς βούληται κατηγορεῖν, εὐθὺς δίδωσι τὴν ψῆφον. καὶ πρότερον μὲν εἷς ἐνέβαλλε τὴν ψῆφον, νῦν δ' ἀνάγκη πάντας ἐστὶ διαψηφίζεσθαι περὶ αὐτῶν, ἵνα ἄν τις πονηρὸς ὢν ἀπαλλάξῃ τοὺς κατηγόρους, ἐπὶ τοῖς δικασταῖς γένηται τοῦτον ἀποδοκιμάσαι. (*5*) δοκιμασθέν<τες> δὲ τοῦτον τὸν τρόπον βαδίζουσι πρὸς τὸν λίθον ἐφ' ο[ὗ] τὰ τόμι' ἐστίν, ἐφ' οὗ καὶ οἱ διαιτηταὶ ὀμόσαντες ἀποφαίνονται τὰς διαίτας καὶ οἱ μάρτυρες ἐξόμνυνται τὰς μαρτυρίας· ἀναβάντες δ' ἐπὶ τοῦτον ὀμνύουσιν δικαίως ἄρξειν καὶ κατὰ τοὺς νόμους, καὶ δῶρα μὴ λήψεσθαι τῆς ἀρχῆς ἕνεκα, κἄν τι λάβωσι ἀνδριάντα ἀναθήσειν χρυσοῦν. ἐντεῦθεν δ' ὀμόσαντες εἰς ἀκρόπολιν βαδίζουσιν καὶ πάλιν ἐκεῖ ταὐτὰ ὀμνύουσι, καὶ μετὰ ταῦτ' εἰς τὴν ἀρχὴν εἰσέρχονται.

(**56**) λαμβάνουσι δὲ καὶ παρέδρους ὅ τ' ἄρχων καὶ ὁ βασιλεὺς καὶ ὁ πολέμαρχος δύο ἕκαστος, οὓς ἂν βούληται, καὶ οὗτοι δοκιμάζονται ἐν τῷ δικαστηρίῳ πρὶν παρεδρεύειν, καὶ εὐθύνας διδόασιν ἐπὰν παρεδρεύσωσιν.

(*2*) καὶ ὁ μὲν ἄρχων εὐθὺς εἰσελθὼν πρῶτον μὲν κηρύττει, ὅσα τις εἶχεν πρὶν αὐτὸν εἰσελθεῖν εἰς τὴν ἀρχήν, ταῦτ' ἔχειν καὶ κρατεῖν μέχρι ἀρχῆς τέλους. (*3*) ἔπειτα χορηγοὺς τραγῳδοῖς καθίστησι τρεῖς, ἐξ ἁπάντων

55. 3. <εἰ> τελεῖ Kaibel & Wilamowitz.

55. 5. δοκιμασθέν<τες> W. G. Rutherford and H. Richards (*CR*).

ἐφ' ο[ὗ] Leeuwen, confirmed by Kenyon, Chambers: ὑφ' ᾧ Kaibel & Wilamowitz[1–2], ἐφ' ᾧ Blass, Kaibel & Wilamowitz[3].

are vetted in the council and again in a lawcourt. Previously anybody who was rejected in the vetting by the council did not serve, but now there is reference to the lawcourt, and that has decisive power in the vetting. (*3*) When they vet them, they ask first, 'Who is your father, and from which of the demes, and who are your father's father and your mother and your mother's father, and from which of the demes?' After that, whether he has a cult of Apollo Patroös and Zeus Herkeios, and where those shrines are; then whether he has family tombs and where they are; next whether he treats his parents well, and whether he pays his taxes, and whether he has performed his military service. After asking these questions, the magistrate says, 'Call the witnesses to these things'. (*4*) When he has provided his witnesses, he asks, 'Does anybody wish to accuse this man?' If there is an accuser, he grants accusation and defence, and then he grants the vote by hand in the council or by ballot in the lawcourt. If nobody wishes to accuse, he grants the ballot immediately; and previously one man used to cast his ballot, but now it is obligatory for all to vote about them, so that if a crooked man has disposed of his accusers it shall be possible for the jurors to reject him in the vetting. (*5*) When they have been vetted in this manner, they proceed to the stone on which the sliced victims have been placed (on which also the *diaitetai* swear before declaring their arbitrations, and witnesses swear when denying their testimony). Climbing on to this, they swear that they will exercise their office justly and in accordance with the laws, and will not accept bribes on account of their office, or if they do accept anything they will dedicate a golden statue. After swearing there they proceed to the acropolis and swear the same again there, and after that they enter on their office.

(**56**) The archon, *basileus* and polemarch each take two *paredroi*, whoever they wish, and these are vetted in the lawcourt before serving and submit *euthynai* after they have served.

(*2*) The archon, as soon as he has entered office, first proclaims that, whatever any people had before he entered office, they shall have and control this until the end of his office. (*3*) Next he appoints three *choregoi*

Ἀθηναίων τοὺς πλουσιωτάτους· πρότερον δὲ καὶ κωμῳδοῖς καθίστη πέντε, νῦν δὲ τούτους αἱ φυλαὶ φέρουσιν. ἔπειτα παραλαβὼν τοὺς χορηγούς τοὺς ἐνηνεγμένους ὑπὸ τῶν φυλῶν εἰς Διονύσια ἀνδράσιν καὶ παισὶν καὶ κωμῳδοῖς, καὶ εἰς Θαργήλια ἀνδράσιν καὶ παισίν (εἰσὶ δ’ οἱ μὲν εἰς Διονύσια κατὰ φυλάς, εἰς Θαργήλια <δὲ> δυοῖν φυλαῖν εἷς· παρέχει δ’ ἐν μέρει ἑκατέρα τῶν φυλῶν), τούτοις τὰς ἀντιδόσεις ποιεῖ καὶ τὰς σκήψεις εἰσ[άγει, ἐά]ν τις ἢ λελῃτουργηκέναι φῇ πρότερον ταύτην τὴν λῃτουργίαν, ἢ ἀτελὴς εἶναι λελῃτουργηκὼς ἑτέραν λῃτουργίαν καὶ τῶν χρόνων αὐτῷ τῆς ἀτελείας μὴ ἐξεληλυθότων, ἢ τὰ ἔτη μὴ γεγονέναι· δεῖ γὰρ τὸν τοῖς παισὶν χορηγοῦντα ὑπὲρ τετταράκοντα ἔτη γεγονέναι. καθίστησι δὲ καὶ εἰς Δῆλον χορηγοὺς καὶ ἀρχιθέω[ρον τ]ῷ τριακοντορίῳ τῷ τοὺς ᾐθέους ἄγοντι. (*4*) πομπῶν δ’ ἐπιμελεῖται τῆς τε τῷ Ἀσκληπιῷ γιγνομένης, ὅταν οἰκουρῶσι μύσται, καὶ τῆς Διονυσίων τῶν Μεγάλων μετὰ τῶν ἐπιμελητῶν, οὓς πρότερον μὲν ὁ δῆμος ἐχειροτόνει δέκα ὄντας, καὶ τὰ εἰς τὴν πομπὴν ἀναλώματα παρ’ αὑτῶν ἀνήλισκον, νῦν δ’ ἕνα τῆς φυλῆς ἑκάστης κληροῖ καὶ δίδωσιν εἰς τὴν κατασκευὴν ἑκατὸν μνᾶς. (*5*) ἐπιμελεῖται δὲ καὶ τῆς εἰς Θαργήλια καὶ τῆς τῷ Διὶ τῷ Σωτῆρι. διοικεῖ δὲ καὶ τὸν ἀγῶνα τῶν Διονυσίων οὗτος καὶ τῶν Θαργηλίων. ἑορτῶν μὲν οὖν ἐπιμελεῖται τούτων. (*6*) γραφαὶ δὲ καὶ δίκαι λαγχάνονται πρὸς αὐτόν, ἃς ἀνακρίνας εἰς τὸ δικαστήριον εἰσάγει, γονέων κακώσεως (αὗται δ’ εἰσὶν ἀζήμιοι τῷ βουλομένῳ διώκειν), ὀρφανῶν κακώσεως (αὗται δ’ εἰσὶ κατὰ τῶν ἐπιτρόπων), ἐπικλήρου κακώσε[ω]ς ([α]ὗ[τ]αι δ’ εἰσὶ κατὰ τῶν ἐπιτρόπων καὶ τῶν συνοικούντων), οἴκου ὀρφανικοῦ κακώσεως (εἰσὶ δὲ καὶ αὗται κ[ατὰ τ]ῶν ἐπιτρό[π]ων), παρανοίας, ἐάν τις αἰτιᾶταί τινα παρανοοῦντα τὰ π̣α̣[τρῷα ἀ]πολλύν[αι], εἰς δατητῶν αἵρεσιν, ἐάν τις μὴ θέλῃ [τὰ] κοινὰ [ὄντα

56. 3. <δὲ> δυοῖν φυλαῖν: <δὲ> Kenyon[1], δυοῖν φυλαῖν Herwerden & Leeuwen, δυεῖν φυλαῖν L.

ἀρχιθέω[ρον τ]ῷ J. H. Lipsius, confirmed as fitting the space Kenyon[4], Chambers: ἀρχιθεώ[ρους C. Torr (*CR*).

56. 6. κακώσε[ω]ς ([α]ὗ[τ]αι Chambers, cf. Kenyon[1]: after κακώσεως unless there was a gap in the papyrus a longer supplement is needed Kenyon[4–5].

αὗται κ[ατὰ τ]ῶν ἐπιτρό[π]ων restored Kenyon[1], read thus by Chambers.

τὰ π̣α̣[τρῷα ἀ]πολλύν[αι] W. Wyse (*CR*), π̣α̣ read by Chambers: ὑπάρχοντα Blass, judged suitable for the space Kenyon[4].

δατητῶν Kenyon[1]: διαιτητ(ῶν) L.

for the tragedians, the richest men from all the Athenians; previously he also used to appoint five for the comedians, but now the tribes supply these. Next he takes over the *choregoi* supplied by the tribes for men, boys and comedians for the Dionysia, and for men and boys for the Thargelia (those for the Dionysia are appointed by tribe; those for the Thargelia one for two tribes, and each of the two tribes supplies the *choregos* in turn). For these he holds *antidoseis*, and he introduces claims for exemption, if anybody states that he has performed this liturgy previously or that he is exempt because he has performed another liturgy and his period of exemption has not yet expired, or that he has not yet reached the age (for a man serving as *chorgeos* for boys must be over forty years old). He also appoints for Delos *choregoi* and the *architheoros* for the triaconter which takes the young men. (*4*) He takes care of processions: that for Asclepius, when the initiates stay at home, and for the Great Dionysia together with the *epimeletai*: previously the *demos* used to elect ten men, and they paid the expenses for the procession from their own resources, but now it allots one for each tribe and gives a hundred minas for the paraphernalia. (*5*) He takes care also of the processions for the Thargelia and for Zeus Soter. Also he administers the competitions at the Dionysia and the Thargelia. Those are the festivals of which he takes care. (*6*) Public and private lawsuits fall to him, and after holding the *anakrisis* he introduces them into the lawcourt: for maltreatment of parents (in these whoever wishes may prosecute without risk of penalty); for maltreatment of orphans (these are against the guardians); for maltreatment of *epikleroi* (these are against the guardians and the husbands); for maltreatment of an orphans's estate (these also are against the guardians); for insanity, if anybody accuses somebody of squandering his ancestral estate; for appointment of distributors, if anybody objects to the administration of property in

νέμε]σ<θαι>, εἰς ἐπιτροπῆς κατάστασιν, εἰς ἐπιτροπῆς διαδικασίαν, εἰς ἐ[μφανῶν κατάστασ]ιν, ἐπίτροπον αὑτὸν ἐγγράψαι, κλήρων καὶ ἐπικλήρων ἐπι[δικασίαι. (*7*) ἐπιμελεῖτ]αι δὲ καὶ τῶν ὀρφανῶν καὶ τῶν ἐπικλήρων, καὶ τῶν γυναικῶν ὅσαι ἂν τελευτή[σαντος τοῦ ἀνδρ]ὸς σκή[πτω]νται κύειν· καὶ κύριός ἐστι τοῖς ἀδικοῦσιν ἐπιβάλ[λειν ἢ εἰσάγειν εἰς] τὸ δικαστήριον. μισθοῖ δὲ καὶ τοὺς οἴκους τῶν ὀρφανῶν καὶ τῶν ἐπικλ[ήρων, ἕως ἄν τις τετταρ]ακαιδε[κέ]τις γένηται, καὶ τὰ ἀποτιμήματα λαμβάν[ει· καὶ τοὺς ἐπιτρόπους], ἐὰν μὴ διδῶσι τοῖς παισὶ τὸν σῖτον, οὗτος εἰσπράττει.

(**57**) καὶ ὁ [μὲν ἄρχων ἐπιμελεῖ]ται τούτων. ὁ δὲ βασιλεὺς πρῶτον μὲν μυστηρίων ἐπιμελεῖτ[αι μετὰ τῶν ἐπιμελητῶν ὣ]ν ὁ δῆμος χειροτονεῖ, δύο μὲν ἐξ Ἀθηναίων ἁπάντων, ἕνα δ᾽ [ἐξ Εὐμολπιδῶν, ἕν]α δ᾽ ἐκ Κηρύκων. ἔπειτα Διονυσίων τῶν ἐπὶ Ληναίῳ. ταῦτα δέ ἐστι [πομπή τε καὶ ἀγών· τ]ὴν μὲν οὖν πομπὴν κοινῇ πέμπουσιν ὅ τε βασιλεὺς καὶ οἱ ἐπιμεληταί, τὸν δὲ ἀγῶνα διατίθησιν ὁ βασιλεύς. τίθησι δὲ καὶ τοὺς τῶν λαμπάδων ἀγῶνας ἅπαντας· ὡς δ᾽ ἔπος εἰπεῖν καὶ τὰς πατρίους θυσίας διοικεῖ οὗτος πάσας. (*2*) γραφαὶ δὲ λαγχάνονται πρὸς αὐτὸν ἀσεβείας, κἄν τις ἱερωσύνης ἀμφισβητῇ πρός τινα. διαδικάζει δὲ καὶ τοῖς γένεσι καὶ τοῖς ἱερεῦσι τὰς ἀμφισβητήσεις τὰς ὑπὲρ τῶν ἱερῶν ἁπάσας

56. 6. [τὰ] κοινὰ [ὄντα νέμε]σ<θαι> Chambers, cf. Blass[4]: κοινὰ [τὰ ὄντα νέμεσθαι] Kenyon[1], perhaps τὰ κοινωνικὰ D. M. Lewis (*ap*. Rhodes, *Comm. Ath. Pol.* 631).
εἰς ἐ[μφανῶν κατάστασ]ιν Kaibel & Wilamowitz[1].
56. 6–7. ἐπι[δικασίαι. ἐπιμελεῖτ]αι Kenyon[1].
56. 7. τελευτή[σαντος τοῦ ἀνδρ]ὸς σκή[πτω]νται Kenyon[1].
ἐπιβάλ[λειν ἢ εἰσάγειν εἰς] J. H. Lipsius.
ἐπικλ[ήρων, ἕως ἄν τις τετταρ]ακαιδε[κέ]τις Blass[1] (τεις with the letter η written above L).
λαμβάν[ει· καὶ τοὺς ἐπιτρόπους] Kaibel & Wilamowitz[1].
57. 1. ὁ [μὲν ἄρχων Blass.
ἐπιμελεῖ]ται τούτων Kenyon[1].
ἐπιμελεῖτ[αι μετὰ τῶν ἐπιμελητῶν Kenyon[1].
ὣ]ν Blass[2].
[ἐξ Εὐμολπιδῶν, ἕν]α δ᾽ ἐκ Κηρύκων Kaibel & Wilamowitz[1]: ἐξ et ἐκ omitted Kenyon[1].
ἐπὶ Ληναίῳ J. E. B. Mayor *et al.* (*CR*): ἐπιληναίων L, retained by Kaibel & Wilamowitz[3], Chambers.
[πομπή τε καὶ ἀγών. τ]ὴν P. N. Papageorgios.

common; for the appointment of a guardian; for the adjudication of a guardianship; for displaying to public view; for registering oneself as a guardian; adjudications of estates and *epikleroi*. (*7*) Also he takes care of orphans and *epikleroi*, and of women who claim to be pregnant at the death of their husband; and he has power to impose a summary penalty on those who do wrong or to introduce a case into the lawcourt. He lets out the estates of orphans, and of *epikleroi* until they reach the age of fourteen; and he receives the valuations; and if guardians fail to provide food for the boys he exacts it.

(**57**) That is what the archon takes care of. The *basileus*, first, takes care of the Mysteries together with the *epimeletai* whom the *demos* elects, two from all Athenians, one from the Eumolpidae and one from the Kerykes. Next, the Dionysia at the Lenaeum. This is a procession and a competition: the procession is dispatched jointly by the *basileus* and the *epimeletai*, and the competition is organised by the *basileus*. He also stages all the torch competitions; and, so to say, he administers all the traditional sacrifices. (*2*) Public lawsuits fall to him: for impiety; and if anybody has a dispute with somebody about a priesthood. Also it is he who adjudicates for *gene* and priests all their disputes about sacred

οὗτος. λαγχάνονται δὲ καὶ αἱ τοῦ φόνου δίκαι πᾶσαι πρὸς τοῦτον, καὶ ὁ προαγορεύων εἴργεσθαι τῶν νομίμων οὗτός ἐστιν. (*3*) εἰσὶ δὲ φόνου δίκαι καὶ τραύματος, ἂν μὲν ἐκ προνοίας ἀποκτείνῃ ἢ τρώσῃ, ἐν Ἀρείῳ πάγῳ, καὶ φαρμάκων, ἐὰν ἀποκτείνῃ δούς, καὶ πυρκαϊᾶς· ταῦτα γὰρ ἡ βουλὴ μόνα δικάζει. τῶν δ' ἀκουσίων καὶ βουλεύσεως, κἂν οἰκέτην ἀποκτείνῃ τις ἢ μέτοικον ἢ ξένον, οἱ ἐπὶ Παλλαδίῳ. ἐὰν δ' ἀποκτεῖναι μέν τις ὁμολογῇ, φῇ δὲ κατὰ τοὺς νόμους, οἷον μοιχὸν λαβὼν ἢ ἐν πολέμῳ ἀγνοήσας ἢ ἐν ἄθλῳ ἀγωνιζόμενος, τούτῳ ἐπὶ Δελφινίῳ δικάζουσιν. ἐὰν δὲ φεύγων φυγὴν ὧν αἴδεσίς ἐστιν αἰτίαν ἔχῃ ἀποκτεῖναι ἢ τρῶσαί τινα, τούτῳ δ' ἐν Φρεάτου δικάζουσιν· ὁ δ' ἀπολογεῖται προσορμισάμενος ἐν πλοίῳ. (*4*) δικάζουσι δ' οἱ λαχόντες ταῦ[τ<α να΄>] ἄ[νδρε]ς πλὴν τῶν ἐν Ἀρείῳ πάγῳ γιγνομένων, εἰσάγει δ' ὁ βασιλεύς, καὶ δικάζουσιν ẹṿ ịẹṛ[ῷ] καὶ ὑπαίθριοι, καὶ ὁ βασιλεὺς ὅταν δικάζῃ περιαιρεῖται τὸν στέφανον. ὁ δὲ τὴν αἰτίαν ἔχων τὸν μὲν ἄλλον χρόνον εἴργεται τῶν ἱερῶν, καὶ οὐδ' εἰς τὴν ἀγορὰν νόμọṣ ἐμβαλεῖν αὐτῷ· τότε δ' εἰς τὸ ἱερὸν εἰσελθὼν ἀπολογεῖται. ὅταν δὲ μὴ εἰδῇ τὸν ποιήσαντα, τῷ δράσαντι λαγχάνει. δικάζει δ' ὁ βασιλεὺς καὶ οἱ φυλοβασιλεῖς καὶ τὰς τῶν ἀψύχων καὶ τῶν ἄλλων ζῴων.

(**58**) ὁ δὲ πολέμαρχος θύει μὲν θυσίας τῇ τε Ἀρτέμιδι τῇ Ἀγροτέρᾳ καὶ τῷ Ἐνυαλίῳ, διατίθησι δ' ἀγῶνα τὸν ἐπιτάφιον ἐπὶ τοῖς τετελευτηκόσιν ἐν τῷ πολέμῳ, καὶ Ἁρμοδίῳ καὶ Ἀριστογείτονι ἐναγίσματα ποιεῖ. (*2*) δίκαι δὲ λαγχάνονται πρὸς αὐτὸν ἴδιαι μόνον, αἵ τε τοῖς μετοίκοις καὶ

57. 3. φαρμάκων Kaibel & Wilamowitz[1] cf. Poll. VIII. 117: φαρμακον L.

αἴδεσίς L, with the letter ρ written above.

57. 4. ταῦ[τ<α να΄>] ἄ[νδρε]ς R. S. Stroud (*CP* lxiii 1968, 212): ταῦ[τ'] ἄ[νδρε]ς Kaibel & Wilamowitz[3], ταῦ[τ'] α . [.] . [.] ς Chambers (but ταῦṭ' ἄν[δ]ρ[ε]ς *TAPA* xcvi 1965, 38–9), ταῦ[τ' ἐφέται] Kenyon. cf. Harp. ε 173 Keaney ἐφέται.

ẹṿ ịẹṛ[ῷ] F. Blass (*NJPhP* cxlv 1892, 574): not read by Chambers.

νόμọṣ Chambers: ν[όμος] Blass[2].

μὴ εἰδῇ τὸν ποιήσαντα, τῷ δράσαντι λαγχάνει: εἰδῇ <τις> P. N. Papageorgios cf. Dem. XXIII. *Aristocrates* 76; lacuna (ἐπὶ πρυτανείῳ *vel sim.*) after λαγχάνει Kaibel & Wilamowitz[1–2], before τῷ δράσαντι Thalheim.

58. 1. ἐπὶ P. N. Papageorgios cf. Philostr. 623 / *Vit. Soph.* II. 30: καὶ L, deleted Kenyon cf. Poll. VIII. 91, retained by Kaibel & Wilamowitz, punctuating not after πολέμῳ but after ἐπιτάφιον.

58. 2. μόνον Kaibel & Wilamowitz: μ(έν) L, retained by some editors.

matters. Also all the private suits for homicide fall to him, and it is he who makes the proclamation of exclusion from the things stipulated by law. (*3*) Suits for homicide and wounding, if anybody kills or wounds from forethought, are held at the Areopagus, and for poisoning, if somebody kills by administering poison, and for arson: only these are the cases tried by that council. Trials for unwilling homicide, for planning, and if anybody kills an attendant, a metic or a foreigner, the court at the Palladium. If anybody admits to having killed, but claims that he has done so in accordance with the laws, for instance by catching an adulterer or in ignorance in war or when competing in a contest, they hold his trial at the Delphinium. If he is in exile in circumstances for which reconciliation is possible and is accused of killing or wounding somebody, they hold the trial for him in Phreatus' sanctuary; and he makes his defence in a boat moored off shore. (*4*) The trial is held by the 51 men picked for this purpose by sortition, except for those held at the Areopagus: the *basileus* introduces the case, and they hold the trial in a sanctuary and in the open air, and the *basileus* when conducting the trial takes off his crown. The man under accusation is excluded from the sanctuaries for the rest of the time, and it is not lawful for him even to encroach on the agora; but on this occasion he goes into the sanctuary to make his defence. When the prosecutor does not know who did the deed, he obtains a hearing against 'the doer'. The *basileus* and the *phylobasileis* also try charges against inanimate objects and other creatures.

(**58**) The polemarch performs the sacrifices to Artemis Agrotera and to Enyalius, and he organises the funeral competition for those killed in war, and he performs heroes' rites for Harmodius and Aristogeiton. (*2*) Private lawsuits only fall to him, those held for metics, *isoteleis* and

τοῖς ἰσοτελέσι καὶ τοῖς προξένοις γιγνόμεναι· καὶ δεῖ τοῦτον λαβόντα καὶ διανείμαντα δέκα μέρη τὸ λαχὸν ἑκάστῃ τῇ φυλῇ μέρος προσθεῖναι, τοὺς δὲ τὴν φυλὴν δικάζοντας τοῖς διαιτηταῖς ἀποδοῦναι. (*3*) οὗτος δ' εἰσάγει δίκας τάς τε {τοῦ} ἀποστασίου καὶ <ἀ>προστασίου καὶ κλήρων καὶ ἐπικλήρων τοῖς μετοίκοις, καὶ τἆλλ' ὅσα τοῖς πολίταις ὁ ἄρχων ταῦτα τοῖς μετοίκοις ὁ πολέμαρχος.

(**59**) οἱ δὲ θεσμοθέται πρῶτον μὲν τοῦ προγράψαι τὰ δικαστήριά εἰσι κύριοι τίσιν ἡμέραις δεῖ δικάζειν, ἔπειτα τοῦ δοῦναι ταῖς ἀρχαῖς· καθότι γὰρ ἂν οὗτοι δῶσιν, κατὰ τοῦτο χρῶνται. (*2*) ἔτι δὲ τὰς εἰσαγγελίας <τοῖς> εἰσαγγέλλουσιν εἰς τὸν δῆμον, καὶ τὰς καταχειροτονίας καὶ τὰς προβολὰς ἁπάσας εἰσάγουσιν οὗτοι, καὶ γραφὰς παρανόμων καὶ νόμον μὴ ἐπιτήδειον θεῖναι καὶ προεδρικὴν καὶ ἐπιστατικὴν καὶ στρατηγοῖς εὐθύνας. (*3*) εἰσὶ δὲ καὶ γραφαὶ πρὸς αὐτοὺς ὧν παράστασις τίθεται, ξενίας καὶ δωροξενίας, ἄν τις δῶρα δοὺς ἀποφύγῃ τὴν ξενίαν, καὶ συκοφαντίας καὶ δώρων καὶ ψευδεγγραφῆς καὶ ψευδοκλητείας καὶ βουλεύσεως καὶ ἀγραφίου καὶ μοιχείας. (*4*) εἰσάγουσιν δὲ καὶ τὰς δοκιμασίας ταῖς ἀρχαῖς ἁπάσαις, καὶ τοὺς ἀπεψηφισμένους ὑπὸ τῶν δημοτῶν, καὶ τὰς καταγνώσεις τὰς ἐκ τῆς βουλῆς. (*5*) εἰσάγουσι δὲ καὶ δίκας ἰδίας, ἐμπορικὰς καὶ μεταλλικάς, καὶ δούλων ἄν τις τὸν ἐλεύθερον κακῶς λέγῃ. καὶ ἐπικληροῦσι ταῖς ἀρχαῖς οὗτοι τὰ δικαστήρια τά ἴδια καὶ τὰ δημόσια. (*6*) καὶ τὰ σύμβολα τὰ πρὸς τὰς πόλεις οὗτοι κυροῦσι, καὶ τὰς δίκας τὰς ἀπὸ τῶν συμβόλων εἰσάγουσι, καὶ τὰ ψευδομαρτύρια <τὰ> ἐξ Ἀρείου πάγου.

58. 2. ἀποδοῦναι: παραδοῦναι P. N. Papageorgios, cf. 53. 2, perhaps rightly.

58. 3. οὗτος δ' J. J. Keaney cf. Harp. α 204 Keaney ἀποστασίου: αὐτὸς δ L, αὐτός τε Harp. π 78 πολέμαρχος Keaney.

{τοῦ} Kaibel & Wilamowitz[1–2].

καὶ <ἀ>προστασίου Kenyon[1] cf. Harp. α 204 Keaney ἀποστασίου: καὶ προστασίου written above in L.

59. 2. <τοῖς> εἰσαγγέλλουσιν εἰς τὸν δῆμον D. M. Lewis (*ap.* Rhodes, *Comm. Ath. Pol.* 658): <ἃς> Blass[4], εἰσαγγέλλουσιν εἰς τὸν δῆμον deleted Kaibel & Wilamowitz.

59. 5. καὶ ἐπικληροῦσι … τὰ δημόσια deleted Kaibel & Wilamowitz[1–2].

τά <τ'> ἴδια Kaibel (*Stil und Text*, 247), perhaps rightly.

59. 6. <τὰ> ἐξ Ἀρείου πάγου Kaibel & Wilamowitz.

proxenoi: he has to take these, divide them into ten sections and assign to each tribe the section picked for it by sortition; and those serving as justices for the tribe have to give them up to the *diaitetai*. (*3*) He introduces for metics private suits for desertion of patron and for having no patron, and for estates and for *epikleroi*; and everything else which the archon does for the citizens the polemarch does for the metics.

(**59**) The *thesmothetai*, first, have the power to prescribe the lawcourts, on which days they must hold trials, and, next, to assign them to the officials: as they assign them, so the officials comply. (*2*) Then it is they who introduce the *eisangeliai* for those who make an *eisangelia* to the *demos*, and all the hostile votes and *probolai*, and the public suits for unlawful proposal and for enactment of an inexpedient law, and those against *proedroi* and against *epistatai*, and *euthynai* for generals. (*3*) Also directed to them are public suits in which a prosecutor's deposit is levied: for being a foreigner; for bribery by a foreigner, when somebody is acquitted of being a foreigner through bribery; and for malicious prosecution; for bribery; for false registration; for false summons; for *bouleusis*; for failure to register; and for adultery. (*4*) Also they introduce the *dokimasiai* for all the officials, and men rejected as citizens by their demesmen, and convictions forwarded from the council. (*5*) Also they introduce private suits: trading suits, mining suits and suits against any slave who maligns a free man. And they allot the private and public lawcourts to the officials. (*6*) Also they ratify the judicial agreements with the cities, and they introduce the suits made on the basis of judicial agreements, and charges of false witness before the Areopagus.

(*7*) τοὺς δὲ δικαστὰς κληροῦσι πάντες οἱ ἐννέα ἄρχοντες, δέκατος δ' ὁ γραμματεὺς ὁ τῶν θεσμοθετῶν, τοὺς τῆς αὑτοῦ φυλῆς ἕκαστος.

(**60**) τὰ μὲν οὖν περὶ τοὺς θ΄ ἄρχοντας τοῦτον ἔχει τὸν τρόπον. κληροῦσι δὲ καὶ ἀθλοθέτας δέκα ἄνδρας, ἕνα τῆς φυλῆς ἑκάστης. οὗτοι δὲ δοκιμασθέντες ἄρχουσι τέτταρα ἔτη, καὶ διοικοῦσι τήν τε πομπὴν τῶν Παναθηναίων καὶ τὸν ἀγῶνα τῆς μουσικῆς καὶ τὸν γυμνικὸν ἀγῶνα καὶ τὴν ἱπποδρομίαν, καὶ τὸν πέπλον ποιοῦνται, καὶ τοὺς ἀμφορεῖς ποιοῦνται μετὰ τῆς βουλῆς, καὶ τὸ ἔλαιον τοῖς ἀθληταῖς ἀποδιδόασι. (*2*) συλλέγεται δὲ τὸ ἔλαιον ἀπὸ τῶν μοριῶν· εἰσπράττει δὲ τοὺς τὰ χωρία κεκτημένους ἐν οἷς αἱ μορίαι εἰσὶν ὁ ἄρχων, τρί' ἡμικοτύλια ἀπὸ τοῦ στελέχους ἑκάστου. πρότερον δ' ἐπώλει τὸν καρπὸν ἡ πόλις· καὶ εἴ τις ἐξορύξειεν ἐλάαν μορίαν ἢ κατάξειεν ἔκρινεν ἡ ἐξ Ἀρείου πάγου βουλή, καὶ εἴ του καταγνοίη θανάτῳ τοῦτον ἐζημίουν. ἐξ οὗ δὲ τὸ ἔλαιον ὁ τὸ χωρίον κεκτημένος ἀποτίνει, ὁ μὲν νόμος ἔστιν, ἡ δὲ κρίσις καταλέλυται· τὸ δὲ ἔλαιον ἐκ τοῦ κτήματος, οὐκ ἀπὸ τῶν στελεχῶν ἐστι τῇ πόλει. (*3*) συλλέξας οὖν ὁ ἄρχων τὸ ἐφ' ἑαυτοῦ γιγνόμενον, τοῖς ταμίαις παραδίδωσιν εἰς ἀκρόπολιν, καὶ οὐκ ἔστιν ἀναβῆναι πρότερον εἰς Ἄρειον πάγον πρὶν ἂν ἅπαν παραδῷ τοῖς ταμίαις. οἱ δὲ ταμίαι τὸν μὲν ἄλλον χρόνον τηροῦσιν ἐν ἀκροπόλει, τοῖς δὲ Παναθηναίοις ἀπομετροῦσι τοῖς ἀθλοθέταις, οἱ δ' ἀθλοθέται τοῖς νικῶσι τῶν ἀγωνιστῶν. ἔστι γὰρ ἆθλα τοῖς μὲν τὴν μουσικὴν νικῶσιν ἀργύριον καὶ χρυσᾶ, τοῖς δὲ τὴν εὐανδρίαν ἀσπίδες, τοῖς δὲ τὸν γυμνικὸν ἀγῶνα καὶ τὴν ἱπποδρομίαν ἔλαιον.

(**61**) χειροτονοῦσι δὲ {καὶ} τὰς πρὸς τὸν πόλεμον ἀρχὰς ἁπάσας, στρατηγοὺς δέκα, πρότερον μὲν ἀφ' <ἑκάστης> φυλῆς ἕνα, νῦν δ' ἐξ ἁπάντων. καὶ τούτους διατάττουσι τῇ χειροτονίᾳ, ἕνα μὲν ἐπὶ τοὺς ὁπλίτας, ὃς ἡγεῖται τῶν ὁπλιτῶν ἂν ἐξίωσι· ἕνα δ' ἐπὶ τὴν χώραν, ὃς

60. 2. συλλέγεται δὲ τὸ ἔλαιον H. Richards (*CR*) *et al.*: σ(υλ)λέγεται τοδ΄ ἔλαιον L, τὸ δ' ἔλαιον συλλέγεται R. D. Hicks (*CR*).

ἐλάαν Herwerden & Leeuwen: ἐλαίαν L.

60. 3. ἀργύριον καὶ χρυσᾶ Kaibel & Wilamowitz: ἀργύρια καὶ χρυσᾶ L (cf. I. Avotins, *CQ*[2] xxxvii 1987, 231–3), ἀργυρᾶ καὶ χρυσᾶ W. G. Rutherford (*CR*), ἀργύρια καὶ χρυσία Herwerden.

61. 1. {καὶ} Kenyon[3]: lacuna before χειροτονοῦσι Kaibel & Wilamowitz cf. 43. 1. <ἑκάστης> Kenyon[1].

(*7*) All the nine archons allot the jurors, with the secretary of the *thesmothetai* tenth, each allotting those of his own tribe.

(**60**) The arrangements for the 9 archons are in that manner. The Athenians also allot as *athlothetai* ten men, one from each tribe. These after undergoing their *dokimasia* hold office for four years, and they administer the procession at the Panathenaea and the competition in music, the competition in athletics and the horse race; and they have the *peplos* made, and with the council they have the amphorae made, and they give the olive oil to the athletes. (*2*) The olive oil is collected from the sacred olives: the archon exacts it from those who own the lands on which the sacred olives grow, one and a half *kotylai* from each plant. Previously the city used to sell the harvest, and if anybody dug up a sacred olive or cut one down he was tried by the council of the Areopagus and if it convicted him they punished him with death; but since the olive oil has been paid by the owner of the land the law has remained in existence but the trial has lapsed: the city obtains the olive oil from the property, not from the particular plants. (*3*) The archon collects what is produced in his term of office, and hands it to the treasurers on the acropolis; and it is not permitted to him to go up to the Areopagus until he has handed it all over to the treasurers. The treasurers keep watch over it on the acropolis for the rest of the time, but at the Panathenaea they measure it out to the *athlothetai*, and the *athlothetai* measure it out to those of the competitors who win. The prizes are gold and silver for winners in music, shields in manliness and olive oil in the athletic competition and the horse race.

(**61**) They elect all the officials for warfare. Ten generals, previously one from each tribe but now from all Athenians. These they assign by their vote: one in charge of the hoplites, who commands the hoplites when they go out; one in charge of the territory, who guards it, and if

φυλάττει, κἂν πόλεμος ἐν τῇ χώρᾳ γίγνηται, πολεμεῖ οὗτος· δύο δ' ἐπὶ τὸν Πειραιέα, τὸν μὲν εἰς τὴν Μουνιχίαν, τὸν δ' εἰς τὴν Ἀκτήν, οἳ τῆς φυλ<ακ>ῆς ἐπιμελοῦνται {καὶ} τῶν ἐν Πειραιεῖ· ἕνα δ' ἐπὶ τὰς συμμορίας, ὃς τούς τε τριηράρχους καταλέγει, καὶ τὰς ἀντιδόσεις αὐτοῖς ποιεῖ, καὶ τὰς διαδικασίας αὐτοῖς εἰσάγει· τοὺς δ' ἄλλους πρὸς τὰ παρόντα πράγματα ἐκπέμπουσιν. (*2*) ἐπιχειροτονία δ' αὐτῶν ἐστι κατὰ τὴν πρυτανείαν ἑκάστην, εἰ δοκοῦσιν καλῶς ἄρχειν· κἄν τινα ἀποχειροτονήσωσιν, κρίνουσιν ἐν τῷ δικαστηρίῳ, κἂν μὲν ἁλῷ, τιμῶσιν ὅ τι χρὴ παθεῖν ἢ ἀποτεῖσαι, ἂν δ' ἀποφύγῃ πάλιν ἄρχει. κύριοι δέ εἰσιν ὅταν ἡγῶνται καὶ δῆσαι τὸν ἀτακτοῦντα καὶ <ἐκ>κηρῦξαι καὶ ἐπιβολὴν ἐπιβαλεῖν· οὐκ εἰώθασι δὲ ἐπιβάλλειν. (*3*) χειροτονοῦσι δὲ καὶ ταξιάρχους δέκα, ἕνα τῆς φυλῆς ἑκάστης· οὗτος δ' ἡγεῖται τῶν φυλετῶν καὶ λοχαγοὺς καθίστησιν. (*4*) χειροτονοῦσι δὲ καὶ ἱππάρχους δύο ἐξ ἁπάντων· οὗτοι δ' ἡγοῦνται τῶν ἱππέων, διελόμενοι τὰς φυλὰς ε´ ἑκάτερος· κύριοι δὲ τῶν αὐτῶν εἰσιν ὧνπερ οἱ στρατηγοὶ κατὰ τῶν ὁπλιτῶν. ἐπιχειροτονία δὲ γίγνεται <καὶ> τούτων. (*5*) χειροτονοῦσι δὲ καὶ φυλάρχους <ι´>, ἕνα τῆς φυλῆς, τὸν ἡγησόμενον <τῶν ἱππέων> ὥσπερ οἱ ταξίαρχοι τῶν ὁπλιτῶν.

(*6*) χειροτονοῦσι δὲ καὶ εἰς Λῆμνον ἵππαρχον, ὃς ἐπιμελεῖται τῶν ἱππέων τῶν ἐν Λήμνῳ. (*7*) χειροτονοῦσι δὲ καὶ ταμίαν τῆς Παράλου καὶ δίχα τῆς τοῦ Ἄμμωνος.

(**62**) αἱ δὲ κληρωταὶ ἀρχαὶ πρότερον μὲν ἦσαν αἱ μὲν μετ' ἐννέα ἀρχόντων ἐκ τῆς φυλῆς ὅλης κληρούμεναι, αἱ δ' ἐν Θησείῳ κληρούμεναι διῃροῦντο εἰς τοὺς δήμους. ἐπειδὴ δ' ἐπώλουν οἱ δῆμοι, καὶ ταύτας ἐκ τῆς φυλῆς ὅλης κληροῦσι, πλὴν βουλευτῶν καὶ φρουρῶν· τούτους δ' εἰς τοὺς δήμους ἀποδιδόασι.

61. 1. πολεμεῖ L: ἡγεῖται Kaibel & Wilamowitz, perhaps rightly.

φυλ<ακ>ῆς ἐπιμελοῦνται {καὶ} Kaibel & Wilamowitz. cf. Kenyon[1] in *apparatus*.

{αὐτοῖς} εἰσάγει Kaibel & Wilamowitz[2–3].

61. 2. <ἐκ>κηρῦξαι Blass.

ἐπιβαλεῖν H. Diels (*ap.* Kenyon[4]): ἐπιβάλλειν L.

61. 4. <καὶ> τούτων Kaibel & Wilamowitz[1].

61. 5. <ι´> H. Richards (*CR*).

<τῶν ἱππέων> Kenyon[1].

61. 7. δίχα Kenyon[4–5], could be read but does not make sense Chambers: δ . . α Wilcken, ἄλλον Kenyon[1–3], fits the traces Chambers, ν[ῦν] Blass[2].

there is war in the territory it is he who wages the war; two in charge of the Piraeus, one for Munichia and one for Acte, who take care of guarding what is in Piraeus; and one in charge of the *symmoriai*, who registers the trierarchs, holds *antidoseis* for them and introduces adjudications for them. The others they send out on current business. (*2*) There is a vote of confidence in them in each prytany, to judge whether they are exercising their office well. If they depose anybody, they try him in the lawcourt, and if he is convicted they assess what he should suffer or pay, but if he is acquitted he holds office again. When they are commanding they have power to imprison a disobedient man, to cashier and to impose a summary penalty; but they are not in the habit of imposing penalties. (*3*) They elect ten taxiarchs, one from each tribe: he commands his tribesmen and appoints *lochagoi*. (*4*) They elect also two hipparchs from all Athenians: these command the cavalry, taking as their share 5 tribes each. They have the same powers as the generals have with regard to the hoplites. There is a vote of confidence in them also. (*5*) They elect also 10 phylarchs, one from a tribe, to command the cavalry as the taxiarchs command the hoplites.

(*6*) They elect also a hipparch to Lemnos, who takes care of the cavalry on Lemnos. (*7*) They elect also a treasurer of the Paralus and separately one of the Ammonos.

(**62**) Of the allotted offices, some used to be allotted with the nine archons from the whole tribe, while others allotted in the Theseum were distributed among the demes. But, since the demes were selling their offices, these too they allot from the whole tribe, apart from the councillors and the guards: they are devolved to the demes.

(*2*) μισθοφοροῦσι δὲ πρῶτον ὁ δῆμος ταῖς μὲν ἄλλαις ἐκκλησίαις δραχμήν, τῇ δὲ κυρίᾳ ἐννέα <ὀβολούς>. ἔπειτα τὰ δικαστήρια τρεῖς ὀβολούς. εἶθ' ἡ βουλὴ πέντε ὀβολούς· τοῖς δὲ πρυτανεύουσιν εἰς σίτησιν ὀβολὸς προστίθεται {δέκα προστίθενται}. ἔπειτ' εἰς σίτησιν λαμβάνουσιν ἐννέ' ἄρχοντες τέτταρας ὀβολοὺς ἕκαστος, καὶ παρατρέφουσι κήρυκα καὶ αὐλητήν. ἔπειτ' ἄρχων εἰς Σαλαμῖνα δραχμὴν τῆς ἡμέρας. ἀθλοθέται δ' ἐν πρυτανείῳ δειπνοῦσι τὸν Ἑκατομβαιῶνα μῆνα, ὅταν ᾖ τὰ Παναθήναια, ἀρξάμενοι ἀπὸ τῆς τετράδος ἱσταμένου. ἀμφικτύονες εἰς Δῆλον δραχμὴν τῆς ἡμέρας ἑκάστης ἐκ Δήλου <λαμβάνουσι>. λαμβάνουσι δὲ καὶ ὅσαι ἀποστέλλονται ἀρχαὶ εἰς Σάμον ἢ Σκῦρον ἢ Λῆμνον ἢ Ἴμβρον εἰς σίτησιν ἀργύριον.

(*3*) ἄρχειν δὲ τὰς μὲν κατὰ πόλεμον ἀρχὰς ἔξεστι πλεονάκις, τῶν δ' ἄλλων οὐδεμίαν, πλὴν βουλεῦσαι δίς.

(**63**) τὰ δὲ {τὰ} δικαστήρια [κ]ληρ[οῦ]σ[ιν] οἱ θ´ ἄρχοντες κατὰ φυλάς, ὁ δὲ γραμματεὺς τῶν θεσμοθετῶν τῆς δεκάτης φυλῆς. (*2*) εἴσοδοι δέ εἰσιν εἰς τὰ δικαστήρια δέκα, μία τῇ φυλῇ ἑκάστῃ, καὶ κληρ[ωτήρι]α εἴκοσι, δύο τῇ φυλῇ ἑκάστῃ, καὶ κιβώτια ἑκατόν, δέκα τῇ φυλῇ ἑκάστῃ, καὶ ἕτερα κιβώτια, [εἰς ἃ ἐ]μβάλλεται τῶν λαχόντων δικαστῶν τὰ πινάκια, καὶ ὑδρίαι δύο. καὶ βακτηρίαι παρατίθενται κατὰ τὴν ε[ἴ]σ[οδον] ἑκάστην ὅσοιπερ οἱ δικασταί, καὶ βάλανοι εἰς τὴν ὑδρίαν ἐμβάλλονται ἴσαι ταῖς βακτηρίαις, ἐγγέγραπται δ' ἐν ταῖς βαλάνοις τῶν στοιχείων ἀπὸ τοῦ ἑνδεκάτου τοῦ Λ {τριακοστοῦ}, ὅσαπερ ἂν μέλλῃ τὰ δικαστήρια πληρωθήσεσθαι. (*3*) δικάζειν δ' ἔξεστιν τοῖς ὑπὲρ λ´ ἔτη γεγονόσιν, ὅσοι αὐτῶν μὴ ὀφείλουσιν τῷ δημοσίῳ ἢ ἄτιμοί εἰσιν. ἐὰν δέ τις δικάζῃ οἷς μὴ ἔξεστιν, ἐνδείκνυται καὶ εἰς τὸ δικαστήριον εἰσάγεται· ἐὰν δ'

62. 2. <ὀβολούς> Kaibel & Wilamowitz[1].

{δέκα προστίθενται} deleted Blass.

<λαμβάνουσι> Kenyon[1].

63. 1. [κ]ληρ[οῦ]σ[ιν] Kenyon[1] cf. 59. 7: [π]ληρ[οῦ]σ[ιν] R. Dareste.

63. 2. κληρ[ωτήρι]α Kenyon[1].

[εἰς ἃ ἐ]μβάλλεται P. N. Papageorgios.

ε[ἴ]σ[οδον] Kenyon[1] (σ read by Chambers): ἔ[ξοδον] Hommel.

{τριακοστοῦ} Kenyon[1]: τοῦ ἑνδεκάτου τοῦ τριακοστοῦ, with the words τοῦ τριακοστοῦ deleted and τοῦ Λ · τριακοστοῦ · written above, L.

(*2*) Stipends are paid, first, to the *demos*, a drachma at the other assemblies but nine obols at the *kyria ekklesia*. Then the lawcourts, three obols. Next the council, five obols; and to the *prytaneis* an obol is added for meals. Then the nine archons receive four obols each for meals; and they support in addition a herald and a piper. Then the archon for Salamis, a drachma a day. The *athlothetai* dine in the *prytaneion* during the month Hecatombaeon, when the Panathenaea occurs, beginning from the fourth of the month. The *amphiktyones* for Delos receive a drachma each day from Delos. Whatever officials are sent to Samos, Scyros, Lemnos or Imbros receive money for meals.

(*3*) It is permitted to hold the offices for warfare several times, but none of the others, except to serve as a councillor twice.

(**63**) The lawcourts are allotted by the nine archons, by tribes, and the secretary of the *thesmothetai* for the tenth tribe. (*2*) There are ten entrances to the lawcourts, one for each tribe; and twenty allotment machines, two for each tribe; and a hundred boxes, ten for each tribe; and further boxes, in which the identity cards of the jurors picked in the sortition are deposited; and two water pots. And there are staves set up by each entrance, as many as there are to be jurors; and acorns are placed in the water pot, equal in number to the staves; and letters are written on the acorns, beginning from the eleventh letter, *lambda*, as many as there are courts to be filled. (*3*) It is permitted to serve as jurors to those who are over 30 years old, as many as are not in debt to the state or *atimoi*. If anybody serves to whom it is not permitted, he is made the subject of an *endeixis* and is introduced into the lawcourt: if he

ἁλῷ, προστιμῶσιν αὐτῷ οἱ δικασταί ὅ τι ἂν δοκῇ ἄξιος εἶναι παθεῖν ἢ ἀποτεῖσαι. ἐὰν δὲ ἀργυρίου τιμηθῇ, δεῖ αὐτὸν δεδέσθαι ἕως ἂν ἐκτείσῃ τό τε πρότερον ὄφλημα ἐφ' ᾧ ἐνεδείχθη καὶ ὅ τι ἂν αὐτῷ προστιμήσῃ τὸ δικαστήριον. (*4*) ἔχει δ' ἕκαστος δικαστὴς τὸ πινάκιον πύξινον, ἐπιγεγραμμένον τὸ ὄνομα τὸ ἑαυτοῦ πατρόθεν καὶ τοῦ δήμου, καὶ γράμμα ἓν τῶν στοιχείων μέχρι τοῦ Κ· νενέμηνται γὰρ κατὰ φυλὰς δέκα μέρη οἱ δικασταί, παραπλησίως ἴσοι ἐν ἑκάστῳ τῷ γράμματι. (*5*) ἐπειδὰν δὲ ὁ θεσμοθέτης ἐπικληρώσῃ τὰ γράμματα ἃ δεῖ προσπαρατίθεσθαι τοῖς δικαστηρίοις, ἐπέθηκε φέρων ὁ ὑπηρέτης ἐφ' ἕκαστον τὸ δικαστήριον τὸ γράμμα τὸ λαχόν.

(**64**) τὰ δὲ [κιβώ]τια τὰ δέκα κ[εῖται ἐ]ν ṭ[ῷ ἔμ]προσθεν ṭῆς εἰσόδου καθ' ἑκάστην τὴν φυλήν· ἐπιγέγραπται δ' ἐπ' αὐτῶν τὰ στοιχεῖα μέχρι τοῦ Κ. ἐπειδὰν δ' ἐμβάλωσιν οἱ δικασταὶ τὰ πινάκια εἰς τὸ κιβώτιον ἐφ' οὗ ἂν ᾖ ἐπιγεγραμμένον τὸ γράμμα τὸ αὐτὸ ὅπερ ἐπὶ τῷ πινακίῳ ἐστὶν αὐτῷ τῶν στοιχείω[ν, τότε] σείσαντος τοῦ ὑπηρέτου ἕλκει ὁ θεσμοθέτης ἐξ ἑκάστου τοῦ κιβωτίου πινάκιον ἕν. (*2*) οὗτος δὲ καλεῖται ἐμ[πήκτ]ης, καὶ ἐμπήγνυσι τὰ πινάκια [τὰ ἐκ το]ῦ κιβωτίου εἰς τὴν κανονίδα [ἐφ' ἧς τὸ α]ὐτὸ γράμμα ἔπεστιν ὅπερ ἐπὶ τοῦ [κιβωτίο]υ. κ[ληροῦται δ'] οὗτος, ἵνα μὴ ἀεὶ ὁ αὐτὸς ἐμπ[ηγνύων] κακουργῇ. εἰσὶ δὲ κανονίδες [πέντε ἐ]ν ἑκάστῳ τῶν κληρωτηρίων. (*3*) ẹ[πειδὰν δ'] ἐμβάλῃ τοὺς κύβους, ὁ ἄρχων τὴν φυλὴν κληρ[οῖ κατὰ κ]ληρωτήριον. εἰσὶ δὲ κύβοι χαλκοῖ, μέλανες καὶ λευκοί· ὅσους δ' ἂν δέῃ [λαχεῖν] δικαστάς, τοσοῦτοι ἐμβάλλονται λευκοί, κατὰ πέντε πινάκια εἷς, οἱ δὲ μέλανες τὸν αὐτὸν τρόπον. ἐπειδὰν δ' ἐ[ξαιρῇ] τοὺς κύβους, καλεῖ τοὺς εἰληχότας ὁ κ[ήρυξ]· ὑπάρχει δὲ καὶ ὁ ἐμπήκτης εἰς τὸν ἀ[ριθμό]ν. (*4*) ὁ δὲ κληθεὶς καὶ ὑπακούσας ἕλκει β[άλανο]ν ἐκ τῆς ὑδρίας, καὶ ὀρέξας αὐτήν, [ἄνω ἔχ]ων τὸ γράμμα, δείκνυσιν πρῶτον μὲν τῷ ἄρχοντι τῷ ἐφεστηκότι· ὁ δὲ ἄρχων, [ἐπειδ]ὰν ἴδῃ, ἐμβάλλει τὸ πινάκιον α[ὐ]τοῦ [εἰς τὸ] κιβώτιον ὅπου ἂν ᾖ ἐπιγεγραμμένον τὸ αὐτὸ στοιχεῖον ὅπερ ἐν τῇ βαλάνῳ, ἵν' εἰς

64. 1. τότε] σείσαντος Kenyon[4–5]: δια]σείσαντος B. Haussoullier (cf. restoration in *IG* ii[3] 292. 36), Chambers, or perhaps ἀνα]σείσαντος (cf. Foucart's restoration in *IG* ii[3] 292.36).

64. 3. ẹ[πειδὰν δ'] B. Haussoullier, Chambers: ὅ[ταν δ'] Wilcken, ὅ[ταν δὲ] Kenyon[4–5], which perhaps fits the space better.

ἐ[ξαιρῇ] Blass, Chambers: ἐ[ξέλῃ] B. Haussoullier, Kenyon[4–5].

is convicted, the jurors assess what they judge he deserves to suffer or pay; if a monetary assessment is made, he must be imprisoned until he has paid both the previous debt on account of which he was subjected to *endeixis* and the sum assessed for him by the lawcourt. (*4*) Each juror has his boxwood identity card, inscribed with his own name, his patronymic and his demotic, and marked with one of the letters up to *kappa*: for the jurors are distributed by tribes into ten sections, about the same number in each letter. (*5*) When the *thesmothetes* allots the letters which are to be attached to the lawcourts, the attendant takes and affixes to each court the letter picked for it by sortition.

(**64**) The ten boxes stand in front of the entrance for each tribe; the letters up to *kappa* are inscribed on them. When the jurors have deposited their identity cards in the box on which is inscribed the same one of the letters as is on their card, then the attendant shakes the boxes, and the *thesmothetes* draws one card from each box. (*2*) This man is called the inserter, and he inserts the cards from his box in the column [on the allotment machine] to which the same letter is applied as to the box. He is allotted, so that the same man shall not insert continually and act dishonestly. There are five columns in each of the allotment machines. (*3*) When he has deposited the cubes [in the machine], the archon performs the allotment for his tribe on the machine. There are bronze cubes, black and white: as many as the jurors who need to be picked in the sortition, the corresponding number of white cubes is deposited, one for five cards; and the black ones in the same way. When the archon has released the cubes, the herald calls on those picked in the sortition; and the inserter is included in the number, (*4*) The man who is called responds, draws an acorn from the water pot, holds it out with the letter on the upper side, and first shows it to the archon in charge. The archon, when he has seen it, deposits the man's card in the box on which is inscribed the same letter as is on his acorn, so that he shall enter the court for which he is picked in

οἷον ἂν λάχῃ εἰσίῃ καὶ μὴ εἰς ο[ἷο]ν ἂν βούληται, μηδὲ ᾖ συναγαγεῖν [εἰς] δικαστήριον οὓς ἂν βούληταί τις. (*5*) πα[ράκει]ται δὲ τῷ ἄρχοντι κιβώτια ὅσαπερ ἂν μέλλῃ τὰ δικαστήρια πληρωθήσεσθα[ι, ἔχο]ντα στοιχεῖον ἕκαστον ὅπερ ἂν [ᾖ τὸ] τοῦ δικαστηρίου ἑκάστου εἰληχός.

(**65**) αὐτ̣ὸ[ς δὲ δείξ]ας πάλιν τ[ῷ ὑ]πηρέτῃ εἶ[τ'] ἐ[ντὸς εἰσέρχετ]αι τῆς κ̣[ι]γκλ̣[ί]δος. ὁ δὲ ὑπηρέτης [δίδωσιν αὐτ]ῷ βακτηρίαν ὁμόχρων τῷ δικαστ[ηρίῳ οὗ τὸ] αὐτὸ γράμμα ἐστὶν ὅπερ ἐν τῇ βαλάνῳ, ἵνα [ἀναγ]καῖον ᾖ αὐτῷ εἰσελθεῖν εἰς ὃ εἴληχε δικαστήριον· ἐὰν γὰρ εἰς ἕτερον εἰ[σ]έλ[θῃ], ἐξε[λέγχετα]ι ὑπὸ τοῦ χρώματος τῆς βακτηρίας. (*2*) τοῖς γὰρ δικαστηρίοις χρῶμα ἐπιγέγραπται ἑκάστῳ ἐπὶ τῷ σφηκίσκῳ τῆς εἰσόδου. ὁ δὲ λαβὼν τὴν βακτηρίαν βαδίζει εἰς τὸ δικαστήριον τὸ ὁμόχρων μὲν τῇ βακτηρίᾳ ἔχον δὲ τὸ αὐτὸ γράμμα ὅπερ ἐν τῇ βαλάνῳ. ἐπειδὰν δ' εἰσέλθῃ, παραλαμβάνει σύμβολον δημοσίᾳ παρὰ τοῦ εἰληχότος ταύτην τὴν ἀρχήν. (*3*) εἶτα τήν τε βάλανον καὶ τὴν βακτηρίαν <ἔχοντες καθίζουσιν> [ἐν τῷ δ]ικαστηρίῳ τοῦτον <τὸν> τρόπον ε[ἰ]σελ[ηλυθό]τες. τοῖς δ' ἀπολαγχάνουσιν ἀποδιδόασιν οἱ ἐμπῆκται τὰ πινάκια. (*4*) οἱ δὲ ὑπηρέται οἱ δημόσιοι ἀπὸ τῆς φυλῆς ἑκάστης παραδιδόασιν τὰ κιβώτια, ἓν ἐπὶ τὸ δικαστήριον ἕκαστον, ἐν ᾧ ἔνεστιν τὰ ὀνόματα τῆς φυλῆς τὰ ὄντα ἐν ἑκάστῳ τῶν δικαστηρίων. παραδιδόασι δὲ τοῖς εἰληχόσι ταῦ[τ]α [ἀπο]διδόναι τοῖς δικασταῖς ἐν ἑκάστῳ τῷ δικαστηρίῳ ἀριθμῷ <πέντε> {τὰ πινάκια} ὅπως ἐκ τούτων καλοῦντες ἀποδιδῶσι τὸν μισθόν.

65. 1. εἶ[τ'] ἐ[ντὸς εἰσέρχετ]αι Kenyon[5] cf. Kenyon[4] in *apparatus*, Chambers.

ἐξε[λέγχετα]ι ὑπὸ τοῦ χρώματος Kaibel & Wilamowitz[3], Kenyon[4–5]: ἐξε[. . . .] . . δ̣ι̣ὰ̣ τὸ χρῶμα τὸ Chambers, judges that the last letter of the first word cannot be ι.

65. 2. χρῶμα Kenyon[4–5] cf. schol. Ar. *Plut.* 278: χρώμα[τ]α L, Chambers.

[ἑκάσ]τῳ L, Kenyon[4–5], Chambers: ἐφ' ἑκάστῳ schol. Ar., but too long for the space.

65. 3. <ἔχοντες καθίζουσιν> Kenyon[4–5] cf. 68. 2, 69. 2: <ἀποτιθέασιν> Thalheim, Chambers.

<τὸν> Kaibel & Wliamowitz[3].

65. 4. ταῦ[τ]α [ἀπο]διδόναι Kenyon[4–5], Chambers (*TAPA* cii 1971, 46): τὸ π̣ά̣λ̣ιν διδόναι Wilcken, Chambers.

ἀριθμῷ <πέντε> {τὰ πινάκια} Kenyon[4–5] (<πέντε> {τὰ πινάκια} cf. 66. 3 Kenyon[4] in *apparatus*): ἀριθμῷ <πέντε> τὰ πινάκια Chambers (who does not read ταῦτα above).

the sortition, and not whichever he wishes, and it shall not be possible to collect whoever somebody wishes in a court. (*5*) There stand beside the archon as many boxes as there are courts to be filled, bearing the letter which has fallen by sortition to each court.

(**65**) The juror shows his acorn again to the attendant, and then goes inside the barrier. The attendant gives him a staff of the same colour as the court which has the same letter as on his acorn, so that he is obliged to enter the court which has fallen to him in the sortition: for if he enters another court he is exposed by the colour of his staff. (*2*) The courts have a colour painted on the lintel of the entrance of each. The juror takes his staff, and proceeds to the court with the same colour as his staff and having the same letter as is on his acorn. When he has entered, he takes an official token from the man to whom that office has fallen by sortition. (*3*) Then, having entered in that way, they retain their acorn and their staff, and sit down in the court. To those rejected in the sortition the inserters return their identity cards. (*4*) The public attendants hand over the boxes from each tribe, one for each court, in which are [the cards with] the names from that tribe of the jurors serving in each of the courts. They hand these over to the men picked by sortition to return them to the jurors in each court, five in number, so that they can call the jurors from these and pay them their stipend.

(**66**) ἐπειδὰν δὲ πάντα πλήρη ᾖ τὰ δικαστήρια, τίθεται ἐν τῷ πρώτῳ τῶν δικαστηρίων β΄ κληρωτήρια, καὶ κύβοι χαλκοῖ ἐν οἷς ἐπιγέγραπται τὰ χρώματα τῶν δικαστηρίων, καὶ ἕτεροι κύβοι ἐν οἷς ἐστιν τῶν ἀρχῶν τὰ ὀνόματα ἐπιγεγραμμένα. λαχόντες δὲ τῶν θεσμοθετῶν δύο χωρὶς ἑκατέρων τοὺς κύβους ἐμβάλλουσιν, ὁ μὲν τὰ χρώματα εἰς τὸ ἓν κληρωτήριον, ὁ δὲ τῶν ἀρχῶν τὰ ὀνόματα εἰς τὸ ἕτερον· ἣ δ' ἂν πρώτη λάχῃ τῶν ἀρχῶν, αὕτη ἀναγορεύεται ὑπὸ τοῦ κήρυκος ὅτι χρήσεται τῷ πρώτῳ λαχόντι δικα[στηρίῳ, ἡ δὲ δευτέ]ρ[α τῷ] δευτέρῳ, καὶ οὕ[τω ταῖς λοιπαῖς, ἵ]να [μηδ]εμία προειδ[ῇ τίνι αὐτῶν χρήσεται], ἀλλ' [οἷο]ν ἂν λάχῃ ἑκάσ[τη τούτῳ χρήσηται. (*2*) ἐπε]ιδὰ[ν δ' ἔλθωσιν καὶ ν[ενεμημένοι ἐπὶ τὰ μέρη ὦ]σιν [οἱ δικα]σταί, ἡ ἀρχὴ ἡ [ἐφεστηκυῖα ἐν τ]ῷ δικαστηρίῳ ἑκάστῳ [ἕλκει ἐξ ἑκάστου τοῦ] κιβωτίου πινάκιον [ἕν, ἵνα γένωνται δέκα], εἷς ἐξ ἑκάστης τῆς φυ[λῆς, καὶ ταῦτα τὰ πινάκ]ια [εἰς] ἕτερον κενὸν κ[ιβώτιον ἐμβάλλει· καὶ] τού[των ε΄] τοὺς πρώτους λα[χόντας κληροῖ, ἕνα μὲν] ἐπὶ τὸ ὕδωρ, τέτταρας δὲ [ἄλλους ἐπὶ τὰς ψή]φους, [ἵνα] μηδεὶς παρασκε[υάζῃ]ι [μήτε] τὸν ἐπὶ τὸ ὕδωρ μήτε τοὺς ἐπὶ τὰς ψήφους, μηδὲ γίγνηται περὶ ταῦτα κακούργημα μηδέν. (*3*) οἱ δὲ ἀπολαχόντες πέντε παρὰ τούτων ἀπολαμβάνουσ[ι . .]ρο̣ γ΄ . [. . . .] . καθ' ὅτι τὸν μισθὸν λα[μβ]ά̣γ̣οντα̣[ι] καὶ ὅπου ἕκασται αἱ φυλαὶ ἐν α[ὐτῷ] τῷ δικαστηρίῳ, ἐπειδὰν δικάσωσι[ν, ὅπως] διαστάντες ἕκαστοι κατ' ὀλίγους [λάβ]ωσι καὶ μὴ πολλοὶ εἰς ταὐτὸ συνκλε[ισθέντες ἀλ]λήλοις ἐνοχλῶσιν.

(**67**) ταῦτα δὲ ποιήσαντες εἰσκαλοῦσι τοὺς ἀγῶνας· ὅταν μὲν τὰ ἴδια δικάζωσι τοὺς ἰδίους, τῷ ἀριθμῷ δ΄, [α΄ ἑκά]στων τ̣ῶν δικῶν τῶν ἐκ τοῦ νόμου, καὶ δ[ιο]μνύ[ουσι]ν οἱ ἀντίδικοι εἰς αὐτὸ τὸ πρᾶγμα ἐρεῖν·

66. 1. οὕ[τω ταῖς λοιπαῖς Blass[3], Chambers: ὡ[σαύτως τοῖς ἄλλοις Kenyon[4–5].

66. 2. ἐπὶ τὰ μέρη cf. 69. 2 (or ἐπὶ τὰ ξύλα cf. Ar. *Vesp.* 90) D. M. MacDowell (*ap.* Rhodes, *Comm. Ath. Pol.* 716), Chambers: ἐφ ἕκαστον Blass[3], Chambers.

ἕνα Blass[2], Chambers: α΄ Kenyon[4–5].

66. 3. . .]ρο̣ γ΄ . [. . . .] . Chambers, cf…] τ̣ὸ̣ γ΄ . . . τ̣α Wilcken, ηρ γ΄ or ηο γ΄ Thomas: τὸ π]ρόγ[ραμμ]α Blass[2], Kenyon[4–5].

λα[μβ]ά̣γ̣οντα̣[ι] Chambers cf. Kenyon[4] in *apparatus*: λ[ήψο]ντ[αι] Kenyon[4–5] ('doubtful reading').

67. 1. [α΄ ἑκά]στων Chambers: [ἕνα ἐ]ξ [ἑκά]στων Hommel, judged too long for the space Thomas: [ἐ]ξ [ἑκά]στων Kenyon[4–5].

δ[ιο]μνύ[ουσι]ν Wilcken, Kenyon[4–5]: δ[ιο]μνύο[ντ]αι Blass[3], . . [.]μ̣υ̣ο̣[. .]ν Chambers.

(**66**) When all the courts are full, 2 allotment machines are placed in the first of the courts, and bronze cubes on which are painted the colours of the courts, and further cubes on which are inscribed the names of the officials. Two of the *thesmothetai* picked by sortition deposit the cubes separately: one deposits the colours in one machine, and the other deposits the names of the officials in the other. Whichever of the officials falls out first, it is proclaimed by the herald that he is to use the court which falls out first; and the second, the second court; and so on with the remainder, so that no official shall know in advance which of the courts he is to use, but each shall use the one which falls to him in the sortition. (*2*) When the jurors have entered and have been distributed in their sections, the official in charge in each court draws from each box one identity card, so that there shall be ten, one from each tribe, and he deposits these cards in another empty box. And of these he allots the 5 which fall out first, one for the water and four others for the ballots, so that nobody can make an arrangement with the man in charge of the water or those in charge of the ballots, and there cannot be any dishonesty in connection with them. (*5*) The five who are rejected recover from them – – – 3 – – – how they are to receive their stipend and where in the court each of the tribes is to do so, when they have completed their trials, so that each tribe can be kept apart and they can receive in small groups and not fall foul of one another by being confined in the same area.

(**67**) After doing that they call in the contests: when they are trying private matters, private suits, 4 in number, one of each of the kinds of suit prescribed by law, and the opposing litigants take an oath to speak

[ὅταν] δὲ τὰ δημόσια, τοὺς δημοσίους, καὶ ἕν[α μόνον] ἐκδικάζουσι. (*2*) εἰσὶ δὲ κλεψύδραι αὐλ[ίσκους] ἔχουσαι ἔκρους, εἰς ἃς τὸ ὕδωρ ἐγχέουσι πρὸς ὃ δεῖ λέγειν {καὶ} τὰς δίκας. δίδοται <δὲ> δεκάχους ταῖς ὑπὲρ πεντακισχιλίας [δραχ]μ̣ὰ̣ς καὶ τρίχους τῷ δ[ευτέρῳ] λόγῳ, ἑπτάχους δὲ ταῖς μέχρι πεντακισχιλίων καὶ δίχους, π[εν]τ̣άχους δὲ τα[ῖς] ἐν[τὸ]ς α̣´ καὶ δίχους, ἑξάχους δὲ ταῖς διαδικασία̣ις [καὶ ὕστ]ερον λόγος οὐκ ἔστιν ο[ὐδ]εί[ς]. (*3*) ὁ δ' ἐφ' [ὕδ]ωρ [εἰ]λη[χ]ὼς ἐπιλαμβάνει τ̣ὸν α[ὐλίσκον ὅταν ψήφισμα ἢ] νόμον ἢ μαρ[τυρίαν ἢ σύμβολον ὁ γραμμ]ατεὺς ἀναγιγ[νώσκειν μέλλῃ. ὅταν δὲ] ἦ̣ [πρὸ]ς διαμεμετρημ[ένην τὴν ἡμέρα] ν ἡ̣ δ̣[ίκη, τό]τε δὲ οὐκ ἐπιλαμβ[άνει αὐτόν, ἀλλὰ δίδοτα]ι τὸ [ἴσο]ν ὕδωρ τῷ τε κατ[ηγοροῦντι καὶ τῷ ἀπο]λογ[ουμ]ένῳ. (*4*) *διαμετ[ρεῖται δὲ πρὸς τὰς ἡμέ]ρας [το]ῦ Ποσιδεῶνος [εἰσὶ γὰρ καὶ ταῖς ἄλλαις σύμμετ]ρ̣ο̣[ι α] ὗ̣τ̣α̣ι̣. χρῶντ[αι δ' ἀμφορεῦσιν ια´, οἳ δ]ια[νέμ]ο̣νται τακτ̣ὰ̣ [μέρη· γ´ μὲν ἀμφορέας ἀ]π̣ο̣τ̣ί̣[θη]σιν ὁ̣ δι[κ]ασ[τὴς τῷ διαψηφισμῷ, τ]ὸ λ[οιπὸν δ']*

67. 2. αὐλ[ίσκους] ἔχουσαι ἔκρους Wilcken, Chambers: αὐλ[ώδεις] H. Diels *ap.* Oppermann, perhaps rightly, ἔχουσ[αι μι]κρούς A. A. Sakellarios, Kenyon[4–5].

{καὶ} secl. Kaibel & Wilamowitz[3] (κ´ Wilcken, Kenyon[4], καὶ Chambers): περὶ (π´) Hommel.

[δραχ]μ̣ὰ̣ς Wilcken, Chambers: rejected Kenyon[4–5].

ἐν[τὸ]ς α̣´ Chambers, cf. [α´] Kenyon[4–5], [χ´] suggested once by B. Keil: [β´] Hommel, ἐ̣ν̣[μήνοις] Kaibel & Wilamowitz[3].

[καὶ ὕστ]ερον Blass[3], Chambers: <αἷς> Kaibel & Wilamowitz[3], Kenyon[4–5].

67. 3. ὅταν ψήφισμα ἢ] νόμον … ἀναγιγ[νώσκειν μέλλῃ. ὅταν Kaibel & Wilamowitz[3], Kenyon[4–5], Chambers: ἐπειδὰν μέλλῃ τινὰ ἢ] νόμον ἢ μαρ[τυρίαν ἢ τοιοῦτόν τι … ἀναγιγ[νώσκειν. ἐπειδὰν Blass[3].

ἡ̣ δ̣[ίκη Blass[2], Chambers: ὁ [ἀγών Kenyon[4–5].

ἐπιλαμβ[άνει αὐτόν Kenyon[4–5]: ἐπιλαμβ[άνει τὸν αὐλίσκον Chambers.

67. 4–68. 1. Extremely uncertain: I print *exempli gratia* the reconstruction of Hommel, but am not convinced that it is right at every point.

67. 4. σύμμετ]ρ̣ο̣[ι α]ὗ̣τ̣α̣ι̣ Hommel: – –]α̣ρ̣ο̣ . . . ντ̣α̣ι̣ Kenyon[4–5], Chambers, α̣ὗ̣τ̣α̣ι̣ not impossible Thomas.

ια´, οἳ δ]ια[νέμ]ο̣νται Hommel: – –]ια . . . τ̣ε̣νται̣ς Kenyon[4–5], cf. Chambers (. . . . ε̣ν̣ταις), ενται without ς Thomas (ο impossible).

τακτ̣ὰ̣ Hommel: τα κλι Kenyon[4–5], perhaps τακλ̣ vel τακτ̣ Thomas, τ̣α̣κλα̣ Chambers.

ἀ]π̣ο̣τ̣ί̣[θη]σιν ὁ̣ Hommel: ἀπ]ο . . . . . ασιν Kenyon[4–5] cf. Chambers, α̣σιν possible but ησιν impossible Thomas.

to the point; when public matters, public suits, and they work through the trial of only one case. (*2*) There are water clocks with outlet tubes, into which they pour the water against which speeches in trials must be timed. The allowance is ten *choes* for cases above five thousand drachmae, and three *choes* for the second speech; seven *choes* for those up to five thousand, and two *choes*; five *choes* for those within 1,000, and two *choes*; six *choes* for *diadikasiai*, and in them there is no subsequent speech. (*3*) The man picked by sortition to take charge of the water clock closes the tube whenever the secretary is going to read a decree or law or testimony or contract. But when the trial is set against the measured-out day, then he does not close it but there is an equal allowance of water for the prosecutor and the defendant. (*4*) *The measuring out is done against the days of Posideon, for they are compatible with the others. They use 11 amphoras, which are distributed in fixed portions: the juror* [*in charge of the water*] *sets aside three amphoras for the voting, and each party*

*ἴσον ἕκαστοι μ̣[έρος λαμβάνουσιν. πρό]τε[ρον] γὰρ ἔσπευδο[ν εἰς πάνυ βραχὺ τοῦ χρόνου μέ]ρος ἐξωθεῖν τοὺς [φεύγοντας, ὥστε τὸ ἐπι]λεῖ[πο]ν ὕδωρ λαμβά[νειν· νῦν δὲ β΄ κάδοι] εἰ[σίν, ὁ] μὲν ἕ̣τερος τοῖς δ[ιώκουσιν, ὁ δ᾽ ἕτερος] το[ῖς] φεύγου[σ]ιν. (5) ἐν δὲ τοῖς [πρότερον χρόνοις ὕδ]α̣τ̣ό̣[ς τι] ἐξεῖλε τῷ διαψη[φισμῷ τῷ δευτέρ]ῳ̣. δ̣ι̣[αιρ]εῖται δ᾽ [ἡ ἡμ]έ[ρ]α ἐπὶ τοῖς [δημοσίοις τῶν ἀγ]ώνω[ν, ὅ]σοις πρόσεστι δεσμ[ὸς ἢ θάνατος ἢ φυγὴ ἢ ἀτι]μία ἢ δήμευσις χρημάτ[ων ἢ τιμῆσαι δ]ε̣[ῖ ὅ] τι χρὴ παθεῖν ἢ ἀποτεῖ[σαι. (**68**) τὰ δὲ δημόσι]α τῶν [δικ]αστηρίων ἐστὶ φ[α΄, οἷς κρίνειν τοὺς ἐλάττου]ς δ̣[ιδό]ασιν· ὅταν δὲ δέ[η̣ τὰς μείζους γραφ]ὰς ε[ἰς ͵α εἰ]σαγαγεῖν, συν[έρχεται β΄ δικαστή]ρια εἰ[ς] τὴν ἡλιαίαν· τα[ῖς δὲ μεγίσταις συνι]κ̣υ̣[εῖται] εἰς φ΄ καὶ ͵α τρία [δικαστήρια.*

67. 4. ὁ δι[κ]ασ[τὴς Hommel: οἱ δ̣ι̣κ̣α̣σ̣[ταὶ Chambers cf. Kenyon[4–5].

τ]ὸ λ[οιπον δ᾽] ἴσον Hommel: ολ[. . . . ε]ἱς ὃν Kenyon[4–5], ολ . . . . . ε̣ ἴσον Chambers.

ἕκαστοι μ̣[έρος λαμβάνουσιν. πρό]τε[ρον] Hommel, Chambers.

εἰς πάνυ βραχὺ τοῦ χρόνου μέ]ρος Hommel: – –]πετ . . ρος Kenyon[4–5], approved Thomas, πετ[. μέ]ρος Chambers.

τοὺς [φεύγοντας, ὥστε τὸ ἐπι]λεῖ[πο]ν ὕδωρ λαμβά[νειν Hommel, Chambers.

νῦν δὲ β΄ κάδοι] εἰ[σίν, ὁ] μὲν ἕ̣τερος τοῖς δ[ιώκουσιν, ὁ δ᾽ ἕτερος] το[ῖς] φεύγου[σ]ιν Hommel: ἀμφορεῖς for κάδοι Chambers.

67. 5. [πρότερον χρόνοις ὕδ]α̣τ̣ό̣[ς τι] ἐξεῖλε Hommel: ατο Kenyon[4–5], Chambers, ὕδ]α̣τ̣ο̣[ς doubtful Thomas; ἐξεῖλε Kenyon[4–5], εξ . . . . Chambers.

διαψη[φισμῷ τῷ δευτέρ]ῳ̣ Hommel, Chambers: τῷ δευτέρ]ῳ̣ not restored by Kenyon[4–5].

δ̣ι̣[αιρ]εῖται δ᾽ [ἡ ἡμ]έ[ρ]α Kenyon[4–5], Hommel, cf. Chambers (who does not read μ]έ[ρ).

[δημοσίοις τῶν ἀγ]ώνω[ν Hommel: [δημοσίοις τῶν not restored by Kenyon[4–5], Chambers.

ὅ]σοις πρόσεστι δεσμ[ὸς … παθεῖν ἢ ἀποτεῖ[σαι Hommel, Chambers: χρημάτ[ων – – – –]μ̣ο̣ι̣ς [ὅ] τι Kenyon[4–5].

68. 1. τὰ δὲ δημόσι]α Hommel: τὰ δὲ πολλ]ὰ Kaibel & Wilamowitz[3], Kenyon[4–5] (but not enough for the space Kenyon[4]), τὰ μὲν οὖν πολλ]ὰ Chambers.

φ[α΄, οἷς κρίνειν τοὺς ἐλάττου]ς δ̣[ιδό]ασιν Hommel: φ[– – – –]σο . . . . ασιν Kenyon[4–5], Chambers (φ[α΄ Chambers), σο not seen by Thomas.

ὅταν δὲ δέ[η τὰς μείζους … εἰ[ς] τὴν ἡλιαίαν Hommel: τὰς δημοσίας Kenyon[4–5], Chambers.

τα[ῖς δὲ μεγίσταις συνι]κ̣υ̣[εῖται] Hommel: not restored by Kenyon[4–5] (κ̣υ̣α̣), κ̣υ̣ possible Thomas, τὰ δ̣[ὲ μέγιστα – – – –]κλ̣ε̣[.] δ᾽ Chambers.

takes an equal share of the remainder. For previously [*the prosecutors*] *were eager to force the defendants into a very small share of the time, so that they had to accept the water which remained; but now there are two jars, one for the prosecutors and one for the defendants.* (5) *In previous times he took out some water for the second vote. The day is divided for those public contests for which there is a penalty of imprisonment or death or exile or* atimia *or confiscation of property, or there has to be an assessment of what the culprit should suffer or pay.* (**68**) *Of the lawcourts the public ones are 501, to which they grant the judging of the lesser suits. When they need to introduce the greater public suits into 1,000, two courts are brought together in the* eliaia*; and for the greatest suits 3 courts are united for 1,500.*

(*2*) ψῆφοι δὲ̣] εἰσιν χαλκαῖ, αὐλίσ̣κον [ἔχουσαι ἐν τῷ μέσῳ, αἱ μ]ὲ[ν] ἡμίσειαι τετρυπ[ημέναι, αἱ δὲ ἡμίσ]ει[αι πλή]ρεις. οἱ δὲ λαχόντες [ἐπὶ τὰς ψήφους, ἐπειδὰν εἰρη]μένοι ὦσιν οἱ [λόγοι, παραδιδόασιν ἑ]κάστῳ τῶν δικαστῶ[ν δύο ψήφους, τετρυπ]ημένην καὶ πλήρη, [φανερὰς ὁρᾶν τοῖς ἀντιδί]κο[ις, ἵνα μήτε πλή[ρεις μήτε τετρυπημένα]ς̣ ἀμφοτέρας λαμβάν[ωσι. τότε δ' ὁ ἐπὶ τοῦτο] εἰληχὼς ἀπολα[μβάνει τὰς βακτηρίας, ἀνθ'] ὧ[ν] εἷς ἕκαστος ψηφιζ[όμενος λαμβάνει σύμβολο]ν [χ]αλκοῦν μετὰ] τοῦ Γ (ἀποδιδοὺς γὰρ γ´ λαμβάνει), ἵνα ψηφίζωνται πάντες· οὐ γὰρ ἔστι λαβεῖν σύμβολον [οὐδεν]ὶ ἐὰν μὴ ψηφίζηται. (*3*) εἰσὶ δὲ ἀμφορεῖς δύο κείμενοι ἐν τῷ δικαστηρίῳ, ὁ μὲν χαλκοῦς, ὁ δὲ ξύλινος, διαιρετοὶ ὅπως μὴ λ̣[άθ]η̣ ὑποβάλλων [τις ψή]φους, εἰς οὓς ψηφίζονται οἱ δικασταί· ὁ μὲν χαλκοῦς κύριος, ὁ δὲ ξύλινος ἄκυρος, ἔχων ὁ χαλκοῦς ἐπίθημα διερρινημένον ὥστ' αὐτὴν μόνην χωρεῖν τὴν ψῆφον, ἵνα μὴ δύο ὁ αὐτὸς [ἐμβάλ]λῃ. (*4*) ἐπειδὰν δὲ διαψηφίζεσθαι μέλλωσιν οἱ δικασταί, ὁ κῆρυξ ἀγορεύει πρῶτον, ἂν ἐπισκή[πτων]ται οἱ ἀντίδικοι ταῖς μαρτυρίαις· οὐ γὰρ [ἔστιν] ἐπισκήψασθαι ὅταν ἄρξωνται διαψηφίζεσθαι. ἔπειτα πάλιν ἀνακηρύττει "ἡ τετρυπημένη τοῦ πρότερον λέγοντος, ἡ δὲ πλήρης τοῦ ὕστερον λέγοντος." ὁ δὲ δικαστὴς λα[βόμενος] ἐκ τοῦ λυχνείου τὰς ψήφους, πιέζων τὸν [αὐλίσκο]ν τῆς ψήφου καὶ οὐ δεικνύων τοῖς ἀγωνιζομένοις οὔτε τὸ τετρυπημένον οὔτε τὸ πλῆρες, ἐμβάλλει τὴν μὲν κυρίαν εἰς τὸν χαλκοῦν ἀμφορέα, τὴν δὲ ἄκυρον εἰς τὸν ξύλινον.

(**69**) πάντες δ' ἐπειδὰν ὦσι διε[ψηφι]σμένοι, λαβόντες οἱ ὑπηρέται τὸν ἀμφορέα τὸν κύριον, ἐξερῶσι ἐπὶ ἄβακα τρυπήματα ἔχοντα ὅσαιπερ εἰσὶν αἱ ψῆ[φοι, καὶ τ]αῦτα ὅπ[ως] αἱ κυρ<ιαι προ>κείμεναι {κ} εὐαρίθμητοι

68. 2. ψῆφοι δέ] εἰσιν … ἀμφοτέρας λαμβάν[ωσι Kenyon[1] cf. Harp.τ 8 Keaney τετρυπημένη.

τότε δ' ὁ ἐπὶ τοῦτο] εἰληχὼς ἀπολα[μβάνει τὰς βακτηρίας Kenyon[4–5], τὰς βακτηρίας P. S. Photiades: ὁ δὲ ταύτην τὴν ἀρχὴ]ν̣ εἰληχὼς ἀπολα[μβάνει τὰ σύμβολα Thalheim, Chambers.

68. 4. λα[βόμενος] Hommel: λα[βὼν ἅμα] Blass[4], Kenyon[4–5], Chambers.

ἐκ τοῦ λυχνείου τὰς ψήφους, πιέζων τὸν [αὐλίσκο]ν Kenyon[4–5] ([αὐλισκὸν]), Chambers, after P. N. Papageorgios: ἐκ τοῦ αὐλίσκου … τὸ [μέσον] Hommel.

69. 1. καὶ τ]αῦτα ὅπ[ως] αἱ κυρ<ιαι προ>κείμεναι {κ} Kenyon[4–5], Chambers: ἵν'] αὖτα[ι φανεραὶ προ]κείμεναι {καὶ} Kaibel & Wilamowitz[3].

(*2*) There are bronze ballots, with a tube through the middle, half hollow and half solid. When the speeches have been delivered, the jurors picked by sortition to take charge of the ballots hand over two ballots to each of the jurors, a hollow and a solid, clear for the opposing litigants to see, so that the jurors shall not receive two solid or two hollow. Then the man picked by sortition for this task takes away the staves, in exchange for which each juror as he casts his vote receives a bronze token marked with *gamma* (for on returning that he receives 3 obols), so that all shall vote; for it is not possible for anybody to receive a token unless he does vote. (*3*) There are two amphoras standing in the court, one of bronze and one of wood, capable of being dismantled so that nobody shall surreptitiously add ballots undetected, and the jurors cast their ballots into these: the bronze amphora is the decisive one and the wooden is not decisive, and the bronze one has a pierced attachment such that only one ballot can pass through it, so that the same man cannot deposit two ballots. (*4*) When the jurors are about to vote, first the herald asks whether the opposing litigants challenge the testimonies; for it is not possible to make a challenge when they have started to vote. Then he proclaims again, 'The hollow ballot is for the man who spoke first, and the solid is for the one who spoke afterwards'. The juror takes his ballots from the lamp-stand, covering the tube of the ballot and not showing the hollow or the solid tube to the contestants, and the deposits the decisive ballot in the bronze amphora and the non-decisive in the wooden.

(**69**) When they have all voted, the attendants take the bronze amphora and empty it on to a board which has as many holes as there are ballots, designed so that the votes which are decisive can be laid out

ὦσιν, καὶ τὰ τρυπητὰ καὶ τὰ πλήρη {δηλονότι τοῖς ἀντιδίκοις}. οἱ δὲ ἐπὶ τὰς ψήφους εἰληχότες δια[ριθ]μ[οῦ]σιν αὐτὰς ἐπὶ τοῦ ἄβακος, [χωρὶ]ς μὲν τὰς πλήρεις, χωρὶς δὲ τὰς τετρυπημένας. καὶ ἀναγορεύει ὁ κῆρυξ τὸν ἀ̣[ριθ]μὸν τῶν ψήφων, τοῦ μὲν διώκοντος τὰς τετρυπημένας, τοῦ δὲ φεύγοντος τὰς πλήρεις· ὁποτέρῳ δ' ἂν πλείων γένηται, οὗτος νικᾷ, ἂν δὲ ἴσαι, ὁ φεύγων. (*2*) ἔπειτα πάλιν τιμῶσι, ἂν δέῃ τιμῆσαι, τὸν αὐτὸν τρόπον ψηφιζόμενοι, τὸ μὲν σύμβολον ἀποδιδόντες, βακτηρίαν δὲ πάλιν παραλαμβάνοντες. ἡ δὲ τίμησίς ἐστιν πρὸς ἥμισυ τοῦ ὕδατος ἑκατέρῳ. ἐπειδὰν δὲ αὐτοῖς ᾖ δεδικασμένα τὰ ἐκ τῶν νόμων, ἀπολαμβάνουσιν τὸν μισθὸν ἐν τῷ μέρει οὗ ἔλαχον ἕκαστοι.

69. 1. καὶ τὰ τρυπητὰ καὶ τὰ πλήρη {δηλονότι τοῖς ἀντιδίκοις} Kenyon[4–5], Chambers, cf. υ . . υ̣π̣ητα Thomas: {καὶ <τὰ> τε[τρ]υπημένα [καὶ] τὰ π[λ]ήρη δηλ(. . .)} [τοῖς ἀν]τιδ[ί]κοις Kaibel & Wilamowitz[3].

69. 2. ἥμισυ τοῦ D. M. MacDowell: ἡμιχοῦν L.

to be counted easily, both the hollow and the solid. The men picked by sortition to take charge of the ballots count them on the board, the solid and the hollow separately. And the herald announces the number of the ballots, the hollow for the prosecutor and the solid for the defendant: whichever has the greater number, he is the winner, and if they are equal the defendant wins. (*2*) Then again they make the assessment, if an assessment is needed, voting in the same way, giving up their token and taking their staff again. Speeches on the assessment are made against a half allowance of water for each. When they have completed the trials prescribed by the laws, they receive their stipend in the section assigned to each by sortition.

COMMENTARY

A. The lost beginning

It has been calculated that the lost beginning, including most of *A.P.*'s account of Cylon (ch. 1, below), should have occupied about five of the chapters into which Kenyon divided the surviving text (cf. Introduction, p. 7). From 41. 2, which lists the 'changes' in the constitution, and the *Epitome of Heraclides* (cf. Introduction, p. 2) we can obtain the following list of items to be supplied before the affair of Cylon: (*a*) Athens was originally ruled by kings; (*b*) Ion settled in Attica and was responsible for the creation of the four tribes; (*c*) Pandion divided the rule among his sons, and that led to *stasis*; (*d*) Theseus moderated the monarchy, making a proclamation of equity; (*e*) the story of Theseus' death was told, with a digression on the recovery of his bones from Scyros by Cimon; (*f*) the kingship was abolished; (*g*) the story of Hippomenes, the last king from the Codridae, was told. *A.P.* will have mentioned episodes which involved a change either in the royal house or in the standing of the people.

(*a*) The kings of Athens (fr. 1). Cf. 3. 1, 3. The legend of the kings was developed from a very meagre tradition. The outline accepted by *A.P.* is that which was acccpted by the later chronographers. After Cecrops I there were fourteen kings of the Erechtheid dynasty from Cranaus to Thymoetes; a new dynasty began with Melanthus; after the death of Melanthus' son Codrus, Codrus' son Medon was the first of a series of archons elected for life from Melanthus' family; after thirteen life archons there was a change to archons elected for ten years; after Hippomenes the office was opened to all eupatrids; annual archons began with Creon (683/2). Few of the kings are mentioned by Herodotus; the list seems originally to have been compiled by Hellanicus (see Jacoby, *Atthis*, 125–7, and commentary on *FGrH* 323a F 23), and *A.P.* had access to a list with some variants.

(*b*) Ion (41. 2, frs 1–2). In the reign of Erechtheus Eleusis and the Thracians attacked Athens, and the defence was successfully led by Ion, son of the Peloponnesian king Xuthus and Erechtheus' daughter Creusa. Ion was not included in the list of Athenian kings, but was considered by *A.P.* to have been the first polemarch (3. 2). He was regarded as the ancestor of the Athenians and all the Ionians, in reflection of the tradition that after the fall of the Mycenaean kingdoms men migrated from other parts of Greece to Athens and from Athens to Asia Minor (e.g. Solon fr. 4a West *ap.* 5. 2; also Hdt. I. 146. 2, 147.2, VIII. 44. 2, IX. 106. 3, Thuc. I. 2. 5–6, 6. 3, 12. 4, II. 15. 4), and the four 'Ionian' tribes found in Athens and elsewhere were said to be named after his sons (e.g. Hdt. V. 66. 2, 69. 1).

41. 2 and fr. 1 report that Ion settled in Attica, and gave it a cult of Apollo Patroios. Fr. 2 was associated with Ion by H. T. Wade-Gery, *CQ* 25 (1931), 2–6 = his *Essays*, 88–92, attributing to him a division of the people not only into four tribes and their subdivisions but also into *georgoi* and *demiourgoi* ('farmers' and 'craftsmen'; but the further separation of a class of *eupatridai* was attributed to Theseus: see §*d*).

Athens' four Ionian tribes were Aigikoreis, Argadeis, Geleontes and Hopletes (e.g. Hdt. V. 66. 2, Eur. *Ion* 1575–81): these and two others, Boreis and Oinopes, are found in other Ionian states, but there is not as much uniformity as is found with the three Dorian tribes in Dorian states. Fr. 2 suggests that each tribe was divided into three *trittyes* = *phratriai*, each of those into thirty *gene*, and each *genos* contained thirty men – and it compares this structure with the seasons, months and days of the year. Cf. the five tribes, sixty demes and 720 phratries of *P. Hibeh* 28 (third century; probably a utopian constitution: see S. R. West, *ZPE* 53 [1983], 79–84); also the 5,040 landholders of Pl. *Leg.* V. 737 E. For the division of the tribes into *trittyes* cf. 8. 3 and 21. 3, and Cleisthenes' division of his new tribes into *trittyes*, 21. 4 (*trittys* might be expected to mean something which was itself divided into three parts, but in Athens it clearly denoted a third of a tribe). On these *trittyes* see N. Papazarkadas, *CQ*[2] 57 (2007), 22–32.

However, *phratriai* were not identical with the *trittyes* but were far more numerous (though it is possible that all the members of a *phratria* belonged to the same tribe); they were kinship groups (fictitious in origin but hereditary); and *gene* were primarily families which provided priests, though it is likely that such families were in fact among the most important socially and politically in early Athens. Every Athenian, it seems, belonged to a *phratria* (cf. Draco's homicide law, ML 86 = *IG* i³ 104 ~ Fornara 15. B. 16–23). Not every Athenian belonged to a *genos* (cf. Philoch. *FGrH* 328 F 35, recording a law which obliged the *phratriai* to accept as members 'the *orgeones* and the *homogalaktes* whom we call *gennetai*', with A. Andrewes, *JHS* 81 [1961], 1–15, but Ch. Theodoridis, *ZPE* 138 [2002], 40–2, has shown that this came from Philochorus' book III and may have been attributed to Solon); but a typical *phratria* may have comprised a *genos* and an outer circle of other members. Andrewes, *Hermes* 89 (1961), 129–40, argued that the classical Greeks' kinship organisations were a creation of the dark age, when it suited the strong to build up bodies of dependants and the weak to attach themselves to a protector. See F. Bourriot, *Recherches sur la nature du génos* (Paris: Champion for U. de Paris I, 1976); D. Roussel, *Tribu et cité* (Ann. Litt. U. Besançon cxciii. Paris: Les Belles Lettres, 1976; S. D. Lambert, *The Phratries of Attica* (U. of Michigan P., 1993); Bourriot and Roussel believe that the 360 *gene* of fr. 3 existed but were different from the *gene* attested in our evidence, but I believe that they are part of a speculative reconstruction which misrepresented the *phratriai* and the *gene.* The old tribes and *trittyes* continued to exist after Cleisthenes' creation of new tribes and *trittyes*, and so did the *phratriai* and *gene* (cf. 21. 2, 6, with commentary). The author of *A.P.* will surely have known that *trittyes* and *phratriai* differed, and that in his time not all Athenians were *gennetai*: he may have thought that in early Athens all citizens were *gennetai*, but he can hardly be responsible for the scheme attributed to him in fr. 3.

Of the two classes, the *georgoi* are farmers. *Demiourgoi* appear in Hom. *Od.* XVII. 383–5, XIX. 135 and later as men who ply specialised crafts; in some states the word was the title of an official, but whatever the origin of the word (perhaps men who worked for the *demos*) in this contrast with farmers they must be craftsmen. §*d* will attribute to Theseus the creation of a third class, the *eupatridai*; and the three classes make their only appearance in the historical period in the problematic 13. 2 (see *ad loc.*). The *eupatridai*, 'well born', existed in historical Athens, as the aristocratic families which in some cases claimed divine ancestry but in practice were the families which had emerged most successful from the upheavals of the dark age, owning the largest tracts of good land and wielding the most political power (cf. C. A. Roebuck, *Hesperia* 43 [1974], 487–90 = his *Economy and Society in the Early Greek World* [Chicago:

Ares, 1979], 87–90). *Eupatridai* and *gennetai* are likely to have been overlapping élite categories within the body of Athenians. However, I suspect that the application of this class division to early Athens rests not on reliable tradition but on philosophers' teaching about what elements ought to be found in the *polis*. Cf. L. Gernet, *RPh*³ 12 (1938), 216–27; Day & Chambers, *Aristotle's History of Athenian Democracy*, 173.

(*c*) Pandion (fr. 1). Erechtheus was succeeded by Cecrops II, and Cecrops by Pandion II. In what became the standard version Pandion was driven out of Athens by the sons of Metion, went to Megara, married the king's daughter and then himself became king of Megara; after his death his four sons recovered Attica and divided the kingdom amongst themselves (Apollod. *Bibl.* III. 205–6, Paus. I. 5. 3–4 cf. 41. 6); but it appears from *Epit.* that *A.P.* followed an alternative version in which Pandion acquired Megara without losing Athens and himself divided the kingdom amongst his sons (cf. Soph. fr. 24 *TrGF ap.* Strabo 392 / IX. 1. 6, schol Ar. *Lys.* 58 cf. schol. *Vesp.* 1223). For discussion of the story and its connection with the quarrels between Athens and Megara in the seventh and sixth century (cf. on 1, 2. 2, 14. 1) see Jacoby on Philoch. *FGrH* 328 F 107, suggesting that in Pandion Athens adopted a figure from Megarian legend while Megara in turn tried to lay claim to Aegeus.

Aegeus as the eldest son obtained Athens and the surrounding plain, Pallas the coast, Lycus the Diacria (the north-east of Attica) – thus foreshadowing the regional divisions of the sixth century (cf. on 13. 4) – and Nisus Megara. Aegeus quarrelled with his brothers: he expelled Lycus, who fled to Asia Minor and became the ancestor of the Lycians (Hdt. I. 173.3 cf. VII. 92, Strabo 573 / XII. 8. 5, 667 / XIV. 3. 10, Paus. I. 19. 3); after recognising Theseus as his son and heir he was attacked by Pallas, whom Theseus defeated (Plut. *Thes.* 13, schol Eur. *Hipp.* 35, which includes Philoch. *FGrH* 328 F 108, cf. Apollod. *Epit.* I. 11); while Nisus was killed and Megara was captured by Minos of Crete (Apollod. *Bibl.* III. 209–11). Thus Attica could be reunited by Theseus.

(*d*) Theseus' proclamation (41. 2; fr. 3). Theseus was believed to have accomplished a *synoikismos* by which the whole of Attica, previously composed of twelve *poleis* (Philoch. *FGrH* 328 F 94 *ap.* Strabo 397 / IX. 1. 20) was attached to the *polis* of Athens (e.g. Thuc. II. 15. 2). He was also said to have been a king with democratic leanings, who somehow gave up the kingship or some of its power and established a form of democracy (e.g. Eur. *Supp.* 399–408, cf. 350–3, 429–41, Isoc. X. *Helen* 34–7, XII. *Panath.* 126–9, [Dem.] LIX. *Neaer.* 74–5, LX. *Epitaph.* 28). In Plut. *Thes.* 25 (= fr. 3) probably only §3 is derived directly from *A.P.*: the proclamation (§1) will have been a standard part of the story, presumably attached to the *synoikismos*; §2 attributes to Theseus the creation of three classes, whereas *A.P.* probably attributed the *georgoi* and *demiourgoi* to Ion and only the separation from them of the *eupatridai* to Theseus (cf. §*b*, above). Theseus' granting of privileges to the *eupatridai* was perhaps seen as the first stage in a development from absolute monarchy to democracy.

As for what actually happened, whatever may have been the state of Attica in the bronze age, it appears from the archaeological evidence that Athens itself was continuously occupied from then until the archaic period but the rest of Attica was not: towards the end of the dark age there was not an attachment to Athens of previously independent settlements but an expansion into Attica from Athens (e.g. C. A. Roebuck, *Hesperia* 43 [1974], 488–9 = his *Economy and Society in the Early Greek World*, 88–9; A. M. Snodgrass, *Archaeology and the Rise of the Greek State* [Cambridge U. P., 1977], 16–21; see also S. Diamant, in *Studies ... Presented to Eugene Vanderpool* [*Hesperia* Supp. 19 (1982)], 38–47); and, while that resulted in settlements across Attica but not in independent *poleis*, the Pisistratid tyranny (chs 14–19) and the reforms of Cleisthenes (chs 20–1) in the sixth century are likely to have created a stronger feeling throughout Attica of belonging to Athens than existed before then. The population was never concentrated in the city, but continued to be dispersed through Attica; the *eupatridai* will for the most part have been families with some property near the city and easy access to the city.

(*e*) The death of Theseus (fr. 4). Theseus' death and the recovery of his bones were not in themselves relevant to the history of the constitution, so we may assume that *A.P.* told the whole story of the events leading to Theseus' death. Theseus and Pirithous captured Helen from Sparta, but were themselves captured when they attempted to carry off Persephone from the underworld (Diod. Sic. IV. 63, Apollod. *Epit.* I. 23–4, Hyg.

Fab. 79; from Epirus, Plut. *Thes.* 31, Ael. *V.H.* IV. 5, Paus. I. 17. 4–5). While Theseus was absent Menestheus roused the Athenians against him and with the help of Helen's brothers was made king in his place; Theseus returned to Athens but failed to regain control, so he sent his children to Euboea and himself sailed to Scyros, where he was lured to his death by Lycomedes (Plut. *Thes.* 32–5, Paus. I. 17. 5–6). The capture of Scyros, in the northern Aegean, perhaps in 476/5, was one of Athens' first achievements after the Persian Wars: Delphi had ordered Athens to bring back the bones of Theseus, and Cimon obtained a suitable skeleton (Plut. *Thes.* 36. 1–3, *Cim.* 8. 3–7, Paus. I. 17. 6). For Scyros in the fourth century see 62. 2 with commentary.

The ousting of Theseus by Menestheus explained why Menestheus was commander of the Athenians in the Trojan War (Hom. *Il.* II. 546–66), and the involvement of Sparta explained why the cult of Heracles was important in Athens but that of Theseus was comparatively late and unimportant (cf. on 15. 4). For those who wanted to attribute the democracy to a later man than Theseus (see particularly E. Ruschenbusch, *Historia* vii 1958, 398–424 = his *Kleine Schriften A. G.*, 59–80, but his view of who was a democratic hero when was too schematic), his removal would also explain the ending of his premature democracy. On Menestheus see M. Valdés Guía, *Incid. Antico* viii 2010, 81–108.

(*f*) The abolition of the kingship (fr. 5). *A.P.* presumably mentioned the recovery of the throne by Theseus' son Demophon, either after Menestheus died at Troy (Plut. *Thes.* 35. 8) or by expelling him after the Trojan War (schol. Thuc. I. 12. 2), and the change of dynasty when Melanthus accepted on behalf of Thymoetes a challenge from Xanthus of Boeotia on condition that he should become king if he won (Hdt. V. 63. 3, Hellanicus *FGrH* 323a F 23, Strabo 393 / IX. 1. 7, Paus. II. 18. 8–9). In what became the standard version Melanthus' son Codrus was the last king and his son Medon was persuaded to be archon for life; 3. 3 quotes a variant, that Medon was the last king and his son Acastus the first life archon. For the alleged softness of the kings cf. 3. 2, where *A.P.* gives the same reason for the appointment of Ion as polemarch.

(*g*) The story of Hippomenes (fr. 5). Although in the standard account the last king was Codrus or Medon, there are traces of an older tradition in which all the rulers down to Hippomenes were kings, and the monarchy was abolished after Hippomenes' cruel punishment of a daughter caught in adultery (*Marm. Par. FGrH* 239 A 27–31, cf. Pl. *Symp.* 208 D 4–5, Paus. I. 3. 3, IV. 13. 7; Hippomenes is king in *Suda* π 655 Adler Πάριππον καὶ κόρην but archon in Diod. Sic. VIII. 22, Nic. Dam. *FGrH* 90 F 49, *Suda* ι 573 Adler Ἱππομένης). *Epit.* suggests that in *A.P.* the family of Codrus had earlier been deprived of the kingship because of its softness, the archons had subsequently had their term reduced from life to ten years, and Hippomenes was 'one of the Codridae' who wanted to retrieve the family's reputation; after his act of cruelty (probably, conveniently, in his tenth year) the office was opened to all the *eupatridai*. For discussion of the different versions see Jacoby on Hellan. *FGrH* 323a F 23 (but he thought that here *A.P.* considered Hippomenes the last of the kings, and ch. 3 was inserted into the original text of *A.P.* at the same time as ch. 4).

The lost beginning of *A.P.* may also have included the change from ten-year archons to annual archons, beginning with Creon (683/2) (cf. 3. 4), and at some point the creation of the council of the Areopagus, since 3. 6 does not look like the first mention of that body.

B. Cylon (fr. 6, ch. 1)

The first surviving words of the preserved text of *A.P.* are the end of a chapter on Cylon. The other main accounts are Hdt. V. 71, Thuc. I. 126. 3–12, Plut. *Sol.* 12. 1–9, schol. Ar. *Eq.* 445 (three accounts).

Cylon, an Olympic victor, married to the daughter of Theagenes the tyrant of Megara, assembled a band of supporters, including a force from Megara, and tried to seize the acropolis. He had consulted Delphi, had been advised to act during the greatest festival of Zeus, and had interpreted that as the Olympic festival rather than Athens' festival, the Diasia (Thuc. §§4–6, schol. §b): this is perhaps contradicting a rival version in which Cylon did act at the Diasia (M. H. Jameson, *BCH* 89 [1965], 167–72).

According to Herodotus the attempt failed, Cylon and his supporters became suppliants at the statue (*sc.* of Athena), they were persuaded to move by 'the *prytaneis* of the *naukraroi*, who then administered Athens', but they were killed and the Alcmaeonid family was blamed for that. For Thucydides Cylon and his supporters occupied the acropolis but the people came in force from the fields (ἐκ τῶν ἀγρῶν: in an alternative version, from Agrae, where they were celebrating the Diasia?) and besieged them; when the people grew weary they entrusted the matter to the nine archons, who 'then conducted most of the political business'; Cylon and his brother escaped, but the others went as suppliants to the altar on the acropolis, and were persuaded to move but were then killed. Plutarch begins with the conspirators as suppliants of Athena; Megacles the archon persuaded them to stand trial; to keep their divine protection they attached a thread to the statue, but the thread broke, Megacles and his colleagues turned against them and they were killed.

Herodotus and the scholia say that those responsible for the killing were cursed. Thucydides says that the accursed were expelled, and were expelled again by Cleomenes of Sparta (in 508/7: see 20. 3), and (apparently on the second occasion) the bones of those who had been buried in Attica were removed too, but later the accursed returned. For Plutarch the surviving Cylonians became strong again and there was *stasis* between them and the descendants of Megacles, until Solon persuaded the accursed to stand trial: Myron of Phlya proscuted, the accursed were convicted, and the living were expelled and the bones of the dead were removed. Athens was plunged into a state of fear when Megara captured Nisaea and Salamis (see on 14. 1), until the Athenians called in Epimenides of Crete, who advised Solon and purified the city. Fr. 6 (*Epit.* 2), mentioning 'those around Megacles', and what survives of ch. 1, indicate that *A.P.* told the same version of the story as Plutarch – but gave only one sentence on Epimenides: we should think of a common source, the one used on Solon and what happened before his reforms (cf. pp. 183, 195), not of Plutarch as following *A.P.*

Tyranny and killing suppliants could both be seen as wrong, so it is not surprising that different versions of the story were told (on this story in oral tradition see expecially R. Thomas, *Oral Tradition and Written Record in Classical Athens* [Cambridge U. P., 1989], 272–80). Herodotus considered the killing of the suppliants wrong, and his invocation of the *prytaneis* of the *naukraroi* (cf. on 8. 3) is usually seen as an attempt to divert blame from the Alcmaeonids. Thucydides was clearly engaging in polemic, and his emphasis on the nine archons as political leaders (probably factually correct) seems to be aimed against Herodotus' *prytaneis* of the *naukraroi*. Only Plutarch (and the lost part of *A.P.*) states that the man particularly responsible was the archon, the Alcmaeonid Megacles. As for Epimenides, there are signs that he was connected with Delphi before the Sacred War of the early sixth century, in which case his purification ought to have been a cleansing of the city for the Cylonians after the expulsion of the Alcmaeonids; but in Plutarch and in Diog. Laert. I. 110 he is associated with Solon, and that should imply (but does not imply in Plutarch) a link with the Alcmaeonids' return. Probably Epimenides' original position was on the Cylonian side, not long after the episode, but he came to be linked with Solon by the kind of fiction which such famous men attracted.

The *coup* and its aftermath had consequences for Athens' relations with Delphi, for the continuing conflict between Athens and Megara (see especially R. J. Hopper, *BSA* 56 [1961], 189–219), and for the Alcmaeonid family as long as its members remained prominent in politics, i.e. to the end of the fifth century (see especially G. W. Williams, *Hermathena* 78 [1951], 32–49, 79 [1952], 3–21, 80 [1952], 58–71). We do not know what combination of factors led Cylon to make his attempt, but the causes of discontent indicated in chs 2–3 cannot yet have been strong enough to gain him widespread support.

A.P. narrates the whole story before proceeding to Athens' problems (2–3), Draco (4) and Solon (5–12), but Myron's prosecution and Epimenides' purification were probably included here for narrative convenience, so their mention here does not imply a date, except that moving the bones of the dead should point to some lapse of time after the original events. Cylon's *coup* must have been in an Olympic year between his Olympic victory in 640 (Euseb. Arm. p. 92 Karst) and Draco's legislation in 621/0 (see on 4. 1), i.e. in 636, 632, 628 or 624. Later dates which some scholars have inferred from such texts as Pl. *Leg.* I. 642 D 4–E 4 (which places Epimenides' visit ten years before the Persian Wars) are not more reliable than the orthodox dating.

Nothing else is known of Myron (he could have come from Phlya, north-east of the city, though he could not have belonged to the deme of Phlya, before Cleisthenes institutionalised the demes: cf. 21. 4). For an oath sworn over (full-grown) victims cf. 29. 5; for the 'aristocratic' nature of the special court cf. 3. 1 with commentary. γένος does not imply that the Alcmaeonids were a *genos* in the technical sense of §A. b, above (and in fact the Alcmaeonids were not strongly connected with any cult). For other stories about Epimenides see Diog. Laert. I. 109–15.

C. Between Cylon and Solon (2–4)

Ch. 2 describes a *stasis* between *gnorimoi* and *plethos* (the 'notables' and the 'masses'), which Solon attempted to resolve; 3 purports to describe 'the structure of the ancient constitution before Draco', and in fact concentrates on the archons; 4 calls the content of 3 'the first constitution' and then describes the organisation which resulted from the *thesmoi* of Draco; 5. 1 introduces the account of Solon by closing the ring and mentioning 'the structure in the constitution' (3) and the enslavement of the many and the *stasis* (2).

Ch. 4 is anachronistic and reminiscent of the intermediate régime of 411/0 (cf. on 33); elsewhere there is no mention of a constitution of Draco apart from a vague reference in [Pl.] *Axioch.* 365 D 7–8, while Arist. *Pol.* II. 1274 B 15–18 explicitly states that Draco enacted laws for the existing constitution; 4. 5, and passages in 3. 1, 41. 2 and perhaps 7. 3, seem to have been written in order to accommodate the constitution of Draco to a text which originally lacked it. A few scholars have defended ch. 4 (e.g. R. Develin, *Athenaeum*[2] 62 [1984], 295–307); others have wanted to reject 3 as well as 4 (e.g. Jacoby, *Atthis*, 387–8 n. 62); but most probably what is neither historically authentic nor a part of *A.P.*'s original text, but an invention of the late fifth or early fourth century, inserted when *A.P.* was revised, runs from 'The structure of his constitution…' (4. 1) to the end of 4. 4, with 4. 5 written to ease the insertion, and may have supplanted material on the *thesmoi* of Draco which was included in the original text. Cf. Introduction, p. 30.

Although variants are noted, as in 3. 3, the careful organisation of these chapters suggests that *A.P.* had one main source; and the extent and nature of agreement between *A.P.* and Plut. *Sol.* in chs 1–12 suggests that that source was a detailed work on Solon and the background to his reforms (cf. pp. 181, 195). Little will have been remembered about Athens before Solon, and what we have in 2–3 will represent later reconstruction rather than authentic tradition: in 2 the reconstruction was based on good material, the poems and laws of Solon (*A.P.* and Plutarch both mention the technical term *hektemoros* as a word which needed to be explained to their readers), but for the institutional development in 3 there is likely to have been little good evidence.

2. 1. After that: The end of ch. 1 continued the story of the Cylonian affair to the purification by Epimenides, implying that that was some time later than the original episode; but the reference here will be to the original episode: Cylon's *coup* is seen as the first incident in a period of *stasis* lasting (probably: cf. 13. 1) until Pisistratus established himself as tyrant.

the notables and the masses: *A.P.* frequently writes of Athens as divided between the upper class (*gnorimoi*, 'notables', here, or various other words) and the lower (*demos*, 'people', or *plethos*, 'mass'), and names individual politicians as *prostatai*, 'champions', of one group or the other (2. 2, etc.; a schematic list in 28. 1–2; on the word see W. R. Connor, *The New Politicians of Fifth-Century Athens* [Princeton U. P., 1971]). This polarisation is absent from Herodotus, but is a commonplace in [Xen.] *A.P.* (1. 2, etc.), Thucydides (III. 27. 2, etc.; *prostatai tou demou* III. 75. 2. etc.) and later writers, and came to be reflected in the facts as men and cities with a range of political standpoints came to label themselves oligarchic or democratic. *Demos* was a conveniently ambiguous word, which could be used of the whole citizen community or of the subject community in contrast to its ruler or rulers or of the lower class in contrast to the upper; and in the last case the line could be drawn differently for different purposes: here *A.P.* writes of oppression of the poor by the rich, but also of the aristocratic monopoly of offices, which impinged not on the poor but on rich non-aristocrats. On the variety of terms used see Kaibel, *Stil und Text*, 51–3; on the uses of *demos* in the archaic period see W. Donlan, *PP* 25 [1970], 381–95.

2. 2. For the constitution … enslaved…: *A.P.* mentions first a political theme, to which he will return in ch. 3, and then an economic theme, with which he deals immediately. *Politeia* in *A.P.* most often, as here, means 'régime', 'constitution', 'government of the state'; but sometimes it means 'control of the government' and so 'citizenship' (e.g. 4. 2), and occasionally it refers to the body of citizens (4. 3, 37. i *fin.*, 38. 2).

the poor were enslaved to the rich Cf. Plut. *Sol.* 13. 4–5. The facts behind *A.P.*'s simple statements have proved far from simple, and there have been many attempts to elucidate the problems of seventh-century Attica: for a survey of modern views see F. Cassola, *PP* 19 (1964), 26–68. The peasants were freed from their troubles by Solon's *seisachtheia*, which both *A.P.* and Plutarch believe involved a cancellation of all existing debts, a ban for the future on loans on the security of the person and a liberation of those currently enslaved for debt. Solon claimed to have liberated the earth by uprooting the *horoi* planted in it, and to have rescued many Athenians sold abroad as slaves (fr. 36. 1–17 West *ap.* 12. 4, Plut. *Sol.* 15. 6; cf. fr. 4. 23–5) – so we can distinguish between men whose condition could be described metaphorically as the enslavement of the earth, and chattel slavery which could involve a man's being sold abroad.

Hektemoros, used by both *A.P.* and Plutarch, seems to be the proper term for dependent peasants in Attica: *A.P.* glosses this as *pelates*, a neighbour and commonly a neighbour who works as a dependant; Plutarch glosses it as *thes*, one who labours for another. The *hektemoroi*, 'sixth-parters', apparently had to give one sixth (clearer in Plutarch than in *A.P.*) of their produce to an overlord: land which they worked on these terms was *epimortos ge*, and the portion which they surrendered was their *morte* (Poll. VII. 151). The three main explanations have been (*a*) that all farming land belonged to one of the aristocratic families and the *hektemoroi* were a hereditary class of dependent serfs; (*b*) that the peasants were former owners of their land, who could dispose of it but whose creditors made them *hektemoroi* when they defaulted on their debts; (*c*) that the *hektemoroi* were owners of their land and could not dispose of it, so their creditors had to retain them as *hektemoroi* when they defaulted on their debts; while Cassola suggested (*d*) that the rich had unlawfully taken over communal and temple lands, driving off the poor, who had depended on them, and who therefore had to work for the rich instead.

It is now generally agreed that land could be disposed of (but for most people it was their main source of livelihood so they would not dispose of it unless they were desperate); it is hard to see why men who defaulted on their debts should first be reprieved as *hektemoroi* and enslaved only when they fell into debt and defaulted again; so the best explanation is probably a version of Cassola's first. In the uncertainties of the dark age it suited both the powerful men and the others that others should become dependants of the powerful (cf. p. 176), and one form which this dependence took was that, as the population began to increase, men were enabled to start working previously uncultivated land as *hektemoroi* of an overlord (cf. W. G. Forrest, *The Emergence of Greek Democracy*

[London: Weidenfeld & Nicolson, 1966], 144–50, comparing Genesis, 47. 13–26 on Egypt). These men could keep their land and pass it to their heirs as long as they paid their *morte*; the overlords were entitled to the *morte* and could reclaim the land if the *morte* was not paid. There were presumably also some independent farmers who were neither *hektemoroi* nor overlords of *hektemoroi*. By the end of the seventh century problems may have been arising from overcropping, division of land between too many heirs, encroachment on public and sacred lands, and the beginning of a change from self-subsistence towards concentration on crops other than grain which did better in Attica. A likely source of debt was inability by the *hektemoroi* to pay their *morte*; though we should not assume that all *hektemoroi* were in difficulties.

he was the first champion of the *demos*: For *demos* and *prostatai* cf. 2. 1. Solon is the first *prostates tou demou* in the list in 28. 2–3, and also in Isoc. XV. *Antid.* 230–6.

2. 3. What was most harsh … was their enslavement: The lower-class Athenians suffered not only from their dependent status as *hektemoroi* but more generally: they 'had a share in nothing' – neither in the wealth of their land nor in justice or political power.

3. 1. The structure of the ancient constitution: This chapter explains the aristocratic basis of the archaic state, which Solon sought to undermine.

before Draco: Inserted when the 'constitution of Draco' was inserted in ch. 4: cf. pp. 30, 183.

on the basis of aristocratic birth and wealth: Repeated in 3. 6; and for what is meant by 'excellence' cf. on 12. 3. That offices had been open only to men who satisfied the double requirement could be inferred from Solon's making wealth the sole requirement (8. 1). No doubt it was at first an understanding which did not need to be formulated; Draco's law on homicide, republished in 409/8, shows that explicit formulation was by his time possible (ML 86. 18–19, Dem. XLIII. *Macartatus* 57). For *A.P.*'s view that before Solon appointments were made by the Areopagus see 8. 2.

at first for life, and afterwards for ten years: Cf. p. 174, and for a variant p. 180. Nothing can be relied on beyond the fact that Athens passed from monarchy to an aristocratic régime with three principal magistrates (archon, *basileus*, polemarch), perhaps in several stages but not necessarily in the stages indicated here. In the second half of the fifth century a list of archons was published on stone (ML 6 = *IG* i[3] 1031 ~ Fornara 23): perhaps beginning with Creon in 683/2; the earliest surviving names are of the 590's.

3. 2. The greatest and first of the offices: When *A.P.* was written there was a college of nine 'archons' – archon, *basileus*, polemarch and six *thesmothetai* – made up to ten with a 'secretary to the *thesmothetai*' so that one could be appointed from each of Cleisthenes' ten tribes (55. 1): the archon was the eponymous official, giving his name to the year, and in the seventh and sixth centuries seems to have been the principal official of Athens (cf. 13. 2). In this chapter we have a good example of fourth-century rationalism, using the standard language of such work (ὅθεν καὶ, 'which is why' … *tekmerion*, 'supporting evidence' … *semeion*, 'indication'…, etc.); and apart from the faith in the story of Ion the reasoning is sensible: though the more specifically named polemarch may have been created later than the archon, it is credible that (not necessarily for the reason given by *A.P.*) the *basileus* who was once king had his civilian power transferred to an archon and his military power to a polemarch but was allowed to retain his religious power, and that the six *thesmothetai* were more recent than the other three. Discussion of who was the first life archon shows that *A.P.* was aware of variants in the tradition.

because some of the kings became soft … warfare: Cf. fr. 5 with p. 179, where a similar reason is alleged for the institution of the archonship. Failure in war may have prompted a change, but resentment of a power which was seen as excessive is as likely as scorn for power held by men who were seen as unworthy of it.

which is why they sent for Ion: Cf. fr. 1 with pp. 174–5 and 41. 2. Since Ion is cited here to account for the institution of the polemarch, *A.P.* presumably believed that he was the first polemarch (cf. Paus. I. 31. 3, schol. Ar. *Av.* 1527) and the office was a regular one from that time onwards (cf. Keaney, *HSCP* 67 [1963], 128).

3. 3. Most say … the time of Medon, but some say the time of Acastus: In the chronographers' scheme Codrus' son Medon was the first of the life archons and Acastus, associated below with the archons' oath of office, the second (cf. p. 179): the rival versions may have been sponsored by different Atthidographers.

the nine archons swear that they will fulfil their oaths as in the time of Acastus: For the archons' oath cf. 7. 1, 55. 5; this clause is not otherwise attested. We may accept that this clause appeared in the oath at the time of *A.P.*, and had probably appeared in it for a long time before then; the Acastus here could be an unknown archon of the seventh or sixth century, but the name is not attested for any historical Athenian until the time of the Roman empire.

it was in his time that the Codridae withdrew … the grants made to the archon: After which they held the life archonship instead of the kingship.

the archon administers none of the traditional matters: Cf. 57. 1 and Pl. *Plt.* 290 E 6–8, [Dem.] LIX. *Neaer.* 74 (where all the traditional sacrifices are assigned to the *basileus*); no doubt *A.P.* is thinking of religious observances here also, and it seems that the texts which ascribe all the traditional sacrifices to the *basileus* (and newer ones both to the archon and to the polemarch) are nearer to the truth, though for a possible exception see on the Thargelia 56. 3..

the added ones: More recent (cf. Isoc. VII. *Areop.* 29); in 25. 2 *A.P.* uses the word in a pejorative sense.

3. 4. *thesmothetai*: *Thesmos* was the oldest Greek word for law (cf. 4. 1, 12. 4, and M. Ostwald, *Nomos and the Beginnings of the Athenian Democracy* [Oxford U. P., 1969], 12–20). A *thesmothetes* like a *nomothetes* ought to be a lawgiver, but the word hardly ever has that sense and is normally used of the office in Athens and similar offices elsewhere; in the fourth century they had a general responsibility not for making laws but for the working of the lawcourts which applied the laws (59. 1, 5). If they existed before Draco and Draco gave Athens its first written laws, they cannot have had the function attributed to them here; some have guessed that they recorded 'judgments' in individual cases (e.g. Ostwald, *op. cit.,* 174–5), but more probably what we have here is a guess by *A.P.* or his source, not reconciled with the tradition about Draco (cf. Mathieu, *Aristote, Constitution d'Athènes*, 7).

when the archons were already appointed annually: The inscribed list (ML 6: cf. above) is of eponymous archons only; but if that was based on written records similar lists of the other archons ought to have survived too.

3. 5. what is now called the *Boukoleion*: The name probably derives from the worship of Dionysus (e.g. Ar. *Vesp.* 9–10, Eur. *Bacch.* 100, 618,

920–2, 1159); and *A.P.* probably thought it was previously called the *basileion*. In the classical period, for at any rate some of his business (Pl. *Euthphr.* 2 A 1–4), the *basileus* used the Stoa of the *Basileus*, in the agora (cf. on 7. 1).

near the *prytaneion*: The *prytaneion* known to Pausanias (I. 18. 3) was situated to the east of the acropolis, near the cave of Aglaurus (on which see G. S. Dontas, *Hesperia* 52 [1983], 48–63); not all are happy to think that the archaic *prytaneion* was there, but the most promising location is a plot running west from 32 od. Tripodon to od. Rangava, due east of the acropolis, where a fragment of a fifth-century inscription has been found which mentions the *prytaneis* and the *prytaneion* (G. Kavvadias & A. P. Matthaiou, in A. P. Matthaiou & R. K. Pitt [eds], *Ἀθηναίων ἐπίσκοπος ... H. B. Mattingly* [Athens: Greek Epigraphic Society, 2014], 51–72, citing other recent discussions; cf. R. K. Pitt, *AR* 61 [2014/5], 50).

the ritual encounter and marriage of the *basileus*' wife with Dionysus: The sacred marriage of the *basileus*' wife (the *basilinna*) and Dionysus took place on 12 Anthesterion (viii) at the *Choes*, the central day of the Anthesteria: see [Dem.] LIX. *Neaera* 73–8, and Parker, *Polytheism*, 303–5. The *symmeixis*, mentioned here before the *gamos*, was the ceremonial meeting of the partners (A. Wilhelm, *Anz. Wien* 74 [1937], 39–57 = his *Akademieschriften zur griechischen Inschriftenkunde* [Leipzig: Zentralantiquariat der D.D.R., 1974], ii. 582–600).

the *prytaneion*: The importance of the *prytaneion* as the religious heart of the city was stressed by N. D. Fustel de Coulanges, *La Cité antique* (Paris: Durand, 1864), liv. III ch. vi. It remained the ceremonial headquarters of the state: it contained the *hestia*, the hearth from which fire was taken to colonies at their foundation, it was the place where the city entertained those whom it wished to honour (cf. on 24. 3), and it was adorned with various statues. It was frequently confused by lexicographers and scholiasts with the *tholos*, the meeting- and dining-place of the *prytaneis*, on the west side of the agora, which was the working headquarters of the state (cf. 43. 2).

the *Epilykeion*: A connection with the Lyceum, a gymnasium outside the city walls to the north-east of the acropolis (*AR* 43 [1996/7], 8–10), which was used as a military training-ground, would be appropriate to the polemarch and has commonly been preferred to *A.P.*'s story of a polemarch called Epilycus (e.g. Kenyon).

In the time of Solon: According to Diog. Laert. I. 58, from Apollodorus, Solon instituted meetings of the nine archons. He is not known to have changed the duties of the archons, so this information, whatever its basis, would not be an obvous inference from any other facts.

they had the power … to hold the preliminary *anakrisis*: αὐτοτελεῖς (cf. 53. 2) reinforces κύριοι, to distinguish between the absolute jurisdiction of the archons in early Athens and their restricted powers in the time of *A.P.* It is normally believed that in early Athens lawsuits were decided by the archons or by the ex-archons in the council of the Areopagus; Solon gave litigants dissatisfied with an archon's verdict the right of appeal to a court (9. 1); by the middle of the fifth century, either by abrupt reform or by gradual development, the archons' jurisdiction in most cases had been limited to a preliminary enquiry (*proanakrinein*), after which cases which were accepted were referred automatically to a court in which the archon in question presided (cf. on 25. 2). Before Solon the archons will have been *autoteleis* in whatever jurisdiction they possessed, but we do not know which cases will have gone to one of the archons and which to the Areopagus.

3. 6. the council of the Areopagites: Probably the kings had had a more or less informal council of aristocratic advisers (as in Homer), that council remained in existence to advise the archons, and its power was increased as the power of the kings / archons was reduced. At some point it became established that each year the retiring nine archons should join the Areopagus unless guilty of misconduct (Plut. *Sol.* 19. 1, cf. *A.P.* 60. 3); even if that was not a fixed rule in early Athens, the archons and the Areopagites will have been drawn from the same restricted class of leading citizens.

It is unlikely that this sentence is *A.P.*'s first mention of the Areopagus: probably the lost beginning stated when it was created (perhaps in connection with Theseus' separation of the *eupatridai* from the other citizens: cf. pp. 175–8, 180) and with what functions (which must have included jurisdiction, especially in cases of homicide: cf. 25. 2 with commentary).

had the task of watching over the laws: On guarding the laws cf. 4. 4, 8. 4, 25. 2 with commentary, where I suggest that at or before the time of Draco the expression was used to describe the Areopagus' powers, and later it was used as a pretext for exercising new powers in new circumstances. Cf. also Aesch. *Eum.* 704–6 (see p. 266), Isoc. VII. *Areop.* 37, 46; also Arist. *Pol.* V. 1308 B 20–2. As a council of ex-archons the Areopagus contained the accumulated political wisdom of Athens, and in the seventh century it will have given advice to the magistrates and have acted as a court of law.

it administered most and the greatest of the affairs in the city: Cf. 8. 4 and the reference to τῶν διῳκημένων in 25. 2. διοικεῖν came to be used of administration in general and financial administration in particular (cf. διοίκησις in 24. 3 *fin.*, 43. 1, with commentary), but in 3. 3 and 57. 1 it is used of religious administration, and here *A.P.* seems to be thinking primarily of judicial activity.

with full power to chastise and punish all the disorderly: *Kolazein* is used of judicial punishments by dramatists, orators and Plato rather than by historians, and it is used of *tous akosmountas* by Isoc. VII. *Areop.* 42 cf. 46; *dioikein* also is a favourite word of Isocrates, and probably this description of the Areopagus is derived ultimately from him (cf. p. 22). He was hardly a good historical source, but what is said here is likely to be essentially correct.

For that reason this alone of the offices has continued to be held for life even now: Despite διὸ, *A.P.* has not explained why membership was for life; but councils of ex-magistrates normally did serve for life. Whether such bodies counted as *archai* was debatable: 3. 5 *fin.* implies not; 62. 3 includes the council of five hundred; Arist *Pol.* III. 1275 A 23–32 wonders whether the term covers assemblies and juries.

4. 1. the first constitution: This echoes 3. 1, but what was 'ancient' there is 'first' here: this seems to have been the first point at which *A.P.* gave an outline of the *politeia* as opposed to a history of events affecting the *politeia*.

after this: The words which follow suggest that *A.P.* is thinking of a definite event, so probably as in 2. 1 the reference is to Cylon's *coup* and its immediate consequences.

in the archonship of Aristaechmus: Aristaechmus is not otherwise attested. The chronographers dated Draco's legislation in Ol. xxxix = 624/3–621/0 (Samuel, *Chronology*, 200), and a possible reading in Diod. Sic. IX. 17 places it twenty-seven years before Solon, i.e. 621/0, so that date should be accepted.

Draco enacted his statutes: For *thesmoi* cf. on 3. 4. There is a reference to the *kyrbeis* of Solon and Draco in Cratinus fr. 300 Kassel & Austin *ap.* Plut. *Sol.* 25. 2 (cf. p. 200); the republication of the laws at the end of the fifth century included Draco's law about homicide (ML 86 = *IG* i³ 104 ~ Fornara 15. B); in 403 the restored democracy was to be based on the *nomoi* of Solon and the *thesmoi* of Draco (Andoc. I. *Myst.* 81–2 with decree *ap.* 83–4); and fourth-century orators tended to attribute the current homicide law to Draco and the remainder of the current laws to Solon. It was believed that there had been laws of Draco on matters other than homicide, which Solon's laws had superseded (cf. 7. 1), and there was a tradition that Draco's penalties had been uniformly severe (Herodicus or Prodicus *ap.* Arist. *Rhet.* II. 1400 B 19–23, Arist. *Pol.* II. 1274 B 15–18, Demades *ap.* Pl. *Sol.* 17. 3).

Doubts have been expressed, both about Draco as a historical figure (e.g. Beloch, *G.G.*², I. ii. 358–62; the name is otherwise attested in Athens in the hellenistic and Roman periods but not in the archaic and classical) and about laws on matters other than homicide (e.g. I. M. Linforth, *Solon the Athenian* [U. of California P., 1919], 68–9, 275–6); Stroud's defence (*Drakon's Law on Homicide* [*U. Calif. Pub. Cl. Stud.* iii 1968], 75–82) was perhaps too optimistic about the Athenians' memory of laws annulled at the beginning of the sixth century. If the affair of Cylon had prompted demands for a publicly accessible statement of the laws, that might well have applied to more than homicide, and E. Ruschenbusch, *Historia* ix 1960, 147–52 = his *Kleine Schriften G. R.*, 47–51, suggested that Draco did not cover all areas of law but did provide a criminal law for offences against individuals, under which the injured party had to obtain a judicial verdict before exercising his right to self-help (punishments under Draco's laws are regularly said to have been death or *atimia*, loss of rights [cf. on 8. 5], and Draco may have made offenders *atimoi* vis-à-vis their victims, whose exercise of self-help may then sometimes have extended to killing the offenders). His laws may have dealt with the status of *hektemoroi*, and with debt; they may well not have dealt with constitutional matters; and their aim was probably to formalise existing practice rather than to change it.

The law of homicide was republished in 409/8 (ML 86 = *IG* i³ 104 ~ Fornara 15. B). The original was written on at least two *axones* (lines 10, 56: cf. 7. 1). The law's text begins (line 11) with the words καὶ ἐὰμ, 'and if', or possibly 'even if', and with 'unwilling' homicide (on which see 57. 3): although Stroud (*op. cit.*, 34–40, 60–4) and others have argued that this was indeed the beginning of Draco's law, I join those who believe that Draco had begun with intentional homicide but that part of his law was not inscribed in 409/8 because it had been superseded by a more recent law (e.g. Ruschenbusch, *op. cit.*).

We do not know who Draco was, or how he came to be given his commission: he was not archon. It is surprising that *A.P.* says no more about his *thesmoi*, and I suspect that the original text did have further material, which was omitted when the 'constitution of Draco' was inserted by the reviser.

The structure of his constitution: Here the insertion begins: for the wording cf. 3. 1.

4. 2. Political rights had been given: On *politeia* cf. 2. 2: here and in some other places the meaning shades into 'political rights' or 'citizenship'.

to those who provided arms: Cf. the intermediate régime of 411/0 (33. 1, Thuc. VIII. 97. 1), and the reference in 411 to those able to serve with their bodies and their wealth (29. 5, Thuc. VIII. 65. 3). In pre-Solonian Athens office-holding was limited to the rich and aristocratic; assemblies probably met rarely, and were in theory open to all free Athenians but in practice only the rich and aristocratic would speak (cf. on 7. 3).

the treasurers: The treasurers of Athena: cf. 7. 3, 8. 1, 47. 1.

owning unencumbered property worth not less than ten minas: This reflects a later date: estates are valued in monetary terms, whereas Solon was to use produce (cf. 7. 3–4 with commentary) and even in his time Athens did not have coinage (cf. on 8. 3, 10), and it sets a higher qualification for *strategoi* and hipparchs than for archons and treasurers.

generals: For *strategoi* before Cleisthenes see on 22. 2; there was probably not a regular office of *strategos* in the time of Draco.

hipparchs: For hipparchs see 61. 4, and for the cavalry in early Athens see on 7. 4.

with legitimate children by a wedded wife: The only other texts containing this kind of requirement are ML 23. 18–22 (the 'decree of Themistocles' purporting to be of 480 but inscribed in the third century) and Din. I. *Demosthenes* 71 (of 323); but cf. Thuc. II. 44. 3 (in the funeral oration attributed to Pericles). It is not impossible that there were such requirements in early Athens.

These had to take guarantors ... until their *euthynai*: For stipulations about the class of the guarantors cf. the quotation of the bouleutic oath in Dem. XXIV. *Timocrates* 144. The institution of *euthynai*, a check on a man's performance at the end of a term of office, was ancient (cf. *IG* i^3 244. *B*, of *c.* 460, Aesch. *Pers.* 828, of 472; and see on 9. 1, 25. 2), but there is no parallel for the rule given here or anything resembling it.

4. 3. The council comprised four hundred and one men: Solon instituted a council of four hundred (8. 4), which Cleisthenes changed to a council of five hundred (21. 3, 43. 2); the extreme oligarchic régime of 411 had a council of four hundred (29. 5, 31. 1). It is not credible that in the time of Draco Athens had any council other than the Areopagus; this council could have been invented in the circles which debated the *patrios politeia* at the end of the fifth century (cf. on 29. 3, 34. 3); 401 as opposed to 400 is reminiscent of the *dikasteria* (cf. 53. 3, 68. 1).

appointed by sortition from those with political rights: Allotment, to share offices 'fairly' among those considered equally eligible, was particularly favoured by democrats (e.g. the Persian debate, Hdt. III. 80. 6; Arist. *Pol.* VI. 1317 B 17–21), but could be used by oligarchs when eligibility was suitably defined (e.g. 30–1, Thuc. VIII. 70. 1). Here *politeia* has to mean 'those possessed of citizenship': cf. 37. 1, 38. 2; but in Arist. *Pol.* (e.g. V. 1302 B 16–17) and in hellenistic inscriptions the normal word for that is *politeuma*.

This appointed by lot...: The subject must be the council, τὴν βουλὴν or conceivably τὴν ἀρχὴν.

the other offices: But probably not the *strategoi* and hipparchs, who were appointed by election even in the classical democracy (cf. 61).

men over thirty years old: In the classical period this was the requirement for *dikastai* (63. 3), *bouleutai* (Xen. *Mem.* I. 2. 35, for the oligarchy of 404/3) and probably most regular officials (cf. p. 344); it is found also in the constitutions of 411 (30. 2, 31. 1).

and the same man could not hold an office for a second time: Cf. 62. 3, with commentary on the exceptions. Like the use of allotment, this rule was particularly associated with democracies (e.g. Arist. *Pol.* VI. 1317 B 17–24), but to safeguard against the emergence of a ruling clique it could be used by régimes of various complexions (e.g. 31. 3; early Drerus, ML 2).

If any of the councillors ... missed the meeting: Cf. the 'future' constitution of 411, 30. 6; there is no evidence that such fines were ever imposed in Athens, but while democracies might offer stipends for attendance oligarchies might impose fines for absence (e.g. Arist. *Pol.* IV. 1297 A 17–B 1, for courts and assemblies).

a *pentakosiomedimnos* had to pay … and a *zeugites* one: Solon's four classes (7. 3–4) make a surprising appearance here (and were probably implied in ἐκ τοῦ αὐτοῦ τέλους for the guarantors in 4. 2), and again the penalties are expressed in monetary terms.

4. 4. The council of the Areopagus: The Areopagus' role of guardian of the laws (cf. 3. 6) seems to have been discussed at the end of the fifth century: cf. Lys. fr. 224 Carey, decree *ap.* Andoc. I. *Myst.* 84.

It was possible for a man who was wronged to make an *eisangelia*: For Solon's institution of *eisangelia* to the Areopagus in cases of attempted tyranny see 8. 4; for fourth-century procedures of *eisangelia* see 43. 4 (for major offences), 45. 2 (against magistrates). It is not clear whether this passage envisages either of those procedures, or denunciations of offenders in general.

4. 5. Loans were on the security of the person: Probably the inserted constitution ends with the previous sentence, and this sentence was written at the time of the insertion to help fit it into its context by recalling ch. 2.

D. Solon (5–12)

Solon is treated slightly by Herodotus, as a sage, lawgiver and poet but not as a reformer (I. 29–33, 86. 3, II. 177. 2, V. 113. 2), and not at all by Thucydides; the most important passage in Arist. *Pol.* (II. 1273 B 35–1274 A 21) reviews current judgments on him; there is an anecdotal account in Diog. Laert. I. 45–67. Otherwise our main source on Solon is Plutarch's *Solon*: that once cites 'Aristotle' (25. 1, citing 7. 1), and has substantial overlaps with *A.P.* (chs 1–3 as well as 5–12), but each has some material which the other lacks (including some of their quotations from Solon's poems and laws), and most probably behind them there lies a common source which dealt with Solon and the half-century before him, which itself quoted from the poems and laws (cf. pp. 12–14, 181, 183). Since Solon's poems and his laws (for which see on 7. 1) were available, there was some reliable information on him – but there may well have been a mistaken tendency to assume that everything established by Solon represented a change from what had gone before.

The outline on which *A.P.* and Plutarch agree is that the Athenians, in a state of tension between rich and poor, chose Solon, a 'middling citizen' to be archon and mediator (*A.P.* 5); he liberated the people by cancelling debts and banning personal security for debts (6); he created four property classes as a basis for political rights (7–8); he laid the foundations of the democracy by banning personal security, by allowing any citizen to prosecute and by allowing appeals from magistrates' verdicts, but did not make his laws deliberately ambiguous (9); he also changed Athens' measures, weights and coinage (10); having pleased neither side, he left Athens for ten years, but there was continuing strife and in due course Pisistratus made himself tyrant (13 sqq.).

It is clear from what Solon did that he was concerned with at any rate two problems: agrarian, resulting from the situation treated in ch. 2, and political, in general because although laws had been published by Draco their administration was not trusted, and among rich non-aristocrats because they were denied the political power to which they aspired. The quotations from his poems suggest that before his reforms he had defended the poor and unprivileged, but he disappointed both them by not doing as much as they had hoped and the rich and privileged by doing more than they had hoped; in the fourth century he could be praised both by those who emphasised his reforms and by those who emphasised his moderation. The best of the older treatments is Linforth, *Solon the Athenian* (including the fragments of the poems and a commentary). There is an Italian translation of the poems and a commentary in A. Masaracchia, *Solone* (Florence: La Nuova Italia, 1958). There is a collection of fragments of the laws by E. Ruschenbusch, *Σόλωνος νόμοι* (*Historia* Einz. 9 [1966]), and a translation of and commentary on some of those fragments in his posthumous *Solon: Das Gesetzeswerke – Fragmente* (*Historia* Einz. 215 [2010]); and there is a new collection, with English translation and commentary, by D. F. Leão & P. J. Rhodes, *The Laws of Solon: A New Edition* (London: Tauris, 2015). There is an edition of the poems and general discussion by M. Noussia Fantuzzi, *Solon the Athenian: The Poetic Fragments* (*Mnemosyne* Supp. 326 [2010]); there is a collection of essays on various problems in J. H. Blok & A. P .M. H. Lardinois (eds), *Solon the Athenian: New Historical and Philological Approaches* (*Mnemosyne* Supp. 262 [2006]).

5. 1. When that was the kind of structure ... against the notables: *A.P.* closes a ring by recapituating 3, 2. 2–3 and 2. 1.

5. 2. They jointly chose Solon as reconciler and archon: Cf. Plut. *Sol.* 14. 3, 16. 5, *Amat.* 763 D. In the chronographic tradition Solon's archonship is dated 594/3 (e.g. Sosicrates *ap.* Diog. Laert. I. 62: see Samuel, *Chronology*, 201), but 14. 1 dates his legislation in the 32nd year before the archonship of Comeas, 561/0 (cf. p. 224), which would imply 592/1. N. G. L. Hammond (*JHS* 60 [1940], 71–83 = his *Studies*, 145–62 + 162–9: cf. the second appointment in Plut. *Sol.* 16) placed the *seisachtheia* in 594/3 and the political reform in 592/1; but these are surely variant dates for the archonship, and the simplest explanation is that (whether or not the chronographers' date is correct) the troubles mentioned in 13. 1–2 led *A.P.* or his source to miscalculate and lose two years. Draco (4. 1) and Cleisthenes (21. 1) were not archons when their laws were enacted, and some sceptics have dated Solon's reforms, with or without his archonship, nearer to Pisistratus' first *coup* (e.g. Hignett, *Constitution*, 316–22), but some of Solon's laws referred to his archonship (*ap.* Plut. *Sol.* 19. 4, [Dem.] XLIV. *Leochares* 68, XLVI. *Stephanus ii.* 14), and the doubts are unjustified.

How long Solon's work needed we cannot say (for Plutarch's two phases see on 10. 1), but there is no reason to think that his archonship was prolonged beyond one year. Likewise we cannot say how he came to be appointed both to the archonship and to a special commission, but the poem quoted in this chapter indicates that he had pronounced on Athens' problems, and other lines (esp. fr. 34. 7–8 West *ap.* 12. 3) confirm the statement of 11. 2 that he could have become tyrant.

I know...: Fr. 4a West, quoted only here.

the eldest land of Ionia: For Athens as the mother city of the Ionians cf. pp. 174–5.

he fights and disputes against each side on behalf of the other side: In the lines quoted in 5. 3 Solon takes the side of the poor, but other fragments are more even-handed, including fr. 5. 5–6 West *ap.* 12. 1 and 37. 9–10 *ap.* 12. 5.

5. 3. Solon was ... one of those in the middle: Cf. Plut. *Sol.* 1–3, esp. 1. 2, and the story in 2. 1 that Solon's father had reduced his property through charitable expenditure; Arist. *Pol.* IV. 1296 A 18–20 says that the best lawgivers come from the *mesoi politai* and Solon's poems show

that he was one of these; for a modern discussion of Solon's family see Davies, *A.P.F.* 322–4 cf. 334–5. In fact his family connections and his appointment as archon make it certain that he was one of the leading citizens; *A.P.* proceeds to a quotation which is said to prove Solon's *mesotes* but does not; possibly verses not now preserved were more informative (cf. next note), but more probably verses in which he expressed his political sympathies were over-interpreted. On what begins but does not end as a balanced sentence see p. 24.
in these verses: *Poiemata* should be 'poems', but what follows is a single extract which does not prove what it is said to prove: this may be a sign that the quotations were present in *A.P.*'s source and he has clumsily abbreviated what he found there.
But you…: Fr. 4c West, quoted only here. These lines and the comment which follows do not either display impartialty or demonstrate Solon's own *mesotes*.
must quieten … in your hearts: Cf. Pl. *Resp.* IX. 572 A 5.
forced your way to an excess: Cf. Tyrt. fr. 11. 10 West.
their love of wealth…: Fr. 4b West. Cf. Plut. *Sol.* 14. 3 (δεδοικὼς τῶν μὲν τὴν φιλοχρηματίαν, τῶν δὲ τὴν ὑπερηφανίαν); also the Delphic oracle *ap.* Diod. Sic. VII. 12. 5. Kenyon's φιλαργυρίαν and θ' yield a pentameter, but φιλ̣[οπλο]υ̣τ̣ίαν is more probably the reading of the papyrus, in which case *A.P.* will have quoted unmetrically and inaccurately.

6. 1. he liberated the *demos* both in the present and for the future: Cf. Pl. *Sol.* 15–16. Solon's economic reform is said to comprise a ban for the future on personal security for debt and the liberation of those already enslaved, and the *seisachtheia*, represented as a cancellation of all private and public debts. We may wonder how many current slaves, particularly outside Attica, were liberated (cf. fr. 36. 8–15 West *ap.* 12. 4); for the future it seems that Solon banned the outright enslavement of defaulters, but not the kind of bondage which was ended when a debt was discharged (cf. E. M. Harris, *CQ*^{2} 52 [2002], 415–30 = his *Democracy and the Rule of Law in Classical Athens* [New York: Cambridge U. P., 2006], 249–69).

It seems unlikely that a man who had borrowed (for instance) a plough before the *seisachtheia* would then become the owner of it. There may have been some other debts which were cancelled also, but probably what Solon cancelled was primarily the obligation of the *hektemoroi*, who were thus made the absolute owners of their land, and what is stated by *A.P.* and Plutarch is an anachronistic reformulation of that (cf. fr. 36. 3–7 West *ap.* 12. 4). Solon says that he abstained from a redistribution of land (fr. 34. 8–9 West *ap.* 12. 3): in the fourth century redistribution of land and cancellation of debts were considered dangerous revolutionary measures (e.g. 40. 3, Isoc. XII. *Panath.* 259), and it was presumably to exempt the good Solon from the charge of being a revolutionary that Androtion reinterpreted the *seisachtheia* (*FGrH* 324 F 34: cf. on 10).

Beyond ending the payment of a sixth of the produce, this will not have made viable a plot of land which was not viable, and the ban on enslavement may actually have made borrowing harder. Solon banned the export of natural products other than olive oil (Plut. *Sol.* 24. 1), and encouraged native and immigrant craftsmen (Plut. *Sol.* 22. 1–3, 24. 4), and we may suspect that some poorer men will have abandoned farming for other livelihoods.

and he enacted laws: These words interrupt the balance of the sentence (Kaibel, *Stil und Text*, 81–2 cf. 134) and the sense. Probably they should not be deleted, but *A.P.* is doing more clumsily here what he did at the beginning of 2. 2, announcing two topics before dealing with the first of them (cf. p. 24).

which they call the *seisachtheia*: Cf. Plut. *Sol.* 15. 2, *Alex. Fort. ii.* 343 c, attributing the name to Solon, *Praec. Ger. Reip.* 807 E; in *Sol.* 16. 5 it is the name of a festival celebrating the achievement. What *A.P.* says suggests that the word was not found in Solon's poems.

6. 2. some people try to slander him: Cf. Plut. *Sol.* 15. 7–9, *Praec. Ger. Reip.* 807 D–E, also *Suda* σ 779 Adler Σόλων. The story was accepted, with disagreement only over whether Solon was naïve and innocent or himself profited from his foreknowledge (cf. p. 14). More probably, however, the whole story is a later invention: it can hardly have been possible, when sales of land were probably rare and coinage did not yet exist, at short notice to borrow capital and buy land on a significant scale. Plutarch names three profiteers: Conon, Cleinias and Hipponicus, descendants of whom (Conon, Alcibiades, Callias) were prominent in the late fifth century. The story may well have been invented to discredit those men (E. Fabricius, *ap.* F. Duemmler, *Hermes* 27 [1892], 262 = his *Kleine Schriften* [Leipzig: Hirzel, 1901], ii. 419), and *A.P.*'s omission of the names may reflect a version friendly to the men accused which suppressed the names of their ancestors.

the democrats: On *A.P.*'s sources and his labelling of them cf. p. 14. We cannot identify the sources on either side of this argument.

6. 3. he could have ... become tyrant of the city: Cf. 11. 2, 12. 3 quoting fr. 34 West; also Pl. *Sol.* 14. 3–15. 1 quoting frs. 32–3, *Comp. Sol. Publ.* 2. 5.

accepted the hatred of both sides: Cf. 11. 2 and the quotations in 12.

7. 1. He established a constitution: Again there are two topics: *A.P.* announces the reform of rhe *politeia* and the legislation, then deals with the legislation in 7. 1–2 and with the *politeia* in 7. 3–8. 5. The political reform did not create a totally new constitution, but if there were any laws of Draco on the constitution (cf. p. 192) they will have been superseded, and Solon's will then have been the only constitutional laws.

and enacted other laws: Possibly other than Draco's laws, but more probably other than the laws about the *politeia*. In contrast to Draco's *thesmoi* (cf. pp. 188, 192), Solon's laws were later called *nomoi* (already in Hdt. I. 29. 1, 2, 2. 177. 2), but Solon himself called them *thesmoi* (cf. on 12. 4).

and they ceased using the statutes ... on homicide: It was later practice to destroy the texts when laws were annulled (e.g. decree *ap.* Andoc. I. *Myst.* 79, *IG* ii^2 43. *A* = RO 22 ~ Harding 35. 31–5); but Solon's laws were a special case, since he produced a corpus of laws, so there is no problem in *A.P.*'s being able to quote obsolete laws of Solon (8. 3). But all Draco's laws were annulled except on homicide, and I doubt the suggestion of Stroud (*The Axones and Kyrbeis of Drakon and Solon* [*U. Calif. Pub. Cl. Stud.* 19 (1979)], 43) that they too were preserved.

They wrote up the laws on the *kyrbeis*: Cf. Plut. *Sol.* 25. 1–2: κατεγράφησαν εἰς ξυλίνους ἄξονας ἐν πλαισίοις †περιέχουσι† στρεφομένους, fragments of which survived in Plutarch's time; 'Aristotle' says they were called *kyrbeis*; the comic poet Cratinus said the *kyrbeis* were used for roasting barley (cf. p. 192); 'some' believe that the *kyrbeis* contained religious matters and the *axones* others. At any rate some sacrifices were recorded in the *kyrbeis* (Lys. XXX. *Nicomachus* 17, 18, 20), and Draco's homicide law (cf. p. 192) and secular laws of Solon (e.g. Plut. *Sol.* 19. 4, 23. 4, 24. 2) were inscribed on numbered *axones*.

Hesychius' list of Aristotle's works includes one 'On the *axones* of Solon' (Hesychius *s.v.* 'Αριστοτέλης = Rose, *Aristotelis ... Fragmenta*, p. 16). In addition to the distinction in content mentioned by Plutarch, some writers distinguished the *kyrbeis* and *axones* by material (but wood is most commonly mentioned for each) or by shape. The etymology of *kyrbis* is unknown. It seems clear that in the hellenistic period the *axones* survived and could be seen by those who wished to see them, and I believe that those who wished to distinguish between laws of Solon and later laws could do so, but there was no longer any knowledge of how if at all the *kyrbeis* had differed from the *axones*.

On modern views see Stroud, *The Axones and Kyrbeis*, and works cited there; recently G. Davis has argued that the original monuments were *kyrbeis* and the (current) laws were reinscribed on *axones* at the end of the fifth century (*Historia* 60 [2011], 1–35). I agree with Ruschenbusch (*Σόλωνος νόμοι*, 14–38) and A. Andrewes (in *Φόρος: Tribute to B. D. Meritt* [Locust Valley: Augustin, 1974], 21–8), against e.g. Stroud, that the two words were alternative names for one set of objects, probably four-sided wooden beams revolving on vertical axles (thus Ruschenbusch: Andrewes supposed them to be horizontal), which would accommodate more text in a limited space than a wall or a set of *stelai*.

placed them in the Stoa of the *Basileus*: The Stoa of the *Basileus* was the northernmost building on the west side of the agora, and is dated to the second quarter of the fifth century (Camp, *Site Guide*, 75–81): it therefore cannot have been the original home of the *axones*, but they were presumably there by 409/8, when Draco's homicide law was obtained from the *basileus* and republished in front of the stoa (ML 86 = *IG* i³ 104 ~ Fornara 15. B. 7–8, cf. Andoc. I. *Myst.* 82 with decree *ap.* 84). According to Anaximenes, *FGrH* 72 F 13, Ephialtes (cf. ch. 25) moved the *axones* and *kyrbeis* down from the acropolis to the *bouleuterion* and the agora (cf. Poll. VIII. 128, with *prytaneion* instead of *bouleuterion*): It is possible that Ephialtes moved the *axones* from the acropolis to the stoa; they had been moved to the *prytaneion* by the beginning of the second century (Eratosthenes *FGrH* 241 F 37c).

and all swore to use them: This, and the oath of the council in Plut. *Sol.* 25. 3, suggest an oath taken afterwards, but Hdt. I. 29. 2 implies an oath taken in advance, when Solon was appointed, and that is more likely. For an oath taken by all the citizens there are parallels, in Athens (e.g. Andoc. I. *Myst.* 90) and elsewhere: it was perhaps administered through the *phratriai*. However, V. J. Rosivach, *Phoenix* 64 (2010), 223–37, believes simply in an oath by members of the élite to accept Solon's laws, and considers everything beyond that fictional embroidery.

The nine archons when swearing at the stone: Cf. the more precise information given in 55. 5. The *lithos* has been found, in front of the north wing of the stoa (Camp, *Site Guide*, 79).

declared: Cf. Plut. *Sol.* 25. 3 (καταφατίζων). The verb is not otherwise attested, but cognates are used in Aristotle's logical works (e.g. *Cat.* 12 B 5–16); Wilamowitz (*A.u.A.* i. 47–8) suggested that it was an archaic Ionian word, appropriate to the solemn declaration.

7. 2. for a hundred years: Cf. Plut. *Sol.* 25. 1; but Hdt. I. 29 has an oath for ten years, linked with Solon's ten year absence (cf. 11. 1). Since those who swore the oath would not live for a hundred years, ten years are more likely.

7. 3. He divided them by an assessment ... divided before: Cf. Plut. *Sol.* 18. 1–2; Arist. *Pol.* II. 1274 A 19–21 places the *hippeis* between the *zeugitai* and the *thetes*. Plutarch does not suggest that the classes existed already; *A.P.*'s formulation is awkward, but this is probably not another of the changes made to fit the 'constitution of Draco' into the work (cf. p. 30). The names suggest that the *pentakosiomedimnoi* are an addition to a structure in which the other three classes existed, and probably what Solon did was distinguish the *pentakosiomedimnoi* from the other *hippeis* and give the classes a new political function.

Most scholars have believed that the names of the three classes reflect economic and social categories, with the *hippeis* men who could keep a horse, *zeugitai* men who could keep a yoke of oxen, and the *thetes* (cf. p. 185) poor labourers, but a minority view looks to military categories, with the *hippeis* the cavalry and the *zeugitai* men yoked together in the hoplite phalanx – in which case the categories will not have been very old in Solon's time (first argued by C. Cichorius, in *Griechische Studien H. Lipsius ... dargebracht* [Leipzig: Teubner, 1894], 135–40; cf. D. Whitehead, *CQ*² 31 [1981], 282–6) – and that seems preferable.

the nine archons: Cf. 8. 1.

the treasurers: The treasurers of Athena, appointed from the *pentakosiomedimnoi* only: cf. 8. 1, 47. 1. On financial offices in the archaic period see H. van Wees, *Ships and Silver, Taxes and Tribute* (London: Tauris, 2013), 39–44.

the *poletai*: The 'sellers', of state contracts and confiscated property: cf. 47. 2–3.

the Eleven: Gaolers and executioners: cf. 52. 1.

the *kolakretai*: 'Collectors of hams' (cf. the original meaning of *tamias*, one who carves or dispenses, e.g. Hom. *Il.* XIX. 44): that suggests that originally they received revenues, but in the latter part of the fifth century they were the paying officers of the state treasury; *c.* 411 the office was abolished and the duty passed to an enlarged board of *hellenotamiai* (cf. 30. 2); in the fourth century there was no longer a central treasury but funds were apportioned among different spending authorities (cf. 48. 2).

To those in the *thetes'* class: The object understood is τέλος. *Telein*, 'pay', was often used of paying taxes, and since Greeks were often divided into classes for paying taxes τελεῖν εἴς τινας came to mean 'belong to a certain class'. Poll. VIII. 129–30 seemed to interpret these Athenian classes in that way and was followed by A. Böckh, *Die Staatshaushaltung der Athener* (Berlin: Reimer, [3]1886), i. 583–91: there is no sign that in the fifth and fourth centuries there was any connection between taxation and these classes (but see A. Moreno, *Feeding the Democracy* [Oxford U. P., 2007], 103–7), but we know so little about the finances of early Athens that we cannot rule out the possibility that there was some connection in the sixth century (cf. van Wees, *op. cit.*, 84–91).

the assembly: Cf. Arist. *Pol.* II. 1274 A 15–21, III. 1281 B 31–4. *A.P.* perhaps implies in 2. 2–3 cf. 4. 2 *init.* that before Solon the *thetes* were excluded from the assembly: that has often been believed (e.g. Busolt, *G.G.* ii[2]. 273 n. 1), but Masaracchia argued that Solon was not granting a new right but confirming an existing one (*Solone*, 164–7), and that is more probably right. Probably all free Athenians had been able to attend the assembly, but as in the case of Thersites (Hom. *Il.* II. 211–77) the lower-class men were not expected to play an active part, and assemblies were held rarely and conducted little business. Solon will have strengthened the assembly not by admitting the *thetes* to it but by giving it a probouleutic council independent of the Areopagus and perhaps by prescribing regular meetings (cf. 8.4).

the lawcourts: Cf. ch. 9.

7. 4. five hundred measures, dry and wet together: We are not told how dry and wet measures, of different crops, were combined in a single scale. The simplest interpretation would be that *medimnoi* (55 l.) of grain and *metretai* (41 l.) of olive oil or wine were added together as 'measures' of produce; the best suggestion of a fairer and more sophisticated kind is that of G. E. M. de Ste. Croix, that quantities of other crops were assessed as equivalent to a quantity of barley (*Athenian Democratic Origins and Other Essays* [Oxford U. P., 2004], 32–46). This still takes no account of other forms of wealth, such as ownership of animals or the proceeds of trade (though in fr. 13. 43–62 West Solon mentions agriculture as one means of livelihood among many), but it was a means of assessing capital, on which later taxes such as the *eisphora* were based.

if they produced three hundred ... able to maintain a horse: Cf. on 7. 3: clearly the question was debated in the fourth century; *A.P.* considers the economic criterion, is silent on the military, and finds it 'more reasonable' that the remaining classes like the highest should have been defined in terms of produce. He does not distinguish between the meanings of the names and the criteria for membership of the classes. Most scholars have accepted his figures as criteria for membership of the classes, and have then tried to assess the significance of the figures: L. Foxhall (in L. G. Mitchell & P. J. Rhodes [eds], *The Development of the Polis in Archaic Greece* [London: Routledge, 1997], 113–36) argued that on these figures even *zeugitai* would be rich, and that the three highest classes were three strata within the rich élite; I think it more likely that *A.P.*'s figures for *hippeis* and *zeugitai* are not authentic Solonian criteria but fourth-century guesses by analogy with the *pentakosiomedimnoi* (in *op. cit.*, 7), and de Ste. Croix (*Athenian Democratic Origins*, 46–51), preferring the military to the economic interpretation of the names, thought that Solon had no quantitative criterion except for the *pentakosiomedimnoi*, and it was left to a citizen's patriotism (and his neighbour's jealousy) to ensure that a man was registered in the correct class – which no doubt would commonly mean that a man registered in the same class as his father.

Diphilus' son Anthemion...: The statue must be of Anthemion. The epigram as quoted in the London papyrus comprises two pentameters: in inscriptions pentameters used otherwise than in elegiac couplets are rare but do occur (cf. P. Ceccarelli, in *Vir Bonus, Docendi Peritus ... G. Garuti* [San Severo, 1996], 47–69, esp. 59–60), so emendation of the first line is not necessary. Almost certainly θητικοῦ ἀντὶ τέλους ἱππάδ' ἀμειψάμενος means 'acquiring hippad in place of thetic rank', though L. H. Jeffery *ap.* Rhodes, *Comm. Ath. Pol.*, 144–5, suggested that Anthemion was a *hippeus* who in 480 volunteered to serve on shipboard (cf. Plut. *Cim.* 5. 2–3). *IG* i³ 831 (*c.* 480–470?) is a dedication of a ζευ]γίτες, who may have risen from being a *thes*.

The statue was presumably standing when *A.P.*'s source was written. It is likely to have been erected after the Persian sack of 480–479, and it is possible (but not certain) that Anthemion is the father of Anytus, a politician active in the late fifth and early fourth centuries (cf. 27. 5, 34. 3: first suggested by W. Aly, *NJA* 16 [1913], 170). Diphilus is a fairly common Athenian name: a Δίπιλος καλός appears on Beazley, *A.R.V.*² i. 371 no. 24 (cf. ii. 1574), by the Brygos painter (*c.* 500–480).

The men belonging to the *zeugitai*'s class ... two hundred measures of the two kinds: Cf. Poll. VIII. 130 and other texts derived from *A.P.*; but in a law *ap.* Dem. XLIII. *Macartatus* 54 the dowry due from a next-of-kin who does not want to marry an *epikleros* is 500 dr. from a *pentakosiomedimnos*, 300 dr. from a *hippeus*, 150 dr. from a *zeugites*.

when a man is about to undergo allotment for any office and is asked: Probably asked by ὁ θεσμοθέτης; the question was presumably asked when men offered themselves as candidates.

nobody would say the *thetes*': In 457/6 *zeugitai* were admitted to the archonship but *thetes* were not (26. 2), and when a colony was sent to Brea in the 430's the colonists were to be drawn from the *thetes* and *zeugitai* (ML 49 = *IG* i³ 46 ~ Fornara 100. 43–6); but by the time of *A.P.* it seems that the law remained but had no serious effect (cf. 8. 1, 47. 1, on the *tamiai*; and for fourth-century invocation of the classes Isae. VII. *Apollodorus* 39, Dem. XXIV. *Timocrates* 144).

8. 1. He had the officials appointed ... pre-elected by the tribes: The reference is presumably, as in the next sentence, to the nine archons. There is no parallel passage in Plut. *Sol.*; Arist. *Pol.* II. 1273 B 35–1274 A 17, III. 1281 B 25–34 claims that Solon retained the 'aristocratic' principle of election. It seems that *A.P.* was written later than *Pol.*, and *A.P.* had a detailed and well-informed source on Solon, so whether *A.P.* was written by Aristotle himself or (as I believe) not, *A.P.* is more likely to be right on this point (cf. pp. 4–6). He quotes as a *semeion* not the law on the archons but the law on the *tamiai*, but here he may be not giving the evidence for his belief but citing a familiar fact to support a less familiar one. If Solon's aim was to admit rich non-aristocrats to the archonship, this method would be appropriate: election to the short list would exclude implausible candidates, while allotment for the second stage would improve the chances for non-aristocrats.

For the appointment of archons later see 22. 5, 26. 2, 55. 1. *Zeugitai* were admitted in 457/6: *A.P.* does not make it clear whether Solon admitted both *pentakosiomedimnoi* and *hippeis* or (as with the *tamiai*) *pentakosiomedimnoi* only.

Each tribe pre-elected ten: That is, each of the four Ionian tribes. *A.P.* says that in his time there were ten candidates from each of the (ten Cleisthenic) tribes, but the coincidence could as well be a product of Athenian conservatism as of a false inference about Solon's rules.

Consequently it still remains the practice ... the lots to be drawn from these: 22. 5 indicates that the survival was not continuous. When the use of *kleroteria* was extended to these appointments, *c.* 370, probably each tribe had to take one of its ten candidates from each of the sections A–K (cf. on 63. 4).

the law about the treasurers: Cf. 47. 1. This confirms the use of allotment and of the four classes, but not the use of an elected short list. A bronze plaque of the mid sixth century was dedicated by perhaps eight *tamiai* (*IG* i^3 510).

8. 2. the council of the Areopagus: The new practice will have been stated in one of Solon's laws, but probably the previous practice will not; it is not unlikely that the ex-archons in the Areopagus should have made the appointments, either directly or by inviting the assembly to confirm their choice, but we can only guess, and probably fourth-century Athenians could do no more.

called up and judged by itself: This seems to envisage interview before appointment, as in the modern world: perhaps *A.P.* or his source is thinking of the *dokimasia* held between appointment and entry into office (cf. 55. 2–4 and commentary on 25. 2).

8. 3. There were four tribes, as before: Cf. pp. 175–6.

and four *phylobasileis*: Cf. 41. 2, Poll. VIII. 111. What duties they performed in early Athens we cannot say; for a fourth-century duty see 57. 4. The revised sacrificial calendar of the end of the fifth century mentions the *phylobasileis* and the formula ἐκ τῶν φυλοβασιλικῶν, which seems to indicate the authority for the sacrifices in question (see S. Dow, *Proc. Mass. Hist. Soc.* 71 [1953–7], 1–35, esp. 15–21, 25–7; S. D. Lambert, *BSA* 97 [2002], 353–99, e.g. fr. 1).

three *trittyes*: Cf. p. 175–6.

there were twelve *naukrariai* in each: Not mentioned in fr. 2. Poll. VIII. 108 deduced, but *A.P.* does not state, that there were four in each *trittys*. The most certain fact about the *naukrariai* is that they no longer existed in the classical period (cf. 21. 5). For the mention of the *prytaneis* of the *naukraroi* in connection with Cylon by Hdt. V. 71. 2 cf. pp. 180–1; the laws quoted here indicate that the *naukrariai* existed in the time of Solon and that their officers, the *naukraroi*, had charge of *argyrion*. The normal etymology interprets *naukraroi* as 'ship-chiefs' (cf. *Anecd. Bekk.* i. 283. 20–1, Poll. VIII. 108), and none of the other etymologies which have been suggested is clearly preferable (cf. inconclusive discussion by V. Gabrielsen, *C&M* 36 [1985], 21–51). They may have had a local basis (cf. *Anecd. Bekk.* i. 275. 20–1, Phot. κ 1300 Theodoridis Κωλιάς), and have been involved in some kind of taxation (cf. Hsch. ν 118 ναύκλαροι). For recent attempts at elucidation see C. Schubert, *Historia* 57 (2008), 38–64; van Wees, *Ships and Silver, Taxes and Tribute*, 44–61.

Athens had no coinage until *c.* 550 (cf. on 10. 1–2), but *argyrion* is mentioned in the law quoted here, and cf. laws quoted in Plut. *Sol.* 23, Lys. X. *Theomnestus i.* 18. By Solon's time a rich man could have gold and silver among his possessions (cf. fr. 24. 1–3 West), and the best explanation is that uncoined weights of silver could be used as a means of reckoning wealth and payments, that that underlies references to *argyrion* and to drachmae in Solon's laws, and that when coins were introduced, pieces of silver of guaranteed weight and purity, they were an improvement on that (cf. Rhodes, *Comm. Ath. Pol.*, 152–3; J. H. Kroll, in *Studies in Greek Numismatics ... M. J. Price* [London: Spink, 1998], 225–32; de Ste. Croix, *Athenian Democratic Origins,* 38).

the income: Probably not the property tax for which *eisphora* became a technical term (e.g. *IG* i³ 52 ~ Fornara 119. *B.* 16–17, Thuc. III. 19. 1), but *eisphorai* and *dapanai* are revenue and expenditure.

in the laws of Solon which they no longer use: On the survival of Solon's laws, including those which were superseded, see pp. 200–1.

8. 4. He created a council of four hundred: Cf. 21. 3, 31. 1, Plut. *Sol.* 19. 1–2. It is possible that Plutarch's comparison of the two *boulai* with a ship's two anchors derives from one of Solon's poems (G. Grote, *A History of Greece*, 'new ed.' in 12 vols. [London: Murray, 1869/84], iii. 122; but this is not included as a 'fragment' of Solon by West or other editors). The existence of this council has been strongly contested, but unnecessarily (against its existence, e.g. Hignett, *Constitution*, 92–6; in favour, e.g. P. Cloché, *REG* 37 [1924], 1–26): the Areopagus would for some time continue to be dominated by the *eupatridai*, and this new council would free the assembly from dependence on it. The emphasis on the people in ML 8 (Chios, first half of sixth century) makes it likely that thc 'popular' council there had been created beside or instead of a more aristocratic council.

According to Plutarch the function of this council was to prepare business for the assembly (cf. 45. 4 on the later council); it may also have had powers of *dokimasia* and discipline over its own members. If it was to justify its existence, we may guess that Solon provided for regular meetings of it and of the assembly (cf. the Great Rhetra in Sparta *ap.* Plut. *Lyc.* 6. 2); and we may guess that, whenever and wherever the decision to count votes was first taken, it was taken in Athens not later than now (cf. J. A. O. Larsen, *CP* 44 [1949], 164–81).

to the council of the Areopagus he gave the task … overseer of the constitution: Cf. 3. 6, 4. 2, 25. 2; also Plut. *Sol.* 19. 2–5. Until there was another council, the council of the Areopagus will not have needed a distinctive name, but Plut. *Sol.* 19. 3–4 rightly rejects the view that it was created by Solon.

it watched over most and the greatest of the city's affairs: Cf. 3. 6.

it called offenders to account, having full power to punish and chastise: Cf. again 3. 6, but the language is less markedly Isocratean here than there. *Euthynein* means 'guide straight', 'direct', and so make the crooked straight (e.g. Solon fr. 4. 36 West) and call to account or punish (e.g. Aesch. *Pers.* 828, Thuc. I. 95. 5). A special instance of that is the *euthynai* of men retiring from office (48. 4–5, cf. 54. 2): according to Arist. *Pol.* II. 1274 A 15–18, III. 1281 B 32–4, Solon gave holding the officials to account to the *demos*; but, whatever Aristotle believed and whatever actually happened (cf. on 25. 2), the reference here is to punishing offenders in general.

and took up the payments to the acropolis: At this date 'payments' for a wrong done to the state probably took the form of a dedication (cf.

7. 1, 55. 5). Probably records which listed penalties without stating the reasons led *A.P.* or his source to suppose that the Areopagus had imposed penalties without stating the reasons. To call the acropolis *polis* was old-fashioned by the fourth century, but the usage persisted in this and some other phrases.

for calling to account: If δ[ιὰ] τὸ [ε]ὐθύ[ν]εσθαι is the reading of the papyrus, there is something wrong with the text.

it tried those who combined for the overthrow of the *demos* ... the law of *eisangelia* concerning them: This formulation is more at home in the late fifth and fourth centuries (e.g. Thuc. VI. 27. 3, decree *ap.* Andoc. I. *Myst.* 96–7, law *ap.* Hyp. IV. *Euxenippus* 7–8, *Agora* xvi 73), but after Cylon and before Pisistratus, when Solon could himself have become tyrant (cf. 6. 3–4, 11. 2, 12. 3). it is credible that he should have enacted a law against tyrants (but contrast Hansen, *Eisangelia*, 17–19, 56–7). The law *ap.* Plut. *Sol.* 19. 4 suggests that previously such charges would have been tried by the Areopagus. On the laws of this kind, which could be invoked only against unsuccessful offenders, see 16. 10 with commentary; on *eisangelia* for major public offences see 25. 2, 43. 4, 59. 2 with commentary.

8. 5. Seeing that the city...: Here we have a new subject, and 9. 1 sums up 7. 3–8. 4 as if 8. 5 did not exist; but probably the Areopagus' jurisdiction has led *A.P.* to the subject of *stasis* and so to Solon's law about *stasis*.

were content with whatever happened: For ἀγαπῶντας cf. Pl. *Resp.* III. 399 C 1; for τὸ αὐτόματον meaning τὸ ἀπὸ τύχης cf. Arist. *M.M.* II. 1199 A 9, Aeschin. III. *Ctesiphon* 167.

he enacted a particular law: Cf. Plut. *Sol.* 20. 1, *Praec. Ger. Reip.* 823 F, *Ser. Num. Vind.* 550 B–C, Cic. *Ep. Att.* X. 1. 2, Gell. II. 12 (citing 'Aristotle'); for disapproval of *apragmones* cf. Pericles in Thuc. II. 40. 2. The authenticity of this has been much debated, with opponents citing Lys. XXXI. *Philon* 27–8 (nobody has legislated against withdrawal from Attica in time of *stasis*); see among those in favour, B. Manville, *TAPA* 110 (1980), 213–21, against, E. David, *MH* 41 (1984), 129–38; see also next note. This became so famous as a law of Solon that it probably is authentic.

did not place his arms at the disposal of one side or the other The basic meaning is 'rest arms' (e.g. Hdt. IX. 52 *fin.*, Thuc. IV. 44. 1), and the meaning here is to place one's arms, literally or metaphorically, at the disposal of one side or the other (e.g. Dem. XXI. *Midias* 145 with W. W. Goodwin [Cambridge U. P., 1906] *ad loc.*). P. E. van 't Wout (*CQ*² 60 [2010], 289–301), has argued that μηδὲ μεθ' ἑτέρων is a separate information unit, whose negative is not affected by the previous μὴ, and that far from meaning 'does not place his arms at the disposal of either side' (as has regularly been assumed) this clause means 'does not ground his arms without allegiance to either side', i.e. that Solon did not forbid neutrality but positively commanded it (as in his own case, in the poems cited in ch. 12) – in which case we should have to suppose that his law was misunderstood not only by modern scholars but by ancient writers subsequent to *A.P.* W. Schmitz, *Klio* 93 (2011), 23–51, sees in this a requirement for members of the Areopagus to vote in trials of men accused of tyranny (8. 4), and regards ostracism with its quorum of 6,000 (22. 3) as a successor to it. These new interpretations seem improbable.

should be *atimos*: On *atimia* as loss of rights see Harrison, *L.A.* ii. 169–76, M. H. Hansen, *Apagoge, Endeixis and Ephegesis against Kakourgoi, Atimoi and Pheugontes* (Odense U. P., 1976), 75–82, and works cited there. In early Athens the *atimos* was an outlaw, with no rights *vis-à-vis* those whom he had injured or the whole community (cf. p. 192); as the scope for self-help was reduced the concept of *atimia* came to be reduced to the loss of civic rights, but the stronger sense did not wholly disappear (cf. Dem. IX. *Phil. iii.* 44; S. Dmitriev, *CQ*² 65 [2015], 35–50, argues that the change was from a moral and social concept to a legal one). Here the stronger sense is intended: breach of this law is treated as equivalent to treachery.

and not participate in the city: Cf. 26. 4, 36. 1, Lys. VI. *Andocides* 48, and μετέχειν τῆς πολιτείας in Lys. XXX. *Nicomachus* 15, etc.; but contrast 21. 2. The *atimos* will be deprived not only of involvement in the city's corporate activities but also of the protection of its laws, including those on homicide: this clause would add nothing to a reader's understanding of *atimon*, and will be an elaboration present in the law, not a comment by *A.P.*

9. 1. These seem to be the three most democratic features...: Cf. the judgment on Solon in 41. 2, and on Cleisthenes in 22. 1, 41. 2. Ruschenbusch found Solon first thus characterised in the 350's (*Historia* vii 1958, 398–424 = his *Kleine Schriften A. G.*, 59–80: cf. p. 179, above). It is true that he is more often thus characterised from then onwards than before; but it is significant that the restored democracy of 403 chose to use the *nomoi* of Solon and the *thesmoi* of Draco after the Thirty had repealed some of Solon's laws (cf. p. 192, 35. 2). Solon is *philodemos* in Ar. *Nub.* 1187, but 29. 3 suggests that Cleisthenes was seen as the founding hero in 411 and the focus moved to Solon as the debate on the *patrios politeia* progressed.

The ban on personal security for loans has been mentioned in 6. 1, but nothing has been said above about the other two features apart from the allusion to *dikasteria* in 7. 3.

the possibility for whoever wished to obtain vengeance for those who were wronged: Cf. Plut. *Sol.* 18. 6–7. Previously only the injured party (or his next of kin) had been able to institute proceedings: Solon instituted a category of cases (*graphai*, as opposed to *dikai*, in which only the injured party could prosecute) in which any citizen with full rights could do so. Probably this was done originally where the injured part was unable in law or for personal reasons to prosecute on his own account (G. Glotz, *La Solidarité de la famille dans le droit criminel en Grèce* [Paris: Fontemoing, 1904], 369–82).

appeal to the lawcourt: Cf. Plut. *Sol.* 18. 2–3, *Comp. Sol. Publ.* 2. 2; also Arist. *Pol.* II. 1273 B 35–1274 A 18. Though *A.P.* and Plutarch both use *dikasterion* it is usually thought that the proper term for Solon's court was *eliaia* (not aspirated in Athens), as in the law *ap.* Lys. X. *Theomnestus i.* 16; and, since cognate words in other dialects denote the assembly (e.g. Hdt. I. 125. 2), and at first cases are not likely to have been so frequent as to need several courts, it is often thought that this was a judicial session of the whole assembly. The word continued to be used in the classical period, sometimes (as in 68. 1) of a building. M. H. Hansen accepts (but aspirates) the name *eliaia* for Solon's court but distinguishes this body from the assembly (*C&M* 33 [1981–2], 9–47). I think it safest to say that we do not know how Solon's court was composed; but a possibility suggested to me by Prof. A. H. Sommerstein is that it was an assembly but open only to men aged thirty and above (cf. the rule for jurors in the classical period, 63. 3). A. L. Boegehold, *The Athenian Agora*, xxviii. *The Lawcourts at Athens* (Princeton: Am. Sch. Class. Stud. Ath., 1995), 3–6, concludes that *eliaia* and *dikasterion* 'are in most senses synonymous'.

Ephesis denotes the removal of a case from one plane to another for a fresh hearing: there were some cases in which *ephesis* was obligatory (e.g. 45. 1–3, 55. 2), but here as in 53. 2 what is envisaged is appeal by a dissatisfied litigant (cf. MacDowell, *Law*, 30–2). However, the law *ap.* Lys. X. 16 suggests that the function of Solon's *eliaia* was not limited to the hearing of appeals.

for when the *demos* has power over the vote ... the political régime: Cf. 41. 1. 41. 2 *fin.*, Arist. *Pol.* II. 1274 A 2–7, Plut. *Sol.* 18. 3: the epigrammatic sentence may well not be original to *A.P.* In the developed democracy the *dikasteria* enjoyed considerable power, particularly through their control of the magistrates (cf. on 25. 2) and political charges such as the *graphai paranomon* and *nomon me epitedeion theinai* (cf. 29. 4, 45. 4, 59. 2), but this power should not be projected back to the sixth century.

9. 2. because his laws were not written simply and clearly: Cf. Plut. *Sol.* 18. 4; also *Sol.* 25. 6 with *A.P.* 11. 1. Solon will not have been intentionally ambiguous: the accusation probably arose in the late fifth century, when the Athenians used the lawcourts on a large scale, experience showed that there were difficult cases not adequately covered by the laws, and his archaic language was beginning to seem obscure (cf. Lys. X. *Theomnestus i.* 15–20). On the attempt of the Thirty to simplify the laws and lessen the power of *dikastai* see 35. 2; fourth-century theorists also wanted to limit interpretation by *dikastai* (Arist. *Rhet.* I. 1354 A 27–B 16, cf. Pl. *Plt.* 294 A 10–295 A 7.

that about inheritance and *epikleroi*: Cf. 35. 2; for a discussion of the law of inheritance see Harrison, *L.A.* i. 122–62. An *epikleros* was a daughter of a man who left no legitimate sons: to prevent the extinction of the family she would be married to a man who would be adopted as son and would hold the property in trust for their sons; otherwise her nearest male relative would have the right to marry her and inherit the property. For further provisions see Plut. *Sol.* 20. 2–4.

it is not just to make conjectures ... what happens now: Cf. Arist. *Pol.* II. 1274 A 5–21, arguing that the present-day democracy was not intended by Solon. Although that passage disagrees with 8. 1 on the appointment of magistrates, this is one of the more striking correspondences between *Pol.* and *A.P.*: cf. pp. 10, 15.

10. 1. before his legislation: After a chapter which seems to conclude the account of Solon's reforms this further chapter is added (cf. p. 27), presumably from a different source. It is unlikely that any evidence survived on the order in which Solon's reforms were enacted (cf. Jacoby, *FGrH*, Supp. i. 147); *A.P.* has not suggested a chronological distinction between the economic reform (6) and the legal and political (7–8), but Pl. *Sol.* 16 has a second appointment after the economic reform to undertake the legal and political; almost certainly what was originally a logical distinction has been misinterpreted as a chronological (but see p. 197).

after that: The reference is uncertain, and the awkwardness presumably results from the addition of this to the main narrative. Pl. *Sol.* 15. 3, arriving at this topic through Androtion's explanation of the *seisachtheia* (below), includes it in the economic reform.

10. 1–2. the increase in the measures, weights and coinage ... in proportion to the stater and the other weights: Cf. Androtion *FGrH* 324 F 34 *ap.* Plut. *Sol.* 15. 3–4. This has been much discussed: I argue for my view in *NC*[7] 15 (1975), 1–11, and 17 (1977), 152.

A.P.'s text implies that the 'increases' were of the measures (of capacity), to make them larger than the Pheidonean, of the weights, to make a heavier mina of 100 drachmae instead of 70, and of the coinage, from a 2-drachmae to a 4-drachmae standard coin; that 63 minas' worth of coins were struck from 60 minas' weight of silver seems to be an additional note (C. M. Kraay, *Essays ... S. Robinson*, [Oxford U. P., 1968], 1–9). Plutarch does not explain measures, suggests that a constant mina was divided into 100 lighter drachmae instead of 70 heavier (for the manuscripts' ἑβδομήκοντα καὶ τριῶν οὖσαν read ἑβδομήκοντ᾽ ἄγουσαν: T. Reinach, *Hermes* 63 (1928), 238–40), and represents this as a change in the coinage, which enabled debtors who owed *x* heavy drachmae to pay only *x* light drachmae (so that Solon was not a revolutionary who cancelled debts but merely by this device reduced them: cf. p. 199). Androtion / Plutarch is evidently engaging in special pleading, whereas *A.P.* is not: *A.P.* should be nearer to the truth.

To establish what actually happened, we must avoid over-sophistacted suggestions of a change from one system to another for commercial advantage (e.g. C. T. Seltman, *Greek Coins* [London: Methuen, [2]1955], 45), and must allow for what seems now to be the certainty that Athens did not issue coins until *c.* 550 (e.g. C. M. Kraay, *Archaic and Classical Greek Coins* [London: Methuen, 1976], 56; J. H. Kroll & N. M. Waggoner, *AJA*[2] 88 [1984], 325–40; but against even lower dates see particularly M. C. Root, *NC* 148 [1988], 1–12), so Solon cannot have changed or even instituted the coinage (but since coins were named after the weights of silver in them it could easily be assumed later that a change in weights was instead or also a change in coinage).

For measures, in the fourth century 8 'Pheidonean' *medimnoi* were equivalent to 5 'Delphic' *medimnoi* (*C. Delphes* ii 4. ii. 2–8): whether Delphi's *medimnos* was the Athenian or the Aeginetan (= 1.5 Athenian), the Athenian will have been larger than the Pheidonean. For weights, there were some places where the mina did consist of 70 drachmae (see M. H. Crawford, *Eirene* 10 [1972], 5–8 at 7 n. 7), and in coinage 70 Aeginetan drachmae were equivalent to 100 Athenian drachmae (*C. Delphes* ii 4. i. 21–3). As for the change in coinage as understood by *A.P.*, it is true that in Athens' earliest coinage (the *Wappenmünzen*) the standard coin was of 2 drachmae but in the 'owls' the standard was 4 drachmae. And, while coin weights remained unchanged, Athens' commercial weights became progressively heavier from the sixth century to the late second, so that the coins were slightly over commercial weight in the sixth century, slightly under weight in the proportion given by *A.P.* in the fifth century and early fourth, and more significantly under weight thereafter (J. H. Kroll, 'Two Inscribed Corinthian Bronze Weights', in *Stephanèphoros ... R. Descat* [Bordeaux: Ausonius, 2012], 111–6, suggesting that Athens already used the 'coin weight' for gold and silver before the introduction of coinage).

For Crawford, it was known in the fourth century that Athens' *medimnos* was larger than the 'Pheidonean' and that 100 Athenian drachmae were equivalent to 70 Aeginetan, but everything beyond that was guesswork. I prefer to be less drastic: if Solon's laws survived, it will have been known that his laws referred to the use of standard measures and weights, which differed from those in use elsewhere, but he may well have been legislating for the use of existing standards rather than changing from one set of standards to another (cf. p. 195).

10. 2. The ancient standard coin was the two-drachmae: The *Wappenmünzen* (cf. above). Philoch. *FGrH* 328 F 200 states that the old 2-drachma coins had a bull stamped on them (which Plut. *Thes.* 25. 3

attributes to Theseus). The bull was just one of the designs used; the significance of the designs is unknown (cf. Kraay, *Archaic and Classical Greek Coins*, 56–60).

11. 1. After he had organised the constitution in the manner which has been stated: This resumptive phrase ignores ch. 10 (cf. on 10. 1) and sums up 7–8(–9).
men took to approaching him and pestering him about his laws: Cf. Plut. *Sol.* 25. 6. Though neither text says so, this statement may be derived (whether reliably or not) from Solon's poems.
he made a foreign journey: Cf. Plut. *Sol.* 25. 6–28. 1, Hdt. I. 29. 1: Herodotus, almost certainly rightly, links this with the period during which Solon's laws were to remain unaltered (cf. 7. 2 with commentary). Solon's travels are discussed by Linforth, *Solon the Athenian*, 297–302; Plutarch's account is based at least partly on Solon's poems. That Solon visited Croesus of Lydia, who became king *c.* 560 (Hdt. I. 29–33), is chronologically not merely difficult (Plut. *Sol.* 27. 1) but virtually impossible; synchronisms with Amasis of Egypt, king from *c.* 570 (Hdt. I. 30. 1, II. 177. 2), and Philocyprus of Cyprus, whose son was alive in 497 (Hdt. V. 113. 2, Plut. *Sol.* 26. 2–4, with a quotation), are possible if Solon did not cease travelling after ten years.
for trade: This is possible, but may be based on no more than the assumption that as one of the 'middling' men Solon must have been a trader (cf. on 5. 3).
to see the sights: Cf. Hdt. I. 29. 1.
he did not think it just that he should remain present and expound the laws: Possibly derived from Solon's poems.
11. 2. both factions had changed their stance: Cf. Plut. *Sol.* 14. 2, 16. 1–4, 25. 4: that Solon displeased both sides is clear from his poems, in ch. 12 and elsewhere; that he failed to resolve Athens' problems sufficiently is shown by the troubles over the archonship (13. 1–2) and the tyranny of Pisistratus.
to make a redistribution of everything: Cf. fr. 34. 8–9 West *ap.* 12. 3, and Plut. *Sol.* 16. 1.
when it was possible … and become tyrant, he chose to be hated by both: Cf. 6. 3–4, fr. 34. 7–8 *ap.* 12. 3; also Plut. *Sol.* 15. 1 quoting frs. 32–3, *Comp. Sol. Publ.* 2. 5. It is more credible that he might have

become tyrant as champion of the poor than of the rich, but fr. 36. 22–5 *ap.* 12. 4 suggests that he could have supported either side against the other, and before his reforms he must have been trusted by both sides.
to save the country and enact laws for the best: Probably a formulation of what Solon thought he was doing rather than an expression of *A.P.*'s approval.

12. 1. all the others agree, and he himself has recorded it in his poetry: Cf. 5. 3, 6. 4.
I gavc the *demos*...: Fr. 5 West, quoted also in Plut. *Sol.* 18. 5; Arist. *Pol.* II, 1274 A 15–16 and Aristid. III. *Quatt.* 547, XXIV. *Rhod. Conc.* 14, are derived from this. The contrast makes it clear that here *demos* refers to the lower class.
or reaching out for it: Not 'nor offering more', in contrast to ἀφελὼν, but reinforcing ἀφελὼν (H. Lloyd-Jones *ap.* Rhodes, *Comm. Ath. Pol.*).
holding my stout buckler against both: Not holding his shield 'over both' (C. Rogge, *PhW* 44 [1924], 797–8).
12. 2. This is how the *demos*...: Fr. 6 West, ll. 1–2 quoted also in Plut. *Comp. Sol. Publ.* 2. 6 (and ll. 3–4 variously quoted and attributed, including Theognis 153–4). We cannot recover the original author of the proverb or the original form of words.
nor constrained: Usually interpreted as passive, as in my translation: the possibility that it is middle, 'allowed to work violence', should be considered (cf. the interpretation of 12. 1), but here the usual interpretation is probably right.
12. 3. They came for plunder...: Fr. 34 West, ll 4–5 quoted also in Plut. *Sol.* 16. 3, ll. 6–7 in Aristid. XXVIII. *παραφθ.* 137. Frs. 4a and 4c *ap.* 5. 2–3 show that not all Solon's words were mild, so if some men had expected him to have a more ruthless purpose they had some grounds for doing so.
or that of the rich land ... equal shares with the bad: As *A.P.* remarks here and in 11. 2, some of the poor had wanted not merely abolition of the obligations of the *hektemoroi* but redistribution of land. κακοῖσιν ἐσθλοὺς uses the terms with reference to social standing rather than moral character (cf. A. W. H. Adkins, *Merit and Responsibility* [Oxford U. P., 1960], 30–40, 75–9, 159–63).
12. 4. Of the things for which...: Fr. 36 West, all except ll. 1–2 quoted

in in Aristid. XXVIII. *παραφθ.* 138–40, ll. 6–7, 11–14, 16 quoted in Plut. *Sol.* 15. 6, 6, 1. In the context of this poem *demos* should refer to the whole people, and the meaning in ll. 1–2 is probably 'Of the purposes for which I brought the people together (*sc* in an assembly)… ' (D. A. Campbell, *Greek Lyric Poetry* [London: Macmillan, 1967], 251, cf. Thuc. I. 120.1, II. 60. 1).

in the justice which time brings: Rather than reference to a court or a trial.

The great mother … Earth: For earth as mother cf. Hes. *Theog.* 116–8, 126–8, *Hymn. Hom.* XXX. *Terr.*, Eur. fr. 839 *TrGF*; and for personification of the soil of Attica cf. Pl. *Leg.* V. 740 A 27, 741 C 1–2.

I | Took up the markers: The *horoi* will have been markers set up by the overlords on land worked by *hektemoroi* (cf. pp. 185–6): by uprooting these Solon abolished the overlords' entitlement and so liberated the land and the *hektemoroi.*

Many men to Athens … who had been sold: It will have been hard for Solon to find such men and redeem them, particularly outside Attica; but to justify this claim there must presumably have been some instances.

under compelling need: From χρεώ, 'from necessity', but the scribe who wrote χρεῶν in the Berlin papyrus was probably thinking of χρέος, 'debt'.

slavery: Referring possibly to the men who had been enslaved but not sold abroad, but more probably to the servile state of the *hektemoroi.*

Harnessing force and justice together: Solon did not seize power by violence, and he claims here that he prevented bloodshed; *bia* and *dike* are normally contrasted as means of resolving a dispute. Here the claim must be not that Solon used physical violence but that he compelled both sides to accept a just settlement.

Statutes: Though later Athenians called his laws *nomoi*, Solon like Draco uses the older word, *thesmos* (cf. pp. 188, 192). Ostwald, *Nomos and the Beginnings of the Athenian Democracy* [Oxford U. P., 1969], 9–59, suggests that the adoption of the word *nomos* was due to Cleisthenes.

for bad and good alike: For the social use of these terms cf. on 12. 3.

like a wolf among many bitches: Cf. Hom. *Il.* XII. 41–2, featuring a boar or lion.

12. 5. If I am to reproach…: Fr. 37. 1–5 West, quoted only here. Presumably the rich aristocrats should praise Solon becaused he saved them from revolution and tyranny.

He would not have restrained...: Fr. 37. 7–10 (*A.P.*'s introductory clause is counted as l. 6); ll. 7–8 are quoted by Plut. *Sol.* 16. 4, and the whole is paraphrased by Aristid. III. *Quatt.* 547. These lines take up the theme of the last lines of fr. 36.
Until he had stirred up the milk and taken off the cream: Best explained by T. C. W. Stinton, *JHS* 96 (1976), 159–60: 'until, by stirring the milk up, he had deprived the milk of its cream (by mixing it with the rest of the milk)', i.e. he had deprived the state of its aristocracy.
as if in the no man's land between them I stood as a boundary marker (?): The image of a *horos* in the space betwen the contenders is difficult, but neither Jaeger's <δ>ορὸς, 'spear' (used of standing in the *metaichmion* in Eur. *Heracl.* 803, *Phoen.* 1361–3: *Hermes* 64 [1929], 22–40 at 31–2 = his *Scripta Minora* [Rome: Ed. di Storia e Letteratura, 1960], ii. 16–18) nor Stinton's τούτων … οὖρος = 'protector' of the aristocrats (cf. Hom. *Il.* VIII. 80: *op. cit.* 161–2) is obviously right.

E. Between Solon and Pisistratus (13)

§§1–2 have no parallel in extant literature: their ultimate source is presumably the archon list, expounded by one of the Atthidographers. §§3–5 deal with the division of Attica into three locally-based factions, which enabled Pisistratus to become powerful: Hdt. I. 59. 3 has a note, significantly different from *A.P.*; Plut. *Sol.* 13. 1–3 has a note on the same lines as *A.P.* but before the appointment of Solon, and 29. 1 names the leaders of the factions after Solon's reforms. For the retrojection of this tripartite division to Pandion see p. 177; almost certainly the factions were a short-lived phenomenon of the time of Pisistratus, and Plutarch's earlier context is mistaken.

13. 1. made his foreign journey: Resuming 11. 1.
the city was still in a state of upheaval: *A.P.* probably regarded the 'upheaval' as running from Cylon's *coup* to the *coups* of Pisistratus: cf. p. 184.
in the fifth year after Solon's archonship they did not appoint an archon: The simplest, and probably the correct, interpretation counts inclusively (as was normal with ordinal numerals) from Solon's archonship in 594/3, takes διὰ τῶν αὐτῶν χρόνων in 13. 2 to mean 'after

the same lapse of time', and obtains *anarchia* in 590/89 and 586/5, and Damasias appointed archon for 582/1 and remaining in office for the whole of 581/0 and the first two months of 580/79. It may be literally true that no archon was appointed for 590/89 and 586/5, or (less probably) that archons were appointed but were subsequently judged to be illegitimate and therefore not included in later lists.

13. 2. Damasias: Δαμασίου τοῦ δευτέρου in *Marm. Par. FGrH* 239 A 38, the first being the archon of 639/8: since the name is rare, the two men were probably related, and both *eupatridai*, in which case the younger Damasias perhaps refused to hand over to a non-eupatrid successor (but T. J. Figueira, *Hesperia* 53 [1984], 447–73, regards him as a populist).

when appointed archon: The verb can have this general meaning, and therefore does not conflict with 8. 1.

to appoint ten archons: *A.P.* seems to envisage a board of ten in place of the eponymous archon, perhaps for the ten remaining months of 580/79, and that is defended by T. J. Figueira, *Hesperia* liii 1984, 447–73. However, no more is heard of the ten archons, and it is an attractive guess of E. Cavaignac, *RPh*[2] 48 (1924), 144–8, cf. H. T. Wade-Gery, *CQ* 25 (1931), 79 = his *Essays*, 102–3, that in fact the ten men were the ten *prokritoi* from each tribe (cf. 8. 1) and that this system continued until allotment was abandoned under the tyranny (cf. on 22. 5).

This is the only appearance in the historical period of the three classes, *eupatridai*, *agroikoi* (that derogatory word is used here) and *demiourgoi*. Since all candidates must have satisfied Solon's class requirement, it is hard to envisage appointments on this basis in the early sixth century: L. Gernet (*RPh*[3] 12 [1938], 216–27) supposed that the whole story was invented by later theorists; I suspect that the theorists elaborated a simpler truth – that Solon's admission of non-*eupatridai* to the archonship was controversial, and here a compromise was provided, that each tribe's ten *prokritoi* should comprise five *eupatridai* and five non-*eupatridai*.

From this it is clear … their dissension was always focused on this office: Probably *A.P.*'s own comment: the archonship was the most important office in early Athens (cf. 3. 2–5) but was no longer so by the mid fifth century (cf. on 22. 5).

13. 3. Altogether they continued … relations between one another: *A.P.*'s reasons are loss of wealth by the rich, loss of power by the *eupatridai*, and personal ambition, perhaps among rich non-*eupatridai*;

he says nothing about the poor who had hoped for a more drastic reform. **the cancellation of debts:** Cf. 6. 1 for this formulation of the *seisachtheia*; probably few if any of the rich land-owners had become seriously poor. **13. 4. The factions were three in number:** For other texts see p. 218; the most thorough modern discussion is by R. J. Hopper, *BSA* 56 (1961), 189–219. The plain (i.e. the plain surrounding Athens) and the coast are unproblematic. The third faction is labelled *hyperakrioi* by Hdt. I. 59. 3 but *diakrioi* by *A.P.* and almost all later texts, and is said by Herodotus to be a group formed by Pisistratus to intervene in the rivalry of the other two. The Diacria was the hilly north-east of Attica, but Pisistratus' base was at Brauron, near the middle of the east coast: probably *hyperakrioi*, the men 'beyond the hills' with respect to Athens, is the correct term, and *diakrioi* was substituted by somebody who did not understand that (H. T. Wade-Gery, *JHS* 71 [1951], 219 n. 40 = his *Essays*, 167 n. 2). The three regions should not be identified with distinct economic classes: most men in all three will have been farmers, though the highest concentration of rich farmers will have been in the plain and the lowest beyond the hills.

For Herodotus the factions are characterised by locality only. For *A.P.* and Plutarch (cf. Arist. *Pol.* V. 1305 A 23–4, 1310 B 30–1) they had distinct ideologies, the men of the plain oligarchic, those of the hills led by the 'most democratic' Pisistratus, those of the coast favouring 'the middle constitution'. Those descriptions are inappropriate to the early sixth century, and the middle (*A.P.*) or mixed (Plutarch) constitution was a philosophers' ideal and particularly an Aristotelian ideal (e.g. *Pol.* IV. 1295 B 34–1296 A 21), but there is some truth behind them, in that the plain is likely to have contained the largest numbers of the ruling class, Pisistratus' party the largest number of discontented poor, and the coastal faction was able at different times to collaborate with each of the others. All three leaders were *eupatridai*, who will have been personal rivals rallying in their support men particularly from the region where they were strongest; and Pisistratus, like other men bidding for tyranny, may well have appealed to supporters with various grounds for discontent.

Megacles son of Alcmeon: Grandson of the Megacles who was archon at the time of Cylon's *coup* (cf. 1), husband of Agariste the daughter of Cleisthenes of Sicyon (Hdt. VI. 126–31), and father of Cleisthenes (cf. on 20. 1). In the classical period the Alcmaeonids are found in demes immediately to the south-east of the city, but there are grounds for thinking that they had land and dependants on the coastal strip running from Phalerum to Sunium (cf. on 21. 4).

Lycurgus: Probably an ancestor of the fourth-century financier Lycurgus, of Butadae, immediately to the north-west of the city, and of the *genos* which when its name was given to the deme took to calling itself Eteobutadae, 'genuine Butadae' (cf. on 21. 5). A conspicuous absentee from the list of three rivals is Miltiades, from Laciadae to the west of Butadae, said by Herodotus to have been powerful in the time of Pisistratus and Croesus (Hdt. VI. 34–38. 1).

Pisistratus: The family claimed to be descended from kings of Pylos (Hdt. V. 65. 3, cf. Hom. *Od.* III. 400–1); a Pisistratus was archon in 669/8 (Paus. II. 24. 7); Solon was related to the family on his mother's side (Plut. *Sol.* 1. 3–4). The family home was at Brauron ([Pl.] *Hipparch.* 228 B 4–5, Plut. *Sol.* 10. 3).

13. 5. There were added to adorn these last: Men additional to Pisistratus' main body of supporters, which *A.P.* presumably saw as the men of his own region. For *proskosmein* = *prostassein* cf. *kosmein* = *tassein* in Hdt. IX. 31. 2.

those who had been deprived of the debts due to them: Rich creditors who had suffered from what *A.P.* believed to be a cancellation of debts (cf. 13. 3).

those of impure ancestry: Solon was said to have encouraged immigrant craftsmen (cf. p. 199), and *A.P.* was perhaps thinking of them and their descendants; it is unlikely that he had direct evidence.

after the overthrow of the tyranny they held a review vote: Cf. *diapsephisis*, of the vetting of citizens in 346/5 (Aeschin. I. *Tim.* 77, Dem. LVII. *Eubulides* 26). *A.P.* presumably thought of an expulsion of men who were not pure Athenians (immigrant craftsmen encouraged by Solon, and men imported by the Pisistratids as mercenaries), afterwards readmitted by Cleisthenes (cf. 21. 4) – and this expulsion would more generally have 'purified' the city after the tyranny (R. Parker, *Miasma* [Oxford U. P., 1983], 262). Some have doubted its authenticity (e.g. Jacoby, *Supp.* i. 158–60); E. Poddighe, *Klio* xcii 2010, 285–304, has argued that this later understanding of the *diapsephismos* was mistaken and it was in fact not an expulsion but the instrument by which Cleisthenes finalised the admission of new citizens, but I doubt that.

F. The tyranny (14–19)

In these chapters we see *A.P.* combining Herodotus and Thucydides with other sources not now preserved. Chs 14–15 cover the rise of Pisistratus: the wording is very close to Hdt. I. 59. 4–64, which *A.P.* must have used as a source (uniquely, he names Herodotus in 14. 4); he has added a series of chronological details which conflict with Herodotus, presumably from an *Atthis*, and some other details from there or elsewhere. Ch. 16 is the fullest account which we have of Pisistratus' rule; there are parallels with Aristotle's *Politics*; we cannot tell whether the material was put together by *A.P.* or by an earlier writer. Chs 17–18 deal with the assassination of Hipparchus, of which there are accounts by Hdt. V. 55–61 (mostly on the family of the killers), VI. 123. 2, Thuc. I. 20. 2, VI. 54–9, both protesting against the standard view that this had ended the tyranny. *A.P.* agrees with them on that, has a problematic passage on the sons of Pisistratus and the love affair which led to the assassination (17. 3–18. 2), then is close to Thucydides but disagrees with him on some details. Ch. 19, on the expulsion of Hippias, is derived mainly from Hdt. V. 62. 2–65; on the involvement of Delphi we can trace the development of the legend from Herodotus to *A.P.* and beyond (cf. on 19. 4).

The chronology of the tyranny has been much discussed: I have treated it in *Phoenix* 30 (1976), 219–33, building particularly on F. Heidbüchel, *Philologus* 101 (1957), 70–89, G. V. Sumner, *CQ*[2] 11 (1961), 37–48. Herodotus' narrative implies that Pisistratus' first two periods of power were short; his first more specific statement is that the third *coup* was 'in the eleventh year' from the second expulsion, before or at the same time as the war which led to the overthrow of Croesus of Lydia (546/5?); Hipparchus was killed at the Panathenaea; Hippias was expelled after four years, and after thirty-six years of tyranny (apparently from the final *coup*). *A.P.* has a complete series of intervals between *coups* and expulsions of Pisistratus, and Pisistratus' death, with the first expulsion in the sixth year after the first *coup* and the second expulsion in the seventh year after the second *coup* (despite the Herodotean narrative implying that those two periods were short), and continues to the killing of Hipparchus at the Panathenaea, the expulsion of Hippias in the fourth year, and further dated events after that; he also has summary figures for Pisistratus, Hippias and the whole tyranny. Thucydides has data for the ending of the tyranny, specifying that Hipparchus' killing was at the Great Panathenaea; and there are summary figures in Arist. *Pol.* V. 1315 B 31–4, diverging from those of *A.P.*

For Pisistratus' *coups* and expulsions *A.P.* can be made to agree with Herodotus only by drastic and arbitrary emendation. It is better to assume that *A.P.*'s figures should be internally consistent, to emend only where necessary to achieve that consistency, and to accept that *A.P.*'s series of figures is incompatible with Herodotus (and was perhaps created by somebody who misunderstood Herodotus' thirty-six years as referring to the years of tyranny between the first *coup* and Hippias' expulsion). The table below summarises my conclusions. Most recently, however, C. Flament has argued that there should be no emendations but *A.P.* tried to reconcile a plurality of sources, including one which gave Pisistratus only two periods in power and one in exile: *REG* 128 (2015), 215–36.

	Implied by Hdt.	*A.P.*	*Actual dates*
First *coup*		561/0	561/0?
First expulsion		556/5	(561/0 or 560/59??)
Second *coup*		552/1	(557/6 or 556/5??)
Second expulsion	557/6 or 556/5	546/5	556/5?
Third *coup*	547/6 or 546/5	536/5	546/5?
Death of Pisistratus		528/7	528/7
Killing of Hipparchus	514/3	514/3	514/3
Expulsion of Hipias	511/0	511/0	511/0

14. 1. seemed to be most democratic: Resuming 13. 4.

had gained a very good reputation in the war against Megara: Cf. Hdt. I. 59. 4. On Athens' war with Megara for the possession of Salamis see Plut. *Sol.* 8–10, 12. 5, and especially R. J. Hopper, *BSA* 56 (1961), 208–17, L. Piccirilli, *ASNP*[3] 8 (1978), 1–13, suggesting that Athens gained and lost Salamis several times; the final award of Salamis to Athens by Spartan arbitrators may not have been made until the end of the sixth century (e.g. M. C. Taylor, *Salamis and the Salaminioi* [Amsterdam: Gieben, 1997], 21–47).

He wounded himself: Cf. Hdt. I. 59. 4, Plut. *Sol.* 30. 1–2 and other texts. This became a favourite device of would-be tyrants: Arist. *Rhet.* I. 1357 B 30–6 cites also Dionysius of Syracuse and Theagenes of Megara.

the proposal was made by Aristion: Cf. Plut. *Sol.* 30. 3. This is not in Herodotus: it may have been either correctly remembered or later invented (but in any case γράψαντος is anachronistic). Many have tried to identify him with the Aristion whose gravestone was found at Belanideza, on the east coast (*IG* i³ 1256, where it is dated *c.* 510[?]: e.g. Wilamowitz, *A.u.A.* i. 261), and / or the Aristion whose name appears on a pre-Cleisthenic *ostrakon* (E. Vanderpool, in *Commemorative Studies ... T. L. Shear* [*Hesperia* Supp. 8 (1949)], 405–8), but the name is a common one.

those who were called club-bearers: Cf. Hdt. I. 59. 5, Plut. *Sol.* 30. 3, 5, and other texts. C. Mossé, *La Tyrannie dans la Grèce antique* (Paris: Presses Universitaires de France, 1969), compares the *korynephoroi* or *katonakophoroi* of Sicyon, and sees them as recruited from Pisistratus' lower-class supporters, J. Boardman, *RA* (1972), 62, suggests a deliberate echoing of Heracles (cf. on 14. 4, 15. 4).

he rose up against the *demos* with these and seized the acropolis: Cf. Hdt. I. 59. 6, Plut. *Sol.* 30. 5. Cylon had tried to seize the acropolis (pp. 180–1), Hippias was expelled from the acropolis in 511/0 (19. 5–6) and Isagoras and Cleomenes occupied the acropolis in 508/7 (20. 3).

in the thirty-second year ... in the archonship of Comeas: 561/0 (cf. p. 197).

14. 2. It is said that ... Solon spoke against it: In Plut. *Sol.* 30. 1–31. 2 and other texts Solon reproached Pisistratus for wounding hmself, opposed the granting of the bodyguard in the assembly and then made the statement given here; after the *coup* he again failed to persuade the people and retired to his house; and Pisistratus respected and even consulted him until he died the next year. In Diog. Laert. I. 49–54 cf. 65–7 and other texts after failing to persuade the citizens and making this statement Solon went on his travels and died in Cyprus. See Wilamowitz, *A.u.A.* i. 261–6, M. Mühl, *RM*² 99 (1956), 315–23. Hardly anything can be confirmed from surviving fragments of Solon's poems; Plutarch's version is probably the older (the alternative assumes that Solon could not have lived under the tyrant); it is possible that Solon lived to 560/59 and witnessed the first *coup* (cf. fr. 11 West *ap.* Diod. Sic. IX. 20. 3), but everything beyond that is probably invention.

he was wiser than some ... braver than those who knew but kept quiet: Plut. *Sol.* 30. 4 supposes that the poor did not understand the consequences of supporting Pisistratus while the rich did but were afraid to oppose him.

he had supported his country: Plut. *Sol.* 30. 7 adds καὶ τοῖς νόμοις, 'and the laws'.

14. 3. Pisistratus … administered public affairs in a citizen's rather than a tyrant's manner: Cf. 16. 2 (on the tyranny as a whole); also Hdt. I. 59. 6 (on the first period of tyranny), Thuc. VI. 54. 5–6 (on the tyranny as a whole). The language is reminiscent of Isocrates, but his only references to Pisistratus are hostile (XII. *Panath.* 148, XVI. *De Bigis* 25–6).

when his rule had not yet taken root … came to an agreement: Cf. Hdt. I. 60. 1; he uses τὠυτὸ φρονήσαντες there, but the compound *homophronein* is a Herodotean word.

in the sixth year … in the archonship of Hegesias: 556/5, but so long a period is hard to reconcile with the narrative (cf. pp. 222–3).

14. 4. In the fifth year after that: Corrected from δωδεκάτῳ, 'twelfth', by Wilamowitz to make *A.P.*'s figures internally consistent; if Pisistratus' first and second periods in power were both very short, this interval could be correct (cf. pp. 222–3).

Megacles, who was under pressure in the factional rivalry: Cf. Hdt. I. 60. 2.

in an archaic and over-simple manner: Cf. Hdt. I. 60. 3; Plut. *Sol.* 3. 6 is probably echoing *A.P.*'s words.

he circulated in advance: This double compound is found only here; there is nothing directly corresponding in Herodotus.

a tall and handsome woman: In Hdt. I. 60. 4, 3 fingers short of 4 cubits (1.715–1.936 m. = 5 ft. 7½ in.–6 ft. 4¼ in., according to the standard used), which is at any rate credible.

as Herodotus says: This is the only place where *A.P.* names a source other than Solon's poems.

from the deme of Paeania: Cf. Hdt. I. 60. 4. Paeania was on the east side of Hymettus, near the main route between the east coast and Athens; the use of the term *demos* with reference to the pre-Cleisthenic period is not problematic (cf. on 21. 4).

as some say … from Collytus: Ath. XIII. 509 C reports from Clidemus *FGrH* 323 F 15 ~ Fornara 30. A that she was Phye the daughter of Socrates (presumably an Athenian) and was married to Hipparchus, and immediately before that states that she was a garland-seller. Collytus was inside the city walls, to the south of the acropolis. Some have rejected the story as a fiction (e.g. Beloch, *G.G.*[2] I. ii. 288, believing that Pisistratus seized power only twice and was expelled only once); J. Boardman compared it to Athena's introduction of Heracles to Olympus (*RA* [1972], 57–72); whether or not Pisistratus was conscious of that parallel, we need not doubt that the charade was performed.

standing at his side: The *para*(*i*)*bates* was the warrior who stood beside the charioteer (e.g. Hom. *Il.* XXIII. 132). The word is not used in Herodotus' account, but is used in that of Clidemus (above): perhaps he and *A.P.* derived it from the same predecessor.

with reverence: Hdt. I. 60. 5 does not use this verb: it refers to an act of homage, 'blowing a kiss' and perhaps also bowing down, which was paid by Persians to human superiors (e.g. Hdt. I. 134. 1) but by Greeks only to the gods.

15. 1. After this he was expelled…: With ὡς ἐξέπεσε the sentence has no main verb, but we should probably blame *A.P.* rather than a copyist.

about the seventh year after his return: In *A.P.*'s scheme 546/5, but as in 14. 3 so long a period is hard to reconcile with the narrative (cf. pp. 222–3).

for he did not hold down his position for a long time: Hdt. I. 61. 1–2 tells the story at greater length but does not make this conclusion explicit.

he became afraid of both factions and withdrew: Herodotus explains that the angry Megacles renewed his alliance with Lycurgus' party.

15. 2. First he joined in settling a place near the Thermaic Gulf: Hdt. I. 61. 2 omits this and takes Pisistratus directly to Eretria, but in I. 64. 1 Pisistratus subsequently received revenues from the Strymon.

Rhaecelus: At the end of the coast running north-west from Potidaea (C. F. Edson, *CP* 42 [1947], 88–91, N. G. L. Hammond, *A History of Macedonia*, i [Oxford U. P., 1972], 186–8, J. W. Cole, *G&R*[2] 22 [1975], 42–3).

the locality around Pangaeum: Near the Thracian coast, east of the Strymon (cf. S. Casson, *Macedonia, Thrace and Illyria* [Oxford U. P., 1926], 63–6. This is the beginning of Athenian attempts to gain a foothold in the region, culminating in the foundation of Amphipolis in 437/6.

hiring soldiers: Herodotus knows that Pisistratus had mercenaries (I. 61. 3–4, 64. 1), but does not mention Thracians. Thrace was a source from which the Greeks freqently obtained mercenaries, and Thracian warriors appear on Athenian vases from *c.* 540 (cf. J. G. P. Best, *Thracian Peltasts and Their Influence on Greek Warfare* [Groningen: Wolters-Noordhoff, 1969], 5–7).
he went to Eretria: Cf. Hdt. I. 61. 2, 62. 1.
in the eleventh year again: Cf. Hdt. I. 62. 1; πάλιν marks this as the latest of *A.P.*'s intervals of time. *A.P.*'s implied date is 536/5, Herodotus', which is to be preferred, is 547/6 or 546/5 (cf. pp. 222–3).
he first tried to recover his rule: Herodotus uses the verb elsewhere, but I. 61. 3 has ἀνακτᾶσθαι.
with the enthusiastic support: Cf. προθυμίην in Hdt. I. 61. 4.
the Thebans: Cf. Hdt. I. 61. 3.
Lygdamis of Naxos: Cf. Hdt. I. 61. 4; he mentions also the Argives, for whom see 17. 4.
the cavalry who controlled the régime in Eretria: Not mentioned by Herodotus; for Eretria's aristocracy of *hippeis* cf. Arist. *Pol.* V. 1306 A 35–6).
15. 3. He won the battle at Pallenis: Cf. the detailed account in Hdt. I. 62–3: Pisistratus landed at Marathon, encountered a force from the city at the temple of Athena Pallenis, attacked at lunch time and was victorious. Pallene and the temple lay in the col between Hymettus and Pentelicon, on the route from Marathon to Athens; for the cult of Athena Pallenis see R. Schlaifer, *HSCP* liv 1943, 35–67.
took control of the city: Here *polis* means the city, not the acropolis.
and then held down the tyranny firmly: Cf. Hdt. I. 64. 1.
he captured Naxos and installed Lygdamis as its ruler: Cf. Hdt. I. 64. 1–2; in the course of the 530's Lygdamis helped Polycrates to size power in Samos (Polyaen. I. 23. 2).
15. 4. He deprived the *demos* of its arms: Cf. Polyaen. I. 21. 2, but contrast Thuc. VI. 56. 2, 58, attributing the disarming to Hippias in 514 (see on 18. 4). Disarming the people was a device of tyrannies and oligarchies (Arist. *Pol.* V. 1311 A 12–13 cf. 1315 A 38), practised by the Thirty in Athens among others (37. 2).
in the Theseum: According to Polyaenus, in the Anaceum (sanctuary of the *Anakes* = Dioscuri). Both were east of the acropolis, near the

prytaneion and the cave of Aglaurus (cf. p. 189), but the Theseum was founded in the time of Cimon whereas the Anaceum was 'ancient' (Paus. I. 17. 2–18. 3); the Anaceum was large enough to hold a cavalry parade (Andoc. I. *Myst.* 45) or a sizeable meeting (Thuc. VIII. 93. 1); and J. Boardman argues that Theseus became popular in Athens only after 510 while the tyrants preferred Heracles (*RA* [1972], 57–72, *JHS* 95 [1975], 1–12). If the story is true, the Anaceum is the more credible location.
the entrance gate: τὸ πρόπυλον rather than τὰ προπύλαια, which would have suggested the grander building of the 430's (Sandys).
in the nearby buildings of the Theseum: In Polyaenus' version, in the sanctuary of Agraulus.
15. 5. go back and focus on their individual affairs: Cf. 16. 3, Hdt. I. 63. 2.

16. 1. that is the series of changes which it underwent: His *coups* and withdrawals. Cf. the list of *metabolai* or *metastaseis* in the constitution, in 41. 2; and *metabolai* of the *politeia* are frequently mentioned in Arist. *Pol.*
16. 2. Pisistratus administered … in a citizen's rather than a tyrant's manner: Cf. 14. 3 (on the first period of tyranny). διῴκει … τὰ περὶ τὴν πόλιν is another Isocratean expression (XII. *Panath.* 124, XV. *Antid.* 158).
humane, mild and disposed to forgive offenders: *Philanthropos* is used by orators and philosophers, and particularly by Isocrates; *praos* by writers of all kinds, and particularly by Isocrates and Plato; *syngnomonikos* particularly by Aristotle, and not by Isocrates or Plato.
he lent funds to the needy for their working: Cf. Ael. *V.H.* IX. 25, where Pisistratus summoned men not working, asked why, and supplied what they lacked. The loans were presumably funded by the tax on produce mentioned in 16. 4.
16. 3. spend their time not in the city … to care for public affairs: Engagement in farming would keep the citizens away from the city (cf. Arist. *Pol.* VI. 1319 A 26–32) and busy (cf. IV. 1292 B 25–9, VI. 1318 B 9–16); cf. also V. 1311 A 13–15, 1313 B 21–5. But a busy peasantry and public works were not necessarily signs of oppression (cf. Isoc. VII. *Areop.* 33, 48–55); and, while Pisistratus may have had the political objective alleged here, he may well also have had the economic objective of helping small-scale farmers for whom life was not easy (cf. p. 199).

16. 4. this resulted in his revenues' becoming greater: *A.P.* writes as if the proceeds went to Pisistratus personally; and in general it is likely that no clear distinction was made between the revenue of a tyrant and the revenue of the state, so that taxes levied by tyrants were particularly resented. This tax may have been abolished on the downfall of the tyranny; but there is no evidence, and P. Cloché supposed that it was already in existence before the tyranny (*La Démocratie athénienne* [Paris, 1951], 3 with n. 2; cf. van Wees, *Ships and Silver, Taxes and Tribute*, 84–91).

for he exacted a tithe of the produce: Cf. Diog. Laert. I. 53 and other late writers, but contrast Thuc. VI. 54. 5 (Pisistratus' sons levied only an *eikoste*). Many have supposed that the sons reduced the tax (e.g. Sandys); but more probably *dekate* is generic and both Pisistratus and his sons levied $^{1}/_{20}$ (e.g. Dover, *H.C.T.*, on Thucydides).

16. 5. he devised the deme justices: Presumably abolished on the downfall of the tyranny: they were revived in 453/2 (26. 3: we cannot infer from that that Pisistratus' justices numbered thirty) and modified at the beginning of the fourth century (53. 1).

so that they should not go down to the city and neglect their work: Cf. 16. 3; but probably small local disputes would previously not have been brought to Athens but have been decided by the local aristocrats, and the new institution will have weakened them.

16. 6. the incident concerning the man ... in the region of Hymettus: Cf. Diod. Sic. IX. 37. 2–3, *Suda* κ 1206 Adler καὶ σφάκελοι ποιοῦσιν ἀτέλειαν, σ 1711 σφακελισμός, and other late texts. There are echoes of *A.P.* in Diodorus, who in the latter part of book IX seems to have been following Ephorus (cf. IX. 26 with *FGrH* 70 F 181, IX. 32 with F 58), and Ephorus may have been the source of both *A.P.* and Diodorus for the story. In *A.P.*'s version, if the farmer did not know that he was talking to Pisistratus, he did not display *parrhesia* except in so far as an unfavourable reference to Pisistratus addressed to anybody might be considered *parrhesia*.

16. 7. always secured peace and was careful to maintain calm: We hear of little military activity, and none in or near to Attica (though our evidence is not plentiful); no doubt the soldiers used in overseas adventures were mercenaries, whether Pisistratus had disarmed the citizens or not (cf. 15. 4–5, 18. 4). Pisistratus installed Lygdamis as tyrant of Naxos (15. 3), 'purified' Delos by removing the graves within sight of the sanctuary (Hdt. I. 64. 2, Thuc. III. 104. 1–2), and reconquered Sigeum from Mytilene and installed his son Hegesistratus as ruler (cf. on 17. 3), while in spite of Hdt. VI. 34–38. 1 Miltiades probably went with Pisistratus' support to rule in the Chersonese.

the age of Cronus: The age of Cronus is a golden age in Hes.*Op.* 109–26; the description is applied to the rule of the sons before the killing of Hipparchus by [Pl.] *Hipparch.* 229 B 3–7, to Aristides' assessment of the Delian League's tribute by Plut. *Arist.* 24. 3, to the generosity of Cimon by Plut. *Cim.* 10. 7 (cf. on 27. 3).

the régime became much harsher: Cf. 19. 1 (deterioration after the killing of Hipparchus); in several cases where a first tyrant was succeeded by one or more sons it was claimed that the first ruler was mild but the son(s) harsh. For those who thought Hipparchus was killed solely for personal reasons (cf. on 18. 2) the tyranny was mild until then and harsh afterwards (Thuc VI. 54. 5–6, 59. 2, cf. Hdt. V. 55, 62. 2, VI. 123. 2; also [Pl.] *Hipparch.* 229 B 3–7), but those who saw the killing of Hipparchus as the act of liberation could regard the rule of Hippias and Hipparchus before 514 as harsh (Ephorus *ap.* Diod. Sic. X. 17. 1, Ideomeneus *FGrH* 338 F 3). *A.P.* agrees with Herodotus and Thucydides that the killing of Hipparchus did not end the tyranny, but has one deterioration after the death of Pisistratus and a second after the killing of Hipparchus.

16. 8. democratic in his character and humane: Cf. 14. 1, 16. 2.

willing to administer everything in accordance with the laws: Cf. Hdt. I. 59. 6, Thuc. VI. 54.6, Plut. *Sol.* 31. 3 (who repeats the story told here), but contrast *A.P.* 22. 1. Tyranny in an established city was an extra-constitutional phenomenon, and tyrants might work through the previous constitution to achieve the results which they wanted or override it as they saw fit; apart from the appointment of archons (ML 6: cf. on 16. 9) and the story which follows, we have no evidence on the extent to which previous institutions continued to function.

when he was summoned to the Areopagus for a homicide trial: Cf. Arist. *Pol.* V. 1315 B 21–2, Plut. *Sol.* 31. 3; in Arist.*Pol.* V. 1315 A 6–8 the 'good' tyrant awards honours himself but allows magistrates and courts to impose punishments. *Proskaleisthai* is the Athenian technical term for a prosecutor's summons to a defendant (cf. 29. 4); this story could be true.

16. 9. For that reason he continued … recovered it easily: Probably the author's own comment.

his friendly dealing with them: Cf. the advice to 'good' tyrants in Arist. *Pol.* V. 1315 B 3–4; but according to Hdt. I. 64. 1 Pisistratus secured the loyalty of some men by depositing their children on Naxos as hostages. The inscribed list of archons (ML 6 = *IG* i³ 1031 ~ Fornara 23) includes those for 527/6–522/1: 527/6 Onetorides, probably from a rich family in Melite, inside the city walls (Davies, *A.P.F.* 421; perhaps already appointed when Pisistratus died); 526/5 Hippias; 525/4 Cleisthenes, of the Alcmaeonids; 524/3 Miltiades, of the Philaids; 523/2 Calliades, unidentified; 522/1 probably Pisistratus, the son of Hippias. Thucydides VI. 54. 6 comments that they took care to have their own men in office: these names indicate that they did not restrict offices to their own family but secured the cooperation of other leading families.

16. 10. the Athenians' laws about tyrants were mild at that time: The point is presumably that the mildness of the laws made it easier for Pisistratus to gain and retain power. Athenian laws against revolution and tyranny are collected and discussed by M. Ostwald, *TAPA* 86 (1955), 103–28, who supposed that the Athenians alternated between 'strong' laws which authorised direct action and 'weak' laws which required offenders to be brought to trial, and that this was a law of Draco, cited *c.* 510 in support of measures taken on the fall of the tyranny. I suspect that from the time of Solon 'strong' and 'weak' laws may have coexisted, that this was an ancient law (cf. next note), and that *A.P.* mistakenly regarded it as mild because he understood *atimia* in its later sense rather than as outlawry (cf. p. 210).

These are statutory and traditional rules of the Athenians: This preamble marks the reaffirmation of what at the time was already regarded as a 'traditional' law (Ostwald, *op. cit.*, 108); J. K. Davies thought that πάτρια pointed to reaffirmation at the end of the fifth century or perhaps at the time of Ephialtes (*CR*² 23 [1973], 225–6), but the word could have been used at another time and we cannot determine when the reaffirmation occurred. The original law can hardly be later than Solon; the formulation of the offence is more appropriate to early Athens than that used by *A.P.* in 8. 4.

if any men rise up for tyranny or he joins: The change from plural to singular is violent. Some have seen it as a sign of antiquity (e.g. Kaibel,

Stil und Text, 165; Ostwald, *op. cit.*, 106); many have emended; it may be a sign that *A.P.* has lost grammatical coherence by abbreviating a longer original (cf. 30–1, 39).

17. 1. grew old in his rule: Cf. Thuc. VI. 54. 2: Pisistratus will have been about seventy-five.

in the archonship of Philoneos ... he had been in exile for the remainder: 528/7 in *A.P.*'s scheme, and that is probably correct. Arist. *Pol.* V. 1315 B 31–4 gives a total of 33 years with 17 in power. Cf. pp. 222–3.

17. 2. For that reason those people are uttering palpable nonsense: An unusually strong rejection, with a verb used by Isocrates and Plato but not by Aristotle. In fact the argument does not justify rejection (cf. below).

who allege that Pisistratus was loved by Solon: Who these were we do not know; despite *A.P.*'s rejection the story is noted as a possibility by Plut. *Sol.* 1. 4–5, Ael. *V.H.* VIII. 16.

and was a general ... for Salamis: Cf. 14. 1 (not mentioning his *strategia*, for which cf. Hdt. I. 59. 4). For *strategoi* before Cleisthenes see on 22. 2: probably there was not yet a regular office but appointments could be made for campaigns outside Attica.

for it does not fit their ages: For this kind of argument cf. Plut. *Sol.* 27. 1 (on Solon's alleged visit to Croesus: cf. p. 215), *Them.* 27. 2.

if one reckons ... the archon under whom each died: *A.P.* does not give the date of Solon's death, but 560/59 (Phaenias fr. 21 Wehrli *ap.* Plut. *Sol.* 32. 3) may be both the date assumed by *A.P.* and correct. More pertinent would be the dates of the men's birth: if Solon was born *c.* 630–625 and Pisistratus *c.* 605–600 (Davies, *A.P.F.* 323–4, 445), on chronological grounds the story is entirely possible.

17. 3. his sons proceeded to hold down the rule: Hdt. V. 55 writes of Hippias the tyrant (but the Pisistratids VI. 39. 1, 103. 3); Thuc. VI. 54. 2 polemically insists that Hippias, not Hipparchus, was ruler (cf. I. 20. 2, VI. 55); Hellanicus seems to have made Hipparchus eldest son and ruler (cf. *Marm. Par. FGrH* 239 A 45); *A.P.* writes of shared rule (cf. 18. 1, Diod. Sic. X. 17. 1). Since tyrant was not an office to which a man was appointed, it may be best to think of shared rule in principle, though it is likely that Hippias as the eldest would be the leading partner.

There were two sons ... the alternative name Thettalus: Herodotus mentions Hippias and Hipparchus without specifying their mother, and (V. 94. 1) Hegesistratus as a *nothos* by the Argive wife; Thuc. VI. 55. 1–2 cf. I. 20. 2 gives Pisistratus three *gnesioi* sons, Hippias, Hipparchus and Thessalus; for *A.P.*'s version cf. Plut. *Cat. Mai.* 24. 8 (Iophon and Thessalus by the Argive wife), schol. Ar. *Vesp.* 502 (four sons altogether). In fact Pisistratus had Hippias, Hipparchus and Thessalus by his Athenian wife and Iophon and Hegesistratus by his Argive wife (Davies, *A.P.F.* 445–50); *A.P.*'s identification of Thessalus with Hegesistratus is simply a product of the disputes over the killing of Hipparchus. The language of legitimacy and illegitimacy has been projected back loosely to the sixth century from Pericles' citizenship law (26. 4).
from his wedded wife: Her identity is unknown. *A.P.* spoils the contrast by using *gamein* in 17. 4 of Pisistratus' union with Timonassa.
Iophon: Nothing more is known about him.
Hegesistratus: Installed as ruler of Sigeum (cf. on 16. 7) and perhaps still ruling when Hippias went there on his expulsion from Athens (Hdt. V. 65. 3, 91. 1, 94. 1, Thuc. VI. 59. 4).
had the alternative name Thettalus: The only attested link with Thessaly is that Thessalians supported Hippias in 511/0 (19. 5).
17. 4. Gorgilus ... of the Cypselids: These details are found only here (except that Plut. *Cat. Mai.* 24. 8 gives the name Timonassa), and we do not know where *A.P.* found them. On Ambracia as a colony of Cypselid Corinth see Strabo 325 / VII. 7. 6, 452 / X. 2. 8.
joined him in fighting: Hdt. I. 61. 4 mentions Argive mercenaries, but not their number or Hegesistratus; *A.P.* 15. 2 omits Argos from Pisistratus' allies at Pallene. Hegesistratus cannot have been older than about fifteen in 546/5 (cf. below), but that does not make the story impossible.
when he was expelled ... obtained his rule for the first time: 561/0–*c.* 556 (cf. pp. 222–3). Since there were two sons, and *c.* 556 Pisistratus was free to marry Megacles' daughter, but he did not lose the support of Argos, probably the marriage was early in that period and Timonassa then died. – unless Pisistratus like some other tyrants did not limit himself to one wife (L. Gernet, in *Éventail de l'histoire vivante ... L. Febvre* [Paris: Colin, 1953], ii. 43–4 = his *Anthropologie de la Grèce antique* [Paris: Maspero, 1968], 346–8).

18. 1. Hippias, being the older: Asserted polemically by Thuc. I. 20. 2, VI. 54. 2, 55. 1, and generally accepted; among those who thought otherwise were Hellanicus (cf. on 17. 3), and [Pl.] *Hipparch.* 228 B 5–6.
by nature politically-minded and sensible: Herodotus and Thucydides say nothing of the sons' characters (except that Hippias was stern in Thuc. VI. 55. 3); but if the tyranny was mild until Hipparchus' death and Hipparchus brought trouble on himself it was natural to see Hippias as a good man and Hipparchus as a bad. In Diod. Sic. X. 17. 1 Hippias and Hipparchus were both violent but Thessalus was virtuous. *A.P.* starts with an account on the same lines as Thucydides', but then switches from Hipparchus to ascribe to Thessalus vicious qualities and love for Harmodius. *A.P.* has added to the Thucydidean account the results of fourth-century revisions of the story, with an incoherent outcome (cf. Davies, *A.P.F.* 448–9).
fond of culture: Hipparchus' patronage of the arts is stressed by [Pl.] *Hipparch.* 228 B 4–229 B 1. One of his herms with verse inscriptions has been found (*IG* i[3] 1023); Herodotus reports that he expelled Onomacritus for forging oracles (VII. 6. 3); he is credited with a lavish wall enclosing the Academy, of which no trace has yet been found (*Suda* τ 733 Adler τὸ Ἱππάρχου τειχίον).
sent for such men as Anacreon, Simonides: Cf. [Pl.] *Hipparch.* 228 C 1–3, Ael. *V.H.* VIII. 2. Paus. I. 25. 1 records a statue of Anacreon in Athens; Simonides' epigrams include one on the death of Hippias' daughter Archedice ('Simonides' fr. xxvi in Page, *F.G.E.*, *ap.* Thuc. VI. 59. 3, attributed to him by Arist. *Rhet.* I. 1367 B 20–1). It is characteristic of Aristotle to use οἱ περὶ τὸν δεῖνα to mean scarcely more than ὁ δεῖνα (H. Bonitz, *Index Aristotelicus* [Berlin: Reimer, 1870], 579 A *s.v.* περί).
and the other poets: Including Lasus of Hermione (cf. Ar. *Vesp.* 1410–1) and Onomacritus (cf. above).
18. 2. Thettalus was much younger, and in his life-style bold and insolent: Cf. above. Hippias was born *c.* 570, Hipparchus and the true Thessalus by *c.* 560, and the sons of Timonassa soon after *c.* 560; νεώτερος πολὺ is part of the deformation of the story.
For he was in love with Harmodius … his affection: In Thuc. VI. 54. 2–4 cf. 56. 1, probably correctly, Hipparchus loved Harmodius and tried but failed to win him from Aristogeiton; in the apologia for Hipparchus in [Pl.] *Hipparch.* 229 C 2–D 7 Aristogeiton imagined that Hipparchus was his rival and Hipparchus won a man loved by Harmodius. Hdt. V.

57–61 concentrates on Harmodius and Aristogeiton as members of the immigrant family of the *Gephyraioi*. Whatever their mixture of personal and public motives, Harmodius and Aristogeiton were afterwards honoured as the men who struck the first blow against the tyranny, and were emphasised by those who did not want to owe Athens' liberation to the Alcmaeonids and the Spartans, until Thucydides protested.

when Harmodius' sister was about to serve as basket-bearer at the Panathenaea: Cf. Thuc. VI. 56. 1–2, where the festival at which Hipparchus was killed is the Great Panathenaea but the festival at which Harmodius' sister was rejected is unidentified; probably *A.P.* or a predecessor has been careless in mentioning the Panathenaea here. For *kanephoroi* (bearers of baskets containing gifts to the gods, commonly daughters of the aristocracy) see e.g. Ar. *Ach.* 241–62 with schol. 242.

he forbade that: Claimed never to have invited her because she was unworthy (Thuc. VI. 56. 1), in effect casting doubt on her chastity (B. M. Lavelle, *AJP* 107 [1986], 318–31).

disparaged Harmodius somewhat as effeminate: Found only in *A.P.*

with many collaborators: Thucydides claimed that Hipparchus was killed for personal reasons only (VI. 54. 1, 59. 1) and that for safety's sake there were not many conspirators (56. 3); but, inconsistently with that, he claimed that the original plan was to kill Hippias (57. 1–3) and overthrow the tyranny (54. 3), and that the conspirators hoped for widespread support when the deed was done (56. 3). Some have inserted οὐ to make *A.P.* agree with Thucydides, but he is not following Thucydides so closely as to justify that.

18. 3. at the Panathenaea … on the acropolis watching Hippias: Thuc. VI. 56. 2 specifies the Great Panathenaea (that of 51<u>4</u>/3: pp. 222–3). VI. 57. 1–3 has Hippias 'outside in the Ceramicus', marshalling the procession, and Hipparchus in the Leocoreum (in I. 20. 2, marshalling the procession), while *A.P.* places Hippias on the acropolis to receive the procession and Hipparchus in the Leocoreum to dispatch it. Perhaps all that was genuinely remembered was the location of Hipparchus, and for Hippias Thucydides and *A.P.* give different guesses (cf. C. W. Fornara, *Historia* 17 [1968], 408–9).

one of their accomplices in the affair: Cf. Thuc. I. 20. 2, VI. 57. 2.

wanting to do something before they were arrested: Cf. Thuc. I. 20. 2, VI. 57. 3.

by the Leocoreum: Commemorating the daughters of Leos (Ael. *V.H.* XII. 28). It was within the city walls (Thuc. VI. 57. 3), 'in the middle of the Ceramicus' (Phanodemus *FGrH*325 F 8). A suggested site east of the south wing of the Stoa of the *Basileus* (e.g. *Agora Guide*[3] [Athens: Am. Sch. Class. Stud. Ath., 1976], 87–90) has been rejected since it has no evidence of cult activity before the second half of the fifth century (J. McK. Camp, II, *The Athenian Agora* [London: Thames & Hudson, 1986], 47–8, 78–81; cf. *Site Guide*, 84–6).

18. 4. Harmodius was killed ... tortured for a long time: Cf. Thuc. VI. 57. 4. In both accounts Hippias has not thc *korynephoroi* of 14. 1 but *doryphoroi*.

he denounced: Not in Thucydides: it was reported by Ephorus (Diod. Sic. X. 17. 2–3) and is repeated in later texts, and is stated of other tyrannicides too.

trace: *Ichnos* is used metaphorically by Plato frequently and by Arist. *H.A.* VIII. 588 A 19, 33, IX. 608 B 4.

the prevalent story: Found in Thuc. VI. 58, cf. 56. 2; consistently with his denial of it, *A.P.* believes that the citizens were disarmed by Pisistratus after Pallene (15. 4–5). We do not know what basis either writer had for his belief, or which is correct.

18. 5. denounced the friends of the tyrants: The 'democratic' version was no doubt the original, to which the other was a rejoinder (cf. Fornara, *Historia* 17 [1968], 407). The first version was given by Ephorus (cf. Diod. Sic. X. 17. 2–3), but in labelling it 'democratic' *A.P.* is probably thinking of more obviously partisan writers.

the tyrants...: *A.P.* continues to use the plural after Hipparchus' death. They would be impious for killing the innocent and weakened by killing their own friends.

18. 6. In the end...: The melodramatic ending corresponds to the 'democratic' version.

19. 1. the tyranny became much harsher: Cf. 16. 7 with commentary. All who knew that the tyranny continued after Hipparchus' death agreed that it then bcame harsher.

his vengeance for his brother and his killing and exiling many men: Thuc. VI. 59. 2–4 mentions killings but not exiles; in fact it seems that the Alcmaeonids went into exile (cf. on 19. 3).

19. 2. About the fourth year: Cf. Hdt. V. 55, Thuc. VI. 59. 4, [Pl.] *Hipparch.* 229 B 3–4: the year is 511/0 (pp. 222–3).
when things in the city were in a bad way: Presumably an inference from the details given.
he tried to fortify Munichia: In *A.P.* only. Munichia is the hill on the east side of the Piraeus, towards Phalerum: it was garrisoned by the Four Hundred in 411 (Thuc. VIII. 92. 5), occupied by Thrasybulus and the democrats in 403 (38. 1), garrisoned by *epheboi* under one of the *strategoi* in the time of *A.P.* (42. 3, 61. 1); Epimenides (cf. 1) is said to have warned the Athenians that Munichia would be a source of trouble to them (Plut. *Sol.* 12. 10, Diog. Laert. I. 144). In Thuc. VI. 59. 2–4 Hippias arranged to be able to withdraw to Lampsacus if forced to leave Athens.
by Cleomenes: Cf. 19. 5–6.
receiving oracles: Cf. 19. 4.
19. 3. The exiles, of whom the Alcmaeonids were the leaders: Cf. Hdt. V. 62. 2, Thuc. VI. 59. 4; also *A.P.* 20. 4. Hdt. I. 64. 3, VI. 123. 1, suggests that they had been in exile since Pisistratus' third *coup* (cf. Isoc. XVI. *De Bigis* 25–6), but the archon of 525/4 was Cleisthenes (ML 6. *c.* 3), the son by Agariste of Sicyon of the Megacles involved in Pisistratus' rise to power, and the reformer of 508/7 (20–1). Probably they went into exile after Pallene, were later reconciled with Pisistratus, and went into exile again after Hipparchus' death (but see the doubts of P. J. Bicknell, *Historia* 19 [1970], 129–31; R. Thomas, *Oral Tradition and Written Record in Classical Athens* [Cambridge U. P., 1989], 147–51).
were not able to bring about ... but always stumbled: Cf. Hdt. V. 62. 2 (also using προσέπταιον, a favourite word of his).
when they had fortified Lipsydrium, in the countryside below Parnes: Cf. Hdt. V. 62. 2 (ὑπὲρ Παιονίης), lexica and scholia. The site is at Karagoupholesa, on the Attic side of Parnes, north of the deme Paeonidae (J. R. McCredie, *Fortified Military Camps in Attica* [*Hesperia* Supp. 11 (1966)], 58–61). Herodotus has given the deme name wrongly, but his ὑπὲρ is acceptable. The papyrus' ὑπὲρ Πάρνηθος cannot be correct in a work written from the Athenian point of view, and the mistake is not likely to be *A.P.*'s: schol. Ar. *Lys.* 666 has περὶ τὴν Πάρνηθον (*sic*), and the manuscripts of *E.M.* 361. 31 ἐπὶ Λειψυδρίῳ μάχῃ have ὑπὸ Πάρνηθος, which is the easiest correction.

Alas…: Quoted also, with variants, by Ath. XV. 695 E, *Suda* ε 2440 Adler, *E.M.* 361. 31 ἐπὶ Λειψυδρίῳ μάχῃ. *A.P.* has added this to his Herodotus-based narrative – perhaps from his own knowledge rather than from an earlier written source (cf. pp. 3, 14).

19. 4. they took the contract to build the temple at Delphi: Cf. Hdt. V. 62. 2–63. 1, Isoc. XV. *Antid.* 232, Dem. XXI. *Midias* 144 with schol., Philoch. *FGrH* 328 F 115 ~ Fornara 40. A; *A.P.*'s narrative is summarised by schol. Ar. *Lys.* 1150. The previous temple was burned in 548/7 (Paus. X. 5. 3); Amasis of Egypt, who died in 526, made a contribution to the funds (Hdt. II. 180). The development of the story is studied by W. G. Forrest, *GRBS* 10 (1969), 277–86. For Herodotus the Alcmaeonids had already done a more expensive job than they had contracted to do; Delphi prefaced every response to a Spartan enquiry with instructions to liberate Athens. Fourth-century writers assumed that the contract was made after Lipsydrium and the Alcmaeonids provided money for hiring mercenaries; *A.P.* combines Herodotus' oracular pressure with misappropriation of the building funds. Philochorus in the third century followed the fourth-century version but had the Alcmaeonids do a more expensive job afterwards out of gratitude.

from which they gained an abundance of funds: Hdt. V. 62. 3 uses similar words, but to make a different point, in a different version of the story.

the Pythia always added … until she convinced the Spartiates: Cf. Hdt. V. 63. 1.

although the Pisistratids were guest-friends of theirs: Cf. Hdt. V. 63. 2, 90. 1.

the Pisistratids' current friendship towards the Argives: Cf. 17. 3–4 on Pisistratus' marriage to Timonassa of Argos. There is no evidence of later dealings between the Pisistratids and Argos, Herodotus does not mention Argos here, and it is unlikely that the Pisistratids maintained simultaenous friendships with Argos and with Sparta.

19. 5. they sent Anchimolus with a force by sea: Cf. Hdt. V. 63. 2 (Ἀγχιμόλιον τὸν Ἀστέρος); schol Ar. *Lys.* 1153 follows *A.P.* No other bearer of the name in either form is known, except that Anchipylus of Elis (Diog. Laert. II. 126) is called Anchimolus by Hegesander *ap.* Ath. II. 44 C; but it is generally thought that *A.P.* has the correct form (e.g. *L.G.P.N.* iiiA *s.n.*: cf. *SEG* xi 667, no. 21). If so, all our manuscripts of

Herodotus have a corrupt form but *A.P.* was using an uncorrupted text. Nothing else is known about him.

When he had been defeated and killed … a thousand cavalry: Hdt. V. 63. 3–4 tells the story in more detail; for the Pisistratids' Thessalian connection see p. 233.

became more angry: Not in Herodotus; the Spartans were already angry with the Pisistratids and this defeat increased their anger (Kaibel, *Stil und Text*, 170).

sent their king Cleomenes with a larger force by land: Cf. Hdt. V. 64. 1 (*stolos* is a favourite word of Herodotus). Cleomenes was Agiad king of Sparta from before 519 (Thuc. III. 68. 5) to *c.* 491/0 (Hdt. VI.85.1 in its context: both dates have been challenged, but I thnk wrongly).

shut Hippias into what was called the Pelargic wall and … laid siege to him: Cf. Hdt. V. 64. 2, *Marm. Par. FGrH* 239 A 45 (τ̣[οῦ Π]ε̣λασγικ̣οῦ τείχους). The story was told by Hecataeus (*FGrH* 1 F 127 *ap.* Hdt. VI. 137. 2) and repeated by the Atthidographers, that the Pelasgians came to Attica, built the wall round the Athenian acropolis and were rewarded with land below Hymetttus, but were later expelled; the wall in question was presumably that dated to Late Helladic IIIB (*c.* 1250–1200). There was also an area called the *Pelargikon*, probably at the north-west corner of the acropolis, left unoccupied for religious reasons until the Peloponnesian War (Thuc. II. 17. 1). Probably the enclosure was called *Pelargikon* from an early date; later the acropolis wall was attributed to the Pelasgians and its name was assimilated to that of the *Pelargikon*. Herodotus was probably thinking of the fortified acropolis as Hippias' refuge (cf. 19. 6), but the good water supply (Hdt. V. 65. 1) may indicate that Hippias controlled the enclosure too.

19. 6. While he was proceeding with the siege: According to Hdt. V. 65. 1 the Spartans had not expected to mount a siege and would have returned home after a few days.

the sons of the Pisistratids when they were trying to escape: Cf. Hdt. V. 65. 1; Hippias is the only son of Pisistratus known to have had children (cf. Thuc. VI. 55. 1).

made an agreement … handed over the acropolis to the Athenians: Cf. Hdt. V. 65. 2. Who went with him we do not know: his grandson Hipparchus son of Charmus stayed in Athens to be archon in 496/5 (Samuel, *Chronology*, 205) and ostracised in 488/7 (22. 4).

in the archonship of Harpactides: 511/0 (cf. pp. 222–3); *A.P.* is the only source for the archon's name

about seventeen years after their father's death From 528/7; Arist. *Pol.* V. 1315 B 31–4 counts inclusively and states eighteen years.

the total with their father's rule being thirty-six: The papyrus has ἑνὸς δεῖ πεντήκοντα, 'forty-nine'. If the interval from Pisistratus' first *coup* to Hippias' expulsion were intended, *A.P.*'s total should in fact be fifty (561/0–511/0); but σὺν οἷς ὁ πατὴρ ἦρξεν points to the years of tyranny within that period, which in *A.P.*'s scheme was thirty-six years (G. V. Sumner, *CQ*² 11 [1961], 41).

G. From Cleisthenes' reforms to Xerxes' invasion (20–2)

A.P. again presents material from Herodotus and material from elsewhere, but here not interwoven but separately: 20. 1–3 is a summary of Hdt. V. 66, 69–73. 1, with close verbal resemblances; 20. 4–5 reverts to the Alcmaeonids' responsibility for ending the tyranny, and quotes a scolium, perhaps from the author's direct knowledge; 21 gives a detailed account of the reforms, dated to the archonship of Isagoras, probably from an *Atthis*. 22 after a general verdict on Cleisthenes gives a dated series of events to the recall of the ostracised at the time of Xerxes' invasion: this again is probably from an *Atthis*; and, since on ostracism *A.P.*'s source can be identified as Androtion (cf. p. 251), he is likely to be the source for the whole of 22 and perhaps for 21 also.

Cleisthenes' laws may have been published permanently, more probably on stone *stelai* than on *axones*; but they may not have survived the Persian sack of 480–479, and Clitophon's amendment in 411 (29. 3) suggests that they might still exist but would have to be searched for. It is less likely that an Atthidographer could have consulted Cleisthenes' laws than that he could have consulted Solon's laws; most though not all of the details in 21 could have been obtained by applying to Cleisthenes' reform knowledge of fourth-century practice.

Except in Herodotus and *A.P.* little material on Cleisthenes survives (a fragment of Clidemus on *naukrariai*, a fragment of Androtion on ostracism and two allusions in Arist. *Pol.*: cf. below), so as a source of material not otherwise available to us chs 21–2 are as valuable as any parts of *A.P.*'s historical narrative. Recent additions to our knowledge have come from topography, revealing how demes were combined to form the new *trittyes* and tribes, and from archaeology, which has yielded many thousands of *ostraka*.

20. 1. Isagoras … and Cleisthenes … engaged in dissension with each other: Cf. Hdt. V. 66. 1–2. For Cleisthenes cf. on 19. 3; Isagoras' family cult (perhaps of Zeus <*I*>*karios*) possibly enables him to be located in Icarium, on the north-east slope of Pentelicon (cf. *IG* i^3 253, with D. M. Lewis, *Historia* 12 [1963], 25–6 = his *Selected Papers*, 81–2, reading *Kar-* in the inscription and in Herodotus).
a friend of the tyrants: Not in Herodotus, and not true of the time of Hippias' expulsion (cf. Hdt. V. 70. 1); probably an inference from Herodotus' narrative rather than independent information (cf. Wade-Gery, *CQ* 27 [1933], 19 = his *Essays*, 138–9).
of the Alcmaeonid family: *Genos* is used of the Alcmaeonids here and in 28. 2, and by Herodotus though not in V. 66. The meaning is simply 'family': the Alcmaeonids were not a *genos* in the technical sense of fr. 2.
since he was getting the worse of the struggle for supporters, tried to win over the *demos* to his side: Cf. Hdt. V. 66. 2: *A.P.*'s rewording does not provide evidence for the existence in the time of Cleisthenes of *hetaireiai* of the kind mentioned in 34. 3 (cf. Wade-Gery, *locc. citt.*). Probably the mark of Cleisthenes' defeat was the election of Isagoras as archon for 508/7 (cf. 21. 1, and for election 22. 5): Cleisthenes, having been archon in 525/4, probably could not have been a candidate but was supporting another, perhaps Alcmeon (archon possibly in 507/6: Poll. VIII. 110 with Davies, *A.P.F.* 382). The initiative is attributed to Cleisthenes, and the offer of political institutions at the local level may well be what gained him his popularity (cf. on 21. 5): the spontaneous popular movement of J. Ober, in C. Dougherty & L. Kurke [eds], *Cultural Poetics in Archaic Greece* [Cambridge U. P., 1993], 215–32 = his *The Athenian Revolution* [Princeton U. P., 1996], [32–]34–52, relied too much on some of the wording of Herodotus' narrative.
offering political power to the masses: Not in Herodotus; perhaps inserted in order to mention the reform at Herodotus' point while delaying the details to ch. 21 (cf. Wade-Gery, *opp. citt.*, 21–2 = 142–3): the meaning is that Cleisthenes gave political power to the ordinary people.

20. 2. Isagoras … among the accursed: Cf. Hdt. V. 70. Herodotus then gives an account of the curse on those who killed the supporters of Cylon (V. 71); *A.P.*, having given an account of Cylon in 1, does not explain the curse here.

falling behind in power: *A.P.* uses the same construction in 27. 4 cf. 34. 3, though it is not found elsewhere (cf. Kaibel, *Stil und Text*, 171).

20. 3. Cleisthenes withdrew … seven hundred Athenian households: Cf. Hdt. V. 72. 1, also Thuc. I. 126. 12. It is surprising that so many families should have been considered subject to the curse (cf. Wilamowitz, *A.u.A.*, i. 31–2).

After completing this … power over the city: Cf. Hdt. V. 72. 1. The council which Cleomenes tried to dissolve must have been Solon's four hundred (8. 4): Cleisthenes' five hundred did not yet exist, and to dissolve the venerable Areopagus would have been unthinkable. R. Sealey, *Historia* 9 (1960), 160 n. 35 = his *Essays in Greek Politics* (New York: Manyland, 1967), 35–6 n. 35, suggested that the three hundred supporters of Isagoras were the Areopagus; but at least one member, Cleisthenes, was opposed to Isagoras.

the council resisted … under a truce: Cf. Hdt. V. 72. 2, also Ar. *Lys.* 274–82. According to Herodotus the truce applied only to the Spartans (though Isagoras survived: V. 74. 1); probably *A.P.* is not consciously disagreeing but has been careless. In *A.P.* the sequel to the reforms is the series of events reported in ch. 22; Herodotus does not report them but reports the further attempts of Sparta to upset the reforms (V. 74–7, 90–6).

recalled Cleisthenes and the other exiles: Cf. Hdt. V. 73. 1.

20. 4. When the *demos* … champion of the *demos*: Without a precise verbal echo, *A.P.* closes the ring opened in 20. 1.

the Alcmaeonids were most responsible for the expulsion of the tyrants: This enlarges on the contrast in 20. 1 between Cleisthenes and Isagoras the 'friend of the tyrants' (cf. J. J. Keaney, *AJP* 90 [1969], 417–20).

for most of the time they had continued in dissension with them: Cleisthenes' archonship of 525/4 is unknown or conveniently forgotten.

20. 5. Even earlier, Cedon of the Alcmaeonids: In the context this is what the words should mean (e.g. Wilamowitz, *A.u.A.*, i. 38), rather than 'before the Alcmaeonids, Cedon'. Nothing else is known of this Cedon:

the author may well have added the reference, and the scolium, from his own knowledge.
sang of him too: In addition to the heroes of Lipsydrium (19. 3).
Pour to Cedon also...: Quoted also by Ath. XV. 695 E.

21. 1. for these reasons: Probably referring to the whole of 20.
Then, as champion of the masses: Resuming 20. 4 (and not implying that he obtained this position only after his return: R. Seager, *AJP* 84 [1963], 289, contr. Hignett, *Constitution*, 332). Cleisthenes is not said to have held any office: probably his proposals were adopted as decrees of the assembly. On the enactment and implementation of the reform see A. Andrewes, *CQ*[2] 27 (1977), 241–8 (but I do not share his view that it was implemented quickly: cf. on 22. 2).
in the fourth year after the overthrow of the tyrants, in the archonship of Isagoras: 508/7 (cf. p. 241). Probably Cleisthenes' proposals were formally approved before, and prompted Isagoras to request, Cleomenes' intervention, but there was no time then to act on them. Probably Isagoras withdrew with Cleomenes, but there is no indication that a replacement archon was appointed for the remainder of the year.
21. 2. first he distributed them all: The abruptness is more probably due to the author's compressing what he found in his source than to a scribal omission. πρῶτον μὲν οὖν marks the first in a series of measures attrbuted to Cleisthenes, interrupted by the author's comments.
in ten tribes instead of the four: Cf. Hdt. V. 66. 2, Arist. *Pol.* VI. 1319 B 19–27. For the four old tribes (which were left in existence with some religious functions) cf. pp. 174–6; for the composition of the new tribes see 21. 4.
wanting to mix them up, so that more men would have a share in political power: For Herodotus Cleisthenes was motivated by dislike of the Ionians, as his grandfather Cleisthenes of Sicyon had been motivated by dislike of the Dorians; in Arist. *Pol.* the creation of additional tribes is a device to facilitate ultimate democracy by mixing up the people and undoing old associations. μετέχειν τῆς πόλεως or πολιτείας often denotes membership of the citizen body (e.g. 8. 5); but here, although *A.P.* believes that more men were admitted to the citizen body (21. 4), the reference is probably not to that but to involving more existing citizens in the running of the state (cf. Wade-Gery, *opp. citt.*, 25 n. 2 = 148 n. 1).

that is why they said, 'Don't judge by tribes' ... men's ancestry: φυλοκρινεῖν should originally have been used with reference to tribal membership but came to be used more generally of over-nice discrimination (e.g. Thuc. VI. 18. 2 with 11. 7); and ἐξετάζειν τὰ γένη could be used either with reference to *gene* in the sense of fr. 2 or more generally of enquiries into men's birth. What *A.P.* says here could refer either to discrimination against new citizens (as in 21. 4) or to distinguishing between the *gnorimoi* and the *demos*, but the latter is more likely.

21. 3. he established the council as a body of five hundred instead of four hundred: For Solon's council of four hundred see 8. 4.

fifty from each tribe: Within each tribal contingent seats were allocated to individual demes (cf. 21. 4, 62. 1) in proportion to their size. Later appointment was for one year, by lot, and no man could serve more than twice in his life (43. 2, 62. 3); probably from men over thirty (Xen. *Mem.* I. 2. 35, referring to the régime of the Thirty), and in theory probably not from the *thetes* (cf. 7. 4). It is possible that allotment and the restriction on repeated service did not apply from the beginning, but they will have been in force when Athens instituted a new council in Erythrae, shortly before 450 (ML 40 = *IG* i^3 14 ~ Fornara 71. 8–12).

The reason why he did not organise them in twelve tribes: It would of course have been possible to create twelve tribes which differed from the twelve old *trittyes*.

21. 4. He distributed them over the countryside by demes ... in all of the regions: Cf. Hdt. V. 69. 2 (δέκαχα [Lolling: δέκα MSS] δὲ καὶ τοὺς δήμους κατένειμε ἐς τὰς φυλάς). The smallest unit was the 'deme' (a special sense of *demos*), a village in the countryside or a part of the city: according to Strabo 396 / IX. 1. 16 there were 170 or 174, but in the fourth century there were 133, six divided into 'upper' and 'lower' sections (cf. J. S. Traill, *The Political Organization of Attica* [*Hesperia* Supp. 14 (1975)], 81–103). Demes were combined to form *trittyes* and *trittyes* were combined to form tribes so that each tribe contained one *trittys* from the 'city' (the city of Athens and the surrounding plain), one from the 'coast' (excluding the part which belonged to the 'city', including the western hills north of Eleusis) and one from the 'inland': these are not the same as the three regions of 13. 4. Men will have been registered in the deme in which they lived, but membership was hereditary: until the

Peloponnesian War most men lived in their demes (cf. Thuc. II. 14. 2, 16), but afterwards a growing number did not.

Many inscriptions list men under their tribes and demes, among them (from the fourth century onwards) lists of members of the council (collected in *Agora* xv), from which it is clear that demes had numbers of councillors assigned to them. There are still a few uncertainties, but in most cases it has become possible to assign demes to their *trittyes* and to place them on the map (see especially Traill, *op. cit.*, with some revisions in his *Demos and Trittys* [Toronto: Athenians, 1986]). Demes, as far as we know, were natural units, and varied in size. *Trittyes* were usually groups of adjacent demes but sometimes more artificial, and they too varied in size (but M. H. Hansen, *C&M* 41 [1990], 51–4, argues that as originally constructed the *trittyes* were approximately equal and each was wholly in one region; see also 44. 1 with commentary). The three *trittyes* of a tribe might meet at a point or on a line, or be totally separate, but in view of the tribal basis of the army and many institutions the tribes ought to have been approximately equal in size. The island of Salamis, and the territory of Oropus when that belonged to Athens, were not included in this system: Athenian citizens who lived there must have been registered elsewhere.

The new system became the basis for Athenian citizenship – to be a citizen a man had to belong to a deme and to the *trittys* and tribe which included that deme – and for Athenian public life, and it required a degree of participation which gave the Athenians practice in and a taste for political involvement. In the assembly men voted as individuals, but the tribes were the basis of the army (22. 2, 61), the council (21. 3, 43. 2, 62. 1) and many offices (e.g. 47. 1, 2, 48. 1: even the nine archons had a secretary added so that one man could be appointed from each tribe, 55. 1), and the lawcourts (63–9). According to *A.P. trittyes* were assigned to tribes by lot, but if *trittyes* were unequal but tribes equal that cannot be right (C. W. J. Eliot, *Coastal Demes of Attika* [*Phoenix* Supp. 5 (1962)], 138–46): true or false, that is a detail which could not be deduced from fourth-century practice.

This complex system will have cut across old loyalties (cf. Arist. *Pol.* VI. 1319 B 19–27). Cleisthenes will at least have 'mixed up the people' by assigning men from different parts of Attica to the same tribe (and it is probably significant that men from the 'city', where most of those active in politics lived, were distributed over all the tribes: D. W. Bradeen, *TAPA* 86 [1955], 22–30). D. M. Lewis, focusing on the more unnatural combinations, suggested that Cleisthenes deliberately undermined old associations, e.g. by separating cult centres from their natural hinterlands (*Historia* 12 [1963], 22–40 = his *Selected Papers*, 77–98, and the reviews in *Selected Papers*, 99–109). The Alcmaeonids were at a disadvantage in the old system, with no major cult centres of their own, but would be at an advantage in the new, with their homes in three demes south-east of the city assigned to the same three tribes as the coastal strip towards Sunium in which they had influence (cf. on 13. 4).

And he made fellow-demesmen … identified by their demes: Already many demes existed as villages though without formal institutions, and men could be identified by their demotic (cf. 14. 4); and by the fourth century the demotic had not supplanted the patronymic but had been added to it (e.g. the politician Δημοσθένης Δημοσθένους Παιανιεύς: see Plut. *Dem.* 20. 3). New demes (or new names for old settlements) might take time to gain currency, and the demotic might be used by, or by other men for, some men more than others. If *A.P.* is right about the intention, Cleisthenes was unsuccessful; more probably he has guessed from the practice of his own time, and in that case his statement of the purpose will be a guess also: suppression of the patronymic could conceal an immigrant's status only when a father with an exotic name gave his son an Athenian name, and even then natural inquisitiveness will usually have exposed the newcomer.

A.P. did not mention in its chronological place the *diapsephismos* after the fall of the tyranny (cf. 13. 5), and here – probably through compression of his material – he does not directly mention the enfranchisement of new citizens. They are mentioned in a difficult passage in Arist. *Pol.* III. 1275 B 34–9, claiming that Cleisthenes πολλοὺς … ἐφυλέτευσε ξένους καὶ δούλους μετοίκους: probably ξένους and δούλους are parallel adjectives qualifying μετοίκους (cf. W. L. Newman, *The Politics of Aristotle* [Oxford U. P., 1887–1902], i. 231 n. 1, iii. 145–6), and foreign immigrants and freed slaves were the two obvious sources of new citizens. When *metoikoi* were defined as a category of registered foreign residents is uncertain: J. Watson, *CCJ* 56 (2010), 259–76, suggests not until the time of Pericles' citizenship law (26. 4). Those enfranchised now will largely have been those disfranchised by the *diapsephismos*:

they will have been a minority in the free population, and Cleisthenes' main appeal must have been to those whose citizenship was not in doubt (e.g. Wade-Gery, *opp. citt.* 25–6 = 148–50).

21. 5. he instituted demarchs: The demes were given a corporate existence, with their own presiding official, the demarch, and assembly; similarly there were to be corporate institutions for the new *trittyes* (about which we hear little) and tribes. This gave the citizens the opportunity to gain political interest and experience on the local as well as the city level, and in due course to challenge the local supremacy of the aristocrats, and may well have played a large part in gaining Cleisthenes his popularity (cf. J. W. Headlam, *Election by Lot at Athens* [Cambridge U. P., 1891], 165–8, D. Kienast, *HZ* 200 [1965], 277–9). Pisistratus' *dikastai kata demous* were probably abolished on the fall of the tyranny (cf. 16. 5, 26. 3): an inscription from Marathon possibly belongs to arrangements for judicial proceedings in the demes (*IG* i^3 2 with E. Vanderpool, *Hesperia* 11 [1942], 329–37).

with the same responsibility … a replacement for the *naukrariai*: On the *naukrariai* and the *naukraroi* see 8. 3 with commentary. *A.P.* probably means that the *naukrariai* were now abolished, but according to Clidemus *FGrH* 323 F 8 ~ Fornara 22. A the ten new tribes were subdivided into fifty *naukrariai*. Some, noting that at the beginning of the fifth century Athens had fifty warships (Hdt. VI. 89 cf. 132), have supposed that Clidemus is right and the *naukrariai* were abolished by Themistocles when he enlarged the navy (22. 7 with commentary: e.g. Wilamowitz, *A.u.A.* ii. 165–6 n. 2); but our evidence is insufficient to decide.

Of the demes he designated … were still known): Many demes were named after local features (e.g. Cephisia) or plants (e.g. Marathon), and many of the names were already in use before Cleisthenes (e.g. Marathon: Hom. *Od.* VII. 80); the potters' quarter in the city was given the name Cerameis. But several demes have names in patronymic form, e.g. Butadae, for the deme north-west of the city where part of the *genos* Butadae lived (to which the *genos* reacted by calling itself Eteobutadae, 'genuine Butadae': cf. on 13. 4). The name Philaidae was given not to the Philaids' home at Laciadae, beyond Butadae, but to the Pisistratids' home at Brauron (cf. on 13. 4); the names Pisistratidae and Alcmaeonidae were not used. Lewis concluded that in cases such as Butadae and Philaidae

Cleisthenes' purpose was to weaken the families whose names were thus used (*Historia* 12 [1963], 26–7 = his *Selected Papers*, 82–3).
still known: The London papyrus' ἔτι is preferable to the Berlin papyrus' ἐν: more literally the meaning is probably, 'There were no longer founders in existence for all the places'.
21. 6. The *gene* … in accordance with tradition in each case: Arist. *Pol.* VI. 1319 B 19–27, referring to Cleisthenes and to Cyrene, writes of new tribes and new *phratriai*, but that does not mean that he thought Cleisthenes had created new *phratriai*. The *gene* with the priesthoods attached to them and the *phratriai* (cf. pp. 174–6) maintained a vigorous existence, and the old tribes and *trittyes* also survived.
For the tribes he created eponymous heroes … pre-elected leaders: Cf. Hdt. V. 66. 2, not mentioning Delphi. On the tribal heroes see U. Kron, *Die zehn attischen Phylenheroen* (*AM* Bhft. 5 [1976]), E. Kearns, *The Heroes of Attica* (*BICS* Supp. 57 [1989]). In view of the Alcmaeonids' connection with Delphi (cf. 19. 4 with commentary) its involvement is not surprising, but it was perhaps asked not to choose from a longer list but to approve Cleisthenes' choices. The ten names adopted (in what became for some purposes an official order) were Erechtheis, Aegeis, Pandionis, Leontis, Acamantis, Oeneis, Cecropis, Hippothontis, Aiantis, Antiochis; Herodotus regarded Ajax, of Salamis, as a neighbour and a foreigner – and it was perhaps about this time that Athens finally gained possession of Salamis (cf. on 14. 1). The statues of the tribal heroes were set up in the agora, and their base served as a state notice board (cf. 53. 4). The monument opposite the *bouleuterion* is now dated after 350, and the earlier monument (Ar. *Pax* 1183–4) was perhaps further south (cf. Camp, *Site Guide*, 66–8).

A.P. and Herodotus say nothing of changes affecting the magistrates or the Areopagus, or affecting the powers of the assembly or council, and there is no need to postulate any such changes, except that direct election of the nine archons may have been changed to allotment of particular posts within an elected college (cf. 22. 5 with commentary). No more is heard of Cleisthenes, but by now he may have been over sixty, and probably he died a natural death (cf. Davies, *A.P.F.* 375).

22. 1. much more democratic than that of Solon: Cf. the summary in 41. 2, and Hdt. VI. 131; but in 462 Cimon was accused of trying to revive

Cleisthenes' aristocracy (Plut. *Cim.* 15. 3), and when in 411 an oligarch evoked Cleisthenes' establishment of the democracy *A.P.* explains that he thought that was not populist but similar to Solon's constitution (29. 3). G. Anderson, in C. Cooper (ed.), *The Politics of Orality* (*Mnemosyne* Supp. 280 [2007]), 103–28, suggests that Cleisthenes represented himself as restoring the old order rather than introducing a new order. From the mid fifth century onwards, he was praised, whether for an advance towards full democracy or for a respectable, limited democracy; in the fifth century he tended to be regarded as the founder of the democracy, but from the end of the century the origins of the democracy were traced back to Solon or even to Theseus and Cleisthenes' role was to restore it after the tyranny (cf. E. Ruschenbusch, *Historia* 7 [1958], 398–424 = his *Kleine Schriften A. G.*, 59–80, on which see p. 179). Probably the word *demokratia* was not coined until the first half of the fifth century, and Cleisthenes used words with the *iso-* root, denoting fairness (e.g. J. A. O. Larsen, in *Essays in Political Theory Presented to G. H. Sabine* [Cornell U. P., 1948], 1–16).

the tyranny had consigned Solon's laws to oblivion by not using them: Contrast 16. 8, and Hdt. I. 59. 6, Thuc. VI. 54. 6, Plut. *Sol.* 31. 8: probably Solon's institutions did on the whole survive but the tyrants used their influence to obtain the results which they wanted.

Cleisthenes enacted other new laws: The only other laws which we know of are the institution of ostracism and of the ten *strategoi*.

among which was his enactment of the law about ostracism: Probably by excessive compression of his material, *A.P.* raises the subject of ostracism here, then drops it and returns to it in 22. 3.

22. 2. in the eighth year after this settlement, in the archonship of Hermocreon: The next archonship mentioned is that of Phaenippus, 490/89 (22. 3): the fifth year after Isagoras, 504/3, is occupied by Acestorides (Dion. Hal. *Ant. Rom.* V. 37. 1), but the twelfth year before Phaenippus, 501/0, is not otherwise occupied, so Hermocreon should belong to that year, the eighth after Isagoras, and to make *A.P.*'s chronology coherent the papyrus' 'fifth' should be emended to 'eighth'.

they created for the council of five hundred the oath which they still swear now: In fact various specific undertakings are known to have been added to the oath later: see H. T. Wade-Gery, *BSA* 33 (1932/3), 113–22; Rhodes, *A.B.* 194–9. Some have seen this as a departure from Cleisthenes' dispensation, by which the council was prevented from doing things which he had allowed it to do (e.g. P. Cloché, *REG* 33 [1920], 28–35); but more probably it marks the culmination of Cleisthenes' dispensation, perhaps introduced in this year because this was the first year in which the new council of five hundred existed (e.g. W. Peremans, *LEC* 10 [1941], 193–201).

Next they elected the generals ... but the leader of the whole army was the polemarch: *Epeita* can as well be logical as temporal, so the chronological problem should not be solved by postulating a lacuna here: again, this may have been the first year for which appointments based on the new system could be made. *Strategoi* earlier are mentioned in 17. 2, 22. 3 (and 4. 2–3), and by Hdt. I. 59. 4, Plut. *Sol.* 11. 2, probably as *ad hoc* appointments in special circumstances (e.g. R. Sealey, *Historia* 9 [1960], 173 = his *Essays in Greek Politics*, 26): what was new was the appointment of ten every year – one from each tribe, but by the assembly as a whole (cf. 61. 1).

The relative powers of the *strategoi* and the polemarch have been disputed. In Herodotus' account of the Marathon campaign of 490 the serious command rested with the *strategoi*, who were equal, but the polemarch was brought in to resolve their disagreement, and in the battle he held the traditional commander's position on the right wing (Hdt. VI. 103–11) – and he is never found with the army again. The *strategoi* were already the commanders in chief, not simply the commanders of their tribal regiments (that fell to the taxiarchs: 61. 3); but on this exceptional occasion when Attica was invaded the full army went to Marathon, with all ten *strategoi* and the polemarch also (cf. N. G. L. Hammond, *JHS* 88 [1968], 48–50 cf. 45, *CQ*[2] 19 [1969], 119–23 = his *Studies*, 229–33 cf. 223–4, 358–64; E. Badian, *Antichthon* 5 [1971], 26 with n. 68, 31–2).

22. 3. In the twelfth year after this ... in the archonship of Phaenippus: 490/89 (cf. p. 249).

After waiting for two years: I.e. 'in the third year', 488/7 (e.g. T. J. Cadoux, *JHS* 68 [1948], 118). The dates of ostracisms will have needed to be recorded, and I believe that *A.P.*'s source, Androtion (cf. next note), recorded each of the ostracisms ἐπὶ — ἄρχοντος, but *A.P.* has avoided the monotony of an annalistic list (cf. pp. 24–5).

22. 3–4. when the *demos* was now confident ... wanting to drive him out: For the first phrase cf. 24. 1, 27. 1, and Isoc. VII. *Areop.* 3, XII.

Panath. 133. For the institution of ostracism cf. Androtion *FGrH* 324 F 6 ~ Fornara 41. A. 1 *ap.* Harp. ι 15 Keaney Ἵππαρχος, which uses very similar words but states that Hipparchus was ostracised τοῦ … νόμου τότε πρῶτον τεθέντος, 'the law having been enacted then for the first time'. Whether ostracism was introduced by Cleisthenes but not used for twenty years or was introduced when it was first used has been much debated (for a review of the discussions see R. Thomsen, *The Origin of Ostracism* [Copenhagen: Gyldendal, 1972], 11–60), but 'then for the first time' makes sense with 'used' as it does not with 'enacted', and the best explanation is that Harpocration has misquoted Androtion, and Androtion said what *A.P.* says and was *A.P.*'s source (e.g. G. V. Sumner, CQ^2 11 [1961], 37 n. 1).

On the purposes of ostracism the various sources agree that it was a democratic institution, intended against those who were too powerful, and in particular to prevent tyranny. In fact it might not be effective in preventing tyranny – a potential tyrant might be able to ensure that another candidate attracted more votes, and ten years' absence from Athens did not prevent Pisistratus from returning (15. 2) – but it could resolve political rivalries such as that between Cleisthenes and Isagoras by removing the less popular rival (e.g. G. R. Stanton, *JHS* 90 [1970], 180–3). Cleisthenes might nevertheless have used the threat of tyranny when proposing the institution: in fact ostracism seems to have been used initially against men under suspicion after Marathon (cf. below), and subsequently to resolve rivalries. After the ostracisms listed in this chapter, the following men were or may have been ostracised: Themistocles *c.* 470 (see on 25. 3), Cimon in 462/1 (see on 25. 1), the elder Alcibiades *c.* 460 (perhaps ostracised twice), Meno son of Meneclides *c.* 457, Callias son of Didymias 440's, Damon 440's or later (see on 27. 4), Thucydides son of Melesias *c.* 443 (see on 28. 2), Hyperbolus probably 415 (see p. 279).

On the mechanism of ostracism see 43. 5 and Diod. Sic. XI. 55. 2, Plut. *Arist.* 7. 5–6, Poll. VIII. 20, schol. Ar. *Eq.* 855, Philoch. *FGrH* 328 F 30 ~ Fornara 41. B. 1. In the sixth prytany of each year the assembly decided whether to hold an ostracism; if it decided in favour, in the eighth prytany there was a special voting session at which each voter submitted a potsherd, *ostrakon*, bearing the name of the man he wished to remove; as long as at least 6,000 votes were cast in total (Plut., rather than 6,000 against one man), the man with the largest number of votes was exiled without loss of property for ten years. Several thousand *ostraka* have been found, most giving simply a man's name, sometimes with patronymic and / or demotic, but a few adding a comment. Many men were voted against, and there was presumably no list of candidates: some voters might vote against a personal enemy, but those who attracted large numbers of votes were public figures being voted against as such. Brenne, *Ostrakismos*, gives the most up-to-date catalogue and discusses various issues.

MS Vat. Gr. 1144. 222^{r-v} is a miscellany including the claim that ostracism was originally held in the council and required at least 200 votes against the victim (cf. J. J. Keaney & A. E. Raubitschek, *AJP* 93 [1972], 87–91): that is totally unparallelled, and I am not inclined to believe it. Ael. *V.H.* XIII. 24 used a familiar *topos* to explain why no more is heard of Cleisthenes: having introduced ostracism, he was himself its first victim. Some late texts, perhaps interpreting literally a metaphorical statement by Theophrastus, described Theseus' exclusion from Athens as ostracism (e.g. *Suda* α 4101 Adler ἀρχὴ Σκυρία: see A. E. Raubitschek, *C&M* 19 [1958], 78 n. 3 = his *The School of Hellas* [New York: Oxford U. P., 1991], 84–5 n. 3).

a demagogue and general: For *demagogos* see on 26. 1, for Pisistratus as *strategos* see 17. 2 and p. 250.

22. 4. one of his relatives, Hipparchus son of Charmus, of Collytus: Probably Charmus was married to a daughter of Hippias (Davies, *A.P.F.* 451). Hipparchus will have been born *c.* 530, is probably the Hipparchus who is *kalos* on vases of the late sixth century (Beazley, *A.B.V.* 667, *A.R.V.*^{2} ii. 1584) and who was archon in 496/5 (Dion. Hal. *Ant. Rom.* VI. 1. 1). We cannot judge the significance of his archonship (some have linked it with the withdrawal of Athens' support for the Ionian Revolt: Hdt. V. 103. 1), but after Hippias had accompanied the Persians to Marathon (Hdt. VI. 107–9) he was naturally suspect.

allowed those of the tyrants' friends … to live in the city: It is not clear whether this is derived from Androtion or is a comment added by *A.P.*; it adds nothing to what is said elsewhere in *A.P.*

the leader and champion of these men was Hipparchus: Doubtless an inference from the fact that of those who remained in Athens he was the closest to Pisistratus and the first to be ostracised.

22. 5. Immediately in the next year, in the archonship of Telesinus: 487/6; *A.P.* is the only source for the name. Possibly the reform was enacted in 488/7 and 487/6 was the first year whose archons were appointed by the new process.
they appointed the nine archons by drawing lots ... the previous archons were all elected: According to *A.P.* this had been introduced by Solon (8. 1 – but Arist. *Pol.* disagreed), and the tyrants had presumably reverted to election. Hdt. VI. 109. 2 has Callimachus appointed by lot as polemarch in 490/89: it has often been supposed that *A.P.* proves Herodotus wrong, but Herodotus seems well informed on Athenian officials then (cf. p. 250), and probably the nine archons were elected as a college but allotted to particular posts (cf. E. Badian, *Antichthon* 5 [1971], 21–6).

The London and Berlin papyri agree on 500 candidates put forward by the demes; but contrast 62. 1, and the 100 in the fourth century in 8. 1, and with the archonship restricted to the highest two classes (cf. 26. 2) it is hard to believe that as many as 500 men would have been eligible. The number and the reference to the demes suggest confusion with the council of five hundred (considered by Kenyon): probably now as later the correct number was 100; at some time election was replaced by allotment for the first stage, and a 'secretary to the *thesmothetai*' was added to make a college of ten (8. 1, 55. 1). This change played a part in the process by which the archons became routine officials and the *strategoi* became the leading officials of Athens, but we cannot tell whether it was a response to a development already under way or a trigger for a development not yet begun; it is often claimed, but without justification, that it was the work of Themistocles, preparing the way for Ephialtes' attack on the Areopagus a generation later (for a version of that see R. J. Buck, *CP* 60 [1965], 96–101).
And Megacles son of Hippocrates, of Alopece, was ostracised: The leading member of the Alcmaeonid family, a nephew of Cleisthenes (Davies, *A.P.F.* 379); his sister was married to Xanthippus (cf. on 22. 6). 4,443 *ostraka* refer certainly to this Megacles, more than twice as many as to any other man, and other Alcmaeonids attracted votes in the 480's: the Alcmaeonids wre accused of colluding with the Persians at Marathon (Hdt. VI. 121–4), and it seems that the earliest victims of ostracism were men with Pisistratid and Alcmaeonid connections, suspected of disloyalty.

According to Lys. XIV. *Alcibiades i.* 39 and (emended) [Andoc.] IV. *Alcibiades* 34 Megacles was ostracised twice: if the Ceramicus deposit, including *ostraka* against him, belongs to the 470's, that is possible, and Brenne argues for 472/1 (*Ostrakismos*, 37–9).

22. 6. For 3 years, then, they proceeded to ostracise the friends of the tyrants: For 486/5 *A.P.* names neither the archon nor the victim: presumably the name of the victim meant nothing to him. If the Ceramicus deposit were dated to the 480's, a possible victim would be Callias son of Cratius, described as 'Mede' on several *ostraka*, but with a date in the 470's he is ruled out and we do not know who was ostracised in this year.

on account of whom the law had been enacted: Cf. 22. 3.

after that, in the fourth year: 485/4.

the first of those unconnected with the tyranny … was Xanthippus son of Ariphron: Of Cholargus. He married Agariste, daughter of Cleisthenes' brother Hippocrates, *c.* 500–496 (Davies, *A.P.F.* 379, 455–6); In 489 he successfully prosecuted Miltiades, the victor of Marathon, after his campaign against Paros (Hdt. VI. 136), and that success suggests that he was not perceived as belonging to the Alcmaeonids and *A.P.* was right to distinguish him from the first three victims (cf. W. G. Forrest, *CQ*[2] 10 [1960], 233–4). In that case, the ostracism of Xanthippus and of Aristides (22. 7), and the votes against Themistocles, suggest that ostracism was now being used to choose between rivals, and that in the 480's Themistocles avoided ostracism while the other two did not. One of the *ostraka* against Xanthippus bears an elegiac couplet which is grammatically open to different interpretations (see the discussions cited by Rhodes, *Comm. Ath. Pol.*, 276–7):

> Χσάνθ[ιππον ?τόδε] φεσὶν ἀλειτερον πρυτανειον
> τὄστρακ[ον ʾΑρρί]φρονος παῖδα μάλιστ᾽ ἀδικε͂ν.

It is possible that the author of this couplet did regard him as tainted by the Alcmaeonid curse (cf. p. 181).

22. 7. In the third year after that, in the archonship of Nicodemus: 483/2; The Berlin papyrus' form of the name is supported by Dion. Hal. *Ant. Rom.* VIII. 83. 1.

when the mines at Maronea were revealed … at Salamis against the barbarians: Cf. Hdt. VII. 144. 1–2, Plut. *Them.* 4. 1–3, Aristid. III. *Quattuor* 236–7; also Thuc. I. 14. 3, Nep. II. *Them.* 2. 2, 8, Polyaen. I.

30. 6, Just. II. 12. 12, Liban. *Decl.* X. 27. It is agreed that the silver mines produced a surplus, and Themistocles was responsible for the decision not to distribute the money among the citizens (cf. Siphnos, Hdt. III.57. 2) but to spend it on ships (cf. Thasos, Hdt. VI. 46), but otherwise the texts disagree on the details. In the other texts Themistocles' plan was public, prompted ostensibly and perhaps in fact by Athens' war with Aegina; *A.P.*'s secret plan is suspect, because other texts ascribe other secret plans to Themistocles, but it may be true that rich men were made responsible each for having one ship built. Athens had 70 ships in 489 and 200 in 480 (Hdt. VI. 132 cf. 89; VIII. 1. 1–2, 14. 1).

the mines at Maronea were revealed: For the Attic Maronea cf. Dem. XXXVII. *Pantaenetus* 4: it was not a deme, but was an area in the far south-east of Attica. The name is presumably borrowed from Maronea in Thrace, north of Samothrace (and not particularly associated with mining): other Thracian names are found in this part of Attica, and perhaps reflect the migration of workmen. Scholars have often thought of a sudden increase in yield, perhaps as a result of finding the 'third contact' seams; but note the caution and stress on continuity of R. J. Hopper, *BSA* 63 (1968), 299–300, 308–9.

Themistocles: Son of Neocles, of Phrearrhii (in south-eastern Attica, near the mining area), and from a family not known to have been active in city politics before, but with a house in Melite, inside the city walls (Plut. *Them.* 22. 2). He was 'recently' prominent in 481 according to Hdt. VII. 143. 1, but he was archon in 493/2 (Dion. Hal. *Ant. Rom.* VI. 34. 1), and it must be to his archonship that Thuc. I. 93. 3 assigns the beginning of work at the Piraeus (see D. M. Lewis / W. W. Dickie, *Historia* 22 [1973], 757–8 / 758–9). He is second to Megacles for the number of surviving *ostraka* against him (and cf. note on 'At this juncture…', below).

with these they fought the naval battle at Salamis against the barbarians: Cf. Thuc. I. 14. 3.

At this juncture Aristides son of Lysimachus was ostracised: Of Alopece. Cf. Plut. *Arist.* 7. He was probably a cousin of Callias son of Hipponicus, of the *Kerykes* (Plut. *Arist.* 25. 4–8 with Davies, *A.P.F.* 48–9, 256–7; that he was a *strategos* at Marathon (Plut. *Arist.* 5. 1–6) is doubtful; that he was archon in 489/8 (Plut. *Arist.* 1. 2–8, 5. 9–10), is likely, though there was another Aristides active at this time. On his rivalry with Themistocles see 23. 3, 28. 2 with commentary; though it is often claimed that his opposition to Themistocles' shipbuilding proposal led to his ostracism (first by Beloch, *G.G.*[2] II. ii. 142), no ancient text states that he opposed it, and we do not know whether the proposal was made before or after he was ostracised.

22. 8. In the third year … in the archonship of Hypsichides: This archon is not attested elsewhere, but the London papyrus' fourth year, 480/79, is occupied by Calliades (Diod. Sic. XI. 1. 2), so here we need the third year, 481/0 (cf. Plut. *Arist.* 8. 1), and probably *A.P.* or a copyist has made a mistake. Aristides and Xanthippus returned and played an active part in the resistance to Persia, both serving as *strategoi* in 479 (Hdt. IX. 28. 6, VIII. 131. 3: probably elected for 480/79 and reelected for 479/8); Megacles probably returned too (cf. p. 254); but Hipparchus probably did not return, and was condemned to death in his absence (Lyc. *Leocr.* 117 emended from Harp. ι 15 Keaney Ἵππαρχος).

for the future they defined … completely *atimoi*: Geraestus is the south-eastern tip of Euboea, Scyllaeum the eastern tip of the Argolid. Many have emended, to require the ostracised to go at least as far from Athens as those points, but in these circumstances it is more likely that they were required not to go beyond those points to the south-east and therefore into the area controlled by Persia. We do not know how long this remained in force; what we have of Philoch. *FGrH* 328 F 30 is corrupt, and he probably wrote the same as *A.P.* καθάπαξ may have been used either by the author of the decree or by a later writer, to emphasise that ἀτίμους was being used to denote total outlawry (cf. on 8. 5).

H. The Mid Fifth Century (23–8)

This section contains an assortment of politically biased anecdotes and comments, and little solid material; in abbreviating and in changing between sources *A.P.* has not produced a coherent account (and lingustic imperfections may be due to that rather than to scribal error). 23. 1–2a and 23. 2b–24 give two accounts of the period after the Persian Wars, the first with an aristocratic and the second with a democratic bias. 25. 1–2 gives a favourable account of Ephialtes' reform (while Plutarch gives an unfavourable); 25. 3–4 gives a story of Themistocles' involvement with Ephialtes which is chronologically impossible and seems to have been added when the text was revised. After a problematic introduction of Cimon in 26. 1, 26. 2–4 chronicles three institutional changes of the 450's. Ch. 27 is a rag-bag of hostile material on Pericles, beginning with his prosecution of Cimon, and ending with his introduction of pay for jurors and the alleged first instance of a jury's being bribed. Ch. 28, having stated that things became worse after Pericles, gives a list of democratic and aristocratic leaders from Solon and Pisistratus to the end of the fifth century, apparently not compiled by our author but repeated from some source, and ending with praise of the last three aristocratic leaders. It will have been hard for our author to find material on the constitution between 478 and 411: the institutional changes of 26. 2–4 probably derive from an *Atthis*; other items probably come from less sober sources, such as partisan writings (there are echoes of old comedy, e.g. in 24. 3, but it does not appear that *A.P.* has made direct use of the plays).

23. 1. So then the city advanced to this point: 41. 2 shows that *A.P.* regarded Athens' constitutional history as a series of changes, some advances towards the final form of democracy and some setbacks. Here the opening words sum up the fifth change, the advance of 20–2, before turning to the sixth change, the ascendancy of the Areopagus.
increasing gradually with the democracy: The verb is often applied metaphorically to a *polis*; Arist. *Pol.* VI. 1319 B 21–2 writes of Cleisthenes' desire to increase the democracy.
the council of the Areopagus became strong again: According to 8. 2 Solon's system for appointing magistrates replaced appointment by the Areopagus, and his creation of the council of four hundred (8. 4) may also have been seen as a weakening of the Areopagus.
gaining its leadership not by any formal decision: This prepares us for the view (25. 2) that the powers taken from the Areopagus by Ephialtes were 'additional' powers, and probably it is based on the assumption that if the Areopagus had to be deprived of powers by Ephialtes it must somehow have increased its powers since the democratic advance of Cleisthenes.
it was responsible for the naval battle near Salamis: Cf. Plut. *Them.* 10. 6–7, citing *A.P.* and then repeating from Clidemus (*FGrH* 323 F 21) a version attributing provision of the money to a decree of Themistocles. Arist. *Pol.* V. 1304 A 17–24 seems to refer to both versions, either of which would prove his point about changes in the constitution; *A.P.* does

not overtly do that, but by citing the 'Areopagite' version of the story here and following it with a democratic account in 23. 2b–24 he makes the move towards oligarchy an immediate consequence of Salamis and the development of Athens' naval power and democracy a long-term consequence. It is possible that money was distributed to the citizens rather than left in Athens for the Persians, and Themistocles as an ex-archon was himself a member of the Areopagus, but both versions have their place in the propaganda battles between Themistocles and Cimon in the 470's (cf. Wilamowitz, *A.u.A.* i. 138–40: he focused on Aristides, but see on 23. 3).

when the generals were unable to cope: In this version of the story the point is that Themistocles was one of the generals.

had proclaimed that everybody should save himself: Cf. Hdt. VIII. 41. 1; Plut. *Them.* 10. 4 assigns similar words to a decree proposed by Themistocles, but there is nothing comparable in the inscribed 'decree of Themistocles', ML 23. 4–12.

23. 2. Athens' politics were in a good condition at this juncture: Cf. 33. 2 (echoing Thuc. VIII. 97. 2), and on individual politicians 28. 5, 40. 2. As we should expect of a pupil of Aristotle, *A.P.* evidently found a moderate democracy or oligarchy most congenial; but where opinions such as this are expressed they are probably repeated with *A.P.*'s approval from a source rather than added as *A.P.*'s own comment on what the source reported as bare fact (cf. Introduction, p. 11).

they gained practice in waging war ... against the wishes of the Spartans: This sentence eases the transition from the theme of the Areopagus' ascendancy to that of Athens' naval power and democracy.

against the wishes of the Spartans: Thuc. I. 95. 7 cf. 75. 2 makes Sparta content to let Athens become leader at sea, Diod. Sic. XI. 50 has a debate which ends unexpectedly with Sparta's not challenging Athens; Hdt. VIII. 3. 2 perhaps implies that Sparta was not content. Sparta seems (or at any rate most Spartans seem) in fact to have been content as long as Cimon was predominant in Athens, but there is no need to emend the text or interpret it unnaturally to make *A.P.* agree with Thucydides.

23. 3. The champions of the *demos*...: *A.P.* has now clearly changed to his democratic view of Athens after the Persian Wars.

Aristides son of Lysimachus and Themistocles son of Neocles: On these in the 480's as two among three or more rivals see p. 254. On their relations after 480 there are conflicting traditions: the main version opposes Aristides the honest aristocrat to Themistocles the wily democrat, with Aristides succeeded by Cimon and Themistocles by Ephialtes (Hdt. VIII. 79. 2, Plut. *Them.*, *Arist.*, *Cim.*, *passim*, cf. 28. 2); but here the two are placed together on the democratic side, and there are traces of this in 24. 3 and in other texts, including those in which Aristides cooperates with or comments on Themistocles' schemes, e.g. 23. 4. This second version seems nearer to the truth: the main rivalry in the 470's seems to have been between Themistocles and Cimon, and Themistocles and Aristides both disappeared from Athenian public life by the end of the decade.

the latter was judged to be a practitioner of warfare and the former to be clever in political matters...: Cf. Plut. *Arist.* 8. 3 (in the context of 480); Arist. *Pol.* V. 1309 A 33–B 14 may intend a reference to Themistocles and Aristides. Themistocles was more commonly admired for intelligence than for strategic skill (e.g. Thuc. I. 138. 3), but that would have given a poorer contrast with Aristides.

to surpass his contemporaries in uprightness: Cf. Hdt. VIII. 79. 1, 95. 1, and many later texts; and 25. 1, on the uprightness of Ephialtes.

23. 4. The rebuilding of the walls, then, they administered together: Cf. Thuc. I. 90–3 and later texts. Sparta wanted to leave Athens unfortified after the Persian Wars; Themistocles went to Sparta and prevaricated while the Athenians rebuilt their walls rapidly; when the walls had reached a sufficient height, Habronichus and Aristides joined him and they acknowledged what had been done.

although they were at variance with each other: The main tradition has been allowed to contaminate the alternative (cf. above).

the defection of the Ionians: For the naval campaign of 478 see Thuc. I. 94–96. *init.*, 128. 3–130, Diod. Sic. XI.. 44–6, Plut. *Arist.* 23, *Cim.* 6. 1–3. For Thucydides the allies offered the leadership to Athens; according to Hdt. VIII. 3. 2, Diodorus and Plutarch Athens took the initiative, and *A.P.* seems to favour that view. Thucydides does not name Athens' commander; Diodorus and Just. II. 15. 16 name Aristides; Plutarch names Aristides and Cimon. Since Aristides assessed the tribute (23. 5) he was probably commander; Plutarch has perhaps added Cimon because he commanded many subsequent campaigns. Even at its foundation not all the members of the alliance (the 'Delian League') were Ionian in the narrow sense of the word, but it suited Ionian Athens, in contrast to Dorian Sparta, to represent it as Ionian.

on account of Pausanias: The Spartan regent Pausanias commanded the Greeks in the naval campaign of 478; he offended the allies and was recalled to Sparta; the Athenians then took over the leadership, and when Dorcis was sent from Sparta he was rejected.

23. 5. fixed the first tribute for the cities: On the organisation of the League see Thuc. I. 96–97. 1, Diod. Sic. XI. 47, Plut. *Arist.* 24–25. 3. Thuc. I does not name any Athenian, but the Peace of Nicias referred to 'the tribute of Aristides' time' (Thuc. V. 18. 5).

in the third year … in the archonship of Timosthenes: The third year from 480/79, 478/7 (cf. Diod. Sic. XI. 38. 1).

he swore the oaths with the Ionians: Cf. Plut. *Arist.* 25. 1.

to have the same enemies and friends: This is the formula for a full offensive and defensive alliance (e.g. Thuc. I. 44. 1); it goes beyond the anti-Persian objectives stated by our other sources, but we have no reason to disbelieve it.

to confirm which they sank the molten iron in the sea: Cf. Plut. *Arist.* 25. 1: this signified that the alliance was to last until the lumps of metal rose to the surface, i.e. indefinitely (cf. Hdt. I. 165. 3). The declared aim of the alliance must therefore have extended beyond the revenge of Thuc. I. 96. 1.

24. 1. when the city was now confident: Cf. 22. 3, 27. 1; in Arist. *Pol.* II. 1274 A 12–15 cf. VIII. 1341 A 30, after the Persian Wars the *demos* thought highly of itself (ἐφρονηματίσθη).

he advised them to grasp the leadership: The subject is Aristides, resumed from 23. 4. Athens had already taken hold of the hegemony (ἀντιλαμβάνεσθαι middle need not imply 'in place of Sparta'): *A.P.* has been careless in excerpting his material.

to go down from the fields and live in the city: Contrast Thuc. II. 14. 2, 16, where most Athenians had stayed in their traditional homes until 431. It must be the result of later theorising that Aristides and public funding created an urban proletariat.

there would be sustenance for all: *A.P.* supposes that the League and the revenue from it would provide maintenance for all the citizens, so they would not need to continue farming their land.

others were attending to public affairs: Cf. Arist. *Pol.* VII. 1324 B 1. The allusion is to the stipends paid to citizens for their civilian duties, of which the earliest instance seems to be jury pay, introduced by Pericles in the 450's (27. 3–4 with commentary).

hold down their leadership: The Athenians would devote themselves to the military and civilian running of the League, and so would maintain control of it, as the Spartans lived off the labour of the helots and so were able to maintain control of them.

24. 2. taking the ruling position: *A.P.* changes from 'hegemony' to 'rule', the word which came to be applied regularly to Athens' control of what became an empire (e.g. Thuc. I. 75. 1, and inscriptions such as *IG* i^3 156): probably his source gave an account of the change from alliance to empire.

apart from the Chians, Lesbians and Samians: According to Arist. *Pol.* III. 1284 A 38–41 Athens humbled those three after it had established its rule forcefully. Samos lost its ships and its original status after the war of 440–439 (Thuc. I. 117. 3); Chios and Lesbos retained a privileged position until the Peloponnesian War (I. 19, II. 9. 5, III. 10. 5); the cities of Lesbos except Methymna lost their ships and their freedom after the revolt of 428–427 (III. 50, VI. 85. 2); Chios though suspect in 424/3 (IV. 51) retained its ships (VI. 43, 85. 2), and so its revolt in 412 was valuable to Sparta (VIII. 5. 4). Retaining ships rather than paying tribute in cash was a sign of comparative independence; but none of the allies were totally free, though none lost its notional autonomy as a separate *polis.*

these they kept as guardians of their rule: In 428 the Mytilenaeans protest that they became allies to free the Greeks from Persia, not to enslave them to Athens (Thuc. III. 10. 3, 11. 3–6).

allowing them to retain the constitutions which they had: Athens came to be associated with democracy and Sparta with oligarchy (e.g. Thuc. III. 82. 1), but even among the other allies Athens interfered with the constitution not systematically but only when provocation and opportunity arose (cf. R. Brock, in J. Ma *et al.* [eds], *Interpreting the Athenian Empire* [London: Duckworth, 2009], 149–66). Athens seems to have tolerated oligarchies in Samos before 440 (cf. I. 115. 3), in Mytilene and the other cities of Lesbos before 428 (III. 27. 2–3, 39. 6, 47. 3), and probably a moderate oligarchy in Chios before 412 (VIII. 9. 3, 14. 2, 24. 4; contrast the narrower oligarchy of 38. 3).

to rule those whom they happened to be ruling: Several island states had a *peraia* on the mainland opposite, of which Athens might deprive them (e.g. Thasos in 463/2: Thuc. I. 101. 3). The war of 440–439 resulted from Athens' supporting Miletus against Samos in a dispute concerning Priene (I. 115. 2); Mytilene in 427 was deprived of its 'Actaean cities' (III. 50. 3 cf. IV. 52. 2–3); Chios was probably left in possession of Atarneus (cf. Hdt. VIII. 106. 1).

24. 3. as Aristides had proposed: *A.P.* turns from the establishment of Athenian rule to the provision of maintenance.

from the tribute, the taxes and the allies: The combination of these three is surprising, and can hardly be what *A.P.*'s source said, but what we read may as well be due to *A.P.* as to a copyist.

more than twenty thousand men received sustenance: The list has been attributed to Stesimbrotus and / or Theopompus, drawing partly on comedy (e.g. A. W. Gomme, *CR* 40 [1926], 8): I do not think the compiler can be identified, or can be assumed (as is regularly done) to have been hostile to democracy. 23. 2b – 24 form a unit, in which the presentation of Aristides and his 'democratic' policies need not be seen as hostile when we recognise that an Athenian could refer to rule over the allies and to *trophe* without disapproval. On the whole list see Wilamowitz, *A.u.A.* i. 153–61, ii. 201–7. On *trophe* for Athenians cf. Thuc. VI. 24. 3, [Xen.] *A.P.* 1. 15–18, 3. 4; in Ar. *Vesp.* 707–11 it is said (with exaggeration) that Athens has 1,000 tribute-paying allies, who could provide maintenance for 20,000 citizens. There was probably never a time when all the men listed here and no others qualified for maintenance; many men, such as jurors, were paid only for the days when they actually served.

six thousand jurors: Cf. Ar. *Vesp.* 662, *Suda* π 2996 Adler πρυτανεία; Andoc. I. *Myst.* 17 (one case tried by 6,000); also the quorum for ostracism (pp. 251–2): probably 6,000 jurors were enrolled each year. On payment for jurors see 27. 3–4, 62. 2.

one thousand six hundred archers: Cf. Thuc. II. 13. 8 (the 1,200 of Andoc. III *De Pace* 7 is probably an error): they were presumably paid when on active service. These citizens are not to be confused with the Scythian archers used in the fifth century to keep order in the city (e.g. Ar. *Ach.* 54 with schol.).

one thousand two hundred cavalry: Cf. Thuc. II. 13. 8, Andoc. III. *De Pace* 7: apparently 1,000 *hippeis* and 200 *hippotoxotai* (cf. Ar. *Eq.* 225).

They possibly received a stipend when on service (but Ar. *Eq.* 576–7 suggests that they did not); they also received a fodder grant for their horses, probably throughout the year (cf. 49. 1 with commentary), and a capital sum (*katastasis*), paid when they joined the force and reclaimed when they left (cf. Lys. XVI. *Mantitheus* 6–7).

five hundred men in the council: Cf. 62. 2. The payment existed by 412/1 (Thuc. VIII. 69. 4), and was more probably instituted before than during the Peloponnesian War.

five hundred guards of the dockyards: Perhaps the *phrouroi* of 62. 1.

50 guards on the acropolis: πόλει probably denotes the acropolis (cf. 8. 4). *IG* i³ 45. 14–17 mentions three archers 'from the tribe in prytany': they may be a part of this force, and if so the whole force may have been part of the body of archers.

internal officials about seven hundred men: For the contrast between internal and external officials cf. Arist. *Pol.* III. 1285 B 14–14, 18. For attempts to find this number of officials see Wilamowitz, *A.u.A.* ii. 202–4; M. H. Hansen, *GRBS* 21 [1980], 153–73 (who thinks the figure about right).

abroad †seven hundred†: With this formulation we should expect a different number. Cf. [Xen.] *A.P.* 1. 19, *IG* i³ 156. 5–7; and on Athenians sent in various capacities to the allied cities R. Meiggs, *The Athenian Empire* (Oxford U. P., 1972), 211–5, J. M. Balcer, *Historia* 25 (1976), 257–87 – but in some cases ἄρχοντες ἐν ταῖσι πόλεσι are better seen as local officials (H. Leppin, *Historia* 41 [1992], 257–71).

when later they set up their arrangements for war: The papyrus' text would most naturally be read as referring to the Peloponnesian War, but the figures are far too low for that: emendation to refer to standing forces before the Peloponnesian War is probably justified (cf. A. W. Gomme, *CR* 40 [1926], 9). On the introduction of military pay at Athens see Pritchett, *War*, i. 7–14.

two thousand five hundred hoplites: Thuc. II. 13. 6 cf. 31. 2 gives Athens in 431 13,000 combat troops and 16,000 on garrison duties; Wilamowitz suggested that *A.P.*'s figure represents the pre-war garrison for Athens and the League (*A.u.A.* ii. 204).

twenty guard ships: There is no other evidence for regular guard ships (except perhaps Plut. *Per.* 11. 4: sixty each year). The normal complement of a trireme was 200 men (e.g. Hdt. VII. 184. 1), so twenty would require

4,000; not all the oarsmen were citizens. It is disputed whether Athens normally paid 1 dr. per day until 413 and 3 ob. after (Thuc. VI. 31. 3 with Dover, *H.C.T. ad loc.*, VIII. 45. 2 with Andrewes, *H.C.T. ad loc.*) or 3 ob. was normal but pay was higher in exceptional circumstances (Pritchett, *op. cit.*, 14–24): the first view is more likely.

†other ships ... two thousand men picked by drawing lots†: It is hard to accept the papyrus' text, which has the accusative τοὺς ... δισχιλίους ἄνδρας unattached, and which conflicts with the evidence that it was normally the allies' duty to send their tribute to Athens (ML 46 = *IG* i³ 34 ~ Fornara 98. 68), though Athens might send to exact money from defaulters (ML 68 = *IG* i³ 68 ~ Fornara 133. 16–18) and commanders might sometimes collect tribute directly for their own expenses (e.g. Gomme, *H.C.T.* i. 277–8). The different kinds of solution are reviewed by Gomme, *CR* 40 (1926), 9–10, but none is obviously right.

then the *prytaneion*: *A.P.*'s language becomes even more condensed. The allusion is to those entitled to the honour of *sitesis en prytaneioi*: *IG* i³ 131 is a decree regulating the honour; for other evidence see R. E. Wycherley, *Agora* iii, pp. 173–4 no. 571.

orphans: 'Orphans' in Athens were men whose fathers had died, whether or not their mothers were still alive. The sons of citizens killed in war were maintained at the state's expense: Thuc. II. 46. 1, Pl. *Menex.* 248 E 6–8, Arist. *Pol.* II. 1268 A 8–11 (first devised for Miletus by Hippodamus), Aeschin. III. *Ctesiphon* 154, Diog. Laert. I. 55 (attributed to Solon), cf. *IG* i³ 6 ~ Fornara 75. *C.* 40–1, [Xen.] *A.P.* 3. 4. See R. S. Stroud, *Hesperia* 40 (1971), 288–90.

guards of prisoners: The Eleven (52. 1, cf. 35. 1 for the régime of the Thirty). The same surprising combination of orphans and gaolers is found in [Xen.] *A.P.* 3. 4, which suggests a common source.

finance: For διοικεῖν and διοίκησις see on 3. 6: the reference is often not simply to administration but to financial administration in particular, and the original meaning of the verb was 'keep house', so the use of the word here in connection with sustenance, i.e. *trophe*, is easily understood.

25. 1. That is how sustenance for the *demos* was provided: *A.P.* sums up first the section on *trophe*, resulting from Aristides' organisation of the Delian League (23. 2b – 24)...

For about seventeen years ... declining gradually: ...and then the previous section on the domination of Athens by the Areopagus (23. 1–2b), thus preparing the reader for Ephialtes' reform of the Areopagus (25).

For about seventeen years: Therefore Ephialtes' reform of 462/1 was in 'the eighteenth year', and the seventeen years are 479/8–463/2. But in 23. 5 and 27. 2 *A.P.* counts from 480/79, and the Areopagus' ascendancy was connected with Salamis in 480/79, so possibly here he has miscounted or a scribe has miscopied.

declining gradually: The same metaphor is used in 36. 1; the usage is originally medical (cf. Kaibel, *Stil und Text*, 48).

As the masses were increasing: That could hardly have occurred in a period of decline and Areopagite domination, but could easily have occurred during the growth of the Delian League and of *trophe*: *A.P.* is now following his democratic source for the reform of Ephialtes.

champion of the *demos*: As in 23. 3 we are given the democratic leader but not his opponent: in 26. 1 Cimon is *prostates* but not *hegemon* of the upper class; in 28. 2 Ephialtes and Cimon form an opposing pair.

Ephialtes son of Sophonides: We know nothing about Sophonides and little about Ephialtes: he commanded one naval expedition (Callisthenes *FGrH* 124 F 16 *ap.* Plut. *Cim.* 13. 4); he opposed Cimon's proposal to help Sparta against the Messenians (Plut. *Cim.* 16. 8–9); he is included in a list of politicians who were not rich (Ael. *V.H.* II.43, XI. 9, XIII. 39).

The reform is ascribed to Ephialtes here, to Ephialtes and Themistocles in 25. 3–4; 27. 1 has a later attack on the Areopagus by Pericles (associated with Ephialtes in Plut. *Per.* and *Cim.*); 35. 2 refers to the laws of Ephialtes and Archestratus; in 41. 2 Ephialtes achieves what Aristides had pointed out. Arist. *Pol.* II. 1274 A 7–8 would be compatible either with successive reforms by Ephialtes and Pericles or with a joint reform. Very probably there was a single reform by Ephialtes, supported by Pericles and with the unknown Archestratus involved somehow: it was enacted while Cimon was in Messenia, and led the Spartans to distrust their Athenian allies (cf. Thuc. I. 102. 3, Plut. *Cim.* 15. 2–3); after his return Cimon tried to upset the reform but was ostracised (Plut. *Cim.* 15. 3, 17. 3, *Per.* 9. 5).

appeared to be incorruptible and upright in his political stance: Cf. Ael. *V.H.* XI. 9, XIII. 39; Aristides in 23. 2 and with Ephialtes in Plut. *Cim.* 10. 8; Solon in 6. 3–4 – but Pericles, incorruptible in Thuc. II. 65. 8

cf. 60. 5, Isoc. VIII. *De Pace* 126, is not similarly upright in *A.P.* (see 27. 3–4).

the council: The Areopagus (still addressed as *boule* in the time of Lysias, e.g. III. *Simon* 1).

25. 2. bringing them to trial in connection with their administration: Cf. Plut. *Per.* 10. 8: probably the main attack was at the *euthynai* of retiring archons, who would join the Areopagus unless sentenced to *atimia* (cf. H. T. Wade-Gery, *BSA* 37 [1936/7], 269 = his *Essays*, 177).

in the archonship of Conon: 462/1 (Diod. Sic. XI. 74. 1) – but Diodorus, whose narrative dates are unreliable, treats Ephialtes under 460/59 (XI. 77. 6).

stripped off … all the additions: 'Additional' powers in contrast to 'traditional' (*patria*): cf. Lys. fr. 224 Carey, and in connection with the archons 3. 3. According to Plut. *Cim.* 15. 2–3 the many, led by Ephialtes, overturned τὸν καθεστῶτα τῆς πολιτείας κόσμον τά <τε> πάτρια νόμιμα οἷς ἐχρῶντο πρότερον, but Cimon on returning to Athens tried to revive the aristocracy of the time of Cleisthenes. Probably the reformers represented the powers taken from the Areopagus as added (and illegitimate), and their opponents represented them as part of the established order. The reform will have been enacted through decrees of the assembly (cf. p. 243, on Cleisthenes), published on the Areopagus (cf. 35. 2), as a copy of the law of 337/6 directed against the Areopagus was published 'at the entrance to the Areopagus' (RO 79 = *IG* ii^3 320 ~ Harding 101).

through which it had acquired its guardianship of the constitution: Cf. what is said of the Areopagus' functions in 3. 6, 4. 4 (the spurious constitution of Draco) and 8. 4; also Aesch. *Eum.* 704–6. A decree (whose authenticity has been doubted by M. Canevaro & E. M. Harris, *CQ*^{2} 62 [2012], 98–129, but defended by M. H. Hansen, *GRBS* 56 [2016], 34–48) ordering the revision of the laws in 403 entrusted the laws to the Areopagus (*ap.* Andoc. I. *Myst.* 84), and perhaps shortly before 323 a board of seven *nomophylakes* was instituted (Philoch. *FGrH* 328 F 64: F 64b[α] ascribes them to Ephialtes, which is defended by G. L. Cawkwell, *JHS* 108 [1988], 12, though they are not otherwise attested during the classical period).

No source specifies what these powers were, though Plut. *Cim.* 15. 2, *Per.* 9. 5, writes of *kriseis*, judicial decisons. I have argued (cf.

pp. 190–1) that the description did not denote any specific power, but was ancient, and over time was used by the Areopagus as a basis for assuming new powers without explicit authorisation (whence the argument over *epitheta* and *patria nomima*). The judicial powers retained by the Areopagus after the reform concerned homicide, wounding and arson (57. 3) and certain religious offences (60. 2). Powers most likely to have belonged to the Areopagus before and to have been removed now are *eisangelia*, for major offences against the state (cf. 8. 4, 43. 4), and control of officials, through *dokimasia* before entering office (cf. 55. 2), *euthynai* on leaving office (48. 4–5, 54. 2), and the possibility of deposition and prosecution during the term of office (cf. 43. 4, 45. 2), which would have given the Areopagus considerable political power. Since 487/6 the archons who joined the Areopagus had been appointed by lot and had been less important men than their predecessors (cf. 22. 5), the working of Cleisthenes' system had given the Athenians experience in and the taste for political involvement (cf. p. 245), and the Areopagus may have provoked Ephialtes and his supporters by condemning Themistocles in an *eisangelia* for medism (cf. 25. 3) and acquitting Cimon in his *euthynai* as *strategos* (cf. 27. 1). Some have suggested that the Areopagus had a right to overrule decisions of the assembly, replaced by the *graphe paranomon* (59. 2: e.g. Wade-Gery, *CQ* 25 [1931], 140, 27 [1933], 24 with n. 3 = his *Essays*, 130–1, 146–7 with 146 n. 4), but the earliest dated instance of that *graphe* is in 415 (Andoc. I. *Myst.* 17).

some to the Five Hundred: On the council in fourth-century Athens see 43. 2–49: if the powers of Cleisthenes' council, as of Solon's (cf. 8. 4), were limited to *probouleusis* and the discipline of its own members, Ephialtes' transfer to it of the oversight of officials will mark the beginning of its development as the most important body in the administration of Athens. I suspect that it was Ephialtes who constituted the tribal contingents within the council as *prytaneis*.

others to the *demos*: Here as often *demos* denotes the meeting of the citizens in the assembly (cf. M. H. Hansen, *GRBS* 50 [2010], 499–536). The assembly was to be involved in *eisangeliai*, and held votes of confidence in the officials (43. 4, cf. 61. 2).

and the lawcourts: The *dikasteria* came to be involved in almost all the procedures mentioned above. Solon had provided for appeals against the verdict of an individual magistrate to a court (9. 1); by the mid fifth century magistrates had strictly limited powers of punishment, beyond which they conducted a preliminary enquiry (56. 6) and then referred cases automatically to a court in which they presided. Wade-Gery argued for an abrupt change by Ephialtes (*BSA* 37 [1936/7], 263–70 = his *Essays*, 171–9; *Essays*, 180–200); more probably there was a gradual development by which appeals grew in frequency until the practice was standardised (cf. R. Sealey, *CP* 59 [1964], 14–18 = his *Essays in Greek Politics* [New York: Manyland, 1967], 46–52), hardly later than the time of Ephialtes but not necessarily by him.

25. 3. with Themistocles as jointly responsible: The only other text which links Themistocles with Ephialtes is the *hypothesis* to Isoc. VII. *Areopagitic*, which cites *A.P.* but gives a different motive. The abrupt ending (25. 4) supports the view that this story was not in the version of *A.P.* which circulated most widely but was added when the text was revised (cf. Introduction, p. 30). Themistocles was ostracised, on accusations from Sparta he was convicted of medism, and he fled to the Persian court (Thuc. I. 135–8 and later texts); the dates are much disputed, but almost certainly he left Athens long before 462/1 (cf. Rhodes, *Historia* 19 [1970], 392–9). He belonged to the same anti-Cimonian circle as Ephialtes and Pericles, but he cannot have been involved in this attack on the Areopagus.

was one of the Areopagites: He had been archon in 493/2 (cf. p. 255).

was about to be tried for medism: Probably by *eisangelia* (Craterus, *FGrH* 342 F 11a), possibly before the Areopagus (cf. p. 267).

he said to Ephialtes ... and to the Areopagites...: This story of Themistocles' cunning is at least *ben trovato*.

combining to overthrow the constitution: For the language cf. 8. 4, 28. 5, 36. 1.

wearing only his undergarment: Cf. οἰοχίτων in Hom. *Od.* XIV. 489: wearing the *chiton* only, and not also the *himation*, a form of abasement presumably thought appropriate to supplication.

25. 4. when the council of the Five Hundred met, and again in the assembly: If Ephialtes' reform was enacted by decree (cf. p. 266), the vote in the assembly must have been preceded by *probouleusis* in the council.

And [*lacuna*] and Ephialtes was removed by being murdered: The transition is abrupt, and probably material on the fate of Themistocles has been lost.

through the agency of Aristodicus of Tanagra: A killer from Boeotia would be presumed to be the agent of an Athenian. Plut. *Per.* 10. 7–8 cites Idomeneus (*FGrH* 338 F 8) for the view that Pericles killed Ephialtes out of envy, and then *A.P.* Antiph. V. *Caed. Her.* 68 says that the killers were never found: either *A.P.* is reporting an unsubstantiated rumour or Aristodicus was known to be the killer but the Athenians behind him were not identified. The reform aroused strong feelings: in addition to Cimon's ostracism and Ephialtes' murder, there are fears of civil war in Aesch. *Eum.* 858–66, 976–87, and the rumour of an oligarchic plot at the time of the battle of Tanagra (Thuc. I. 107. 4, 6).

26. 1. the constitution became more loosened: The verb is used particularly of loosening the strings of a bow or musical instrument, and in music some *harmoniai* were *syntonoi* (taut) and others *anieimenai* (slack) or *malakai* (soft); for the application to political constitutions cf. Arist. *Pol.* IV. 1290 A 13–29, V. 1301 B 13–17, 1304 A 20–1. For Aristotle the ideal was a mean between excessive tautness and excessive slackness, but the association of tautness with manliness and slackness with effeminacy led some to prefer taut to slack (e.g. Pl. *Resp.* III. 398 C 1–399 E 4). Here the slackening is clearly seen as worsening.
those engaging enthusiastically in demagogy: On the word *demagogos* see R. Zoepffel, *Chiron* 4 (1974), 69–90. The older word for a political leader was *prostates* (cf. p. 186). *Demagogos* is used by Aristophanes of the leadership which is practised by Cleon and is to be taken over by the sausage-seller (*Eq.* 191–3, 213–22, cf. *Ran.* 416–21), occasionally by Thucydides and Xenophon of democratic leaders (e.g. Thuc. IV. 21. 3, of Cleon); in the fourth century orators use the word occasionally as one among the words for 'politician', while historical and political writers use it of the great political leaders; Plato does not use it at all; Aristotle is distinctive in using it pejoratively of democratic leaders (esp. *Pol.* IV. 1292 A 4–37). *A.P.* uses the term regularly of democratic leaders, and usually but not always with hostile implications. The argument in 26–28. 1 is: after Ephialtes' reform the opposition was weak (26. 1) and the democracy made further progress (26. 2–4); Pericles' introduction of jury pay had a corrupting effect (27); after his death the democratic leaders became worse (28. 1).

the more respectable men had no leader, but the man who acted as their champion: The intention is to belittle Cimon (and explain why the democratic advance was not prevented: the source was perhaps an oligarchic pamphlet). The distinction between *hegemon* and *prostates* is a fine one: many have inserted an adjective, but probably mistakenly. *Epieikes* is used here in opposition to *demos*, but at the end of this section to denote the 'respectable' men in both classes.

Cimon son of Miltiades: Of Laciadae; his mother was the Thracian Hegesipyle (Plut. *Cim.* 4. 1). Athenian politics in the 470's are best explained in terms of opposition between him and Themistocles, culminating in the ostracism and condemnation of Themistocles (cf. p. 259). Cimon's opposition to Ephialtes led to his ostracism (cf. p. 265): in *A.P.* he has not been mentioned before but makes a belated and inauspicious appearance here (but in 28. 2 Ephialtes succeeds Themistocles on the democratic side and Cimon succeeds Aristides on the aristocratic).

was fairly young and had only recently come forward to political engagement: Untrue after Ephialtes' reform, of a man who was born *c.* 510 (Davies, *A.P.F.* 302) and had been active in public life since 479 (Plut. *Arist.* 10. 10), but there are stories of his youth and stupidity at the time of Miltiades' death in 489 (e.g. Plut. *Cim.* 4. 4). Many editors have rejected νεώτερον, but more probably the word is sound and *A.P.* is misapplying here (as perhaps his source had done before him) what was originally written about Cimon in an earlier context.

many of these men had perished in war: To make sense in its context this must mean that many of the upper class had died, but that can hardly be true of the early campaigns of the Delian League, and the end of this section may be a sign that *A.P.* realised that.

For campaigns at that time were based on registers: Cf. Arist. *Pol.* V. 1303 A 8–10 (referring to the Peloponnesian War). Citizen army service was always based on a register of eligible men, so editors have seen a contrast between the citizen forces of the fifth century and the mercenary forces increasingly (though not exclusively) used in the fourth; but more probably the contrast is between the fourth-century system based on age groups (53. 7) and a selective fifth-century system which made willing and experienced men more likely to be enlisted (e.g. Thuc. VI. 26. 2, 31. 3: see A. Andrewes, in *Classical Contributions ... M. F. McGregor* [Locust Valley: Augustin, 1981], 1–3).

the generals in command were inexperienced ... but honoured...: Down to the generation of Pericles the leading men were still from the aristocratic families which had dominated Athens in the archaic period, but afterwards men from new families rose to prominence (cf. 28. 1). This would have enabled a hostile writer to suggest that fifth-century leaders did not live up to their forebears' reputations; but *strategoi* were elected by the assembly, and we have no reason to think that those elected before Pericles' death were either better or worse than those elected later.

the result was that repeatedly two or three thousand of the men who went out were killed: Cf. Isoc. VIII. *De Pace* 87–8. We do not know how many the casualties were, but the existence of published casualty lists from the fifth century may have encouraged the belief that Athens' wars were prodigal of Athenian lives.

the respectable men both among the *demos* and among the well-off: Here the reference is to the 'better' men in both classes, who would be more likely to serve and to risk their lives.

26. 2. did not pay heed to the laws as they had done previously: While fifth-century sophists contrasted *nomos* (human convention) with *physis* (nature), fourth-century thinkers tended to contrast *nomoi* (laws with wide validity) with *psephismata* (ephemeral decrees of an assembly or council), and that underlay the distinction in fourth-century Athens between *nomoi* and *psephismata*, enacted in different ways. Aristotle regarded it as characteristic of extreme democracy that *psephismata* prevail over *nomoi* (*Pol.* IV. 1292 A 4–37, cf. *A.P.* 41. 2 *fin.*). The rest of this chapter will chronicle three laws which do not provide instances of that; but this passage marks the transition from the military disasters of 26. 1 to the legal changes of 26. 2–4.

they did not interfere with the appointment of the nine archons: Changed to *klerosis ek prokriton* in 487/6 (22. 5); αἵρεσιν here means 'appointment', by whatever means. *A.P.*'s point must be that, although they departed from the laws in other respects, the democrats did keep to the law about the appointment of the archons, apart from relaxing the class qualification.

in the sixth year ... and the first from these to hold office was Mnesithides: *A.P.* has not given a date for Ephialtes' death (25. 4), but must be counting from 462/1 (25. 2), and the sixth year from that is

457/6, when Mnesitheides was archon (Diod. Sic. XI. 81. 1). If he was the first archon under the new system, the change must have been enacted in 458/7 or late 459/8 (cf. on 22. 5); that Mnesitheides was himself a *zeugites* may have been recorded or may be an inference.

Before him they had all been from the *hippeis* and *pentakosiomedimnoi*: *A.P.* has not stated whether *hippeis* were admitted to the archonship by Solon or later (cf. p. 206).

the *zeugitai* had held the routine offices: ἐγκύκλιος means 'recurring' or 'ordinary': here the contrast is with the major offices from which the *zeugitai* had been excluded; in 43. 1 routine civilian offices are contrasted with military offices.

except when some stipulation in the laws had been neglected: This comment may be prompted by what is stated above about not keeping to the laws, or by the later tendency to overlook class qualifications for offices (cf. 7. 4).

26. 3. In the fifth year after that, in the archonship of Lysicrates: 453/2 (cf. Diod. Sic. XI. 88. 1).

the thirty justices called deme justices were re-instituted: Cf. 16. 5, on the justices (not necessarily thirty) appointed by Pisistratus and presumably abolished on the fall of the tyranny; the thirty may have been one for each *trittys*. Perhaps now the extra business resulting from Ephialtes' reform and the growing complexity of Athens' administration was over-burdening the *dikasteria*; in any case, local settlement of local disputes would be convenient. The thirty's successors in the fourth century decided suits for sums up to 10 dr. (53. 1–3), and that may have been true of the thirty in the fifth century.

26. 4. And in the third after that, under Antidotus: 451/0 (cf. Diod. Sic. XI. 91. 1).

because of the large number of citizens … born from two citizens: Athenian laws on mixed marriages and *nothoi* are assembled by Harrison, *L.A.* i. 24–8, 61–8. For Pericles' law cf. Plut. *Per.* 37. 3, Ael. *V.H.* VI. 10, XIII. 24, fr. 68 = *Suda* δ 451 Adler δημοποίητος. It seems to have been annulled or ignored towards the end of the Peloponnesian War, but was reenacted to affect those born in or after 403/2 (Dem. LVII. *Eubulides* 30, Eumelus *FGrH* 77 F 2, Carystius fr. 11 Müller *ap.* Ath. XIII. 577 B–C) and strengthened with a positive ban on mixed marriages ([Dem.] LIX. *Neaera* 16, 52). Plut. *Per.* 37. 4 links with the law an expulsion of many wrongly registered citizens when a gift of corn was received from Egypt (dated 445/4 by Philoch. *FGrH* 328 F 119 ~ Fornara 86). Before this law, whether or not entitlement to citizenship was formally defined (C. B. Patterson, *Pericles' Citizenship Law of 451–50 BC* [New York: Arno, 1981], 8–39, suggests that it was not), sons of foreign mothers such as Cleisthenes (p. 237) and Cimon (p. 270) were able to become citizens.

That Athens should be democratic but restrict the range of men entitled to share in the democracy is not problematic. *A.P.*'s explanation of the law is 'because of the number of the citizens' (cf. Arist. *Pol.* III. 1278 A 26–34): that does not fit the picture in 26. 1 of heavy losses in war, or the reenactment of the law after the Peloponnesian War, and if as I believe bastards were not legally entitled to citizenship (cf. on 42. 1), the law would limit citizens' choice of wife but would not limit the number of their citizen sons. The growth of the Delian League increased the opportunities for mixed marriages, but as the benefits of Athenian citizenship increased it was seen as desirable to restrict those benefits to genuine Athenians. The question continues to be debated: see J. H. Blok, *Historia* 58 (2009), 141–70 (numbers were not a problem, and the aim was to make all citizens pure Athenians eligible for priesthoods and other offices); J. Watson, *CCJ* 56 (2010), 259–76 (easy access to citizenship produced such dramatic growth in Athens' citizen numbers during the first half of the century that numbers had become a problem).

Pericles was born about the mid 490's to Xanthippus and the Alcmaeonid Agariste (p. 254); he was Aeschylus' *choregos* in 473/2 (*hypothesis* to Aesch. *Pers.* with *IG* ii^2 2318. 9–11); this is the earliest dated measure attributed to him, though the introduction of jury pay (27. 3–4) may be earlier.

27. 1. After that…: What follows begins with an episode earlier than Ephialtes' reform: ch. 27 is a rambling and anecdotal collection of hostile material on Pericles, and this is a linking phrase without a genuine chronological reference.

first gained a good reputation when, while still young: Plut. *Cim.* 14. 3–5 cf. *Per.* 10. 6 provides the context: after the siege of Thasos (465/4–463/2) Cimon was accused of taking bribes to spare Macedon; Pricles was one of a board of elected prosecutors, and after intervention by Cimon's sister Elpinice was mild in his attack; Cimon was acquitted. Only *A.P.* refers to Cimon's *euthynai*, but that may well be right (cf. p. 267).

the constitution became still more democratic: Cf. 22. 1, on Cleisthenes.

For he stripped off some powers of the Areopagites: Probably not a further reform, but a misapplied attribution to Pericles of a share in Ephialtes' reform (cf. p. 265).

particularly steered the city towards naval power: Cf. 23. 4–24, on Aristides, 41. 2, linking naval power with the régime introduced by Ephialtes; in Thuc. I. 93. 3–4, 7, Plut. *Them.* 19. 3–7 the policy of concentrating on naval power is attributed to Themistocles, and in Thuc. II. 13. 2, 62. 2–3, 65. 7 Pericles stresses the advantages of naval power for his strategy in the Peloponnesian War.

the many became confident: Cf. 22. 3, 24. 1.

27. 2. In the forty-ninth year … in the archonship of Pythodorus: 432/1 (Diod. Sic. XII. 37. 1, cf. Thuc. II. 2. 1).

the *demos* was shut up in the city: Cf. Thuc. II. 13. 2, 14–17, also 52. 1–2, VII. 27. 2–28.

grew accustomed to earning stipends on campaign: Cf. 24. 3; the war increased the amount of service required and therefore the amount of *misthophoria*.

intentionally … unintentionally … it chose to administer the state itself: Politicians such as Cleon were ostentatiously populist (cf. 28. 3), but it is hard to establish a direct connection between the Peloponnesian War and the advance of democracy.

27. 3. it was Pericles who was first to provide a stipend for the lawcourts: Cf. Pl. *Grg.* 515 E 2–7, Arist. *Pol.* II. 1274 A 8–9, Plut. *Per.* 9. 2–3, Aristid. III. *Quatt.* 98, 106–7. The emphasis on this suggests that it was the first instance of payment for civilian service: such payments were important if ordinary citizens were to play a part in the democracy, and they came to be seen as characteristic of democracies (though for a non-democratic instance see *Hell. Oxy.* 19. 4 Chambers; on other non-Athenian instances see G. E. M. de Ste. Croix, *CQ*[2] 25 [1975], 48–52). They were never lavish (cf. 62. 2).

an act of demagogy to counter the lavishness of Cimon: Cf. Plut. *Per.* 9. 2; and Cimon's generosity was notorious (cf. Davies, *A.P.F.* 310–2, suggesting that he used up his capital for political gain). Pericles was rich, though no doubt unable to rival Cimon in expenditure (cf. *A.P.F.* 459–60): while *A.P.* represents jury pay as use of the state's wealth to outdo Cimon's use of his own wealth, the democrats will have been opposed in principle to Cimon's kind of aristocratic patronage. What *A.P.* states might imply that jury pay was introduced while Cimon was based in Athens (before 462/1 or 451 to his death shortly afterwards, if despite Theopomp. *FGrH* 115 F 88 ~ Fornara 76, Plut. *Cim.* 17. 8, *Per.* 10. 4 he spent ten years out of Athens when ostracised), but probably the period of his ostracism should not be ruled out (and V. J. Rosivach, *ZPE* 175 [2010], 145–9, doubts the inference from Cimon altogether).

whose property was like that of a tyrant: Ath. XII. 532 F – 533 C cites Theopomp. *FGrH* 115 F 135 on Pisistratus' generosity immediately before F 89 on Cimon's generosity: the comparison may have been made by a common source of Theopompus and *A.P.*, and reduced to a generalisation by *A.P.*

was outstanding in his performance of the public liturgies: On *leitourgiai* as public services required from the richer citizens see 56. 3, 61. 1. We do not know of any *leitourgiai* performed by Cimon; public bulldings attributed to him are listed by W. Judeich, *Topographie von Athen* (Munich: Beck, ²1931), 73–4.

sustained many of his fellow-demesmen: The citizens in general, according to Theopompus; *A.P.*'s more focused generosity is more likely to be right.

all his land was unfenced: According to Plut. *Cim.* 10. 1, *Per.* 9. 2 he removed the fences.

27. 4. for that service: Strictly *choregia* is the *leitourgia* of supporting a chorus in a festival; it could be extended to civilian *leitourgiai* in general, and here Cimon's support for his demesmen is represented as a kind of *leitourgia*.

on the advice of Damonides of Oë: Cf. Plut. *Per.* 9. 2 (with Οἴηθεν in **S** and most manuscripts). In fact Pericles' adviser was the musician Damon son of Damonides (e.g. Isoc. XV. *Antid.* 235, Plut. *Per.* 4. 1–4, ostraca [see below]), and he was Ὄαθεν (from Oa, not Oë: Steph. Byz. Ὄα = 37 A 1 DK); but since the error was present in the edition of *A.P.* used by Plutarch it should perhaps be blamed on *A.P.* or his source rather than a copyist. See Davies, *A.P.F.* 383, with bibliography 369 (citing some dissenters); R. W. Wallace, *Reconstructing Damon* (Oxford U. P., 2015).

who seems to have suggested most of Pericles' measures to him: Cf. the story that Themistocles was shown by Mnesiphilus that the Greek fleet needed to stay at Salamis (Hdt. VIII. 57–8). The purpose here is probably malicious: Pericles was not capable of devising his own demagogic manoeuvres.
because of that they later ostracised him: Cf. Brenne, *Ostrakismos*, 130–2.
careful to present themselves for allotment: When more than 6,000 applied for registration as jurors (cf. p. 262), some would have to be eliminated.
27. 5. judicial bribery: *Dekazein* is used particularly of bribing jurors, and perhaps refers to a particular form of bribery. If the occasion referred to was indeed the first, payment of jurors is hardly to be blamed: [Xen.] *A.P.* 3. 7, probably written in the 420's (cf. the edition of J. L. Marr & P. J. Rhodes [Oxford: Oxbow, 2008]), was aware of the word and the possibility.
Anytus after his generalship at Pylos: Anytus was one of the politicians of the late fifth century from a non-aristocratic background (cf. Davies, *A.P.F.* 40–1). In 410 or 409 the Spartans attacked the Athenian fort at Pylos in Messenia, he was sent with thirty ships to relieve it but was prevented by bad weather, and on returning to Athens he was prosecuted but acquitted (Diod. Sic. XIII. 64. 5–7 and later texts, cf. Xen. *Hell.* I. 2. 18); D. Lenfant, *Historia* 65 (2016), 258–74, suggests that the charge of bribery began as a malicious story in comedy but afterwards was believed as serious history. For Anytus' later career see 34. 3.

28. 1. While Pericles was champion of the *demos* ... but after Pericles' death...: For Pericles as the last of Athens' good leaders cf. Isoc. VIII. *De Pace* 124–8, XV. *Antid.* 230–6, and earlier Lys. XXX. *Nicomachus* 28, Thuc. II. 65. 5–13.
not of good repute among the respectable men: Shown by the next clause to be equivalent to 'not a member of the upper class'. For a modern version of the change after Pericles' death see W. R. Connor, *The New Politicians of Fifth-Century Athens* (Princeton U. P., 1971), with J. K. Davies, *Gnomon* 47 (1975), 374–8; but C. Mann, *Die Demagogen und das Volk* (*Klio* Bhft. [2]13 [2007]), begins a new era with Alcibiades rather than Cleon. To Pericles' death most of the leading men belonged

to or married into the old aristocracy, but from then to the end of the fifth century the old aristocracy is represented only by Alcibiades and Critias (and perhaps Conon).

28. 2. For from the beginning it was Solon who was the first champion of the *demos*: On *prostatai* cf. p. 184. For precedents for this list see Isoc. XV. *Antid.* 230–6, Pl. *Grg.* 503 C 1–3 cf. 515 C 5–D 1, Theopompus' digression on the demagogues at Athens (Ath. IV. 166 D = *FGrH* 115 F 100) and Stesimbrotus on Themistocles, Thucydides and Pericles (Ath. XIII. 589 E = *FGrH* 107 F 10a), and before them perhaps Eupolis' comedy *Demes* (Connor, *Theopompus*, 165–6 n. 69). This list begins with Solon and (perhaps) Pisistratus as *prostatai tou demou*, followed by (inevitably over-simple) pairs of *prostatai* of the *demos* and (under different labels) the upper class, apparently based on known conflicts. It is brief, sometimes obscure, and does not wholly match the narrative in the rest of *A.P.*'s first part: probably it is a summary of what *A.P.* found in some earlier work. For Solon as *prostates tou demou* cf. 2. 2, and the summary judgment in 9.

secondly Pisistratus: Cf. 13. 4–5, where Pisistratus 'seemed to be most democratic'.

and Lycurgus of the well-born and notable: If the papyrus' text is essentially sound, *A.P.* is emphasising that Solon and Pisistratus, though on the democratic side, were themselves of good families; but, whereas Solon is presented as a mediator accepted by all, Pisistratus did have opponents. The shortest of three suggestions by A. W. Gomme, naming Lycurgus but not Megacles (*HSCP* Supp. 1 [1940], 238 n. 2 = his *More Essays in Greek History and Literature* [Oxford: Blackwell, 1962], 62–3 n. 49), is the best.

After the overthrow of the tyranny it was Cleisthenes ... the circle of Isagoras had gone into exile: If we add Lycurgus as *prostates* of the aristocrats above, the statement that Cleisthenes had no opponent makes more sense; on the other hand, that addition makes the failure to state that Cleisthenes was *prostates tou demou* more awkward (though not impossible). That Cleisthenes was an Alcmaeonid is probably a simple biographical note (cf. the notes on some of the other *prostatai*, below), not an insertion to make the point that he was not himself of the lower class.

After this Xanthippus ... and Miltiades...: This is historically unsatisfactory, since there is no evidence that Athenian politics were polarised in this way at the beginning of the fifth century; but the facts that Xanthippus prosecuted Miltiades (p. 254) and that their sons Pericles and Cimon appear later in the list, will have been a sufficient basis for this pairing. *A.P.* does not mention Miltiades elsewhere except as the father of Cimon.

then Themistocles and Aristides: Although Themistocles and Aristides are together on the democratic side in 23. 3, the natural interpretation here, indicated by the addition of 'respectively' in my translation, is that Themistocles was the democratic *prostates* and Aristides the aristocratic (Gomme, *HSCP* Supp. 1 [1940], 238 n. 2 = his *More Essays* 62–3 n. 49), in accordance with the main tradition that the two men were opponents: *A.P.* has not reconciled material from different sources. Democracy was not an issue in the 470's, but men associated with Themistocles were supporters of democracy when it became an issue in the 460's.

after them Ephialtes ... and Cimon son of Miltiades...: In 25–6 the introduction of Cimon was perversely delayed, but here he is given his due, and this is one of the better pairings.

then Pericles ... and Thucydides...: Pericles is associated with democracy in 27; despite Thuc. II. 65. 9 he was not unopposed either before or after the ostracism of Thucydides. Thucydides son of Melesias is not mentioned elsewhere in *A.P.* except in 28. 5: he was related to Cimon, possibly as brother-in-law, and was possibly maternal grandfather of Thucydides the historian (but Davies, *A.P.F.* 232–6, is agnostic). He became the leading opponent of Pericles after Cimon's death *c.* 450, but was ostracised *c.* 443 (see particularly Plut. *Per.* 11–14). If the papyrus' text is correct, *A.P.* here exhausted his list of synonyms for the upper class, and Thucydides and Theramenes are labelled *prostatai* of the 'others'.

28. 3. After Pericles' death ... Nicias ... Cleon...: This will be based on the clash between them over Pylos in 425 (Thuc. IV. 26–8). Thucydides in some sense admired Nicias (VII. 86. 5), but he detested Cleon (III. 36. 6, etc.); in the fourth century Nicias' reputation was good and Cleon is rarely mentioned; 28. 5 praises Nicias as a *kalos k'agathos* with the elder Thucydides and Theramenes. In fact both men seem to have been sons of newly-rich fathers and the first men from their families to aspire to a leading position (Davies, *A.P.F.* 318–9, 403–4, Connor, *The New Politicians of Fifth-Century Athens*, 151–63); but while Nicias adopted a traditional style (e.g. frequently serving as *strategos* and performing *leitourgiai*) Cleon was ostentatiously populist (cf. below).

seems particularly to have correupted the *demos* by his wild impulses: *Hormai* are violent impulses; cf. Thucydides' description of Cleon as 'most violent of the citizens' (III. 36. 6). As caricatured by Aristophanes he was given to making wild promises and wild accusations, of which the promise to finish the affair at Pylos within twenty days (Thuc. IV. 28. 4) was typical. *A.P.* omits to underline here the point that after Pericles' death things became worse.

was the first to shout and utter ... in an orderly manner: Cf. Plut. *Nic.* 8. 6, *Ti. Gracch.* 2. 2, schol. Lucian *Tim.* 30 = Theopomp. *FGrH* 115 F 92 + Philoch. 328 F 128b. Aeschin. I. *Timarchus* 25–6 comments on the modesty of ancient *rhetores* and cites a statue of Solon, to which Dem. XIX. *F.L.* 251 objects that the statue was less than fifty years old; Plut. *Praec. Ger. Reip.* 800 C comments on the modest stance of Pericles. Cleon shouted and uttered abuse, and spoke with his *himation* unfastened in order to gesticulate wildly. *Anakrazein* is a favourite word of Aristophanes, which suggests that the ultimate source of this description is comedy.

Then after these ... Theramenes ... Cleophon...: The need to provide pairs of *prostatai* has led to the omission of Alcibiades (aristocratic but populist: absent also from the account of 411–410, in 29–33), his clashes over policy with Nicias (Thuc. V. 43–6, VI. 8–26), and the ostracism of 415 (?) which led to the removal not of one of them but of the *demagogos* Hyperbolus (Plut. *Nic.* 11. 1–8, *Alc.* 13. 4–9). Theramenes was prominent in setting up the oligarchic régimes of 411 (32. 2) and 404 (34. 3), but each time fell out with the extremists (33. 2, 36–7); his father Hagnon had a distinguished public career from the 440's to the 410's. Cleophon, often as here referred to as 'lyre-maker', was said to be of low or foreign origin (e.g. Ar. *Ran.* 678–82 with schol. 678), but it is now known from the *ostraka* cast against him in Athens' last ostracism that his father was Cleïppides, a *strategos* in 428 (Thuc. III. 3. 2) and himself a candidate for ostracism in the 440's (see Brenne, *Ostrakismos*, 197–200). He was a *demagogos* in the manner of Cleon and Hyperbolus, in the last years of the war opposed to peace with Sparta (cf. 34. 1) whereas it was Theramenes who finally negotiated the peace.

the first man to provide the two-obol grant: The records of the treasurers of Athena include many payments 'for the *diobelia*' from 410/09 onwards (e.g. ML 84 = *IG* i³ 375 ~ Fornara 154. 10); in 406/5 a man called Archedemus was a *prostates* of the *demos* and in charge of the *diobelia* (Xen. *Hell.* I. 7. 2). What this 2-obol payment was remains uncertain: J. J. Buchanan, *Theorika* (Locust Valley: Augustin, 1962), 35–48, and J. H. Blok, *ZPE* cxciii 2015, 87–102, review the evidence and modern theories; the best suggestion is a form of that made in a too-modernistic way by Wilamowitz (*A.u.A.* ii. 212–6), that it was a subsistnce grant paid to citizens not otherwise supported by the state. The verb ἐπόρισε calls to mind the office of *poristes* ('provider', *sc.* of funds), attested between 419 (Antiph. VI. *Chor.* 49 and 405 (Ar. *Ran.* 1505), which may have been held at some time by Cleophon.

it was abolished by Callicrates of Paeania ... to the two obols: In Athens' straitened circumstances towards the end of the war the increase could not be afforded (cf. W. K. Pritchett, *Anc. Soc.* 8 [1977], 45); distributions of grain recorded for 405/4 (*IG* ii² 1686. *B*) may have replaced the *diobelia*. Nothing else is known of this Callicrates.

Both of these were afterwards condemned to death: For Cleophon's death see on 34. 1.

for it was the masses' custom ... to do anything improper: The fickleness of the Athenian assembly is a commonplace in writers who were not fond of the democracy (e.g. Thuc. II. 59. 1–2, 61. 2–3, 65. 3–4, [Xen.] *A.P.* 2. 17).

28. 4. After Cleophon: The politicians of the fourth century are dismissed collectively and anonymously: cf. Isoc. VIII. *De Pace* 75.

there was a continual succession in demagogy: Cf. schol. Ar. *Pax* 681: the thought is that there was a continuous succession of democratic *prostatai*.

who most wanted to be outrageous and to gratify the masses: Cf. Isoc. XII. *Panath.* 132–3.

28. 5. It seems that the best ... were Nicias, Thucydides and Theramenes: It is surprising that these three should be singled out for praise: Nicias was over-cautious, and by his obstinacy made disaster in Sicily in 413 certain; Thucydides was unsuccessful in his opposition to Pericles, and no positive achievements of his are known; Theramenes is admitted to be controversial. They are men of whom we should expect *A.P.* to disapprove, but probably as elsewhere he is not commenting spontaneously but repeating a comment from his source (cf. p. 11; but contr. P. Harding, *Phoenix* 28 [1974], 110–1).

fine gentlemen: Cf. above: Thucydides was a *kalos k'agathos*; Nicias was not, but made himself acceptable to the *kaloi k'agathoi*.

civic-minded, and treated the whole city in a fatherly manner: Echoed by Plut. *Nic.* 2. 1.

Theramenes: Cf. above. He was described as a *kothornos*, a boot capable of fitting either foot (Plut. *Nic.* 2. 1, cf. Xen. *Hell.* II. 3. 31, 47, Ar. *Ran.* 534–41); he may sincerely have held the 'moderate' views attributed to him in Xen. *Hell.* II. 3. 18–19, 48–9; Lys. XII. *Eratothenes* 62–78 is hostile to him. Modern judgments have been mostly hostile, but he was defended by B. Perrin, *AHR* ix 1903/4, 649–69. The weakest point in his career was his willingness to risk oligarchy again in 404 when he had seen what happened in 411/0: he had defeated the extremists then, and presumably hoped that since the Athenians remembered that episode he would be able to do so again.

because in his time there were disturbances with regard to the constitution: The meaning must be that in his time there was confusion as to how the state should be goverened, as Athens alternated between democracy and oligarchy.

those who do not express their opinions casually: γνώμην or some such word is to be understood as object. Lys. XII. *Eratosthenes* and the 'Theramenes papyrus' (cf. p. 13) show that Theramenes' part in the upheavals of the period was debated after his death, and *A.P.*, aware of this, realised that his judgment needed to be justified.

as his detractors allege: Cf. Critias *ap.* Xen. *Hell.* II. 3. 30–1, Lys. XII. *Eratosthenes* 78.

supported them all: Cf. Arist. *Pol.* II. 1274 A 9–11.

as long as they did nothing illegal … but when they did act illegally…: Pl. *Plt.* 302 C 1–303 B 7 distinguished good forms of constitution as those which rule according to law from bad forms as those which rule unlawfully (but Arist. *Pol.* III. 1279 A 22–B 10 distinguished those which seek the common interest from those which seek the ruler's interest). Theramenes may well have objected to the illegalities of the oligarchs in both periods, and perhaps also to the illegality of the democracy after Aegospotami, but it is hard to think that he accused the democracy before 411 of illegality.

which is the duty of a good citizen: Aristotle does not praise adaptability to different régimes; [Xen.] *A.P.* criticises those who do not belong to the *demos* but choose to live under a democratic régime.

I. The Four Hundred and the Five Thousand (29–34. 1 init.)

On the revolutions of 411 we have two detailed sources, Thuc. VIII and *A.P.* Thucydides wrote shortly after the events, but as an exile was dependent on what others told him; his account emphasises intrigue and violence, and often contrasts men's publicly professed motives with what he believed to be their real motives. *A.P.*'s account concentrates on technical details and the formalities of the constitutional changes: the effect of that is more favourable to the oligarchs, but that effect was perhaps not intended by *A.P.* As on Pisistratus' rise to power *A.P.* combined Herodotus with another source (14—15), here he has combined Thucydides with another source, which quoted documents, in which the oligarchs tried to appear respectable by democratic criteria of respectability (on that cf. E. David, *Eirene* 50 [2014], 11–38): possibly the *Atthis* of Androtion, whose father Andron was probably the man who under the intermediate régime proposed the trial of Antiphon and others (Craterus *FGrH* 342 F 5 *ap.* Harp. α 133 Keaney Ἄνδρων, [Plut.] *X Or.* 833 E), and / or Antiphon's speech in his defence (cf. p. 13; and on the question in general, A. Andrewes, *PCPS*² 22 [1976], 14–25). The constitutional documents in 30–1 have no parallel in Thucydides; otherwise, despite differences in detail, it is better to assume that Thucydides and *A.P.* report the same episodes, albeit incompletely and sometimes inaccurately, than that each reports episodes which the other omits (contr. M. L. Lang, *AJP* 69 [1948], 272–89, 88 [1967], 176–87).

Diod. Sic. XIII. 34. 1–3, 36 (carelessly repeating what is stated in 34), 38. 1–2, presumably derived from Ephorus, is very brief; there are allusions to these events in Arist. *Pol.* V. 1304 B 7–15, 1305 B 22–7.

29. 1. While affairs were evenly balanced in the war: *A.P.* plunges abruptly into the new topic, which has not been foreshadowed in the preceding chapters.

after the disaster which occurred in Sicily: Cf. Thuc. VIII. 24. 5, Isoc. XVI. *De Bigis* 15, Dem. XX. *Leptines* 42; schol. Ar. *Lys.* 421 and *Suda* π 2355 Adler πρόβουλοι are probably derived from *A.P.* Athens' failed expedition to Sicily left it short of men and money, enabled the Spartans to establish their fort at Decelea (cf. p. 303), and suggested to members of the Delian League that defiance might succeed.

their alliance with the King: For a series of Spartan agreements with Persia in 412–411 see Thuc. VIII. 17. 4–18, 36. 2–37, 57–8: Persian support enabled Sparta to persist in the war and challenge the Athenians at sea.

they were compelled: Voluntarily, but in despondency, Diod. Sic. XIII. 34. 2. For the exculpation of the *demos* cf. 34. 1, 3; in Arist. *Pol.* V. 1304 B 7–15 the oligarchs were deceitful in offering Persian support for Athens (not claimed by Thucydides: cf. below); but in Xen. *Hell.* II. 3. 45 Theramenes emphasises that the *demos* voted for the régime of the Four Hundred. M. C. Taylor notes that in Thucydides' narrative the *demos* did not in fact strenuously resist the oligarchy (*JHS* 122 [2002], 91–108).

The speech introducing the decree was made by Melobius: πρὸ means 'before', the speech introducing the proposal: this information is without parallel, and suggests that *A.P.* found his information not in a bare document but in a narrative containing the document. The reason for a speaker other than the formal proposer may be that Pythodorus was a member of the council but Melobius was not. Melobius is probably the man of that name who was later a member of the Thirty (Lys. XII. *Eratosthenes* 12, 19, Xen. *Hell.* II. 3. 2), though another Melobius appears in a casualty list of 409 (*IG* i³ 1191. 270).

the formal proposal was made by Pythodorus of Anaphlystus: Possible identifications are the member of the Four Hundred who had prosecuted Protagoras (Diog. Laert. IX. 54) and the archon of 404/3 (35. 1), but the name is a common one. In inscribed decrees of the fifth century proposers are not identified by patronymic or demotic, but the information may have been included in the archival text; γνώμην γράφειν is a common literary formula for proposing a decree, but inscribed texts regularly use εἰπεῖν.

they thought that the King would be more likely to fight on their side: Cf. the detailed account of Alcibiades' intrigues and the hopes that he could divert Persian support from Sparta to Athens in Thuc. VIII. 45–56. By the time the oligarchic régime was set up it will have been public knowledge that the Persians had reaffirmed their commitment to Sparta, but hopes that they would support Athens continued, at any rate at some times among some Athenians, until 407. *A.P.*'s account is condensed, and probably does not mean to imply that there was general expectation of Persian support or that the failure of the negotiations was unknown to the citizens in Athens at the time of Pythodorus' motion.

There were other motives for the change of constitution, which no doubt affected different men in different proportions. Some hoped that under an oligarchic régime Alcibiades could return to Athens (e.g. Thuc. VIII. 47: he is noticeably absent from this account, as from 28. 3, on which see p. 279), but Phrynichus supported the oligarchs only when they had ceased supporting Alcibiades (Thuc. VIII. 68. 2); some hoped to save money by abolishing Athens' civilian stipends (cf. below); some hoped that a change of government would lead to more successful prosecution of the war (supported by Persian money), but others hoped to put an end to the war (cf. 32. 3); some may genuinely have believed that democracy was a bad form of government (cf. [Xen.] *A.P.*), while others wanted to seize power for themselves (e.g. Thuc. VIII. 66. 1).

if they based the constitution on a few men: Thucydides writes of abolishing the democracy in connection with Alcibiades (VIII. 48. 1), but attributes more ambiguous language to Pisander (VIII. 53. 1, 3).

29. 2. of this nature: τοιόνδε is less specific than τάδε (30. 1), ταύτην … τήνδε (31. 1); the text here is close to the language of a decree but shows some signs of editing.

together with the ten *probouloi* already in existence: Not explained or mentioned elsewhere in *A.P.*: they were a board of ten older (probably over forty, as here) men appointed in 413 after the disaster in Sicily to take over some of the functions of the council and *prytaneis* (Thuc. VIII. 1. 3, Ar. *Lys.* 387 etc.); the two known are Hagnon the father of Theramenes (cf. p. 279: Lys. XII. *Eratosthenes* 65), born before 470, and Sophocles the tragedian (Arist. *Rhet.* III. 1419 A 26–30), born *c.* 496 (but this identification has been doubted: H. C. Avery, *Historia* xxii 1973, 509–14). προϋπαρχόντων betrays the viewpoint of a narrator: the motion would have used ὑπαρχόντων.

twenty others: Cf. Androtion *FGrH* 324 F 43, Philoch. 328 F 136 ~ Fornara 148; schol. Ar. *Lys.* 421 and *Suda* π 2355 Adler πρόβουλοι are probably derived from *A.P.*; but Thuc. VIII. 67. 1, cf. Harp. σ 56 Keaney συγγραφεῖς, makes the *syngrapheis* ten in all. Probably *A.P.* is right; agreement with Androtion does not prove that he is *A.P.*'s source.

those over the age of forty: Men who had reached their fortieth birthday (cf. on 42. 1).
should swear … best for the city: Cf. the oaths of the *bouleutai* (22. 2) and the archons (55. 5); an oath was sworn also by the *katalogeis* (29. 5), and arrangements for an oath appear in 31. 1.
to draft … should draft proposals for their salvation: Cf. Thuc. VIII. 67. 1. In the fifth century *syngrapheis* were sometimes appointed to draft complex proposals (e.g. ML 73 = *IG* i^3 78 ~ Fornara 140); the Thirty in 404 were another such board (cf. p. 313); but the use of *syngrapheis* to introduce oligarchic régimes discredited the practice (cf. Isoc. VII. *Areop.* 58), and in the fourth century matters which needed careful consideration were referred to the council (e.g. *IG* ii^2 125 + RO 69 ~ Harding 66. 6–9). For περὶ τῆς σωτηρίας cf. 29. 4 and Thuc. VIII. 72. 1, 86. 3: while the literal meaning was appropriate, this seems to have been a recognised formula for an open debate (cf. Rhodes, *A.B.* 231–5); and αὐτοκράτορας in Thuc. VIII. 67. 1 may likewise mean that they were free to recommend whatever they thought appropriate.
anybody else who wished could make proposals: This invitation to volunteer citizens was in conformity with democratic practice: cf. *IG* i^3 64. 5–9, decree *ap.* Andoc. I. *Myst.* 83–4, RO 58 = *IG* ii^3 292 ~ Harding 78. A. 16–54.
29. 3. Cleitophon: Probably the Cleitophon of Pl. *Clit.*, mentioned with Theramenes in 34. 3 and Ar. *Ran.* 967.
in other respects as Pythodorus: τὰ μὲν ἄλλα καθάπερ, the standard formula for introducing an amendment, points to a documentary original, but the placing of εἶπεν and the later use of ἔγραψεν reflect modification by a narrator. If Pythodorus was a member of the council (cf. p. 283), a normal document would have used καθάπερ τῇ βουλῇ rather than καθάπερ Πυθόδωρος, but even if this did so a subsequent narrator could have modified it.
also search out: This is the only instance of the double compound: probably the word could denote either looking at something which was known to exist or looking for something which was hoped to exist; but these events showed that the laws were confused and uncertain, and the restored democracy of 410 set about a new codification (cf. pp. 306, 315–6), so the second is more likely.
the traditional laws which Cleisthenes enacted when he established

the democracy: On the appeal to the *patrios politeia*, 'traditional constitution', see particularly A. Fuks, *The Ancestral Constitution* (London: Routledge, 1953), associating it particularly with Theramenes and the 'moderates'. More probably it was at first used by oligarchs of all kinds to represent their régime as a return to the respectable past rather than a dangerous novelty, and the rift between extremists and moderates opened only when they had gained power; subsequently oligarchs and democrats advanced rival claims to be champions of the traditional constitution (cf. Rhodes, in G. Herman [ed.], *Stability and Crisis in the Athenian Democracy* [*Historia* Einz. 220 (2011)], 16–23).

His point was that Cleisthenes' constitution was ... much like that of Solon: As indicated in the translation, not a part of Cleitophon's amendment, but a comment by *A.P.* or his source, to explain why a man involved in introducing the oligarchy cited Cleisthenes' democracy.

29. 4. Those who were elected proposed first... Then...: The *syngrapheis* reported to an assembly held outside the city, at Colonus (Thuc. VIII. 67. 2–68. 1 *init.*): with the countryside of Attica in the hands of the Spartans, that may have deterred some poorer citizens from attending, but some more innocent reason must have been given for the decision.

proposed first ... for the *prytaneis* to put to the vote all proposals...: Cf. Thuc. VIII. 67. 2: any citizen could make a proposal (Thuc.), and every proposal must be put to the vote (*A.P.*). *A.P.*'s account is narrative in form, and has some non-documentary usages (e.g. οἱ ἐθέλοντες rather than οἱ βουλόμενοι), but still has a documentary flavour.

Then they suspended the *graphai paranomon*, the *eisangeliai* and the *proskleseis*: Cf. Thuc. VIII. 67. 2 (specifying only the *graphe paranomon*). For that *graphe*, by which a decree could be attacked as unlawful or otherwise improper, cf. p. 267; *eisangeliai* here might be either charges of treason (cf. 8. 4, 43. 4) or charges against an official (e.g. if the *prytaneis* put an improper proposal to the vote: 45. 2); *prosklesis* is the prosecutor's summons to a defendant to appear before a magistrate (see Harrison, *L.A.* ii. 85–8). Some decrees contained an 'entrenchment clause' which sought to make repeal harder or impossible, and ἐὰν δέ τις..., below, may be described as 'an entrenchment clause against entrenchment clauses' (cf. D. M. Lewis, in *Φόρος: Tribute to B. D. Meritt* [Locust Valley: Augustin, 1974], 81–9 = his *Selected Papers*, 136–49).

The *syngrapheis*' intention was no doubt to suspend all impediments to the assembly's freedom to decide.

what was laid before them: The matters put forward for discussion: there is no instance in fifth-century Athenian inscriptions, but cf. Ar. *Eccl.* 401; also Hdt. I. 207. 3, Pl. *Grg.* 457 D 4–5, *Lach.* 184 C 8.

on account of this: There is no prepositional use of χάριν in Athenian inscriptions before the Roman period, but it is popular with Plato and Aristotle, and used in *A.P.* 16. 3, 18. 6, 22. 6, 35. 3.

imposed a penalty or made a *prosklesis* or brought a man before a lawcourt: The *prytaneis* could probably impose fines on the spot (cf. the fourth-century laws in Aeschin. I. *Timarchus* 35), a volunteer prosecutor would summon an offender (cf. above), a magistrate accepting a prosecution would introduce the case into court (cf. 56. 6 etc.).

he should be liable to *endeixis* and *apagoge* … the death penalty: For *endeixis* (bringing the authorities to an offender) and *apagoge* (taking an offender to the authorities) and summary punishment of criminals caught *in flagrante delicto* cf. 52. 1. Under the democracy the *strategoi* had judicial responsibilities only in military cases (cf. Harrison, *L.A.* ii. 31–4): their use here perhaps reflects the oligarchs' dislike of salaried civilian officials, perhaps is intended to heighten the sense of crisis.

29. 5. After that they organised the constitution: In 29. 4 and 30. 1 the *syngrapheis* are the subject, but *diatattein* should be used of those competent to decide, in this case the assembly, rather than of those who made the proposal. Probably *A.P.* has written carelessly, and means that the assembly decided on the recommendation of the *syngrapheis*; Thuc. VIII. 67. 2 states emphatically that the *syngrapheis* only withdrew the safeguards and the positive proposals were made by Pisander – but probably he was one of the *syngrapheis* and claimed or implied that he was speaking for all.

A.P. reports the abolition of almost all non-military stipends for the duration of the war, the entrusting of the state to five thousand or more men, empowered to make treaties, and the appointment of a hundred men to register the Five Thousand and (30. 1) a hundred to write up the constitution. Thuc. VIII. 67. 3 reports the abolition of existing offices and stipends, the appointment of five *proedroi* to appoint a hundred men who will coopt a further three hundred, and the institution of these Four Hundred as a council to rule *autokratores* and convene the Five

Thousand when they see fit. Probably both are incomplete accounts of the same set of decisions: *A.P.* omits Thucydides' on-the-spot appointment of the Four Hundred because it conflicts with 31. 1, Thucydides omits the appointment of the Five Thousand because he has already mentioned them in his account of the oligarchs' programme (VIII. 65. 3) and because at this stage their appointment did not take effect (89. 2, 92. 11, 93. 2).

it should not be permitted ... other than the war: Cf. the oligarchs' programme in Thuc. VIII. 65. 3: oligarchs disliked the lower-class civilian participation which civilian stipends facilitated, and after the disaster in Sicily Athens was short of money.

all the officials ... whatever *prytaneis* there might be: Cf. Thuc. VIII. 67. 3. *A.P.*'s qualifications are no doubt a part of what was formally decided: the abolition of stipends was an emergency measure for the duration of the war (cf. Pisander in Thuc. VIII. 53. 3); the nine archons were the formal heads of state, and had been more important in the past to which the oligarchs were appealing (those of 412/1 were probably left in office for what remained of the year); 'whatever *prytaneis* there might be' would be the effective heads of state, the men on full-time duty.

three obols: This was the current rate for jurors, probably raised from 2 ob. in the 420's by Cleon and still paid in the time of *A.P.* (cf. 62. 2); oarsmen were now paid 3 ob. per day but had earlier been paid 1 dr. (cf. p. 264); for the archons and *prytaneis* in the time of *A.P.* se 62. 2.

All the remaining political power ... as long as the war continued: Not directly mentioned by Thucydides (cf. above), but cf. Lys. XX. *Polystratus* 13, 16: this will denote the institution of the Five Thousand as the assembly, the residual sovereign body of the state. Nothing is said about the judiciary: R. W. Brock, *LCM* 13 (1988), 136–8, suggests that the Five Thousand were to be jurors as well as assembly-men.

most able to serve with their bodies and their possessions: Cf. the oligarchs' programme in Thuc. VIII. 65. 3; also Xen. *Hipparch.* 1. 9 and *A.P.* 49. 2 on the cavalry. On the public services called *leitourgiai* see 27. 3, 56. 3, 61. 1. Here the concept of public service is extended; for 'performing *leitourgia*' with one's body cf. Dem. XXI. *Midias* 165, X. *Phil. iv*. 28. The reference must be to men of hoplite status and above (cf. 33. 1 and Thuc. VIII. 97. 1; also the 'constitution of Draco' in 4. 2). It is not clear what the oligarchs' attitude was to men too old to fight: Arist. *Pol.* IV. 1297 B 1–34 shows awareness of that problem; it may have been left unresolved now, but must have been resolved under the intermediate régime which followed.

not fewer than five thousand: Five thousand as a maximum will reflect the oligarchs' ambitions in Thuc. VIII. 65. 3; as a minimum will reflect the formal proposal put to this assembly. The oligarchs alleged that attendance at assemblies was never as high as five thousand (Thuc. VIII. 72. 1): that might have been true after 415, when a substantial proportion of the citizens were first in Sicily, afterwards with the navy at Samos, but it will not have been true that all who were attended were of hoplite status and above. It is hard to estimate the numbers of citizens, above and below the line between hoplites and *thetes*, at particular dates in the war: for an attempt see M. H. Hansen, *Three Studies in Athenian Demography* (Copenhagen: Munksgaard for Royal Danish Academy, 1988), 14–28: he reckons that there were still about 30,000 adult male citizens in 411, and it is not credible that as few as 5,000 would have been above the line.

should have power to make treaties with whoever they wanted: Some may still have been hoping for Persian support (cf. pp. 283–4), others may already have been thinking of making peace with Sparta (cf. 32. 3). If this is an authentic part of what was decided, it confirms that the Five Thousand were intended to function as an assembly: even where little business was referred to an assembly, that business included peace, war and alliances (cf. Arist. *Pol.* IV. 1298 B 5–8).

There should be elected … to register the Five Thousand: Lys. XX. *Polystratus* comprises parts of two speeches in defence of a man who belonged both to the Four Hundred and to the *katalogeis*: he was appointed, apparently to the Four Hundred, by members of his tribe (§2); he served reluctantly as *katalogeus* and registered as many as 9,000 men (§§13–14); after eight days as a member of the Four Hundred he went to Eretria and did not return until after their overthrow (§§14–16). This confirms that *katalogeis* existed early in the régime of the Four Hundred. Altogether we read of three groups of a hundred at this stage: Thucydides' nucleus of the Four Hundred (above), the *katalogeis*, and the *anagrapheis* (30. 1, 32. 1): possibly all three were appointed on the spot at Colonus; some have argued that they were identical in membership (e.g. Busolt, *G.G.* III. ii. 1481–2 n. 1, 1486), but even if that is not true there was probably a considerable overlap. For the minimum age of forty cf. the *syngrapheis* (29. 2).

swearing an oath over full-grown victims: Cf. p. 182, and, e.g., ML 73 = *IG* i³ 78 ~ Fornara 140. 39, Thuc. V. 48. 8. It is not clear whether the oath of Lys. XX. *Polystratus* 14 concerned membership of the Four Hundred or of the *katalogeis*.

30. 1. That, then, is what was drafted by those who had been elected: This implies that the positive proposals, as well as the removal of safeguards, were the work of the *syngrapheis*: cf. p. 287.

When it had been ratified ... to write up the constitution: Cf. 32. 1 *init.* According to Thucydides the proposals at Colonus were ratified without opposition and later the Four Hundred took over the council house without opposition (VIII. 69–70. 1); under this régime the list of the Five Thousand was not completed or published (89. 2, 92. 11, 93. 2; cf. *A.P.* 32. 3). Yet here the *anagrapheis* are appointed by the Five Thousand and in 32. 1 their proposals are ratified by the *plethos*. Some have rejected the *anagrapheis* and their documents altogether (cf. next note); those who are less drastic have resorted to various explanations, of which the best is that they were appointed by the assembly at Colonus and reported shortly afterwards (e.g. Busolt, *G.G.* III. ii. 1486: I suggest that they reported at the formal inauguration of the régime): the assembly decided in principle that there should be a powerful council of Four Hundred and a residual assembly of Five Thousand, and appointed the *katalogeis* to register the Five Thousand and the *anagrapheis* to work out the constitutional details. It was supposed (perhaps officially, at the time) that the body which appointed the *anagrapheis* had been the Five Thousand; almost certainly, in spite of 32. 1, their draft was not approved by any body larger than the Four Hundred.

Anagraphein and *anagrapheus* are normally used of recording what has already been decided (e.g. Lys. XXX. *Nicomachus* 2, 4, ML 86 = *IG* i³ 104 ~ Fornara 15. B.. 4–6), and here we should expect *syngraphein* and *syngrapheus*, as in 29. 2.

those who were elected wrote up and brought forward the following: Some have supposed that the *anagrapheis*, their documents and the ratification of their documents are simply a fraud perpetrated in or soon after 411 to help legitimise the oligarchy (e.g. A. Andrewes, *PCPS*² 22 [1976], 20–1, and in *H.C.T.* v. 242–6: a fraud put about by the Four Hundred). Unless it was the constitution of the intermediate régime (cf. below), the ‘future’ constitution of 30 was never put into effect; the ‘immediate’ constitution of 31 may embody the propaganda of the Four Hundred rather than reflect the facts of their rule. The documents are incoherent and incomplete, and it is hard to decide how much of the fault lies in the original documents and how much in *A.P.*’s condensation of the material.

The ‘immediate’ consitution could be a document issued officially at the beginning of the régime of the Four Hundred, not as a complete instrument of government but as an announcement to the Athenians of how the state was to be run in the short term – essentially, by giving full power to the council and the *strategoi*. Provisions within this for ‘now’ and ‘the future’ could be for the remainder of 412/1 and for 411/0 (for dates see 32. 1–2). V. L. Ehrenberg thought that the ‘immediate’ constituion was Pisander’s proposal at Colonus and the ‘future’ constitution was that put into effect by the intermediate régime (*Hermes* 57 [1922], 613–20 = his *Polis und Imperium* [Zurich & Stuttgart: Artemis, 1965], 315–21): his view of the ‘future’ constitution was popular for a time and more recently has been championed by E. M. Harris, *HSCP* 93 (1990), 243–80, but more probably that was a theorist’s sketch, owing something to the constitutions of the Boeotian cities, and never put into practice. Perhaps, when the *anagrapheis* met, a distinction between ‘moderates’ and ‘extremists’ emerged, and led to the production of the ‘extremist’ constitution for immediate use, while the ‘moderates’ were allowed to outline a constitution for the future; the last sentence of 31. 3 may represent an amendment to the ‘immediate’ constitution by a ‘moderate’, calling on the *katalogeis* to include in their registration a subdivision of the Four Hundred to facilitate the introduction of the ‘future’ constitution in due course.

30. 2. The council year by year: *A.P.* plunges *in medias res*, and we discover only in 30. 3 and 31. 1 that this is a constitution for the future. It must have been assumed that men other than the Five Thousand would be excluded from the council and all offices.

This must be read with the rotation of the ‘four councils’ in 30. 3: the text begins with eligibility for the council, then comes eligibility for various offices, and appointment follows at αἱρεῖσθαι δὲ πάντας…; all who were eligible would serve in the council, but not all in the same year.
those over the age of thirty: This was the age requirement for jurors

under the democracy (63. 2), for councillors under the Thirty (Xen. *Mem.* I. 2. 35), and cf. 4. 3, 31. 1; and probably it was Athens' standard requirement whenever no other requirement was set (cf. forty in 29. 2, 5).
without stipend: Contrast 29. 5, where the abolition of civilian stipends is said to be for the duration of the war.
From these: The contrast with μὴ ἐκ τῆς βουλῆς below indicates that this denotes the (quarter) council currently in office.
the generals: The number is not specified, but ten as under the democracy was probably intended. If they had to be appointed from the current (quarter) council, a man could not hold this or any other major office more than one year in four: that would not make for efficient waging of war, but it was not only democracies which liked offices to rotate among men considered equally eligible, and this is defended as an application of that principle by J. A. O. Larsen, *Representative Government in Greek and Roman History* (Sather Lectures xxviii. U. of California P., 1955), 197 n. 30.
the *hieromnemon*: This was the title of the voting representative sent by Athens to the council of the Delphic Amphictyony (Aeschin. III. *Ctesiphon* 115, Dem. XVIII. *Cor.* 148–9): Arist. *Pol.* VI. 1321 B 34–40 notes that the title is given in some cities to a legal official, but there is no evidence that that was ever true of Athens.
the taxiarchs and hipparchs and phylarchs: The commanders of the tribal regiments of hoplites, the commanders in chief of the cavalry and the commanders of the tribal regiments of cavalry (61. 3–5). Here the hipparchs are plural but the number is not stated, but in 31. 3 there is one; for practice at other times see 61. 4 with commentary.
garrison commanders: At this time the countryside was overrun by the Spartans, and the only garrisons inside Attica can have been inside the fortifications of Athens and Piraeus (for a garrison on the acropolis see 24. 3). However, if there were eight of these commanders and two hipparchs (for two hipparchs cf. 61. 4) the officials here would number 100, which may have been intended.
ten treasurers of the sacred funds of the Goddess and the Other Gods: In Athens Athena is regularly ἡ θεός, so in the absence of certainty θε[ῷ] is the more likely text. For the long-standing board of treasurers of Athena cf. 8. 1; probably in 434/3, other sacred treasuries were combined and entrusted to a board of treasurers of the Other Gods (ML 58 = *IG*

i^3 52 ~ Fornara 119). The amalgamation of those boards, foreshadowed here, occurred at the beginning of 406/5; they were separated again at the beginning of 385/4 (W. S. Ferguson, *The Treasurers of Athena* [Harvard U. P., 1932], 104–6, 14); for their further history see 47. 1 with commentary.

twenty *hellenotamiai* to handle also all the other proper funds: Previously ten *hellenotamiai* had received and disbursed the funds of the Delian League, ten *apodektai* had received (cf. 48. 1–2) and ten *kolakretai* had disbursed (cf. 7. 3) the non-sacred funds of the city; but, while the *apodektai* still existed in the late fifth (ML 91 = *IG* i^3 117 ~ Fornara 161. 6–7, restored) and the fourth century, the *kolakretai* are last attested in 418/7 and probably 413/2 (*IG* i^3 84. 28, 136. 36), and in and after 410 the *hellenotamiai* did number twenty and make payments which would previously have been made by the *kolakretai* (two *hellenotamiai* per tribe in ML 84 = *IG* i^3 375 ~ Fornara 154, payments for inscription in ML 85 = *IG* i^3 102 ~ Fornara 155. 11–12, 35–6, both 410/09). This draft either reflects a change made slightly earlier or proposes a change which the restored democracy accepted. However it came about (see J. H. Blok, cited on 43. 6), the word *hosios* came to be used of public business and funds which were not *hieros*, 'sacred'.

***hieropoioi* and *epimeletai* ten each:** On the titles of religious officials in general see Arist. *Pol.* VI. 1322 B 19–25. Boards of *hieropoioi*, usually ten and often from the council, cooperated with priests in various festivals (for two boards see 54. 6–7); *epimeletes* is a title borne by various officials with religious duties (e.g. 56. 4, 57. 1) and also various with secular duties (e.g. 51. 4). Wilamowitz suggested that it would fit the centralising tendency of this draft if there were only one board of *hieropoioi* and one of (religious) *epimeletai* (*A.u.A.* ii. 120).

All of these should be elected from pre-elected candidates: In contrast with κληρωτὰς below, αἱρεῖσθαι here should mean not merely 'appoint' but specifically 'elect': this is a two-stage procedure with election used at both stages.

pre-electing a larger number from those currently in the council: But the number is not specified, and it is not stated who are to make nominations, elect to the short list or finally appoint. Appointment is to be made from the current (quarter) council, but the division of the qualified citizens into quarters is not expounded until 30. 3.

The *hellenotamiai* ... should not join in deliberation: This is a particularly difficult sentence, apparently meaning that the *hellenotamiai*, though appointed from the current (quarter) council (above), are not to sit with the council – though it is not clear why this should apply to them but not to the other major officials. Some have read οἳ ἂν διαχειρίζουσι τὰ χρήματα as describing the whole board (e.g. U. Kahrstedt, *Forschungen zur Geschichte des ausgehenden V. und des IV. Jahrhunderts* [Berlin: Weidmann, 1910], 251; it was read thus by Harp. ε 40 Keaney ἑλληνοταμίαι), others as defining a section of the board (e.g. Wilamowitz, *A.u.A.* ii. 117 n. 12), but if the text is sound οἱ διαχειριοῦσιν above and the phrase here should both describe the whole board.

30. 3. Four councils should be created ... should serve as council: If the text is sound, it envisages a division of qualified citizens (members of the Five Thousand over thirty years old) into four (quarter) councils, to serve in turn, as in the cities of Boeotia (*Hell. Oxy.* 19. 2 Chambers, cf. the subdivision of the federal council of 660, *Hell. Oxy.* 19. 4 with Thuc. V. 38. 2–4). E. M. Harris argues that for βουλὰς we should read φυλὰς, and that four tribes were to be created, each of which would provide 100 members of a council of four hundred (*HSCP* 93 [1990], 251–5); but it is not clear that this draft envisaged (or that the intermediate régime used) a council of four hundred, and if the oligarchs wanted four tribes they would surely use the four still-existing old tribes (the 'immediate' constitution retains the ten tribes: 31. 1). This is the first indication that we are here in a constitution for the future, and the words presumably are meant to emphasise that the form of government just established is not to be superseded immediately.

The other men also should be distributed to each section: *Lexis* can denote either the process of allotment (e.g. Pl. *Critias* 113 B 8) or what is allotted (e.g. Pl. *Critias* 113 C 1); but here and in 31. 3 we obtain a better sense if we take it to denote the four divisions (e.g. Wilamowitz, *A.u.A.* ii. 116). 'The other men' are perhaps members of the Five Thousand who are not yet aged thirty.

the hundred men should distribute ... and make an allotment: The hundred men are presumably the *katalogeis* of 29. 5 (Wilamowitz, *A.u.A.* ii. 116), and in this sentence 'the others' should be all of the Five Thousand except the *katalogeis*: here the *katalogeis* are to divide into four sections themselves and the rest of the Five Thousand, and in 31. 3 they are to subdivide the Four Hundred (presumably to provide continuity between the 'immediate' and the 'future' constitution). ὡς ἰσαίτατα may mean either 'as equally as possible' (the translation which I give) or, by criteria which are not indicated, 'as fairly as possible'.

the council should serve for a year: Presumably each quarter was to serve for a year (e.g. Busolt, *G.G.* III. ii. 1487).

30. 4. with regard to the funds: Cf. pp. 292–3.

spent on what was necessary: Money is to be spent on what is necessary and not on what is not. Pericles was alleged to have paid 10 tal. to induce the Spartans to withdraw from Attica in 446, and to have included this in his accounts as εἰς τὸ δέον (Ar. *Nub.* 859 with schol., Plut. *Per.* 23. 1–2, cf. Thuc. II. 21. 1).

if they wanted to deliberate … from the same age range: Each member of the current (quarter) council would be able to coopt one further member; but this draft contains no provision for meetings of all four quarters, or of all the Five Thousand including those aged under thirty (contrast the Boeotian cities, *Hell. Oxy.* 19. 2 Chambers).

each member should coopt one coopted member: No other instance is known of the verb or the adjective in the sense 'invite(d) in addition'.

from the same age range: Probably 'with the same age qualification', i.e. over thirty.

hold meetings of the council … unless they needed more: κατὰ πενθήμερον is probably inclusive, i.e. every four days as we should reckon. Probably in the late fifth century as in the fourth, under the democracy the council met every day except holidays and the assembly had forty regular meetings a year (43. 3–6): this body, intermediate in size between the two, is to be intermediate in the frequency of its meetings. Nothing is said of a smaller body which would meet more frequently and be able to deal with urgent business.

30. 5. The council should be convened by the nine archons: (§5 begins here in Kenyon's O.C.T. and Chambers' Teubner ed., but many editions follow the original division of Kaibel & Wilamowitz, in which it begins at κληροῦν δὲ τοὺς λαχόντας, below.) If πληροῦν is right, the archons are to convene (more literally, 'man') the council, as they probably convened the council and assembly in early Athens: for the democracy's practice see 43. 3, 44. 2.

the votes by hand should be judged … to put motions to the vote:

In the time of *A.P.* this duty fell to nine *proedroi*, of whom one was *epistates*; earlier it had been the duty of the fifty *prytaneis*, of whom one was *epistates* (44. 2–3). Thucydides uses *proedroi* of the five men forming the nucleus of the Four Hundred (VIII. 67. 3), but says that the Four Hundred proceeded to appoint *prytaneis* (70. 1); ML 80 = *IG* i^3 98 ~ Fornara 149, apparently a decree either of the régime of the Four Hundred or of the intermediate régime which followed, appears to have an *epistates* with four colleagues whose title is not given. It is best to say that we do not know what the title of these men would have been.

pick by lot those who wanted to appear before the council: It would not seem strange to an Athenian that the topics for debate should be picked by lot. 43. 6 records a quota of topics for certain kinds of debate at certain meetings of the assembly.

first on sacred matters … fourthly on other matters: The same order, but with ὁσίων for the fourth category, is found in Aeschin. I. *Timarchus* 23; the same as in Aeschines, but with κήρυξιν and πρεσβείαις conflated as a single item, in *A.P.* 43. 6. In each case the first and fourth items appear in the genitive but the second and third in the dative: that presumably reflects the democratic law.

on matters of war … without allotment: In [Xen.] *A.P.* 3. 2 περὶ τοῦ πολέμου heads the list of topics debated by the council; Aristotle twice lists περὶ πολέμου καὶ εἰρήνης, without article, among topics for debate (*Pol.* IV. 1298 A 3–7, *Rhet.* I. 1359 B 21–3).. Even with the article the expression can be used generally, as in 58. 1; but in this context, with provision for special access when the generals need it, the reference may be more specifically to the Peloponnesian War. There is some evidence that during the Peloponnesian War the *strategoi* enjoyed a privileged position *vis-à-vis* the council and assembly (Rhodes, *A.B.* 43–6): in this régime they would in any case be members of the council, but what is at issue here is a privileged opportunity to initiate debate.

30. 6. did not go to the council house: Cf. the 'constitution of Draco', 4. 3. Neither the old *bouleuterion*, built in the late sixth or early fifth century, nor the new, built at the end of the fifth century, could easily accommodate a council of about 1,000 members.

the time: This means 'the time' in general, not necessarily 'the hour' (a hellenistic usage) or 'the time of day'.

received leave from the council: We do not know what the procedure would be, or what the procedure was when Polystratus, a member of the Four Hundred, left Athens after eight days (p. 289). *Apheinai* and cognates are used to mean 'release' in various contexts: cf. 43. 3, Dem. XXIV. *Timocrates* 26 (days with no meeting of the council).

31. 1. That is the constitution ... for the time to come, but for the present juncture the following: The two draft constitutions are separated by a sentence in narrative form: if the two were published together, there must have been a corresponding statement in the original, that what precedes was for use in the future and what follows was for use in the immediate crisis.

There should be a council of four hundred in accordance with tradition: For Solon's council of four hundred cf. 8. 4: even if that is not authentic (though I believe it is), it was accepted as authentic in later Athens, and 'in accordance with tradition' is part of the oligarchs' propaganda claim that they were not instituting a dangerous novelty but returning to a better past (cf. p. 286).

forty from each tribe: Cleisthenes' ten tribes are retained: Solon's council comprised 100 men from each of the four old tribes.

from pre-elected candidates ... from those over thirty years old: Cf. 30. 2, in the 'future' constitution. It was perhaps envisaged that this procedure would be used for the council of 411/0 (for the appointment of the original Four Hundred see pp. 287–8), but there seems to have been only one body of Four Hundred, which held office from late 412/1 to early 411/0: possibly they reappointed themselves for the new year; more probably by then they were less interested in a show of legitimacy.

institute the officials: Only the *strategoi* and the other military officials are dealt with in 31. 2–3.

†make a proposal about the oath which was to be sworn†: Presumably an oath taken by the officials, but the formulation of the papyrus' text cannot be right in a sentence which gives the Four Hundred full power. I suggest καὶ τὸν ὅρκον..., 'and they are to draw up the oath which people must swear'.

***euthynai*:** The holding to account of officials retiring from office: for the democratic system see 48. 4–5, 54. 2.

do what they thought advantageous: This gives them full power, and it is no accident that there is no mention of the Five Thousand.

31. 2. The laws which they enacted … or to enact others: The subject should be 'the Athenians' (F. Sartori, *La crisi del 411 a.C. nell'Athenaion Politeia di Aristotele* [Padua: C.E.D.A.M., 1951], 92–3), and 'which they enacted' should cover the laws already enacted and any further laws (supplementary, rather than modificatory); περὶ τῶν πολιτικῶν here must, as in my translation, mean 'about constitutional matters', though the usage is without parallel. If taken seriously, this would make peaceful transition to the 'future' constituion or any other régime impossible.

For now the election of the generals … the Five Thousand: Athens was at war, and could not manage without *strategoi* even for a short period: presumably 'now' is the remainder of 412/1 and 'the incoming year' is 411/0, still seen as falling under this 'immediate' constitution (but A. Andrewes thought the contrast was between the period of the 'immediate' and that of the 'future' constitution: *H.C.T.* v. 230–1). If what is said here is to be taken literally, this régime did not exclude men under thirty from the *strategia*.

when the council had been established: The Four Hundred were probably appointed on the spot at Colonus (cf. pp. 287–8); I argue that they formally inaugurated their rule on 22 Thargelion (the later of the dates in 32. 1), and that these drafts were compiled betwen those two occasions. The drafters are here referring to the installation of the Four Hundred as an event still in the future.

secretary: There is no evidnce for a secretary to the *strategoi* in democratic Athens.

with full power: When men were made *autokratores* they were given the freedom to do a job with less interference or need to secure approval than would otherwise be the case, but as here the extent of that freedom was not always made clear.

31. 3. one hipparch and ten phylarchs: Cf. 30. 2 (where, as under all other régimes, there is a plurality of hipparchs). It is surprising to find no mention of the taxiarchs, and perhaps with Wilamowitz we should insert them.

for the future … what had been written: Presumably, as with the *strategoi*, there was to be an immediate appointment for the remainder of 412/1, followed by a more regular appointment on the same lines as for the *strategoi* for 411/0 (cf. Sartori, *La crisi del 411 a.C.*, 97–8).

For the other officials … more than once: For the democracy's rule, that there was no limit to repetition in military offices, but civilian offices could be held only once except that two years in the council were allowed, see 62. 3. The 'future' constitution limits repetition by requiring appointment from the current (quarter) council (cf. p. 292).

either to these or to anybody else: This, following an exception for the council and *strategoi*, is totally obscure: perhaps the fault lay with *A.P.* in condensing his material.

For the rest of the time: This sentence, with its reference to the four *lexeis*, looks ahead not to 411/0 but to the 'future' constitution (cf. M. Cary, *JHS* 72 [1952], 57): cf. p. 291.

so that the Four Hundred should be distributed into the four sections: If the constitution of 31 were eventually to be succeeded by the constitution of 30, it might be thought desirable, for the sake of continuity (or perhaps to split the Four Hundred), to distribute the Four Hundred through all four *lexeis*, and the purpose of this clause (I suggest, added to the draft by a 'moderate') is apparently to do that as a preparatory measure towards the transition.

when it became possible for them to deliberate with the others: The papyrus' τοῖς ἀστοῖς does not make sense in the circumstances of 411, when all Athenians in Attica were inside the city and subject to the new régime: Sandys' text, referring to the time when 'they' (the Four Hundred) can join 'the rest' (of the Five Thousand) in deliberation, is the best solution.

were to distribute: The change from infinitive to imperative may confirm (but is not enough to prove) that this is an addition to the draft.

the hundred men: The *katalogeis* of 29. 5 (cf. p. 294).

32. 1. That constitution ... the hundred men elected by the Five Thousand: Closing the ring which was opened in 30. 1.

When that had been ratified by the masses, put to the vote by Aristomachus: I have argued that the *anagrapheis* were appointed by the assembly at Colonus and did their work before the formal inauguration of the Four Hundred (p. 290). After Colonus there can have been no assembly open to all whom the democracy regarded as citizens, and Thucydides' narrative makes it very unlikely that there was one even of the the Five Thousand; yet *A.P.*'s naming of the man who put the motion (though that was not the formulation used in fifth-century documents), followed by dates, suggests that his ultimate source was a document. The least difficult explanation is that Aristomachus presided in the assembly at Colonus, and the documents were not approved by any body larger than the Four Hundred (cf. E. Meyer, *Forschungen zur alten Geschichte* [Halle: Niemeyer, 1892/8], ii. 432), or else he presided in the meeting of the Four Hundred which approved them. Aristomachus cannot be identified.

the council of the year of Callias: That of 412/1 (archon Callias of Scambonidae; but another Callias was archon in 406/5: 34. 1). He was probably left in office for the remainder of the year (as perhaps were the treasurers of Athena: ML 81 = *IG* i^3 373 ~ Fornara 150 records expenditure by the treasurers of the early part of 411/0).

without completing its term of office: This use of the active is unique: the middle is used to mean 'debate to the end' (e.g. Thuc. II. 5. 5).

the fourteenth of the month Thargelion: Thargelion was the eleventh month, and this date was approximately 9 June (B. D. Meritt, *The Athenian Year* [Sather Lectures xxxii. U. of California P., 1959], 218). This will be the date of the democratic council's actual dismissal, probably a few days after the assembly at Colonus (A. Andrewes, *PCPS*^{2} 22 [1976], 22–3 with 25 n. 22): for a narrative see Thuc. VIII. 69–70. 1.

the twenty-second of Thargelion: Approximately 17 June (the Athenian calendar divided each month into three decades, and counted days backwards to the end of the month in the last decade). Athens will not have had no government at all after 14 Thargelion, but this will be the date of the Four Hundred's formal entry into office (Thuc. VIII. 70. 1: cf. below on the democratic council's formal entry).

The council appointed by lot ... 14 Scirophorion: The democratic council is thus characterised in Thuc. VIII. 66. 1, 69. 4, and the decree of Demophantus *ap.* Andoc. I. *Myst.* 96 (authenticity challenged by M. Canevaro & E. M. Harris, *CQ*^{2} 62 [2012], 98–129, Harris, *τεκμήρια* 12 [2013–4], 121–53; but defended by A. H. Sommerstein, *CQ*^{2} 64 [2014], 49–57, M. H. Hansen, *GRBS* 55 [2015], 898–901). 14 Scirophorion (xii) in this year was approximately 9 July, and 1 Hecatombaeon (i) 25 July; this is one of the texts which indicate that in the second half of the fifth century (perhaps from Ephialtes' reform in 462/1), perhaps until the democratic restoration in 403, the council worked not to the archon's year of twelve or thirteen lunar months but to a solar year of 366 days (cf. Samuel, *Chronology*, 61–3, and for the date of the change J. D. Morgan *ap.* S. D. Lambert, *Attic Inscriptions Online Papers* [https://www.atticinscriptions.com/papers/] 5 [2014], 3 n. 5).

32. 2. about a hundred years after the expulsion of the tyrants: Cf. Thuc. VIII. 68. 4 (ἔτει ἑκατοστῷ μάλιστα): by the inclusive reckoning appropriate to Thucydides' ordinal numeral 412/1 is exactly the hundredth year after 511/0; *A.P.* has retained μάλιστα while changing to a cardinal numeral.

The men particularly responsible … intelligence and judgment: Cf. Thuc. VIII. 68, placed at the end of his account of the assembly at Colonus: he lists Pisander, Antiphon, Phrynichus and Theramenes, praising the intelligence and oratorical ability of Antiphon and Theramenes in particular and of the revolutionaries in general. *A.P.* is clearly following Thucydides; and, since there is no obvious reason why he should omit Phrynichus, that omission may well be due to a copyist. Thucydides does not say that the leaders were well born: that may be simply an inference by *A.P.*, and in fact, while Theramenes was the son of Hagnon (himself distinguished but without distinguished forebears), none of the others is known to have belonged to a rich or aristocratic family.

Pisander was a member of the council in 416/5 (Andoc. I. *Myst.* 43 with K. J. Dover, *H.C.T.* iv. 273–6); in 415 he was prominent in investigating the religious scandals and attributing them to opponents of the democracy (Andoc. I. *Myst.* 36); in Thucydides' narrative he was the leader of the men who travelled between Samos and Athens and organised the revolution; and in Lys. XXV. *Overthrowing Democracy* 9 Phrynichus and he are the leading *demagogoi* who changed sides and set up the oligarchy. On the fall of the Four Hundred he fled to the Spartans at Decelea (Thuc. VIII. 98. 1), and his property was confiscated (Lys. VII. *Olive Stump* 4).

Antiphon was Athens' first professional orator; whether he was identical with 'Antiphon the sophist' is disputed, but probably he was not (see in favour of the identification M. Gagarin, *Antiphon the Athenian* [U. of Texas P., 2002]; against, G. J. Pendrick, *Antiphon the Sophist* [Cambridge U. P., 2002]). According to Thucydides, while Pisander was the most conspicuous Antiphon was active in the background; he and Phrynichus were the most prominent of those who tried to make peace with Sparta (Thuc. VIII. 90. 2); on the fall of the Four Hundred he stayed in Athens but was brought to trial, condemned and executed (Craterus *FGrH* 342 F 5 *ap.* Harp. α 133 Keaney Ἄνδρων, [Plut.] *X Or.* 833 D – 834 B), and Thucydides and others knew and admired his speech in his defence (cf. p. 13).

Phrynichus is alleged to have come from a poor family and to have become a *sykophantes*, a habitual prosecutor (Lys. XX. *Polystratus* 11–12); it is probably he who is linked with Antiphon in a list in Ar. *Vesp.* 1301–2. He was a *strategos* in 412/1, opposed to the revolution while Alcibiades was associated with it but in favour when he was not (Thuc. VIII. 48–51, 54. 3, 68. 3). After the failure of the attempt to make peace with Sparta (cf. above) he was murdered, but later he was judged to be a traitor and those involved in his murder were honoured (Thuc. VIII. 92. 2, Lys. XIII. *Agoratus* 71–6, ML 85 = *IG* i³ 102 ~ Fornara 155, Lyc. *Leocr.* 112–5).

On Theramenes cf. pp. 279, 281. Although his aims were different from those of the extremists, and he helped to overthrow the régime which he had helped to set up (cf. 33. 2), it seems clear that the difference between them did not become apparent until after the institution of the Four Hundred.

32. 3. the Five Thousand were elected only in name: Thuc. VIII. 92. 11, 93. 2, cf. 89. 2, makes it clear that the list of the Five Thousand was never completed or published; this passage, 33. 2, and Lys. XX. *Polystratus* 13, XXX. *Nicomachus* 8, are compatible with that; for the claim that the *anagrapheis* who produced the drafts of 30–1 were appointed by the Five Thousand see p. 290 (but A. Andrewes thought that *A.P.* wrongly believed that the Five Thousand did exist: *H.C.T.* v. 238–9).

the ten men with full power: The generals (cf. 31. 2).

were inaugurated in the council house and began ruling the city: Cf. Thuc. VIII. 70. 1.

they sent envoys to Sparta: For a detailed account see Thuc. VIII. 70. 2–71, 86. 9, 90. 2, 91. 1.

on the basis of what each side possessed … their rule of the sea: This does not correspond to anything in Thucydides' narrative: in VIII. 90. 2, 91. 1. He suggests that the extremists were willing to make peace on whatever terms they could obtain; this stage in the negotiations may be authentic, and those who were later brought to trial would no doubt have insisted (whether truthfully or not) that they would not have accepted terms detrimental to Athens' interests. J. M. Moore, *Aristotle and Xenophon on Democracy and Oligarchy* (London: Chatto & Windus, [2]1983), 265, suggests that the negotiations failed because the oligarchs could not answer for the fleet at Samos.

33. 1. about four months: Repeated by Harp. τ 6 Keaney τετρακόσιοι. If they ruled for two months of 411/0 (below), their rule in fact spanned three and a half months.

Mnasilochus was archon for two months in the archonship of Theopompus: Callias was probably allowed to serve to the end of 412/1 (cf. on 32. 1), but on the fall of the Four Hundred Mnasilochus was replaced by Theopompus, who came to be regarded officially as the archon of 411/0 (cf. Diod. Sic. XIII. 38. 1). Mnasilochus is presumably the Mnesilochus who was a member of the Thirty (Xen. *Hell.* II. 3. 2).

defeated in the battle near Eretria: For a detailed account see Thuc. VIII. 91. 2–96.

the whole of Euboea had defected apart from Oreus: Cf. Thuc. VIII. 95. 7. Oreus, earlier known as Hestiaea, was at the north end of Euboea, and had been occupied by Athenian cleruchs since 446 (Thuc. I. 114. 3).

they were dejected at this disaster to a greater extent than at what had gone before: Cf. Thuc. VIII. 96. 1.

for they happened to be deriving more benefit from Euboea than from Attica: Cf. Thuc. VIII. 96. 2; also II. 14, VII. 28. 1. The Spartan occupation of Decelea in Attica, from 413 onwards (cf. p. 283), made Athens more dependent than ever on friendly territory which could be reached by sea.

they overthrew the Four Hundred … the hoplite qualification: Cf. Thuc. VIII. 97. 1 (the decision was formally taken at an assembly on the Pnyx, the democracy's assembly-place). For the Five Thousand as men of hoplite status and above cf. p. 288; no more is heard of rhe *katalogeis*, and we are not told whether a list was now produced or those who claimed to belong to the Five Thousand were simply accepted as members of the Five Thousand.

Thuc. VIII. 97. 2 mentions many other assemblies and the appointment of *nomothetai*, but neither he nor *A.P.* (nor Diod. Sic. XIII. 38. 1) gives details of the organisation of the state under this intermediate régime. The documents of Craterus *FGrH* 342 F 5b *ap.* [Plut.] *X Or.* 833 D – 834 B reveal a council divided into prytanies, with a secretary and an *epistates* who could belong to the same tribe (as they could not in the democracy of the late fifth and early fourth centuries), *strategoi*, a *dikasterion* and *thesmothetai* to organise it, the Eleven (cf. 52. 1) and demarchs. ML 80 = *IG* i^{3} 98 ~ Fornara 149 perhaps belongs to the régime of the Four Hundred rather than to this régime (cf. p. 296). The decree of 410/09 *ap.* Andoc. I. *Myst.* 96 (on its authenticity see above, p. 300) refers emphatically to 'the council of five hundred appointed by lot', and we may guess that under this régime the council was of five hundred but elected. It has usually been believed that 'entrusted their affairs' means that an assembly of the Five Thousand became the effective sovereign body in the state: G. E. M. de Ste. Croix argued that the assembly and lawcourts of the democracy were restored and only the right to hold office was limited to the Five Thousand (*Historia* 5 [1956], 1–23); I have defended the usual view (*JHS* 92 [1972], 115–27); and in fact *thetes* were excluded from offices in the fifth century even under the democracy. The rule of the Four Hundred had become unpopular not because they came from a limited class but because they seized unlimited power for themselves.

decreeing that no office should attract a stipend: Cf. Thuc. VIII. 97. 1: this was a reaffirmation of one of the decisions taken at Colonus (29. 5).

33. 2. The men most responsible for the overthrow were Aristocrates and Theramenes: Cf. Thuc. VIII. 89. 2, 91–2 (Theramenes, Aristocrates and others); also Lys. XII. *Eratosthenes* 66–7 (when Theramenes lost influence among the oligarchs he decided to cooperate with Aristocrates), Diod. Sic. XIII. 38. 2 (naming only Theramenes). Aristocrates son of Scellias was from a family prominent over several generations (cf. Davies, *A.P.F.* 56–7): he swore to the Peace of Nicias and the alliance with Sparta in 421 (Thuc. V. 19. 2, 24); he was *strategos* in 413/2 (VIII. 9. 2), taxiarch under the Four Hundred (VIII. 92. 4), *strategos* with the fleet in and after 410 (ML 84 = *IG* i^{3} 375 ~ Fornara 154. 35), and in 407/6 and 406/5 (Xen. *Hell.* I. 4. 21, 5. 16) when Theramenes was not; and he was one of the *strategoi* condemned after the attle of Arginusae (Xen. *Hell.* I. 7. 2: cf. *A.P.* 34. 1).

A.P. does not name the leaders of the extremists at this stage: Thuc. VIII. 90. 1 names Phrynichus, Aristarchus, Pisander and Antiphon; Xen. *Hell.* II. 3. 46 names Aristoteles (a member of the Thirty), Melanthius and Aristarchus.

not satisfied … referred nothing to the Five Thousand: According to Thuc. VIII. 89. 2–4 they expressed alarm over Alcibiades and the fleet, and the negotiations with Sparta, and demanded the disclosure of the Five Thousand and a fairer constitution, but were really motivated by ambition and a sense that the extreme oligarchy would fail: the Four Hundred offered discussion, but as the Peloponnesian fleet approached no discussions were held. *A.P.*'s acceptance of the dissidents' professed reason need not imply conscious disagreement with Thucydides, and what he says about the Five Thousand need not imply a belief that the list had been published.

Their political affairs seem to have been run well … based on the hoplites: Cf. Thuc. VIII. 97. 2 (praising a 'reasonable mixture with regard to the few and the many'). Here as elsewhere the favourable verdict is not original to *A.P.* but is repeated (in this case with a different slant) from a source with which he found himself in agreement (cf. Introduction, p. 11). The meaning of Thucydides' judgment need not be discussed here. *A.P.*'s explanation is clear: it was good to limit political rights to men of hoplite status and above in time of war, when the safety of the state depended on its soldiers (the importance of the navy is conveniently ignored) and there was no money for civilian stipends.

34. 1. The *demos*, then, soon deprived these of their political control: This is best seen as an allusion to the replacement of the intermediate régime ('these' will be the Five Thousand, or, less probably, Aristocrates and Theramenes) by the full democracy (which *A.P.* otherwise omits here (41. 2 mentions the Four Hundred and then the democracy, but not the intermediate régime). However, von Fritz & Kapp, 180–1 n. 117, argued that this is a resumption of the overthrow of the Four Hundred in 33. 1, and does not refer to the later ending of the intermediate régime.

Thucydides' narrative ends in autumn 411, and there is no mention of the democratic restoration in Xen. *Hell.* or Diod. Sic. The best evidence for the change is the decree of Demophantus *ap.* Andoc. I. *Myst.* 96–8, dated to the first prytany of 410/09 (on its authenticity see above, p. 300), and probably what prompted the change was the victory of the fleet over the Spartans in the battle of Cyzicus (Xen. *Hell.* I. 1. 11–21, Diod. Sic. XIII. 49–51). B. D. Meritt argued from the financial records of 410/09 that the council's year began artificially early, before the archon's year, and marked a new start under the democracy (ML 84 = *IG* i³ 375 ~ Fornara 154, with *Athenian Financial Documents of the Fifth Century* [U. of Michigan P., 1932], 105–7, and most recently *PAPS* 122 [1978], 289–90), which may be true but the basis of his argument was insecure.

J. The Thirty and the Ten (34–41. 1)

34. 1–2 provides a brief and inaccurate bridge between 411–410 and 404–403 – perhaps, even for the dates, based not on a written source but on what the author thought he knew. One item which could have been included but is not is the beginning in 410 of a recodification of Athens' laws (cf. pp. 315–6).

On 404–403 we have some information in speeches (especially Lys. XII. *Eratosthenes*, XIII. *Agoratus*, Isoc. XVIII. *Callimachus*), one allusion in Arist. *Pol.* (see p. 311), and four narratives: Xen. *Hell.* III. 3. 11–4. 43; Diod. Sic. XIV. 3–6, 32–3; Just. V. 8. 5–10. 11; *A.P.* 34–40 (see table in Rhodes, *Comm. Ath. Pol.*, 416–9). Diod. Sic. and Justin are sufficiently similar to make it likely that both are derived ultimately from Ephorus, so in essence we have three narratives (arguments that one was derived from another are various but unconvincing). Xenophon wrote from first-hand knowledge, and his order of events is commonly believed to be correct (e.g. Hignett, *Constitution*, 384–9; but *A.P.*'s order is preferred by Krentz, *Thirty*, 131–52). However, the Ephoran version postpones the attack on metics to after Theramenes' death, and postpones the expulsion from the city of the citizens not included in the privileged category of the Three Thousand to after Thrasybulus' occupation of Phyle; and *A.P.* disagrees with the consensus of the others in placing Thrasybulus' occupation of Phyle, the killing of Theramenes, the disarming of the unprivileged (omitted by Diodorus and Justin) and the arrival of the Spartan garrison in that order, which is the reverse of theirs. The Ephoran version is favourable to Theramenes, and *A.P.* is more so, with most of the outrages of the Thirty placed after his death (but the point is lost in *A.P.*'s presentation of the narrative, since he does not admit that Theramenes was one of the Thirty). Among the other peculiarities in *A.P.*'s account is his having two successive boards of Ten after the deposition of the Thirty (38), apparently a device to protect the reputation of Rhinon. One man conspicuously absent from *A.P.*'s account is Critias, an absence which perhaps reflects the influence of Critias' relative Plato (cf. pp. 310–1).

To set against the distortions, some of the material in *A.P.*'s account suggests a documentary origin, but we have few fragments from the *Atthides* on this period and cannot identify a source. In spite of the amnesty of 403, what a man had done in this period was often mentioned in lawsuits of the next twenty years, and there were probably several pamphlets also. There will have been ample material available to *A.P.*, but there is little to suggest that he has uneasily combined conflicting sources.

34. 1. The *demos*, then, soon deprived these of their political control: On this sentence see p. 305.

In the seventh year … in the archonship of Callias of Angele: Callias is given his demotic to distinguish him from the archon of 412/1 (32. 1). The year of his archonship and of the battle of Arginusae was 406/5 (Diod. Sic. XIII. 80. 1, *Marm. Par. FGrH* 239 A 64), the sixth year from 411/0 by inclusive counting; but the inaccurate note which follows may have been written from memory, and this error may be due to *A.P.* rather than a copyist.

the naval battle at Arginusae occurred: For the battle, in which an Athenian reserve fleet defeated the Spartan Callicratidas but owing to bad weather did not afterwards pick up survivors or corpses, and for the repercussions in Athens, see Xen. *Hell.* I. 6. 25–7, Diod. Sic. XIII. 98–103. 2, and P. Cloché, *RH* 130 (1919), 5–68, A. Andrewes, *Phoenix* 28 (1974), 112–22. The fact that Socrates was one of the *prytaneis* who tried to enforce lawful procedure in the assembly added to the notoriety of the episode.

first, that the ten generals … on another man's ship: In fact eight *strategoi* fought at Arginusae, and of them six returned to Athens and were put to death, and two did not return and were condemned in absence: the error appears also in Plat. *Ap.* 32 B 2–3 and some later texts. χειροτονίᾳ probably means 'vote' without implications for the means of voting: according to Xenophon the first votes were taken by show of hands but the final condemnation was by ballot (*Hell.* I. 7. 9, 34).

the *demos* was deceived by those who inflamed its anger: In Xenophon's account the condemnation results from a malicious attack by Theramenes; in Diodorus' preferable version it results from a more innocent misunderstanding. Subsequently Callixenus, who had proposed the condemnation, and four others were charged with *apate* ('deceit') and arrested, but in the turmoil at the end of the war they were not brought to trial (Xen. *Hell.* I. 7. 35, Diod. Sic. XIII. 103. 1–2). In both of the episodes here the *demos* was deceived, and in 29. 1 and 34. 3 the *demos* was 'compelled' to set up the oligarchic régimes: it suited oligarchs to stress that their régimes had been instituted by the *demos*, and it suited democrats to claim that the *demos* went astray only because it was led astray.

the Spartans were willing to withdraw from Decelea: Peace offers by Sparta are recorded after Cyzicus by Diod. Sic. XIII. 52–3 and in 411/0 by Philoch. *FGrH* 328 F 139 (both attributing the rejection to Cleophon), in 408/7 by Androtion *FGrH* 324 F 44 ~ Fornara 157 (resulting in an exchange of prisoners), after Arginusae by *A.P.* and schol. Ar. *Ran.* 1532 (derived from *A.P.*), and without context by Aeschin. II. *F.L.* 76 (attributing the rejection to Cleophon: his threat is most appropriate after Aegospotami); and Cleophon was opposed to peace after Athens' defeat at Aegospotami (Lys. XIII. *Agoratus* 5–12 cf. XXX. *Nicomachus* 10–13). Cyzicus is more likely to have prompted Sparta to offer peace than Arginusae, and probably *A.P.* has misdated the offer of Diodorus and Philochorus (not following a different source or trying to make a point, but simply recording what he thought he knew). For Sparta's occupation of Decelea, at the southern end of a pass through Parnes, from 413 to the end of the war see Thuc. VII. 19. 1–2, Xen. *Hell.* II. 3. 3, and for its effects on Athens Thuc. VII. 27–8, *Hell. Oxy.* 20. 3–5 Chambers.

make peace on the condition that each side should possess what it currently had: Diodorus mentions retaining cities, closing guard-posts (presumably Pylos and Decelea) and exchanging prisoners; Aeschines, less credibly, that Athens should retain Lemnos, Imbros and Scyros (which probably first became an issue in 392) and should live under democracy in accordance with the laws (presumably invented after the peace was in fact followed by the ending of the democracy).

the masses refused it, since they were deceived by Cleophon: For the deceit cf. above (and, in this case, Diodorus); on Cleophon see p. 279.

going into the assembly drunk and wearing a breastplate: Found only in *A.P.* The verb θωρήσσεσθαι seems sometimes to mean 'fortify oneself with drink', but here the literal meaning is appropriate: Wilamowitz thought this detail was due to an eye-witness (*A.u.A.* i. 130 n. 15), but it could easily be an embellishment.

unless the Spartans relinquished all the cities: This is appropriate only after Aegospotami: before then the cities were in theory voluntarily supporting a Sparta which proposed to free them from Athens.

34. 2. They did not manage affairs well … recognised their error: Cf. Diod. Sic. XIII. 53. 3–4, Aeschin. II. *F.L.* 76–7.

in the next year, in the archonship of Alexias: 405/4 (cf. Diod. Sic. XIII. 104. 1).

they failed in the naval battle at Aegospotami: See Xen. *Hell.* II. 1. 20–32, Diod. Sic. XIII. 105. 2–106. 7, Plut. *Alc.* 36. 6–37. 5, *Lys.* 9. 6–13.

Lysander gained power over the city: After Athens had accepted Sparta's peace terms the Spartan commander Lysander entered the city (Xen. *Hell.* II. 3. 22–3, Lys. XIII. *Agoratus* 34: Plut. *Lys.* 15. 1 dates this 16 Munichion [x], *c.* late April); if he then went to Samos (Lys. XII. *Eratosthenes* 71–2, Diod. Sic. XIV. 3. 4), he returned to Athens before the institution of the Thirty (34. 3).

34. 3. Peace was made for them … the traditional constitution: This requirement is absent from what seem to be the best-informed accounts of the terms (Xen. *Hell.* II. 2. 20, Diod. Sic. XIII. 107. 4, Andoc. III. *De Pace* 11–12, Plut. *Lys.* 14. 8), but is included in Diod. Sic. XIV. 3. 2 cf. 6, Just. V. 8. 5); Lys. XII. *Eratosthenes* 70 is not evidence for a clause in the treaty. After the democracy had lost the war and Theramenes had played a large part in negotiating the peace, it was very likely that the democracy would collapse, and Lysander's presence when the Thirty were instituted would have encouraged the view that there was a formal requirement, but probably there was not. However, the different invocations of the *patrios politeia* ('traditional constitution': cf. p. 286) point to a contemporary dispute, and as Fuks suggested (*The Ancestral Constitution* [London: Routledge, 1953], 52–63) the treaty could have contained a clause such as Ἀθηναίους εἶναι αὐτονόμους κατὰ τὰ πάτρια ('the Athenians shall be autonomous in accordance with tradition'), which was not intended to refer to the constitution but was exploited as if it did.

The democrats … those of the notables in the clubs … those who were not involved in any of the clubs…: For *A.P.*'s polarisation cf. especially 2. 1, 28. 2–3. Diod. Sic. XIV. 3. 3 has a twofold division in which each party invokes a form of *patrios politeia*; the interpolator of

Xen. *Hell.* II. 3. 2 has the Thirty appointed 'to draft the traditional laws;. *A.P.* subdivides the *gnorimoi* and makes the *patrios politeia* the objective of Theramenes and his supporters, intermediate between oligarchy and democracy; and Lys. XII. *Eratosthenes* 75–6 makes the Thirty comprise three groups of ten, one group nominated by Theramenes, one by the five 'ephors' (agents of the oligarchic *hetaireiai*) and one chosen from those present (perhaps falsely supposed to represent democrats). Presumably oligarchs, of one kind or more, first claimed as in 411 that they wanted a return to the *patrios politeia*, and democrats responded by claiming that Athens' *patrios politeia* was democracy.

The democrats were trying to save the *demos*: Lys. XIII. *Agoratus*, esp. 15–43, reports a democratic conspiracy, which seems in fact to have been formed and betrayed between the acceptance of the peace terms and the overthrow of the democracy, but whose participants were condemned under the Thirty (cf. Busolt, *G.G.* III. ii. 1637 n. 1). *A.P.* does not name any leaders of the 'democrats' or 'oligarchs': the leading democrats are likely to have been men put to death by the Thirty.

those of the notables in the clubs: Cf. Lys. XII. *Eratosthenes* 43–4. On *hetaireiai* in the late fifth century, associations of upper-class young men which could have a political dimension, see Andoc. I. *Myst.* 49, 54, 61–2, 67 (415), Thuc. VIII. 54. 4, 65. 2 (411), and G. M. Calhoun, *Athenian Clubs in Politics and Litigation* (U. of Texas P., 1913), F. Sartori, *Le eterie nella vita politica ateniese del VI e V secolo a.C.* (Rome: L' Erma di Bretschneider, 1957).

In Xenophon's and Diodorus' accounts the leader of the extreme oligarchs is Critias, related tenuously to Solon and more securely to Plato and to Andocides (cf. Davies, *A.P.F.* 322–35). There is no good evidence for his involvement in the régime of the Four Hundred; either under the intermediate régime or under the restored democracy he proposed the posthumous trial of Phrynichus (Lyc. *Leocr.* 113), under the democracy he proposed the recall of Alcibiades (Plut. *Alc.* 33. 1); but when Alcibiades withdrew into exile again after Notium Critias was exiled on the prosecution of Cleophon and became involved in a democratic movement in Thessaly (Xen. *Hell.* II. 3. 36, cf. *Mem.* I. 2. 24). He was among the exiles who returned to Athens in 404, was one of the five 'ephors' (Lys. XII. *Eratosthenes* 43) and became one of the Thirty. He notoriously clashed with Theramenes (cf. 37. 1), but was killed in the battle of 38. 1; his cousin Charmides was one of the Piraeus Ten (cf. 35. 1). *A.P.* never mentions him; the only allusion to the Thirty in Arist. *Pol.* (V. 1305 B 22–7) mentions Charicles as using demagogic methods within the Thirty as Phrynichus had done within the Four Hundred; and the connection with Plato may be responsible for the silence on Critias of the Aristotelian school. Charicles was a democrat with Pisander in 415 (Andoc. I. *Myst.* 36) and a *strategos* in 414/3 (Thuc. VII. 20. 1, 26. 1); probably a member of the Four Hundred and exiled on their downfall (Isoc. XVI. *De Bigis* 42 with MacDowell on Andoc. I. 36); a member of the Thirty, and mentioned with Critias by Lys. XII. *Eratosthenes* 55.

those of the exiles who had returned after the peace: At the beginning of 405 Aristophanes had urged the reinstatement of the *atimoi* (*Ran.* 686–705), and that was done after Aegospotami (Andoc. I. *Myst.* 73–9); the return of exiles was stipulated in the peace terms (Xen. *Hell.* II. 2. 20, Plut. *Lys.* 14. 8, Andoc. III. *De Pace* 12).

those who were not involved in any of the clubs: Cf. Socrates' claim to have taken no part in *synomosiai* and *staseis* (Pl. *Ap.* 36 B 8–9). It is unlikely that every *hetaireia* was implicated with extreme oligarchy, but Lys. XII. *Eratosthenes* 43–7 with 76 confirms that some were, and the attempt to separate Theramenes from the extremists leads to a separation of him from the *hetaireiai*.

who otherwise seemed not to be inferior to any of the citizens: It is not made clear in what respect they seemed inferior to none.

Archinus: Before 405 he had combined with Agyrrhius (cf. 41. 3) to reduce the payments made to comic poets (Ar. *Ran.* 367 with schol.); he was not a member of the Thirty, but was with Thrasybulus at Phyle (Dem. XXIV. *Timocrates* 135, Aeschin. III. *Ctesiphon* 187, 195), and in 40. 1–2 he is praised for his moderation after the restoration of the democracy.

Anytus: Cf. 27. 5. He too was not a member of the Thirty but was with Thrasybulus at Phyle (Xen. *Hell.* II. 3. 42, 44, Lys. XIII. *Agoratus* 78, 82), and was influential at the restoration of the democracy (Isoc. XVIII. *Callimachus* 23, Pl. *Men.* 90 B 2–3). He was a defender of Andocides in 400 (Andoc. I. *Myst.* 150) and a prosecutor of Socrates in 399 (e.g. Pl. *Ap.* 23 E 3–24 A 1), and an associate of Thrasybulus in 396 (*Hell. Oxy.* 9. 2 Chambers); but he ended his life in exile in Heraclea Pontica (Diog. Laert. II. 43).

Cleitophon: Cf. 29. 3. He was not a member of the Thirty; nothing is known of him later.
Phormisius: In Ar. *Ran.* he is a disciple of Aeschylus whereas Theramenes and Cleitophon are disciples of Euripides. He was not a member of the Thirty, but was one of the returning democrats though presumably not at Phyle (Dion. Hal. 526 / *Lys.* 32); after the restoration he proposed that citizenship should be limited to men who owned some land, Lys. XXXIV. *Traditional Constitution* was written in opposition and the proposal failed. His later career included an embassy to Persia on which he was accused of taking bribes (Pl. Com. frs. 127–30 Kassel & Austin, Plut. *Pelop.* 30. 12, Ath. VI. 251 A–B) and support for Thebes when it was occupied by Sparta in 382 (Din. I. *Demosthenes* 38–40).

Theramenes' alleged supporters are a surprising set of men: none was a member of the Thirty, though ten of the Thirty are said to have been nominated by Theramenes (p. 310); and three were returning democrats, two of them men of Phyle, though none was vindictively anti-oligarchic. It is possible that they were associated with Theramenes before the institution of the Thirty, but defenders of Theramenes afterwards might have wrongly linked him with men who honourably survived 404–403. It is unfortunate that we do not know whether this information is true, or where *A.P.* obtained it.
Theramenes: Cf. 28. 3–5 (Theramenes the last *prostates* of the upper class), 32.3, 33. 2 (411–410). In 404 as in 411 he helped to overthrow the democracy but found the resulting oligarchy too extreme for his tastes, but *A.P.* by distinguishing between oligarchs and supporters of the *patrios politeia* and by not mentioning that he was one of the Thirty minimises his responsibility. Diod. Sic. XIV. 4. 1 alleges that he was elected to the Thirty to counteract the influence of the extremists.
When Lysander gave his support … to vote for the oligarchy: Xen. *Hell.* II. 3. 11 reports the appontment of the Thirty laconically, with no mention of Lysander or any other individual. Diod. Sic. XIV. 3. 2–7 places Theramenes on the democratic side of his twofold division: as the dispute progressed the oligarchs summoned Lysander from Samos, and at an assembly Lysander spoke for oligarchy and Theramenes against; Lysander claimed that by not demolishing their fortifications in time the Athenians were in breach of the treaty, and Theramenes and the *demos* were compelled to overthrow the democracy. In Lys. XII. *Eratosthenes*

71–7 (claiming the support of Theramenes' own defence) Theramenes summoned Lysander, Theramenes spoke for oligarchy, Lysander supported him and claimed that the Athenians were in breach of the treaty, and no opposition was expressed. Lysias is seeking to show that a man who supported Theramenes was still a supporter of oligarchy, but probably on this matter he is correct and Diodorus and *A.P.* have both distorted the truth to conceal Theramenes' responsibility.

the *demos* was terrified and was compelled to vote for the oligarchy: Cf. Diod. Sic. XIV. 3. 7, and on 411 *A.P.* 29. 1. Probably as in 411 (29. 4) safeguards against bad decision-making were suspended.

the proposer of the decree was Dracontides of Aphidna: Cited by schol. Ar. *Vesp.* 157, and for the information cf. Lys. XII. *Eratosthenes* 73. For the naming of the proposer cf. 29. 1 (411), likewise with demotic. Dracontides was a member of the Thirty, but is not necessarily the Dracontides of Ar. *Vesp.* 157, 438. According to Lysias the city was to be entrusted to thirty men and to use the constitution indicated by Dracontides; in Xen. *Hell.* II. 3. 11 cf. 2 the Thirty were to draft laws for the constitution; in Diod. Sic. XIV. 3. 7–4. 1 they were to administer the city, appoint a council and other officials and draft laws for the constitution, and that is probably right: they were to draft a new constitution and to act as a provisional government until that could be brought into being.

The Thirty are listed in Xen. *Hell.* II. 3. 2 (which is interpolated but seems to be correct); Lys. XIII. *Agor.* 74 alleges that all were members of the Four Hundred who had been exiled, which is untrue at any rate of Theramenes. R. Loeper, in an article published in Russian in 1896, argued that they were three from each tribe and one from each *trittys*, listed in official tribal order; D. Whitehead has shown that at any rate they were not one from each *trittys*, and has suggested that they were not even three from each tribe, though the list may yet have been arranged in tribal order (*JHS* 100 [1980], 208–13); but at a time when a façade of regularity was being maintained three from each tribe is possible, and (if plotters had lists prepared) is compatible with Lysias' three groups of ten. Some, noting the five 'ephors' (cf. p. 310), have argued that the Thirty were intended to echo the Spartan *gerousia* (e.g. Krentz, *Thirty*, 63–8), but the thirty *syngrapheis* of 411 (29. 2) are a sufficient explanation of the number. The later Ten were one from each tribe (p. 322).

35. 1. That is the way in which the Thirty were installed: Closing a ring opened at the end of 34. 2; but, perhaps by condensing his material, *A.P.* has said nothing directly about the Thirty.

in the archonship of Pythodorus: 404/3 (Pythodorus is possibly but not necessarily the Pythodorus of 29. 1). Cf. 41. 1, Lys. VII. *Olive Stump* 9, and some inscriptions; but according to Xen. *Hell.* II. 3. 1 (interpolated) and Diod. Sic. XIV. 3. 1 the year was later deemed to be one of *anarchia*. Lysander's entry into Athens on 16 Munichion (x) (p. 309) would allow the appointment of the Thirty to fall either in late 405/4 (implied by Xenophon's interpolator) or in early 404/3 (implied by *A.P.*). How long the demolition of the fortifications (Xen. *Hell.* II. 3. 11) took is uncertain, but no other text indicates appointment in 405/4; on the other hand, arguments for placing the appointment as late as the autumn are unconvincing (cf. p. 325). R. Stem (*Phoenix* 57 [2003], 18–34) has revised a suggestion of J. A. R. Munro that a board of thirty *syngrapheis* was originally appointed in the spring, but when it failed to reach conclusions Lysander was brought to Athens in the autumn and refashioned it as a board of thirty oligarchs; but that is not the best way to handle the conflicting evidence. Probably in the uncertainty the democracy had not appointed an archon for 404/3 but Alexias continued in office; the Thirty were appointed early in 404/3, and they appointed Pythodorus as archon as they appointed a council and other officials (cf. Hignett, *Constitution*, 378–83).

they overlooked the other decisions … about the constitution: Xen. *Hell.* II. 3. 11 and Diod. Sic. XIV. 4. 2 both write of their procrastinating; for one innovation see 37. 1; for the Thirty's terms of reference see p. 313.

appointed five hundred councillors and the other officials: Cf. Xenophon and Diodorus. Only *A.P.* says that the council was of five hundred, but that need not be doubted. Lys. XIII. *Agoratus* 20 says that the previous year's council was corrupted and oligarchic, and many of its members served again this year; the Thirty will not have felt bound by the democracy's rules about reappointment.

from a thousand pre-elected men: If the papyrus' text were correct, it would imply a well-known or previously-mentioned body of men: Herwerden's deletion of ἐκ τῶν is the best solution.

ten governors of the Piraeus: Cf. Pl. *Ep.* VII. 324 c 3–5, Plut. *Lys.* 15. 1; one of them was Charmides, related to Critias and Plato (Pl. *Chrm.*

154 B 1–2, Xen. *Hell.* II. 4. 19). They seem to have been the deputies of the Thirty in the Piraeus (Plato regards them as comparable to the Eleven in Athens), and they were among those excluded from the amnesty of 403 (39. 6).

eleven guards of the prison: Cf. Xen. *Hell.* II. 3. 54, Pl. *Ep.* VII. 324 C 3–5, and for the Eleven under the democracy 24. 3, 52. 1. These too were excluded from the amnesty.

three hundred attendants armed with whips: These are the *hyperetai* who took Theramenes to his death (Xen. *Hell.* II. 3. 23, 54–5 [armed with daggers], Diod. Sic. XIV. 5. 1 [but *stratiotai* in 4. 6]), and perhaps the *tria milia ... satellitum* of Just. V. 8. 10–11: we do not know what their status was or how they were recruited.

35. 2. At first they were moderate towards the citizens: Cf. Diod. Sic. XIV. 4. 2.

pretended that their goal was the traditional constitution: Schol. Aeschin. I. *Timarchus* 39 (82 Dilts) says that they abolished the *patrios politeia* and defiled the laws of Draco and Solon. What *A.P.* says here is hard to reconcile with 34. 3 (linking the *patrios politeia* with Theramenes) and 35. 1 (neglect of the Thirty's duty to draft a constitution); but, since the mild beginning of the régime was too well known to be suppressed, it is represented as a pretence.

They took down ... the laws of Ephialtes and Archestratus about the Areopagites: Cf. 25 (Ephialtes) and 27. 1 (Pericles): no other text mentions an Archestratus in this connection, and the man cannot be identified, but there is no reason to suspect invention here. The laws were annulled by the physical removal from the Areopagus of the *stelai* on which they were inscribed (cf. *IG* ii² 43. *A.* = RO 22 ~ Harding 35. 31–5, and for the placing at the Areopagus of laws affecting the Areopagus RO 79 = *IG* ii³ 320 ~ Harding 101. 22–7).

they cancelled those laws of Solon which contained scope for disputes: For the democratic viewpoint of schol. Aeschin. see above. The *axones* containing Solon's laws were now housed in the Stoa of the *Basileus* (cf. 7. 1 with commentary), and although the Thirty were willing to modify the laws it is unlikely that they tampered with the *axones*.

Revision of the laws was a task inherited by the Thirty from the democracy. The upheavals of 411–410 had revealed or emphasised the uncertainty of the laws, and so in 410/09 a board of *anagrapheis* had been appointed to republish 'the laws of Solon and the homicide statute of Draco' (which seems to have meant the laws currently in force): the task proved complicated, and was unfinished when the Thirty came to power (Lys. XXX. *Nicomachus* 2–3, cf. ML 86 = *IG* i³ 104 ~ Fornara 15. B, and *IG* i³ 105). After the reconciliation of 403 a board of Twenty was appointed to act as a provisional government under 'the laws of Solon and ordinances of Draco', a procedure for revising the laws was instituted (Andoc. I. *Myst.* 81–9), and the code, including the religious calendar, was completed and published in 400/399 (Lys. XXX. *Nicomachus* 4; on the epigraphic fragments see especially S. D. Lambert, *BSA* 97 [2002], 353–99). The Thirty had their own view of desirable revisions; we have no inscribed text of their laws, but two are mentioned in 37. 1 in connection with the execution of Theramenes, and in Xen. *Hell.* II. 3. 51 one is cited as 'in the new laws'.

in the case of bequeathing property to whoever one wants: Plut. *Sol.* 19. 3 states that previously there had been no freedom of bequest but Solon granted it where there were no children; part of the law is quoted in [Dem.] XLVI. *Stephanus ii.* 14. Probably what later came to be regarded as freedom of bequest was originally freedom for a man with no legitimate sons to adopt an heir (who if there were daughters would have to marry one of them: see L. Gernet, *REG* 33 [1920], 123–68, 249–90 = his *Droit et société dans la Grèce ancienne* [Paris: Sirey, 1955], 121–49, Harrison, *L.A.* i. 82–4, 149–50). By the fourth century there was some freedom of bequest not tied to adoption and marriage (Harrison, 131–2).

they gave men absolute power: In the sense that the qualifications mentioned were withdrawn. It is clear from fourth-century speeches that the democracy reinstated the qualifications.

the attached difficulties: Difficulties of interpretation give rise to lawsuits and the exercise of discretion by jurors.

'unless under the influence of insanity or senility, or induced by a woman': The law is quoted in [Dem.] XLVI. *Stephanus ii.* 14, and paraphrased in various places. Writers could be selective and make small verbal changes: it is hazardous to insist that *A.P.* should conform totally to the wording of the law or to one particular statement of it, but I have accepted one emendation to match [Dem.], and suspect that *A.P.*'s aorist πιθόμενος should be restored there. For another law on insanity see 56. 6. Solon's law left it to a jury to decide whether a man had for any reason been incompetent when he made a will: removing that possibility would remove the possibility of disputes, but would not necessarily lead to greater justice; and it is not in fact possible to produce a code of laws so clear and so complete that there will be no circumstances in which the interpretation can be disputed (cf. Pl. *Plt.* 294 A 6–295 B 2, Arist. *Pol.* II. 1269 A 9–12).

so that there should be no way in for malicious prosecutors: Cf. Theramenes' speech in Xen. *Hell.* II. 3. 38. *Sykophantes* ('[contraband-] fig-revealer') is applied by Aristophanes and later writers to men who took advantage of the opportunity for prosecution by *ho boulomenos* (cf. 9. 1) to make a profession of prosecuting, often in order to win the rewards offered to prosecutors or to be bought off by defendants; but Athens' judicial system depended on such volunteers, and needed to deter the malicious while encouraging the public-spirited (cf. 35. 3, 43. 5, 59. 3; Ar. *Ach.* 860–958, *Plut.* 850–950, Lyc. *Leocr.* 3–4; and R. Osborne and D. Harvey, in P. Cartledge *et al.* [eds], *Nomos* [Cambridge U. P., 1990], 83–102 and 103– 21).

in all the other cases: We do not know in what other ways they modified existing laws.

35. 3. That is how they acted … evildoers and wicked: Cf. Xen. *Hell.* II. 3. 12, Diod. Sic. XIV. 4. 2, Lys. XII. *Eratosthenes* 5, XXV. *Overthrowing Democracy* 19.

those who associated with the *demos* … contrary to what was best: Cf. Arist. *E.N.* X. 1173 B 33–4. In Xen. *Hell.* II. 3. 15 Theramenes says to Critias that both have often said and done things to please the *polis*; Thuc. II. 65. 8–10 claims that Pericles did not rely for his power on improperly gratifying the people but those who followed him competed in doing that.

evildoers: Cf. Isoc. XV. *Antid.* 224, 225 (both in conjunction with *sykophantai*), 236, Xen. *Hell.* V. 2. 36.

the city was glad that that was happening: Cf. Xen. *Hell.* II. 3. 12, Diod. Sic. XIV. 4. 2, both (but differently) specifying who within the *polis* was pleased.

35. 4. when they had a stronger grip on the city: Xen. *Hell.* II. 3. 13–14, Diod. Sic. XIV. 4. 3–4, Just. V. 8. 11 and Plut. *Lys.* 15. 6 all place here the Thirty's obtaining a garrison from Sparta, which *A.P.* defers to 37. 2: cf. p. 306.

they held off from none of the citizens … possessions, family and reputation: Cf. Xen. *Hell.* II. 14, 15, 17 (killing their personal opponents), 21 (after the selection of the Three Thousand killing many out of enmity and many for their money), 38, Diod. Sic. XIV. 4. 4 (killing the rich). Later we hear of an attack on rich metics: Xen. *Hell.* II. 3. 21–2, 41 (before the killing of Theramenes), Diod. Sic. XIV. 5. 6 (after the killing of Theramenes), Lys. XII. *Eratosthenes* 6–7 cf. fr. LXX / 164–73 Carey. No doubt the Thirty were motivated both by the need for money and by the wish to be rid of actual or potential opponents.
no fewer than one thousand five hundred: Confirmed by *Epit.* 7; and cf. Isoc. VII. *Areop.* 67, XX. *Lochites* 11, Aeschin. *Ctes.* 235; schol. Aeschin. I *Timarchus* 39 (82 Dilts) gives this as the figure of 'some' and 2,500 as that in a speech by Lysias. This is probably intended as the total number put to death by the Thirty.

36. 1. When the city was declining in this way Cf. 25. 1.
Theramenes, annoyed at what was happening: Cf. Xen. *Hell.* II. 3. 15, Diod. Sic. XIV. 4. 5, Just. V. 9. 2.
to give a share in affairs to the best men: Cf. Xen. *Hell.* II. 3. 17. In this part of the narrative but not elsewhere *A.P.* is close to Xenophon: perhaps a common source lies behind them.
They opposed him at first: Not stated by Xenophon, but probably true.
when the news had seeped out … they were afraid: In Xen. *Hell.* II. 3. 18 Critias and the Thirty were afraid that this would happen.
that he would become champion of the *demos* and overthrow their clique: Cf. Thuc. VIII. 89. 4 on the men opposed to the Four Hundred in autumn 411: the extremists were afraid that Theramenes would again help to overthrow the régime which (as *A.P.* never admits) he had helped to set up. This is *A.P.*'s last use of *prostates tou demou*, and his only use of *dynasteia*, denoting the despotic rule of a small clique (cf. Thuc. III. 62. 3).
they proceeded to enrol three thousand … a share in political power: Cf. Xen. *Hell.* II. 3. 18, Lys. XXX. *Nicomachus* 15. Defenders of the papyrus' δισχιλίους suppose that the 1,000 of 35. 1 were now augmented by a further 2,000. The significance of 3,000 is explored by R. Brock, *JHS* 109 (1989), 160–4. μεταδιδόναι / μετέχειν τῆς πολιτείας / τῶν πραγμάτων refers to granting / possessing citizenship in a normal régime (cf. 8. 5, 26. 4), and here as in 411–410 to granting / possessing full

rights within a restricted régime (cf. 33. 1) – but in Lys. XVI. *Mantitheus* 3 the reference is to playing a part in the régime. In fact the right to a trial before the council was limited to the Three Thousand, and other Athenians were disarmed and expelled from the city (37, not mentioning the expulsion); the Three Thousand were used to condemn the men of Eleusis, and presumably those of Salamis (Xen. *Hell.* II. 4. 9–10), but the laws which made Theramenes' condemnation possible are said to have been enacted by the council (37. 1).

36. 2. first … as if good qualities were limited to that number: Cf. Xen. *Hell.* II. 3. 19; in II. 3. 49 Theramenes claims that he never joined either extreme in depriving *kaloi k'agathoi* of their citizenship. *Epieikes* is one of the words used of the upper class in 28; we do not know by what criteria the Three Thousand were chosen.

next because they were doing two totally incompatible things … those whom they were ruling: Cf. Xen. *Hell.* II. 3. 19: they were making the rulers weaker than their subjects.

They took no notice of this: Possibly true, but possibly contaminated by the history of the Five Thousand in 411. Xen. *Hell.* II. 3. 20 proceeds directly to the disarming of the other Athenians (which presumes knowledge of who had been listed), which *A.P.* delays to 37. 2.

the register of the Three Thousand: Cf. Xen. *Hell.* II. 3. 51, 52, 4. 1.

they deleted some of the men written in it: For *exaleiphein* cf. Xen. *Hell.* II. 3. 51, 52 (Critias' deletion of Theramenes), *A.P.* 49. 2. 47. 5–48. 1 uses *apaleiphein* and *proexaleiphein*.

37. 1. Once winter had set in: This is the only indication of season in *A.P.*'s account: it may be simply a deduction from the snowstorm of Xenophon and Diodorus, but it may still be correct, and unless the phrase is mistranslated 'at the beginning of winter' it causes no chronological problem.

Thrasybulus with the exiles seized Phyle: Thrasybulus of Steiria (see Davies, *A.P.F.* 240–1: another Thrasybulus, of Collytus, was active at this time too) was prominent in the return to democracy in the Athenian fleet at Samos in 411 (Thuc. VIII. 73–6), in the naval campaigns which followed was a *strategos* closer to Alcibiades and Theramenes than to the strongest democrats (A. Andrewes, *JHS* 73 [1953], 3–4), and with Theramenes was a trierarch at Arginusae given the task of collecting bodies and survivors (Xen. *Hell.* I. 6. 35, 7. 5, Diod. Sic. XIII. 101. 2). When the Thirty came to power he went into exile, and set out from Thebes to occupy Phyle, on the south side of Parnes (Xen. *Hell.* II. 3. 42, 44, 4. 2, Diod. Sic. XIV. 32. 1, Plut. *Lys.* 27. 5–7). After successfully leading the returning democrats he was prominent in Athenian politics until *c.* 390, when he was killed while commanding an expedition to Asia Minor. Hitherto *A.P.* has mentioned executions but not exiles; in Xen. *Hell.* II. 3. 42, 44, exiles including Thrasybulus are mentioned in Theramenes' defence; II. 4. 1 and Diod. Sic. XIV. 5. 6–6, Just. V. 9. 3–5 after the expulsion of those other than the Three Thousand. It is generally agreed that *A.P.* is wrong in placing the occupation of Phyle before the execution of Theramenes: it is not impossible that for tidiness' sake Xenophon has mentioned together all that happened at Phyle, and the occupation was earlier than he suggests (O. Armbruster, *Über die Herrschaft der Dreissig zu Athen, 404/3 v. Chr.* [Freiburg im Breisgau thesis, 1913], 18–22), but it might have seemed unwise to the Thirty after the occupation to drive out men who might then support Thrasybulus.

had a bad outcome with the expedition which they sent out: Xenophon and Diodorus mention two failures of the Thirty: one in a snowstorm (Xen. *Hell.* II. 4. 2–3, Diod. Sic. XIV. 32. 3–3) and one when Thrasybulus attacked their camp (Xen. *Hell.* II. 4. 4–7, Diod. Sic. XIV. 32. 6–33. 1); Just. V. 9. 10 like *A.P.* conflates the two. Diod. Sic. XIV. 32. 5–6 and Just. V. 9. 12–14 add an unsuccessful attempt to corrupt Thrasybulus. The killing of the men of Eleusis and Salamis, in case the Thirty needed either as a refuge, is reported by Xen. *Hell.* II. 4. 8–10 (Eleusis only), Diod. Sic. XIV. 32. 4, Lys. XII. *Eratosthenes* 52, XIII. *Agoratus* 44.

to deprive the others of their arms: 37. 2 shows that the reference is to the men other than the Three Thousand.

to destroy Theramenes in the following way: Cf. Xen. *Hell.* II. 3. 23–56, Diod. Sic. XIV. 4. 5–5. 4, Just. V. 9. 2. Xenophon and Diodorus both report a clash between Critias and Theramenes in the council; *A.P.* reports what the Thirty presumably wished to be known.

They introduced two laws to the council: The second was no doubt a device aimed at Theramenes, either at the time or (Hignett, *Constitution*, 389) subsequently to provide a retrospective justification, but the first may have been enacted when the Three Thousand were instituted, with no *ad hominem* intent (Hignett).

one of these … not included in the register of the Three Thousand: Cf. Xen. *Hell.* II. 3. 51.

other banned from participating in the current régime: Not mentioned in Xen. *Hell.* II. 3. 51, where Critias deletes Theramenes from the Three Thousand. The text of the law is more likely to have stated μὴ μετέχειν τῆς πόλεως (cf. 8. 5, 26. 4, 36. 1), or perhaps μὴ εἶναι τῶν τρισχιλίων.

those who happened to have demolished the fort at Eëtionea: Cf. Thuc. VIII. 90–2: in the autumn of 411 the Four Hundred were fortifying Eëtionea, on the north side of the Piraeus, and on the approach of a fleet from the Peloponnese some men, with Theramenes' support, mutinied and began to demolish the walls. *A.P.* did not mention that in its place, but mentions it here as if no explanation were needed.

he was outside the régime: Cf. 38. 2; also 4. 3 ('constitution of Draco'), Arist. *Pol.* VI. 1321 A 30–1.

37. 2. they deprived all except the Three Thousand of their arms: Cf. Xen. *Hell.* II. 3. 20, 41 (after the arrival of the Spartan garrison, before the elimination of Theramenes: cf. p. 306): the disarming is omitted by Diod. Sic., Just. For the disarming of the people by Pisistratus or his sons see 15. 4–5.

in other respects advanced a long way in the direction of savagery and wickedness: Much less specific than what *A.P.* has said above.

They sent envoys to Sparta: Some editors proposed to move this sentence earlier, but, in view of his other distortions of the chronology, we should accept *A.P.*'s placing of the appeal to Sparta at this late stage in the narrative.

denounced Theramenes: In *A.P.*'s narrative Theramenes is already dead, but they may have thought that the execution needed to be justified to Sparta.

asked the Spartans to come to their support: Diod. Sic. XIV. 32. 6–33. 1 has an appeal to Sparta before his second battle near Phyle (p. 317), and Just. V. 9. 14 has one before the battle of Munichia (38. 1), and there may be some truth behind that; but *A.P.* is alluding to the appeal which elicited the Spartan garrison, placed earlier by the other sources.

the Spartans sent Callibius: Cf. Xen. *Hell.* II. 3. 13–14, Diod. Sic. XIV. 4. 3–4, Just. V. 8. 11, Plut. *Lys.* 15. 6.

as *harmostes*: Cf. Xenophon and Plutarch: the word was used of

Spartiates commanding a garrison or a non-Spartiate army. See H. W. Parke, *JHS* 52 (1932), 42–6, G. Bockisch, *Klio* 46 (1965), 129–239.
about seven hundred soldiers: Cf. Justin.
to the acropolis: Cf. Plutarch; also Lys. XII. *Eratosthenes* 94, XIII. *Agoratus* 46.

38. 1. the men from Phyle seized Munichia: Cf. Xen. *Hell.* II. 4. 10 (the fourth night after the attack on Phyle), Diod. Sic. XIV. 33. 2, Nep. VIII. *Thras.* 2. 5. Munichia, the hill on the east side of the Piraeus, had been fortified by Hippias (19. 2) and garrisoned by the Four Hundred in 411 (Thuc. VIII. 92. 5): the move was made possible by the demolition of the long and Piraeus walls after the peace.
defeated in battle those who rallied against them with the Thirty: Cf. Xen. *Hell.* II. 4. 10–19, Diod. Sic. XIV. 33. 2–3, Just. V. 9. 15–10. 1, Nep. VIII. *Thras.* 2. 5–6 (two battles in Diodorus and Nepos). Among the oligarchs killed were Critias and Charmides.
The men from the city withdrew ... and the next day...: Xen. *Hell.* II. 4. 22–3 has the Thirty in the council-house while the Three Thousand debate the matter; Diod. Sic. XIV. 33. 4 has (probably wrongly) many from the city as well as many exiles joining Thrasybulus.
overthrew the Thirty ... to resolve the war: Cf. Xen. *Hell.* II. 4. 23–4, Diod. Sic. XIV. 33. 5, Just. V. 10. 4, Lys. XII. *Eratosthenes* 54–5. The surviving members of the Thirty retired to Eleusis (Xenophon, Justin), with two exceptions (Lysias). The Ten were one from each tribe (Xenophon), including men thought to be opposed to the extremists (Lysias), *autokratores* to end the war (Diodorus, cf. Lys. §§53, 58). That they were instructed to work for a settlement has been accepted by some (e.g. A. Fuks, *Mnemosyne*[4] vi 1953, 198–207), but probably mistakenly (cf. Cloché, *Restauration*, 61–136), though it may be that the democrats expected the overthrow of the Thirty to result in a change and were disappointed when it did not.
they did not do the task for which they had been elected: Cf. Diod. Sic. XIV. 33. 5, Lys. XII. *Eratosthenes* 55–60.
sent to Sparta: Cf. Diod. Sic. XIV. 33. 5, Just. V. 10. 6, Plut. *Lys.* 21. 3–4. In the detailed account of Xen. *Hell.* II. 4. 24–9, while the men at the Piraeus grew in confidence, both the Thirty and the men in the city sent to Sparta and Lysander arranged for himself and his brother Libys to be sent; in Lys. XII. *Eratosthenes* 55–60 the Ten first made war both on the

Thirty and on Thrasybulus but later one of them obtained a force under Lysander. That version is defended by Cloché (*Restauration*, 186–8).

borrow money: Cf. Xen. *Hell.* II. 4. 28, Lys. XII. *Eratosthenes* 59, Isoc. VII. *Arop.* 68, Plut. *Lys.* 21. 4, all specifying 100 talents. On debts incurred by both sides see 39. 6 cf. 40. 3.

38. 2. were dejected at this: Consistent with 38. 1: most of the men in the city wanted peace.

afraid: As in my translation, the subject must be the Ten.

arrested and executed Demaenetus: Nothing else is known of him and his execution

some men among the cavalry: The cavalry were loyal supporters of the oligarchy (Xen. *Hell.* II. 4. 2–10, 24–7, 31–2); the wording of §2 should not be pressed to argue that they were a separate group of privileged men, not included in the Three Thousand (separate group, e.g. Bugh, *Horsemen*, 123–4; against, e.g. Cloché, *Restauration*, 7–9). In autumn 400, when the Spartans asked the Athenians for cavalry to fight in Asia Minor, they sent men who had served under the Thirty, hoping to be rid of them (Xen. *Hell.* II. 1. 4); for the Thirty's cavalry under the restored democracy see also Lys. XVI. *Mantitheus* 3–8, XXVI. *Evandrus* 10, fr. 130 Carey.

38. 3. the whole *demos* defected: Diod. Sic. XIV. 33. 4 has Thrasybulus joined both by deserters from the city and by more of the exiled democrats: it is not clear whether δήμου here refers to the Three Thousand (δῆμον below does not, but it would be consistent with the tendency of this part of *A.P.*'s narrative), but it is unlikely that significant numbers of the Three Thousand did in fact join the democrats, either immediately after the battle or later.

got the upper hand in the war: The Ten's appeal to Sparta was mentioned in 38. 1, the arrival of Lysander and Libys is not mentioned, Pausanias' arrival is mentioned below. In Xen. *Hell.* II. 4. 24–9 the appeal to Sparta follows Thrasybulus' successes; Lysander and Libys arrive, blockade the Piraeus and enable to oligarchs to gain the upper hand again. Probably in *A.P.*'s chronology Lysander and Libys have now arrived, but are passed over so that Thrasybulus' successes can lead to the appointment of the second Ten.

they overthrew the Ten … judged to be the best men: No other text reports this (Androtion *FGrH* 324 F 10 ~ Fornara 170. A should mean 'the Ten and what happened afterwards'), while many including *A.P.* 39. 6 write of 'the Ten' as if there was only one such board. The second Ten continue to have their defenders (e.g. Krentz, *Thirty*, 97; E. M. Carawan, *The Athenian Amnesty and Reconstructing the Law* [Oxford U. P., 2013], 147, thinks of a single body modified by 'some shake-up'), but are surely a fiction: in particular Rhinon, named by *A.P.* among the second Ten, was certainly a member of the Ten who succeeded the Thirty, and acquiesced in their acts (e.g. Cloché, *Restauration*, 170–85; and on Rhinon see below). If they result from distortion rather than outright invention, we should look to the provisional government of Twenty appointed after the reconciliation (Andoc. I. *Myst.* 81), who may well have comprised ten men from the city and ten from the Piraeus (Wilamowitz, *A.u.A.* ii. 223).

helped by these men's efforts and enthusiasm: Referring to the second Ten.

Rhinon of Paeania: A recipient of money in 417/6 (ML 77 = *IG* i^3 370 ~ Fornara 144. 26); probably the eponym of the *Rhinon* of Aeschines Socraticus (Diog. Laert. II. 61) and of Archippus (frs. 42–4 Kassel & Austin). In Isoc. XVIII. *Callimachus* 5–8, he is one of the Ten who followed the Thirty, not at odds with his colleagues; but his acceptance by the restored democracy shows that he must have become amenable to the democrats.

Phaÿllus of Acherdus: His son was a *choregos* and a trierarch in the fourth century (*ΑΔ* 25 [1970], μελ. 146 no. 5, *IG* ii^2 1624. 71–2): see Davies, *A.P.F.* 53–4.

before Pausanias arrived they made overtures to those at Piraeus: *A.P.* mentions Pausanias but in such a way as to give most of the credit for the reconciliation to Rhinon and Phaÿllus, but his statement is unlikely to be true. In Xen. *Hell.* II. 4. 29–37 Pausanias, jealous of Lysander, gained the support of three out of five ephors, took an army to Athens, and first attacked the Piraeus but afterwards encouraged the two parties to seek a settlement. The other sources are briefer: in Lys. XII. *Eratosthenes* 60 this Spartan force was again invited by the Ten, in Diod. Sic. XIV. 33. 6 Pausanias was jealous of Lysander and concerned for Sparta's reputation, in Just. V. 10 7 he pitied the exiles, in Plut. *Lys.* 21. 4–7 his intervention was the policy of both kings, who were afraid of Lysander, in Paus. III. 5. 1–2 he went τῷ λόγῳ to support Lysander but after winning a battle returned home and was put on trial but acquitted. We need not rule out jealousy of Lysander (defended by Cloché, *Restauration*, 200–13), but probably Pausanias was led to change his mind by the situation which he found in Attica (Krentz, *Thirty*, 98–101; P. Harding, *Hermes* 116 [1988], 186–93).

38. 4. the ten reconcilers who arrived afterwards from Sparta: Fifteen according to Xen. *Hell.* II. 4. 38; and in view of *A.P.*'s proliferation of boards of ten fifteen is more likely to be right.

their good will towards the *demos*: Cf. above.

they received their charge under the oligarchy ... under the democracy: The contrast ἐν ὀλιγαρχίᾳ ... ἐν δημοκρατίᾳ ... became a common one (e.g. Lys. XII. *Eratosthenes* 78, Andoc. I. *Myst.* 99). The Ten were among those not covered by the amnesty unless they satisfactorily underwent *euthynai* (39. 6); since Rhinon subsequently held office, he at least must have done so.

Rhinon was immediately elected general: Not confirmed; but he is possibly to be restored among the treasurers of Athena for 402/1 in *SEG* xxiii 81. 10, 82. 4. G. Rudberg, *Eranos* 22 (1924), 217–19, points out that this last sentence is a piece of rhetoric in the manner of Gorgias, presumably repeated by *A.P.* from his source.

39. 1. The settlement was made in the archonship of Euclides: Euclides was the archon of 403/2 (e.g. Diod. Sic. XIV. 12. 1), presumably appointed after the reconciliation had taken effect (cf. references to Pythodorus in 41. 1 and Lys. VII. *Olive Stump* 4 with 9). The first attempt to dislodge Thrasybulus from Phyle was frustrated by a snowstorm (p. 320); the battle of Munichia was fought on the fifth day from the second battle near Phyle (p. 322) and it was then said that more Athenians had been killed by the Thirty in eight months than by the Peloponnesians in ten years of war (Xen. *Hell.* II. 4. 21); shortly after that men gathered *opora* ('fruit'), which should point to early June (Xen. *Hell.* II. 4. 25); Plut. *Glor. Ath.* 349 F dates the return of the men from Phyle to 12 Boedromion (iii), *c.* September. The easiest solution is to date the institution of the Thirty early 40<u>4</u>/3 (cf. p. 314) and to count the eight months not from then but from the beginning of the reign of terror (Hignett, *Constitution*, 383). The reconciliation will have been arranged early 40<u>3</u>/2, with Pythodorus retained in office as Alexias had been retained the year before (Krentz, *Thirty*, 151–2), and 12 Boedromion will be the date of the procession of Xen. *Hell.* II. 4. 39 and Lys. XIII. *Agoratus* 80 (Cloché, *Restauration*, 247 with n. 1).

A.P. uses *dialyseis* and cognates; Xenophon, Diodorus and the orators use *diallagai* ('reconciliation') and cognates; we also find *synthekai* ('agreement') used by *A.P.* and the orators, and oaths mentioned in *A.P.* 39. 4 and elsewhere (*synallagenai* and oaths in the final reconciliation of 401/0, Xen. *Hell.* II. 4. 43). *A.P.*'s account of the terms is in places obscure, and other evidence shows that it is incomplete (Lys. fr. 165. 38–48 Carey, Isoc. XVIII. *Callimachus* 20). *A.P.* may himself be responsible for some or all of the condensation, but he probably found the material in a narrative source rather than the original document.

There is a detailed and in some respects controversial analysis of the problems associated with the original settlement and its subsequent working-out by Carawan, *The Athenian Amnesty*.

those who wished to emigrate should occupy Eleusis: Cf. Xen. *Hell.* II. 4. 38, Diod. Sic. XIV. 33. 6. The Thirty had occupied Eleusis (pp. 319–20, 322), and were presumably not a party to the reconciliation between the democrats and the oligarchs of the city: it was easiest to leave them there and to allow other oligarchs to join them.

retaining their civic rights … receiving their revenue: See Cloché, *Restauration*, 251–3: these men remain citizens (subject to certain limitations, below), with full power and authority over themselves and the affairs of their own community, and in possession of and entitled to the revenues from their own property. Difficulties could arise over the legitimacy of recent transactions: judicial decisions given under the democracy were to be valid but those given under the Thirty were not (Andoc. I. *Myst.* 87–8); Lys. fr. 165. 38–48 Carey quotes a ruling on sales of movable property. Cf. p. 330.

39. 2. The sanctuary should be the common property of both parties: For the purposes of the Eleusinian cult the split in the state was to be ignored.

the Kerykes and Eumolpidae should have care of it in accordance with tradition: The two *gene* which supplied the principal officials of the Eleusinian cult (cf. 57. 1).

It should not be permitted … to go to Eleusis: To reduce the likelihood of conflict: the men at Eleusis were forbidden to visit the city, and if they had property there would have to attend to it through an agent; but they were presumably free at their own risk to visit the rest of Attica and property which they had there.

except to each party for the Mysteries: If the Mysteries, with ceremonies in Athens and in Eleusis, were to be celebrated and both communities were to participate, the principle of isolation had to be suspended.

should contribute to the alliance … the other Athenians: By the peace treaty of 404 Athens had become a subordinate ally of Sparta (Xen. *Hell.* II. 2. 20, Diod. Sic. XIII. 107. 4: not mentioned at *A.P.* 34. 3), and for the purpose of this alliance as for the Eleusinian cult the split in the state was to be ignored.

39. 3. If any of those departing … they must persuade the owner: Those who go to Eleusis must not expropriate property but must negotiate with the owner; but after the earlier massacre (pp. 319–20, 322) it might well be hard to find legitimate owners.

Those of the Eleusinians whom the migrants wished: As in my translation, οὗτοι will be the new settlers, and συνοικεῖν will denote living at Eleusis, not sharing a house (cf. Carawan, *The Athenian Amnesty*, 70). It is not clear how many of the previous inhabitants had survived the massacre.

39. 4. The registration: Those who wish to join the community at Eleusis are to register (cf. Lys. XXV. *Overthrowing Democracy* 9): if already in Athens they must register within ten days of taking the oath (but this text does not state how or with whom), and must go within twenty days (it is not clear from when); if they are not in Athens the days will be counted from the date of their return. Oligarchs known already to be at Eleusis were perhaps registered *in absentia*. 39. 5 shows that any who had gone to Eleusis could cancel their registration and return to Athens.

39. 5. It should not be permitted … until he had registered to live in the city again: It is a natural consequence of the split that men at Eleusis are debarred from holding offices in Athens.

until he had registered to live in the city again: Cf. on 39. 4. According to Lys. XXV. *Overthrowing Democracy* 9 some men who had registered for Eleusis (stayed in or returned to Athens and) joined in the attack on the oligarchs in 401/0 (cf. 40. 4).

Trials for homicide should be in accordance with tradition: It has normally been assumed that the purpose of this sentence is to state an exception to the amnesty which follows in 39. 6: the amnesty could not wipe out the pollution associated with murder (R. J. Bonner, *CP* 19 [1924], 175–6). However, E. M. Harris, *ap.* C. J. Joyce, *Antichthon* 49 (2015), 45–9, argues that it is concerned with cases in which a member of the community in Eleusis kills a member of the community in Athens or *vice versa*, and that the corrupt phrase beginning εἴ τίς τινα, which seems to refer to doing the deed in person, 'may have been a marginal comment that crept into the text'. Men are accused of responsibility but not of killing in person in Lys. XII. *Eratosthenes* and XIII. *Agoratus*: Eratosthenes probably was not prosecuted but was accused as a member of the Thirty who submitted to *euthynai* (cf. S. C. Todd, *Lysias* [U. of Texas P., 2000], 113–4); Agoratus denied that he was guilty ἐπ' αὐτοφώρῳ ('flagrantly', a requirement for *apagoge* [cf. on 52. 1]: §§85–7), and claimed that he was protected by the oaths and *synthekai* (but the detail is not spelled out: §§88–90). Since *A.P.*'s report of the agreement is condensed (cf. on 39. 1), it is not certain though it is possible that this sentence belongs with what precedes it and concerns the withdrawal to Eleusis; if the decision to apply the laws with effect from 403/2 (Andoc. I. *Myst.* 87–8) applied to all the laws, the prosecution of Agoratus does seem to have been a breach of the agreement.

39. 6. For past actions nobody should be permitted to recall wrongs against anybody: 'Past actions' here, τῶν κατεληλυθότων ('the men who have returned') in 40. 2; neither should be emended. Cf. Andoc. I. *Myst.* 90–1, Nep. VIII. *Thrasybulus* 3. 2; Xen. *Hell.* II. 4. 43 and Just. V. 10. 11 mention this in an oath after the final settlement of 401/0. Isoc. XVIII. *Callimachus* 20 shows that the full text of the agreement was more detailed. E. M. Carawan, *JHS* 122 (2002), 1–23, cf. *The Athenian Amnesty*, 21–65, has argued that *me mnesikakein* denoted not a blanket obliteration of past wrongs but a specific ban on reopening what had been agreed with regard to reinstated *atimoi*; C. J. Joyce, CQ^2 58 (2008), 507–18, and subsequent articles, has defended the traditional view of a blanket obliteration. Carawan's limit to the scope of the amnesty, and of the application of the laws to acts committed in and after 403/2, seems mistaken; so we should believe in a blanket obliteration.

except against the Thirty … ruled the Piraeus: Cf. Xen. *Hell.* II. 4. 38 (omitting the Ten), Andoc. I. *Myst.* 90 (omitting the Ten and the Piraeus Ten). See Cloché, *Restauration*, 259–62: *A.P.*'s list of exclusions should be correct, and what was intended was that any Athenian might be prosecuted for killing or wounding in person (if the usual interpretation of 'Trials for homicide…' in §5 is correct), and members of these four boards might be prosecuted on any other charge (but men at Eleusis would not be obliged to leave Eleusis and face a court in Athens). The reference to 'the Ten' here conflicts with the two boards of Ten at 38. 3–4.

not even against these if they submitted *euthynai*: Cf. Andoc. I. *Myst.* 90: if they wished to remain in Athens, they had to undergo *euthynai* (cf. the regular *euthynai* of retiring officials, 48. 4–5, 54. 2); if they were cleared they could remain, but if they were found guilty they would be punished.

***Euthynai* should be submitted by those who had ruled Piraeus … by those in the city…:** This is condensed to the point of obscurity: see Cloché, *Restauration*, 269–72. The Piraeus Ten were to be judged by the men domiciled at (or the demesmen of) Piraeus; we should expect the others to be judged by the whole citizen body (it is not clear whether we should envisage juries, or assemblies of all qualified men willing to participate). τοῖς τὰ τιμήματα παρεχομένοις is an unparallelled expression, but presumably means those possessing a property qualification (perhaps *zeugitai* and above): there was no property qualification for democratic jurors (63. 3), but perhaps the intention was to avoid strong bias against the oligarchs (Cloché, 312–3). We should expect this rule to apply both in the Piraeus and in the city, but the failure to specify that may be due to *A.P.* or to his source rather than to a later copyist. (However, E. M. Carawan, *CQ*^{2} 56 [2006], 65–9, *The Athenian Amnesty*, 144–50, suggests that the *euthynai* in the Piraeus were for returning democrats and were without property qualification.)

those who did not want to comply should emigrate: Those who migrated to Eleusis were those who did not wish to undergo *euthynai* and stay in Athens. T. C. Loening, *The Reconciliation Agreement of 403/402 BC in Athens* (*Hermes* Einz. 53 [1987]), 49–50, reads εἴθ' … τοὺς ἐθέλοντας and translates, 'or let those emigrate who wish to do so'.

The funds … each party should repay separately: Cf. 40. 3. For money borrowed by the Thirty cf. Dem. XX. *Leptines* 11; by the Ten, 38. 1; by the democrats, Lys. XXX. *Nicomachus* 22, Dem. XX. *Leptines* 149.

On the observance of the amnesty see Cloché, *Restauration*, 296–404, A. P. Dorjahn, *Political Forgiveness in Old Athens* (Northwestern U., 1946), 24–53, Loening, *The Reconciliation Agreement*. As far as we know, nobody was convicted on a charge on which the amnesty ought to have protected him. Lys. frs. LXX / 164–73 Carey show Lysias attempting to recover property; but Isoc. XVIII. *Callimachus* 23 claims that Thrasybulus and Anytus endured the loss of their property rather than bring lawsuits to recover it, and we may suspect that fear of breaking the amnesty benefited the oligarchs in other cases also. For fragments from the records of property confiscated from the oligarchs see M. B. Walbank, *Hesperia* 51 (1982), 74–98. The amnesty could not prevent men from citing their and their opponents' behaviour in suits which did not formally break it, and the *dokimasiai* of men appointed to offices provided a particular opportunity for that.

A.P. says nothing about the government of the state after the reconciliation. Thrasybulus is said to have demanded the restoration of the *patrios politeia* between the two battles near Phyle (Diod. Sic. XIV. 32. 5–6 cf. Just. V. 9. 13–14), and to have talked of the ancient laws after the return procession from the Piraeus (Xen. *Hell.* II. 4. 40–3). Phormisius proposed a property qualification for citizenship, and was supported by Sparta but successfully opposed by Lysias (XXXIV. *Traditional Constitution ap.* Dion. Hal. 525–33 / *Lys.* 32–3). In fact an interim government of Twenty was followed by the restoration of the democracy (cf. pp. 316, 324).

40. 1. were afraid ... but delaying their registration until the final days: There must have been doubts about the effectiveness of the amnesty, during which men on the oligarchic side hesitated over migration to Eleusis.

as everybody is apt to do: This comment on human nature is unusual in *A.P.*

Archinus: Cf. 34. 3. In addition to what is stated here, he instituted perhaps late in 401/0 the procedure of *paragraphe*, by which a defendant could have a prosecution in breach of the amnesty ruled inadmissible (Isoc. XVIII. *Callimachus* 1–3: see Harrison, *L.A.* ii. 106–24, this date D. M. MacDowell, *RIDA*^{3} 18 [1971], 267–73; somewhat earlier, D. Whitehead, *MH* 59 [2002], 71–96), and was responsible for Athens' official adoption of the Ionic alphabet, to replace its local alphabet (Theopomp. *FGrH* 115 F 155), though that change was in fact already in progress.

conscious of the numbers and wishing to keep the men back: The semi-independent state at Eleusis would cause less embarrassment and danger if only a few Athenians joined it.

withdrew the remaining days for the registration: For the period within which registration was allowed see 39. 4: how Archinus cut short the period is not stated.

until they grew confident: Until they realised that the amnesty was working and they were safe in Athens.

40. 2. It seems that Archinus followed a good policy in this respect: Cf. 23. 2, 28. 5, 33. 2; and for praise of Archinus Dem. XXIV. *Timocrates* 135: this approval of moderation is what we should expect of the Aristotelian school, but probably here as elsewhere *A.P.* is repeating with his agreement what he found in his source.

when he attacked in a *graphe paranomon* the decree of Thrasybulus: There are many references to proposals to reward men who had supported the returning democrats, but they are hard to fit together (cf. Rhodes, *Comm. Ath. Pol.*, 474–7). Other mentions of a *graphe paranomon*, probably all against this proposal though some specify citizenship for Lysias, are [Plut.] *X Or.* 835 F – 836 A, Aeschin. III. *Ctesiphon* 195 and schol. (438 Dilts), *P. Oxy.* xv 1800, frs. 6–7: the decree was allegedly *aprobouleuton*, not covered by a *probouleuma* of the council (cf. 45. 4); according to Planudes (C. Walz, *Rhetores Graeci*, v. 343) there was not yet a council which could pass it to the assembly. For honours for men who were at Phyle see Aeschin. III, *Ctesiphon* 187–90; *Hesperia* x 1941, 284–95 no. 78 (revised and dated 401/0 by G. E. Malouchou, *hóρος* 22–5 [2010–3], 115–44; abridged English version *Γραμματεῖον* 4 [2015], 89–98; cf. R. K. Pitt, *AR* 61 [2014/5], 51). For a decree of 401/0 and list of honorands probably in three categories see M. J. Osborne, *Naturalization in Athens* (Brussels: Royal Academy, 1981–3), D 6 + *SEG* xliv 34 = RO 4.

some of whom were blatantly slaves: On the names and occupations of the men in Osborne D 6 see D. Hereward, *BSA* 47 (1952), 113–7.

thirdly … to execute him without trial: For *apagoge* as a technical term see 52. 1; this haling before the council is very close to the technical usage. Certainly in the fourth century and probably in the fifth also the council was not competent to sentence to death (cf. 45. 1 with commentary); immediately after the reconciliation it may not have been clear what was lawful. Isoc. XVIII. *Callimachus* 1–3 credits Archinus with the institution of *paragraphe* against prosecutions in breach of the amnesty (cf. p. 330): probably he first secured this summary execution and afterwards instituted *paragraphe*.

nobody ever afterwards recalled wrongs: At any rate, nobody obtained a court verdict which was directly in breach of the amnesty (cf. pp. 329–30).

40. 3. they seem to have dealt ... in the finest and most civic-minded way of all: This is *A.P.*'s most fulsome expression of praise, and unlike the others: here if anywhere we might look for an Aristotelian judgment, but there are several non-Aristotelian features in the language.

not only did they wipe out accusations about previous matters: The verb is used in its literal sense in 36. 2, 49. 2; here it is used in a sense very close to the literal.

they collectively repaid ... should repay separately: Cf. 39. 6; and for this decision Lys. XXX. *Nicomachus* 22, Dem. XX. *Leptines* 11–12 (both claiming pressure from Sparta, which schol. Dem. [32 Dilts] plays down), Isoc. VII. *Areop.* 67–9.

in other cities ... they engage in a redistribution of the land: Cf. the generalisations in Pl. *Resp.* VIII. 565 E 3–566 A 4, *Leg.* III. 684 D 1–E 5, Arist. *Pol.* V. 1305 A 3–7, 1309 A 14–20; Solon at the beginning of the sixth century had resisted demands for redistribution (11. 2, 12. 3). Demands for social revolution including redistribution of land became frequent from the mid fourth century, but Athens escaped such demands. This comment is more likely to have originated then than near the time of these events.

40. 4. They made a settlement with those who had gone to live at Eleusis: According to Xen. *Hell.* II. 4. 43 the Athenians heard that the men at Eleusis were hiring mercenaries, marched out against them, killed the *strategoi* who came to negotiate with them and persuaded the others to accept a reconciliation and oath of amnesty; cf. Just. V. 10. 8–11, Lys. XXV. *Overthrowing Democracy* 9. Probably the amnesty of 403 was extended to the men at Eleusis, and members of the Thirty, the Ten, the Eleven and the Piraeus Ten had to undergo *euthynai* or go into exile.

in the third year after their emigration, in the archonship of Xenaenetus: In 401/0 (Diod. Sic. XIV. 19. 1, giving the name as Ἐξαίνετος; but other texts confirm *A.P.*'s form of the name), the third year by inclusive counting from 403/2. Only *A.P.* dates this episode; Diod. Sic. XIV. 32–3 dates the events from Phyle to the first reconciliation 401/0 and omits this episode. In 400/399 the sacred treasurers took charge of objects ['Ἐλευσ]ινόθ[εν]: *IG* ii² 1375. 28 with D. M. Lewis & A. M. Woodward, *BSA* 70 (1975), 183–9.

41. 1. That is what happened at a later juncture: Rounding off 40. 4, after which *A.P.* returns to the original restoration of the democracy.
at this point the *demos* gained power over affairs: In 34–9 *A.P.* followed a source sympathetic to Theramenes (cf. p. 306), and 40 emphasised the moderation of the restored democracy; but here the author is looking forward to the summary of Athens' constitutional development, which will culminate (41. 2 *fin.*) in ἁπάντων γὰρ αὐτὸς αὑτὸν πεποίηκεν ὁ δῆμος κύριον.
in the archonship of Pythodorus: It is possible that Pythodorus' archonship was prolonged beyond the end of 404/3 (cf. p. 325), but *A.P.* dates the reconciliation to Euclides in 39. 1 cf. 40. 4. Some have suspected corruption, but more probably *A.P.* after turning away from the source of the previous chapters (cf. above) has failed to achieve consistency.
†when the *demos* seemed to be justified … by its own action.†: This is grammatically incoherent, and the correct text is irrecoverable, but the meaning is clear: the downfall of the oligarchy and the restoration of the democracy was the *demos*' own achievement – and that is consistent with 39. 3–4, which minimises the role of Pausanias.

K. Conclusion to first part (41. 2–3)

41. 1 describes the restored democracy as the present constitution, and the last of the (originally) eleven 'changes' which follows is that restoration. Whereas the list of *prostatai* in 28. 2–3 seems to be an imported list, this seems to be *A.P.*'s own compilation (and the comments at the end of 41. 2 form one of the most Aristotelian passages in the work: cf. p. 10), showing how by some changes towards democracy and some away from it Athens arrived at its final form of democracy. After 403, though there were piecemeal changes, there was not another major change in the constitution until the suppression of the democracy in 321 (p. 29).
41. 2. That was…: The restoration of 403.
Ion and those who settled with him: Cf. fr. 1 with pp. 174–5, 3. 2.
that was when they were first distributed through the four tribes: Cf. frs. 1–2 with pp. 175–6.

they instituted the *phylobasileis*: Cf. 8. 3, 57. 4.

The second, and first after that, involving a structuring of the constitution: Probably the clumsiness results from the addition of καὶ πρώτη μετὰ ταύτην, and possibly of ἔχουσα πολιτείας τάξιν, to mask the addition of Draco (below).

under Theseus, inclining slightly away from the kingly: With ἡ understand μετάστασις, and with τῆς βασιλικῆς understand πολιτείας *vel sim.*

After that, the change under Draco, in which they first wrote up laws: The original numbered list passed directly from Theseus to Solon; the reference to Draco will have been added when the 'constitution of Draco' was added to 4 (cf. *ad loc.* and p. 30), but here what is mentioned is authentic, Athens' first written laws.

after the dissension: Cf. 2. 1, 5. 1–2.

under Solon, from which came the beginning of democracy: Cf. 5–12.

the tyranny under Pisistratus: Cf. 13–17.

after the overthrow of the tyrants: Cf. 17–19.

that of Cleisthenes, which was more democratic than that of Solon: With ἡ here understand πολιτεία (more easily after τυραννίς above). Cf. 20–2, with 22. 1 and 23. 1 on its democratic character.

that after the Persian Wars, with the council of the Areopagus presiding:· Cf. 23. 1–2a.

Seventh and after that: A strange expression, but probably the result of an attempt at variety.

pointed to by Aristides: Cf. 23. 2b – 24.

completed by Ephialtes when he overthrew the Areopagite council: Cf. 25. Here *A.P.* exaggerates: Ephialtes reduced the powers of the Areopagus, but did not abolish it.

through the demagogues ... its rule of the sea: Cf. 26–7: despite δημοτικωτέραν ἔτι in 27. 1, *A.P.* does not assign a separate change to Pericles.

establishment of the Four Hundred: Cf. 29–32.

after that, ninth, democracy again: This is startling Greek, but probably ought not to be emended. 33 recorded the fall of the Four Hundred and the institution of the intermediate régime of the Five Thousand; 34. 1 begins with the supplanting of τούτους, probably the Five Thousand. Probably here *A.P.* thinks of an oligarchic revolution and a return to democracy, without deliberately including the intermediate régime either under the oligarchy or under the restored democracy.

the tyranny of the Thirty and the Ten: Cf. 34–8: here in agreement with the other sources but in disagreement with 38. 3 *A.P.* implies that there was only one board of Ten after the deposition of the Thirty. The expression 'Thirty Tyrants' seems due particularly to Ephorus (e.g. Diod. Sic. XIV. 2. 1: see Krentz, *Thirty*, 16 n. 2): in Athens they are normally 'the Thirty' or 'the oligarchy', but see Xen. *Hell.* II. 3. 16, 49, 4. 1.

after the return from Phyle and Piraeus: Cf. 37–40.

from which it has persisted until that in force now: *A.P.*'s focus has shifted from changes to constitutions (cf. above), and probably we should understand καθόδου with ἧς and ἡ πολιτεία with διαγεγένηται.

continually extending the competence of the masses: The text is problematic (cf. Kaibel, *Stil und Text*, 203–4), but the meaning is clear: the restoration of 403 was the last abrupt change (or the restored democracy was the last new constitution), but since then the power of the *demos* has continued to increase – which would not have pleased Aristotle and here seems not to please *A.P.* Whether that is true is doubtful: some scholars believe that the power of the *demos* was made less in the fourth century than in the late fifth (e.g. Hansen, *Democracy*, 300–4); I have argued that changes made early in the fourth century were in the spirit of the fifth-century democracy but changes made later were not (e.g. *C.A.H.* vi^{2}. 565–72).

has itself made itself master of everything: Cf. 41. 1.

it administers everything through decrees and lawcourts … has the power: It was believed in fourth-century Athens that *nomoi* were or should be of higher status and wider application than *psephismata* (cf. p. 271), and after the revision of the laws completed in 400/399 (p. 316) a separate procedure for enacting further *nomoi* was established (cf. p. 345). For the way in which the *dikasteria* kept power in the hands of the people see 9, 35. 2; and they exercised political power through such procedures as *eisangelia* (43. 4) and the *graphai paranomon* and *nomon me epitedeion theinai* (45. 4, 59. 2). Athenians would not normally say that the courts were representative of or embodied the *demos*, because that word was associated particularly with the assembly, but they might say that the courts were representative of or embodied the *polis* (see M. H. Hansen, *GRBS* 50 [2010], 499–536, the latest instalment in a long debate).

also the judgments of the council have come to the *demos*: *Kriseis* are primarily judicial decisions. Cf. 45. 1 with commentary (where I argue that the council had never had unlimited power), 45. 3, 49. 3; Arist. *Pol.* IV. 1299 B 38–1300 A 3, VI. 1317 B 30–5, remarks that when there is an abundance of stipends power passes from the council to the assembly.

in this they seem to be acting rightly: This kind of judgment is particularly reminiscent of [Xen.] *A.P.*, e.g. 3. 10; but cf. also Arist. *Pol.*, e.g. II. 1270 A 18–20.

for the few are more easily corrupted than the many: Cf. Arist. *Pol.* III. 1286 A 26–35; also Dem. XXIV. *Timocrates* 37.

by profit and favours: If the support of individuals has to be bought, the fewer the easier; but it is also possible for a mass of people to be corrupted *en masse*, as *A.P.* suggests with the financial benefits of the Delian League (24) and jury pay (27. 3–4).

41. 3. At first: In the fifth century, when stipends were provided for jurors (27. 3–4), councillors (Thuc. VIII. 69. 4) and various officials (24. 3). *A.P.* here adds one post-403 detail to illustrate the continuing advance of the *demos*.

when men were not gathering ... various devices: Aristophanes reports one device: a rope dyed red, used to herd men from the agora to the Pnyx, after which men marked but absent were fined (*Ach.* 21–2 with schol., Poll. VIII. 104). The number of adult male citizens was perhaps *c.* 60,000 before the Peloponnesian War and 25,000–30,000 after (M. H. Hansen, *Demography and Democracy* [Herning: Systime, 1985]; *Three Studies in Athenian Demography* [Copenhagen: Munksgaard for Royal Danish Academy, 1988], 14–28). In 411 the oligarchs alleged that attendance at the assembly never exceeded 5,000 (cf. p. 289); but in the fourth century the quorum for the ratification of citizenship grants points to regular attendance in excess of 6,000 (Hansen, *GRBS* 17 [1976], 115–34 esp. 127–30 = his *The Athenian Ecclesia* [Copenhagen: Museum Tusculanum P., 1983], 1–20[–23] esp. 13–16). On the capacity of the Pnyx see Stanton / Hansen in B. Forsén & G. R. Stanton (eds), *The Pnyx in the History of Athens* (Helsinki: Finnish Institute at Athens, 1996), 7–21 / 23–33. P. Gauthier, who has re-edited the fourth-century decree concerning assembly pay at Iasus (*SEG* xl 959 = RO 99), noting that there only men who arrived before a certain time were paid, and that in Athens also there was a limit of some kind (Ar. *Eccl.* 186–8, 289–93), suggests that the concern was with punctuality rather than with numbers (in M. Piérart [ed.], *Aristote et Athènes* [Paris: De Boccard for U. de Fribourg, 1993], 231–50).

for the ratification of the votes: Voting in general, not only voting by show of hands: decisions requiring a quorum required a secret ballot (e.g. [Dem.] LIX. *Neaera* 89–90).

first Agyrrhius A man with particular financial interests. Before 405 he combined with Archinus to reduce the payments made to comic poets (cf. p. 311); he was presumably on the democratic side in 404/3, was one of the secretaries in 403/2 (*IG* ii^2 1 = RO 2 ~ Harding 5. 41–2), and his continuing career included heading a tax-collecting syndicate (Andoc. I. *Myst.* 133–6), and was interrupted by time in prison after he was convicted of embezzlement (Dem. XXIV. *Timocrates* 134–5); he is last attested as proposer of the grain-tax law of 374/3 (*SEG* xlvii 96 = RO 26). Attribution to him of the theoric fund (Harp. θ 19 Keaney θεωρικά: cf. p. 346) is probably a mistaken allusion to his institution of assembly pay. This must be dated soon after 403.

Heraclides of Clazomenae, known as 'king': For Athens' (conferment of citizenship on him and subsequent) election of him as *strategos* cf. Pl. *Ion* 541 D 1–4, Ath. XI. 560 A, Ael. *V.H.* XIV. 5. The identification of an additional fragment has made it virtually certain that he is the Heraclides of ML 70 = *IG* i^3 227 ~ Fornara 138, honoured probably in the late 420's for helping in negotiations with Persia, and that may explain the nickname *basileus*.

Agyrrhius again three obols: This stage had been reached by the time of Ar. *Eccl.* (289–311, 392), in the late 390's; by the time of *A.P.* there had been a further increase, to 1½ dr. at the *kyria ekklesia* and 1 dr. at other meetings (62. 2).

L. Beginning of second part: registration and training of citizens (42)

The first part of *A.P.* outlined the history of the *politia* to its last 'change', at the end of the fifth century; the second part sets out 'the present form of the constitution' (42. 1) For its organisation, and derivation from the laws of Athens, see Introduction, pp. 16–21.

Ch. 42 is devoted to citizenship: the requirement of two citizen parents, the *dokimasia* and registration of citizens, and their two years of training as *epheboi*. *A.P.*'s summary leaves unanswered various questions which will be discussed below. This chapter does not contrast earlier with current practice for the *epheboi* (as 53. 4 does), but other evidence indicates that the system described here was instituted *c.* 335/4: Lycurgus mentioned a man called Epicrates who was honoured for a law about the *epheboi* (Lyc. fr. 20 Conomis *ap.* Harp. ε 101 Keaney Ἐπικράτης), and the series of inscriptions for *epheboi* begins with perhaps nine for those registered in 334/3 and 333/2 (collected by O. W. Reinmuth, *The Ephebic Inscriptions of the Fourth Century BC* [*Mnemosyne* Supp. 14 (1971)]; the second decree of his no. 1 has commonly been dated 333/2, but A. S. Chankowski, *BCH* cxxxviii 2014, 15–78, argues that it is earlier and reflects the *ephebeia* before Epicrates' law). (This provides a *terminus post quem* for the writing of *A.P.*: cf. Introduction, pp. 29.) However, some provision for *epheboi* existed earlier: Aeschin. II. *F.L.* 167 refers to his *synepheboi*, and Dem. XIX. *F.L.* 303 refers to the oath of the *epheboi* (cf. p. 342); the *dokimasia* of young citizens is attested in Ar. *Vesp.* 578; and both in the 450's and in the Peloponnesian War the *neotatoi* ('youngest') were a separate category in the Athenian army (Thuc. I. 105. 4, II. 13. 7). H. van Wees, *Greek Warfare: Myths and Realities* (London: Duckworth, 2004), 94, argues from a contrast between Aeschin. II. *F.L.* 167 and Xen. *Poroi* 4. 52 that some degree of compulsion was introduced *c.* 360. The word *ephebos* belongs to the series of words for age classes found throughout the Greek world.

We should accept that the *dokimasia* of young citizens and the imposition of an oath on them were ancient Athenian institutions, and that it was an ancient practice to give the title *ephebos* to men in their first two years after *dokimasia* and to treat them differently from older citizens, but it was Epicrates in the 330's who converted the *ephebeia* into a period of full-time service for all young citizens (except the unfit and the *thetes*: below). Cf. Reinmuth, *TAPA* 83 [1952], 34–50, *The Ephebic Inscriptions*, 123–38; Ch. Pélékidis, *Histoire de l' éphébie attique des origines à 31 avant J.-C.* (Paris: De Boccard, 1962), 7–79. By 305/4 service had been reduced to one year, and lower numbers suggest that it was no longer compulsory: *IG* ii^2 478 = Reinmuth 17, with Reinmuth *ad loc.*

42. 1. The present disposition of the constitution is in the following manner: This sentence introduces the second part of *A.P.*: there are some larger and smaller rings within this part (cf. pp. 25–6), but there is no resumptive expression corresponding to this at the end of the whole work. For *katastasis* cf. Pl. *Leg.* VIII. 832 D 4–5; in the first part *A.P.* wrote of the *taxis* of the *politeia* (3. 1 etc.).
Men participate in the citizen body: Similarly in Arist. *Pol.* IV. 1296 B 13–1297 B 34 the discussion of the best form of constitution begins with the citizen body. For the expression cf. on 8. 5.
born of two citizen parents: This was first required by Pericles' law of 451/0; towards the end of the Peloponnesian War it was annulled or ignored; after the war it was reenacted, and strengthened by a positive ban on mixed marriages (cf. on 26. 4). *Astos* means 'citizen', but in respect of birth rather than of political rights (M. H. Hansen, in Hansen [ed.], *The Polis as an Urban Centre and as a Political Community* [*C.P.C. Acts* 4. Copenhagen: Munksgaard for Royal Danish Academy, 1997], 10–11); *A.P.* does not think it necessary to state that women could not be *politai*. *A.P.* also does not state whether men had to be born in wedlock to be citizens: it is clear from Arist. *Pol.* III. 1278 A 26–34, VI. 1319 B 8–10, that neither the inclusion nor the exclusion of bastards was unthinkable in Greece; in Athens bastards were excluded from the *phratriai* (cf. *IG* ii² 1237 = RO 5. 109–11), and probably they were excluded from the demes and from citizenship (cf. Rhodes, *CQ*² 28 [1978], 89–92; for the contrary view see D. M. MacDowell, *CQ*² 26 [1976], 88–91).
they are registered among their demesmen: There was no central register of all citizens (but there was of men eligible for military service: 53. 4–5, 7): each deme kept the *lexiarchikon grammateion* of its members, and those who were members of a deme were thereby citizens. Metics were regarded as 'living in' a deme (e.g. *IG* i³ 476. 6–7), and probably the demes registered their metics also.
when they have reached the age of eighteen: There was an annual ceremony of *dokimasia* and registration, probably early in the new year (cf. Lys. XXI. *Bribery* 1). The forty-two years of service, and the different formulation of 53. 4 (οἷς ἂν ἑξηκοστὸν ἔτος ᾖ) make it clear that the reference here is to men who have passed their eighteenth birthday and there is to men 'in their sixtieth year', i.e. between their fifty-ninth and their sixtieth birthday. In that case what Demosthenes says in XXVII.

Aphobus i is misleading; perhaps the status of men with birthdays (cf. M. Golden, *Phoenix* 33 [1979], 25–38) between the beginning of the year and the day of registration was ambiguous.

the demesmen vote over them after swearing an oath: There is a tendency to use *psephizesthai* and *cheirotonein* of different kinds of decision rather than different methods of voting, but all votes in connection with citizenship do seem to have been taken by ballot (e.g. Dem. LVII. *Eubulides* 13–14 cf. 61); *dia-* is used of deciding between alternatives (cf. 55. 4). For the oath, perhaps required because this was seen as a quasi-judicial activity, cf. Isae. VII. *Apollodorus* 28, Dem. LVII. 26, 61, 64.

whether they are judged to have reached the age: Since Athenians were not registered in any way at birth, there might be no good evidence of a man's age (cf. Pl. *Lys.* 207 B 8–C 2).

they revert to the rank of boys again: The demesmen may be penalised if they accept a man but the council rejects him (42. 2); nothing is said here of penalties for the father or guardian, but the 'Demotionid decrees' (*IG* ii^2 1237 = RO 5) suggest that they existed.

if he is free: I.e. not a slave. Some have thought that what is meant here is not only freedom but citizen birth, but that is covered by the next clause.

has been born in accordance with the laws: This means 'in accordance with the laws about citizenship', so does not explicitly denote born in wedlock, but it will implicitly include that if that was one of the requirements for citizenship.

if they vote to reject him as not being free: If *A.P.*'s text is accurate and complete, candidates rejected by the deme as unfree could appeal to a *dikasterion*, candidates approved by the deme were reconsidered by the council on grounds of age, and there was no further check on birth in accordance with the laws. This is improbably haphazard, and probably candidates rejected by the deme on any criterion could appeal to a *dikasterion* and candidates accepted were reviewed on all criteria by the council. In 346/5 candidates rejected as foreign appealed to a *dikasterion* (Isae. XII. *Euphiletus*, Dem. LVII. *Eubulides*).

he appeals: Until he was accepted as a citizen a man could not initiate proceedings: presumably the appeal was made by the father or guardian.

the demesmen elect five men … as prosecutors: Accusers who would state the deme's case for rejection (cf. for 346/5 Aeschin. I. *Timarchus*

114; praise of *kategoroi*, *IG* ii^2 1205). Contrast *IG* ii^2 1237 = RO 5. 30–8, where the *synegoroi* sit and vote with the Demotionidae.

if he is judged ... the city sells him as a slave: Some commentators have been indignant, but probably, if a man rejected as free but foreign accepted his rejection, he was registered as a metic, but if he appealed and the rejection was upheld, he could then be sold as a slave (cf. for 346/5 Isae. XII. *hyp* = Dion. Hal. 617–8 / *Isae.* 16, Dem. LVII. *hyp.*); it would be possible for his sponsor to buy him and free him.

42. 2. the council vets those who have been registered: If the demesmen conspired to accept an unqualified candidate nobody might appeal, so acceptance was followed by compulsory reference to the council. Cf. the *dokimasia* of [councillors and] archons, 45. 3, 55. 2–4, and *IG* ii^2 1237 = RO 5. 78–94.

if anybody is judged to be below the age of eighteen: Probably the council considered all criteria: cf. above.

it punishes the demesmen who registered him: Cf. *IG* ii^2 1237 = RO 5. 88–94, where members of the *thiasos* who opposed acceptance do not have to contribute to the fine.

When the *epheboi* have been vetted: *A.P.* has not used the word *epheboi* before. It is implied, here and for the *diaitetai* at 53. 4–5, that all newly registered citizens became *epheboi* and underwent training (cf. Lyc. *Leocrates* 76). Those physically unfit must have been exempted from the training (cf. Pélékidis, *Histoire de l'éphébie attqiue*, 97 with n. 5). Since the training was primarily hoplite training, I am among those who believe that the *thetes* were exempted too (e.g. Reinmuth, *The Ephebic Inscriptions*, 106), but others believe that the *thetes* were included (e.g. Reinmuth, 126–7); and M. H. Hansen suggests that the *thetes* were included in principle but the number who actually served increased over time (*Studies in the Population of Aigina, Athens and Eretria* [Copenhagen: Munksgaard for Royal Danish Academy, 2006], 33–8).

their fathers assemble: No other text mentions these tribal meetings of fathers (and, presumably, guardians), but cf. *IG* ii^2 1159 = Reinmuth 19. 11–14.

elect three of the tribesmen over forty years old: For the age, to reduce the risk of corrupting the young, cf. the *choregoi* of boys' choruses (56. 3). The positions were quasi-military, and required skill or moral fitness, so supervisors and instructors were appointed by election.

the best and most suitable to take care of the *epheboi*: Cf. *IG* ii² 1006. 56 (122/1).

the *demos* elects from these one man from each tribe as *sophronistes*: A *sophronistes* makes *sophron*, especially by chastising those who fall short (cf. Thuc. III. 65. 3, VI. 87. 3, VIII. 48. 6, Pl. *Resp.* V. 471 A 6–7, Dem. XIX. *F.L.* 285). *Sophronistai* are found in the inscriptions of the late fourth century, but then disappear until the second century AD. Probably they and the *kosmetes* served for two years with one contingent of *epheboi* (cf. K. Clinton, *'Αρχ. 'Εφ.* [1988], 28–9).

from the rest of the Athenians a *kosmetes* over all of them: *Kosmos* ('orderliness') was a virtue more associated with Sparta (e.g. Hdt. I. 65. 4) and with Crete (where there were officials entitled *kosmoi*: e.g. Arist. *Pol.* II. 1272 A 6), but is not wholly alien to Athens in the second half of the fourth century (cf. the council, 44. 3; the theatre, e.g. *IG* ii³ 306. 24–5). This title was used for the principal supervisor of the *epheboi* at all dates; the appointment should have been from all citizens, not from the thirty short-listed to be *sophronistai*; and here too there was probably an age requirement of forty.

Inscriptions show that some of the *epheboi* were given 'cadet' appointments as *taxiarchoi* and *lochagoi* (e.g. Reinmuth 9. i. 20–31: see F. W. Mitchel, *TAPA* 92 [1961], 347–57).

42. 3. These take the *epheboi*: *Sc.* the *kosmetes* and *sophronistai*.

first make a tour of the sanctuaries: The purpose was presumably to instil in the *epheboi* a devotion to the cults of Athens. It was presumably at this stage, before beginning their military training, that the *epheboi* took their oath – in the sanctuary of Aglaurus (Dem. XIX. *F.L.* 303: cf. p. 189), who is the first deity invoked in the inscribed version of their oath (RO 88. 17).

then proceed to Piraeus … some guard Acte: Cf. 61. 1, where of the two *strategoi* assigned to the Piraeus one is given Munichia, the hill on the east side towards Phalerum, and one Acte, the peninsula to the south of the main, westward-facing harbour.

two physical trainers: Gymnastic trainers (Antiph. III. *Tetr. ii.* γ. 6), perhaps involved with the *epheboi* in their first year only. Later there was only one: e.g. *IG* ii² 478 = Reinmuth 17. 26 (305/4).

teachers: *A.P.* does not say how many, but proceeds to mention four skills, hoplite-fighting, archery, javelin-throwing and catapult-firing: in the fourth century there seem to have been separate instructors for each tribe (e.g. Reinmuth 9. i. 33–6).

who teach: Rutherford's future, διδάξουσιν, should not be restored here but was probably used in the law which lies behind *A.P.*

For sustenance: For contemporary stipends see 62. 2. The instructors, not necessarily Athenian, were presumably paid more.

each *sophronistes* ... (for they eat together by tribes): In this scheme ephebic service was a full-time occupation; eating together by tribes was perhaps a conscious imitation of the Spartan messes.

takes care of everything else: This is disappointingly vague.

42. 4. an assembly is held in the theatre ... their skills in manoeuvring: The theatre of Dionysus, south of the eastern half of the acropolis, rebuilt in the time of *A.P.* (cf. Travlos, *Pictorial Dictionary*, 537–52; J. Hanink, *Lycurgan Athens and the Making of Classical Tragedy* [Cambridge U. P., 2014], 95–103); presumably this was used in preference to the Pnyx (also remodelled about this time: cf. Travlos, 466–76; S. I. Rotroff & J. McK. Camp, *Hesperia* 65 [1996], 263–94) because its *orchestra* was convenient for the *epheboi*'s display (J. Dillery, *CQ*[2] 52 [2002], 462–70, thinks even the theatre would not suffice and the stadium was used).

receive a shield and spear from the city: This was presumably an innovation of the 330's: earlier the state presented arms to the sons of men killed in war (Pl. *Menex.* 248 E 6–249 B 2).

42. 5. wearing short cloaks: The *chlamys* was a short cloak, worn originally by horsemen, and used by *epheboi* in Athens and elsewhere; until AD 165/6 those of the Athenian *epheboi* were black (symbolising their marginal status: P. Vidal-Naquet, *Le Chasseur noir* [Paris: La Découverte / Maspero, [2]1983], 123–207 = trans. A. Szegedy-Maszak, *The Black Hunter* [Johns Hopkins U. P., 1986], 83–156). They also wore the broad-brimmed hat called *petasos* (Philemon I fr. 34 Kassel & Austin *ap.* Poll. VIII. 164).

they are free from all impositions: They were clearly not exempt from military service, and it is not clear what they were exempt from, apart from involvement in lawsuits: possibly from festival liturgies, or from all liturgies (on the grounds that they would not have time to perform them), possibly from *eisphorai* and other direct taxes.

concerning inheritance: When a man was registered as a citizen he became κύριος ... τῆς οὐσίας (Aeschin. I. *Timarchus* 103). Before

A.P.'s ephebic system was introduced, Demosthenes had prosecuted his guardians immediately after his *dokimasia* (e.g. XXX. *Onetor i.* 15).
***epikleroi*:** The son of an *epikleros* (cf. 9. 2) became *kyrios* of the property but perhaps not of the woman when he came of age: ([Dem.] XLVI. *Stephanus ii.* 20).
if a priesthood in his *genos* falls to anybody: This is presumably an exception from the ban on absence rather than from exemption from lawsuits: for priesthoods hereditary in *gene* cf. p. 175).

M. Offices, sortitive and elective: the council (43–9)

Chs 43–62 are devoted to Athenian offices, within which there is a recognisable sub-section on the council (cf. Introduction, pp. 16–17).

43. 1 has an introductory note on offices, and there is more on offices in general in 62, but there are some matters on which *A.P.* is silent. Candidates had to be citizens, from the three higher Solonian classes (but in *A.P.*'s time that was not taken seriously: 7. 3–8. 1, 47. 1); probably when no higher minimum is stated they had to have reached the age of thirty (cf. on 30. 2, 63. 3), though it is possible that younger men could hold military offices (cf. Pritchett, *War*, ii. 63 n. 17). Naturalised Athenians could not hold archonships or priesthoods, though their sons could if born of Athenian mothers ([Dem.] LIX. *Neaera* 92, 104–6); archons at their *dokimasia* were asked questions about household cults which imply membership of a *phratria* (55. 3), normal but possibly not universal for fourth-century citizens. For the sake of her ritual marriage to Dionysus (3. 5) the wife of the *basileus* had to be an Athenian who had not previously been married to anybody else ([Dem.] LIX. *Neaera* 75). Din. I. *Demosthenes* 71 claims that *rhetores* (regular speakers in the assembly) and *strategoi* had to have a stake in Athens by having children and owning land within Attica, cf. the 'constitution of Draco' (4. 2) and the 'decree of Themistocles' (ML 23. 18–22); also Pericles in Thuc. II. 44. 3: possibly this is a survival from the archaic state (though *rhetores* indicates a fourth-century reformulation), not enforced unless a man invoked it to attack an enemy. We are not told how men became candidates for office: texts such as Lys. VI. *Andocides* 4, XXXI. *Philon* 33, suggest that they volunteered; compulsion may have been possible if there were too few volunteers (cf. E. S. Staveley, *Greek and Roman*

Voting and Elections [London: Thames & Hudson, 1972], 39–40, 51), but when appointments were made by *kleroterion* (cf. on 63. 4) they could not be made without the candidates' consenting and supplying their *pinakia*.

Discussion of the council begins with its organisation, to which *A.P.* attaches material on the meetings of the council and the assembly (43. 2–44). Then follow the powers of the council: jurisdiction (45. 1–3), *probouleusis* (45. 4), the navy (46. 1), public works (46. 2), financial offices (47–8) and *dokimasiai* (49). The council was involved in all of Aristotle's 'three parts of all constitutions': deliberation (i.e. decision-making), 'offices' (i.e. administration) and justice (*Pol.* IV. 1297 B 35–1301 A 15). *A.P.*'s analysis, probably following the organisation of Athens' laws, is based on offices: this perhaps explains why the assembly is treated with the council, the fourth-century distinction of *nomoi* from *psephismata* of the assembly (where the council and assembly initiated the procedure to enact *nomoi* but the final decision was taken by a separate board of *nomothetai*: cf. p. 335 and Hansen, *Democracy*, 161–77) is not treated at all, and the financial offices supervised by the council are treated with the council, separately from other offices (cf. p. 17).

43. 1. That is the manner … and for the *epheboi*: *A.P.* summarises the two topics treated in ch. 42…
The officials for the regular administration: …and introduces the theme of chs 43–60(–62). *Dioikesis* in *A.P.* normally refers to the administration of the state's affairs (cf. on 3. 6); the word was particularly associated with finance, but its sense is not limited to that here. *Enkyklios* means 'recurring', and so 'regular' or 'ordinary': in 26. 2 the *enkyklioi archai* are the routine as opposed to the major offices of the state; here the *enkyklios dioikesis* is the day-to-day administration of the state, civilian as opposed to military. *A.P.* treats civilian offices to ch. 60, military in 61, and ends the treatment of offices in ch. 62.
they appoint by allotment: In 42. 2–4 *A.P.* wrote of ὁ δῆμος: with the plural verbs here we must understand οἱ Ἀθηναῖοι. Allotment was used, especially but not only by democracies, to distribute fairly among those eligible posts which were thought to require loyalty rather than particular ability (cf. on 4. 3). Some other elected offices are mentioned in 54. 3–5.
apart from the treasurer of the stratiotic fund: The fourth-century

budgeting procedure (cf. 48. 2) recognised a plurality of spending authorities: the stratiotic (military) fund is first attested in 374/3 (*SEG* xlvii 96 = RO 26. 54–5) but could be older, and its treasurer in 344/3 (*IG* ii^2 1443. 12–13). The post was presumably made elective because it was thought of as military; its involvement in supervising the old financial boards (47. 2) and preparing prizes for the Panathenaea (49. 3) I suspect to be due to the reduction in the 330's of the power of the theoric treasurers.
the men in charge of the theoric fund: The ostensible purpose of the fund was to pay grants to citizens to cover the cost of theatre tickets at the major festivals (e.g. Harp. θ 19 Keaney θεωρικά, quoting *inter alios* Philoch. *FGrH* 328 F 33, Philinus fr. 3 Sauppe). Theoric payments are ascribed to Pericles in general passages in Plut. *Per.* 9. 1, 34. 2; to Agyrrhius by Harp. *loc. cit.*; to a Diophantus e.g. by Hesychius δ 2351 δραχμὴ χαλαζῶσα. Pericles instituted jury pay (27. 3–4), and Agyrrhius assembly pay (41. 3): there is no mention by Aristophanes that men were paid to go to his plays, and I suspect that the attributions to Pericles and Agyrrhius are falsely derived from the payments which they did introduce. A Diophantus was archon in 395/4 (*L.G.P.N.* ii *s.n.* 4); but Diophantus of Sphettus (*L.G.P.N.* ii *s.n.* 54) was an associate in the 350's and 340's of Eubulus, under whom the theoric treasurers became powerful (below), and the theoric fund is best seen as a creation of those men, probably in the late 350's after the Social War (cf. J. van Ooteghem, *LEC* 1 [1932], 388–407, relying on Just. VI. 9. 1–5, schol. Aeschin. III. *Ctesiphon* 24 [65 Dilts]).

According to Aeschin. III. *Ctesiphon* 25, because of the Athenians' trust in Eubulus, before the law of Hegemon the men in charge of the theoric fund had powers in various areas amounting to virtually the whole *dioikesis* of the city. *A.P.*'s language here points to a board, presumably of ten, but Aeschines' language would be compatible either with a board or with a single man, and *IG* ii^3 306. 38–9 (343/2) points to a single man. I have argued that at first the fund was controlled by a single man, elected and capable of being re-elected; that by receiving not only a regular allocation but also any surplus revenue (e.g. Dem. I. *Ol. i.* 19–20 with *hyp.* 4–5) the fund became substantial enough to pay for various projects, and that its treasurer came to be involved in supervising the old financial boards (cf. 47. 2 with commentary); in the 330's by Hegemon's law the single man was replaced by a board, tenure was limited and the stratiotic treasurer joined in the supervisory role (*A.B.* 235–40).

A.P. does not mention the comparably powerful position held by Lycurgus for τρεῖς πενταετηρίδας in the 330's and 320's ([Plut.] *X Or.* 841 B–C cf. decree *ap.* 852 B, Diod. Sic. XVI. 88. 1): probably this was the position ἐπὶ τῇ διοικήσει, which, held possibly at first by a single man but later by a board, was one of the major financial positions in hellenistic Athens (cf. Rhodes, *A.B.* 107–10); and possibly it was originally instituted by *psephisma* and therefore overlooked by *A.P.*

the *epimeletai* of the fountains: Cf. *IG* ii³ 338 and perhaps 301; these are among the offices which a city needs in Pl. *Leg.* VI. 758 E 5–6, Arist. *Pol.* VI. 1321 B 26. It is not clear why this office should have been made elective.

hold office from Panathenaea to Panathenaea: This means not for four years from one Great Panathenaea to the next, but (together with some other officials) for one year beginning at the Panathenaea on 28 Hecatombaeon (i) rather than 1 Hecatombaeon (W. S. Ferguson, *Hellenistic Athens* [London: Macmillan, 1911], 474–5).

They also elect all the officers for warfare: Cf. 61. 1 and, on their election 44. 4; also Aeschin. III. *Ctesiphon* 13.

43. 2. The council is of 500 appointed by lot, 50 from each tribe: The council of five hundred comprising fifty from each tribe was instituted by Cleisthenes (21. 3); appointment by lot, if not original, was presumably used by the late 450's, when Athens imposed a council appointed by lot on Erythrae (ML 40 = *IG* i³ 14 ~ Fornara 71. 8–9); in the various tribal changes of post-classical Athens the principle of fifty per tribe was retained until the second century AD (Rhodes, *A.B.* 1, 241). 62. 1 reports that, while appointment to most offices by demes had been abandoned, it was retained for councillors. There are many inscriptions which list members from a single tribe or all the tribes under their demes (collected in *Agora* xv), and which show that at any time between *c.* 400 and *c.* 200 BC there were normal quotas for the representation of individual demes, though on occasions there might be small adjustments; if there were quotas for the fifth century (which is likely, but we lack evidence), they were probably different from those of the fourth century (M. H. Hansen, *GRBS* 24 [1983], 230–2 = his *The Athenian Ecclesia II* [Copenhagen: Museum Tusculanum P., 1989], 76–8 cf. 85–6). ἐπιλαχόντες (reserves) are attested occasionally in the late fifth and fourth centuries (cf. Rhodes, *A.B.* 7–8).

serves in turn as prytany: The prytany played the same role with regard to the whole council as the council did with regard to the assembly (cf. below).
as determined by sortition: Inscriptions, particularly *IG* ii² 553. 16–17, show that it was not known except during the ninth prytany of a year which tribe would hold the next prytany: there must have been nine occasions each year when the next prytany was allotted (cf. W. S. Ferguson, *The Athenian Secretaries* [New York: Macmillan for Cornell U., 1898], 19–27).
the first four … (for the year is regulated by the moon): For κατὰ σελήνην … ἄγουσιν cf. Ar. *Nub.* 626, Diog. Laert. I. 59.

For most purposes Athens used a year of twelve or thirteen lunar months, each of 29 or 30 days, i.e. *c.* 354 or *c.* 384 days in all, so some prytanies will have been longer than others: what *A.P.* states here would apply to a twelve-month year of 354 days. It was long disputed between B. D. Meritt (e.g. *The Athenian Year* [Sather Lectures xxxii. U. of California P., 1959], esp. 72–134) and W. K. Pritchett (e.g. W. K. Pritchett & O. Neugebauer, *The Calendars of Athens* [Harvard U. P., 1947], 34–67) whether *A.P.*'s formulation, with the longer prytanies at the beginning of the year, was a binding rule (Pritchett, who also postulated a comparable rule for thirteen-month years and for the period before 403 when the council used a solar year: cf. on 32. 1) or merely an illustration (Meritt). There is no text which proves Pritchett wrong; I think that what *Ath. Pol.* states may well be what the law stated, but since the calendar suffered various irregularities in other respects I think it would be dangerous to insist that it can never have suffered an irregularity in this respect (cf. S. D. Lambert, in *φιλαθήναιος ... M. J. Osborne* [Athens: Greek Epigraphic Society, 2010], 91–102, focusing on 352/1–322/1).
43. 3. first eat together in the *tholos*: The *tholos* , a circular building, was built on the west side of the agora, south of the (old) *bouleuterion*, *c.* 465 (Camp, *Site Guide*, 48–50) – I suspect, after the tribal contingents were constituted as *prytaneis* by Ephialtes (cf. on 25. 2). The state secretaries dined in the *tholos* with the *prytaneis* (Dem. XIX. *F.L.* 249 with schol. [475 Dilts], 314); the archons dined in the *thesmotheteion* (schol. Pl. *Phdr.* 235 D: cf. 3. 5, 62. 2); those whom the state honoured dined in the *prytaneion* (24. 3).
receiving money from the city: Cf. 62. 2.

then convene both the council and the *demos*: They announce when meetings are to be held and what business is to be transacted. They are honoured for this in hellenistic inscriptions (e.g. *Agora* xv 89. 15–16); in the fourth century there were three councillors entitled *syllogeis tou demou* from each tribe, but there is not yet any evidence of their performing duties to match their title (cf. Rhodes, *A.B.* 129–30). Until the early fourth century the *prytaneis* presided at meetings, but that duty then passed to the *proedroi* (44. 2–3).

the council every day, except when there is a day of exemption: Cf. εὑρισκόμενος ἄφεσιν in 30. 6; in 44. 3 *apheinai* is used of closing a meeting. The days of exemption comprised holidays and days of ill omen (cf. Lucian, *Pseudol.* 12); for the courts there were about sixty a year (Ar. *Vesp.* 660–3 with schol. 663); for the council J. D. Mikalson argues for annual festivals (about sixty) but not monthly festivals (*The Sacred and Civil Calendar of the Athenian Year* [Princeton U. P., 1975], 196–8).

the *demos* four times in each prytany: Details are given below. We may guess that earlier the *kyria ekklesia* was the only regular meeting in a prytany, and the likeliest time for the increase is between 462/1 and 431 (cf. G. T. Griffith, in *Ancient Society and Institutions ... V. Ehrenberg* [Oxford: Blackwell, 1966], 124 with 136 n. 43); additional meetings could be summoned when necessary. However, M. H. Hansen has argued that before the 340's there were only three regular meetings, and that an *ekklesia synkletos* was not an additional meeting but a meeting summoned in an irregular manner (the most recent items in a long debate: E. M. Harris, defending the view given here, *AJP* 112 [1991], 325–41 = his *Democracy and the Rule of Law* [New York: Cambridge U. P., 2006], 103–20; Hansen, *GRBS* 47 [2007], 271–306).

prescribe: *Prographein* is a technical term for such announcements; the written announcement was a *programma* (44. 2).

where it is to meet: The 'old' *bouleuterion*, on the west side of the agora, was built perhaps at the end of the sixth century, after the institution of the council of five hundred by Cleisthenes (e.g. Camp, *Site Guide*, 60–3; but because of reused material in it H. A. Thompson preferred a date *c.* 460, e.g. in *Πρακτικά τοῦ XII διεθνοῦς συνεδρίου κλασικῆς ἀρχαιολογίας, 1983* [Athens: Ministry of Culture and Sciences, 1988], 198–204); a new *bouleuterion* was built to the west of the old at the end of the fifth century (e.g. Camp, 58–9). Meetings in many other places are attested, especially for business which could be dealt with only in a particular place, such as the transfer of sacred treasures, on the acropolis (47. 1): see Rhodes, *A.B.* 35–6.

43. 4. prescribe the assemblies: According to *Anecd. Bekk.* i. 296. 8, Phot. π 1281 Theodoridis πρόπεμπτα, five days' notice was given. The *programma* would be based on the rules given below and on the *probouleumata* of the council.

One is the *ekklesia kyria*: 'Principal': on its significance in Athens see above. It handled the most essential business; in the time of *A.P.* a higher payment was given for attendance at it (62. 2); from the mid 330's the titles *ekklesia* and *ekklesia kyria* are sometimes included in the prescripts of decrees, and show that the *ekklesia kyria* was not necessarily held early in the prytany (the thirty-[second] day, *IG* ii^3 353). The assembly did not meet on annual or monthly festivals, and at some times in the year not many days will have been available (cf. Mikalson, *The Sacred and Civil Calendar*, 182–204).

hold a vote of confidence ... conducting their offices well: *Epicheirotonein* is to vote in approval (cf. 37. 1), here and in 55. 4, to uphold appointments already made: presumably the vote was preceded by a debate in which objections to particular officials could be raised. Further details are given in connection with the *strategoi* in 61. 2. For an occasion when the *thesmothetai* were deposed in the *epicheirotonia* see [Dem.] LVIII. *Theocrines* 27.

about grain: Athens was heavily dependent on imported grain, and the grain supply was a subject of great importance (cf. Xen. *Mem.* III. 6. 1–13; but it is not mentioned explicitly in Arist. *Pol.* IV. 1298 A 3–7, *Rhet.* I. 1359 B 21–3). For officials regulating the grain trade see 51. 3–4.

about the defence of the territory: This could appropriately mean what it says: cf. one of the generals' posts in 61. 1, and Xen. *Mem.* III. 6. 1–13, Arist. *Rhet.* I. 1359 B 21–3 cf. 1360 A 6–11 (but not *Pol.* IV. 1298 A 3–7). However, some decrees from the time of *A.P.* and later use the phrase *phylake tes choras* to label, and presumably claim privileged status for, a decree which was not concerned with the defence of the country (e.g. *IG* ii^2 435. 13, RO 100 = ii^3 370. 270–1, ii^2 1631. 401–3). See Rhodes, *A.B.* 231–5.

those who wish are to make *eisangeliai*: Harp. ε 7 Keaney and *Suda* ει 222 Adler εἰσαγγελία distinguish three technical uses: for major public offences, to the council or assembly; for maltreatment of parents and wards, to the archon (cf. 56. 6); for misconduct by a *diaitetes*, to the *dikastai* (cf. 53. 6). I identify as a fourth category *eisangelia* for misconduct by officials, to the council (cf. 45. 2). For my views see *A.B.* 162–71; *JHS* 99 (1979), 106–14; for an alternative Hansen, *Eisangelia*; *JHS* 100 (1980), 89–95.

Eisangelia for major public offences is mentioned in 8. 4; I believe that it was transferred from the Areopagus to the council and assembly by Ephialtes (cf. p. 267). Extracts from the *nomos eisangeltikos* of the fourth century are quoted by Hyp. IV. *Euxenippus* 7–8, 29, 39: the three main heads are overthrowing the democracy, treason, and being a *rhetor* and taking bribes to speak contrary to Athens' interests. There may also have been provision for major wrongful acts not covered by any law (e.g. Harp., *Suda*). Business for the assembly had to be submitted first to the council (45. 4), but it may be that this clause allowed cases to be presented to the assembly directly. The final hearing of a case took place either in the assembly or in a *dikasterion* (in a *dikasterion*, with the *thesmothetai* as *eisagousa arche*: 59. 2), but no final hearings in the assembly are attested after 362, and Hansen suggests that the assembly lost this right (*Eisangelia*, 51–7).

read out schedules of confiscated property: Cf. 47. 2, 3, 52. 1: the purpose was presumably to allow any one who knew of property wrongly omitted or included to draw attention to it; this presumably preceded the judgment in the court of the Eleven (52. 1).

applications for the assignment of inheritances and *epikleroi*: Claimants to an estate other than direct or adopted descandants had to register their claim with the archon (cf. 56. 6): see Harrison, *L.A.* i. 10–11, 158–62, and on the law of succession 9. 2, 35. 2.

so that none should go unclaimed without anybody's noticing: Again the purpose is publicity, so that a man with a weak claim shall not succeed through the ignorance of a man with a stronger claim. Claims were published on the archon's *sanis* (cf. Isoc. XV. *Antid.* 237), and when a claim had been decided a herald made a proclamation (Dem. XLIII. *Macartatus* 5).

43. 5. in addition to what has been stated: *A.P.* proceeds to business which occurs only once a year.

a vote on ostracism ... to hold one or not: Cf. 22. 3; if an ostracism was held it took place in the eighth prytany (Philoch. *FGrH* 328 F 30 ~

Fornara 41. B. 1), but none had been held since that of Hyperbolus in 415 (?) (cf. p. 279). Presumably the institution was not formally abolished, and the assembly still voted each year whether to hold an ostracism.
***probolai* against *sykophantai* ... up to three of each:** There is no obvious reason why these should be allowed only in the sixth prytany, and G. Gilbert suggested that they could be presented at any *ekklesia kyria* (*The Constitutional Antiquities of Sparta and Athens* [London: Sonnenschein, 1895], 303 n. 3). In addition to *A.P.*'s two categories, *probolai* could be made for offences connected with major festivals (Dem. XXI. *Midias* 1–2, 8–11). *Probolai* had only advisory force: if the assembly accepted the charge the complainant was not bound to proceed further, while if the assembly rejected the charge the complainant was not forbidden to proceed further. If he did proceed further, the *thesmothetai* were the *eisagousa arche* (59. 2).

As with *eisangeliai*, this rubric may have allowed direct submission to the assembly without prior submission to the council, but the limit on numbers may point to submission to the council, which would choose which cases should go forward. Complainants did not have to be citizens (cf. Dem. XXI. *Midias* 175), but non-citizens would need special permission to address the assembly.
whether anybody has made a promise ... failed to keep it: Another charge on which *probolai* could be made; it could also (assimilated to speaking contrary to the people's interests) be the subject of an *eisangelia*. For the offence as a form of *apate* cf. Hdt. VI. 136, Dem. XX. *Leptines* 100, 135, [Dem.] XLIX. *Timotheus* 67.
43. 6. supplications ... addresses the *demos*: On supplication as a religious and social act see J. P. A. Gould, *JHS* 93 (1973), 74–103; F. S. Naiden, *Ancient Supplication* (Oxford U. P., 2006). Here we have a civic version of the act: a petitioner places an olive branch bound with wool on the altar, as a sign that he is not claiming a right but asking a favour, and then makes his plea (cf. Andoc. I. *Myst.* 110–6, Aeschin. I. *Timarchus* 104, II. *F.L.* 15, Dem. XVIII. *Cor.* 107, XXIV. *Timocrates* 12, 53); several fourth-century decrees contain a statement that a man has been judged to be making a lawful supplication (e.g. *IG* ii^3 302. 7–9). Supplications could also be made to the council (cf. Aeschin. I. 104), which if they concerned a matter within its competence would not have to be referred to the assembly.

The other two: Poll. VIII. 96 divides these, assigning heralds and embassies to the third assembly and sacred and secular business to the fourth.

the laws prescribe: This is the first of a number of passages in which *A.P.* states that the laws prescribe something (cf. pp. 19–20).

three sacred items ... heralds and embassies ... proper: Cf. 30. 5 (where the final category is 'other matters'), Aeschin. I *Timarchus* 23 (where heralds and embassies are not conflated into a single item: possibly *A.P.* or a copyist has been careless, but for the conflation cf. Dem. XIX. *F.L.* 185). Sacred business took priority: many inscriptions state that business is to be raised πρῶτον μετὰ τὰ ἱερά (e.g. *IG* ii^2 107 = RO 31 ~ Harding 53. 15–16) and some state that business is to be raised ἐν ἱεροῖς (e.g. *IG* ii^3 914. 16). On *kerykes* (heralds) and *presbeis* (envoys) see F. E. Adcock & D. J. Mosley, *Diplomacy in Ancient Greece* (London: Thames & Hudson, 1975), 152–5: *kerykes* were considered to be under divine protection, and were used to make formal proclamations rather than to negotiate. ὅσια has often been interpreted as 'secular' business; but J. H. Blok argues that it denotes human business of concern to the gods and that the categories mentioned here do not cover the whole of the assembly's business (in V. Azoulay & P. Ismard [eds], *Clisthène et Lycurgue d'Athènes* [Paris: Publications de la Sorbonne, 2011], 233–54 at 252–3). My rendering 'proper' attempts to span the usual interpretation and Blok's interpretation.

sometimes they transact business without a *procheirotonia*: *A.P.* has condensed his material and says only this about *procheirotonia*. The procedure is mentioned by Aeschin. I. *Timarchus* 23, Dem. XXIV. *Timocrates* 11–12; the lexicographers supplying Lys. fr. 227 Carey state that when a *probouleuma* was presented to the assembly the assembly first voted whether to debate the *probouleuma* or accept it. Wilamowitz, *A.u.A.* ii. 254–6, considered that senseless, and suggested that when too many items in a category were submitted the assembly decided which to consider; J. H. Lipsius, *LSKP* 17 (1896), 405–12, thought that the choice was between debate and outright rejection; but the lexicographers' explanation has been defended, as a means of dispatching a lengthy agenda, by M. H. Hansen, *The Athenian Ecclesia* [Copenhagen: Museum Tusculanum P., 1983], 123–30: a *probouleuma* incorporating a specific recommendation would be debated only if in the *procheirotonia* somebody voted against automatic acceptance.

Heralds and envoys ... deliver them to them: Since the *prytaneis* prepared business for the council and the council prepared business for the assembly, all messages and deputations had first to go to the *prytaneis*: cf. Dem. XVIII. *Cor.* 169–70. Dem. XIX. *F.L.* 185 shows that the council also had designated sessions for heralds and embassies.

44. 1. There is a chairman of the *prytaneis* ... for the same man to serve twice: This is the *epistates* named in decrees of the fifth and early fourth century. Limitation to one day is a special instance of the rule in 62. 3, that men might serve twice in the council but only once in other civilian offices (comparison with 44. 3 suggests service as *epistates* one day in a man's life – in which case the Antiphanes of 337/6 and of 330/29 must be different men: thus *L.G.P.N.* ii *s.n.*, 40, 41), but if it was common to serve two years in the council we may wonder if there were always enough councillors eligible under that rule.

He keeps watch over the keys ... are kept: Cf. Dem. XXII. *Androtion*, *hyp.* ii. 7. Treasures were kept in various sacred buildings: see D. Harris, *The Treasures of the Parthenon and Erechtheion* (Oxford U. P., 1995); T. Linders, *The Treasurers of the Other Gods in Athens and their Functions* (Meisenheim an Glan: Hain, 1975), 3–7, 46–8, 53–4. There were also the secular funds of the Athenian state, in the fifth century kept in a central treasury (we do not know where) and in the fourth divided between different spending authorities (cf. 48. 1–2). Official records were kept in various places by various authorities, but after the old *bouleuterion* was replaced by a new (cf. p. 349) the old came to be used as a record-house, known as the Μητρῷον from the middle of the fourth century and replaced by a new building in the second century (cf. Camp, *Site Guide*, 60–3; J. P. Sickinger, *Public Records and Archives in Classical Athens* [U. of North Carolina P., 1999]).

the public seal: He is called on to use it in RO 58 = *IG* ii^{3} 292 ~ Harding 78. A. 39–40; Xen. *Vect.* 4. 21 refers to slaves σεσημασμένα τῷ δημοσίῳ σημάντρῳ.

it is obligatory to remain in the *tholos* for him: Presumably when his duties did not take him elsewhere: until the institution of the *proedroi*, with his fellow *prytaneis* he presided in the council and assembly.

a *trittys* of the *prytaneis* ordered by him: A *trittys* is a third part of a tribe; Cleisthenes' tribes were divided into *trittyes* unequal in size (cf.

pp. 175, 245). Since neither 50 nor 49 is divisible by 3, the *trittys* here cannot have been an exact mathematical third: many have thought that it was the councillors of one Cleisthenic *trittys*; some have detected in the arrangement of fourth-century lists for some tribes a more nearly equal threefold division which might have been used for this purpose (e.g. W. E. Thompson, *Historia* 15 [1966], 1–10); some have suspected that in Cleisthenes' original scheme the *trittyes* were more nearly equal than in the fourth century (e.g. M. H. Hansen, *C&M* 41 [1990], 51–4).

44. 2. when the *prytaneis* convene the council or the *demos*: Cf. 43. 3.

he picks by lot nine *proedroi*, one from each tribe except the tribe in prytany: I.e. a board of *proedroi* was appointed on each day when there was to be a meeting of the council or assembly. This is confirmed by inscriptions (in particular, several decrees from the late fourth century to the late third list all the *proedroi*: S. Dow, *Hesperia* 32 [1963], 335–65), and repeated in some scholia and lexica, but other scholia and lexica give erroneous accounts (e.g. schol. Aeschin. III. *Ctesiphon* 3, 4 [10, 13 Dilts], schol. Dem. XXII. *Androtion* 5 [22a Dilts]). In later Athens the number of *proedroi* remained one fewer than the number of tribes (e.g. eleven in *IG* ii^2 502. 5–11). The *nomothetai* of the fourth century had their own *proedroi* and *epistates*: (*IG* ii^3 452. 48–52 with Rhodes, *A.B.* 28).

again from these one chairman: Decrees down to 403/2 name an *epistates* who belongs to the tribe in prytany (e.g. *IG* ii^2 1 = RO 2 ~ Harding 5. 41–2); decrees from 379/8 name an *epistates* who does not belong to the tribe in prytany and who in what eventually became the standard formula is explicitly said to be *epistates* of the *proedroi* (first in *CSCA* 5 [1972], 164–9, no. 2. 9–11). The old system is reflected probably in Lys. XIII. *Agoratus* 37 (399), and possibly in Ar. *Eccl.* 86–7 (late 390's); F. X. Ryan, *JHS* 115 (1995), 167–8, sees the old system in [Dem.] LIX. *Neaera* 89–90, and argues for a change after 384. The allotment of juries was modified about the same time, so that nobody could know in advance which jurors would try which case (cf. p. 423 and chs 63–5), and Dr. N. Sato has suggested to me that similarly the purpose was to ensure that nobody could know in advance who would preside in the council and assembly on a particular day. Both *epistatai* have duties in RO 58 = *IG* ii^3 292 ~ Harding 78. A. 30–41.

he gives the agenda to them: Cf. 43. 3.

44. 3. they take care of good order: Cf. Ar. *Thesm.* 853–4, 920–46, Dem. XXV. *Aristogeiton i.* 9, Aeschin. I. *Timarchus* 34 (but the laws inserted in §35 are generally regarded as a forgery). On *kosmos* in fourth-century Athens cf. 42. 2 with commentary.

they judge the votes by show of hands: Cf. 30. 5. Probably when voting was by show of hands votes were estimated but not precisely counted (M. H. Hansen, *GRBS* 18 [1977], 123–37).

they have the power of dismissal: To close the meeting: cf. Ar. *Eq.* 674, *Vesp.* 595; *Ach.* 169–73 uses *lyein.*

it is not permitted ... to be *proedros* once in each prytany: Cf. 44. 1, on the *epistates* of the *prytaneis.* During a year, if there were meetings on *c.* 300 days, a councillor might serve as *proedros* five or six times, more than half would have to serve once as *epistates* of the *proedroi* and likewise as *epistates* of the *prytaneis*, so that some would have to serve in both capacities.

44. 4. They also hold elections: Cf. 43. 1, 61; also Xen. *Mem.* III. 4. 1, Dem. XXIII. *Aristocrates* 171, Aeschin. III. *Ctesiphon* 13, Plut. *Phoc.* 8. 1–2; we do not know whether the civilian officials of 43. 1 were elected on the same occasion. This section would more naturally be placed with the regular business of the assembly in the latter part of ch. 43.

in accordance with whatever the *demos* decides: The law should have specified that ten generals should be elected 'from all Athenians' and five assigned to particular posts (61. 1), one taxiarch and one phylarch should be elected from each tribe (61. 3, 5), and so on; it may have specified a minimum age and other qualifications (see p. 344). It is not clear in what respect the assembly might have had discretion: we need an explanation applicable to other officers as well as to generals; M. Piérart suggests that the assembly might have been free to receive nominations at the meeting (*BCH* 98 [1974], 140).

this is done ... in whose term there are good omens: *Eusemos* usually means 'clear', but here the reference is more probably to good omens (cf. B. D. Meritt, *Klio* 52 [1970], 277–8) than to good weather (Sandys), which would not be particularly necessary for this meeting). For the importance of good omens for military activity see Y. Garlan trans. J. Lloyd, *War in the Ancient World* (London: Chatto & Windus, 1975), 42–3; Pritchett, *War*, i. 109–26. It is not clear whether this was one of the regular assemblies or an additional assembly; but by the second century it

was at any rate possible for other business to be transacted at an electoral assembly (*IG* ii^3 1272, 1276, ii^2 955). These men's year of office was presumably the archontic year, beginning in mid summer: the Athenians did not find it intolerable that the change occurred in the middle of the campaigning season (H. B. Mayor, *JHS* 59 [1939], 45–64, who did, was answered by W. K. Pritchett, *AJP* 61 [1940], 469–74).
There has to be a *probouleuma* about this also: *A.P.* has not yet mentioned *probouleumata*, on which see 45. 4. A *probouleuma* for an election might read, e.g., 'The *demos* shall elect forthwith ten taxiarchs, one from each tribe, from those Athenians who are eligible'.

45. 1. The council formerly had the power … and to execute: On this section see P. Cloché, *REG* 23 (1920), 1–50; Rhodes, *A.B.* 179–207. It has proved hard to find any occasion when the council had the absolute power which is here claimed for it, and I believe that the council first acquired judicial powers (apart from the *dokimasia* and discipline of its own members) through Ephialtes' reform of the Areopagus (25. 1–2), that those powers were limited from the start, and that the story here was invented or misapplied to illustrate a ficitious reduction in the council's powers. This is the first of several passages in the second part of *A.P.* which contrast current with earlier practice (cf. pp. 20, 29), but the anecdote is unique in the second part.
Lysimachus: The name is common in Athens, and we cannot tell who is intended.
to the public servant: The noun δοῦλον is to be understood. This was the public executioner: cf. Lys. XIII. *Agoratus* 56 (emended), Ar. *Eccl.* 81, Aeschin. II. *F.L.* 126 (some MSS).
sitting and waiting to be executed: Lysimachus was to be killed by *apotympanismos* (cf. below). Sitting is not the most obvious posture for a man awaiting that, and L. Gernet considered but did not adopt καθη<λω>μένον, 'nailed down; (*AC* 5 [1936], 333–4, cf. *REG* 37 [1924], 267 n. 1 = his *Anthropologie de la Grèce antique* [Paris: Maspero, 1968], 295–6, cf. 307 n. 23).
Eumelides of Alopece: The demotic suggests that a known man is intended, but nothing is known about him now.
saying … without the judgment of a lawcourt: In fact there were various circumstances in which men could be executed without being

condemned by a *dikasterion*: murderers condemned by the Areopagus (cf. 57. 3), major offenders condemned by the assembly after an *eisangelia* (cf. 43. 4), *kakourgoi* by the Eleven (52. 1), adulterers caught in the act by the wronged husband (57. 3). Eumelides should have claimed not that only a *dikasterion* could sentence to death but that the council could not sentence to death.

when judgment was passed in a lawcourt: What is envisaged is what happened in the fifth and fourth centuries when the council wanted a penalty beyond its competence: the hearing in court will have been a fresh trial (cf. below), and either the same man prosecuted again or somebody prosecuted on behalf of the council (cf. Harrison, *L.A.* ii. 56).

the man who came back from the garrotte: *Eponymia* is a derived name; ὁ ἀπὸ τοῦ τυπάνου is 'the man who came back from the garrotte', i.e. who escaped execution by *apotympanismos*. A collection of skeletons found at Phalerum suggests that the victims were fastened to a plank and perhaps slowly strangled by a collar round the neck (cf. Gernet, *REG* 37 [1924], 261–93 = his *Anthropologie de la Grèce antique*, 302–29).

the *demos* took away from the council … punish with fines: In fact, as late as the mid fourth century the council could impose fines up to 500 drachmae ([Dem.] XLVII. *Evergus & Mnesibulus* 43) and could order precautionary though not penal imprisonment (Dem. XXIV. *Timocrates* 63; 144, 147–8; cf. for the time of *A.P.* 48. 1). Some have thought that penalties within the council's competence were subject to appeal (e.g. J. H. Lipsius, *Das attische Recht und Rechtsverfahren* [Leipzig: Reisland, 1905–15], 196–8), but more probably the council like other authorities had absolute power up to the prescribed limit and what *A.P.* says here is wrong (the same issue arises in other cases, below).

if the council convicted anybody of wrongdoing: Cf. ML 46 = *IG* i^3 34 ~ Fornara 98. 37–41, Aeschin. I. *Timarchus* 111.

the convictions and proposals … to the lawcourt: Cf. 59. 4. *Epizemiosis* is not found elsewhere, and in cognate forms the prefix seems not to import a special shade of meaning; I doubt the view of Wilamowitz (*A.u.A.* ii. 196) that the word refers specifically to fines beyond the council's competence.

whatever the jurors voted that should be definitive: This would be a fresh trial, with verdict as well as sentence to be decided (cf. above).

45. 2. The council judges most of the officials ... handle funds: The council tried men accused of misconduct in office, especially misappropriation of public money. This accompanied the council's administrative supervision of officials (cf. 47. 1, 49. 5): a committee of the council examined their accounts each prytany (48. 3); the council was less involved in the financial examination at the end of the year (54. 2), but the *euthynoi*, who received general complaints at the end of the year, were members of the council (48. 4). Aeschin. III. *Ctesiphon* 14 quotes on accountability a law referring to 'all who handle the city's business for more than thirty days', so for the purposes of this section *arche* will include not only ordinary officials but other men with public duties to perform, such as trierarchs and tax collectors. For the suggestion that the council acquired these responsibilities by the reform of Ephialtes see p. 267.

the judgment is not decisive ... to the lawcourt: Probably, as in 45. 1, the council had the absolute right to impose penalties within its own competence but had to refer cases to a *dikasterion* if it wanted a heavier penalty.

It is also permitted to private individuals: The trial of an official might result either from the council's own supervision (47–8) or from an accusation by a private citizen. The speaker of Antiph, VI. *Chor.* made a private accusation in 420/19 (§35), and uncovered further malpractices as a member of the council and of the first prytany in 419/8 (§§49 with 45).

an *eisangelia* ... on a charge of not complying with the laws: Cf. Antiph. VI. *Chor,* 35, *SEG* xxvi 72 = RO 25. 33–4 (εἰσαγ[γελλέτω μὲ]|ν Hansen, *Eisangelia*, 28 n.). Although the same word is used, and some offences might fall into either category, I distinguish *eisangelia* against officials from *eisangelia* for major public offences: cf. pp. 350–1.

there is reference ... if the council convicts: This confirms that we are dealing with compulsory reference (when the council wanted a penalty beyond its own competence), not with a right of appeal, which we should expect to be available to whoever was the unsuccessful litigant.

45. 3. vets the councillors ... in the following year: It was standard Athenian practice for officials to be subjected to vetting before they entered offices to which they had been appointed (55. 2): formally this was to check their qualifications (cf. 55. 3, for the archons), but men who were opposed might have to justify their career and demonstrate that they were good citizens (cf. p. 330). In classical Athens most *dokimasiai* took place in the *dikasteria* (55. 2), but in early Athens some may have been conducted by the Areopagus (cf. p. 267), and the council may always have conducted the *dokimasia* of its successors (cf. Rhodes, *A.B.* 178). Lys. XVI. *Mantitheus* and XXXI. *Philon* were written for the *dokimasiai* of councillors. For other *dokimasiai* conducted by the council see 49.

the nine archons: Cf. 55. 2–4. This *dokimasia* is mentioned here also because it was conducted by the council and subject to *ephesis*.

previously it had the power … reference to the lawcourt: Cf. 55. 2. What is said here suggests that *ephesis* took place only after a rejection, but the more detailed account in 55 shows that in the time of *A.P.* for archons there was compulsory reference to a *dikasterion* whether the council accepted or rejected. But it is hard to believe that that cumbersome procedure was followed each year for five hundred councillors, and for them I suspect that *ephesis* occurred (whether as optional appeal or as compulsory reference) only when the council rejected (cf. Rhodes, *A.B.* 178). *A.P.* does not state when the change took place.

45. 4. In these matters the council lacks definitive power: *Akyros* is the opposite of *kyrios*. With μὲν οὖν … δὲ we should expect a transition to an area in which the council was *kyrios* (cf. J. D. Denniston, *The Greek Particles* [Oxford U. P., [2]1954], 472), but in fact §4 deals with the council's submission of *probouleumata* to provide a basis for debate and final decision in the assembly.

it conducts *probouleusis* … not prescribed by the *prytaneis*: In Plut. *Sol.* 19. 1 (but not in *A.P.* 8. 4) Solon's council of four hundred is characterised in this way. On the principle of *probouleusis*, prior consideration by a smaller council leading to decision by a larger body, see A. Andrewes, *Probouleusis* (Oxford: inaugural lecture, 1954); Rhodes, *A.B.* 52–81; R. A. de Laix, *Probouleusis at Athens* (U. of California P., 1973), 3–139. As far as we know, the rule was normally observed at Athens, in that debate in the assembly was preceded by a *probouleuma* which might make a recommendation or invite the assembly to decide for itself, and the assembly could accept a recommendation or modify it or decide otherwise. Some other cities interpreted the principle so as to make the council more powerful and the assembly less powerful: see, e.g., Arist. *Pol.* II. 1273 A 6–13 on Carthage, Crete and Sparta.

In the fifth century some complicated measures were drafted by *ad hoc* boards of *syngrapheis* (e.g. ML 73 = *IG* i^3 78 ~ Fornara 140. 3–4), and in that inscription Lampon had himself commissioned to *syngraphein* and the council required to submit his draft to the assembly (ll. 59–61); but the *syngrapheis* who prepared the way for the régimes of the Four Hundred (29. 2) and the Thirty (34. 3) discredited that instituion, and in the fourth century instead the council was sometimes commissioned by the assembly to submit a *probouleuma* to a subsequent meeting (e.g. RO 69 = *IG* ii^3 399 ~ Harding 66. 6–10). For some special cases see 43. 4–6, 44. 4, with commentary; for *probouleusis* and *procheirotonia* see 43. 6 with commentary. Three occasions are known when a proposal was said to be *aprobouleuton*: by Thrasybulus in 403 (p. 331), by Androtion *c.* 355 (pp. 362–3), and by Aristogeiton *c.* 345–331 (Dem. XXV. *Aristogeiton i, hyp.* 1–2: see Rhodes, *A.B.*, 53).

not prescribed by the *prytaneis*: On the *programma* see 43. 4, 44. 2.

the man who succeeded: ὁ εἰπὼν or ὁ γράψας, 'the proposer', would be more appropriate, since proceedings could be started before the assembly voted (e.g. Dem. XXIV. *Timocrates* 11–14), but the text need not be doubted. If proceedings were not started within the year, the proposal could still be challenged but not the proposer (Dem. XX. *Leptines* 144, with reference to a *nomos*, cf. *hyp. 2.* 3, with reference to both *nomoi* and *psephismata*).

***graphe paranomon*:** Listed (with the *graphe nomon me epitedeion theinai*) in 59. 2. The *graphe paranomon*, first clearly attested in 415 (cf. p. 267), suspended in 411 and 404 to facilitate the overthrow of the democracy (29. 4, p. 313), was a prosecution for illegally proposing a decree; by analogy the *graphe nomon me epitedeion theinai* was provided against proposing an inexpedient law; and in practice either illegality or inexpediency could be alleged in either. M. H. Hansen, *The Sovereignty of the People's Court in Athens in the Fourth Century BC* (Odense U. P., 1974), collects instances of both and uses them to argue that the courts rather than the assembly were the ultimate sovereign body in the fourth century.

46. 1. The council also takes care … the shipsheds: Cf. [Xen.] *A.P.* 3. 2, using *neoria*: strictly *neoria* are dockyards and *neosoikoi* are ship-sheds, but the distinction is not always observed. For a review of recent work on these installations see C. Papadopoulou, *AR* 60 (2013/4),

50–4. The dockyards and their contents were controlled directly by the *epimeletai ton neorion*, not mentioned in *A.P.*, best known for the records which they published in the second and third quarters of the fourth century (*IG* ii^2 1604–32). Decisions regarding ships and equipment were taken commonly by the council but sometimes by the assembly; routine lawsuits in naval matters were tried by the *dikasteria*, but some came to the council, and serious matters could be pursued through an *eisangelia* against an official (45. 2) or for a major public offence (43. 4).

and it builds new: Diod. Sic. XI. 43. 3 credits Themistocles with a target of twenty ships a year after the Persian Wars, but no figure is given by Dem. XXII. *Androtion*, *hyp. 1.* 1 and *hyp. 2.* 8, and the evidence is not sufficient to support a regular quota. Ship-building programmes are discussed by D. J. Blackman, *GRBS* 10 (1969), 202–16 (who thinks there was a fixed quota but would not restore a numeral here).

triremes or quadriremes, whichever the *demos* votes: Above and below *A.P.* mentions only triremes; here he mentions triremes and quadriremes; he does not mention quinqueremes. The list of 330/29 has 18 quadriremes, that of 326/5 an uncertain number of quadriremes and still no quinqueremes, that of 325/4 50 quadriremes and 2 quinqueremes (*IG* ii^2 1627. 275–8, 1628. 495–7, 1629. 808–12, with N. G. Ashton, *GRBS* 20 [1979], 237–42, on 1629). This suggests that *A.P.* was originally written in the 330's and mentioned only triremes here, and that quadriremes were added *c.* 328–325 (cf. A. Tovar, *REC* 3 [1948], 153–9, and p. 29).

equipment and shipsheds for these: Here *neosoikoi* are to be taken strictly, as ship-sheds. For expenditure on ship-sheds and equipment in this period see *IG* ii^2 1627. 49–51 and later lists, 505. 7–17, 1668; Aeschin. III. *Ctesiphon* 25, Philoch. *FGrH* 328 F 56a ~ Harding 96. A, Hyp. fr. 118 Jensen = Kenyon, [Plut.] *X Or.* 852 c cf. *IG* ii^2 457. *b*. 5–8.

The *demos* elects architects for the ships: In the fourth century lists ships are commonly identified as τοῦ δεῖνος ἔργον (e.g. *IG* ii^{2}1612. 100–213); in that list *architekton* is once used of the men responsible for repairing ships (ll. 151–213). It is not known whether the *architektones* had to be re-engaged each year.

If they do not hand over ... to take their award: Cf. 60. 3, on the archon and olive oil. Androtion proposed that the council in which he had served his second term (probably 356/5: e.g. G. L. Cawkwell, *C&M*

23 [1962], 40–5) should be rewarded, although it had not satisfied this requirement, and he was prosecuted, apparently unsuccessfully, in a *graphe paranomon* (Dem. XXII. *Androtion* 8–20, cf. *hyp. 1, 2.* 8, 10: cf. p. 361). The *dorea* was a gold crown (Aeschin. I. *Timarchus* 111–2, Dem. XXII. *Androtion* 36, 38–9).

they take it under the subsequent council: The law changed between the prosecution of Androtion and the time of *A.P.*: earlier the council put the proposal to the assembly late in its own year (Dem. XXII. *Androtion* 8–9); the council of 343/2 was certainly honoured in its own year for managing the Dionysia, and may also have received the general reward in its own year (*IG* ii^3 306. 21–2, 24–5; 1–3). Aeschin. III. *Ctesiphon* 9–12 (330) claims that for individuals, when it was found that honours were prejudicing their *euthynai*, it was forbidden to honour men while still *hypeuthynoi*: provisional honours, to be conferred after the *euthynai*, are found in inscriptions from the late 340's to the early 320's, and that was perhaps a response to the prosecution of Androtion, itself forbidden in the 320's (Rhodes, *A.B.*, 15–16).

It builds the triremes ... *trieropoioi*: Inscriptions of the late fifth century mention *naupegoi* (shipwrights) and *treieropoioi* (ML 91 = *IG* i^3 117 ~ Fornara 161. 4–16, *IG* i^3 182. 9–13); Dem. XXII. *Androtion* 17–20 refers to a ταμίας τῶν τριηροποιικῶν (emended from τριηροποιῶν) who is said to have been appointed illegally by the council, and to have absconded with 2½ talents (see Rhodes, *A.B.* 121–3). Aeschin. III. *Ctesiphon* 30 (330) gives building triremes as one of the jobs assigned 'now' to the tribes.

46. 2. it inspects all the public buildings: *A.P.* does not state whether this refers to existing buildings, new buildings or both: in the fifth century new buildings were supervised by boards of *epistatai*, probably elected by the *demos* (cf. the Eleusinian *epistatai*, *IG* i^3 32. 7–13); in the fourth century *IG* ii^3 429 attests both elected supervisors and the involvement of the council. See also 49. 3.

if it judges anybody guilty ... hands him over to a lawcourt: We should expect the same kind of procedure as in 45. 1–3. In the time of *A.P.* the Areopagus made *apophaseis* to the assembly, and the assembly then decided whether to prosecute in a *dikasterion* (cf. p. 409). Here, if the papyrus' text is right, the council referred the case to a *dikasterion* (presumably, if it wanted a penalty beyond its own competence) and the report to the assembly was an additional requirement; if the καταγνόντος (*sc.* τοῦ δήμου) of Kaibel & Wilamowitz were right, the council would hold a first hearing and report to the assembly, the assembly would hold a second hearing, and if it condemned the council would refer the case to a *dikasterion* – but that is procedurally more difficult than the papyrus' text.

47. 1. It also joins in administration … for the most part: This opens a ring, which is closed in 49. 5: since 47–8 deals with financial officials and 49 with *dokimasiai*, the concluding sentence would be better placed at the end of 48. Cf. also 45. 2.
the treasurers of Athena: For the history of these treasurers and those of the Other Gods to 385/4 (when an amalgamated board gave way to two separate boards) see pp. 292–3. They were amalgamated again in the 340's, perhaps in 344/3 or 343/2 (N. Papazarkadas, *Sacred and Public Land in Ancient Athens* [Oxford U. P., 2011], 30), but this time the Other Gods disappeared from the title, and they were called ταμίαι (τῶν) τῆς θεοῦ (e.g. *IG* ii³ 429. 37); they are not attested after 299/8. (The text of *c.* 200 or later which mentions the Other Gods appears to be a reinscription of a fourth-century decree: *SEG* lii 104. 9–10, cf. Rhodes, *G&R*² 60 [2013], 215 with n. 85). The affairs of the gods were a part of the concerns of the Athenian state, and the state took decisions for them as it took decisions for its other concerns. The treasury of Athena was Athens' richest sacred treasury: during the Peloponnesian War the state borrowed money from it (e.g. ML 72 = *IG* i³ 369 ~ Fornara 134), and towards the end of the war dedications had to be melted down (Philoch. *FGrH* 328 F 141a *ap.* schol. Ar. *Ran.* 720). In the fourth century the stock of dedications was built up again, and the treasury was used as a bank by the state only exceptionally (cf. Ferguson, *The Treasurers of Athena*, 128–40).
are ten in number: Presumably since the creation of Cleisthenes' ten tribes: there appear to be eight in *IG* i³ 510 (*c.* 550?).
from the *pentakosiomedimnoi* … (for the law is still valid): Cf. 8. 1; the only other cross reference from the second part to the first is in 55. 1.
the man picked in the sortition … even if he is really poor: Because the assignment of citizens to classes was now wholly unrealistic (as it was not yet in the 450's, when the archonship was opened to *zeugitai*

but not to *thetes*: cf. 26. 2) and / or because the law was only nominally observed, and any one who wanted to be treasurer would claim to be a *pentakosiomedimnos* and would not be challenged (cf. 7. 4). A fragment of Theophrastus criticises property qualifcations as a basis for appointments (MS Vat. Gr. 2306. B. 17–36: pp. 96–115 Szegedy-Maszak).

They take over ... in the presence of the council: The statue was that made by Pheidias between 447/6 and 438/7 (*IG* i³ 453–60 [extracts ML 54 ~ Fornara 114], Philoch. *FGrH* 328 F 121 ~ Fornara 116. A): in 431 Pericles mentioned the gold plates as a source of emergency funds (Thuc. II. 13. 5), but the statue survived intact until 296/5 (*P. Oxy.* xvii 2082. iv = *FGrH* 257a F 4. 1–16). All but one of the fifth-century gold *Nikai* were melted down in and after 407/6 (schol. Ar. *Ran.*. 720), but new ones were made in the fourth century, particularly at the instance of Lycurgus (e.g. [Plut.] *X Or.* 841 D, 852 B); these also were destroyed in 296/5: see particularly D. B. Thompson, *Hesperia* 13 (1944), 173–209. τὸν ἄλλον κόσμον will include other dedications, and equipment for religious ceremonies; χρήματα will be money. The council met on the acropolis to witness the transfer (e.g. ML 58 = *IG* i³ 52 ~ Fornara 119. *A*. 18–21); the *paradoseis*, records of the annual transfers, were inscribed on stone (*IG* i³ 292–362, ii² 1370–1513).

47. 2. the *poletai*: 'Sellers' of state contracts and of confiscated property (*polein* is used below of both activities): they are mentioned among Solonian officials in 7. 3 and are attested epigraphically from the mid fifth century (e.g. *IG* i³ 23. 11). Like the treasurers of Athena (47. 1) they probably became ten after the creation of the ten tribes. Their office, the *poleterion*, was probably in the south-western part of the agora (e.g. Dem. XXV. *Aristogeiton 1*. 57: see M. K. Langdon, *Agora* xix, pp. 65–7; Camp, *Site Guide*, 51–2). There is a dedication by two *poletai* of 324/3 (*'Αρχ. 'Εφ.* [1973], 175–6 no. 1).

together with the treasurer ... the theoric fund: Cf. 43. 1. In 307/6, the last year in which the *poletai* are attested, *ho epi tei dioikesei* is found working with them (*IG* ii² 463. 36).

in the presence of the council: Cf. Andoc. I. *Myst.* 134, Aeschin. I. *Timarchus* 119.

they ratify for whoever the council votes: The arrangement of the text applies this specifically to mining contracts (though some have moved the statement to the end of the sentence to make it apply more generally).

If mining contracts were given not to the highest bidder but at fixed rates (cf. below), a vote of the council may have been particularly important; and mine leases bear prytany dates (e.g. *Agora* xix P5. 40), whereas sales of confiscated property bear calendar dates (e.g. P26. 460–1). Two inscriptions, perhaps both later than 322, mention the placing of contracts for public works in a *dikasterion* (*IG* ii² 1669. 8, 21, etc., 1678. *aA*. 27–8).

the mines which are sold: On the Athenan silver mines see R. J. Hopper, *BSA* 48 (1953), 200–54, 63 (1968), 293–326; C. E. Conophagos, *Le Laurium antique et la technique grecque de la production de l'argent* (Athens: Ekdotike Hellados, 1980); R. G. Osborne, *Demos: The Discovery of Classical Attica* (Cambridge U. P., 1985), 111–26. Mine leases form the largest item in the records of the *poletai* published as *Agora* xix P1–56. The state let out the rights for mining, while at least some and perhaps most of the land in question remained in private ownership (Hopper 1953, 205–9, 227–8); for two suggestions as to what then happened to the silver see P. G. van Alfen, in F. de Callataÿ (ed.), *Quantifying Monetary Supplies in Greco-Roman Times* (Bari: Edipuglia, 2013), 143–6; G. Davis, *Historia* 63 (2014), 263–74 (for Lusitania under the Roman empire see *FIR* 113 = *FIRA* i. 104. 3–4, 5–7, 11–12).

those which are in working order … sold for 7 years: The leases use three catgeories: ἐργάσιμα, 'working', καινοτομίαι, 'new cuttings', and (παλαιὰ) ἀνασάξιμα, which are probably equivalent to *A.P.*'s συγκεχωρημένα, 'conceded', i.e. given up by a previous lessee but now attempted again (Hopper 1953, 201–3). The longer leases, probably for the second and third categories, were in fact for seven years (M. Crosby, *Hesperia* 19 [1950], 199–200): probably *A.P.* wrote ζ′ but a scribe mistakenly repeated γ′. K. M. W. Shipton, *ZPE* cxx 1998, 57–63, argues that the prices attested in the leases are best interpreted as pointing to different periods of time, at a standard rate of 5 dr. per prytany (cf. *Agora* xix P26. 474–5: 20 dr. for many of the *anasaxima* would represent an exploratory four prytanies) – in which case either there was an extremely large number of concessions or the state also had some other means of deriving profits from the mines.

they sell the properties … in the presence of the council: It is not clear why 'exiles from the Areopagus' who had not waited for the result of their trial for homicide (cf. Dem. XXIII. *Aristocrates* 45, 69) are distinguished from 'the others'. Apart perhaps from a few fragments, the earliest published documents of the *poletai* are the 'Attic *stelai*', listing property confiscated after the scandals of 415 (*IG* i³ 421–30 [extracts ML 79 ~ Fornara 147. D]: see especially W. K. Pritchett, *Hesperia* 22 [1953], 225–99, 25 [1956], 178–328, D. A. Amyx, *Hesperia* 27 [1958], 163–310). Published records protected the purchasers' right to what they bought (cf. the reading of inventories in the assembly: 43. 4).

the 9 archons ratify them: It is not clear why they did this or what their ratification amounted to. In *Agora* xix P26 we have only a *kyrotes* from the *prytaneis* (e.g. l. 462), but in P4. 1–2 ἐννέ' ἄρχοντε[ς ἔφηναν κυ|ρώσα]ντε[ς ἐ]ν τῆι βουλῆι τοῖς πεντακοσ[ίοις].

the taxes sold for a year: Such as the *pentekoste* of Andoc. I. *Myst.* 133–4; in *Agora* xix P26. 470–2 one man is μετ|ασχόντα τέλους μετοικίου ἐπὶ Πυθοδότου ἄ|ρχοντος.

they hand to the council: Cf. 47. 5–48. 1.

writing up on whitened boards: Charcoal on whitened boards was the normal medium for temporary notices (cf. 47. 4, 53. 4; πινάκιον λελευκωμένον 48. 4; σανίς 48. 2; λεύκωμα e.g. Lys. IX. *Soldier* 6). The *poletai* seem not to have published permanent records of tax contracts.

47. 3. They write up separately … to pay in the ninth prytany: *Kataballein* and *katabole* are the standard terms. We do not know how it was decided into which category a contract should fall (for payments each prytany in mine leases see above); Dem. XXIV. *Timocrates* 98 confirms that much of the revenue from *tele* was not received until near the end of the year, and complains that Timocrates' law would worsen this situation.

They write up also … for they sell these also: This return to confiscated property suggests that *A.P.* is relying on clauses in the law about the terms of payment and the records to be kept,

For houses … in ten years: Cf. *Agora* xix P2. 5.

47. 4. The *basileus* introduces the leases of sacred lands: *Sc.* εἰς τὴν βουλήν (cf. 47. 5). *A.P.* does not say that the *poletai* were involved also, but we should expect that, and in *IG* i³ 84. 4–18 that is stated in the amendment though not in the original proposal (cf. M. B. Walbank, in *Agora* xix, pp. 149–51, 154–5, 166–7, but contrast M. K. Langdon, in *Agora* xix, pp. 64–5).

the lease of these also is for ten years: The last reference to a ten-year period was to the ten annual instalments at the end of 47. 3; but that is not a good parallel, and we may wonder if a better parallel was given in the law but omitted by *A.P.*

for ten years, and the payment is made in the 9th prytany: The *temenos* of *IG* i^3 84 was let for twenty years with payment in the ninth prytany. For ten-year leases see *IG* i^3 402, *Agora* xvi 75. 9 (restored), *IG* ii^2 2498, 1241 (each of the last two payable in two instalments). A. Williams, *Hesperia* 80 (2011), 261–86, argues that *Agora* xix L6 is from four different *stelai* and not all sacred leases came up for renewal at the same time.

For that reason most of the money is collected in this prytany: Cf. Dem. XXIV. *Timocrates* 98, cited above. This will not have been in the laws but is an observation added by *A.P.*: cf. 54. 3, and see Introduction, p. 20.

47. 5. The boards ... and the public slave keeps watch over them: The *poletai* made the records (above), the *apodektai* cancelled them when payment was made (48. 1), in the meantime the records were in the custody of a public slave. On the old *bouleuterion* as a record-house see p. 354.

When there is a payment of money: For the expression cf. *SEG* xxvi 72 = RO 25. 7. Presumably the day was fixed by the *prytaneis* (cf. 43. 3).

to the *apodektai*: Cf. 48. 1–2.

taking down from the racks: The normal meaning of *epistylion* is 'architrave' (e.g. *IG* i^3 474. 33–9); here they must be objects to which the different *grammateia* relevant to different dates for payment can be attached.

wiped off: Cf. 48. 1; 36. 2 and 49. 2 use *exaleiphein* for deleting a name from a register; Ath. IX. 407 c uses *dialeiphein* in a story of Alcibiades' destroying the record of an impending trial.

48. 1. *apodektai*: 'Receivers' of state revenue, including revenue destined for the sacred treasuries. Androtion *FGrH* 324 F 5 says that they were created by Cleisthenes to replace the *kolakretai*, but the *kolakretai* in the fifth century were paying officers, and make their last dated appearances in 418/7 (*IG* i^3 84. 28, 136. 6), while the *apodektai* make their first dated appearance in 418/7 (*IG* i^3 84. 15–18: cf. p. 293). On their involvement in Androtion's collection of arrears of *eisphora* in the 350's see Dem. XXIV. *Timocrates* 162, 197; they also acted as *eisagousa arche* for lawsuits concerning tax-collecting (52. 3). Aeschin. III. *Ctesiphon* 25 includes them among the officials whose office the theoric treasurers ἦρχον (cf. p. 346): this probably denotes supervision rather than supersession, and can be compared with what is said of the *poletai* in 47. 2.

These take over the boards, and wipe off the monies paid: Cf. 47. 2–5.

in the presence of the council in the council house: As the *poletai* made contracts in the presence of the council (47. 2, 5); cf. RO 25 = *SEG* xxvi 72. 4–8. Payments in the navy lists are said sometimes to be εἰς βουλευτήριον (e.g. *IG* ii² 1622. 524–5), sometimes ἀποδέκταις (e.g. *IG* ii² 1627. 215).

they give back the boards: Payments due later will have been recorded on separate tablets (47. 5), so the tablets given back should have been blank (and available for reuse).

he is written in there: Cf. Dem. XXV. *Aristogeiton 1.* 4, XLIII. *Macartatus* 71; *A.P.* uses the verb also in 42. 1, 49. 1.

he is obliged to pay double … to be imprisoned: On public debts see Rhodes, *A.B.* 148–51: men who became debtors by making a contract had to provide guarantors; if they defaulted the debt was doubled and they became *atimoi* until it was paid, and the council could imprison them and confiscate the guarantors' property; men from whom immediate payment was due were treated as contractors already in default; for some instances of doubled debts see *Agora* xix P26. 490–1, 510–1. Under the law proposed in the 350's by Timocrates and attacked in Dem. XXIV. *Timocrates*, men in the second category were treated as if they were under contract to pay by the ninth prytany; cf. 54. 2.

the council has the power … in accordance with the laws: This was done through another board of ten, the *praktores* (e.g. [Dem.] LVIII. *Theocrines* 20, 48).

48. 2. On the first day: Since some payments fell due each prytany (47. 3), presumably two days were provided for this business each prytany.

they receive all the payments: καταβολάς is to be understood.

make the *merismos* to the officials: In the fifth century Athens had a central state treasury, but in the fourth it made regular allocations (for which *merizein* and *merismos* are technical terms) to separate spending authorities; this system is first attested in *IG* ii² 29 = RO 19. 18–22 (386): see Rhodes, *A.B.* 99–101. The practice is reflected in Arist. *Pol.* VI. 1321 B 31–3.

on the next day ... writing it on a tablet: For *eispherein* cf. 47. 4, 5: there seems to be no difference in meaning betwen *grammateion* and *sanis*. What has to be checked is that the *apodektai* in their distribution have complied with the *merismos*; nothing is said of receipts which would assist a check that the payments listed on the second day matched those made on the first.

read it out in the council house: Cf. 43. 4, 54. 5 (where *anagignoskein* is used).

in the council they call ... they put to the vote proposals: The subject of these verbs should be the *proedroi*, perhaps omitted here through *A.P.*'s condensation of his material.

48. 3. Also the councillors allot from themselves ten *logistai* ... in each prytany: These interim 'reckoners' are not to be confused with the annual *logistai*, treated in 54. 2. They were presumably one from each tribe, but from the councillors, as the officials in 47–8 were not. There will have been more need for such checks in the fourth century after the institution of the *merismos* (cf. above), but the interim check is mentioned in Lys. XXX. *Nicomachus* 5 (399), without any suggestion that it was new. For detailed studies of accounting in Athens see Wilamowitz, *A.u.A.* ii. 231–51, M. Piérart, *AC* 40 (1971), 526–73.

48. 4. They also allot *euthynoi* ... and 2 *paredroi* for each of the *euthynoi*: On the meaning of *euthynein* cf. p. 208. The final examination of retiring officials comprised a financial *logos* (54. 2) and general *euthynai*, but the two words are not always distinguished. In *A.P.*, and presumably in the laws, the two are treated separately, because the *euthynoi* were appointed from the council but the *logistai* were not. A *paredros* is one who sits beside, and so an assistant (cf. Pind. *Ol.* 2. 76, 8. 22, Hdt. VII. 147. 2). In Athens some other officials had *paredroi*, including the three senior archons (56. 1); the annual *logistai* were assisted by *synegoroi* (54. 2); the *paredroi* of the *euthynoi* are found in *IG* i^3. 18–19, decree *ap.* Andoc, I. *Myst.* 78, RO 100 = *IG* ii^3 370. 238–9; cf. the deme decree *IG* ii^2 1174, but in 1183, from another deme, the *euthynos* is assisted by a committee of ten).

by the eponymous hero of each tribe: For the tribal *eponymoi* cf. 21. 6 with commentary. Each team sat perhaps by the statue of the *eponymos* of a tribe other than its own, to receive complaints against officials from that tribe (cf. 53. 2 with commentary).

against any of those who have submitted *euthynai* in the lawcourt: Despite the word used, the allusion is probably to the presentation of the financial *logos*.
in market hours: Kenyon's restoration ταῖς ἀ[γορ]αῖς has been accepted *faute de mieux* by most editors. Some indication of time seems needed, though perhaps a longer word; Efstathiou's <ἐπὶ> ταῖς σ[τήλ]αις, 'by the *stelai*' mentioned in 53. 4, is ingenious but seems an unnecessary addition to 'by the eponymous hero'.
to invoke either a private or a public *euthyna*: *Embalesthai* is used of submitting a document in various legal contexts (e.g. 53. 2, 3).
within 30 days: Cf. the thirty days allowed for submission of the *logos* (54. 2; 30 days, Harp. λ 24 Keaney, *Suda* λ 651 Adler, λογισταὶ καὶ λογιστήρια); but it seems more likely that '3 days' is the reading of the papyrus.
he writes on a whitened tablet … the offence of which he accuses him: Notices of *graphai* were similarly posted by the tribal *eponymoi* (e.g. Dem. XXI. *Midias* 103).
the assessment which he judges right: Cf. Ar. *Plut.* 480, Aeschin. I. *Timarchus* 16. Here and in 53. 2 a *timema* is an assessment of a sum at issue or a penalty (so that lawsuits were categorised as *timetoi* or *atimetoi* according to whether the penalty was assessed or fixed: 69. 2 cf. 67. 5).
48. 5. reads it: ἀν[αγνοῦ]ς is preferable to ἀν[ακρίνα]ς, since what the *euthynos* does is not analogous to the *anakrisis* made by the *eisagousa arche* (56. 6).
he hands private matters to the deme justices who are serving for that tribe: For these cf. 16. 5, 26. 3; and 53. 1–2, where they are given their fourth-century title, the Forty: probably the older term survived in the law which *A.P.* used here. The scribe wrote εἰσάγουσιν, probably under the influence of the following sentence.
reports public matters to the *thesmothetai*: Cf. 59. 2, for the *euthynai* of generals. *A.P.* omits to mention that the *euthynoi* could themselves impose fines (RO 100 = *IG* ii^3 370. 233–42).
if they take it over: The *euthynoi* have already judged the man guilty: we should not expect the *thesmothetai* to have discretion, so Kontos' ἐπὰν (cf. 42. 2, 56.1) may be right. But A. A. Efstathiou, *Dike* 10 (2007), 113–35 esp. 114–24, accepts 'if' with the implication that the *thesmothetai* do have discretion.

49. 1. vets the horses: *Sc.* of the cavalry: cf. Xen. *Oec.* 9. 15, *Hipparch.* 1. 13, and Rhodes, *A.B.* 174–5. This is illustrated on the name vase of the δοκιμασία Painter, *c.* 480–470 (Berlin, Antikensammlung, F 2296; Beazley, *A.R.V.*^{2},. 412 no. 1; Beazley Archive 204483), and other vases: see H. A. Cahn, *RA* (1973), 3–22. On a series of lead tablets giving various details including the values of the horses see K. A. I. Braun, *AM* 85 (1970), 129–32, 198–269; J. H. Kroll, *Hesperia* 46 (1977), 83–140.
fines him the fodder grant: For the fodder grant, presumably paid throughout the year, cf. ML 84 = *IG* i^3 375 ~ Fornara 154. 4, ii^2 1264. 5–8, schol. Dem. XXIV. *Timocrates* 101 (202 Dilts); there was also a capital sum (*katastasis*: cf. pp. 262–3).
the horse to which this is done is rejected: One who is *adokimos* is one rejected in a *dokimasia*: cf. [Dem.] L. *Polycles* 36, and for coins Pl. *Leg.* V. 742 A 6.
the *prodromoi*: Cf. Xen. *Hipparch.* 1. 25, Philoch. *FGrH* 328 F 71 *ap.* Harp. α 91 Keaney ἅμιπποι: They were a special body of light-armed cavalry, successors to the *hippotoxotai* of the fifth and early fourth centuries (po. 262–3): see Bugh, *Horsemen*, 221–4.
the *hamippoi*: Light infantry who fought with the cavalry, best known in Boeotia (e.g. Thuc. V. 57. 2). Athens had none at Mantinea in 362 (Xen. *Hell.* VII. 5. 23); their use is recommended by Xen. *Hipparch.* 5. 13, and Harp. *loc. cit.* cites Isaeus (= fr. 125 Sauppe), so they were probably instituted soon after 362.
49. 2. The cavalrymen: A force of 1,000 (cf. pp. 262–3).
the *katalogeis*, ten men elected by the *demos*: Cf. *IG* ii^3 1281. 26–7 (187/6). They were probably one from each tribe, elected by analogy with other military appointments. They are not attested elsewhere, presumably their duty was to list those who were qualified but not already registered.
the hipparchs and the phylarchs: Cf. *SEG* xxi 525. 2–7 (282/1), *IG* ii^3 1281. 26–7. The hipparchs were commanders in chief of the cavalry and the phylarchs commanders of the tribal regiments: cf. 61. 4–5.
They open the tablet: The sealed tablet listed those who had served in the previous year, the *katalogos* those newly registered by the *katalogeis*.
swear an oath of exemption: Probably their claim was accepted unless somebody challenged it. Doubtless they could also claim that their

property was so diminished that they were financially unable to serve (cf. below), but it is better not to insert <ἢ ταῖς οὐσίαις> here.
those who have been enrolled: Those newly listed by the *katalogeis*.
unable to serve either with his body or with his property: Cf. Xen. *Hipparch.* 1. 9, and the formulation of the requirement for membership of the Five Thousand in 411 (29. 5).
the councillors vote on whether he is fit to serve or not: If there was a quota of 1,000, the council will have needed to approve a fixed number from those listed. *Diacheirotonein* is regularly used of deciding between alternatives (e.g. ML 65 = *IG* i[3] 61 ~ Fornara 128. 5) – not necessarily by show of hands, but probably that was done here.
49. 3. used to judge the patterns and the *peplos*: It is disputed whether the *paradeigmata* here are plans for public works in general (e.g. Wilamowitz, *A.u.A.* i. 212–3) or for the *peplos* in particular (e.g. Blass[1], reading παραδείγματα τὰ εἰς τὸν): we cannot be sure, but I think the latter more likely.

The *peplos* is the robe taken in procession at the Great Panathenaea (Pl. *Euthyphr.* 6 C 2–3, Harp. π 51 Keaney πέπλος) and given to the priestess of Athena to clothe (probably) the old cult statue of the goddess: see Deubner, *Attische Feste*, 11, 29–31, 35–6; H. W. Parke, *Festivals of the Athenians* (London: Thames & Hudson, 1977), 38–43; Parker, *Polytheism*, 264–5, 269 n. 71; and cf. 60. 1.
a lawcourt picked by sortititon: We are not told when the change was made, or who acted as *eisagousa arche*.
joins with the treasurer of the stratiotic fund: See 43. 1 and 47. 2 with commentary. For his involvement with the dedications of this period cf. *IG* ii[2] 1493.
the making of the Victories: Cf. 47. 1. Decisions about the *peplos* were presumably mentioned here because analogous to *dokimasiai*, and *A.P.* digresses from them to other religious objects.
the prizes for the Panathenaea: Cf. 60. 1.
49. 4. the invalids … cannot do any work: *A.P.* returns to *dokimasiai*: for this cf. Lys. XXIV. *Pens. Inv.* (an invalid's reply to a challenge, delivered before the council, arguing both that he needs support and that he is physically disabled), Aeschin. I. *Timarchus* 103–4 with schol. (222–4 Dilts). Grants to war invalids are attributed to Solon or Pisistratus (Plut. *Sol.* 31. 3–4), and the maintenance of orphans of the war dead is

attributed to Solon by Diog. Laert. I. 55 (cf. p. 264): this institution is attributed to Solon by schol. Aeschin. I. 223 Dilts, but must be a creation of the Periclean or post-Periclean democracy.

each given two obols per day: 1 obol in Lys. XXIV. 13, 26; Aeschin. I. 104 might mean that (in 361: §109) one instalment was paid each prytany, or simply that there was one opportunity for *hiketeriai* each prytany (cf. 43. 6); if the former, 9 drachmae per month (Philoch. *FGrH* 328 F 197a) is probably a commutation made in the twelve-tribe period. The grant was less than an unskilled but able-bodied man could earn (cf. 62. 2).

they have an allotted treasurer: This would more naturally refer to a treasurer of a special fund (cf. Kaibel, *Stil und Text*, 25–6), but there is no supporting evidence, and more probably it refers to the treasurer of the council and payment came from the council's expense account (see Rhodes, *A.B.* 141 with nn. 3–4). The council had two treasurers in 343/2 (*IG* ii³ 306. 40–2, cf. ii² 120. 20–2), but one in and after 335/4 (*IG* ii² 1700. 218 = *Agora* xv 43. 232).

49. 5. It also joins in administration … so to say: This would be better placed at the end of 48 (cf. p. 364), but clumsiness by *A.P.* is more likely than corruption by a scribe.

N. Sortitive officials (50–4)

For the arrangement of the material on offices see Introduction, pp. 16–17. Between the council and the archons *A.P.* treats offices concerned with city facilities (50–1), with justice (52–3) and with some other matters (54). Most awkward is the treatment of the *hodopoioi* in 54. 1 rather than 50–1; it is strange that 54. 3–5 mentions three of the six secretaries attested in contemporary inscriptions, and 54. 6–7 two of the many boards of *hieropoioi*; the treatment of the *diaitetai* in 53 seems excessive, but probably reflects the Athenians' pride in their elaborately fair judicial processes.

50. 1. That, then, is the administration done by the council: This closes a ring opened in 43. 2.

There are also allotted ten men as *hieron episkeuastai*: Presumably, for this and other such boards, one from each tribe (cf. 47–8). Cf. *'Αρχ.*

'Εφ. (1923), 36–42 no. 123 (dated 369/8 by D. Knoepfler, *Chiron* 16 [1986], 71–98), law *ap.* Ath. VI. 235 D, and the *epimeletai* of Arist. *Pol.* VI. 1322 B 19–22. In the hellenistic period Athens had a στρατηγὸς ἐπὶ τὴν παρασκευήν and an ἀρχιτέκτων ἐπὶ τὰ ἱερά: see Rhodes, *A.B.* 125–6.

take thirty minas from the *apodektai*: I.e. receive this as their allowance in the *merismos* (cf. 48. 1–2). ½ talent would not pay for much: a decree of (probably) 434/3 authorised expenditure up to 10 talents a year (ML 58 = *IG* i³ 52 ~ Fornara 119. *B.* 5–12).

50. 2. And ten *astynomoi*: On offices of this kind see in general Arist. *Pol.* VI. 1321 B 18–27, VII. 1331 B 6–13; also a hellenistic law on the *astynomoi* of Pergamum, *OGIS* 483 (re-edited by G. Klaffenbach, *Abh. Berlin* [1953], vi). In particular, the *astynomoi* had to see that sanctuaries and roads used by processions were in a fit state: cf. *IG* ii² 380 (320/19), transferring the duties in the Piraeus to the *agoranomoi*, ii³ 879 (283/2), showing *astynomoi* still or again working in the city.

5 hold office in Piraeus and five in the city: Cf. the offices in 51. 1–3, and the two testers of silver coins (*SEG* xxvi 72 = RO 25).

the pipe-girls, harp-girls and lyre-girls: Cf. Pl. *Prt.* 347 C 3–E 1, Xen. *Symp.* 1. 1, 2. 1: both mention *orchestrides* (dancing-girls) also; *A.P.*'s list is doubtless incomplete.

to see that they are not hired for more than two drachmae: Cf. *Suda* δ 528 Adler διάγραμμα; Hyp. IV. *Euxenippus* 3 mentions prosecutions for breaking this regulation. Rich men will have had entertainers attached to their households or regularly available; this regulation deals with those available for casual hire.

if several men … hire her to the man picked by sortition: This implies that there were fixed times and places for hiring.

none of the dung-collectors deposits the dung within 10 stades of the wall: Cf. Ar. *Vesp.* 1184, *Pax* 9; *IG* ii² 380; *OGIS* 483. 36–47 (Pergamum); and see E. J. Owens, *CQ*² 33 (1983), 44–50.

building to encroach on the streets: Cf. [Xen.] *A.P.* 3. 4.

extending balconies over the streets: Elsewhere *dryphaktoi* are railings (cf. Rhodes, *A.B.* 33–4); here they must be balconies projecting from houses (cf. schol. Ar. *Eq.* 675, *Vesp.* 386). In [Arist.] *Oec.* II. 1347 A 4–8, Polyaen. III. 9. 30, threats to their balconies are used as a device to obtain money from house-owners.

creating overhead drainpipes which discharge into the street: Cf. *OGIS* 483. 60–78.
opening shutters into the street: The reference should be to outward-opening window-shutters, which if not secured might fall into the street.
And those who pass away in the streets they retrieve: *Sc.* for burial: cf. Ar. *Vesp.* 386, Xen. *An.* VI. 4. 9, *IG* ii^2 1672. 119.

51. 1. There are also allotted 10 *agoranomoi*: They maintained order in the agora (Ar. *Ach.* 968), and collected market dues (schol. Hom. *Il.* XXI. 203) and probably the tax paid by foreign traders (Dem. LVII. *Eubulides* 31, 34). They could have non-citizens flogged (cf. Ar. *Ach.* 724, Cratin. fr. 123 Kassel & Austin, *IG* ii^2 380. 40 sqq.), and probably could fine citizens or prosecute them for a heavier penalty; but in *SEG* xxvi 72 it is the *syllogeis tou demou* (cf. p. 349) who discipline the *dokimastes* and receive notice of offences. They had an office, the *agoranomion* (office in the Piraeus, *IG* ii^2 380. 10–12); for lead tokens which they issued see *Agora* x. 79–81 with L170, L194.
to take care of everything that is sold ... pure and genuine: A law prescribing ἀψευδεῖν ἐν τῇ ἀγορᾷ is cited by Dem. XX. *Leptines* 9, Hyp. III. *Athenogenes* 14. Earlier their responsibilities had included bread (Xen. *Symp.* 2. 20); for the division of duties in *A.P.*'s time see 51. 3–4.
51. 2. There are also allotted 10 *metronomoi*: For Athens' standard weights and measures see 10 with commentary; there is a decree of the late second century on the enforcement of standards (*IG* ii^2 1013). There is a document of the *metronomoi* of 211/0, *SEG* xxiv 157.
51. 3. There used to be 10 allotted *sitophylakes* ... but now...: This is one of the places where *A.P.* distinguishes between earlier and current practice (cf. Introduction, pp. 20, 29): the change was perhaps made during the grain shortage from which Greece suffered in the 330's–320's (cf. B. D. Meritt, *Hesperia* 13 [1944], 245); Harp. σ 19 Keaney σιτοφύλακες has only the earlier number but Phot. σ 253 Theodoridis σιτοφύλακες has a corrupt version of the later, so perhaps this was noted when *A.P.* was revised, Harpocration used the original edition and Photius the revised (cf. p. 29). In Lys. XXII. *Corn-Dealers.* 8 before mentioning Anytus the manuscripts read οἱ μὲν δύο, T. Bergk suggested δ´, which with Anytus would yield half of a board of ten, T. Thalheim νῦν, contrasted

with Anytus as serving in the previous year, C. Carey ἄλλοι. In the third century the twelve tribes supplied ten *sitophylakes* and two secretaries (cf. *Agora* xvi 127, 194).

For the importance of imported grain and the state's interest in it cf. 43. 4 with commentary; Arist. *Pol.* IV. 1299 A 23 mentions *sitometrai* as commonly-found officials. In the fourth century both citizens and metics were forbidden to transport grain or to lend money for its transport to any destination outside Attica (e.g. Dem. XXXIV. *Phormio* 37, XXXV. *Lacritus* 50–1, Luc. *Leocr.* 27); in the 380's laws regulated the stock which retail *sitopolai* might hold and the profit which they might make (Lys. XXII. *Corn-Dealers* 5, 8).

now there are twenty for the city and fifteen for Piraeus: Probably there was a scheme by which each year five tribes supplied four men and five supplied three.

unground: Cf. Hippocr. *V.M.* 13.

the breadsellers: For female *artopolides* see Ar. *Vesp.* 238, *Ran.* 858: *artopolai* are found in *SEG* xviii 36. *B.* 6 (*c.* 335–325), cf. Osborne, *Naturalization*, D 6. ii. 60, iii. 23 (401/0).

at the weight which the *sitophylakes* fix: The weight of loaves, rather than their price, would vary with the price of grain: C. Ampolo, *Opus* iii 1984, 115–20, v 1986, 143–51.

51. 4. They allot ten *emporiou epimeletai*: To their general responsibility *A.P.* adds ensuring that two thirds of imported grain was sent to the city; they also had to enforce the ban on transporting grain to destinations outside Attica (Dem. XXXV. *Lacritus* 51, [Dem.] LVIII. *Theocrines* 8–9 with *hyp.*; cf. above). They are first attested in *SEG* xxvi 72 = RO 25. 18–23, which suggests that in the 370's the *sitophylakes* controlled the wholesale as well as the retail trade in grain.

to the grain market: Cf. *sitos* in *SEG* xxvi 72 = RO 25. 18, 22–3.

52. 1. They appoint by lot the Eleven: See Lipsius, *A.R.* 74–81, Harrison, *L.A.* ii. 17–18. The reason for the number is unknown, but they presumably antedate Cleisthenes' ten tribes (cf. 7. 3). They were gaolers and executioners; those who served under the Thirty were considered so implicated in that régime that they were excluded from the amnesty of 403 (cf. 35. 1, 39. 1). They are mentioned as as an instance of separating the exaction of (financial) penalties from the custody of prisoners by

Arist. *Pol.* VI. 1322 A 19–20. Isae. IV. *Nicostratus* 28 reports that all the members of one board were condemned for letting prisoners escape.

to take care of those in the prison: Athens certainly used precautionary imprisonment for some men awaiting trial, men awaiting execution and men with outstanding public debts (e.g. Pl. *Phd.* 58 C 4–5, proposal of Timocrates *ap.* Dem. XXIV. *Timocrates* 39–40); whether it ever used penal imprisonment has been debated but should be accepted (cf. I. Barkan, *CP* xxxi 1936, 338–41; Harrison, *L.A.* ii. 177). Athens seems to have had only one prison (cf. R. E. Wycherley, *Agora* iii, pp. 149–50; H. A. Thompson & R. E. Wycherley, *Agora* xiv. 125 n. 48): for a possible identification, to the south-west of the agora, see Camp, *Site Guide*, 176–8. The Eleven presumably had subordinates, whether slave or free (cf. Pl. *Cri.* 43 A 5–6).

to punish with death ... put them to death: See Lipsius, *A.R.* 317–38; Harrison, *L.A.* ii. 221–32; M. H. Hansen, *Apagoge, Endeixis and Ephegesis against Kakourgoi, Atimoi and Pheugontes* (Odense U. P., 1976). *Apagoge*, taking the accused to the authorities, and *ephegesis*, taking the authorities to arrest the accused, were available against common criminals (*kakourgoi*) caught ἐπ᾽ αὐτοφώρῳ (not necessarily in the act, but flagrantly guilty: Hansen, 48–53; E. M. Harris, *Symposion 1993* [*AGR* 10 (1994)], 129–46 = his *Democracy and the Rule of Law in Classical Athens* [New York: Cambridge U. P., 2006], 373–89[–90]), and against *atimoi* and exiles who exercised rights of which they had been deprived (e.g. 63. 3). It was a distinctive feature that if the accused admitted their guilt they could be executed without trial.

if they confess: Cf. Aeschin. I. *Timarchus* 113, Dem. XXIV. *Timocrates* 65.

introduce them into the lawcourt: The Eleven are the *eisagousa arche* and preside in the court. For their court cf. Ar. *Vesp.* 1108, Antiph. fr. 43 Sauppe *ap.* Harp. π 21 Keaney παράβυστον, and A. L. Boegehold & M. Crosby, *Agora* xxviii. 178–83.

lands and houses registered for confiscation: If a man's property was forfeit, it was sometimes the duty of his demarch (e.g. [Plut.] *X Or.* 834 A), sometimes left to *ho boulomenos* (e.g. *Agora* xix P26. 460–541), to *apographein* the items to be seized. The *apographe* was read out at a *kyria ekklesia* (43. 4), and was taken to court as a quasi-prosecution; a man who claimed that an item was not liable to forfeiture would enter a defence; if there was no defence within a certain time the Eleven could probably accept the *apographe*. See Lipsius, *A.R.* 299–308, Harrison, *L.A.* ii. 211–7.

hand over to the *poletai*: Cf. 47. 2–3.

introduce the *endeixeis*: *Endeixis*, denouncing the accused to the authorities, was available for the same offences as *apagoge* and *ephegesis*, but did not require guilt ἐπ' αὐτοφώρῳ; it was possible but not obligatory for the accused to be arrested (cf. Hansen, 11–17).

the *thesmothetai* introduce some of the *endeixeis*: *A.P.* generalises, where the laws will have specified which cases were handled by the *thesmothetai*; Hansen, 20–1, suggests that they handled cases where the accused had not been imprisoned. *Endeixeis* are not mentioned among the *thesmothetai*'s lawsuits in 59.

52. 2. *eisagogeis*, who introduce the monthly suits, five men, each one for two tribes: Kaibel, *Stil und Text*, 223, insisted that the meaning must be that each was responsible for the lawsuits of defendants (cf. 53. 2) from two tribes; but it may also be true that each was appointed from two tribes, and that *A.P.* is thinking of that too. Cf. 54. 1, 56. 3, 62. 2; also the thirty-five *sitophylakes* in 51. 3. An *eisagogeus* is an *eisagousa arche* (cf. on 52. 1). The title is found in *IG* i^3 71. 7, 12, 13. The fourth-century *eisagogeis* are mentioned only here and in Poll. VIII. 101; probably they were instituted after 347/6 (when Dem. XXXVII. *Pantaenetus* 33–4 used the word in a general sense), at the same time as or shortly after the *dikai emmenoi* (L. Gernet, *REG* li 1938, 2–9 = his *Droit et société dans la Grèce ancienne* [Paris: Sirey, 1955], 174–8).

the monthly suits: These have usually been seen as cases in which a decision was to be given within a month (e.g. Lipsius, *A.R.* 901, Harrison, *L.A.* ii. 16, 21, 154); but it has been argued convincingly by E. E. Cohen that, while by by-passing the *diaitetai* these were decided quickly, the meaning is that there was an opportunity to institute proceedings every month (*Ancient Athenian Maritime Courts* [Princeton U. P., 1973], 9–59).

The monthly suits are: Poll. VIII. 101 mentions three categories, including *emporikai*, which with *metallikai* are assigned by 59. 5 and Poll. VIII. 88 to the *thesmothetai*. *A.P.*'s assignment of *emporikai* is confirmed by Dem. XXXII. *Apaturius* 1, XXXIV. *Phormio* 45: possibly there was a change at some date, but more probably Poll. VIII. 101 is mistaken. Some categories of 'monthly' case can be explained by commercial or military need for haste, but not all: probably the procedure was instituted for some cases and others were added piecemeal.

for a dowry, if a man owes it and fails to pay: Certainly available to the *kyrios* to whom a woman returned after divorce or her husband's death, or to the head of her family if she predeceased her husband and had no children. It may also have been available to the husband against the head of his wife's family if he did not receive the promised dowry (for, Lipsius, *A.R.* 496–7; against, H. J. Wolff, *RE* xxiii. 144–5; non-committal, Harrison, *L.A.* i. 50–2). Dem. XL. *Boeotus ii* and XLI. *Spudias* reflect earlier procedure.

if anybody borrows at a drachma interest and defaults: 1 drachma per mina per month: this was considered a reasonable rate (cf. Dem. XXVII. *Aphobus i.* 23, 35, Aeschin. III. *Ctesiphon* 104); higher rates were sometimes charged (and 1½ dr. per month was prescribed on dowries to be returned to the wife's *kyrios*: Dem. XXVII. *Aphobus i.* 17, [Dem.] LIX. *Neaera* 52), but presumably could not be claimed through this suit.

if anybody wishing to work in the agora borrows capital from somebody: In this case there was presumably no limit to the rate of interest.

battery: An assault less serious than *trauma* (57. 3). Dem. XXXVII. *Pantaenetus* 33 and LIV. *Conon* 26–9 reflect earlier procedure.

friendly loans: That is what is meant here: *eranoi* as 'friendly associations' are not attested before the mid third century (M. I. Finley, *Studies in Land and Credit in Ancient Athens, 500–200 BC* [Rutgers U. P., 1952], 100–6).

associations: Concerning associations, but probably not suits by or against associations (e.g. Lipsius, *A.R.* 771), since it is not certain that an association was a person capable of suing and being sued (Harrison, *L.A.* i. 242, ii. 22).

concerning slaves and yoke-animals: Perhaps concerning damage done by or to slaves and animals, rather than property in them (Harrison, *L.A.*. ii. 22 n. 10, against Lipsius, *A.R.* 640, 682, 745).

trierarchic suits: Probably not public disputes for which other procedures were available but private suits entered by or against trierarchs (e.g. Harrison, *L.A.* ii. 22 n. 9). If [Dem.] L. *Polycles* was written for a suit of this kind (which is possible but not necessary), it reflects earlier procedure.

banking suits: Suits entered by or against bankers (e.g. Harrison, *L.A.*

ii. 22 n. 7). The actions concerning Pasion's bank in the 360's seem not to have been *emmenoi*.

52. 3. try them: Commonly used of the men who decide the verdict, but here it is used of those who preside and presumably state the jury's verdict (cf. 57. 4, of the *basileus*).

the *apodektai* introduce suits by and against tax-collectors: Cf. 47. 2, 48. 1–2.

having definitive power up to ten drachmae: For such *epibolai* cf. 53. 2, *SEG* xxvi 72 = RO 25. 23–6; also 56. 7, 61. 2, and Arist. *Pol.* IV. 1300 B 32–5; but 45. 1–3, 46. 2, does not distinguish between penalties which were and which were not within the competence of the council. Probably there was no direct right of appeal, but a man could in practice gain a hearing in court by refusing to pay.

53. 1. plaintiffs obtain their hearing in the other private suits: οἱ διώκοντες must be understood as subject. When the plaintiff summons the defendant and the authority allots a day for the *anakrisis*, the authority κληροῖ and the plaintiff λαγχάνει δίκην (cf. Lipsius, *A.R.* 817–8, Harrison, *L.A.* ii. 88–9). These will be private suits other than those mentioned in 52. 2–3; but *A.P.* is simplifying, since cases which went to one of the nine archons (56. 5, 57. 2–4, 58. 3, 59. 5–6) probably did not go also to the Forty and the *diaitetai* (cf. R. J. Bonner, *CP* 2 [1907], 407–18).

Previously they were thirty ... have become forty: This is one of the places where *A.P.* contrasts earlier and later practice (cf. pp. 20, 29): here he gives a date and a reason. *Dikastai kata demous* were instituted by Pisistratus (16. 5), abolished presumably on the fall of the tyranny and revived in 453/2 (26. 3): thirty was convenient for Cleisthenes' tribes and *trittyes* and was presumably the number chosen in 453/2. Probably they ceased travelling in the last years of the Peloponnesian War, and the Thirty of 404/3 made that an inauspicious number. Lys. XXIII. *Pancleon* implies that the change had been made when the hearing of *dikai* resumed after the war, perhaps in 401/0; but the first *diaitetai* served perhaps in 399/8 (D. M. MacDowell, *RIDA*^{3} 18 [1971], 267–73; earlier dates for both D. Whitehead, *MH* 59 [2002], 71–96).

53. 2. The cases up to ten drachmae they have independent authority to try: Probably this was true also of their fifth-century predecessors; cf. the competence of the *apodektai* in 52. 3.

the *diaitetai*: Cf. 53. 4–6.
take them over: When they accepted a case they took an oath in front of the Stoa of the *Basileus* (55. 5).
if they are not able to make a settlement they decide: They were not an *arche* but resembled private arbitrators, and so first tried to bring about an agreement; *gignoskein* and *gnosis* are regularly used of their judgments (e.g. Dem. XXI. *Midias* 92).
if both parties are satisfied . .. if either of the opposing litigants appeals...: In contrast to cases where reference to a court was required (45. 1–2, 46. 2, and 45. 3, 55. 2), the *diaitetai*'s judgment was final if both parties accepted it, but either could appeal.
they insert in jars: The subject is probably οἱ ἀντίδικοι. They place in the jars all the evidence in the broadest sense which they cite; for a longer list see Arist. *Rhet.* I. 1375 A 22–1377 B 12 with Harrison, *L.A.* ii. 133–4. Written testimony was required in lawsuits from about the 370's (G. M. Calhoun, *TAPA* 50 [1919], 177–93). *Echinoi* are frequently mentioned by the orators, apparently always in connection with arbitration (e.g. [Dem.] XLVII. *Evergus & Mnesibulus* 16); but a surviving fragment suggests that they were used more widely (A. L. Boegehold, *Agora* xxviii. 79–91).
attach the decision of the *diaitetes* written on a board: Presumably the tablet containing the judgment was attached to both jars.
to the 4 who are trying cases for the defendant's tribe: Probably they were assigned to a tribe other than their own: cf. pp. 379 (*eisagogeis*), 384 (*diaitetai*), and for the expression 48. 5, 58. 2.
53. 3. those up to a thousand ... those over a thousand...: *Sc.* δραχμῶν, δραχμάς. For the size of juries cf. 67. 6–68. 1, where this information is not repeated.
It is not permitted ... inserted in the jars from the *diaitetes*: To this extent the principle that what followed *ephesis* was a fresh trial was limited. For problems in this regard see Dem. XXXIX. *Boeotus i.* 17, XLV. *Stephanus i.* 57–60.
53. 4. The *diaitetai* are those in their sixtieth year: The link to their registration guarantees that this means men 'in their sixtieth year', whose sixtieth birthday will fall during the year in question. Some scholia and lexica say ὑπὲρ πεντήκοντα ἔτη, and some scholars have suggested a change by Demetrius of Phalerum (e.g. Harrison, *L.A.* ii. 67 n. 1), but probably these texts are wrong and the *diaitetai* were abolished after 322/1

(Wilamowitz, *A.u.A.* i. 224). The first board of *diaitetai* served in 399/8 or slightly earlier (cf. p. 381): if the Forty and their predecessors were already limited to cases up to 10 drachmae, this will have extended the range of lawsuits which could be decided cheaply without a jury. As *A.P.* does not state in 42 that the *thetes* were excluded from the *ephebeia*, here he does not state that they were excluded from service as *diaitetai*, but I believe both to be the case.

This is clear from the archons and the eponymous heroes: From the fact of the forty-two year-classes.

there are ten eponymous heroes of the tribes: Cf. 21. 6. They are mentioned here to distinguish them from the forty-two; and *A.P.* will not have needed any source for these facts.

the age-classes: The men registered in each year formed a separate *helikia*.

The *epheboi* when they were entered used ... but now...: On their registration see 42. 1–2; the change may plausibly be associated with the reorganisation of the *ephebeia*, *c.* 335/4. This passage is quoted by Harp. σ 41 Keaney στρατεία ἐν τοῖς ἐπωνύμοις; and Keaney, noting that Harpocration used an unrevised version of 51. 3 (cf. *ad loc.*), suggested that the same is true here and this contrast was included in the original version (*Historia* 19 [1970], 330–6: cf. Introduction, p. 29).

whitened boards: Cf. 47. 2.

the names were written ... the previous year's *diaitetai*: Imperfect tense: the forty-two-year system was older than the reorganisation of the *ephebeia*. The hero of the men who were *diaitetai* in 336/5 was used again for the *epheboi* registered in 335/4; and to provide an absolute date the archontic year of the registration was added to each list (cf. 53. 7). This provided a simple way of ensuring that those who had completed their forty-two years were exempted from further service.

now they are written up on a bronze *stele*: None of these bronze *stelai* has been found, but we have inscriptions on stone concerning both *epheboi* (cf. p. 338) and *diaitetai* – which use archontic years but not *eponymoi*.

in front of the council house by the eponymous heroes: The statues of the ten tribal heroes (cf. p. 248): limestone bases for triangular bronze *stelai* which might be these *stelai* have been found near there (R. S. Stroud, *The Axones and Kyrbeis of Drakon and Solon* [U. Calif. Pub. Cl. Stud. xix 1979], 49–57).

53. 5. take the last ... which cases each is to arbitrate: These heroes are those of the age-classes. There will have been differing numbers of *diaitetai* from different tribes, but (like the Forty: 53. 2) each will have been assigned to defendants of a tribe other than his own (cf. [Dem.] XLVII. *Evergus & Mnesibulus* 12); particular cases will then have been assigned to particular *diaitetai*.
it is obligatory ... whichever cases fall to him: Either they had to continue beyond their year of service if necessary to complete cases or they were not allowed to take new cases so late in the year that that might happen (for the latter cf. Wyse, ed. of Isaeus, 721–2).
he is to be *atimos*: Cf. p. 210. Here the weaker sense, loss of civic rights, is intended: cf. Dem. XXI. *Midias* 83–102, where the *atimos* Strato can be exhibited but cannot give evidence in court.
unless ... only these are exempt: We are not told how long a period of absence was needed to qualify, or whether the absence had to be for good cause. If the *thetes* did not serve as *epheboi* or as *diaitetai* (cf. pp. 341, 383), they will not have been included in the lists so will not have required further exemption.
53. 6. to make an *eisangelia* to the *diaitetai*: For other procedures called *eisangelia* see 43. 4, 45. 2, 56. 6; for this procedure, at the end of the year, see Dem. XXI. *Midias* 83–102.
it is possible for these to appeal: A dissatisfied litigant could appeal from the board of *diaitetai* to a *dikasterion*; we do not know what had happened in the case of Strato.
53. 7. They use the eponymous heroes also for military campaigns: After digressing from the Forty as sortitive officials to the *diaitetai*, *A.P.* digresses further to explain the military use of the forty-two age-classes.
when they send out an age range: In the time of *Ath. Pol.* the members of specified age-classes were called up for service: cf. Dem. III. *Ol. iii.* 4, Aeschin. II. *F.L.* 133; but the reference in Aeschin. II. *F.L.* 168 to service ἐν τοῖς μέρεσιν may be to a different, earlier practice (cf. A. Andrewes, in *Classical Contributions ... M. F. McGregor* [Locust Valley: Augustin, 1981], 1–3).

54. 1. They allot also the following officials: *A.P.* returns from the digression to the main theme of 50–4.
five road-builders: The tribes were perhaps grouped in pairs: cf.. 52. 2,

56.3, 62. 2; also 51. 3. Arist. *Pol.* VI. 1321 B 18–27 gives this duty to *astynomoi*, and schol. Aeschin. III. *Ctesiphon* 25 (70a Dilts) makes them responsible for the cleanliness of the streets, which was in fact a duty of Athens' *astynomoi* (50. 2); and the *hodopoioi* would more logically have been mentioned in 50–1. When Aeschin. *loc. cit.* says that the controllers of the theoric fund ἦσαν ... ὁδοποιοί he means that they provided funds for road-building, not that they supplanted the *hodopoioi* (cf. 47. 2, 48. 1).

54. 2. And ten *logistai* and ten advocates for them ... to bring their accounts: These are the auditors who examined officials' financial accounts at the end of the year (cf. Aeschin. III. *Ctesiphon* 17–24): they were not *bouleutai*, unlike the *logistai* who made an interim financial examination each prytany (48. 3) and the *euthynoi* who conducted the non-financial part of the annual examination (48. 4–5). Officials' assistants are elsewhere entitled *paredroi* (48. 4, 56. 1); while Arist. *Pol.* VI. 1322 B 7–12 makes this a title of financial examiners, in Athens *synegoroi* are usually advocates (cf. L. Rubinstein, *Litigation and Cooperation* [*Historia* Einz. 147 (2000)]), and these *synegoroi* perhaps acted as public prosecutors when the *logos* was taken to court (e.g. MacDowell, *Law*, 61). These *logistai* appear in ML 58 = *IG* i³ 52 ~ Fornara 119. *A*. 25–7, but the *logistai* of ll. 7–9 and ML 72 = *IG* i³ 369. 1 cf. i³ 259. 2 are different; an inscription of the deme Myrrhinus mentions a *logistes* and *synegoroi* (*IG* ii² 1183. 13–16).

it is these alone ... introduce their *euthynai* into the lawcourt: If the text is correct, this is surprisingly emphatic. Strictly the financial account was the *logos* and the general examination was the *euthynai*, but the distinction was not always observed; the *eisagousai archai* for *euthynai* in the strict sense were the Forty and the *thesmothetai* (48. 5). The *logos* had to be taken to court even if no objections were raised (e.g. Dem. XVIII. *Cor.* 117, XIX. *F.L.* 211).

if they establish that a man is an embezzler, the jurors convict him of embezzlement: Here rather than paraphrasing the laws *A.P.* uses the language of narrative (cf. Introduction, pp. 19–20). The same three charges are mentioned in connection with the prosecution of Pericles in Plut. *Per.* 32. 4; for *klope* (embezzlement) cf. Ar. *Vesp.* 836–1008, Antiph. II. *Tetr. i.* α. 6, β. 9, Dem. XIX. *F.L.* 293, XXIV. *Timocrates* 112, 127.

the amount decided is repaid tenfold: Ten times the amount he is found to have taken (cf. Dem. XXIV. *Timocrates* 112, 127).

if they demonstrate that a man has taken bribes … this also is repaid tenfold: For a tenfold penalty for taking bribes cf. Din. I. *Demosthenes* 60, II. *Aristogeiton* 17, Hyp. V. *Demosthenes* col. xxiv. Dinarchus' alternative death penalty (I. 60) could be obtained by means of an *eisangelia*.

if they convict him of misdemeanour … this is repaid simply: For the simple repayment cf. Hyp. *loc. cit.*; the double restitution of Din. I. 60 reflects the doubling of overdue debts (for which cf. 48. 1). This points to venial wrongs; MacDowell suggests accounting errors with no intent to defraud (*Law*, 171).

if a man pays before the 9th prytany: For the significance of the ninth prytany of the year cf. 47. 3. This provision is in accordance with the law attacked in Dem. XXIV. *Timocrates*, by which the state would not treat debtors as defaulters unless they failed to pay by the ninth prytany.

The tenfold payment is not doubled: No other text states this.

54. 3. the secretary called the secretary by the prytany: On the secretaries see Rhodes, *A.B.* 134–41; A. S. Henry, *Hesperia* 71 (2002), 91–118. *A.P.* mentions only three secretaries, but others are attested in inscriptions, including one ἐπὶ τὰ ψηφίσματα (cf. on 54. 4). This first was the principal secretary of the Athenian state, named in prescripts and ordered to publish both decrees and laws. His older title was γραμματεὺς τῆς βουλῆς; between 363/2 and 322/1 both that and *A.P.*'s title were used (both within four lines in *IG* ii^2 120. 11–19); after that *A.P.*'s title until in the second century AD it was replaced by περὶ τὸ βῆμα, except that for two short periods in the late fourth and early third centuries the principal secretary was entitled ἀναγραφεύς. *A.P.*'s title seems to have been introduced when the mode of appointment was changed (on that cf. below), and it denotes 'prytany by prytany (through the year)', not 'serving for one prytany'.

has power over the documents: He presumably had general responsibility for the state's records. On the Μητρῷον, where records were kept in the fourth century, see p. 354.

guards the decrees which are enacted: Presumably he kept an official copy of the text, both of decrees and of laws, whether or not they were inscribed on stone.

copies everything else: Probably the actual writing was done by a *demosios* under his direction (cf. *IG* ii² 120. 11–19). *Antigrapheus* was the title of a financial official superseded or encroached on by the theoric officials (Aeschin. III. *Ctesiphon* 25: cf. p. 346); the title appears in inscriptions both before and after the time referred to by Aeschines, and it is most likely that it was used of a financial official earlier in the fourth century and reused for a secretary later.

sits in attendance on the council: He must also have attended meetings of the assembly and the *nomothetai*; and when they referred matters to a court he had to give the relevant documents to the *eisagousa arche* (e.g. ML 69 = *IG* i³ 71 ~ Fornara 136. 51–4). In Ar. *Thesm.* 383–432 a speaker outlines her general proposal and offers to work out the details with the secretary.

Previously this man was elected … But now he has become allotted: No other text mentions this change, but inscriptions attest to other associated changes: until at any rate 366/5 the secretary served for one prytany, and was a member of the council, from a tribe other than the current prytany, each tribe providing one secretary during the year (W. S. Ferguson, *The Athenian Secretaries* [New York: Macmillan for Cornell U., 1898], 14–27; date Henry, *op. cit.*, 92); but from at any rate 363/2 one secretary served for the whole year, and did not have to be a member of the council, and from 356/5 the appointment rotated among the tribes in their official order (Ferguson, 32–8; but the survival of the old system in 366/5 rules out a less regular tribal rotation 366/5–357/6).

they used to elect the most distinguished … this man is written up: Secretaries were regularly named in prescripts both before and after the change; some decrees have a heading in larger letters before the prescript, and during the fourth century first secretaries and later archons ceased to be mentioned in these headings. *A.P.* may be thinking of the fact that by his time secretaries were no longer named in headings, but his point seems to be that under the new system less distinguished men were appointed. Some of the secretaries under the old system were men otherwise distinguished (e.g. Agyrrhius and Cephisophon in 403/2), but by no means all; presumably under the new system secretaries were more likely to be men attracted by this kind of work than men with political ambitions.

54. 4. another secretary, in charge of the laws: Included in some lists from the late fourth century onwards (first in *Agora* xv 53. 19, of 324/3;

absent from *Agora* xv 43, of 335/4); ἐπὶ τὰ ψηφίσματα, not mentioned by *A.P.*, is first mentioned in *Agora* xv 34. 3, of 343/2. It is not clear how the work was divided between these two and *A.P.*'s first secretary.

he sits in attendance on the council, and he also copies them all: *Sc.* τοὺς νόμους. The council and assembly set the machinery in motion, but the final decision to enact laws was taken by a board of *nomothetai*, whom *A.P.* never mentions (cf. p. 345).

54. 5. the *demos* elects the secretary who is to read documents to itself and the council: Cf. Thuc. VII. 10, Dem. XX. *Leptines* 94; he is most economically identified with the inscriptions' γραμματεὺς (τῆς βουλῆς καὶ) τοῦ δήμου / (τῇ βουλῇ καὶ) τῷ δήμῳ (e.g. *Agora* xv 12. 64); cf. 67. 3 on the secretaries who read out documents in the courts. This was an important job when multiple copies of documents could not be produced, so election was appropriate, but it seems to have been subject to the rule of 62. 3, that tenure was limited to one year (cf. *Agora* xv, p. 15).

54. 6. allots ten *hieropoioi*: *Hieropoioi* are among the religious officials reviewed by Arist. *Pol.* VI. 1322 B 18–19; and there were various boards of *hieropoioi* in Athens who cooperated with priests in administering festivals, usually boards of ten and often appointed from the council. It is unclear why *A.P.* mentions these two boards. Athens' religious officials are surveyed by R. S. J. Garland, *BSA* 79 (1984), 75–123,

in charge of expiatory sacrifices: For *ekthymata* as expiatory sacrifices cf. e.g. Hdt. VI. 91. 1: these *hieropoioi* are not attested elsewhere.

the sacrificial rites ordered by oracles: When an oracle has been consulted after some misfortune.

if there is a need to seek good omens: Before going to war, founding a colony or embarking on some other major undertaking.

together with the soothsayers: For *manteis* in Athens cf. *IG* i³ 1147. 128–9, Thuc. VIII. 1. 1.

54. 7. ten others, those called yearly … except the Panathenaea: *Hieropoioi* with this title are mentioned in an Eleusinian document of the 320's (*IG* ii² 1672. 251), and earlier, involved with the Great Panathenaea, in a document of 410/09 (ML 84 = *IG* i³ 375 ~ Fornara 154. 6–7), whereas a decree of *c.* 335 mentions a separate board of *hieropoioi* for the annual Panathenaea (RO 81. 31–2 = *IG* ii³ 447. 57–8). Presumably the Panathenaea was transferred from the 'annual' *hieropoioi* to the separate board in the 330's or earlier.

The five-yearly festivals are: first, that to Delos: The counting is inclusive: these were quadrennial, as we reckon. The Athenians revived the Ionian festival of Apollo after their 'purification' of Delos in winter 426/5 (the third year of an Olympiad), but after interruptions at the beginning of the fourth century the festival fell in the spring of the second year (e.g. *IG* ii^2 1635. 30–40). For the festival cf. 56. 3; for Athens' control of Delos cf. 62. 2.

there is also a seven-yearly festival there: This should mean that there were both a quadrennial and a sexennial festival at Delos (as there were a biennial and a quadrennial Eleusinian festival: below). The sexennial festival is not attested elsewhere, and it has been suggested that the one festival was made sexennial after 330 (C. Torr, *CR*. 5 [1891], 277); but what the text states is not necessarily wrong.

second, the Brauronia: A festival of Artemis Brauronia (Parker, *Polytheism*, 230–1, 463), of Brauron, in eastern Attica (Hdt. VI. 138. 1: cf. pp. 220–1, 247). There was also a Βραυρώνιον on the acropolis, adjoining the south side of the Propylaea (Paus. I. 23. 7: cf. Travlos, *Pictorial Dictionary*, 124–5), and the festival incorporated a procession from Athens to Brauron (Ar. *Pax* 874). This fell in the fourth year of an Olympiad, if *IG* ii^2 1480. *A* may be dated 313/2 (D. M. Lewis, in *Comptes et inventaires dans la cité grecque ... J. Tréheux* [Geneva: Droz, 1988], 298 n. 7).

third, the Heraclea: Harp. η 14 Keaney Ἡράκλεια remarks that there were several local festivals of Heracles, the most important being at Marathon and at Diomea (perhaps north of the city wall: Parker, *Polytheism*, 472–3, and in *Tria Lustra ... J. Pinsent* [Liverpool: *Liverpool Classical Monthly*, 1993], 25–6). If the festival held inside the city in 346/5 (Dem. XIX. *F.L.* 125) and *A.P.*'s festival are the same, the year will be the third of the Olympiad.

fourth, the Eleusinia: See Parker, *Polytheism*, 201–2, 328–9, 468–9. *IG* ii^2 1672. 258–62 refers to offerings for a biennial and a quadrennial festival. The festivals were held at Eleusis, in late summer: thanks to work on the Athenian calendar by J. D. Morgan (briefly, *AJA*^{2} 100 [1996], 395), it now seems likely that in both the classical and the hellenistic period the major, quadrennial festival was held in the third year of the Olympiad and the lesser, 'biennial', in the first year (K. Clinton, *O.C.D.*^{4} 500).

5th, the Panathenaea: The Panathenaea (cf. 60; Parker, *Polytheism*, 329–37) was celebrated in the city, in Hecatombaeon (i), the Great Panathenaea in the third year of the Olympiad and the Little Panathenaea every year.

none of these falls in the same year: That none were celebrated in the same place is true, but would be a surprising comment: that none, or none of the first four, were celebrated in the same year, which *A.P.* probably means, now appears to be untrue.

Now there has been added also the Hephaestia, in the archonship of Cephisophon.: The date, 329/8, is the latest in *A.P.* and the only date in the second part; this clause is clearly an addition to the original text (cf. Introduction, pp. 20, 29). The Hephaestia is a festival with which *hieropoioi* were concerned (*IG* i^3 82. 21–3: *hieropoioi* from the council), but we have no other evidence for a quadrennial festival and know no reason for instituting one in 329/8. On the other hand, we do know that the quadrennial Amphiarea at Oropus was revived in 329/8 (*IG* ii^3 348, 355): Ἀμφιάραια was not written in the London papyrus, but it remains possible that that was written by *A.P.* and subsequently corrupted and wrongly emended.

54. 8. They allot also an archon for Salamis: Salamis, though continuously Athenian from the end of the sixth century, was never incorporated into Attica but ruled as subject territory (cf. pp. 229, 245). So too were the Aegean islands possessed by Athens in the fourth century (cf. 62. 2), and Oropus when it was in Athenian hands (as it was when *A.P.* was written, but *A.P.* does not mention it).

a demarch for Piraeus: Other demarchs were appointed by their demes (e.g. *IG* ii^2 1194: Eleusis *c.* 300), but Piraeus as the harbour town of Athens was not an ordinary deme, and this was a *polis* appointment. We do not know whether he had to be a demesman of Piraeus.

who conduct the Dionysia … and appoint the *choregoi*: Dionysia κατ' ἀγρούς are attested in several demes and at any rate in some included dramatic performances, which were financed as deme liturgies. See Deubner, *Attische Feste*, 134–8; A. W. Pickard-Cambridge rev. J. P. A. Gould & D. M. Lewis, *The Dramatic Festivals of Athens* (Oxford U. P., 1968), 42–56; and for Thoricus D. Whitehead, *ZPE* 62 (1986), 231–20. At Piraeus there was a theatre before the end of the fifth century (Thuc. VIII. 93. 1, Lys. XIII. *Agoratus* 32, Xen. *Hell.* II. 4. 32); from Salamis a fourth-century dedication records a dithyrambic victory and names the archon (*IG* ii^2 3093), and tragedies are attested in the hellenistic period. These officials will have had secular as well as religious duties, but it is because of their religious duties that they are mentioned here, after the *hieropoioi*.

In Salamis in addition the name of the archon is written up: The archon was the eponymous officer, who would be named in documents (e.g. *IG* ii^2 1227. 1), as the demarch was the eponymous officer in a deme (e.g. *IG* ii^2 2498. 1, from Piraeus); but this sentence ought to state something which is true of Salamis but not of Piraeus, and the allusion may be to a list of *archontes*.

O. The archons (55–9)

A law *ap.* Dem. XXIV. *Timocrates* 20 has laws 'for the nine archons' as one of four categories of laws, and the archons form a substantial subsection within *A.P.*'s treatment of officials, but would be better placed before 50–4 (cf. p. 18). *A.P.* begins with their appointment and *dokimasia*, and then lists the duties of particular archons, ending with the duty of the whole college to assign jurors to courts. These chapters show the close relationship between *A.P.* and the laws of Athens (cf. pp. 18–21): Dem. XLIII. *Macartatus* 75 quotes the law on orphans which lies behind 56. 7, and XXIII. *Aristocrates* 22 with 24, 53, 77, quotes parts of the homicide law which lies behind 57. 3.

55. 1. Those offices are allotted … all the matters stated: This rounds off the section on sortitive officials, begun in 50. 1.

the so-called nine archons: This distinguishes the 'nine archons' from the (eponymous) archon, and from *archontes* in the broader sense (as in 55. 2).

the manner in which they were appointed … has been stated: Their institution was dealt with in 3. 2–4, and their manner of appointment at different times in 8.1, 22. 5, 26. 2. This is the only place where *A.P.* refers to the first part to contrast current with earlier practice, and the only place except 47. 1 where the second part refers to the first.

Now they allot … in turn from each tribe: *A.P.* has not previously mentioned the secretary, added to the nine to make a college of ten, or the distribution of the offices among the tribes; he said in 8. 1 and does not repeat here that election for the first stage of the appointment (cf. 22. 5) had by his time been replaced by sortition. We do not know when these changes occurred (but see on 55. 2); in *IG* ii^2 2811 the archon of 394/3 has one *paredros* and a secretary.

κατὰ μέρος ought to mean that the posts within the college went to different tribes in rotation, by tribal order or by lot over a ten-year period (cf. N. G. L. Hammond, *CQ*^{2} 19 [1969], 131 = his *Studies*, 375–6). For most years we know the eponymous archon only by personal name and the others not at all, but no kind of regularity can be found in the instances in which we do know the archon's tribe.

55. 2. These are vetted … in the council and again in a lawcourt: Cf. 45. 3, and for *dokimasiai* in the courts 59. 4; Dem. XX. *Leptines* 90. Lys. XXVI. *Evandrus* was written for the *dokimasia* of a prospective archon, probably the man who held office in 382/1.

the secretary. He like the other officials is vetted in a lawcourt only: *Archontes* here are officials in general (cf. above). The difference may indicate that the secretary's post was not created until it was normal for *dokimasiai* to be held in the courts.

for all allotted and elected officials serve after being vetted: Cf. Aeschin. III. *Ctesiphon* 14–15. This parenthesis is *A.P.*'s own comment; and *archontes* here refers to officials in general as opposed to the 'nine archons'.

Previously … that has decisive power in the vetting: Cf. 45. 3. *Ephesis* is used of appeal by a dissatisfied litigant in 53. 2 and probably 53. 6; of compulsory reference from the council to a court in 45. 1–2 and 46. 2. Here and in 45. 3 *A.P.*'s language might suggest appeal against rejection, but the details in this account, and Dem. XX. *Leptines* 90, indicate that in the time of *A.P.* there was compulsory reference for archons (e.g. Bonner & Smith, *Administration of Justice*, ii. 243–4); but for councillors see on 45. 3.

There has been discussion both of the current practice and of the earlier practice with which it is contrasted (see, for instance, M. Just, *Historia* 19 [1970], 132–40). *A.P.* seems to envisage three stages: the earliest, in which the council's was the only hearing; a second, in which the Athenians were afraid of unjust rejection, and required reference to a court but the court's hearing was a formality when there was no accuser

(55. 4); and a third, when they also feared unjust acceptance and required two serious hearings. The second stage would be surprising: possibly it represents the weakening of an original proposal by an amendment; or possibly the history has been distorted, these *dokimasiai* were originally held in the Areopagus and were a formality there if there was no accuser, and after they were taken from the Areopagus by Ephialtes (cf. p. 267) the hearing by the council of five hundred was from the beginning subject to compulsory reference.

55. 3. they ask: Cf. Xen. *Mem.* II. 2. 13, Dem. LVII. *Eubulides* 66–70, Din. II. *Aristogeiton* 17–18. The nature of the questions suggests an ancient institution, though in the archaic period, when candidates and examiners came from a limited class and were well known to one another, they are likely to have been a matter of formal confirmation rather than genuine enquiry.

'Who is your father … and from which of the demes?': Cf. Dem. LVII. 66. The nine archons had to be the sons of citizens by lawful marriage to citizen wives ([Dem.] LIX. *Neaera* 92, 104–6), and the proof that a woman was a *politis* was that her father was registered as a citizen. The father's paternity was not strictly necessary (for *phratria* membership *IG* ii^2 1237 = RO 5. 114–25 omits the paternal grandfather), but despite the intention attributed to Cleisthenes (21. 4) the patronymic remained part of a man's full designation. (However, M. J. Osborne, *Naturalization in Athens*, iii–iv. 175, argues that citizen grandparents were required at the time of *A.P.* though not at the time of [Dem.] LIX.)

whether he has a cult … and where those shrines are: Cf. Dem. LVII. 54, 67. It was confirmation that a man was an Athenian that he had in Athenian territory household cults of Apollo Patroios (Apollo being through Ion the common ancestor of all the Athenians).

whether he has family tombs and where they are: An *erion* is a mound, and by extension any kind of tomb: to provide further confirmation candidates were asked about their family tombs. Cf. Xen. *Mem.* II. 2. 13, Dem. LVII. 67, Din. II. 17 (where Valesius emended ἱερὰ to ἠρία).

whether he treats his parents well: Cf. Xen. *Mem.* II. 2. 13, Dem. LVII. 70, Din. II. 17–18. A man who failed to support his parents or grandparents was liable to prosecution (56. 6, cf. Ar. *Av.* 1353–7).

whether he pays his taxes: Cf. Cratinus Jun. fr. 9 Kassel & Austin *ap.* Ath. XI. 460 F, Din. II. 17 with 18. Pol.. VIII. 86 has καὶ εἰ (τί Koch) τὸ τίμημα ἔστιν αὐτοῖς, seeing a reference to membership of a Solonian class, and we should expect membership to be checked at the *dokimasia* (cf. 7. 4, 26. 2), but it is clear from Cratinus and Dinarchus that this question was about paying taxes.

whether he has performed his military service: Cf. Din. II. 17–18; also Lys. XVI. *Mantitheus* 12–18.

After asking these questions: *A.P.* changes from plural to singular; the subject is presumably the *epistates* in the council or the presiding magistrate in the court.

'Call the witnesses to these things': Cf. Dem. LVII. 67. Written testimony replaced spoken in the courts from about the 370's (cf. p. 382), but witnesses still had to appear to acknowledge their depositions.

55. 4. When he has provided his witnesses: *Sc.* the candidate.

'Does anybody wish to accuse this man?' In the formal interrogation the candidate was a defendant without an accuser; then an opportunity to object was provided, presumably to all citizens, and if anybody did object the candidate could reply. We have prepared speeches of defence in Lys. XVI. *Mantitheus* and XXV. *Overthrowing Democracy*, and accusation in XXVI. *Evandrus*.

he grants the vote ... grants the ballot immediately: The council voted by show of hands, the court by ballot; the use of ψῆφον alone at the end of the sentence is due to condensation.

previously one man used to cast his ballot ... to reject him in the vetting: This refers to the court: the token vote would be appropriate to a body which voted by ballot but not to one which voted by show of hands. For this stage in the development of the procedure see pp. 392–3.

to vote about them: Cf. the use of *diapsephizesthai* in the *dokimasia* of eighteen-year-old citizens (42. 1).

55. 5. When they have been vetted: There must have been a lapse of time either between the *dokimasia* and the oath or between the oath and entry into office; more probably the oath immediately preceded the entry into office.

they proceed to the stone: Cf. 7. 1 with commentary.

on which the sliced victims have been placed: *Tomia* are victims cut up for sacrifice: cf. Dem. XXIII. *Aristocrates* 68.

on which also the *diaitetai* swear before declaring their arbitrations: Cf. 53. 2–6 (where this is not mentioned), and Isae. V. *Dicaeogenes*

32. This was probably a promissory oath, sworn when accepting a case (Bonner & Smith, *Administration of Justice*, ii. 156–7).

witnesses swear when denying their testimony: After the introduction of written testimony (cf. p. 382) witnesses had to attend the trial, to acknowledge their testimony or to deny it on oath (cf. Isae. IX. *Astyphilus* 18, Aeschin. I. *Timarchus* 45–7, 67, Dem. XIX. *F.L.* 176, Lyc. *Leocr.* 20, and Harrison, *L.A.* ii. 139–45).

Climbing on to this: The stone was *c.* 0.4 m. = 1 ft. 4 in. high, with a surface *c.* 1 m. × 3 m. = 3 ft. × 10 ft.

they swear … they will dedicate a golden statue: Similar undertakings were sworn by members of the council (Xen. *Mem.* I. 1. 18) and by jurors (oath *ap.* Dem. XXIV. *Timocrates* 150, likely to contain authentic elements though the document itself is suspect).

or if they do accept anything they will dedicate a golden statue: Cf. 7. 1: this passage, linking the dedication with bribe-taking, is the more likely to be correct.

they proceed to the acropolis and swear the same again there: No other text mentions this. Since the Stoa was not built until the fifth century (cf. p. 201), they may orignally have sworn on the acropolis only (E. Will, *RPh*^{3} 42 [1968], 135).

after that: See first note on 55. 5.

56. 1. The archon … take two *paredroi*, whoever they wish: Cf. 48. 4, on the *paredroi* of the *euthynoi*; schol. Aeschin. I. *Timarchus* 158 (319 Dilts) wrongly states that each archon had a *paredros*. The *paredroi* make various appearances in literature and inscriptions of the fourth century and later. It is striking that the archons were allowed to choose their own assistants (perhaps a survival from early times), but having been chosen the *paredroi* were subject to the normal procedures of *dokimasia* and *euthynai*. See S. Dow, in *In Memoriam O. J. Brendel* (Mainz: von Zabern, 1976), 80–1; K. A. Kapparis, *Historia* 47 (1998), 383–93.

56. 2. The archon: *A.P.* proceeds to the duties of the different archons, first religious and then judicial (on the origins of the offices see 3. 1–5); a duty of the archon not mentioned here is to collect olive oil for prizes at the Panathenaea (60. 2–3).

first proclaims … until the end of his office: Presumably the proclamation was made by the herald of the nine archons (62. 2). In the classical period the archon had little opportunity to enforce it, or himself to break it, so it is likely to be early, but it is not likely to have been instituted until the possibility of *ges anadasmos* had arisen. Solon's *seisachtheia* might be considered a breach of it: perhaps after proclaiming the *seisachtheia* he enacted that future archons should proclaim the security of property.

have and control: Cf. *IG* ii^{2} 2758. 3–4, 2759. 6 (hellenistic).

56. 3. he appoints three *choregoi* ... the richest men from all the Athenians: On *choregoi* see P. Wilson, *The Athenian Institution of the Khoregia* (Cambridge U. P., 2000). *Choregia*, financial and general responsibility for a chorus at a festival, was one of the responsibilities which the state (or a deme) imposed on its richer citizens; for the range of festival liturgies see J. K. Davies, *JHS* 87 (1967), 33–40. The archon presumably had to call on the richest of the men not temporarily or permanently exempt (but a man could volunteer: cf. Lys. XXI. *Bribery* 1–5, Dem. XXI. *Midias* 13). Aristotle disliked these impositions (*Pol.* V. 1305 A 4–5, 1309 A 14–20). Probably *c.* 316–315, festival liturgies were abolished by Demetrius of Phalerum, after which the people elected an *agonothetes* who was provided with some public money but could add to it. However, P. J. Wilson & E. G. Csapo in D. S. Rosenbloom & J. Davidson (eds), *Greek Drama IV* (Oxford: Oxbow, 2012), 300–18, argue that the *choregia* continued longer, perhaps even to the fall of Demetrius in 307. Three tragedians competed each year at the Great Dionysia (and there was also a tragic competition at the Lenaea); the archon had also to 'grant a chorus' to the poets whom he accepted as contestants.

previously ... but now the tribes supply these: Both at the Lenaea and at the Great Dionysia five comedians competed. The change in procedure appears to be earlier than 348/7 (Dem. XXXIX. *Boeotus i.* 7 with J. J. Keaney, *Historia* 19 [1970], 330 and n. 19); in spite of it, comic choruses like tragic remained non-tribal. The Lenaea was among the responsibilities of the *basileus*, and he should have appointed the *choregoi* for that (cf. Dem. XXXV. *Lacritus* 48, XXXIX. 9).

he takes over the *choregoi* supplied by the tribes: He also supervised the drawing of lots between *choregoi* for poets and pipers (Dem. XXI. *Midias* 13).

for men, boys: For the dithyrambic contests.

those for the Dionysia ... those for the Thargelia one for two tribes...: At the Dionysia each tribe competed both in the men's and in the boys' class, so two *choregoi* will have been needed from each (J. K. Davies, *JHS* 87 [1967], 33). For the Thargelia, in the late fifth century tribes were paired by lot each year (Antiph. VI. *Chor.* 11); but some time between 380/79 (*IG* ii^3. 4. 1 476) or 375–373 (Hyp. IV. *Euxenippus* 16 with D. Knoepfler, *REG* 129 [2016], 453–87) and 372/1 (478) a regular pairing was introduced. Cf. 52. 2, 54. 1, 62. 2; also 51. 3.

he holds *antidoseis*: On *antidoseis* see Harrison, *L.A.* ii. 236–8; MacDowell, *Law*, 162–4; V. Gabrielsen, *C&M* 38 (1987), 7–38. A man who was called on to perform a liturgy but claimed that a richer man had been passed over could call on that man either to perform the liturgy or to exchange property with him; if that man would do neither, the case went to court. There is no clear instance in which an exchange was completed, but see Lys. IV. *Wound* 1, Dem. XLII. *Phaenippus* 5–7. Cf. 61. 1, on *antidoseis* and *diadikasiai* for the trierarchy.

he introduces claims for exemption: A *skepsis* was a claim that a man was legally exempt from a liturgy to which he was appointed (cf. Harrison, *L.A.* ii 232–6). In addition to the grounds listed by *A.P.*, hereditary exemption had been given to various distinguished Athenians; a law of Leptines proposed to ban that except for the descendants of Harmodius and Aristogeiton, but the attack on it by Dem. XX. *Leptines* seems to have succeeded. Probably men with less than a stated amount of property were exempt (cf. Dem. XX. 19); minors were exempt (Lys. XXXII. *Diogeiton* 24) and possibly in the time of *A.P. epheboi* also (cf. 42. 5 with commentary).

he has performed this liturgy previously: Cf. the ban on holding a civilian office more than once (62. 3). Presumably a man could voluntarily perform a liturgy which he had performed before, but I do not know any instance of that.

he is exempt … has not yet expired: By performing a liturgy in one year, a man was exempt in the following year (Dem. XX. 8), and *a fortiori* from other liturgies in the same year ([Dem.] L. *Polycles* 9). Some expensive liturgies might earn a longer period of exemption (e.g. Isae. VII. *Apollodorus* 38).

that he has not yet reached the age … over forty years old): Cf. Aeschin. I. *Timarchus* 11; also Pl. *Leg.* VI. 764 E 6–765 A 1, and the requirement for the *sophronistai* and probably the *kosmetes* of the *epheboi* (42. 2). This was an innovation of the fourth century (cf. e.g. Lys. XXI. *Bribery* 1–5, Dem. XXI. *Midias* 147).

He also appoints for Delos ... takes the young men: Cf. 54. 7. A *theoria* was sent to Delos every year (cf. Pl. *Phd.* 58 A 6–C 2: Socrates was tried in 400/399 [Diog. Laert. II. 44, Diod. Sic. XIV. 37. 7], the first year of an Olympiad and not the year of a quadrennial festival). According to *L.R.C.* ἐπώνυμος ἄρχων (emended) the archon was responsible for *theoriai* both to Delos and elsewhere. For the diminutive τριακοντόριον cf. *IG* ii^2 1627. 16, 1631. 426; and for this and other sacred ships see 61. 7. *Eitheoi* are unmarried young men, the male equivalent of *parthenoi* (cf. Hdt. III. 48. 3).

56. 4. He takes care of processions ... when the initiates stay at home: This was on the day of the Epidauria, 17 or 18 Boedromion (iii), before the procession to Eleusis for the Mysteries. See Parker, *Polytheism*, 347–8 nn. 87–8. The initiates spent the day in the temple of Asclepius (cf. Ar. *Plut.* 411, 621), possibly fasting (W. Burkert, *Greek Religion, Archaic and Classical* [Oxford: Blackwell, 1985], 287) According to 3. 3 the archon administered only the more recent festivals: the quadrennial festival on Delos was revived in 426/5 (cf. p. 389); the cult of Asclepius was introduced into Athens in 420/19 (*IG* ii^2 4960. 10–13).

the Great Dionysia: This is one of the earliest uses of that expression; the festival was otherwise known as the City Dionysia (e.g. Thuc. V. 20. 1). The procession leading to the sacrifices in the precinct of Dionysus was held on the first day of the festival, 10 Elaphebolion (ix), after the *proagon* and Asclepiea on the 8th and the *eisagoge apo tes escharas* on the night of the 8/9th or 9/10th (see Parker, *Polytheism*, 317–8). This was generally considered one of the more recent festivals: the bringing of the image of Dionysus from Eleutherae to Athens and the acquisition of Eleutherae by Athens cannot be firmly dated (see R. Parker, *Athenian Religion: A History* [Oxford U. P., 1996], 8, 93–5); the Dionysia in its classical form is conventionally dated *c.* 534 from *Marm. Par. FGrH* 239 A 43, *Suda* θ 282 Adler Θέσπις, and that is not conclusive but still seems preferable to the dating to the end of the sixth century by W. R. Connor (*C&M* 40 [1989], 7–32 = Connor *et al.*, *Aspects of Athenian Democracy* [Copenhagen: Museum Tusculanum P., 1990], 7–32).

together with the *epimeletai* ... a hundred minas for the paraphernalia: Cf. *IG* ii^3 359. 15–19, and (hellenistic) 920. 13–15, 22–31, ii^3 1284. 34–8. In the middle of the century they were still elected (Dem. XXI. *Midias* 15): the change was presumably part of the reorganisation of festivals associated with Lycurgus (cf. *IG* ii[3] 447), and will have been very recent when *A.P.* was written – but there is no sign that this was not part of the original text.

56. 5. He takes care also of the processions for the Thargelia: πομπῆς must be understood. This was a festival of Apollo (see Parker, *Athenian Religion*, 95–6): on 6 Thargelion (xi) the city was purified by the driving out of scapegoats, and on the 7th first-fruits of unripe corn were offered and there were a procession and choral contests (see Parker, *Polytheism*, 181–2, 203–4). The festival will have been established before the month gained its name, so this will not be a recent addition (cf. Parker, *Athenian Religion*, 8); but Parker suggests that dithyrambs were added in the Pisistratid period or later.

for Zeus Soter: The Diisoteria was a festival of Zeus Soter and Athena Soteira (Saviours), held in Piraeus in Scirophorion (xii) (*IG* ii[2] 380. 19–21, 30–2), and presumably established after Piraeus had become Athens' harbour town. See Parker, *Athenian Religion*, 237–8, *Polytheism*, 466–7.

Those are the festivals of which he takes care: *A.P.* rounds off the religious part of the archon's duties…

56. 6. Public and private lawsuits fall to him: …and proceeds to the judicial part. For λαγχάνειν cf. 53. 1.

after holding the *anakrisis*: Cf. Dem. XLVIII. *Olympiodorus* 31. The *anakrisis* was the preliminary enquiry conducted by the *eisagousa arche*, to check that the case was in order and prepare it for the trial in court: see Harrison, *L.A.* ii. 94–105.

maltreatment of parents … maltreatment of orphans … maltreatment of *epikleroi* … maltreatment of an orphan's estate…: These prosecutions could be referred to either as *eisangelia* or as *graphe*, and Isae. XI. *Hagnias* uses both. Some lexica use *dike*, but as Harp. κ 12 Keaney κακώσεως states prosecution was certainly open to *ho boulomenos*. See Harrison, *L.A.* i. 117–9.

maltreatment of parents: Athenians were required to care for their parents while alive and give them proper burial when dead: cf. 55. 3. Hyp. IV. *Euxenippus* 6 confirms that these cases fell to the archon.

in these whoever wishes may prosecute without risk of penalty: *A.P.* notes the exception but not the rule, that prosecutors in *graphai* who withdrew or failed to obtain a fifth of the votes were fined and subjected to a form of *atimia* (cf. Harrison, *L.A.* ii. 83 with n. 2). Originally this did not apply to any *eisangeliai*, but not long before 330 the fine was introduced for *eisangeliai* of major public offences (Hyp. I. *Lycophron* 8, 12: see Harrison, *L.A.* ii. 51 with n. 3). The full exemption survived for all *eisangeliai* of *kakosis*.

maltreatment of orphans (these are against the guardians): These were available against anybody who wronged orphans and *epikleroi* (Dem. XXXVII. *Pantaenetus* 45: Harrison, *L.A.* i. 118).

for maltreatment of *epikleroi* (these are against the guardians and the husbands): On *epikleroi* cf. 9. 2, 35. 2, 42. 5, 43. 4. Offences include failure by the next of kin to marry the *epikleros* or find her a husband, *hybris* and failure by the husband to have intercourse with her as prescribed (cf. Plut. *Sol.* 20. 2–4). *Synoikein* came to be used of living together in wedlock (Harrison, *L.A.* i. 2 with n. 4). That these cases fell to the archon is confirmed by Isae. III. *Pyrrhus* 46, 62, Dem. XXXVII. *Pantaenetus* 46.

maltreatment of an orphan's estate (these also are against the guardians): Charges under this head could also be made by *phasis* (Dem. XXXVIII. *Nausimachus and Xenopithes* 23). See Harrison, *L.A.* i. 115–7.

insanity … squandering his ancestral estate: See Harrison, *L.A.* i. 80–1. This was probably a *graphe*; for another law on insanity see 35. 2.

for appointment of distributors … the administration of property in common: A *datetes* is a distributor: according to Harp. δ 6 Keaney, *Suda* δ 88 Adler δατεῖσθαι καὶ δατηταί, if some members wanted to dissolve a partnership but others did not, those who did could sue for the appointment of *datetai*. This was perhaps introduced for inheritance disputes and later extended: see Harrison, *L.A.* i. 243. It and the suits which follow will have been *dikai*, not available to *ho boulomenos*.

the appointment of a guardian … the adjudication of a guardianship: The first will be a suit to appoint a guardian for an orphaned minor, the second a dispute between potential guardians (*diadikasia* is used of deciding between two or more claimants to something). See Harrison, *L.A.* i. 99–104.

displaying to public view: A suit to secure the production of an object, to enable the claimant to lay hands on it (cf. *Anecd. Bekk.* i. 246. 4): see Harrison, *L.A.* i. 207–10.

registering oneself as a guardian: Thought by Kenyon[1] to belong with the previous phrase, but more probably a separate lawsuit, by which a man interested in a guardianship could intervene without making a claim: see Harrison, *L.A.* i. 103.

adjudications of estates and *epikleroi*: Claimants to an estate other than direct descendants or adopted sons had to register their claim with the archon: the claim was read out at a *kyria ekklesia* (43. 4), and anybody who disputed it could enter an *epidikasia*. See Harrison, *L.A.* i. 10–11, 158–62.

56. 7. of orphans and *epikleroi* ... at the death of their husband: Cf. what purports to be the text of the law, *ap.* Dem. XLIII. *Macartatus* 75: *A.P.* described where the law prescribes; he paraphrases and abbreviates. In the archaic period the archon's responsibility may have involved substantial executive duties; in the classical period it is not clear what it involved beyond acting as *eisagousa arche* for relevant lawsuits.

to impose a summary penalty ... or to introduce a case into the lawcourt: The law quoted by Demosthenes is mor specific. For officials' *epibolai* cf. 52. 3 with commentary, and see Harrison, *L.A.* ii. 4–7.

He lets out the estates ... until they reach the age of fourteen: A guardian might be instructed or might choose to lease out the property until the heir came of age: see Isae. VI. *Philoctemon* 36–7, and Harrison, *L.A.* i. 105–7. τετταρακαιδεκέτις is feminine: presumably an orphaned girl with no brothers was treated as an orphan until she reached fourteen, and as an *epikleros* thereafter. Male orphans entered on their inheritance at eighteen (cf. 42. 5).

he receives the valuations: The lessee had to provide land as security, and the archon sent *apotimetai* to value the land and ensure that it was sufficient: see Isae. VI. 36, and Harrison, *L.A.* ii. 293–6.

if guardians fail to provide food for the boys he exacts it: Wards as minors were not legally in a position to complain, so perhaps here the archon had the right of initiative. For *sitos* as maintenance cf. Dem. XXVII. *Aphobus i.* 15, XXVIII. *Aphobus ii.* 11 (62. 2 uses *sitesis*). The article suggests a recognised level of maintenance.

57. 1. That is what the archon takes care of: *A.P.* rounds off his treatment of the archon…

The *basileus*, first, takes care of the Mysteries: …and passes to the *basileus*, beginning with religious duties. For the evolution of this official see 3. 1–3; for his responsibility for the Eleusinian Mysteries cf. Lys. VI.

Andocides 4, Andoc. I. *Myst.* 111, and for a modern discussion of the Mysteries see Parker, *Polytheism*, 342–60.

together with the *epimeletai* ... one from the Eumolpidae and one from the Kerykes: *Epimeletai* of the Mysteries are not attested in the fifth century, but are instituted in a law of the mid fourth century (*Agora* xvi 56. 30–7 – but in l. 29 I restore ἱεροποιοὺ]ς, not ἐπιμελητὰ]ς). In the hellenistic inscriptions which praise them there are only two (e.g. *IG* ii³ 915): either there was a change, or these inscriptions praise only the two elected from all Athenians (and the other two were perhaps not then elected). For the Eumolpidae (who supplied the *hierophantes* and other officials of the cult) and the Kerykes (who supplied the *daidouchos* and others) cf. 39. 2, and see K. Clinton, *The Sacred Officials of the Eleusinian Mysteries* (*TAPhS* 64. 3 [1974]).

the Dionysia at the Lenaeum: The Lenaea was held in the month Gamelion (vii): see Pickard-Cambridge rev. Gould & Lewis, *The Dramatic Festivals of Athens*, 25–42. The location of the sanctuary remains uncertain (see Pickard-Cambridge, 37–40); the name is probably derived from *lenai*, a term used of the maenads who worshipped Dionysus.

This is a procession and a competition ... organised by the *basileus*: At the Lenaea there were contests for comedy (five comedians) and tragedy (in the fifth century two tragedians); a third-century inscription attests a dithyrambic victory (*IG* ii² 3779. 7–8). The involvement of the *epimeletai* of the Mysteries is surprising, but confirmed by inscriptions (*IG* ii² 1496. 74–5, 1672. 82)

He also stages all the torch competitions: Torch races are attested at several festivals: see J. Jüthner, *RE* xii. 569–77; Parker, *Polytheism*, 472. The teams competing were entrusted to *gymnasiarchoi*, analogous to *choregoi* (e.g. Andoc. I. *Myst.* 132), appointed by their tribes like dithyrambic *choregoi* (Dem. XXXIX. *Boeotus i.* 7; cf. 56. 3); the *basileus* was the *eisagousa arche* for *antidoseis* and *skepseis* (Dem. XXXV. *Lacritus* 48).

so to say, he administers all the traditional sacrifices: Cf. Pl. *Plt.* 290 E 6–8: this seems nearer to the truth than the statement of 3. 3 that the *basileus* and polemarch but not the archon administered traditional festivals (cf. p. 407).

57. 2. Public lawsuits fall to him: for impiety: Cf. Dem. XXXV. *Lacritus* 48, Hyp. IV. *Euxenippus* 6. Other procedures were available too (cf. Dem. XXII. *Androtion* 27), e.g. *eisangelia* against the men accused in 415, *endeixis* against Andocides in 400; but a *graphe* was used against Socrates in 399. See Lipsius, *A.R.* 358–68.

if anybody has a dispute with somebody about a priesthood: Presumably, if there were rival claims to hold a hereditary priesthood.

adjudicates for *gene* and priests all their disputes about sacred matters: *Diadikazein* (cf. *diadikasia*, in 56. 6) is used of the *basileus* as *eisagousa arche*, as *dikazein* is used in 52. 3, 57. 4: it does not imply that the *basileus* gave a personal ruling in these cases.

all the private suits for homicide fall to him: These cases were all *dikai*, in which only the relatives of the deceased could prosecute. For the different categories of homicide see what follows; in all cases the accusation was lodged with the *basileus*, who made a proclamation against the accused, held three *prodikasiai* in separate months, and in the fourth month brought the case to trial. See MacDowell, *Homicide*, 34–7. On Athens' homicide courts see Dem. XXIII. *Aristocrates* 65–81, Paus. I. 28. 5, 8–11; and for the philosophers' categories see Pl. *Leg.* IX. 865 A 1–874 D 1, Arist. *Pol.* IV. 1300 B 24–30.

it is he who makes the proclamation of exclusion from the things stipulated by law: Other texts mention a proclamation made in the agora by the relatives of the deceased (Antiph. VI. *Chor.* 35, [Dem.] XLVII. *Evergus & Mnesibulus* 69), but exclusion from 'the things prescribed by the laws' (MacDowell, *Law*, 111) had force only after the *basileus*' proclamation: the effect is spelled out by Dem. XX. *Leptines* 158. The killer was polluted, and would defile other people by associating with them, and in this respect the accused was presumed guilty until proved innocent.

57. 3. Suits for homicide and wounding … and for arson: Cf. Dem. XXIII. 22, 24: Demosthenes gives direct quotations from the law; as elsewhere *A.P.* has replaced prescription of what should happen with description of what happens, and here his version is clearer than the law. On trials before the Areopagus see MacDowell, *Homicide*, 39–47. Killing and wounding 'from forethought' are contrasted with 'unwilling', below; the prosecutor had to decide which charge to press, and in hard cases a court might have to decide where the line between these should be drawn. *Trauma* appears to be wounding of a more serious kind than *aikeia* (52. 2); the reason for the separate mention of poisioning may be that *phonos* was originally limited to violent killing (MacDowell, *op. cit.*, 44–5); arson was presumably included here because of the danger to life.

unwilling homicide … the court at the Palladium: Cf. Dem. XXIII. 71, and see MacDowell, *Homicide*, 58–69. The Palladium is usually located south-east of the acropolis and west of the temple of Olympian Zeus (e.g. Travlos, *Pictorial Dictionary*, 412–6); A. L. Boegehold argues that there was another Palladium at Phalerum and homicide trials were held there (*Agora* xxviii. 47–8), but a location in the city seems more likely. The charges tried there were less serious than those tried at the Areopagus: 'unwilling' homicide, 'planning' and killing somebody other than an Athenian citizen or the wife or child of a citizen. The scope of 'planning' has been disputed and perhaps could be disputed at the time; if somebody was killed but by a person acting as the agent of another, the prosecutor would have to decide whom to prosecute on which charge, and the court would then have to decide whether the accused was guilty on that charge.

If anybody admits to having killed … at the Delphinium: Cf. Dem. XXIII. 53, 60–1, 74, and see MacDowell, *Homicide*, 70–81. The Delphinium has been located south of the temple of Olympian Zeus (e.g. Travlos, *Pictorial Dictionary*, 83–90). A man who accepted that a killing was lawful ought not to prosecute (Pl. *Euthrphr.* 4 B 8–10); there would be a trial at the Delphinium when a man was accused of unlawful killing but pleaded in defence that the killing was lawful. *A.P.* has shortened and rephrased the list of lawful acts in Dem. XXIII. 53, and even that list is not complete.

If he is in exile in circumstances for which reconciliation is possible … in Phreatus' sanctuary: Cf. Dem. XXIII. 77–8, and see MacDowell, *Homicide*, 82–4: reconciliation with the family of the deceased was possible in cases of unwilling homicide. The connection with a hero named Phreatus is at any rate as old as Theophrastus (*Leg.* fr. 13 Szegedy-Maszak). This court is located at Piraeus by Paus. I. 28. 11; for these cases *Anecd. Bekk.* i. 311. 17–22 has a court 'at Zea' followed by a court 'at Phreatto'. However, A. L. Boegehold, *CSCA* 9 (1976), 7–19, cf. *Agora* xxviii. 49–50, has argued from ballots found there that in the fourth century there was an ordinary court at Zea, with which the court in Phreatto or of Phreatus (which rarely had to meet) was mistakenly identified.

and he makes his defence in a boat moored off shore: Cf. Dem. XXIII. 87 (not a quotation from the law). The purpose was to protect the land of Attica from pollution (cf. R. Parker, *Miasma* [Oxford U. P., 1983], 119).

57. 4. The trial is held by the 51 men … those held at the Areopagus: (§4 should begin here, as with e.g. Kaibel & Wilamowitz, Chambers, rather than at ὁ δ' ἀπολογεῖται.) The jury in homicide trials other than *A.P.*'s first category was a body of fifty-one *ephetai* (ML 86 = *IG* i³ 104 ~ Fornara 15. B. 13, Dem. XLIII. *Macartatus* 57), chosen ἀριστίνδην (Poll. VIII. 125) and perhaps over fifty years old (Phot. ε 2416 Theodoridis, *Suda* ε 3877 Adler, ἐφέται). Some argue from Androtion *FGrH* 324 F 4a = Philoch. 328 F 20b that they were appointed from the Areopagus (e.g. J. W. Headlam, *CR* 6 [1892], 252); and that they were thus appointed is perhaps more likely than not (cf. Harrison; MacDowell is agnostic). Some have argued that in the fourth century, though the title persisted, ordinary jurors were used (e.g. Lipsius, *A.R.* 40–1), but the evidence cited for a change is insufficient. See in general MacDowell, *Homicide*, 48–57; R. S. Stroud, *Drakon's Law on Homicide* [U. Calif. Pub. Cl. Stud. iii 1968], 47–9; Harrison, *L.A.* ii. 36–43.

they hold the trial in a sanctuary and in the open air: Out of doors because of the pollution with which the killer was tainted.

the *basileus* when conducting the trial takes off his crown: Here *dikazein* refers to the *basileus* as *eisagousa arche*, and does not imply a personal verdict (cf. 52. 3, 57. 2). All the archons wore a myrtle crown as a badge of office (e.g. Lys. XXVI. *Evandrus* 8, Aeschin. I. *Timarchus* 19); removal of the crown is probably due to the killer's pollution.

The man under accusation … goes into the sanctuary to make his defence: As an exception to the ban imposed on him (cf. 57. 2) the accused enters a sanctuary for his trial.

When the prosecutor does not know … against 'the doer': ὁ διώκων must be understood as subject. *A.P.* now mentions trials held at the *prytaneion* (cf. Dem. XXIII. 76, and see 3. 5): the omission of the court is probably due to compression by the author rather than error by a scribe. See in general MacDowell, *Homicide*, 85–9; Harrison, *L.A.* ii. 42–3.

The *basileus* and the *phylobasileis*: For the *phylobasileis* cf. 8. 3, 41. 2; they were probably associated with the *basileus* in all homicide cases (this is the better understanding of *basileis* in ML 86 = *IG* i³ 104 ~ Fornara 15. B. 12). In the amnesty law *ap.* Plut. *Sol.* 19. 4 the *ephetai* and the *prytaneion* should cover all homicide courts: the Areopagus is mentioned there in connection with tyranny, and did not try homicide cases before Solon (e.g. Ruschenbusch, *Historia* ix 1960, 129–54 at 132–5 = his *Kleine Schriften G. R.*, 34–7); the *prytaneion* could have condemned only unknown killers. In the decree of Patroclides *ap.* Andoc. I. *Myst.* 78 (authenticity challenged by M. Canevaro & E. M. Harris, *CQ*[2] 64 [2014], 49–57; defended by M. H. Hansen, *GRBS* 55 [2015], 884–97) the Areopagus is rightly included among homicide courts. The Delphinium (included in the manuscript text) was manned by the *ephetai* and would not have made anybody *atimos*. Probably a jury was thought unnecessary in cases where there was no defendant, and *dikazein* here means that the *basileus* and *phylobasileis* decided the cases without the *ephetai* (e.g. MacDowell, Harrison; contr. Harp. ε 173 Keaney ἐφέται, Poll. VIII. 125).

inanimate objects and other creatures: Cf. Dem. XXIII. 76; an inanimate object (and probably an animal) if judged guilty was removed from Attica (e.g. Aeschin. III. *Ctesiphon* 244).

58. 1. The polemarch performs the sacrifices to Artemis Agrotera and to Enyalius: Either at a single festival of the two deities (Deubner, *Attische Feste*, 209) or on separate occasions (Parker, *Polytheism*, 398 with n. 43); *enyalios*, 'warlike', is an epithet of Ares (e.g. Hom. *Il.* II. 651), but is also the name of a separate god (e.g. Ar. *Pax* 457, Plut. *Sol.* 9.7). The Athenians vowed at Marathon to sacrifice a goat to Artemis Agrotera for every barbarian killed, but in view of the large number settled on an annual sacrifice of five hundred (Xen. *An.* III. 2. 12, Plut. *Her. Mal.* 862 B–C): whatever the date of the battle, the festival was celebrated on 6 Boedromion (iii) (Plut. *Glor. Ath.* 349 E, cf. *Her. Mal.* 862 A emended), the 6th of each month being sacred to Artemis (Diog. Laert. II. 44), and 5 Boedromion the day of the Genesia, a festival of the dead (Philoch. *FGrH* 328 F 168). See Parker, *Polytheism*, 400, 461–2.

he organises the funeral competition for those killed in war: Cf. Pl. *Menex.* 249 B 3–6, Lys. II. *Epit.* 80, Philostr. 623 / *Vit. Soph.* II. 30; ἐπὶ is supported by inscribed bronze vases (E. Vanderpool, *ΑΔ* 24 [1969], μελ. 1–5). A date after the end of the campaigning season is likely (Parker, *Polytheism*, 469–70, thinks it might vary). When the *patrios nomos* of Thuc. II. 34. 1 was instituted is much discussed (see e.g. Parker, *Athenian*

Religion, 131–5); the *agon* (not mentioned by Thucydides) and oration are dated 479 by Diod. Sic. XI. 33. 3, which is possible but not certain.

performs heroes' rites for Harmodius and Aristogeiton: Hdt. II. 44. 5 distinguishes *thyein* to the gods and *enagizein* to heroes. Dem. XIX. *F.L.* 280 states that Harmodius was given honours equal to those of heroes and gods; I. Calabi Limentani, *Acme* 29 (1976), 9–27, compares them with those who died in war, but apart from those who died at Marathon there is no evidence that the war dead were treated as heroes. Unless we punctuate with Kaibel & Wilamowitz, *A.P.* distinguishes this cult from that of the war dead. The cult (for which cf. p. 235) cannot have been instituted before the expulsion of Hippias in 511/0, so with the possible exception of Enyalius all the polemarch's religious observances were introduced after that date, and 57. 1 is to be preferred to 3. 3.

58. 2. Private lawsuits only fall to him: ἴδιαι emphasises that here *dikai* are private suits, contrasted with *graphai* (cf. 59. 5). In the fifth century the polemarch handled all lawsuits (except for homicide) in which metics and privileged foreigners were involved, but in the fourth century such public suits were handled by the same magistrates as when both parties were citizens, and that may apply also to some private suits (MacDowell, *Law*, 243–4).

those held for metics, *isoteleis* and *proxenoi*: Metics were non-citizens registered as residents in Attica (cf. p. 339); *isoteleis* (foreigners allowed in some respects to rank with citizens) and *proxenoi* (originally men looking after Athenian interests in their own cities, but the title was increasingly used to honour men who might live in Attica and want to appear before Athenian courts) were privileged non-citizens. Foreigners outside these categories perhaps had no right to appear in Athenian courts (except in *dikai emporikai*: 59. 5), unless their state had a judicial treaty with Athens (cf. 59. 6), but might as a favour be allowed to do so (see Harrison, *L.A.* i. 189–95, ii. 10–16; MacDowell, *Law*, 222–4). Metics and privileged foreigners could appear either as prosecutors or as defendants, though *A.P.* seems to be thinking of them primarily as defendants, and they did not normally prosecute in *graphai*.

he has to take these ... give them up to the *diaitetai*: On *dikai* between citizens see 53. 1–3; since foreigners were not members of the tribes, a special assignment had to be made when they appeared as defendants. Cf. Harrison, *L.A.* ii. 19–21.

58. 3. private suits for desertion of patron: Cf. Dem. XXXV. *Lacritus* 48, and see Harrison, *L.A.* i. 165, 182. This was a suit against a freedman (who in Athens became a metic) who deserted his former master for another *prostates* or failed to comply with conditions imposed at his manumission (e.g. Harp. α 204 Keaney ἀποστασίου).
for having no patron: Cf. Dem. XXXV. 48. This was a suit against a metic who had no *prostates* (e.g. Harp. α 218 Keaney ἀπροστασίου); unlike the other suits listed here it must have been a *graphe*. How far in the time of *A.P.* a metic still needed a *prostates* is unclear (see e.g. Harrison, *L.A.* i. 189–93); MacDowell, *Law*, 78, suggests that this was a prosecution for failing to register as a metic.
for estates and for *epikleroi*: Cf. [Dem.] XLVI. *Stephanus ii.* 22. Since a citizen could not marry a non-citizen (cf. pp. 272–3, 339), in these suits both prosecutor and defendant(s) would be metics. Citizens' suits in these matters were handled by the archon (56. 6–7).
and everything else ... the polemarch does for the metics: I.e. such charges as *goneon kakosis* (56. 6–7); in the case of a metic family, the prosecutor would normally be a metic.

59. 1. The *thesmothetai*, first, have the power ... to assign them to the officials: Allocation of courts to magistrates is repeated in 59. 5. The six *thesmothetai* will not have had direct knowledge of all current judicial business, and the *eisagousai archai* must have told them what they needed; they will then have told a particular magistrate that he was to have a court on a stated day, with a jury of a stated size (cf. *SEG* xxvi 72 = RO 25 ~ Harding 45. 25–8, RO 100 = *IG* ii^3 370 ~ Harding 121. 204–17). For the further allocation of juries to courts see 63–6. Ar. *Vesp.* 661–3 calculates the money paid to jurors on the assumption that all 6,000 were required on 300 days in the year; in fact it can be estimated that the courts met on 175–225 days and employed up to 2,000 men (Hansen, *Democracy*, 186–8).
as they assign them, so the officials comply: A loose sentence, which adds nothing.
59. 2. Then it is they who introduce the *eisangeliai* for those who make an *eisangelia* to the *demos*: We should expect *A.P.* to say that they were the *eisagousa arche* when an *eisangelia* was referred to a *dikasterion*, and a text is needed which makes τὰς εἰσαγγελίας the object of εἰσάγουσιν below.

all the hostile votes: This has usually been understood as referring to cases of deposition from office, but the usual word for that is *apocheirotonia* (cf. 61. 2), and *A.P.* probably subsumed these under *eisangeliai*. A better suggestion is that these are cases referred to a *dikasterion* by the assembly after an *apophasis* by the Areopagus (Hansen, *Eisangelia*, 39–40, 44: that procedure is not mentioned elsewhere in *A.P.*).

***probolai*:** Cf. 43. 5. That the *thesmothetai* were the *eisagousa arche* is confirmed by Dem. XXI. *Midias* 1 with 32 (cf. Lipsius, *A.R.* 213).

the public suits for unlawful proposal and for enactment of an inexpedient law: Cf. 45. 4 with commentary.

those against *proedroi* and against *epistatai*: Harp. ρ 3 Keaney ῥητορικὴ γραφή, *Anecd. Bekk.* i. 299. 21–6, mention *graphai prytanike* and *epistatike*: if they were concerned with the presidency of the council and assembly, the *graphe proedrike* will have been needed when the *proedroi* took over that duty from the *prytaneis* (cf. 44. 2). See Harrison, *L.A.* ii. 14.

***euthynai* for generals:** Cf. 48. 4–5 (but for the financial *logos* the *logistai* were the *eisagousa arche*: 54. 2). It is not clear why here *A.P.* refers specifically to the generals.

59. 3. a prosecutor's deposit: In many *dikai* fees called *prytaneia* were paid by both parties (Harrison, *L.A.* ii. 92–4); in some property suits the plaintiff paid a *parakatabole* (Harrison, *L.A.* ii. 179–83); the *parastasis* was paid by the prosecutor in many *graphai*, and probably refunded if he won his case (Harrison, *L.A.* ii. 94). See also on court fees A. C. Scafuro, in *ἄξων ... R. S. Stroud* (Athens: Greek Epigraphic Society, 2015), i. 363–92.

A.P.'s list of *graphai* is incomplete. For others handled by the *thesmothetai* see Harrison, *L.A.* ii. 15–16; probably those also attracted a *parastasis*. He also omits the *endeixeis* handled by the *thesmothetai* (cf. 52. 1).

being a foreigner: Accusing a man who poses as a citizen of being a foreigner (cf. *L.R.C.* ξενίας γραφὴ καὶ δωροξενίας). *A.P.* does not mention a change, but in the fifth century this was handled by *nautodikai* (Craterus *FGrH* 342 F 4 and Ar. fr. 237 Kassel & Austin *ap.* Harp. ν 5 Keaney ναυτοδίκαι). Inscriptions mention also *xenodikai* (e.g. *IG* i³ 439. 75), but there is no evidence that they were concerned with the *graphe xenias*. See E. E. Cohen, *Ancient Athenian Maritime Courts* (Princeton U. P., 1973), 162–76.

bribery by a foreigner: Explained by *A.P.* in the words that follow.
malicious prosecution: On *sykophantai* see 35. 2, 43. 5; Isoc. XV. *Antid.* 314 mentions this *graphe* among various procedures against them. See Lipsius, *A.R.* 401–4.
bribery: Bribery likewise could be dealt with by various procedures. In Poll. VIII. 42 the *graphe doron* was aimed at receivers of bribes and the *graphe dekasmou* at givers (cf. law *ap.* [Dem.] XLVI. *Stephanus ii.* 26); in *Anecd. Bekk.* i. 237. 3–7 the *graphe doron* was aimed at both (cf. Dem. XXI. *Midias* 104–7). *Dekazein* is used particularly with reference to jurors (cf. 27. 5), and perhaps later than the institution of the *graphe doron* the *graphe dekasmou* was instituted for judicial bribery. See Lipsius, *A.R.* 410–4.
false registration: Falsely entering a man's name on a list of public debtors. See Lipsius, *A.R.* 443–6.
false summons: To initiate most lawsuits the prosecutor in the presence of witnesses summoned the defendant before the relevant authority; this was a prosecution for falsely testifying to such a summons (Poll. VIII. 44). See Lipsius, *A.R.* 446–8, 804–7; Harrison, *L.A.* ii. 85–6.
***bouleusis*:** Failing to delete a discharged debtor from the list (*IG* ii^2 1631. 385–98). See Lipsius, *A.R.* 443–6; it is not clear why this offence should be termed *bouleusis* (for a more straightforward use of the term see 57. 3).
failure to register: *Sc.* a debtor. According to [Dem.] LVIII. *Theocrines* 51–2 this was used for the deletion of an undischarged debtor, while failure to register a debtor was dealt with by *endeixis*; but the name points rather to the second category, and this *graphe* may have been available for both. See Lipsius, *A.R.* 410–2.
adultery: Probably *moicheia* was originally intercourse with a man's wife, but it came to be extended to intercourse with other free women in a man's household; again various procedures were available (for one cf. 57. 3). See Lipsius, *A.R.* 429–34, Harrison, *L.A.* i. 32–6.
59. 4. they introduce the *dokimasiai* for all the officials: For members of the council the *dokimasia* was in the council, with *ephesis* to a *dikasterion* (45. 3); for archons there was a first stage in the council and a second in a *dikasterion* (45. 3, 55. 2–4); for other *archai* it was in a *dikasterion* (55. 2).
men rejected as citizens by their demesmen: Cf. 42. 1.

convictions forwarded from the council: Probably this refers to all cases referred by the council to a *dikasterion* for a penalty beyond its own competence (cf. 43. 4, on *eisangeliai*; 45. 1–2). Timocrates' *habeas corpus* law *ap.* Dem. XXIV. *Timocrates* 63 provides that if men have been imprisoned and the council's *katagnosis* has not been transmitted to the *thesmothetai* the Eleven are to introduce the case into court within thirty days: perhaps the Eleven took over as *eisagousa arche* if the council had failed to instigate action by the *thesmothetai.*

59. 5. private suits: trading suits: For ἰδίας cf. 58. 2. *Dikai emporikai* were availble to captains and traders in cases of trade to or from Athens where there was a written contract (Dem. XXXII. *Zenothemis* 1: both trade and contract required, but probably it was simply assumed that at least one party would be a captain or trader: Cohen, *Ancient Athenian Maritime Courts*, 100–29). Such cases did not have to be brought in Athens under Athenian law (if the defendant lived elsewhere it might be more effective to sue there). These suits were available to all men, whatever their status (e.g. Dem. XXI. *Midias* 176); because they were not all Athenian residents, the plaintiff could require the defendant to produce guarantors (e.g. Dem. XXXII. 29), and defeated litigants could be kept under arrest until their debt was discharged (e.g. Dem. XXXIII. *Apaturius* 1, XXXV. *Lacritus* 46–7).

These were 'monthly' suits (cf. 52. 2). Early in the fourth century the *nautodikai* (cf. on 59. 3) had jurisdiction in some cases concerning *emporoi* (Lys. XVII. *Eraton* 5). Xen. *Vect.* 3. 3 (*c.* 355) recommends a rapid procedure for commercial suits, Dem. XXI. *Midias* 176 (347/6?) uses the term *dike emporike*, and [Dem.] VII. *Halon.* 12 (343/2) refers to a time when 'monthly' *dikai emporikai* did not yet exist, so these were instituted in the late 350's or early 340's. Poll. VIII. 101 includes these among the 'monthly' suits handled by the *eisagogeis* (cf. 52. 2), but speeches confirm that at any rate for his own time *A.P.* is right to assign *dikai emporikai* to the *thesmothetai* (Cohen, 158–98, suggests that they were first handled by the *eisagogeis* and later transferred to the *thesmothetai*).

mining suits: Cf. Dem. XXXVII. *Pantaenetus* 34–6 (§34 confirms that they fell to the *thesmothetai*); and 2 (indicating that these were 'monthly').

suits against any slave who maligns a free man: *Dikai kakegorias* in which a slave was accused of maligning a free man; other *dikai* *kakegorias* followed the normal procedure for *dikai* (53, and cf. Dem. XXI. *Midias* 81 with 83); it is not clear why a different procedure was used in these cases. See Lipsius, *A.R.* 627–8.

And they allot the private and public lawcourts to the officials: This repeats what was said in 59. 1, adding the detail of allotment. It interrupts the list of *dikai*, and Kaibel & Wilamowitz[1–2] deleted it, but more probably its presence is due to *A.P.*'s carelessness.

59. 6. they ratify the judicial agreements with the cities: *Symbola* are the complementary parts of a tally retained by the parties to an agreement, and by extension the agreement itself, especially between states on the resolution of conflicts between their citizens (cf. Arist. *Pol.* III. 1275 A 8–11, 1280 A 34–B 5): in Athens they had to be ratified in a *dikasterion* under the presidency of one of the *thesmothetai* ([Dem.] VII. *Halon.* 9, *IG* ii² 466. 32–5). See in general P. Gauthier, *Symbola: les étrangers et la justice dans les cités grecques* (Nancy: Annales de l'Est, Mém. 42 [1972]).

they introduce the suits made on the basis of judicial agreements: Here *dikai* is used in its wider sense and includes *graphai*. Probably these were handled by the *thesmothetai* because of their involvement in ratifying the *symbola*; and probably such cases were tried in the city where the dispute arose, commonly that of the defendant (Gauthier, 174–83). In the fifth century the *thesmothetai* handled cases transferred from member states of the Delian League (e.g. ML 52 = *IG* i³ 40 ~ Fornara 103. 71–6), and in the fourth century they are mentioned in the fragmentary *IG* ii² 179. *a*. 10, 17.

charges of false witness before the Areopagus: See Harrison, *L.A.* ii. 127–31, 192–7, and cf. 68. 4. Normally such a charge would be handled by the same magistrate as the original suit (but on a later day, so with a different jury). Witnesses in homicide cases swore an oath as witnesses in other cases did not (e.g. Antiph. V. *Caed. Her.* 12), and Prof. A. H. Sommerstein suggests to me that this may be why there was a special procedure in these cases; but there is no obvious reason why, when the original court was the Areopagus and the *eisagousa arche* was the *basileus*, these cases should fall to the *thesmothetai*.

59. 7. All the nine archons allot the jurors … those of his own tribe: *A.P.* ends his section on the archons with a duty shared by all of them (for the addition of the secretary to create a tribally-based board of ten cf. 55. 1). This fact is repeated in 63. 1 at the beginning of the account of the *dikasteria*.

P. The athlothetai (60)

After various categories of allotted annual officials, *A.P.* passes to the *athlothetai* (allotted, for four years), and then in 61 to military officials (elected, for one year). From the *athlothetai* he digresses to olive oil and prizes at the Panathenaea.

60. 1. The arrangements for the 9 archons are in that manner: *A.P.* rounds off the section on the archons, begun in 55. 1, …
allot as *athlothetai* ten men, one from each tribe: …and turns to the *athlothetai*. The subject to be understood is 'the Athenians', but Poll. VIII. 87 wrongly took it to be the archons.
These after undergoing their *dokimasia* hold office for four years: For the *dokimasia* cf. 55. 2. The Panathenaea was celebrated annually in Hecatombaeon (i), but more elaborately in the third year of each Olympiad as the Great Panathenaea (cf. pp. 347, 390). The principal responsibility of the *athlothetai* was for the Great Panathenaea, but we do not know how their term of office was defined.
they administer the procession at the Panathenaea: There was a procession at the Little Panathenaea (RO 81. *B.* 3–7, 31–5 = *IG* ii^3 447. 28–33, 57–61) as well as the Great, but at the time of *Ath. Pol.* it was only at the Great that a new *peplos* was brought for Athena (cf. 49. 3 and below). The procession at the Little Panathenaea was administered by *hieropoioi*, and we may guess from the title that originally the *athlothetai* were responsible only for contests, and later acquired general responsibility for the Great celebration (cf. J. A. Davison, *JHS* 78 [1958], 29–33 = his *From Archilochus to Pindar* [London: Macmillan, 1968], 41–8).
the competition in music: For contests and prizes in the first half of the fourth century see *IG* ii^2 2311. 1–22. Plut. *Per.* 13. 9–11 attributes to Pericles the Odeum (south-east of the acropolis: Travlos, *Pictorial Dictionary*, 387–91) and musical contests at the Panathenaea, but Panathenaic amphorae and literary texts suggest that musical contests were held from *c.* 560, and Vitruv. V. 9. 1 says that Themistocles 'roofed'

the Odeum. There is no evidence for *c.* 470–450, and Davison 33–42 = 48–66 suggested that Pericles rebuilt the Odeum and revived the contests after a period of disuse; but the gap may be fortuitous.

the competition in athletics: See *IG* ii^2 2311. 23–50; amphorae attest athletic contests from *c.* 560. Earlier they were held in the agora (H. A. Thompson, *AA* [1961], 227), but *c.* 330 the stadium was built for them (east of the city: Travlos, *Pictorial Dictionary*, 498–504; cf. RO 94 = *IG* ii^3 352 ~ Harding 118. 15–20).

the horse race: See *IG* ii^2 2311. 51–70 and Xen. *Symp.* 1. 2; they are again attested by amphorae from *c.* 560. They were held at Echelidae, in the deme Xypete between Piraeus and Phalerum (*E.M.* 340. 53 ἐν Ἐχελιδῶ<ν>).

Contests are attested also in *euandria* (cf. below), in the war-dance called *pyrriche*, a torch-race and a contest for ships.

they have the *peplos* made: They presumably supervised the work: the weaving was done by *ergastinai* under the immediate direction of two *arrhephoroi*; for the *paradeigmata* see 49. 3.

with the council they have the amphorae made: Cf. 49. 3, mentioning the council and the treasurer of the stratiotic fund. The prizes for athletic and equestrian contests were olive oil (cf. below), supplied in distinctive amphorae for which a particular style had become standard by *c.* 530, featuring Athena with the inscription τõν Ἀθένεθεν ἄθλον, and an event from the games (see J. Boardman, *Athenian Black Figure Vases* [London: Thames & Hudson, 1974], 167–77).

they give the olive oil to the athletes: Presumably, they present the prizes: this is stated more clearly in 60. 3 after the digression on the oil. They were responsible also for crowns awarded at the festival: RO 64 = *IG* ii^3 298 ~ Harding 82. 26–9.

60. 2. The olive oil is collected from the sacred olives: The sacred olives from which the oil was taken were called *moriai* (Ar. *Nub.* 1005 with schol., Lys. VII. *Ol.* 7).

the archon exacts … one and a half *kotylai* from each plant: *C.* 400–450 c.c. = ¾ imperial pint. Sacred olives, allegedly offshoots of the tree planted by Athena, existed throughout Attica, and whoever acquired land with a sacred olive acquired the obligation. This duty of the archon is not mentioned in 56. 3–5.

Previously the city used to sell the harvest: Probably this means that previously the right to collect the oil was farmed like a tax (cf. 47. 2) but in *A.P.*'s time the oil was collected directly by the archon (Gernet & Bizos on Lys. VII. 2)

if anybody dug up a sacred olive ... they punished him with death: *Exoryttein* is used in Lys. VII. 26, but that speech uses other verbs too. §§3, 32, 41 show that at the beginning of the fourth century the penalty was exile and confiscation of property, and §§25, 29 indicate lesser penalties for lesser offences.

since the olive oil has been paid ... the trial has lapsed: The law has become a dead letter: this information will be due to *A.P.*'s direct knowledge.

the city obtains the olive oil from the property, not from the particular plants: Probably so many sacred olives had died that the older practice had become impracticable, and with the oil levied as a tax on the property it no longer mattered if sacred olives were damaged.

60. 3. The archon collects what is produced in his term of office: Some fourth-century amphorae bear the archon's name. Cf. Boardman, *Athenian Black Figure Vases*, 169–70; and for a catalogue of inscribed amphorae A. Smets, *AC* 5 (1936), 87–104.

hands it to the treasurers on the acropolis: To the treasurers of Athena (in the time of *A.P.* to the single board using that title: cf. p. 364).

it is not permitted to him ... to the treasurers: Cf. the statement in 46. 1 that the council cannot receive its award unless it has built the ships required; we do not know whether recently an archon had failed in his duty. Passages such as this make it clear that archons did not join the Areopagus until they had satisfactorily completed their year (cf. p. 190).

they measure it out to the *athlothetai*: This suggests interim storage in large containers; but the use of archons' names on fourth-century amphorae suggests that the oil was placed in them in the year of collection.

the *athlothetai* measure it out to those of the competitors who win: Cf. 60. 1 *fin.*

The prizes are gold and silver for winners in music: Cf. *IG* ii^2 2311. 1–22; but at first and during the Peloponnesian War olive oil was used (Davison, *JHS* 78 [1958], 36–8 = his *From Archilochus to Pindar*, 54–8).

shields in manliness: *Euandria* was omitted from 60. 1. *IG* ii^2 2311. 75 shows that it was a tribal competition, with an ox as prize; but *IG* ii^2

1461. 10–11, 18–20, appears to record *aspides* from 346/5 and 330/29 (cf. *addenda*, fasc. 2. 2. 809), perhaps unawarded prizes. The essence of the competition was military prowess.
olive oil in the athletic competition and the horse race: Cf. *IG* ii^2 2311. 23–70.

Q. Elective military offices (61)

Command of the army and navy was thought to require skill as well as loyalty, so for these offices election was used (cf. 44. 4; for a cynical comment see [Xen.] *A.P.* 1. 3). Knowledge of the men elected makes it clear that appointment was for one year but with no restrictions on reappointment. A fragment from Theophrastus (MS Vat. Gr. 2306. B, pp. 96–115 Szegedy-Maszak) reports advice by Hagnon to have a mixture of younger and older generals (ll. 105–71) and suggests that generals ought previously to have been taxiarchs or phylarchs (ll. 172–83), but there is no evidence that either was ever a requirement in Athens.

61. 1. They elect all the officials for warfare: *A.P.* nowhere treats elective civilian offices (cf. 43. 1), and καὶ might suggest that they were treated between 60 and 61 but have been lost in copying; but more probably *A.P.* has been remiss (though καὶ may be deleted).
Ten generals, previously one from each tribe but now from all Athenians: For one from each tribe cf. 22. 2, Plut. *Cim.* 8. 8; the claim that as many as four of the generals of 323/2 were from one tribe (J. Sundwall, *Klio* Bhft. 4 [1906], 23–5) is insecure. It seems likely that from 441/0 (Androtion *FGrH* 324 F 38 ~ Fornara 110) or earlier to 357/6 (*IG* ii^2 124 = RO 48 ~ Harding 65. 19–23) or later one general per tribe was normal but one exception, or perhaps occasionally more than one, was permitted: for a recent discussion see L. G. Mitchell, *Klio* 82 (2000), 344–60 (suggesting that a tribe with no strong candidate could adopt a candidate from another tribe). The tribal link was so far abandoned that in later Athens the number of generals remained ten through the various tribal changes. The generals had an office in the agora, the *strategeion* (*testimonia*, R. E. Wycherley, *Agora* iii, pp. 174–7; a possible location, Camp, *Site Guide*, 51–2).
These they assign by their vote: one in charge of the hoplites … when

they go out: When they go out of Attica. There is still no sign of such appointments in 357/6 (*IG* ii[2] 123 = RO 52 ~ Harding 69. 13–15, 48 = 124 ~ 65. 19–23), but the *strategos epi ten choran* appears soon after that (cf. next note), and these two posts may well have been created together. This one, in inscriptions regularly ἐπὶ τὰ ὅπλα (on *A.P.*'s and epigraphic titles see p. 22), is not epigraphically attested before the third century; in Roman Athens he became one of the chief officers of state. It is not clear whether men were elected generals first and then assigned to particular posts, or directly elected to particular posts.
one in charge of the territory ... it is he who wages the war: First found in 356/5 (*SEG* xlvii 159. 2–4: restored) or 352/1 (RO 58 = *IG* ii[3] 292 ~ Harding 78. A. 19–20). In fourth-century ephebic inscriptions the title is regularly ἐπὶ τῆι χώραι (and this should be restored in *SEG* xlvii 159). On *phylake tes choras* in decrees see 43. 4. πολεμεῖ is startling, and ἡγεῖται may well be right.
two in charge of the Piraeus ... guarding what is in Piraeus: For Munichia and Acte cf. 42. 3. Ephebic inscriptions of the 330's mention one general for the Piraeus (to Reinmuth 9. ii. 9–10), but a later one has two, for 'Piraeus' and Acte (Reinmuth 15. r.h.s. 2–3). This passage was written after the change (or else was rewritten without any sign of the change): cf. p. 29.
one in charge of the *symmoriai* ... introduces adjudications for them: Men liable to *eisphora* were organised in *symmoriai* in 378/7 (Philoch. *FGrH* 328 F 41 cf. Clidemus 323 F 8 ~ Fornara 22. A); and *c.* 357 the 1,200 richest citizens were organised in *symmoriai* to contribute to trierarchic expenses ([Dem.] XLVII. *Evergus & Mnesibulus* 21–2), though individual trierarchs, with the liturgy of responsibility for individual ships, were still appointed: see V. Gabrielsen, *Financing the Athenian Fleet* (Johns Hopkins U. P., 1994), 182–99. This general performed for trierarchs the same functions as the relevant archon for men with festival liturgies (cf. 56. 3). *A.P.* uses *skepseis* there and *diadikasiai* here: in connection with the trierarchy both words can be used of claims to exemption and of suits arising from loss or damage; here the first sense is intended, as in RO 100 = *IG* ii[3] 370 ~ Harding 121. 204–17 (325/4, mentioning this general). There were some exemptions from the trierarchy, but fewer than from festival liturgies (cf. Dem. XX. *Leptines* 18, 27–8, XIV. *Symm.* 16); men who had served were exempt for two years afterwards (Isae. VII. *Apollodorus*

38), but did not always claim their exemption. In *IG* ii^2 1623. 147–59 (334/3) and some speeches trierarchs are appointed by 'the generals', so the institution of this post must have been very recent when *A.P.* was written. The classical trierarchy was probably abolished by Demetrius of Phalerum along with the festival liturgies (cf. p. 396), but the title *trierarchos* was still used of the man responsible for a ship (e.g. *IG* ii^2 1491. *B*). There will then have been no need for this general; but a *strategos epi to nautikon*, to command the fleet, is first found *c.* 321 or 315 (*IG* ii^3 985. 4–7).

The others they send out on current business: By the end of the third century there were probably regular postings for all ten generals: see W. S. Ferguson, *Klio* 9 (1909), 314–23; Th. Ch. Sarikakis, *Ἀθηνᾶ* 57 (1953), 254–61.

61. 2. There is a vote of confidence … whether they are exercising their office well: Cf. 43. 4, on *archai* in general; 61. 4, on hipparchs. The procedure was perhaps instituted for military officials and subsequently applied to others.

If they depose anybody, they try him in the lawcourt: Probably as in other cases where a vote in the assembly was the first stage the *thesmothetai* were the *eisagousa arche* (cf. 59. 2). There may have been distinct rules for depositions, but often the resulting trial took the form of an *eisangelia*. MacDowell, *Law*, 169, doubts whether deposition automatically led to trial, or acquittal automatically led to reinstatement.

if he is convicted they assess what he should suffer or pay: I.e. the trial was an *agon timetos*, not one with a fixed penalty (cf. 69. 2). If the trial took the form of an *eisangelia*, the council or assembly could state its choice of penalty, but in some cases the law seems to have prescribed the death penalty (cf. Dem. XX. *Leptines* 100, 135). See Hansen, *Eisangelia*, 33–6.

When they are commanding they have power to imprison a disobedient man: Cf. [Dem.] L. *Polycles* 51. Earlier generals had put to death: Lys. XIII. *Agoratus* 67, cf. Front. *Strat.* III. 12. 2 (where the victim was a mercenary and Iphicrates may not have been an Athenian general).

to cashier: Cf. Lys. III. *Simon* 45.

to impose a summary penalty; but they are not in the habit of imposing penalties: Cf. Lys. IX. *Soldier* 6–12, XV. *Alcibiades ii.* 5; and for *epibolai* cf. p. 381. For a practice which has become obsolete cf. 60. 2.

61. 3. They elect ten taxiarchs, one from each tribe: he commands his tribesmen: These and the hipparchs are mentioned with the generals in Dem. IV. *Phil. i.* 26. They are attested from the time of the Peloponnesian War (e.g. Ar. *Ach.* 569, Thuc. IV. 4. 1); and if from their creation the generals were commanders not of their tribal regiments but of the whole army (cf. p. 250) they should have been created at the same time as the generals. We should have expected their number to change with the number of the tribes in the hellenistic period, but in 272/1 there were still ten (*IG* ii^3 907. 37–56).
appoints *lochagoi*: There are a few fourth-century references to *lochagoi*, but we have no information on how the tribal regiments were divided into *lochoi*; for a guess see P. J. Bicknell, *Studies in Athenian Politics and Genealogy* (*Historia* Einz. 19 [1972]), 21 with n. 67.
61. 4. two hipparchs from all Athenians ... with regard to the hoplites: Cf. Xen. *Hipparch.* 3. 11, Dem. IV. *Phil. i.* 26; but a fifth-century dedication names three hipparchs (*IG* i^3 511), and there is a plurality in 30. 2 but only one in 31. 3. The parallel with the generals is imperfect: both had tribal commanders under them, but the generals were commanders of all Athens' forces, not only of the hoplites. For the involvement of the hipparchs and phylarchs in registering the cavalry see 49. 2. The hipparchs had an office, the *hipparcheion* (*IG* ii^3 1281.41), possibly in the north-west of the agora (H. A. Thompson & R. E. Wycherley, *Agora* xiv. 73 n. 199).
There is a vote of confidence in them also: Cf. 61. 2 (generals), 43. 4. Mention here suggests that taxiarchs and phylarchs may not have been subject to it.
61. 5. 10 phylarchs ... as the taxiarchs command the hoplites: Cf. Ar. *Lys.* 561–2, Isae. XI. *Hagnias* 41, Men. *Sam.* 15; but the phylarchs of Hdt. V. 69. 2 can hardly be cavalry officers.
61. 6. a hipparch to Lemnos: Lemnos and Imbros were acquired for Athens perhaps in the 490's (Hdt. VI. [137–]140), and remained in Athenian hands to 318 except for a short period after the Peloponnesian War (and were again Athenian at some times in the hellenistic and Roman periods). ἱππαρ]χõντος would be a possible restoration in *Agora* xix L3. 5 (but editors prefer ἄρ]χοντος); clay tablets found in the Athenian agora have seals naming Pheidon, hipparch to Lemnos (see J. H. Kroll & F. W. Mitchel, *Hesperia* 49 [1980], 87–96). On this officer and his cavalry see Bugh, *Horsemen*, 209–18.

a treasurer of the Paralus and separately one of the Ammonos: Classical Athens had two special 'sacred' triremes, used to convey *theoriai* and on formal state business; originally they were named Paralus and Salaminia (e.g. Thuc. III. 77. 3), but at some time in the fourth century Ammonias (which seems to be the correct form of the name, though Ammonos in the papyrus may be what *A.P.* wrote) replaced Salaminia, and some further ships were added in the hellenistic period. There was also a triaconter sent to Delos (56. 3). The commissioning of Ammonias to replace Salaminia, and the institution of *tamiai* for the sacred ships to replace their trierarchs, are perhaps to be dated 363/2 (W. Bubelis, *Historia* 59 [2010], 385–411); on Midias as treasurer of the Paralus see Dem. XXI. *Midias* 171–4.

R. Concluding note on offices (62)

Discussion of the *archai*, begun in 43, ends with notes on the *archai* in general: on allotment, stipends and repetition of office; *A.P.* then passes to the *dikasteria*, without any indication that a major section has been ended. The material in this chapter will be based on the laws, but has probably been assembled from various laws by *A.P.*

62. 1. Of the allotted offices … distributed among the demes: *A.P.* does not state which appointments used to be made through the demes, how that was done or when the change was made. In the light of a hoard of inscribed clay tokens bisected by a jigsaw cut (H. A. Thompson, *Hesperia* 20 [1951], 51–2), E. S. Staveley suggested that particular offices were allotted to particular demes (*Greek and Roman Voting and Elections* [London: Thames & Hudson, 1972], 48–51, 69–72). *Kleroteria* were introduced for the allotment of jurors soon after 388 and adopted also for the appointment of officials *c* 370; on the *pinakia* used with them men were assigned to a tribe and to one of ten sections within the tribe (cf. 63. 4), and the older system will have been abandoned at or before the adoption of these for appointing officials. Aeschin. III. *Ctesiphon* 13 (in 330, at the time of *A.P.*'s current practice) distinguishes officials allotted in the Theseum (on which see pp. 227–8) from elected officials (in the assembly: 44. 4), and *A.P.* has perhaps been careless in connecting the Theseum specifically with deme-based appointments.

apart from the councillors and the guards: they are devolved to the demes: For members of the council see on 43. 2. The *phrouroi* may be the 500 *phrouroi neorion* of 24. 3: it would be easy to use council quotas for 500 or any multiple.

62. 2. Stipends are paid … at the *kyria ekklesia*: See on fifth-century stipends 24. 3, on assembly pay 41. 3 and on *kyriai* and other *ekklesiai* 43. 4–6. In the Erechtheum accounts of 409–407 unskilled workers are paid 3 obols and skilled 1 drachma (*IG* i^3 475–6); in the accounts of the Eleusinian *epistatai* for 329/8 unskilled workers are paid 1½ drachmae and skilled 2 or 2½ (*IG* ii^2 1672), so the increase in assembly pay to the time of *A.P.* will have matched the increase in wage rates.

Then the lawcourts, three obols: Jury pay (27. 3–4) was 2 obols at first, raised to 3 obols in the 420's (Ar. *Eq.* 797–800, schol. *Vesp.* 88 [emended], 300) and not raised again afterwards: presumably enough men volunteered to make an increase unnecessary, but by the time of *A.P.* those most attracted will have been those rich enough not to need the money and those so poor that even 3 obols was better than nothing.

Next the council, five obols: Cf. 24. 3; the council was being paid in 411 (Thuc. VIII. 69. 4), and this civilian payment was more probably introduced before than during the Peloponnesian War. We may guess that earlier the rate was lower.

to the *prytaneis* an obol is added for meals: For the *prytaneis*' meals cf. 43. 3. Probably *misthos* was paid only for days of attendance, while *sitesis* was paid to officials who ate together or who spent time away from Athens (cf. below) for every relevant day (cf. M. H. Hansen, *SO* 54 [1979], 7–10; for an alternative suggestion by D. M. Pritchard see below, p. 422). For the exemption of *prytaneis* and archons from the general abolition of stipends in 411 see 29. 5.

Then the nine archons receive four obols each for meals: Their headquarters was the *thesmotheteion* (3. 5), and they ate there (schol. Pl. *Phdr.* 235 D cf. Hes. πρυτανεῖον).

they support in addition a herald and a piper: Cf. lists of archons from the Roman period (e.g. *IG* ii^2 1717. 17–20, 1721. 16–19); these are distinct from the *keryx* and *auletes* attached to the council (B. D. Meritt & J. S. Traill, *Agora* xv, pp. 7–15). It is not clear whether these were covered by the archons' payments or there was an additional payment for them.

Then the archon for Salamis, a drachma a day: Cf. 54. 8.

The *athlothetai* dine in the *prytaneion* … beginning from the fourth of the month: The day of the procession at the Great Panathenaea was τρίτη φθίνοντος, the 27th or 28th (Procl. 9 B *ad* Pl. *Ti.* 17 B, schol. Pl. *Resp.* I. 327 A). Sandys thought this provision applied in the years of the Great Panathenaea only; but the *athlothetai* had some responsibility for the Little festival too, so possibly it applied every year and ὅταν ᾖ τὰ Παναθήναια does not refer to the Great festival but explains why this provision was made in Hecatombaeon.

The *amphiktyones* for Delos receive a drachma each day from Delos: On festivals at Delos see 54. 7, 56. 3. The *amphiktyones* were the officials with financial responsibility for the sanctuary: after changes earlier, from *c.* 367 there was an annual board of five Athenian *amphiktyones* (in 374/3 there were five Athenians, from tribes VI–X, and five Andrians [*I. Délos* 98], but there is no sign of tribal rotation later except for the secretary). For other appointments of five men see 52. 2, 54. 1, 56. 3; also 51. 3.

Whatever officials are sent … receive money for meals: Samos was taken by Athens from the Persians in 366–365 and became an Athenian cleruchy (Dem. XV. *Lib. Rhod.* 9, Isoc. XV. *Antid.* 111, Arist. *Rhet.* II. 1384 B 32–5): it was left in Athens' hands after Chaeronea in 338 but threatened by Alexander's order for the restoration of exiles in 324 and freed in 322 (Diod. Sic. XVIII. 56. 7, 8. 7, 18. 9). On the route from the Hellespont, Scyros was acquired by Athens *c.* 476/5 (p. 179), and Lemnos and Imbros perhaps in the 490's (p. 419). We find a general on Scyros and two on Lemnos in 329/8 (*IG* ii^2 1672. 275–7); and the cleruchs had their own officials (see especially from Samos *IG* XII. vi 262).

The list of salaried officials given here is probably not complete: the argument that many officials paid in the fifth century were not paid in the fourth (M. H. Hansen, *SO* 54 [1979], 5–22; *C&M* 32 [1971–80], 105–25) rests on silence and is probably not to be trusted (V. Gabrielsen, *Remuneration of State Officials in Fourth Century BC Athens* [Odense U. P., 1981]). See most recently D. M. Pritchard, *GRBS* 54 (2014), 1–16, supporting Gabrielsen; Hansen, *GRBS* 54 (2014), 404–19, in reply; Pritchard, *Public Spending and Democracy in Classical Athens* (U. of Texas P., 2015), 63–80 – where he suggests that officials were paid once a prytany but at a lower 'daily' rate for those who did not have to work every day.

62. 3. It is permitted to hold the offices for warfare several times: For military offices cf. 43. 1, 61. 1; but in Sparta, notoriously, after navarch became an annual office *c.* 409 reappointment to that was not permitted (Xen. *Hell.* II. 1. 7, Diod. Sic. XIII. 100. 8, Plut. *Lys.* 7. 3). Reappointment may also have been permitted to the few elective civilian offices; Hegemon's law of the 330's may then have limited tenure of the theoric and similar offices to four years (cf. pp. 346–7).

but none of the others, except to serve as a councillor twice: In civilian offices citizen participation was considered more important than finding the best men, and allotment and the ban on reappointment both served that end (while the potential inefficiency was mitigated by the fact that many of the officials each year would have held other posts in previous years). That two years in the council were allowed suggests that without this concession there would not have been enough men eligible and willing to fill five hundred places each year (in the council imposed on Erythrae *c.* 450 one year in four was allowed: ML 40 = *IG* i³ 14 ~ Fornara 71. 12); it now seems that there was a further relaxation in the third century (S. V. Tracy, in O. Palagia & S. V. Tracy [eds], *The Macedonians in Athens, 322–229 BC* [Oxford: Oxbow, 2003], 60). For the purposes of this rule the college of nine archons and secretary was considered a single office (Tracy, *CP* 86 [1991], 201–4).

S. Jury-courts (63–9)

A.P. turns abruptly to a detailed account of some aspects of the working of the *dikasteria*: the assignment of jurors and magistrates to courts, the appointment of courtroom officials, the timing of speeches, the size of juries in public lawsuits, the voting procedure, the second vote in *agones timetoi* and the payment of jurors. This is limited to the mechanical side of procedure on the day of the trial: nothing is said about what preceded that day, or about speeches by litigants and their *synegoroi*, the presentation of evidence and so on. By the time of *A.P.* extremely elaborate procedures had been devised to make the procedures as impartial and as immune to bribery as possible, so that nobody could know in advance which jurors would try which case, or which jurors would try the same cases. Presumably the Athenians were proud of these procedures and *A.P.* himself (whether an Athenian or not) was fascinated by them; cf. his detail on the *diaitetai* and the forty-two year-classes in 53. However, V. Bers, in *Polis and Politics ... M. H. Hansen* (Copenhagen: Museum Tusculanum P., 2000), 553–62, plays down fears of malpractice and focuses rather on the use of solemn ceremonies which some Athenians might see as divinely backed. For an up-to-date account of the procedures see Boegehold, *Agora* xxxviii. 36–41.

It is difficult to decribe elaborate procedures to readers who are not familiar with them, and *A.P.* has not always succeeded. Several times he makes a statement which cannot be understood without information not yet provided, and has to digress to provide it (64. 2, 3, 4, 67. 3). There are places where he does not give enough information: e.g. the purpose of the *symbolon* in 65. 2; to which cases the time allowances of 67. 2 and of 67. 3 applied; how secret voting was achieved in *diadikasiai*, to which there might be more than two parties. Except in the fragmentary 67. 4–5, he concentrates on the procdures of his own day, without remarking on earlier procedures (the most recent change incorporated in his account is the daily allotment of magistrates to courts, after the late 340's: 66. 1). As elsewhere, his account is based on the laws but is descriptive rather than prescriptive; and it has no doubt been influenced by his own direct knowledge, whether as a citizen participant or as a non-citizen observer.

Chapters 64–69. 1 are the least well preserved part of the surviving text, particularly col. xxxiv (67. 3–68. 2). I normally do not annotate or discuss readings and restorations on which Kenyon[4–5] and Chambers agree; for the particularly difficult 67. 4–68. 1 see p. 433.

63. 1. The lawcourts are allotted ... for the tenth tribe: Repeats what was said in 59. 7: the allotment is that described in detail in 63–5. *Dikasteria* refers to courts as collections of men in this sentence, but to courtrooms in the next.

63. 2. There are ten entrances to the lawcourts: Dow's identification of the *kleroteria* as allotment machines (cf. below) has made the procedures more intelligible than they were before. Readers might suppose from *A.P.*'s account that all the courts were physically connected in a single complex, but that was certainly not the case before the time of *A.P.* It is possible that a group of buildings in the north-east of the agora was used for this purpose in the time of *A.P.*, and that the 'square peristyle' which replaced them *c.* 300 was intended to provide a more coherent location, though some courts may still have met elsewhere (see A. L. Boegehold and R. F. Townsend, *Agora* xxviii. 10–16, 91–113). In my Penguin translation, 159 fig. 2 shows schematically the court complex with the items of equipment provided at the entrances.

twenty allotment machines: *A.P.* begins a list of equipment needed for the allotments. S. Dow identified blocks of stone with columns of slits in one face as hellenistic versions of an allotment machine, and realised that this is what *kleroterion* denotes (*Prytaneis* [*Hesperia* Supp. 1 (1937)], 198–215, *HSCP* 50 [1939], 1–34; refinements by J. D. Bishop, *JHS* 90 [1970], 1–14). For a reconstruction see, e.g., my large commentary, 707 fig. 2, or my Penguin translation, 161 fig. 4, based on Dow's reconstruction but with Bishop's refinements. The word is first found in Ar. *Eccl.* 681, but the allotment was simpler then than in the time of *A.P.* (cf. Harrison, *L.A.* ii. 240–1).

a hundred boxes: One for each of the sections A–K of each tribe (63. 4; their use 64. 1).

further boxes, in which the identity cards ... are deposited: The *pinakia* (63. 4) will have been dropped into the appropriate box when the jurors were allotted to their courts (64. 4–5, 65. 4). 66. 2 mentions another *kibotion* in each courtroom.

two water pots: Presumably two for each tribe: they hold the *balanoi* used to allot jurors to particular courts.

staves ... as many as there are to be jurors: Cf. Dem. XVIII. *Cor.* 210. The staves bore the colours of the different courts (65. 1–3). ε[ἴ]σ[οδον] is correct for the procedure envisaged by Dow.

acorns ... equal in number to the staves: Cf. above. By the time of *A.P.* they were probably manufactured tokens replacing acorns.

letters are written on the acorns ... as many as there are courts to be filled: The courts are identified by letters (beginning with Λ) as well as colours (63. 5), and jurors are allotted to courts by drawing a lettered *balanos* from a water-pot. A copyist misinterpreted Λ as 30.

63. 3. It is permitted to serve as jurors ... or *atimoi*: Logically this would be better placed at the beginning of 63. In the fifth century there was a panel of 6,000 jurors (24. 3); for the time of *A.P.* the frequently reused *pinakia* suggest annual registration, and probably 6,000 were registered each year (J. H. Kroll, *Athenian Bronze Allotment Plates* [Harvard U. P., 1972], 69–86). Thirty was the normal age requirement for office-holding (cf. pp. 194, 344); public debtors were automatically *atimoi* until their debt was discharged (cf. Dem. XXIV. *Timocrates* 123), so what follows means 'or *atimoi* on other grounds'.

If anybody serves ... the sum assessed for him by the lawcourt: For *endeixis* cf. 52. 1, and an *endeixis* on this charge Dem. XXI. *Midias* 182. The council could but did not have to imprison public debtors (cf. Rhodes, *A.B.* 150), but a defaulting debtor who broke this rule had to be imprisoned.

63. 4. Each juror has his boxwood identity card ... in each letter: *A.P.* does not mention a change, but Dem. XXXIX. *Boeotus i.* 10–12 (*c.* 348) mentions bronze *pinakia*. No boxwood *pinakia* survive, but there are nearly two hundred bronze *pinakia*, and the stamps on many include the design used on 3-obol coins, regarded as appropriate to jurors (cf. 62. 2). They measure *c.* 11 × 2 × 0.2 cm. = 4⅓ × ¾ × 1/12 in.; some but not all include the patronymic; for their use with *kleroteria* see below. See Kroll, *Athenian Bronze Allotment Plates* (supplemented in *Studies ... S. Dow* [GRBMon. x 1984], 165–71; also M. L. Lang, *Agora* xxviii. 59–64 and pls. 7–8), who argues that *pinakia* with the 3-obol stamp were introduced for dicastic allotments soon after 388 (he favoured 378/7); later the *pinakia* were used for allotting officials also, and men eligible for offices were given a *pinakion* which also bore a *gorgoneion* stamp; *c.* 350 boxwood replaced bronze for jurors, while bronze was retained for offices but now without stamps. Men became members for life of one of the tribal sections A–K.

63. 5. When the *thesmothetes* ... letter picked for it by sortition: Presumably any of the 'ten archons' might perform this task; probably he was picked by lot (cf. 66. 1). The colours were presumably assigned to courts permanently (63. 2, 65. 1–3); allotting a letter seems unnecessary, but may be a survival from a time before magistrates were allotted to courts (66. 1). Various *hyperetai* are mentioned in these chapters: it will be sufficent for all passages except 69. 1 if each of the ten had his own *hyperetes*.

64. 1. The ten boxes ... the *thesmothetes* draws one card from each box: This refers to the first set of boxes mentioned in 63. 2. In front of each tribal entrance there are ten boxes, each man drops his *pinakion* into the box bearing his section letter, then the *hyperetes* shakes the boxes, the archon from that tribe draws one *pinakion* from each box, and the man whose *pinakion* is drawn serves as *empektes*.

64. 2. This man is called the inserter ... in each of the allotment machines: Each tribe has two *kleroteria*; each of them has five columns of slots, labelled A–E and Z–K (made clear at the end of this section), and the 'inserter' inserts the remaining *pinakia* from his box into the appropriate column, working downwards from the top.

He is allotted ... act dishonestly: Commonly more men will have been present from some sections than from others, and those whose *pinakia* were placed lower than the bottom of the shortest column will have had no chance of being selected: an unscrupulous inserter might see and leave until last his enemies' *pinakia*.

When he has deposited the cubes ... in the same way: The order of exposition is again not ideal. Each *kleroterion* has a tube with a funnel at the top and a release mechanism at the bottom. After the *pinakia* have been inserted, black and white 'cubes' (but spherical ballots in cylindrical tubes will have been most practical) are poured into the funnel, and fall into the tube in a random order: as many white as jurors are needed from each section, and as many black as are needed to make up a total equal to the number of *pinakia* in the shortest column. The archon releases one cube at a time: if the first is white, the men whose *pinakia* are in the first horizontal row are selected, if the second is black, the men whose *pinakia* are in the second row are rejected, and so on. Men whose *pinakia* are below the bottom of the shortest column are automatically rejected: the use of two *kleroteria* for each tribe was perhaps a compromise between the unfairness of performing the procedure once for the tribe and the inconvenience of performing it separately for each section. We are not told what would be done if fewer men than were needed were present, altogether or in some tribes or some sections.

When the archon has released ... the herald calls on those picked in the sortition: There is a single herald of the archons in 62. 2; the courts require a herald for each tribe in the allotments, and a herald for each court during the trials (68. 4–69. 1, cf. 66. 1).

64. 4–5. The man who is called responds ... with the letter on the upper side: ὁ δὲ at the beginning of 64. 4 is ὁ εἰληχώς. When a man is selected, he goes to the water pot, one of which presumably stands near each *kleroterion* (63. 2), draws out an acorn and holds it up to show the letter on it.

first shows it to the archon ... the letter which has fallen by sortition to each court: Again the reader needs to look ahead. Near the *kleroteria* are as many boxes as there are courts to be manned (63. 2), labelled with the letters designating the courts (63. 5). When a juror has drawn his acorn, he shows it to the archon, who takes his *pinakion* from the *kleroterion* and drops it into the box for his court; he then proceeds to the barrier and shows his acorn to the *hyperetes*. The boxes of *pinakia* are taken to the courts, and the *pinakia* are returned to their owners when they are paid at the end of the day (65. 4, 66. 3, 69. 2).

65. 1. The juror shows his acorn again ... goes inside the barrier: A *kinklis* is a gate in a barrier; if the allotments took place outside the tribal entrances to the court complex (63. 2), the *kinklides* will have been at those entrances. On the *hyperetai* cf. 63. 5 with commentary.

The attendant gives him a staff ... the colour of his staff: Again the reader needs to look ahead. Each courtroom is designated permanently by a colour (65. 2); each is also given a letter for the day (63. 5), and the acorns are marked with those letters (64. 4–5); at the *kinklis* each juror is given a staff of the colour which that day corresponds to the letter on his acorn. This was unnecessarily complicated: it should have been as easy to check acorns as to issue staves and check staves, and errors could occur at the extra stage.

65. 2. The courts have a colour painted on the lintel of the entrance of each: In a building a *sphekiskos* is usually a rafter, but here it seems to be a lintel.

When he has entered ... that office has fallen by sortition: *A.P.* does not explain enough. This *symbolon* must be different from that of 68. 2; and *A.P.* does not explain its purpose or, if the text which I accept in 65. 3 and 68. 2 is correct, mention it again. Boegehold suggests that these were the bronze tokens of his series A–E, marked with letters of the alphabet and used to assign jurors to seats (*Agora* xxviii. 67–76 and pls. 9–11; for other tokens which have been considered see on 68. 2). It is not clear why *A.P.* chose to emphasise the public nature of these particular objects. The man 'to whom that office has fallen by sortition' (presumably not a slave but one of the jurors, despite *Suda* β 49 Adler βακτηρία καὶ σύμβολον) was possibly the man similarly described in 68. 2, and the man who made up the jury to one more than the round hundred (A. L. Boegehold, 'Aristotle and the Dikasteria' [Harvard thesis, 1957], 50–2).

65. 3. Then, having entered in that way ... sit down in the court: A verb is needed to take τήν τε βάλανον καὶ τὴν βακτηρίαν as object. In Kenyon's text, which I print, the jurors retain their acorn and staff when they enter the court, and surrender their staff when they receive their ballots (cf. 68. 2); in the alternative text proposed by Thalheim, the jurors surrender their acorn and staff when they receive the *symbolon* of 65. 2 and enter the court, and surrender that *symbolon* when they receive their ballots (cf. 68. 2). Thalheim's reconstruction is the more elegant procedurally. However, the fact that, when after voting on the verdict the jurors have to vote on assessment of the penalty, they surrender the *symbolon* of 68. 2 and are again given staves (69. 2), is decisive in favour of Kenyon's (cf. A. W. Gomme, *CR* 44 [1930], 65, K. K. Carroll, *Philologus* 118 [1974], 274–6; but Thalheim's is defended by M. H. Chambers, in *Mazzo di fiori ... H. Hoffmann* [Ruhpolding & Mainz: Rutzen, 2010], 90–6).

To those rejected in the sortition the inserters return their identity cards: *A.P.* returns to the place where the allotments have been held: unsuccessful applicants may have their *pinakia* returned either as soon as their black ball emerges or after allotments have been completed.

65. 4. The public attendants hand over ... in each of the courts: For the boxes cf. 63. 2, 64. 4–5, and for the *hyperetai* cf. 63. 5. The boxes containing the *pinakia* are taken to the courts; each tribe is represented in each jury, and the *pinakia* are already sorted by tribes for the payment of the jurors (66. 3 cf. 69. 2). To provide ten officials in each court, the presiding magistrate draws one *pinakion* from each of the ten boxes in his court (66. 2–3).

They hand these over ... pay them their stipend: The insertion of πέντε (cf. 66. 3) is the only way to save ἀριθμῷ; if Kenyon's ταῦ[τ]α is right, the awkwardly placed τὰ πινάκια is best deleted as a gloss on that.

66. 1. When all the courts are full ... the names of the officials: Which magistrates and cases are to appear on a particular day has already been decided (59. 1, 5), but magistrates and their cases have to be assigned to courtrooms. This further allotment seems to have been a recent innovation: [Dem.] LIX. *Neaera* 52 cf. 54 (*c.* 340) cites a law under which *dikai* *sitou* are to be tried in the Odeum. So that there shall be witnesses, the allotment is made in 'the first of the courts' (the one designated Λ?); on a *kleroterion* which might have been used for this see J. D. Bishop, *JHS* 90 (1970), 5–9. It would have been possible to create courts of different sizes on the same day, but this allotment implies that any magistrate might be assigned to any of the day's courts. As a compromise, which would lessen the risk of bribery in the most important cases, Hommel distinguished between days for private and days for public suits (cf. ὅταν in 67 1) and suggested that there would otherwise be only one size of jury on each day but when there was a public suit requiring a large jury that could coexist with juries of 501 in other courts (*Heliaia*, 72–8).

Two of the *thesmothetai* ... the one which falls to him in the sortition: Probably the two men could be any of the 'ten archons' (cf. 63. 5, 64. 1). With unnecessary elaboration two *kleroteria* are used to produce a random order both of magistrates and of courts. There is a herald in each court (68. 4, 69. 1): probably the herald here is that of the court in which the allotments are made.

66. 2. When the jurors have entered ... there cannot be any dishonesty in connection with them: MacDowell suggested ἐπὶ τὰ μέρη or ἐπὶ τὰ ξύλα because with Blass's ἐφ' ἕκαστον the second thing mentioned would occur before the first. To pick courtroom officials (ten so that each tribe shall supply one) the magistrate draws one *pinakion* from each of the ten tribal boxes (cf. 65. 4); probably the man whose *pinakion* is drawn first is assigned to the clock (cf. 67. 2–4) and the next four to the ballots (cf. 68. 2, 69. 1). There is one epigraphic reference to these men: *SEG* xxv 180. 12–19.

66. 3. The five who are rejected ... being confined in the same area: This section is concerned with the responsibility of the other five men for the payment of stipends, and if γ´ is rightly read as a numeral that will refer to the 3-obol payment; the π]ρόγ[ραμμ]α of Blass and Kenyon we should expect to refer to the schedule of cases to be tried (cf. προγράψαι in 59. 1, the assembly's *programma* in 44. 2) rather than to the arrangements for payment.

67. 1. After doing that they call in the contests: It was known in advance which magistrates would introduce which cases on a particular day, but not in which courtroom (and possibly not in what order): there must have been an area where all litigants, *synegoroi* and witnesses waited until these matters were decided.

when they are trying private matters ... one of each of the kinds of suit prescribed by law: The restoration of α´ gives the best sense; the reference will be to the four categories of 67. 2 (and this perhaps represents the maximum which could be required of one court in one day). Elsewhere *A.P.* distinguishes between *dikai* (*idiai*) and *graphai* (in which *ho boulomenos* might prosecute – and there were other forms of public prosecution, such as *eisangelia*); here he refers to *idioi* and *demosioi agones*; but although lawsuits could be categorised on other grounds (e.g. 67. 5, Dem. XXI. *Midias* 42–6) *A.P.* should be using aspects of a single distinction between private and public (Lipsius, *A.R.* 238–46, contr. Harrison, *L.A.* ii. 75–8).

the opposing litigants take an oath to speak to the point: The speaker of Dem. LVII. *Eubulides* frequently insists that he is speaking εἰς αὐτὸ τὸ πρᾶγμα (7 etc.); according to Arist. *Rhet.* I. 1354 A 22–3 litigants before the Areopagus were forbidden to speak ἔξω τοῦ πράγματος. Scholars have regularly accepted the implication of the positioning of this, that the oath applied only to private suits, but I doubt if we can rely on *A.P.* in this way. For a discussion of relevance in lawcourt speeches see Rhodes, in E. M. Harris & L. Rubinstein (eds), *The Law and the Courts in Ancient Greece* (London: Duckworth, 2004), 137–58.

when public matters ... they work through the trial of only one case: Cf. 67. 3. It would have been hard to reassemble the same jury on a second day, and it appears that every trial had to be completed within one day (note Pl. *Ap.* 37 A–B, and cf. D. M. MacDowell, in *Polis and Politics ... M. H. Hansen* [Copenhagen: Museum Tusculanum P., 2000], 563–8).

67. 2. There are water clocks ... speeches in trials must be timed: For *auliskoi* in ballots see 68. 2; *ekrhous* as a noun is used in Hdt. VII. 129. 2, Arist. *Meteor.* I. 351 A 10, and Diels proposed the unattested αὐλ[ώδεις] to make it a noun here. The use of *klepsydrai* as waterclocks in the courts is attested for the fifth century by Ar. *Ach.* 693, *Vesp.* 93, 857–8. For a *klepsydra* of that period see M. L. Lang, *Agora* xxviii, pp. 77–8 and pl. 13: it is a bowl with a hole near the rim, fixing the level to which it was filled, and a bronze-lined hole at the foot, through which the water flowed out; it is marked XX (= δίχους) and ’Αντιοχ[ίδος] (for one of the ten tribes), holds 6.4 litres and empties itself in 6 minutes. It is possible that the lawcourt *klepsydrai* of *A.P.*'s time were more sophisticated and / or that the time which they took was different.

What follows, to ἀναγιγ[νώσκειν μέλλῃ in 67. 3, concerns private suits; *A.P.* then turns to the tripartite day, which was used for public suits. **The allowance is ten *choes* ... there is no subsequent speech:** The four categories seem to be three of *dikai* according to the sum at issue, and *diadikasiai* (to which there might be more than two parties). 1,000 drachmae is the one dividing-line mentioned in 53. 3; Hommel restored β′ because he supposed that *A.P.* was here dealing only with suits for more than 1,000 drachmae, tried by juries of 401.

The *klepsydra* mentioned above implies a time allowance of 3 minutes per *chous* = 36 minutes per *amphora*; earlier Keil had argued for 4 minutes per *chous* = 48 minutes per *amphora* (*Anonymus Argentinensis* [Strassburg: Trübner, 1902], 246–63). If a court tried one case in each category, and there were two parties to the *diadikasia*, speeches would take 3 hours 30 minutes or 4 hours 40 minutes, plus a few more minutes in *agones timetoi* (cf. 69. 2), and more time would be required for reading documents, which in *dikai* were not included in the litigant's allowance (67. 3). On first and second speeches see Harrison, *L.A.* ii. 160–1. It is not certain that litigants were allowed a second speech in all *dikai*; but Dem. XLIII. *Macartatus* 8 (probably late 340's) mentions a *diadikasia* in which each litigant was allowed 1 *amphora*, and 3 *choes* for a second speech, so there must have been at least one change shortly before *A.P.* was written. Second speeches seem not to have been allowed in *graphai*; supporting speeches by *synegoroi* were included in the litigant's allowance.

67. 3. The man picked ... a decree or law or testimony or contract: If the text which I print is correct, it is surprising to find *psephisma* mentioned before *nomon*. For the juror assigned to the clock see 66. 2; for a secretary who read out documents cf. 54. 5 for the council and assembly. Probably the measured-out day was used for all public suits (cf. 67. 1: e.g. Hommel, *Helaia*, 86–7, Harrison, *L.A.* ii. 161–2), and in view of the more generous allowance the clock was never stopped in them: references to stopping the clock are frequent in speeches in private suits, but there are none in what are certainly public suits.

when the trial is set against the measured-out day ... for the prosecutor and the defendant: The principal references to the measured-out day are Xen. *Hell.* I. 7. 23, Aeschin. II. *F.L.* 126, III. *Ctesiphon* 197–8.

Xenophon, and scholia and lexicographers, assign the third part of the day to the jurors (but there is no evidence that they were allowed time to consider their verdict, and voting should not have taken that long; for Xenophon this period covers the setting-up of the court and the voting); Aeschin. III, which can hardly be wrong about contemporary procedure, assigns it to the assessment of penalty in cases where that was needed.

67. 4–68. 1. The text of col. xxxiv, and particularly of these sections, is extremely uncertain. Only G. Colin (*REG* 30 [1917], 20–87) and H. Hommel (*Heliaia*) have attempted a complete reconstruction; *exempli gratia*, I print and translate the reconstruction of Hommel, with the warning that it may well not be right at every point (and at several points it does not match the traces read by Kenyon and Chambers).

67. 4. *The measuring out ... one for the defendants*: Having mentioned the measured-out day *A.P.* realises that it needs to be explained. It is based on the length of days in Posideon (vi), the mid-winter month: the shortest day in Athens is slightly under 9 hrs. 30 min.; the eleven *amphoreis* are mentioned by Aeschin. II. *F.L.* 126; Keil's 48 minutes per *amphora* (above) imply 8 hrs. 48 min. for the timed proceedings, which probably leaves too little for the allotment of jurors at the beginning of the day and voting and payment at the end, but may be considered a maximum; 36 minutes per *amphora* imply 6 hrs. 36 min. The next part of Hommel's reconstruction is problematic, since allocating the final three *amphoreis* to the voting seems too generous, and follows Xenophon rather than Aeschines. At the end of this section the imperfect ἔσπευδο[ν supports πρό]τε[ρον] and a contrast between earlier and current practice, and a single allowance from which the prosecutor might take more than his fair share is plausible. κάδοι was restored from Philoch. *FGrH* 328 F 187, which states that *kados* was an ancient word for *amphora*; Chambers restores ἀμφορεῖς; either word must here denote a large vessel, not the *amphora* measure mentioned above.

67. 5. *In previous times ... what the culprit should suffer or pay*: Hommel begins this section with another contrast between previous and current practice, but an imperfect would have been more appropriate than the aorist ἐξεῖλε, and it is hard to see why a change should have been made. Following that, more reliably, there seems to be a belated explanation that the measured-out day is used in public cases, i.e. those which there is a fixed penalty of some kind (*agones atimetoi*: Hommel understood νόμῳ with πρόσεστι: *Heliaia*, 24, 95) or (*agones timetoi*) in which the penalty has to be assessed (cf. p. 418).

68. 1. *Of the lawcourts ... 3 courts are united for 1,500*: Here it is reasonably certain that *A.P.* stated that the normal size of jury in public suits was 501, but two panels could be combined to make 1,00(1) or three to make 1,50(1) (and still larger juries are attested: a full 6,000 in 415, Andoc. I. *Myst.* 17; 2,500 in the 330's or 320's, Din. I. *Demosthenes* 52). Dem. XXIV. *Timocrates* 9 writes of 1,001 as 'two *dikasteria*'; the odd one, often omitted in references to juries, was supposed to avoid a tie (schol. Dem. XXIV. 9 [25 Dilts]), though 69. 1 makes provision for a tie. We are not told how the odd one was appointed (he was possibly the official of 65. 2 and 68. 2), or how it was decided what size of jury should try each case. By the middle of the fourth century the name *eliaia* was used for a particular courtroom, possibly the largest in the complex in the north-east of the agora (Boegehold, *Agora* xxviii, pp. 10–15).

68. 2. There are bronze ballots ... shall not receive two solid or two hollow: Without mentioning any aspect of the hearing of the cases except the timing, *A.P.* passes to the voting. A number of the ballots have survived: they are discs of bronze with a solid or hollow axle (*auliskos*) which enabled the jurors after taking them to feel but not to show to others which was which (cf., e.g., M. L. Lang, *Agora* xxviii. 82–90 and pls. 13–22). Earlier each juror had a single ballot, to place in one of two vessels (Harrison, *L.A.* ii. 164–5). For the men *epi tas psephous* cf. 66. 2.

Then the man picked by sortition for this task takes away the staves: For the objects taken cf. 65. 3, 69. 2; however we restore this passage, the man who takes them is probably the same as the man mentioned at the end of 65. 2.

in exchange for which ... unless he does vote: Cf. Ar. *Vesp.* 752–3. Prsumably the jurors left their seats, gave up their staves and took their ballots, voted and then received their new *symbola*. They will not have been marked Γ (alphabetic numerals were not yet in use); they may have been marked III (A. L. Boegehold, *Hesperia* xxix 1960, 394 with n. 5; but either possible, *Agora* xxviii. 39, 72); but I should not rule out the possibility of tokens with a triobol design, such as those which used to be considered the *symbola* of 65. 2 (e.g. Hommel, *Heliaia*, 69–70), though surviving specimens are of lead.

68. 3. There are two amphoras … the same man cannot deposit two ballots: Precautions are taken against two kinds of malpractice: the vessels (by the time of *A.P.* specially made) can be dismantled, to show that no ballots have been inserted in advance, and the bronze vessel has a lid with a hole small enough to prevent the insertion of more than one ballot. Earlier each juror had a single ballot, to be inserted in one of two amphorae (probably then ordinary vases), and a wicker *kemos*, through which the ballots were dropped, perhaps covered the two (Boegehold, *Agora* xxviii. 28–9). *A.P.* says nothing of *diadikasiai* to which there were more than two parties: perhaps each juror had as many ballots as there were parties, one with a hollow axle for a favourable vote (Harrison, *L.A.* ii. 165–6).
68. 4. When the jurors are about to vote … when they have started to vote: An *episkepsis* is a declaration of intent to prosecute a witness for perjury (cf. Harrison, *L.A.* ii. 192–7, and 59. 6). For *episkepseis* before the vote cf. Pl. *Leg.* XI. 937 B 3–7; but in hellenistic Alexandria they followed the verdict (*P. Hal.* 1. 24–6). For the heralds cf. 64. 3.
Then he proclaims again … for the one who spoke afterwards': Cf. Aeschin. I. *Timarchus* 79.
The juror takes his ballots … and the non-decisive in the wooden: The juror takes his ballots from a stand resembling a lamp-stand, with two pans to hold the two kinds of ballots.

69. 1. When they have all voted … both the hollow and the solid: The sense is clear: *hyperetai* empty the bronze vessel and arrange the ballots on a board which has holes into which the axles are pegged.
The men picked by sortition … he is the winner: Presumably the same men count the ballots as issued them (66. 2, 68. 2). The result of one count is reported in *IG* ii^2 1641. 30–3 = *I. Délos* 104–26. *C.* 7–10, *I. Délos* 104–26 *bis. C.* 1–3.
if they are equal the defendant wins: If the courts were fully manned and every juror voted, ties ought not to have occurred (cf. p. 434); possibly a rule was retained which was more necessary earlier.
69. 2. Then again they make the assessment, if an assessment is needed: If the suit is an *agon timetos*, without a fixed penalty, if the jury finds for the prosecutor there follow a pair of speeches and a vote on the penalty: each litigant makes a proposal and the jury decides between them (cf. Pl. *Apol.* 35 E 1–38 B 9)

voting in the same way, giving up their token and taking their staff again: This reverses the procedure of 68. 2 (and confirms the restoration of the text there and in 65. 3); presumably the same procedure was followed with private suits when the court had another case to try.

Speeches on the assessment ... a half allowance of water for each: The papyrus' ἡμιχοῦν ὕδατος would be 1½ minutes by the agora *klepsydra*, 2 minutes by Keil's calculations (cf. p. 432). There was no need for such brevity in public suits (cf. pp. 432–3), and D. M. MacDowell (*CQ*[2] 35 [1985], 525–6) persuasively argued from Dem. XXX *Onetor* 32 that it is implausible even in private suits: half the allowance for the principal speeches would allow private suits to match public suits.

When they have completed the trials ... assigned to each by sortition: For 'prescribed by the laws' cf. 67. 1. The jurors responsible for the payments receive instructions on the logistics (66. 3), take the box containing rhe *pinakia* of each tribe's jurors, call the men by name, and give them their payment and *pinakion* in exchange for the 'triobol' token of 68. 2. The significance of 'in the section' is uncertain: it refers possibly to an allotment of two tribes to each of the five men (P. S. Photiades, *Ἀθηνᾶ* 15 [1903], 25–6), possibly to parts of the courtroom (e.g. Sandys[2]). If the reconstruction of the text which I accept is correct, the jurors must now have surrendered (if they had not done so earlier) the acorn of 64. 4 and the *symbolon* of 65. 2.

Here the scribe ends, in the middle of a line and in the middle of col. xxxvi of the papyrus, and with a flourish in the left-hand margin. This is an abrupt ending of the text, but we have no reason to believe that there was further material which has been lost.

INDEX

This index is not exhaustive: in particular, it omits some persons, places and subjects mentioned only in a context in which there are other names or words for which readers are more likely to search. References are to pages, mostly in the Introduction and translation; references to the Commentary are sometimes added to guide readers to discussions of a subject or to references which could not be inferred from the translation. In some cases a principal reference is given first, in bold type.